# RETROSPECTIVE SUPPLEMENT I

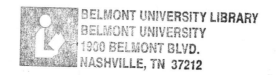

# AMERICAN WRITERS
## A Collection of Literary Biographies

### A. WALTON LITZ
### MOLLY WEIGEL
### General Editors

# RETROSPECTIVE SUPPLEMENT I

**Charles Scribner's Sons**
Macmillan Library Reference USA
Simon & Schuster Macmillan
New York

Simon & Schuster and Prentice Hall International
London   Mexico City   New Delhi   Singapore   Sydney   Toronto

Charles Scribner's Sons
An imprint of Simon & Schuster Macmillan
1633 Broadway
New York, New York 10019

1   3   5   7   9   11   13   15   17   19      20   18   16   14   12   10   8   6   4   2

Printed in the United States of America

Library of Congress Cataloging-in-Publication Data

American writers: a collection of literary biographies.
American writers: retrospective supplement I edited by A. Walton Litz and Molly Weigel.
The 4-vol. main set consists of 97 of the pamphlets originally published as the
University of Minnesota pamphlets on American writers; some have been rev. and
updated. Supplements I to IV cover writers not included in the original series.
Includes bibliographies.
Contents: v. 1. Henry Adams to T. S. Eliot — v. 2. Ralph Waldo Emerson to
Carson McCullers — [etc.] — Supplement[s] — [etc.] — Retrospective supplement I.
Willa Cather to William Carlos Williams.
1. American Literature — History and criticism. 2. American literature — Bio-
bibliography. 3. Authors, American — Biography. I. Unger, Leonard, ed. II. Baechler,
Lea. III. Litz, A. Walton. IV. Weigel, Molly. V. University of Minnesota. Pamphlets on
American writers.

PS129.A55          810′.9          73-1759

ISBN 0-684-80494-8

Acknowledgment is gratefully made to those publishers and individuals who have permitted the use of the following material in copyright.

"Emily Dickinson"
Excerpts reprinted by permission of the publishers and the Trustees of Amherst College from THE POEMS OF EMILY DICKINSON, Thomas H. Johnson, ed., Cambridge, Mass.: The Belknap Press of Harvard University Press, Copyright © 1951, 1955, 1979, 1983 by the President and Fellows of Harvard College.

Excerpts from THE COMPLETE POEMS OF EMILY DICKINSON by T. H. Johnson. Copyright 1929, 1935 by Martha Dickinson Bianchi; copyright © renewed 1957, 1963 by Mary L. Hampson. By permission of Little, Brown and Company.

"T. S. Eliot"
Excerpt from SELECTED ESSAYS by T. S. Eliot, copyright 1950 by Harcourt Brace & Company and renewed 1978 by Esme Valerie Eliot, reprinted by permission of the publisher.

Excerpts from "The Waste Land," "The Hollow Men," "Ash Wednesday," "Journey of the Magi," and "Sweeney Agonistes" in COLLECTED POEMS 1909–1962 by T. S. Eliot, copyright 1936 by Harcourt Brace & Company, copyright © 1964, 1963 by T. S. Eliot, reprinted by permission of the publisher.

# Editorial and Production Staff

# Contents

# Contents of Other Volumes
# in the American Writers Series

# Introduction

Between 1961 and 1972 the University of Minnesota Press published nearly one hundred Minnesota Pamphlets on American writers, a series of "introductory essays . . . aimed at people (general readers here and abroad, college students, etc.) . . . interested in the writers concerned, but not highly familiar with their work." The challenge was to produce an extended, jargon-free essay that would serve the general reader and be of use to the specialist. Many of the finest scholar-teachers of the generation after World War II rose to this challenge, and the names of some contributors to the Minnesota Series are still familiar ones: Philip Young (author of the first full-length critical study of Ernest Hemingway) on Hemingway; Lawrance Thompson (the official biography of Robert Frost) on Frost; Leon Edel (the official biographer of Henry James) on James; and Denis Donoghue on Emily Dickinson.

The Minnesota pamphlets reflected the postwar consensus on the history of American literature and enshrined the canon established in the magisterial *Literary History of the United States* published by Macmillan in 1948. This canon was dominated by white males and, from the perspective of the later 1990s, it looked strikingly out of date. The half-century that passed since the first Minnesota pamphlets appeared witnessed a remarkable widening of the canon to include women, African Americans, members of other ethnic groups, and writers of the nineteenth century whose work had been reassessed. More striking, these years witnessed rapid changes in methodology, from archetypal criticism, through post-structuralism and deconstruction, to feminism and cultural studies. The New Criticism, with its suspicion of historical and biographical evidence, no longer informs our critical writing.

In 1974 Scribners published the texts of the Minnesota pamphlets (with some revisions) in four large hardbound volumes. Supplements devoted to more recent authors and to earlier authors not included in the Minnesota series appeared in 1979, 1981, 1991, and 1996. (A complete listing of the contents of the American Writers series precedes this introduction.)

The present volume contains essays on nineteen classic American writers most often addressed by students; teachers at all levels and librarians were consulted in drawing up the list. At first we thought of revising the original essays and updating their bibliographies, but this would have threatened the integrity of essays that have an enduring critical and historical value. So we decided to let the original essays stand as written—they are permanent and still useful monuments to a great period in American literary study—and to commission entirely new essays that would reflect not only the rich lode of new information that has been uncovered over the latter half of the century but the fruitful and varied critical approaches of the 1990s. And so this Retrospective Supplement can either stand alone as a new look at nineteen classic writers or supplement and update the original essays. The overriding aim is the same—a fresh view of the writer cast in accessible form—but the critical assumptions are current today. This strikes us as an appropriate way to end the century and to round off one of its most influential critical enterprises.

A. WALTON LITZ
MOLLY WEIGEL

# Contributors

**Ronald Bush.** Professor of Literature, California Institute of Technology. Author of *The Genesis of Ezra Pound's Cantos; T. S. Eliot: A Study in Character and Style;* and *T. S. Eliot: The Modernist in History;* coeditor of *Prehistories of the Future: The Primitivist Project and the Culture of Modernism.* T. S. ELIOT.

**Evan Carton.** Professor of English, University of Texas at Austin. Author of *The Rhetoric of American Romance: Dialectic and Identity in Emerson and Dickinson, Poe, and Hawthorne* and *The Marble Faun: Hawthorne's Transformations.* NATHANIEL HAWTHORNE.

**Scott Donaldson.** Louise G. T. Cooley Professor of English emeritus, University of Virginia. Author of biographies of Winfield Townley Scott, Ernest Hemingway, F. Scott Fitzgerald, John Cheever, and Archibald MacLeish; articles on American writers and culture. ERNEST HEMINGWAY.

**C. K. Doreski.** National Endowment for the Humanities Fellow. Author of *Elizabeth Bishop: The Restraints of Language* and *Writing America Black: Race in the Public Sphere.* F. SCOTT FITZGERALD.

**William Doreski.** Professor of English, Keene State College. Author of *The Modern Voice in American Poetry* and *The Years of Friendship: Robert Lowell and Allen Tate.* ROBERT FROST.

**Dean Flower.** Professor of English, Smith College. Advisory Editor of *The Hudson Review.* Author of essays and reviews in *The New England Quarterly, The Massachusetts Review, Essays in Criticism,* and *The Hudson Review.* Editor of works by Henry James and Henry David Thoreau. JOHN UPDIKE.

**David Fogel.** Professor of English, Executive Vice Chancellor and Provost, Louisiana State University. Author of *A Companion to Henry James Studies; Daisy Miller: A Dark Comedy of Manners;* and other books and articles on Henry James. Editor of *The Henry James Review.* Executive Director of the Henry James Society. HENRY JAMES.

**Janet Gray.** Editor of *She Wields a Pen: American Women Poets of the 19th Century.* EMILY DICKINSON.

**T. Walter Herbert.** Brown Professor of English and University Scholar, Southwestern University. Author of *Moby-Dick and Calvinism: A World Dismantled; Marquesan Encounters: Melville and the Meaning of Civilization;* and *Dearest Beloved: The Hawthornes and the Making of the Middle-Class Family.* HERMAN MELVILLE.

**Jennie Kassanoff.** Assistant Professor of English, Barnard College. Author of articles on Edith Wharton and Pauline Elizabeth Hopkins. EDITH WHARTON.

**A. Walton Litz.** Holmes Professor of Literature, Princeton University. Author of books on Ezra Pound, James Joyce, T. S. Eliot, and Wallace Stevens among others. Editor of poems of Pound and William Carlos Williams. EZRA POUND.

**James Longenbach.** Joseph Henry Gilmore Professor of English, University of Rochester. Author of *Modernist Poetics of History; Stony Cottage: Pound, Yeats, and Modernism;* and *Wallace Stevens: The Plain Sense of Things.* WALLACE STEVENS.

**Christopher MacGowan.** Professor of English, College of William and Mary. Coeditor of *Collected Poems of William Carlos Williams.* WILLIAM CARLOS WILLIAMS.

**Veronica Makowsky.** Professor of English, University of Connecticut. Author of books on Caroline Gordon and Susan Glaspell and of numerous critical essays on American literary figures. EUDORA WELTY.

**David Minter.** Libbie Shearn Moody Professor of English, Rice University. Author of *The Interpreted Design: A Study in American Prose; William Faulkner: His Life and Work;* and *A Cultural History of the American Novel.* WILLIAM FAULKNER.

**Tenney Nathanson.** Associate Professor of English, University of Arizona. Has published poetry in such journals as *Social Text, The Massachusetts Review, Ironwood,* and the on-line poetry journal RIF/T. WALT WHITMAN.

**Sharon O'Brien.** James Hope Caldwell Professor of American Cultures and Professor of English and American Studies, Dickinson College. Author of *Willa Cather: The Emerging Voice,* and editor of the works of Willa Cather in the Library of America. WILLA CATHER.

**David Roessel.** Lecturer in English, Princeton University. Associate editor of *The Collected Poems of Langston Hughes.* LANGSTON HUGHES.

**Michael Wood.** Charles Barnwell Straut Professor of English, Princeton University. Director, Christian Gauss Seminars in Criticism. Author of *America in the Movies* and *The Magician's Doubts: Nabokov and the Risks of Fiction.* VLADIMIR NABOKOV.

# RETROSPECTIVE SUPPLEMENT I

# Willa Cather
## 1873–1947

"*L*IFE BEGAN FOR me," Willa Cather once said, "when I ceased to admire and began to remember." Her artistic power was also born when she moved from admiration to memory, but this was a long process. Cather began writing fiction as an undergraduate at the University of Nebraska in the early 1890s; in her first novel, *Alexander's Bridge,* published in 1912, she was still an admirer, patterning her story after the high-toned psychological fiction of Henry James—whom she described as the "mighty master of language." But in *O Pioneers!*—published just a year later, in 1913—Cather "hit the home pasture," as she told her friend Elizabeth Sergeant. Now her creative process had tapped into the deep wellspring of memory, and after that, her fiction would soar.

*O Pioneers!* was her literary breakthrough: in it she returned to the Nebraska cornfields of her childhood and invented a character new to American fiction, a strong, creative woman who is not rebuked for her independent-mindedness, unlike the heroines created by Nathaniel Hawthorne and Henry James. Cather continued to take what she called the "road home" in *The Song of the Lark* (1915), her novel of a woman artist's emergence from a Western background much like Cather's own, as well as in *My Ántonia* (1918), the novel that most extensively draws on, and explores, the creative power of memory.

Cather's early novels were hailed as bringing a fresh voice to American fiction by such prominent critics as H. L. Mencken and Edmund Wilson. She kept writing and her literary reputation continued to rise throughout the 1920s: she won the Pulitzer Prize in 1923 for *One of Ours* (1922), received honorary degrees from major universities, and was elected to the National Institute of Arts and Letters. In the 1930s, when left-wing critics attacked her for "escapism," Cather's literary reputation slipped momentarily. But her creativity continued to flow, and she published a novel or a collection of short stories every two or three years until 1940, an extraordinary record of productivity coupled with continuing literary excellence. She suffered no dry spells, not even when politically motivated critics slighted her work, confounding F. Scott Fitzgerald's famous dictum, "There are no second acts in American lives." Cather's discovery of the deep force of her creative powers in *O Pioneers!*—after twenty years of apprenticeship—had opened the floodgates.

CATHER'S REPUTATION AND APPEAL

The novels she wrote during those years are not only still valued, they are read. What is extraordinary about Willa Cather is her continued enjoy-

*1*

ment of critical esteem combined with a wide popular readership. After suffering slightly during the 1930s and 1940s, Cather's literary reputation began to rise again in the 1970s and 1980s as new critical approaches—feminist criticism, cultural studies, gay and lesbian studies, among others—found new depths and resonances in her fiction. Her complete works were published by the Library of America in the 1990s.

Her work appeals to different kinds of readers because it can be read on so many levels—her prose is supple, pure, and readable, always in the service of the story, and yet resonant with what Cather called "the inexpressible presence of the thing not named." Some readers believe that this beautifully ambiguous phrase refers to the lesbian narrative she could not tell directly. It also suggests the power given the text by what has been omitted—and by those ineffable truths that can only be suggested by language, not directly captured.

Once viewed simply as a celebrator of the American landscape and the heroic past, Cather is now considered a writer who employs a complex and shaded emotional palette and whose work explores the darker tones of American life—violence, greed, change, loss—as well as the power of the creative imagination, which she sees possessed by pioneers as well as artists, women as well as men. Cather's fiction, even when somber, is not pessimistic. Against the forces of pettiness, materialism, and mortality, she places the human desire to make meaning through work, family, religion, art, domestic crafts, and—perhaps most important to her—storytelling.

NEBRASKA GIRLHOOD AND EDUCATION

Willa Cather was first introduced to storytelling during her rural Virginia childhood. Although we associate her with Nebraska, she was born on December 6, 1873, in the small farming community of Black Creek in Virginia's Shenandoah Valley,

the eldest child of Charles and Mary Virginia Cather. She eventually would be the older sister to six brothers and sisters. She recalled her earliest delight with narrative taking place when women came to the Cathers' farmhouse, Willow Shade, to help out with canning, preserving, and quilting, and told stories that enthralled Cather as a listening child. Later, Cather would pay tribute to this first exposure to women's creativity in her last novel, *Sapphira and the Slave Girl* (1940).

In 1883, when Willa was nine years old, Charles Cather decided to leave sheep farming behind, and the family left Willow Shade to join Charles' brother and parents, who were farming on the Nebraska Divide. Cather at first found the transition from Virginia's green, sheltered landscape to the raw openness of the Nebraska prairies a painful one. She almost died, she later said, from homesickness and did not know how she had survived being "thrown out" into a country as "bare as a piece of sheet iron."

Eventually Cather came to love her new home, which proved to be a rich source of material for soul-making. The prairies' wide expanses gave her a sense of freedom rather than annihilation, and her exhilaration with the West's open spaces lasted a lifetime. "When I strike the great open plains, I'm home," she would say. "That love of great spaces, of rolling open country like the sea—it's the grand passion of my life."

Helping Cather to feel at home were the immigrant farmers who had come to the American Midwest to start over; like the young Cather, they were surviving the trauma of uprooting and resettlement. She was surrounded by a far more varied ethnic mix of people than in the more homogenous culture of the Shenandoah Valley, Scandinavians, French, Russians, Germans, and Bohemians farmed alongside native-born Americans. European settlers "spread across our bronze prairies like the daubs of color on a painter's palette," she said later, bringing vitality and shading to a "neutral new world."

In many of her novels and short stories she recorded the lives of Nebraska's immigrant settlers, who introduced her to the cultures and histories that first directed her gaze from America to Europe. Throughout her life, Cather remained sensitive to the processes of uprooting, transplantation, and resettlement: the move to Nebraska stamped her creative imagination forever. Time and again, her novelist's imagination was drawn to individuals and groups who leave one home for another: a slave girl who escapes to Canada; a professor who finds himself unable to leave his old house; the immigrants who settle the Nebraska Divide; the French settlers in seventeenth-century Quebec; the Spanish and French missionaries in the American Southwest; the Native Americans who migrated to the Southwest and built their homes into the cliffs of Arizona and New Mexico. When she wrote these stories, she was concerned not with simple survival but with the capacity of human beings to create spiritual and emotional meaning in their new landscapes—to make the strange become familiar and to make houses become homes.

Charles Cather did not take to farming, and in 1884 the family moved into the small prairie town of Red Cloud, where he found work in real estate. Willa Cather's awakening imagination found many resources in the town; she attended a school where she found supportive teachers, acted in amateur theatricals, attended plays, studied Greek and Latin with a town storekeeper, apprenticed herself to the town's two doctors, and found neighbors who introduced her to European literature. She formed close friendships with the Miner girls, Carrie and Irene, and found herself drawn to the daughters of the immigrant farm women, "hired girls" like Annie Sadilek (later the model for Ántonia) who found work in town.

But even as she formed such friendships, Willa Cather herself was repudiating Victorian girlhood. In 1888, when she was fourteen years old, she rejected the constraints of "namby-pamby" femininity by cropping her hair to crew-cut length, donning male attire, and proclaiming herself "William Cather, Jr.," and "William Cather, M.D.," reflecting her ambition to be a doctor. "The old country doctor and I used to talk over his cases," she said. "I was determined then to be a surgeon."

Cather's desire to be a doctor illustrates her repudiation of conventional gender roles: she scorned the nineteenth century's "cult of true womanhood," which celebrated the supposedly innate female virtues of purity, piety, submissiveness, and domesticity. As "William," she could envision a heroic future for herself and imagine leaving the domestic sphere her culture assigned to women. Given the fact that Victorian society imagined "woman" and "artist" as conflicting, incompatible identities, Cather was also clearing space for her creative emergence.

Ultimately, Willa Cather would leave William Cather behind and manage to integrate the identities of woman and artist by redefining "woman." This was a necessary part of her artistic journey, since as long as she repudiated women she was repudiating herself, and denial is not a powerful source of creativity. Had Cather never moved beyond male identification, she would not have become the writer we read today—one who does not imitate male writers but who speaks in her own voice.

Although the teachers and mentors Willa Cather found in Red Cloud offered support for a gifted rebel, the town was limited and confining, the source for the repressive Black Hawk in *My Ántonia* where the "tongue of gossip" keeps people in line. Cather's burning need to escape gave her another theme to explore in her fiction, the story of an unconventional self, at war with confining, soul-numbing mediocrity, the story she tells in "Paul's Case," *The Song of the Lark,* and *One of Ours.*

In September 1890 Cather happily moved to Lincoln and enrolled as a second-year student in the Latin School, the two-year preparatory school of the University of Nebraska. She eventually graduated from the university in 1896. In Lincoln, Cather found her interests moving from medicine to literature, and she began writing book and drama reviews for local newspapers; she also published her first short story, "Peter," in a Boston magazine. She also wrote several stories that appeared in the college literary magazine.

Although discovering herself as writer, as a critic the young Cather declared that womanhood and art were incompatible. She wrote contemptuous dismissals of women writers and declared her fondness for the "manly" ideology of masculinity that was popular during the 1890s. "As a rule," she wrote, "if I see the announcement of a new book by a woman, I—well, I take one by a man instead. . . . I have noticed that the great masters of letters are men, and I prefer to take no chances when I read." Cather did acknowledge some exceptional women writers. She admired "the great Georges, George Eliot and George Sand, and they were anything but women, and there was Miss [Charlotte] Bronte who kept her sentimentality under control, and there was Jane Austen who certainly had more common sense than any of them and was in some respects the greatest of them all." Even here, however, Cather suggests that femininity and literary greatness are incompatible, since the "great Georges" were "anything but women." And her literary advice to young women writers reveals her connection of aesthetic excellence with masculine values: "When a woman writes a story of adventure, a stout sea tale, a manly battle yarn, anything without wine, women and love, then I will begin to hope for something great from them."

Among her friends and fellow students at the university were Dorothy Canfield (later Dorothy Canfield Fisher) and Louise Pound. Canfield became a novelist and judge for the Book-of-the-Month Club, and remained Cather's personal and literary confidante over the years. Cather's friendship with Pound was more important to her emerging romantic nature. Cather did not remain friends with Pound, who became a well-known folklorist and linguist, perhaps because this was a love relationship which, once broken, could not be repaired.

Although not all Cather's biographers and critics regard her as lesbian, some do, often approaching Cather's writing from the critical frameworks offered by feminist and queer theory. Some readers of Cather's fiction concentrate on her need to conceal her lesbian desire by writing heterosexual "cover" stories that hide the subversive homosexual subtext. These readers argue for example, that in *My Ántonia* the narrator, Jim Burden, is a mask for a female consciousness, and unable to develop or express his love for Ántonia because he is really a stand-in for the lesbian author. Certainly camouflage has a place in Cather's writing, but we need to be careful, as we explore the impact of concealment on her creative process, not to minimize her imaginative reach. Like all great writers, she possessed a creative imagination that allowed her to create a variety of characters different from herself; the connection between any writer's life and art is never simple or direct.

When she first began writing fiction in the 1890s, however, Willa Cather did not yet possess a great novelist's transformative power. Her apprenticeship fiction in general cannot be distinguished from the average fiction of the day. Many of her early stories are based on popular formulas or are derived more from her reading than from her own observations. Occasionally, however, signs of the mature Willa Cather appear, as in her first published story, "Peter," which was based on the first tragic tale Cather heard when she came to Nebraska: disheartened by a long, cold winter, Francis Sadilek, a Bohemian immigrant farmer, killed himself. Later Cather would rework "Peter" in describing the death of Mr. Shimerda in *My Ántonia*, but her first fiction has its own grim power: "In the morning Antone found him stiff, frozen fast in a pool of blood. They could not straighten him out enough to fit a coffin, so they buried him in a pine box."

## EARLY STORIES

Ironically enough—given her views of women's sentimental writing—Cather's first job was editing a woman's magazine, the Pittsburgh *Home Monthly,* which she took over in the summer of 1896. She did a good job, but still enjoyed satirizing the magazine's domestic content in her letters home: it was the worst trash in the world, she wrote a Lincoln friend, all babies and mince pies. During her ten years in Pittsburgh, she worked as editor, newspaper woman, and high school teacher of English and Latin. These were productive years, professionally and personally. Cather wrote book and drama reviews for the Lincoln and Pittsburgh papers, placed several short stories in national publications (among them *Scribner's, McClure's,* and *Cosmopolitan*), and in 1903 published a collection of poems—largely languid, imitative verse—called *April Twilights.* Her fiction caught the attention of the powerful S. S. McClure, editor of *McClure's* magazine, who published her short story collection *The Troll Garden* in 1905.

Some of the stories in *The Troll Garden* are in her Jamesian mode, such as "The Marriage of Phaedra" and "Flavia and Her Artists," in which the young writer shows off her familiarity with classical references and gives her two-dimensional characters stilted dialogue. (" 'I meant, madam,' said the novelist conservatively, 'intellectual in a sense very special, as we say of men in whom the purely intellectual functions seem almost independent.' ") But two stories with Western settings, "A Wagner Matinee" and "The Sculptor's Funeral," foreshadow Cather's return to her Nebraska material in *O Pioneers!*

In the brilliant "Paul's Case," Cather looks back at an earlier self—William Cather, Jr.—as she portrays another imaginative, sensitive youth at odds with a repressive society. Paul's enemy is Presbyterian Pittsburgh, an emotionally and aesthetically bankrupt world that he flees, preferring the fairy-tale beauty of the concert hall and theater. Forbidden these realms by his father and put to work as a bank messenger, Paul steals money to finance a trip to New York, the Waldorf, and the Metropolitan Opera, but he cannot escape "the tepid waters of Cordelia Street." "Paul's Case," the high-water mark of Cather's early fiction, reflects her training with such writers as Gustave Flaubert and Anton Chekhov. Long the favorite of critics, this was Cather's first choice as well, and in later years the only story she allowed to be anthologized.

Cather's maturing craft and steady productivity were owed in part to the happy domestic life she found in Pittsburgh. In 1899, she met Isabelle McClung, the daughter of a wealthy and prominent judge. The two women were drawn together by their shared interests in literature, the arts, and the theater. They began a lifelong intimacy; Isabelle remained the romantic love of Cather's life, even after they separated in 1916. In 1901, Cather began living with Isabelle and her family, and the McClung home became a nurturing space where she could combine intimacy with creativity, taking over an unused sewing room as a study and writing room.

Just as Isabelle fostered Cather's writing, so she helped her to reconcile creativity with womanhood. Isabelle was a beautiful, elegant woman who enjoyed wearing fine clothes as well as buying them for her friend. Under Isabelle's tutelage, Cather became more interested in elegant styles of women's dress. In later years Cather would purchase fabrics, furs, and hats from Bergdorf Goodman and have dresses custom-made. She preferred royal and theatrical clothing—velvets and silks, turbans and feathers, which became signs of female power to her.

## JEWETT'S ADVICE

In 1906, Cather accepted a job offer from S. S. McClure and moved to New York City to begin work at *McClure's* as a staff writer. In 1908, she became managing editor and began sharing an apartment with Edith Lewis, a Nebraska acquaintance who was working in advertising, although she made frequent trips back to Pittsburgh to stay with Isabelle. These were years of heady accomplishment during which Cather succeeded in the male world of publishing and journalism. But they were also years of exhaustion and eventual depression when she feared her literary powers, drained by the work of editing, were not maturing. Although she struck others as energetic, confident, and self-assured, she progressively felt depleted and unsure of her literary talents. Because her work involved securing and editing other people's manuscripts, she was enabling other people to write while she was silencing herself. McClure had ceased to flatter Cather as a fiction writer, suggesting to her that her true talents were in journalism—vocational wisdom that would keep her working for him.

In 1908, Cather wrote a discouraged and depressed letter to Sarah Orne Jewett, the Maine author of *The Country of the Pointed Firs,* who would be the maternal mentor of Cather's fiction. With all her energy absorbed by work she did not want to be doing, after a day in the office she simply did not have the resources to write, she told Jewett. She was in her thirties and should be a better fiction writer than she was—her literary talents, she feared, were declining, not advancing. (Cather decided to turn the clock back for her 1909 *Who's Who* entry, listing her birth date as 1875, as if that way she could give herself more time to develop as a writer.)

In December 1908, Jewett sent Cather the most important letter she ever received. "I think it became a permanent inhabitant of her thoughts," Edith Lewis observed. It is a wonderful letter—a letter of both encouragement and warning. The older writer was concerned that Cather's demanding work was impeding her literary development, and she had the delicate task of letting the younger woman know she was concerned about her literary growth without disheartening her.

My dear Willa,—
I have been thinking about you and hoping that things are going well. I cannot help saying what I think about your writing and its being hindered by such incessant, important, responsible work as you have in your hands now. I do think it is impossible for you to work so hard and yet have your gifts mature as they should. . . . In the "Troll-Garden" the Sculptor's Funeral stands alone a head higher than the rest, and it is to that level you must hold and take for a starting-point. You are older now than that book in general; you have been living and reading and knowing new types; but if you don't keep and guard and mature your force, and above all, have time and quiet to perfect your work, you will be writing things not much better than you did five years ago. This you are anxiously saying to yourself! but I am wondering how to get at the right conditions.

The "right conditions," Jewett thought, were a protective and nurturing solitude: "To work in silence and with all one's heart, that is the writer's lot; he is the only artist who must be a solitary, and yet needs the widest outlook on the world." So Jewett encouraged Cather to find a "quiet place near the best companions (not those who admire and wonder at everything one does, but those who know the good things with delight!)."

Jewett ended her letter with a lovely reassurance that could hearten any writer: she assured Cather that she had been "growing" even when she felt "most hindered." Later Cather would dedicate *O Pioneers!* to Jewett, acknowledging her maternal role in her literary emergence.

Cather took a leave of absence from the magazine in 1911 and spent three months in a quiet farmhouse in Cherry Valley, New York, with Isabelle McClung, always the guardian of her friend's creativity. There she revised the manuscript of what was to be her first novel, *Alexander's Bridge.* But this novel was still in her Jamesian mode, an "external" story, she said later, that did not spring from her deepest self.

In later years Cather liked to disown *Alexander's Bridge*, viewing it as a failed, conventional beginning. But she was too hard on her first work. Not only was the novel more self-expressive than she acknowledged, but also its acceptance for publication by Houghton Mifflin bolstered her self-confidence and helped her to take a creative risk with her next novel. The seeds of her Western fiction were already flowering during her Cherry Valley sojourn: "The Bohemian Girl" is a story of adulterous love and defiance of convention set on the Divide, its protagonists drawn from the immigrant groups who peopled Cather's home landscape. And "Alexandra," the story of a Swedish woman farmer, would lead directly into *O Pioneers!*.

### O PIONEERS!

Cather's restorative vacation at Cherry Valley, where she had found the "quiet center of life" Jewett had hoped for her, gave her the courage to take an even longer break from *McClure's* in 1912. She decided to take a journey to the Southwest, and this would be the turning point in her creative life.

While visiting her brother Douglass, exploring canyons and Indian cliff dwellings, hiking and camping, Cather spent a good deal of time with a young Mexican named Julio who told her local legends and myths and took her to the Painted Desert. Cather's letters to her friend Elizabeth Sergeant describing Julio show her romantic infatuation with him—they are joyous, glowing, exuberant. Later he would contribute to the portrait of Spanish Johnny in *The Song of the Lark*.

Cather was always captivated by the Southwest's desert landscape and the Indian cultures she found there. Like other writers and artists who gravitated to New Mexico and Arizona during the first decades of the twentieth century—the novelists D. H. Lawrence and Mary Austin, the pho-

tographer Laura Gilpin, the writer and literary figure Mabel Dodge Luhan—Cather admired Pueblo civilization. Communal, religious, and mystic, the Southwest Indians' culture seemed a healthy counterpoint to the increasing materialism and isolation of American life.

Cather was particularly moved by the pots and vessels the Indian women had shaped to hold grain and water. She felt inspired by "women who, under conditions of incredible difficulty and fear of enemies had still designed and molded . . . beautiful objects for daily use out of river-bottom clay." In the cliff-dweller's civilization, unlike her own, woman and artist were not conflicting identities. Following so soon after her creative inheritance from Sarah Orne Jewett, Cather's discovery of the Indian women potters strengthened her association of femaleness with creativity, and helped her to create the artist-heroines of her next two novels, Alexandra Bergson and Thea Kronborg.

On her way back East, Cather stopped off in Red Cloud to see friends and family. She was in time for the wheat harvest, a communal activity she had not witnessed in several years. She enjoyed this return to her homeland, soaking herself "in the scents, the sounds, the colours, of Nebraska, the old memories."

By October Cather was resettled in Isabelle McClung's house in Pittsburgh, ready to begin writing. Stories began to emerge that she had not planned, a sign that she was letting material emerge from her unconscious. She began a short story set in Nebraska called "The White Mulberry Tree," a tale of tragic love, and all of a sudden something seemed to explode inside her and this new story entwined itself with "Alexandra," the Cherry Valley story, giving her the novel she had not known she was going to write.

When she left Pittsburgh for New York she had a draft of *O Pioneers!* with her. Later Cather described this submission to her creative intuition as "the thing by which our feet find the road home on a dark night, accounting of themselves for roots and stones which we had never noticed by day." In composing *Alexander's Bridge*, Cather had consciously shaped the story, but this time she found she had "less and less power of choice" in determining the direction of her narrative: "It seem[ed] to be there of itself, already molded."

Even at the time, Cather knew this novel marked her breakthrough into literary originality. She sent a copy of *O Pioneers!* to her childhood friend Carrie Miner in Red Cloud, writing this inscription on the flyleaf:

> This was the first time I walked off on my own feet—everything before was half real and half an imitation of writers whom I admired. In this one I hit the home pasture and realized I was Yance Sorgeson and not Henry James.

The novel begins with a section called "The Wild Land," evoking the harshness of the Nebraska Divide in the 1880s, before white settlers have made their mark:

> The dwelling-houses were set about haphazard on the tough prairie sod; some of them looked as if they had been moved in overnight, and others as if they were straying off by themselves, headed straight for the open plain. None of them had any appearance of permanence, and the howling wind blew under them as well as over them. . . . But the great fact was the land itself, which seemed to overwhelm the little beginnings of human society that struggled in its sombre wastes.

Recalling the harsh landscape of "A Wagner Matinee" and her early *Troll Garden* stories—as well as the grim land "as bare as a piece of sheet iron" the young Cather confronted in 1883—this "disheartening" country is one where human beings have not been able to write their story:

> The roads were but faint tracks in the grass, and the fields were scarcely noticeable. The record of the plow was insignificant, like the feeble scratches in stone left by prehistoric races, so indeterminate that they may, after all, be only the markings of glaciers, and not a record of human strivings.

Cather begins her next section, "Neighboring Fields," after a sixteen-year gap. Now we see the cultivated, inscribed land:

> From the Norwegian graveyard one looks out over a vast checker-board, marked off in squares of wheat and corn; light and dark, dark and light. . . . From the graveyard gate one can count a dozen gayly painted farmhouses; the gilded weather-vanes on the big red barns wink at each other across the green and brown and yellow fields. . . . The Divide is now thickly populated.

Taking her title from Whitman's poem of settlement, "Pioneers! O Pioneers!," Cather tells the bold, epic story of emigration, westward expansion, and manifest destiny, and, despite her fascination with Southwestern native culture, fails to recognize that Nebraska was not a blank, uninscribed land before white settlement in the 1870s and 1880s. And yet hers is a story with a difference: to use Adrienne Rich's term, *O Pioneers!* is a "re-vision" of the male-authored American story of the pioneer experience. The novel's hero, and the person responsible for this transformation of the land is a woman, Alexandra Bergson—a woman who wants to work with the land rather than against it.

Alexandra's father does not succeed in his pioneer venture, Cather suggests, because he has no sympathy for Nebraska's landscape: he has come to conquer, not cultivate, and so he makes "little impression upon the wild land he had come to tame." Alexandra succeeds as a farmer because she combines traits her society divided between "female" and "male." Unlike her father and brothers, she loves the land, coming to sense poetry and beauty in its soil. Yet even while giving Alexandra a maternal, even erotic connection with the land, Cather grants her shrewd business sense and agricultural pragmatism. Alexandra experiments with new farming techniques, confers with other farmers, buys up the land others are deserting and expands her holdings. Alexandra's successful use of both "male" and "female" traits reflects

Cather's own challenging of the polarized gender identities.

If the novel had ended with Alexandra's success, it would have been interesting enough, a kind of feminist rewriting of the westward expansion story—the national myth that ascribed the creation of culture and the conquering of the frontier to men—and a reassessment of the violence and greed that often accompanied the land's settlement. But when Cather intertwined "The White Mulberry Tree" with "Alexandra," she produced an even richer, darker novel than that, complicating the American myth of progress with the tragic lovers' subplot.

Some of Cather's readers have criticized her for writing an episodic novel in which the lovers' subplot is imperfectly integrated into the whole, but she had good reasons for intertwining the two stories—both are stories about passion. Alexandra channels her passionate energies into the land; her younger brother Emil and Marie, the Bohemian wife of the disgruntled farmer Frank Shabata, channel theirs into romantic love, with disastrous results.

The novel ends on a muted note: Alexandra, grieving and depressed after the lovers' murder, will marry her childhood friend Carl Linstrum, but this is not the romantic ending of the sentimental women's fiction Cather disliked. "When friends marry, they are safe," Alexandra observes, and the reader is left wondering about the submerged emotions the protagonist is still guarding.

Alexandra's last words are unusual ones in an American novel of that era: "I am tired," she tells Carl. "I have been very lonely." Fatigue and loneliness are very much part of American life, but generally are not acknowledged by a protagonist at a novel's end. Cather, as the narrator, goes on to conclude her novel with a paean to the Nebraska Divide—"Fortunate country, that is one day to receive hearts like Alexandra's into its bosom, to give them out again the yellow wheat, in the rustling corn, in the shining eyes of youth!"—but

this odd spiritual recycling does not outweigh the sadness and loss with which Cather concludes Alexandra's story, and which give the novel its depth and resonance.

Cather's editor at Houghton Mifflin, Ferris Greenslet, was impressed with the novel and told his colleagues it would establish Cather as a "novelist of the first rank." Most reviewers agreed, singling out her use of American materials and settings. A *New York Times* critic praised Cather for creating a "new mythology" with this story of a "goddess of fertility" who is "American in the best sense of the word," and the Lincoln *Sunday State Journal* reviewer, Celia Harris, commended Cather's "extraordinary" and "beautiful" book, particularly applauding Cather's move from her denser, more convoluted early style to simple, unaffected prose.

In drawing on her own memory and imagination, Cather had indeed taken more command of the language, leaving her stilted Jamesian structure behind. Writing of her own country and people, she knew what words to use. When a college professor criticized Cather's use of the word "globule" instead of "dewdrop," Cather was not intimidated. She defended her choice "stoutly," remembered her friend Elizabeth Sergeant, saying that dewdrops "could be of several shapes," but only "globule" described the "firm round drop found on prairie grass."

### THE SONG OF THE LARK

Willa Cather never returned to the staff of *McClure's*. After *O Pioneers!* was published, she wrote a few freelance articles for the magazine and ghostwrote S. S. McClure's autobiography, which appeared in the magazine under his name with the acknowledgment "I wish to express my indebtedness to Miss Willa Sibert Cather for her invaluable assistance in the preparation of these memoirs." This was the last time Cather would publish something for which she did not receive full recognition.

One of Cather's freelance articles, "Three American Singers," gave her an idea for her next novel, *The Song of the Lark* (1915). Cather had long been interested in opera and considered the divas who dominated the stage the epitome of the female artist. She interviewed three of America's most famous divas—Louise Homer, Geraldine Farrar, and Olive Fremstad, a Swedish-born immigrant who had also grown up in the Midwest. Cather and Fremstad became friends, and the singer helped the writer to imagine the character of Thea Kronborg.

Cather sensed the connection between her own recent transition from the short story to the novel and Fremstad's bold decision to extend her vocal range from contralto to soprano—thereby preparing herself to take on opera's most central and dramatic female roles. Fremstad's strength was supposed to be in her lower tones, according to music critics, but she believed that the "Swedish voice is always long" and extended her upper range "tone by tone, without much encouragement." "I do not sing contralto or soprano," Fremstad told Cather. "I sing Isolde. What voice is necessary for the part, I will produce."

As the author of *O Pioneers!* who had also produced the voice she needed for the part, Cather delighted in the correspondences she saw between herself and Fremstad, as well as the similarities between Fremstad and the immigrant farm women she had known in childhood. In *The Song of the Lark*, Cather combined her story and Fremstad's in creating Thea, the singer who discovers the power of her voice after a liberating sojourn in the Southwest. The strongest autobiographical source for the novel, though, was the emergence of Cather's own voice as a writer in *O Pioneers!*: Cather's new self-confidence allowed her to see the parallels between herself and Fremstad, and in a sense *Song* is the story of Cather's creative journey to *O Pioneers!*

*The Song of the Lark* is a *künstlerroman*, the story of an artist's awakening to her own talent, traditionally a male story—but here the portrait is of the artist as a young woman. At the time Cather was writing her novel—the fall of 1914 and spring of 1915—she was exuberant and self-confident, telling Ferris Greenslet that she thought so well of her book that she had better not give him her opinion, but she knew he would not be publishing a novel like it every day.

In 1932, when Cather wrote a new preface for an English edition to the novel, she was less happy with it. *The Song of the Lark* is Cather's longest novel: she describes not only Thea's artistic emergence, but also devotes a lengthy section to her artistic life after she becomes an acclaimed opera singer. Cather felt she had made a mistake in doing so: "Success is never so interesting as struggle," she wrote, "not even to the successful." In the latter half of the novel, she acknowledged, her story becomes "paler," and she wished she had "disregarded conventional design" and ended the novel with Thea's discovery of her voice, rather than with her triumphs at the Metropolitan Opera. Later in her career Cather endorsed the values of understatement and suggestion—"the novel démeublé," or the unfurnished novel—and *The Song of the Lark* struck her as too heavily upholstered, given the sparer literary aesthetic she adopted.

Although the latter part of the novel, showing the professional success brought by Thea's spiritual revelation, is too naturalistically detailed, it does show Cather rewriting earlier patterns in American fiction that had kept "woman" and "artist" separated, or that had punished the woman artist with silence or death (as in Kate Chopin's *The Awakening*, published just sixteen years earlier). Cather was engaging in re-vision in *The Song of the Lark*, just as she had in *O Pioneers!*, creating a new story for the gifted female protagonist, suggesting the comfort she had attained in reconciling womanhood with art. Cather was well aware that she was writing an inspiring woman's story: she urged Ferris Greenslet to advertise the novel in women's colleges like Smith, Mount Holyoke, and Bryn Mawr, knowing that the students would admire Thea's defiant success.

Cather dedicated *The Song of the Lark* to Isabelle McClung, including a poem evoking the nurturing, creative space Isabelle had created for her in Pittsburgh, and in their relationship:

> On uplands,
> At morning,
> The world was young, the winds were free;
> A garden fair,
> In that blue desert air,
> Its guest invited me to be.

But shortly after the novel was published, Isabelle's father died, the Pittsburgh house was sold, and Cather lost both a home and a creative sanctuary. She liked her New York apartment, she told a friend, but it did not feel like home in the way Isabelle's house did—a safe, protected space. Then, a few months later, came even more terrible news: Isabelle announced her upcoming marriage to violinist Jan Hambourg. Cather at first was devastated by this apparently unexpected turn of events. Writing to her friend Dorothy Canfield, she said that the change in her life was irrevocable, the loss overwhelming. When she talked with Elizabeth Sergeant about Isabelle's marriage, her eyes were "vacant," her face "bleak." "All her natural exuberance had drained away," Sergeant remembered.

The winter of 1915–1916 was grim: marked by the "loss of old friends by death and even by marriage," Cather admitted to a friend. Isabelle's marriage was a kind of death. Throughout the winter and spring Cather remained grieving and depressed. She had an idea for a new novel—a novel that would become *My Ántonia*—but she had no interest or desire to begin it. Her creative force seemed as vacant as Nebraska's winter landscape would to Jim Burden.

In the summer of 1916 she traveled west, staying in New Mexico—always a landscape of renewal for her—and visiting her brother Roscoe in Wyoming. Isabelle's marriage was still hard, she wrote a friend, but the rest of the world was still there. Then she returned to Red Cloud for several months, feeling that she had left the grim winter of her soul behind in the Rockies. In Red Cloud she renewed attachments to family and friends, including Annie Sadilek—once one of the "hired girls" who had worked for American-born families, now a farm woman with several children, and the inspiration for Cather's next novel.

## MY ÁNTONIA

When Cather returned to New York in the fall of 1916, *My Ántonia* was ready to emerge, and she wrote steadily and well for several months. Then she found a new summer retreat to replace Pittsburgh—the Shattuck Inn in Jaffrey, New Hampshire. She and Edith Lewis spent several weeks there in the summer of 1917. Cather pitched a tent in a friend's meadow, and this became the morning retreat where she wrote.

*My Ántonia* was the most aesthetically daring novel Willa Cather had yet written. In returning to memories of her childhood and youth in Nebraska, she crafted a novel that was experimental in both form and content. "I knew I'd ruin my material if I put it in the usual fictional pattern," Willa Cather said. *My Ántonia* is a drama of memory. Narrated by Jim Burden—who, like Cather, was transplanted in childhood from Virginia to Nebraska—the novel tells the story of Ántonia Shimerda, the Bohemian immigrant girl who preoccupies Jim's imagination throughout his life.

Retrospectively narrated, the novel evokes the intensity of his frontier childhood and of Ántonia's vitality, but always with a sense of loss, for Jim has not found emotional or spiritual fulfillment in his adult life. Because, according to Cather's narrative design, Jim not only narrates but also *writes* the story we read, we sense that for Jim loss is a spark for creativity.

During the act of recalling Ántonia and "the country, the conditions, the whole adventure of our childhood," the past comes alive for Jim, as he often tells us. "I can remember exactly how the country looked to me," he says, and "All the years that have passed have not dimmed my memory of that first glorious autumn." Phrases like "I can see them now" or "they are with me still" recur throughout the novel. "They were so much alive in me," Jim says, speaking of the memories of Black Hawk friends that remain vivid after he has left for Lincoln, "that I scarcely stopped to wonder whether they were alive anywhere else, or how."

Like memory, which is a collection of separate and sometimes unconnected images, *My Ántonia* is told through vignettes (sometimes widely separated in time), inset stories, and word pictures that, taken as a whole, make up a photograph album of the past. There is no conventional love story (Ántonia deserved better than that *Saturday Evening Post* treatment, Cather said), no linear dramatic action, no single conflict and resolution.

While early readings of the novel tended to view it as an elegiac, nostalgic narrative of the frontier, later readings have taken account of the novel's darker, more disturbing material—such as the suicide of Mr. Shimerda, Peter and Pavel's story of the bride fed to the wolves, Wick Cutter's attempted rape of Jim (posing as Ántonia), Ántonia's seduction and "disgrace" as an unwed mother, Jim's erotic fantasy of Lena carrying a "curved reaping hook," and, winding its way through the novel, the sexual allure of the working-class, immigrant "hired girls" who distract Black Hawk's middle-class young men.

Some critics see sexual fear underlying the novel, pointing to the fact that Jim, although preoccupied with Ántonia and Lena, never achieves a satisfactory sexual and emotional relationship with either one. Others see the novel as a feminist critique of male-authored stories and myths about women, pointing out that Jim, as the narrator, has the power to silence the female characters and to represent them in limiting ways. His celebration of Ántonia as a stereotypic Earth Mother, a "rich mine of life" who produced "sons that stood tall and straight" is an example of his restricted representation of the women in the novels. Still other readers see Cather as perpetuating, rather than challenging, limiting male views of women. And others regard Cather as the lesbian writer who uses Jim as the unconvincing mask to hide her own desire.

*My Ántonia* has attracted such contradictory interpretations because of its unusual narrative structure. In contrast to Cather's three previous novels, which were all narrated in the third person, *My Ántonia* has a first-person narrator, Jim Burden, who not only tells the story but also *writes* it. We find out that he is the author in the unusual preface, in which an unnamed narrator—a writer who is assumed by most critics to be a stand-in for Willa Cather—meets Jim Burden on a train. The narrator and Jim are childhood acquaintances and "old friends," having grown up in the same Nebraska town, and their conversation drifts back to "a central figure, a Bohemian girl whom we had known long ago and whom both of us admired. . . . To speak her name was to call up pictures of people and places, to set a quiet drama going in one's brain." At the end of the trip, the two agree to write down their memories of Ántonia, and months later Jim brings the narrator his manuscript. "My own story was never written," the narrator of the preface tells us, "but the following narrative is Jim's manuscript, substantially as he brought it to me."

The narrative ambiguities here, given the autobiographical nature of the novel, are intense. Are we supposed to think that the narrative reflects Jim's views, and so are we to distinguish Cather from her narrator? Or is Cather to be identified with Jim? And just what does "substantially" mean: has the narrator of the preface, who can be read as Cather, made editorial alterations that we are supposed to catch? Because critics' decisions about authorial distance have varied so much—some believing that Cather is identified with Jim, others that she is ironically distant—they have constructed such contradictory readings.

My own view is that Cather's authorial distance wavers in this narrative: at times she seems merged with Jim, as when he evokes the beauty of the Nebraska landscape; at times she is the author self-consciously detaching herself from a fictional character with limited, unreliable views. This complex relationship between author and narrator gives us a novel that is rich with ambiguity and that yields no simple or unified interpretation.

In addition to the biographical details they share—the Virginia homeland, the Nebraska childhoods, the move East in adult life—Jim and Cather are most similar in the sources of their creativity—loss, change, memory. "Some memories are better than anything that will happen to you again," Jim says, and many of his memories, like Cather's, are the stories he recalls, and shapes, from his past. In addition to the novel Cather creates and the story Jim writes, there are several inset stories—the Bohemian folktales Ántonia tells; the story of Pavel and Peter that she tells him; the Widow Steavens' narrative of Ántonia's romantic betrayal; the stories Ántonia and her children tell while they are looking at photographs of the past. Without loss and absence, the novel suggests, these stories would not come into being.

Of all her fiction, *My Ántonia* was the novel about which Cather cared the most deeply; she invested herself from the start in the book's production, stating her preferences for the colors of the cover and the book jacket, the typeface, the weight of the paper. Even more important, she commissioned a series of line drawings from the Bohemian artist W. T. Benda to illustrate her manuscript, and fought to keep them in the text when Houghton Mifflin balked at the price. She also gave her publisher strict instructions about design and placement, and when Houghton Mifflin dropped the illustrations for a cheap 1930 reprint, Cather considered this an unauthorized edition. Later she fought to keep her novel out of paperback and away from the movies: she did not want mass production to cheapen "her" Ántonia.

In her correspondence with Greenslet over the next several years, much of it concerned with defending the novel's integrity, Cather invariably refers to *My Ántonia* as "she" rather than "it." Her novel appears in these letters as a living, breathing woman, vulnerable to being exploited by a publisher who views her as a commercial object. She was particularly outraged when Houghton Mifflin wanted to publish excerpts from the novel in an anthology and produced a reduced text for classroom use—such cutting and packaging was a brutal trade, she told Greenslet, and in 1938 she won his agreement to continue protecting Ántonia's integrity.

### ONE OF OURS

Houghton Mifflin's stinginess with the Benda illustrations—they agreed to pay only for eight, not the twelve Cather wanted—convinced her that it was time to leave her publisher. Like many authors, at first Cather was thrilled to be published by such a venerable house, but soon came to feel that her work was not being sufficiently promoted, advertised, and valued. As good reviews accrued for *O Pioneers!* and *The Song of the Lark*, she thought Houghton Mifflin was refusing to acknowledge her growing literary stature, a belief not dispelled when her editor told her that *My Ántonia* might have significant sales as a children's book.

Cather's growing belief in the literary power and commercial potential of her fiction led her to leave Greenslet and Houghton Mifflin after the publication of *My Ántonia* for Alfred A. Knopf, who was just starting a new publishing company. In Knopf, Cather found a man who believed that novels should be beautifully designed, aesthetically rich, and commercially successful; like Cather, he did not see why art and financial reward should be contradictory. Cather's confidence in her new publisher was justified: throughout the 1920s and 1930s her satisfaction with the appearance and marketing of her novels increased along with their sales and her royalties. *My Ántonia* had been published in 1918 in a first edition of only 3,500 copies, and Cather earned only $1,300 in the first year of publication, $400 in the second. In September 1922, by contrast, Knopf published *One of Ours* in an edition of 15,000 copies; 40,500 copies were in print by November. The following year Cather earned $19,000 in royalties, quite a sum for 1923.

In the fall of 1920, Knopf published *Youth and the Bright Medusa*, a short story collection that included the *Troll Garden* stories—with some revisions—as well as four new stories with New York settings. Meanwhile Cather was working on a manuscript she called *Claude*. When she finished it a year later, she reluctantly agreed with Knopf's suggestion that it be retitled *One of Ours.*

In *One of Ours* (1922), Willa Cather took the risk of writing a war novel, inspired not by her former advice to write a "manly battle yarn," but by loss—the novel originated in the death of her nephew G. P. Cather, killed in 1918 at Catigny. After reading his letters to his mother Cather felt compelled to tell his story; as she wrote her friend Dorothy Canfield, she felt a kind of blood-identity with her nephew, and she spent the next four years in what she later termed a perfect companionship with the novel's protagonist Claude Wheeler, an imaginative rendering both of her nephew and of a male figure whom she came to regard as her other self. Some of her was buried with her nephew in France, she told Canfield, and some of him was living in her. Given her psychic bond with her fallen nephew, Cather felt that she pos-

sessed the authority, as well as the inspiration, to invade male literary territory and write a war novel. Although she knew this was a problematic genre for a woman writer, she felt claimed by her subject, claimed by a story that demanded to be told.

Her nephew, who had seemed to her to be a discontented country boy, found dignity and purpose in his death, she thought—testimony to the transforming power of war. David Hochstein, a young violinist whom she knew slightly, likewise seemed to have been mysteriously ennobled by his experience in battle. After reading Hochstein's letters to his mother, published after the war, Cather observed that "something very revolutionary had happened in Hochstein's mind; I would give a good deal to know what it was!"

*One of Ours* was in part inspired by Cather's desire to "know what it was" that happened to her nephew and soldiers like Hochstein. In addition to reading her nephew's and Hochstein's letters to their mothers, she had many conversations with returned soldiers, some of whom she interviewed in the hospital, some of whom she invited to her Bank Street apartment; and, one summer in Jaffrey, she came across a military doctor's journal that became the source of book 4, "The Voyage of the *Anchises.*"

Although as a woman and a civilian Cather was removed from the experience of war, her letters to Dorothy Canfield show how strongly she identified with G. P. Cather and, by extension, with the American soldier. In addition to describing her sense of empathy with her nephew, Cather stressed their shared dislike of Nebraska's constricted life and desire for escape. She invested Claude with her own desire to flee bourgeois oppression, her distaste for materialism, and her quest for authentic, creative selfhood. Cather did not feel that by augmenting her character with her own motivations she was falsifying the experience of her cousin or other American farm boys who believed they would play more exciting parts in the theater of war than in the fields at home.

Although Cather won the Pulitzer Prize in 1923 for *One of Ours,* it is not her best novel, and has attracted criticism from male writers and critics who found the novel to be a woman writer's romanticized, inauthentic view of modern combat.

But such critics of the novel miss an antiromantic subtext: scattered around the margins, among the minor characters we find weakness, infantilization, disease, amputation, and dismemberment as Cather surrounds Claude with disfigured and mutilated men. Near the end of the novel Cather introduces her most grotesque image of dismemberment, the hand of a German corpse that keeps reaching out of the earth, refusing to stay buried.

The imagery of mutilation undercuts the surface plot of heroic masculinity, and may also have reflected Cather's awareness that she was a woman writer venturing into hostile literary territory. Throughout her life Cather associated creative power with the hand—she wrote all her drafts by hand, employing a secretary to type them for her, in turn correcting typed drafts by hand. Yet she frequently suffered from pain and paralysis in her right hand, which at times prevented her from writing. Images of mutilation in her fiction frequently occurred at times of professional and personal stress, so the soldiers lacking fingers, hands, and arms that we find in the margins of the text may not just reflect the realities of war, but also the woman author's anxiety about attempting the male-defined genre of the war novel.

Cather had anticipated criticism before the novel came out, and in a letter to Canfield imagined rescuing Claude from the text. Even if the book fell down, she told Canfield, she would want to save Claude: he could jump from the book as from a burning building, and she would catch him in a blanket. All her letters to Canfield reveal her deep emotional connection with Claude: when she finished proofreading, she wrote, she felt as if she were putting away a dead lad's things.

She was distressed by negative reviews: she had been deeply involved with this novel, with Claude, and with G. P. Cather and the American soldier. The Pulitzer, welcome as it was, did not fully make up for the criticism. In the summer of 1923, Cather went to France to visit Isabelle and her husband, hoping to work on a new novel, but she suffered a painful attack of neuritis in her right arm and shoulder and was unable to write.

## *A LOST LADY* AND *THE PROFESSOR'S HOUSE*

In 1922 Cather published "The Novel Démeublé," (the unfurnished novel) in the *New Republic,* her statement of aesthetic principles of selection and refinement that would guide all her later fiction: "Out of the teeming, gleaming stream of the present [the novel] must select the eternal material of art."

*A Lost Lady,* published in the fall of 1923, was such a novel. It tells the story of the charm, decline, and resilience of Marian Forrester, the "lost lady" of the title, wife of Sweet Water, Nebraska's captain of industry, the banker Captain Forrester. The novel is narrated in the third person, but located squarely in the center of consciousness of Niel Herbert, a local boy who becomes entranced with Marian's magical grace. Niel's narrative presence is not always reliable. Some readers of the novel have assumed Cather's identification with Niel's perspective—in particular, when he links Marian Forrester's decline, after her husband's death, into sexual and economic dependence on the evil realtor Ivy Peters with the decline of the West from pioneer splendor to commercial squalor.

But such readings do not take into account the irony with which Cather surrounds the romantic, rhapsodizing Niel, showing us how his seemingly pure worship of his "lady" conceals a sexual urge he does not acknowledge. When he embarks on a morning pilgrimage to Marian's bedroom, carrying flowers as a sacred offering, Cather surrounds him with an eroticized nature—"wild roses, with flaming buds, just beginning to open"—that tells the reader the story of his unconscious yearnings. When Niel, holding his bouquet of "half awake" roses finds his lost lady, half awake, in bed with her lover Frank Ellinger and throws the roses into the mud, thinking "Grace, variety, the lovely voice . . . all this was nothing," we are not supposed to join him in his castigation of Marian, but to see how, in his limited emotional repertoire, he has turned the virgin into the whore.

In contrast to the heroines of Cather's pioneer novels who did devote themselves to what she called "something complete and great" *My Ánto-nia*—the land, art, the family—Marian Forrester seems weaker, given her dependence on men's economic protection, and Cather seems to be retreating from an earlier, more feminist, stance. But in fact she was enlarging her canvas and her sympathies. Her later novels, beginning with *A Lost Lady*, show her ability to understand the mixture of power and dependence in women who could not leave the marriage plot behind, women more like her mother than like herself.

Throughout 1924 Cather was hard at work on *The Professor's House*, a novel drawing on her experience of the Southwest as well as her own entrance into mid-life. She turned fifty in 1923, and her protagonist, Godfrey St. Peter, is trapped in what we would now call a mid-life depression, a time when the structures and relationships that have defined him have lost their savor and yet he is unable to move on.

Published in 1925, *The Professor's House* reflects Cather's penchant for narrative experimentation. The novel is structured like a triptych. The first section, "The Family," describes the professor's reluctance to leave the comfortable house where he and his wife have raised their family and where he has written his books in an attic study. His thoughts keep going back to Tom Outland, his brilliant and charismatic student who was killed in

the war, and with whom he seems to have shared the most profound relationship of his life. In the second section, Outland's diary tells the story of the summer he spent on the Blue Mesa in Colorado in the cliff-dweller ruins. Cather wanted this section—set in the light and air and space of the Southwest, in sharp contrast to the professor's dark, enclosed study and confining life—to open her novel outward, letting the fresh air from the Blue Mesa blow away the cobwebs and the trivialities. In the final section, Godfrey St. Peter reminisces in his attic study, drawn by the lure of Tom Outland's memory and the freer aspirations of his own younger self. He forgets to turn off an old, defective gas heater and falls asleep, nearly dying from the fumes. He is rescued by the housekeeper, Augusta, a primal woman of the earth. Cather then gives *The Professor's House* an unusual ending for an American novel: the protagonist is neither renewed nor destroyed, but accepts his need to live "without delight," and lets go of his yearning for passionate intensity, whether joy or grief.

Some critics of the novel find its three-part structure unsuccessful, finding "Tom Outland's Story" to be an unintegrated disruption. But Tom's evocation of the cliff-dwellers' houses reminds the reader of what the professor's contemporary American life is missing—houses that were homes, meant for shelter, not status, and grouped together to signify and create community.

## DEATH COMES FOR THE ARCHBISHOP

Both *A Lost Lady* and The *Professor's House* show Cather more and more concerned with the issues of the second half of life—not with issues of achievement, but with issues of meaning. Cather followed this direction in her novella *My Mortal Enemy* (1926), a sharp, bleak little book that gives us a woman who believes, too late in life for change, that she has taken the wrong path. Myra

Henshawe eloped with a German "freethinker" and was disinherited by her wealthy uncle. When she is old and ill, living in a shabby rented apartment, she regrets her choices: "It's been the ruin of us both," she tells her still-devoted husband. "We've destroyed each other. I should have stayed with my uncle. It was money I needed. We've thrown our lives away." In *My Mortal Enemy* Cather delivers the death-blow to the sentimental love plot perpetuated by nineteenth-century women writers: the fairy-tale story of courtship and marriage that ended, always, happily. Here Cather begins her story years after the ending of the romance and shows her heroine suffering the consequences of a romantic gesture—all very well when she was young, but not satisfying when she is old. The stories that give hope in the first half of life, Cather suggests, may not be adequate for the second.

At this time Cather was encountering the dark fact that while the first half of life ends, if we are lucky, in some sort of individual accomplishment, whether marriage, motherhood, or professional success, the second half of life ends in death. In 1926 she spent time with her sick mother in Red Cloud, and although her mother did not die for five more years, the long process of her decline had begun. Cather was now fifty-three, and in her mother's illness she could see foreshadowed her own death. In 1922 she and her parents had been confirmed in the Episcopal Church in Red Cloud (the family had been Baptist) and Cather grew more and more interested in the ways in which the Catholic Church had preserved spiritual stories over time, stories that offered people a meaningful connection to something larger than the self.

In 1925, when she was staying in Santa Fe, Cather came across a rare book, *The Life of the Right Reverend Joseph P. Machebeuf* by a priest named William Howlett. Father Machebeuf had been the boyhood friend and co-worker of Archbishop John Baptist Lamy, the first Roman Catholic bishop of New Mexico, and his biography told the story of the missionary priests in the Southwest. The discovery of this book—like the intertwining of "Alexandra" and "The White Mulberry Tree"—was an inner catalyst, sparking Cather's growing interest in matters spiritual. She stayed up late reading Howlett's book and by the next day she could see the design of *Death Comes for the Archbishop* in her mind. "Without these letters in Father Howlett's book to guide me, I would certainly never have dared to write my book," she said later. Writing her book, returning to the purity and danger of pioneer times, was like "going back and playing the early composers after a surfeit of modern music." In a sense, *Death Comes for the Archbishop* was an open window—as if Cather wanted to dwell, for an extended period, in the bracing spiritual landscape of "Tom Outland's Story."

The novel itself is like a series of saints' legends, lacking the principles of conflict and resolution thought essential to the novel. The greatest mystery in this novel is not human motivation, but the link between the visible and invisible worlds; Cather returns to an earlier time when even the land is read spiritually, when signs are taken for wonders. When the Bishop is taking a solitary journey by horseback through the red hills of New Mexico, he comes upon a juniper in the shape of a cross. Understanding it to be a message from God, he concludes that it is time to pray.

If the novel can be said to have a plot, it is the plot of a spiritual Western—the bishop gradually brings the order and civilization of European Catholicism to this land of mixed cultures, a transformation signified by the building of his French-inspired cathedral in Santa Fe. And yet this novel, like *My Ántonia*, has elements of unintegrated darkness, suggesting Cather's awareness that Native American religions and cultures are not so easily erased by Catholicism, the religion of the colonizers. We see this subterranean resistance to spiritual colonization most clearly in the "Stone Lips" sequence, when the archbishop and his Indian guide Jacinto take refuge in a cave to escape a blizzard. The archbishop feels uncomfortable in this underground refuge, which is, he suspects, a chamber used by the Indians for "pagan" rituals. As in *My Ántonia*, Cather is interested in what stories are told, and what stories are silenced. The stories told by Native American religions are literally driven underground by the triumph of the archbishop's cathedral, and the economic, social, and religious power it signifies.

But this observation of the silencing power of a dominant religion itself seems underground in the novel. Cather did not consciously set out to remind us of the stories that were lost by the victories of the missionary priests; the story of Jacinto's cave seems a tale told by her unconscious, and it is not fully integrated into the novel. This subversive undercurrent only makes *Death Comes for the Archbishop* more interesting and complex, riven with chasms and fissures like the New Mexico soil itself. "Trust the tale, not the teller" is D. H. Lawrence's guide to reading American literature, and this dictum seems especially helpful in the case of this novel.

*Death Comes for the Archbishop* was published by Knopf in September 1927, the fifth novel Cather had completed since her move to Knopf in 1922. Her new publisher nourished her creativity, but equally important was the supportive life that she and Edith Lewis had fashioned together. After Isabelle McClung's marriage, Cather shared more and more of her life with Lewis. The two developed a social life as a couple, hosting Friday afternoon open houses at their Bank Street apartment. Gradually, Bank Street became the creative sanctuary Cather needed, and Lewis the companion to her creativity, accompanying her on summer writing sojourns in Jaffrey, and later to the cottage Cather had built on Grand Manan Island. Lewis was the ideal writer's partner—supportive when needed, deferential to her friend's talent, offering

her companionship as well as "solitude without loneliness."

### ART AND POLITICS

*Death Comes for the Archbishop* gained glowing reviews, but Cather did not have long to relish them. The next few years would be hard ones, marked by death and loss and grieving. In the summer of 1927 her father suffered a heart attack, and he died in March of 1928. At the same time Cather's apartment building on Bank Street was torn down to make room for a subway, and she and Edith Lewis moved to the Grosvenor Hotel on Fifth Avenue, a move intended to be temporary but one that lasted for five years. Then, near the end of 1928, her mother had a stroke that left her partially paralyzed. During the spring of 1929 Cather stayed with her mother in Long Beach, California, and she found it painful and sad to be with this once-powerful woman, now dependent and speechless. She tried to work on *Shadows on the Rock*, but found it hard to concentrate. She was beginning to feel, she told Dorothy Canfield, a good deal like a ghost. Her mother died in August 1931; a month later, *Shadows on the Rock* was published. Reviews were unenthusiastic, but sales reached 160,000 by Christmas.

Although *Shadows* is set in seventeenth-century Quebec, the central relationship—between the apothecary Euclide Auclair and his daughter Cécile—evokes Cather's lost bond with her father. At the same time we see her reflecting on the power of mother-daughter inheritance in Cécile's fidelity to her dead mother's housekeeping traditions, "all the little shades of feeling which make the common fine." The French settlers in Quebec have much in common with Cather's Nebraska pioneers and artists: they too are bringing their culture to a remote, inhospitable place, keeping alive the past through story, legend, and ritual. Given Cather's interest in cultural continuity and emotional connection, the recipes Cécile's mother passes on have as much weight in maintaining civilization as do the legends of the martyrs.

Many of Cather's reviewers, however, were not pleased with her juxtaposition of domestic and religious ritual, what Lionel Trilling termed her "mystical concern with pots and pans." Although Cather's novels continued to be praised in journals such as *Saturday Review* and *Commonweal*, during the 1930s they found increasing disfavor with left-wing critics who believed that art should grapple with the stern social, political, and economic realities of the time. Newton Arvin complained in *The New Republic* that Cather wrote as if "mass production and technological unemployment and the struggle between the classes did not exist" and so she failed to "come to grips with the real life of her time."

Such attacks on Cather reflect a conflict over art and politics: her critics were judging her work using a 1930s standard of politically correct writing, one that Cather ignored. Sexual politics were also at work: her critics were male, and throughout the 1930s and 1940s they not only referred to her as a "feminine" writer, as if that made her second-rate. They also established a set of metaphoric equivalences among "feminine," "romantic," and "small," a circle of associations that led them, seemingly inevitably, from "woman" to "minor."

Faced with such criticism, Cather could have tried to please the reviewers and write against her own grain. But she kept to her own course, as Sarah Orne Jewett might have advised. In 1932 she published *Obscure Destinies*, a collection of three lovely Nebraska stories that are among her best writing. One of them, "Old Mrs. Harris," is the most autobiographical story Cather ever wrote. In this story, concerned with the legacy of love and power and misunderstanding that connects a grandmother, mother, and daughter, Cather portrays her female relatives, and her own younger self, with compassion and reflective understanding. Doubtless prompted by her mother's death,

the story shows Cather coming to terms with her own past.

In the fall of 1932 Cather and Lewis finally moved from the Grosvenor Hotel to an apartment on Park Avenue, and Cather was happy to be reunited with all the belongings she had kept in storage for five years. Shortly after they moved in their former French housekeeper came back to cook for them: "It was like beginning to really live again," Lewis recalled. Soon after they were settled, Alfred and Blanche Knopf gave Cather a phonograph and she bought dozens of records, enjoying this return to the pleasures of music. "Perhaps it was in part the happiness of living again in an atmosphere of music—she heard scarcely any music during the Grosvenor period—that gave Cather the theme of *Lucy Gayheart*," Edith Lewis speculates. Cather's story of a musically gifted young girl who subordinates her talent to her romantic infatuation with a famous singer seems like a pale revisiting of *The Song of the Lark*. Cather began writing the novel in a state of fatigue and "she did not attack it with any great vigour or enthusiasm," Lewis remembers, and *Lucy Gayheart* does read like a novel she decided to write rather than one she *had* to write. The novel was published in 1935, a difficult year for Cather— Isabelle McClung Hambourg, ill with a kidney disease, was in New York for medical treatment, and Cather devoted most of her time to her ailing friend, who did not have long to live.

### SAPPHIRA AND THE SLAVE GIRL

Cather was now in her late sixties, not sure how much longer she would live herself and thinking about beginnings and endings. Perhaps inevitably, her imagination began to drift back to her Virginia origins. In the spring of 1938 she visited her childhood home in Black Creek with Edith Lewis. The trip had a particular poignancy, Lewis remembers, as if Cather were seeing into the past itself. Willow Shade, her old home, had become "so ruinous and forlorn that she did not go into it," but this sad transformation, "instead of disheartening her, seemed to light a fierce inner flame that illumined all her pictures of the past." When she returned to New York, the story of *Sapphira and the Slave Girl*, her only novel set in Virginia, came flooding out. "She could have written two or three *Sapphiras* out of her material," Lewis recalls, "and in fact she did write, in her first draft, twice as much as she used. She always said it was what she left out that counted."

More deaths and losses blocked her progress on the novel—her brother Douglass and Isabelle McClung Hambourg both died in October 1938. But Cather kept working, finding it even more urgent to listen to the lost voices of the past. Knopf published *Sapphira and the Slave Girl* on December 6, 1940, Cather's sixty-seventh birthday.

Set in 1850s Virginia, the novel concerns the tangled relationships among a group of women— a slaveholding mother, her daughter, and the slave girl whose escape the daughter aids. Reading the novel now, when we are attuned to questions of race and gender, we can see how daring a novel *Sapphira* was for its time, as well as the ways in which Cather still perpetuates demeaning racial stereotypes. But in the face of her critics Cather was publishing a novel centered on women and set in the nineteenth century, a decision she must have known would not please the left-wing reviewers.

The independence Cather showed in writing *Sapphira* during her decade of trouble with critics is evident also in the novel's unusual form. This apparently conventional historical novel ends with an unusual epilogue. Instead of continuing the novel's fiction, the epilogue is a personal essay in which Cather tells the story of the real-life event that gave rise to her novel—the reunion she, as a child, had witnessed between an African American mother and daughter. The daughter had

escaped from slavery, fleeing to Canada, and in the late 1870s the young Cather was present when the daughter returned and saw her mother for the first time in more than fifteen years.

In a sense, Cather ends her last novel by telling, in her own voice, the story of her creative process: the childhood memory of a mother-daughter reunion giving rise to her last novel. This mixing of the genres of fiction and memoir, although common today, was unusual in 1940. And because Cather was criticized for being too limited and feminine, it was also a daring move to end her novel with a self-exposing autobiographical narrative. Yet it seemed to her that her fiction demanded a personal conclusion, and she did what she felt her material required.

THE FORMER HALF

"The world broke in two in 1922 or thereabouts," Willa Cather once said, saying she belonged to the "former half." She was referring to her increasing distaste for a modernizing American culture that she found materialistic and soulless. But if we take the phrase another way, it can help us understand the difference between the first and the second halves of Cather's life, as well as the shift in her fiction that began with *A Lost Lady*, her first novel published after the turning point in 1922.

During the first half of life, she was living what we might call the child's story. Looking ahead toward individual accomplishment, she saw life as an ascending curve, seemingly without end, or ending in the drama of personal success. But once Cather entered the second half of life—a period that began after Isabelle's marriage in 1916 and became entrenched in the early 1920s—she recognized that the end of life was not individual accomplishment but the obliteration of the self in death. Earlier novels like *O Pioneers!*, *The Song of the Lark*, and—to an extent—*One of Ours* tell versions of the hero's plot: linear, chronological narratives in which a sensitive individual triumphs over limiting circumstances. But beginning with *A Lost Lady*, Cather was telling more muted, darker stories, creating novels in which individual achievement is far more qualified. Myra Henshawe faces a lonely and poverty-ridden old age; Godfrey St. Peter resigns himself to a limited domestic existence; the archbishop does not live to see his cathedral built.

But Cather's later novels in a way are more satisfying than her early ones, which partake too much of the American myth of progress. Her later novels acknowledge the darkness that is part of human life but they also celebrate the light—the human ability to make meaning from experience, often in the form of stories. Stories take many guises in Cather's fiction: they can be the simple conversations farm people have with each other; the myths and religions that structure the worlds of Native Americans, Mexicans, and Anglos in New Mexico; the rituals of cooking and housekeeping that are passed down from mother to daughter in Quebec; the music that inspires Lucy Gayheart; and the inherited folktales and legends that Cather received from the old women in Virginia that underlie *Sapphira and the Slave Girl*.

There are common threads, however, that weave together Cather's more optimistic early fiction and her darker later fiction. Dorothy Canfield Fisher declared that the theme of all Cather's work was escape, and Cather agreed. By "escape" the two writers meant transcendence, or the escape from limiting circumstances to a purer realm of spirit and meaning. What Cather meant by "escape" is perhaps best expressed in *Death Comes for the Archbishop*. Cather is describing Archbishop Latour's love for the air of desert countries—dry, light air that one "could breathe only on the bright edges of the world, on the great grass plains or the sage-brush desert." The desert air for the archbishop is what the creative process was for

Willa Cather—a force larger than the self, into which the soul expands.

> That air would disappear from the whole earth in time, perhaps; but long after his day. He did not know just when it had become so necessary to him, but he had come back to die in exile for the sake of it. Something soft and wild and free, something that whispered to the ear on the pillow, lightened the heart, softly, softly, picked the lock, slid the bolts, and released the prisoned spirit of man into the wind, into the blue and gold, into the morning, into the morning!

Willa Cather's last years, which coincided with the outbreak of World War II, were not easy ones. Subject to failing health, the deaths of family and friends, painful neuritis in her right arm, fearing for the survival of European civilization, she confessed to a friend that sometimes she just did not want to live in the world. She could only write infrequently, given the pain in her right arm. Dictating was impossible: she needed the physical act of writing in order to see the pictures the words made. Trying to dictate a novel, she said, was like trying to play solitaire without looking at the cards.

But she and Edith Lewis maintained some of the old rhythms of their life together. They could not travel to Grand Manan during World War II, so they spent summers at the Asticou Inn at Northeast Harbor, Maine, sharing a "charming cottage" with a fireplace. It often rained torrents, Lewis remembered, but Cather was happy to sit by the fire and read.

During this last period Cather's life was diminished, as it is for most people in old age. But she still could take satisfaction from small pleasures. As Lewis recalled,

> In the last year, it was the little things one lived in; the pleasure of flowers; of a letter from an old friend in Red Cloud, the flying visit of a young niece . . . the glory of great poetry, filling all the days. She turned

almost entirely to Shakespeare and Chaucer that last winter, as if in their company she found her greatest content, best preferred to confront the future.

Willa Cather died from a cerebral hemorrhage on April 24, 1947, in her New York City apartment. Edith Lewis carried out her wishes, and she was buried in Jaffrey, New Hampshire, within sight of Mount Monadnock, close to the field where she had written much of her fiction. On her gravestone is a quote from *My Ántonia*: "That is happiness, to be dissolved into something complete and great."

## Selected Bibliography

### WORKS OF WILLA CATHER

POETRY
*April Twilights.* Boston: Gorham Press, 1903.
*April Twilights and Other Poems.* New York: Knopf, 1923.

NOVELS AND SHORT STORIES
*The Troll Garden.* New York: McClure, Phillips, 1905.
*Alexander's Bridge.* Boston: Houghton Mifflin, 1912.
*O Pioneers!* Boston: Houghton Mifflin, 1913.
*The Song of the Lark.* Boston: Houghton Mifflin, 1915.
*My Ántonia.* Boston: Houghton Mifflin, 1918.
*Youth and the Bright Medusa.* New York: Knopf, 1920.
*One of Ours.* New York: Knopf, 1922.
*A Lost Lady.* New York: Knopf, 1923.
*The Professor's House.* New York: Knopf, 1925.
*My Mortal Enemy.* New York: Knopf, 1926.
*Death Comes for the Archbishop.* New York: Knopf, 1927.
*Shadows on the Rock.* New York: Knopf, 1931.
*Obscure Destinies.* New York: Knopf, 1932.
*Lucy Gayheart.* New York: Knopf, 1935.
*Sapphira and the Slave Girl.* New York: Knopf, 1940.
*The Old Beauty and Others.* New York: Knopf, 1948.

ESSAYS
*Not under Forty.* New York: Knopf, 1936.

*Willa Cather on Writing.* New York: Knopf, 1949.
*Willa Cather in Europe: Her Own Story of the First Journey.* Lincoln: University of Nebraska Press, 1984.

COLLECTIONS
*Willa Cather's Collected Short Fiction, 1892–1912.* Introduction by Mildred R. Bennett. Lincoln: University of Nebraska Press, 1965.
*The Kingdom of Art: Willa Cather's First Principles and Critical Statements 1893–1896.* Edited by Bernice Slote. Lincoln: University of Nebraska Press, 1966.
*The World and the Parish: Articles and Reviews, 1893–1902.* 2 volumes. Edited by William M. Curtin. Lincoln: University of Nebraska Press, 1970.
*Uncle Valentine and Other Stories: Willa Cather's Uncollected Short Fiction 1915–1929.* Edited by Bernice Slote. Lincoln: University of Nebraska Press, 1973.
*Early Novels.* New York: Library of America, 1987.
*Later Novels.* New York: Library of America, 1990.
*Stories, Poems, and Other Writings.* New York: Library of America, 1992.

OTHER WORKS
Bohlke, L. Brent. *Willa Cather in Person: Interviews, Speeches, and Letters.* Lincoln: University of Nebraska Press, 1986.

### BIBLIOGRAPHY

Arnold, Marilyn. *Willa Cather: A Reference Guide.* Boston: G. K. Hall, 1986.
Crane, Joan. *Willa Cather: A Bibliography.* Lincoln: University of Nebraska Press, 1982.
Lathrop, JoAnna. *Willa Cather: A Checklist of Her Published Writing.* Lincoln: University of Nebraska Press, 1975.
O'Connor, Margaret Anne. "A Guide to the Letters of Willa Cather," *Resources for American Literary Study* 4: 145–172 (Autumn 1974).

### CRITICAL AND BIOGRAPHICAL STUDIES

Bennett, Mildred R. *The World of Willa Cather.* Lincoln: University of Nebraska Press, 1961.

Bloom, Harold, ed. *Willa Cather.* New York: Chelsea House, 1985.

Brown, E. K., and Leon Edel. *Willa Cather: A Critical Biography.* New York: Knopf, 1953.

Carlin, Deborah. *Cather, Canon, and the Politics of Reading.* Amherst: University of Massachusetts Press, 1992.

Daiches, David. *Willa Cather: A Critical Introduction.* New York: Collier, 1962.

Fischer, Mike. "Pastoralism and Its Discontents: Willa Cather and the Burden of Imperialism," *Mosaic: A Journal for the Interdisciplinary Study of Ideas* 23: 31–44 (Winter 1990).

Fryer, Judith. *Felicitous Space: The Imaginative Structures of Edith Wharton and Willa Cather.* Chapel Hill: University of North Carolina Press, 1986.

Gelfant, Blanche H. "The Forgotten Reaping-Hook: Sex in *My Ántonia.*" *American Literature* 43: 60–82 (March 1971).

Harrell, David. *From Mesa Verde to* The Professor's House. Albuquerque: University of New Mexico Press, 1992.

Lee, Hermione. *Willa Cather: Double Lives.* New York: Pantheon, 1990.

Lewis, Edith. *Willa Cather Living.* New York: Knopf, 1953.

Middleton, Jo Ann. *Willa Cather's Modernism: A Study of Theme and Technique.* Rutherford, N.J.: Fairleigh Dickinson University Press, 1990.

Millington, Richard H. "Willa Cather and 'The Story-teller': Hostility to the Novel in *My Ántonia.*" *American Literature* 66: 689–718 (December 1994).

Murphy, John, ed. *Critical Essays on Willa Cather.* Boston: G. K. Hall, 1984.

O'Brien, Sharon. *Willa Cather: The Emerging Voice.* New York: Oxford, 1987.

O'Brien, Sharon. "Becoming Non-Canonical: The Case against Willa Cather." *American Quarterly* 40: 110–26 (1988).

Reynolds, Guy. *Willa Cather in Context: Progress, Race, Empire.* New York: St. Martin's Press, 1996.

Robinson, Phyllis. *Willa: The Life of Willa Cather.* New York: Doubleday, 1983.

Rosowski, Susan. *The Voyage Perilous: Willa Cather's Romanticism.* Lincoln: University of Nebraska Press, 1986.

Schroeter, James, ed. *Willa Cather and Her Critics.* Ithaca, N.Y.: Cornell University Press, 1967.

Schwind, Jean. "The 'Beautiful' War in *One of Ours.*" *Modern Fiction Studies* 30: 53–72 (1984).

Sergeant, Elizabeth Shepley. *Willa Cather: A Memoir.* Philadelphia: Lippincott, 1953.

Skaggs, Merrill Maguire. *After the World Broke in Two: The Later Novels of Willa Cather.* Charlottesville: University Press of Virginia, 1990.

Slote, Bernice, and Virginia Faulkner, eds. *The Art of Willa Cather.* Lincoln: University of Nebraska Press, 1974.

Stouck, David. *Willa Cather's Imagination.* Lincoln: University of Nebraska Press, 1975.

Urgo, Joseph R. *Willa Cather and the Myth of American Migration.* Urbana: University of Illinois Press, 1995.

Woodress, James Leslie. *Willa Cather: A Literary Life.* Lincoln: University of Nebraska Press, 1987.

Woods, Lucia. *Willa Cather: A Pictorial Memoir.* Text by Bernice Slote. Lincoln: University of Nebraska Press, 1973.

*—SHARON O'BRIEN*

# *Emily Dickinson*
## *1830–1886*

$O$NE IMAGE OF Emily Dickinson is found on T-shirts and coffee mugs and in the ever-growing number of studies of her life and work. She is seventeen, a student at a rigorous school for young women. No effort has been spared in standardizing her appearance. Her hair, which she described as brash like a chestnut burr, must have tended to wildness; in the school photograph, her hair lies obedient. She gazes unsmilingly at the camera, or if there is a smile, it is suppressed into one corner of her mouth.

No American poet—and no woman poet writing in English—has enjoyed wider circulation, greater popularity, or more secure canonicity than Dickinson. Critics have celebrated her body of short poems as if they encapsulate structures of the psyche that transcend time and place. Yet she wrote during a time of dramatic social change and national trauma. Sequestering herself in an upper-middle-class private life, Dickinson fended off historical forces, encoding events such as the Civil War with cryptic metaphysical symbols. She wrote for her own purposes, "publishing" her poems by copying them into personal correspondence. By avoiding the literary marketplace, she exercised strict control over who would read her poems and protected her sensibility from commercialism. Yet in the ways she organized and

stored her poems, and in their preoccupation with the vocation of the poet, Dickinson seems to have anticipated what would become of them after her death: they would be taken from their hiding place, published, read, loved, and immortalized.

"And once you begin, how to tell the story of a life that had no story?" Richard Sewall asked himself this question as he prepared a two-volume biography of Dickinson in the 1970s. Because of her reclusiveness and her refusal to publish, Dickinson's life and poems were continually reinvented long after her death. The posthumous publication of her poems and letters occurred in several phases, under different editorial hands, and spanned more than half a century. Her letters are nearly as enigmatic as her poems and do not provide clear windows onto her life. Firsthand reports of her life came from relatives and family friends who had their own secrets to hide. The story seemed to be one of genius, with little of what is usually called experience. She made trips to Philadelphia, Washington, D.C., and Boston, but otherwise spent most of her life in her father's house in Amherst, Massachusetts. Dickinson was a nearly blank screen receptive to projected myths.

Sewall recalled that when he first taught Dickinson's poetry to college classes in the 1930s, she was summed up in clichés: Frustrated Lover, Great Renunciation, Queen Recluse, New England Nun, Moth of Amherst. The myth of a mad, mystical, diminutive genius began to take shape in her lifetime. An often-cited account of her comes from Thomas Wentworth Higginson, a correspondent who met her in 1870. In a letter to his wife, he described Dickinson as a little, plain woman in a white dress whose puzzling chatter and childlike anxiety drained his nerves.

Because Dickinson did not write in order to publish, readers have been tempted to see in her poems an extreme honesty free from social repression. Yet many critics have found her to be a versatile poseur. Writing to Higginson, she strikes the pose of a giddy pupil, while in letters to the writer Helen Hunt Jackson she is a warm, respectful colleague. Jackson's fictionalized impressions of Dickinson in *Mercy Philbrick's Choice* (1876) fall just short of linking the truthful Dickinson to the poseur. The novel's heroine, modeled after Dickinson, suffers pangs of conscience about the lies one must tell for the sake of social decorum. It is a sin, she believes, to act in such a way that people "think you're glad to see them when you're not. . . . A lie's a lie, let whoever will call it fine names, and pass it off as a Christian duty." Mercy's conflicts leave her "morally bruised, and therefore abnormally sensitive to the least touch. She was in danger of becoming either a fanatic for truth, or indifferent to it."

Dickinson's poems, like her life, tend to be treated as reflections of the concerns and convictions of their readers. Grammatical distortions and startling word choices make variant readings equally plausible. "So much Summer" illustrates qualities common to much of her verse:

> So much Summer
> Me for showing
> Illegitimate—
> Would a Smile's minute bestowing
> Too exorbitant

> To the Lady
> With the Guinea
> Look—if She should know
> Crumb of Mine
> A Robin's Larder
> Would suffice to stow—          (P 651)

(Selections from the poems of Emily Dickinson are taken from the 1955 edition edited by Thomas H. Johnson and are indicated in this essay by the letter P, followed by the number of the poem.) Like most of Dickinson's poems, "So much Summer" consists of altered ballad stanzas. Conventionally each stanza would have four lines, the first and third lines would have four beats, and the second and fourth would rhyme and have three beats. The poem begins with vastness ("So much Summer") and ends with something small ("A Robin's Larder"); the interplay of such natural extremes is frequent in Dickinson's imagery. The language is hyperbolic, dramatizing the voice of the speaker, who seems to be experiencing an inner struggle.

What is going on in this poem? It encrypts a recognizable experience. Someone has given the speaker a strange look that makes her feel out of place. She wonders if a tiny smile would have been too much to expect. If only that woman knew how little it took to satisfy me; she could have just tossed me a crumb. But what does the line "So much Summer" have to do with this situation? Suppose it's a busy summer in Amherst, the summer of 1862. Much is occurring that makes Dickinson feel how improper others consider her increasingly frequent retreats to her room. Someone gives her a look that reminds her of a gold coin or of a guinea fowl demanding to be fed: the woman wants something from her, perhaps a donation to a charitable cause, or a loaf of bread to sell at a church bazaar to raise funds for the Union cause. It's not that Dickinson would be satisfied with a crumb but that she has little to give, or nothing appropriate; she finds feeding birds more gratifying than submitting to community obligations. And who failed to smile, the other woman or Dickinson? Perhaps the speaker is not Dickinson at all but a knight out of an old romance wooing an elusive lady, with the summer stimulating his ardent desire. Or is the lady's suitor a woman? Maybe the speaker *is* the lady sequestered in an upper room, looking down at the suitor and wondering if it would cost her too much to smile.

## CHILDHOOD AND EDUCATION

Emily Dickinson was born in Amherst, Massachusetts, on December 10, 1830. She was the middle child in a prominent family whose male members helped to establish and run the town and its institutions. Her ancestor Nathan Dickinson was among those who founded the town in 1745, and her grandfather, Samuel Fowler Dickinson, took part in the founding of Amherst Academy in 1814 and Amherst College in 1821. Emily's father, Edward Dickinson, a lawyer and treasurer of Amherst College, served in state public offices during her childhood and was elected to Congress in 1852. Her mother, Emily Norcross Dickinson, tended to charitable duties in the community as well as the care of the household. The Dickinson home, known as the Homestead, was a center of Amherst society. Emily's brother, William Austin Dickinson, born in 1829, married her close friend Susan Gilbert and built a house called the Evergreens next to the Homestead. He followed in his father's footsteps, becoming a lawyer and college treasurer and also serving on corporate and civic boards. Lavinia Dickinson, born in 1833, remained unmarried like her sister, and the two grew old together in the Homestead after their parents' deaths.

Nostalgic illustrations of old New England towns show tranquil places where church spires sanctify the wilderness and modest homes promise protection against rough weather. Dickinson's life did not fit neatly into such a simple, harmonious setting. Helen Hunt Jackson, born in Amherst the same year as Dickinson, found a virulent tedium at the heart of "the ordinary New England town." In *Mercy Philbrick's Choice* she wrote:

> The community is loosely held together by a few accidental points of contact or common interest. The individuality of individuals is, by a strange sort of paradox, at once respected and ignored. This is indifference rather than consideration, selfishness rather than generosity; it is an unsuspected root of much of our national failure, is responsible for much of our national disgrace. . . . Our people are living, on the whole, the dullest lives that are lived in the world, by the so-called civilized.

Jackson gives her heroine a passion for beauty and truth that makes her a misfit in this place. For pathos, Jackson portrays Mercy as an impoverished widow. Dickinson was never poor, but social and economic change did threaten her family's status. Edward Dickinson, like his father, was a town squire. He functioned as a justice of the peace but the title conveyed the social status of an English country gentleman. During the 1830s and 1840s Amherst and other New England towns became increasingly dependent on the wider industrialized economy. The rising class of merchants and manufacturers began to displace New England's old aristocracy at the top of local social hierarchies.

The fortunes of the Dickinson house illustrate the family's vulnerability to such change. The Homestead's alternate names, the Manor and the Mansion, signify the borrowing of status from English feudalism for an American setting. It was the first brick house built in Amherst. Its double parlors, high ceilings, large bedrooms, and extensive landscaping on Main Street bespoke money and success. Yet soon after Samuel Fowler Dickinson built it in 1813, he had to sell it to relatives, who leased it back to him. Edward Dickinson bought half of the house in 1830, and in 1833 David Mack, an industrialist, foreclosed on the half that Samuel Fowler Dickinson occupied. Having lavished his wealth on public projects, the house's builder moved to Ohio in a state of financial ruin. Edward Dickinson's family, with three small children and only two bedrooms, was crowded in their half of the house. By 1840 Edward's financial condition allowed him to sell his half to Mack and move the family to a nearby wood frame house spacious enough to accommodate social gatherings. It was not until 1855, when Emily was twenty-five, that the Dickinson family took possession of the entire Homestead.

In private letters Edward Dickinson wrote of his fears about "democratic mixing," the opening of civil-service jobs to lower-class workers, the prospect of losing property and falling in the social hierarchy. In 1835 he wrote anxiously to his wife about the need to make money. Soon afterward he entered politics. When other members of the Whig party defected to the antislavery Republican Party, Edward Dickinson stayed in the conservative ranks, resisting the fervor of abolitionism. His daughter, too, would resist the rising social impulses of democratization, protest, and reform.

Emily Dickinson's upbringing was divided between an exceptionally serious education and an induction into domestic duties. She began attending primary school before her fifth birthday and at nine entered Amherst Academy, where she earned a reputation as school wit. In letters written during her teens, she reports studying grammar, composition, and a wide range of subjects in the humanities and natural sciences. At age sixteen she entered Mount Holyoke Female Seminary in nearby South Hadley. Mount Holyoke offered the nearest thing to a college education that was then available to women. Its founder, Mary Lyon, directed instruction toward producing young women who would subordinate their personal desires to the social good. Such notions of a woman's role in society were much in the air during the decades before the Civil War. Seeking to raise women's status without challenging male dominance in public life, writers and educators articulated a philosophy that saw women's special mission as one of improving the nation by exerting a moral influence in the home and community.

Confining as this philosophy may seem today, it inspired many women to become writers, speakers, and activists for social reform. Dickinson, however, mocked efforts to mold her character. In a letter to her brother, Austin, she writes that she pondered whether she should present his letter to Lyon's assistant for approval before reading it herself:

> The result of my deliberation was a conclusion to open it with moderation, peruse it's contents with sobriety becoming my station, & if after a close investigation of it's contents I found nothing which savored of rebellion or an unsubdued will, I would lay it away in my folio & forget I had ever received it. (L 22)

(Selections from the letters of Emily Dickinson are taken from the 1958 edition edited by Thomas H. Johnson and Theodora Ward and are indicated in this essay by the letter L, followed by the number of the letter.)

Dickinson withdrew from Mount Holyoke after two terms and became immersed in domestic responsibilities. In a letter to her childhood friend Abiah Root, she described her duties with flippancy and exasperation:

> I am yet the Queen of the court, if regalia be dust, and dirt, have three loyal subjects, whom I'd rather releive from service. Mother is still an invalid tho' a partially restored one—Father and Austin still clamor for food, and I, like a martyr am feeding them. Would'nt you love to see me in these bonds of great despair, looking around my kitchen, and praying for kind deliverance. (L 36)

In Paula Bennett's 1990 study of female creativity, *My Life a Loaded Gun*, she argues that Dickinson believed her mother tried to coerce her into accepting a life of drudgery that would destroy her individuality. As Joanne Dobson has pointed out in *Dickinson and the Strategies of Reticence*, the sheer amount of domestic labor needed to sustain an entertainment schedule like the Dickinsons' would have been formidable. Servants did the heavy work, but Emily and Lavinia would have shopped, cooked, mended, and cleaned. Eventually Emily specialized in baking bread and creating extravagant desserts, which she gave to neighbors' children. (Local legend has it that at her most reclusive she lowered a cream puff from her window to a waiting child.)

That growing up was difficult for Dickinson is evident from the letters she wrote during her teens, particularly those to Abiah Root. Abiah formed part of an intimate circle Dickinson called "the five" and attended school with her until they were fifteen. The early letters to Abiah are full of news and questions about mutual friends. Quickly, though, Emily begins to sound fearful that Abiah no longer cares about her. From Mount Holyoke, where she was the only student who resisted the wave of Christian revivalism sweeping the region, she confessed to Abiah her regret that she did not "give up & become a Christian." Now, she thought, it was too late, and she could not honestly say that her only desire was to be good (L 23). In a letter written late in 1850, Emily contrasted herself with Abiah and another childhood friend. They were becoming women, engaging in good works and learning "control and firmness," but Emily loved "to be a child" and to let her imagination wander: "Oh I *love* the *danger*!" (L 39). Yet a letter Dickinson wrote to Susan Gilbert in 1852 suggests that she saw a greater danger in being a wife. "You have seen flowers at morning, *satisfied* with the dew," she writes. At noon those same flowers bow their heads "in anguish before the mighty sun." The sweet romance of youthful female friendships gives way to addiction to male power: "They will cry for sunlight, and pine for the burning noon, tho' it scorches them, scathes them; they have got through with peace—they know that the man of noon, is *mightier* than the morning, and their life is henceforth to him" (L 93).

In November 1855 the Dickinson family moved into the Homestead, an event that Emily jokingly called a "catastrophe." Her mother was ill again, so a great deal of the work of settling into the new home must have fallen on Emily. The following summer Austin and Susan married and moved into the Evergreens, an elegant Italianate-style house linked to the Homestead by a flower-lined path. Few records remain of Dickinson's life during this time, and although her earliest poem can be dated to around 1850, there is no evidence that she wrote poems between 1854 and 1858. By the end of the decade, however, she had begun her lifework as a poet.

## THE POET AT WORK

In 1858 Dickinson started to make fascicles or manuscript books. R. W. Franklin, who edited a facsimile edition of these booklets in 1981, reconstructed her composition habits from the evidence provided by the manuscripts. She would draft a poem on any piece of paper that came to hand—a shopping sack, a used envelope, the back of a recipe. Later she would rework the poem, make a fair copy on a folded piece of stationery, and usually destroy the draft. She filled all four sides of the folded sheet with poems, attaching a partial sheet with a pin if a poem extended beyond the available space. She selected four or five sheets, stacked them rather than setting them inside one another, and bound them by stitching a cotton string along the left margin with a darning needle, then tying the ends in a bow.

At first she treated the bound poems as completed drafts. Starting around 1861, however, many of the fascicles include alternate wordings, some added long after she copied the poem. Franklin speculates that as she leafed through her poems, perhaps searching for just the right one to send to a friend, she would start composing again, turning a fair copy into a working draft that could be altered for different purposes or recipients. In 1862 she began leaving some copied poems unbound, and she stopped binding them altogether in 1864, having created forty fascicles containing over eight hundred poems. From 1867 on her practice of making fair copies became intermittent. During the last years of her life she left poems on the odd bits of paper on which she had first drafted them.

From 1858 to 1862 Dickinson's productivity increased. The fair copies of 366 poems have been dated to 1862 based on an analysis of the manuscripts. Whether she actually composed all these poems during this remarkable year or copied some of them from earlier drafts is not known since she did not date the poems herself. In any case, she must have devoted time each day to her poems, writing, revising, copying, and organizing them. The burst of productivity continued in 1863 (141 poems) and 1864 (174 poems), and in later years it leveled off to an average of 50 poems annually.

From her letters and poems it is evident that Dickinson attained a new sense of seriousness about her calling as a poet during these years. It was also during this time that a few of her poems appeared in print. Karen Dandurand has found ten Dickinson poems published during her lifetime, six of them reprinted one or more times, totaling twenty publications. The poems are " 'Sic transit gloria mundi' " (P 3), "Nobody knows this little Rose—" (P 35), "I taste a liquor never brewed—" (P 214), "Safe in their Alabaster Chambers—" (P 216), "Success is counted sweetest" (P 67), "These are the days when Birds come back—" (P 130), "Flowers—Well—if anybody" (P 137), "Blazing in Gold and quenching in Purple" (P 228), "Some keep the Sabbath going to Church—" (P 324), and "A narrow Fellow in the Grass" (P 986). All were published anonymously with varying degrees of editing. They appeared in periodicals published in Springfield (a city near Amherst), Boston, New York, and Brooklyn, as well as in an anthology.

### RESISTING PUBLICATION

The paucity of works published during her lifetime enhanced the fascination of readers who discovered her through the posthumously published books of poems. She seemed to have been a genius who was neglected or suppressed, either because she was a woman or because she was far ahead of her time. Recent studies, however, have shown that she had ample opportunity to publish but regarded the literary marketplace as an anxiety-provoking diversion from her purposes in writing. Friends tried to persuade her to send her work to publishers, and literary figures such as Samuel Bowles, editor of the *Springfield Republican*, repeatedly urged her to give them poems for publication. When Bowles did print "A narrow Fellow in the Grass" without her permission, Dickinson complained to Higginson on February 14, 1866, that it was robbed from her (L 316).

Resisting publication out of modesty was a conventional stance for women, and yet the nineteenth century saw unprecedented numbers of women making successful careers as writers. For much of the century they dominated the literary marketplace. From the 1830s on, women writers and editors built a flourishing female print culture, extending their belief in women's special mission to enter the field of public discourse. Some of these writers avoided controversy by concentrating on genteel subjects, while others tackled injustice. Helen Hunt Jackson, for example, documented the United States' breach of trust with Native Americans and distributed copies of her book *A Century of Dishonor* to every member of Congress. As Joanne Dobson has shown, although Dickinson had little interest in social issues, few of her poems would have been out of place in the literary culture of her time. The need to earn money was a commonly accepted justification for women publishing. Although she herself had no need to earn an income, Dickinson begrudgingly allows this exception in "Publication—is the Auction" (P 709): "Poverty—be justifying / For so foul a thing // Possibly." Comparing the literary marketplace to a slave auction, she declares, "Publication—is the Auction / Of the Mind of Man," generalizing the degradation regardless of gender. To publish was to reduce the human spirit to a price.

Dickinson's attitude toward publishing reflects fears that some mid-nineteenth-century critics expressed as American publishing grew into a thriving industry, namely, that literature would become just another trade—mechanical, commercial, and subject to the laws of supply and demand. Given her reservations about publishing, why Dickinson chose to send poems to Thomas Wentworth Higginson during her most productive year is a mystery. Higginson, then editor of the *Atlantic Monthly*, was a leading liberal who crusaded for women's rights and the abolition of slavery. Perhaps Dickinson wanted to test her estimate of her writing against that of an influential arbiter of taste, or perhaps she was testing her negative idea of the literary marketplace against Higginson's optimistic view. In an article entitled "Letter to a Young Contributor," published in the April 1862 issue of the *Atlantic*, Higginson promoted an idea of poetry as a craft of expressive language that Dickinson would have found compatible with her own practice. However, he also asserted his faith in the judgment of the literate public, suggesting that their expecting "the same dash and the same accuracy" from literature as they did from

the providers of goods and services would benefit the craft of poetry.

Two weeks after the issue was published, Dickinson sent Higginson four poems with a note asking him "to say if my Verse is alive" (L 260). She did not ask him to consider publishing the poems, and he recommended that she learn to control the "spasmodic" movement of her lines before submitting poems for publication. Dickinson rejected his editorial advice and never accepted any instruction he tried to give her, but he became a trusted friend. She sent him a hundred poems over the course of their twenty-three-year correspondence, and they met twice. Perhaps combining an ironic pose with real gratitude, she signed her letters "Your pupil" and said he had saved her life.

Of the people who urged Dickinson to publish, none was more emphatic than Helen Hunt Jackson. Like Higginson, Jackson believed that placing a market value on the quality of a literary work did not detract from it but rather encouraged writers to develop their skill. The daughter of an Amherst professor, Jackson became acquainted with Dickinson in 1860. Jackson, herself a highly regarded poet, probably appreciated Dickinson's poetry more fully than did any other literary figure of the time. She copied Dickinson's poems in her notebooks and from them learned to pay close attention to the formal qualities of her own verse. One difference between Dickinson and Jackson's fictional heroine Mercy Philbrick is that Mercy publishes her poetry, attaining a saintlike status because of her ability to comfort readers through her poems. From 1876 on, Jackson repeatedly pressured Dickinson to publish, even offering strategies for protecting her anonymity.

At one point an exasperated Dickinson solicited Higginson's help in getting Jackson to stop pressuring her, but she did agree to allow "Success is counted sweetest" (P 67) to appear in *A Masque of Poets*, an anthology published by Roberts Brothers of Boston in 1878. The poem was well received, quoted in a review of the anthology, and was attributed by many readers to Emerson. With the title "Success," added by her editors, it would play a prominent role in the unfolding of Dickinson's works to a wider readership after her death; it was placed first in collections of her poems published between 1890 and 1937. The poem's aphoristic lines declare that victory is apprehended most fully by someone

defeated—dying—
On whose forbidden ear
The distant strains of triumph
Burst agonized and clear!

Read as an introduction to Dickinson's works, the poem seems to invite readers to join in vanquishing her unjust obscurity.

During the last year of her life, Jackson wrote to Dickinson from California, "What portfolios of verses you must have.—It is a cruel wrong to your 'day & generation' that you will not give them light." For Jackson publishing was a moral obligation: "I do not think we have a right to with hold from the world a word or a thought any more than a *deed*, which might help a single soul" (L 937a). Dickinson may have partly agreed with Jackson; she generously offered up her words to people known to her, but she firmly resisted releasing them to the wider public.

RECLUSIVENESS AND COMMUNITY

During her period of tremendous productivity, Dickinson began to withdraw from the social world. She no longer attended church, stopped visiting friends and relatives, and eventually refused to see people in her home. Reclusiveness is central to the legend of Emily Dickinson that developed when her poems were posthumously published, but even before her death it was rumored that she was eccentric, misanthropic, ill, mad, or lovelorn. Lavinia insisted that Emily was not withdrawn; she was always glad when someone "rewarding" would come to the house, but she was very busy: "She had to think." In her obituary of Emily, Susan Dickinson also attributed Emily's retreat to that of a brilliant mind with a sense of mission.

Dickinson did maintain a sense of community through her abundant correspondence. She wrote many of her poems to send to friends on special occasions: to mourn the loss of a loved one or mark the anniversary of a death, to congratulate or sympathize, or to accompany gifts of dried flowers. Parts of the letters themselves have the same meter that she used in most of her poems. The letters that have been published—numbering well over a thousand—represent only a fraction of what she wrote. Several important groups of letters, such as those to Charles Wadsworth, a clergyman with whom she corresponded for at least twenty years, were destroyed. There are dozens of addressees for the surviving correspondence, some names appearing on one or two brief notes and others on letters that cover many years, giving evidence of strong, enduring attachments. There are letters addressed to her childhood schoolmates, close and distant relatives, friends and their relatives, associates of her father and grandfather, and people she met through other family members. Among her frequent correspondents were Samuel Bowles and his wife, Mary; Elizabeth Holland and her husband, Josiah, an associate of Bowles; Judge Otis Phillips Lord, with whom Dickinson formed a romantic attachment after he was widowed in 1877; and her younger cousins Louise and Frances Norcross.

Three letters found in draft form among Dickinson's papers have attracted much attention because of their apparent relevance to her reclusiveness. They are addressed to an unknown recipient whom Dickinson calls "Master." Their estimated dates are 1858, 1861, and 1862. The third letter sounds especially anguished:

Oh, did I offend it— ~~Did'nt it want me to tell it the truth~~ Daisy—Daisy—offend it—who bends her smaller life to his/it's meeker/lower every day— who only asks—a task— ~~who~~ something to do for love of it—some little way she cannot guess to make that master glad— (L 248)

The "Master" letters have fueled speculation that an unfulfilled love for someone inaccessible (probably married) caused an emotional crisis that prompted Dickinson's withdrawal and ignited her creativity. That Dickinson did experience a life-altering crisis is evident from the available documents. In her second letter to Higginson, for instance, she hints: "I had a terror—since September—I could tell to none" (L 261). Guesses as to the object of her injured love have included Higginson, Wadsworth, Bowles, Lord, Susan Dickinson, and Susan's friend Catherine Anthon. She clearly had strong feelings for all of these people, but there is no solid evidence as to who the Master was or even that the Master was a real person. In *My Emily Dickinson* the poet and critic Susan Howe reads the letters as literary exercises, noting that the fallen women in Elizabeth Barrett Browning's *Aurora Leigh* and Charles Dickens' *David Copperfield* are likely sources. Rather than reflecting emotional desperation, Howe argues, the letters show Dickinson experimenting with distorted language, "forcing, abbreviating, pushing, padding, subtracting, riddling, interrogating, re-writing—," in other words practicing the techniques of her craft.

## FAMILY MATTERS

Dickinson's biographers have struggled with the apparent eventlessness of her life. Yet her family's intrigues could have inspired a work of modern fiction. The texture of the Dickinsons' family life was one of secrets not revealed but recycled, masked in conflicting reports. As the Dickinsons'

story unfolded long after the poet's death, Austin's marriage proved a bitter failure, with Susan perceived as a destructive influence who caused a rift in the family—grandiosely referred to as "The War between the Houses." Yet Susan may be a scapegoat in this account. Stories of her depravity were filtered through the prism of class prejudice and largely based on an aging Austin's complaints to his young lover, Mabel Loomis Todd—who would become the first editor of Emily's poems— about how unhappily married he was.

Smith, Bennett, and other critics have called attention to Dickinson's relationship with her sister-in-law, arguing that it was her most powerful bond and had the strongest influence on her writing. As different as they appeared, Susan was Emily's intellectual match and their lives complemented each other. In *Mercy Philbrick's Choice* Jackson predicted that the time would come when the dullness of New England towns "will have crystallized into a national apathy, which will perhaps cure itself, or have to be cured, as indurations in the body are, by sharp crises or by surgical operations." Both Susan and Emily conducted their lives on the fringes of Amherst's conventions, generating crises in the dullness and performing surgery on its rigidities.

Susan Gilbert's marriage to Austin Dickinson was a step up for her socially; she was the orphaned daughter of a tavern keeper. The Dickinson family approved of the match, but years later Susan's class origins became the favored explanation of family and friends for the unhappiness prevailing in the Dickinson households. Austin told Mabel Todd that he once believed that a vigorous, lower-class woman would strengthen the Dickinson line, but that Susan had disappointed him. He reported that his wife feared sex and childbearing and had had several abortions before giving birth to their first son.

Susan managed the household in a manner antithetical to the puritanism of the Dickinsons' forebears. Preceding her as the family hostess, Emily Norcross Dickinson, like many other women of her class, worked hard until she collapsed with vague but disabling illness. Susan, by contrast, spent money, exercised her good taste, and enchanted rooms of people with her presence. Accounts of gatherings at the Evergreens describe fine meals, luscious decor, and conversation ranging over limitless topics, often with such visiting luminaries as Ralph Waldo Emerson or Harriet Beecher Stowe in attendance. Austin, who paid the bills for these events, eventually found this way of life distasteful. He complained in his diary that his house was his wife's tavern, a place of riotous hedonism. Other Amherst citizens praised her brilliance and taste, albeit with a note of distrust, as if expecting her to veer into impropriety. As the austere ways of the old elite class passed into anachronism, however, Susan's gift for staging "sprees" (as Austin called them) revitalized the Dickinson family's social prominence.

Susan and Emily met in early adulthood as Emily's childhood friends were marrying and moving away from Amherst. Emily's letters display a sense of jealousy and grief over the loss of Susan to Austin during their courtship, but during their early years in the Evergreens Emily joined the couple for laughter-filled evenings. What became of the friendship in later years is uncertain because of contradictory reports. Mabel Todd claimed that when she arrived on the scene in 1881 the most notorious story in Amherst concerned Susan's turning against Lavinia and Emily. Lavinia's complaints against Susan were extreme; she asserted that her sister-in-law's cruelty shortened Emily's life by ten years. Yet the correspondence shows that Susan visited Emily often until 1883, the year that Austin and Todd began meeting secretly at the Homestead. If sheer quantity is an indicator of the value Dickinson placed on a reader of her poetry, then Susan must have been Emily's ideal audience. She sent Susan over four hundred pieces of correspondence—most including poems—during

their thirty-five-year relationship. Emily expressed high regard for Susan's literary taste; she once wrote her that she had learned more from her than she had from anyone excepting Shakespeare.

From the beginning of their friendship, Emily's letters show that her love for Susan was passionate and intense. Intimate romantic friendships between women were common in the nineteenth century; it was not until the end of the century that these relationships were understood to have a sexual dimension and were stigmatized. Sometime after Dickinson's death, someone at the Evergreens—possibly Austin—went through her letters to family members and disguised expressions of praise or love for Susan. The poem "One Sister have I in our house" (P 14), for example, was cut into two pieces and blacked out, with the last line ("Sue—forevermore!") marked up especially heavily. The poem acknowledges that Susan is different from the rest of the family: "She did not sing as we did— / It was a different tune." But the speaker commits herself to this second sister with sensual, romantic images:

> I spilt the dew—
> But took the morn—
> I chose this single star
> From out the wide night's numbers—
> Sue—forevermore!

Edward Dickinson died in 1874. The following year Emily Norcross Dickinson was stricken with paralysis. Her daughters nursed her until her death in 1882. In 1884 Emily Dickinson made a now uncustomary trip along the path to the Evergreens to see her young nephew Gilbert, who was dying of typhoid. She had not been well since an attack of flu in 1882, and after Gilbert's death she became weaker, suffering bouts of unconsciousness—early symptoms of the progressive kidney disease of which she died on May 15, 1886. She left instructions for her correspondence to be destroyed. Lavinia was carrying out her instructions when she came across the locked wooden box in which Emily kept her poems. No one had known of this box, nor had she given anyone any idea how much she wrote.

### EARLY EDITIONS OF THE POETRY

The task of introducing Emily Dickinson's poetry to the public fell to Mabel Loomis Todd and Thomas Wentworth Higginson. Just thirty when Dickinson died, Todd had begun her own literary career with the publication of several short stories; later she wrote books on her travels with her husband David, an astronomer. Although Todd visited the Homestead regularly after 1881 and exchanged poems and drawings with Dickinson, she never met the poet face to face. While Mabel and Lavinia visited in the parlor—with Mabel sometimes performing on the piano—Emily eavesdropped from the next room.

Dickinson's readers are often horrified to learn that Todd and Higginson altered her poems. Yet they were not meddling with the words of a famous and revered poet; they were preparing new material by an unknown author. If Dickinson was to be read, they needed to create a niche for her in the current marketplace, and they were pressed to believe their efforts would fail. The editors at Houghton Mifflin, the first publisher Higginson approached, ridiculed him for promoting Dickinson's work. Thomas Niles at Roberts Brothers expressed reluctance to "perpetuate" the poems; he thought them "quite as remarkable for defects as for beauties [and] generally devoid of true poetical qualities." When the poet Arlo Bates reviewed Todd and Higginson's first selection of Dickinson's poems, he disagreed with Niles but thought half of the poems needed careful editing. Together Todd and Higginson edited two volumes, with the poems arranged under such headings as "Life," "Love," "Nature," and "Time and Eternity." *Poems by Emily Dickinson* (1890) and *Poems by Emily Dickinson, Second Series* (1891) met with mixed reviews but unanticipated commercial success. Todd next spent several years collecting Dickinson's letters, from which she prepared a two-volume edition, which was published in 1894; later, without Higginson's help (he was seventy-one and unwell), she edited *Poems by Emily Dickinson, Third Series* (1896).

Todd's work on Dickinson's manuscripts ended with the "War between the Houses" embroiling her in a lawsuit. At Austin's insistence, Lavinia agreed that a strip of land owned by the Dickinsons would be deeded to Todd in partial payment for her work. In 1895 Austin died; the following year Lavinia signed the deed over to Todd, but while the Todds were away on an astronomical expedition, Lavinia changed her mind and filed suit to recover the property, alleging that she did not know the paper she had signed was a deed. Despite a weak case, Lavinia won the suit and the Todds lost an appeal. Mabel Todd returned the land but accused Lavinia of fraud and renounced their friendship.

Emily Dickinson's manuscripts were divided up between Todd and Lavinia. When Lavinia died in 1899, her portion went to Susan Dickinson, and when Susan died in 1913, it went to Susan's daughter, Martha. For over twenty years Martha Dickinson Bianchi controlled the release of her aunt's poems to the public. *The Single Hound* (1914) included poems Emily had sent to Susan and her family. These were collected with the first three volumes and published as *The Complete Poems of Emily Dickinson* (1924), supposedly exhausting the manuscripts. But Susan's portion of the divided manuscripts had yet to be published. Some appeared in *Further Poems of Emily Dickinson* (1929), incorporated in *The Poems of Emily Dickinson* (1930). Still more new poems appeared in *Unpublished Poems of Emily Dickinson* (1935), followed by another collected edition, *Poems of Emily Dickinson* (1937).

In their introductions, Bianchi and her collaborator, Alfred Leete Hampson, portrayed Dickinson as a modern mystic who renounced her love for a married man and became obsessed with death and immortality. They also defended the continuing arrangement of the poems by topic, as opposed to a more scholarly chronological arrangement, insisting that the poems could not be dated with certainty. When Bianchi died in 1943, all the poems that Lavinia had kept when the manuscripts were divided up had been published. In 1945 Mabel Todd's daughter, Millicent Todd Bingham, released *Bolts of Melody*, which included the previously unpublished poems from Todd's portion of the manuscripts. In her introduction Bingham indirectly denounces the "false legends" about the poet as a result of Bianchi's cultivation of the Dickinson mystique. She devotes most of her discussion to the manuscripts. Not denying the difficulty of the task, she concluded that the poems should be arranged chronologically.

Thomas H. Johnson, the first scholar to edit Dickinson's work, undertook the dating of Dickinson's manuscripts, beginning in 1950. In the three-volume variorum edition published in 1955, Johnson listed Dickinson's alternate wordings for each poem. For the reader's edition published in 1960, he made choices among alternative wordings but tried to base them on Dickinson's preferences. He replicated Dickinson's capitalization and punctuation, though Dickinson's intention frequently was far from obvious. The marks he usually transcribed as dashes, for instance, sit short or long, high or low, angled upward or downward on the manuscript pages. His editions contain 1,775 poems.

Johnson's chronological arrangement of the poems and restoration of Dickinson's stylistic eccentricities made it possible for readers to discover an unfolding story of rebellion against literary and social authority. For some readers the new editions exploded the myth that Bianchi had promoted. According to the poet and critic Louise Bogan ("A Mystical Poet"), Johnson's work made accessible an exceptionally full picture of a poet's development:

> We ourselves can discover, in the index to the three volumes, that her favorite subject was not death, as was long supposed; for life, love and the soul are also recurring subjects. But the greatest interest lies in her progress as a writer, and as a person. We see the young poet moving away, by gradual degrees, from her early slight addiction to graveyardism, to an Emersonian belief in the largeness and harmony of nature. Step by step, she advances into the terror and anguish of her destiny; she is frightened, but she holds fast and describes her fright. . . . Nature is no longer a friend, but often an inimical presence. Nature is a haunted house. And—a truth even more terrible—the inmost self can be haunted.

For the poet Adrienne Rich, the legend of Dickinson's life had been disturbing "because it seemed to whisper that a woman who undertook such explorations must pay with renunciation, isolation, and incorporeality." Johnson's collected edition of the poems, however, revealed a mind so powerful that, for Rich at least, the myth became unimportant.

## THE CRITICAL RECEPTION

During the decades when Dickinson's poems were first published, the social factors shaping reading in the United States changed greatly, but they proved continually hospitable to her canonization. In the 1890s popular magazines and women's literary clubs largely determined American reading habits, but starting in the 1920s academic influences played an increasingly important role. The methods and goals of teaching literature in schools also changed. The old system was to have students study literary language in order to acquire refined habits of speech developed through oral performance. The new approach, which became known as New Criticism, emphasized the interpretation of texts. Poetic language was conceived of as something apart from educated Standard English, and authentic poetry was seen as complex—figurative, ironic, paradoxical. Strongly influenced by the modernist poet and critic T. S. Eliot, the New Critics concentrated on texts that supported these precepts.

In the 1930s and 1940s, the field of American studies took shape as critics began to formulate a literary canon. Seeking to transform a vast, heterogeneous cultural history into an academic discipline, scholars organized the new field around key myths, one of which concerned the centrality of the Puritans in the nation's intellectual life. The simultaneous development of New Criticism and American studies subjected literary works to conflicting standards. According to the former, a work should reward formal aesthetic readings disengaged from historical contexts; according to the latter, a work should contribute to an account of the nation's cultural history.

The influential critic Allen Tate succeeded in linking these two academic approaches in his praise of Emily Dickinson. Historically, according to Tate, Dickinson wrote at a time when a balance existed between the old and the new, a cultural context that produces "a special and perhaps the most distinguished kind of poet." The work of such a poet meets the aesthetic requirement of complexity because it reflects a mind held in "lucid tension." Indebted to Puritanism for her habit of internal discipline, Dickinson nevertheless overturned the Puritan code of absolute truth: "Her poetry is a magnificent personal confession, blasphemous and, in its self-revelation, its honesty, almost obscene. It comes out of an intellectual life towards which it feels no moral responsibility. Cotton Mather would have burnt her for a witch." Dickinson's ambiguous, difficult poems suited the methods of New Criticism, and her Puritan background appealed to the codifiers of the American literary canon. Nonacademic reading practices had laid the groundwork for her canonization, and the inclusion of her work in academic texts reflected and reinforced her canonicity.

In the early 1990s William Harmon used the ninth edition of a venerable reference work (*Granger's Index to Poetry*) to produce an anthology of the five hundred most frequently published poems in the English language. Harmon's project proved that Dickinson is by far the most established woman poet in the English language, but it also reveals that the Dickinson canon—the list of her most frequently read poems—had begun to take shape before the academy's cultural influence took hold. With the exception of "After great pain, a formal feeling comes" (P 341), all fourteen of the Dickinson poems in Harmon's collection first appeared in print either during her lifetime or in the 1890s. The two linked themes of isolation and death dominate these poems, portraying a Dickinson much like the heartbroken mystic whose legend Bianchi promoted. Only four of the poems depart from these topics: "A Bird came down the Walk" (P 328), "I like to see it lap the Miles" (P 585), "A narrow Fellow in the Grass" (P 986), and "I never saw a Moor" (P 1052).

In four poems isolation is associated with an individual's distinctiveness or superiority over the majority. "I taste a liquor never brewed" (P 214) represents the poet's distinctiveness with a parodic play on spiritual inebriation. When the bee is evicted for drunkenness and the butterfly takes a temperance oath, the speaker keeps drinking until even heaven is scandalized:

Till Seraphs swing their snowy Hats—
And Saints—to windows run—
To see the little Tippler
Leaning against the—Sun—

"The Soul selects her own Society" (P 303) presents isolation as a matter of choice, absenting oneself from the "divine Majority" and holding back feeling and attention to all but one. "Much

Madness is divinest Sense" (P 435) distinguishes the exceptional individual with a paranoid note:

> 'Tis the Majority
> In this, as All, prevail—
> Assent—and you are sane—
> Demur—you're straightway dangerous—
> And handled with a Chain—

"Success is counted sweetest" (P 67) links isolation to death, singling out the special awareness of a dying person who hears someone else's triumph being trumpeted in the distance.

Many critics consider Dickinson's poems about death and despair to be among her greatest works, modern in their resistance to sentimental consolation. A common comfort presented in nineteenth-century verse was the anticipation of meeting loved ones in heaven. Dickinson skeptically inverts this hope in "My life closed twice before its close—" (P 1732): whether death represents a loss as terrible as those she has experienced in life remains to be seen, but the experience of parting blurs the difference between heaven and hell. In "There's a certain Slant of light" (P 258), despair is projected onto outward images to describe a sense of inward disruption: " We can find no scar, / But internal difference, / Where the Meanings, are." The landscape and its shadows, rather than any human subject, notice the arrival of this terrible feeling, and when it leaves, " 'tis like the Distance / on the look of Death—." Death is a metaphorical frame for "After great pain, a formal feeling comes—" (P 341). Here, as in other poems, Dickinson does little more than exquisitely capture an instance of anguish. "The Nerves sit ceremonious, like Tombs—," the heart vaguely questions Christian precept, the feet become mechanical. The hour of the "formal feeling" is "Remembered, if outlived, / As Freezing persons, recollect the Snow—/ First— chill—then Stupor—then the letting go—." In "I felt a Funeral, in my Brain" (P 280), as in many of Dickinson's poems about death, the voice speaks from beyond the grave. Sensational and Poe-like,

the poem ends with the speaker crashing through world after world, as if the very scaffolding of existence were collapsing. The posthumous voice speaks with irreverent humor in "I heard a Fly buzz—when I died—" (P 465). While mourners wait for God to appear in the death room, a fly "With Blue—uncertain stumbling Buzz—" occupies the last of the dying person's consciousness.

## "BECAUSE I COULD NOT STOP FOR DEATH—"

For all these poems, the versions that circulated in anthologies and textbooks and inspired literary critics for several decades contained editorial changes that went beyond punctuation, changes made to appeal to the reader's taste and comprehension rather than according to scholarly standards. Three poems were drastically altered. The last stanza of "I felt a Funeral, in my Brain" was omitted, leaving the poem less extreme in its irrationality, and five lines of "I heard a Fly buzz— when I died—" were altered to smooth the rhythm and rhyme scheme.

The publication history of "Because I could not stop for Death—" (P 712), Dickinson's most anthologized poem, makes a revealing case study. For the 1890 edition of the poems the editors altered the wording of the third stanza from:

> We passed the School, where Children strove
> At Recess—in the Ring

to:

> We passed the school, where children played
> Their lessons scarcely done.

The change creates a rhyme for the stanza but eliminates the paradox that leisure involves effort. For the 1924 edition Bianchi and Hampson restored "strove" but rewrote the next line as "At wrestling in a ring," carrying through the sense of effort but still avoiding the paradox. In the fifth stanza Dickinson rhymes "Ground" with itself; the editors replaced "in the Ground" with "but a mound" to eliminate the repetition. Most drastically, in the 1890 edition Todd and Higginson eliminated the fourth stanza altogether, so that the poem read:

> Because I could not stop for Death,
> He kindly stopped for me;
> The carriage held but just ourselves
> And Immortality.
>
> We slowly drove, he knew no haste,
> And I had put away
> My labor, and my leisure too,
> For his civility.
>
> We passed the school where children played,
> Their lessons scarcely done;
> We passed the fields of gazing grain,
> We passed the setting sun.
>
> We paused before a house that seemed
> A swelling of the ground;
> The roof was scarcely visible,
> The cornice but a mound.
>
> Since then 'tis centuries; but each
> Feels shorter than the day
> I first surmised the horses' heads
> Were toward eternity.

The missing stanza, finally restored in Johnson's editions, blocks the motion of the poem while adding hints of carnality.

> Or rather—He passed us—
> The Dews drew quivering and chill—
> For only Gossamer, my Gown—
> My Tippet—only Tulle—

The carriage seems to stop as the sun passes, leaving the air damp and cold. Clad in gauzy fabrics, the speaker is ready for a wedding or a sexual encounter but not for the night air. The "Dews" take on characteristics of flesh passing into death.—

For fifty years the poem appeared in anthologies in the edited versions. The history of its selection for inclusion closely parallels reading trends in the United States throughout the twentieth century; it is as if at every stage the poem's canonicity were assured—as if, in fact, it helped to set the standards of canonicity rather than being subject to them. The first *Granger's Index of Poetry*, published in 1904, lists forty of Dickinson's poems as having been included in collections. "Because I could not stop for Death—" was chosen for two songbooks, reflecting the era's use of poetry in performance. By 1940 it was included in collections with titles reflecting the efforts of both the New Critics and the scholars of American studies to define their respective fields.

By 1973 nearly five hundred of Dickinson's poems—now in Johnson's transcriptions—were included in anthologies. The collections in which "Because I could not stop for Death—" appeared from the 1950s through the early 1970s further secured the poem's place in the fields of American, modern, and world literature. Two publication trends became especially prominent during this period: an explosion of inexpensive paperback anthologies, part of a broad effort to make literature accessible to readers from all economic classes; and the proliferation of school and college textbooks. From the end of the 1960s through the 1990s, poetry textbooks surpassed paperback anthologies and dominated the list of those works that included "Because I could not stop for Death." In his 1992 survey of American studies, *Redrawing the Boundaries*, Phillip Fisher commented: "No cultural fact is more decisive in the past fifty years than the wholesale movement of every component of our literary life, past, present, and future, into the universities." Dickinson's poems followed this trend, their audience becoming increasingly defined as students with reading assignments and academics with professional obligations to fulfill.

One reason for the prominence of "Because I could not stop for Death—" in the Dickinson canon may be that the situation it reenacts epitomizes the critic's engagement with the Dickinson mystique. In the textbook *Understanding Poetry,* by Cleanth Brooks and Robert Penn Warren, whose editions spanned the era of New Criticism, students were asked to ponder Tate's comments on "Because I could not stop for Death—." Despite its appearance in 1960 after the restored text of this poem was published, the third edition of *Understanding Poetry* retained the version that omitted the fourth stanza. Tate's comments also refer to the shortened version: "If the word great means anything in poetry, this poem is one of the greatest in the English language."

Tate discusses the technical proficiency of the rhythm, the synthesis of image and idea, and the restraint that prevents the poem from becoming "ludicrous." Death "is a gentleman taking a lady out for a drive," he remarks. He highlights "the subtly interfused erotic motive" and associates the pairing of love and death with Romanticism. Having invoked the story of a "genteel driver" who embodies the terror of death, Tate ignores the implied seduction scene and praises Dickinson for showing readers a juncture of immortality and physical dissolution without telling us what to think. Brooks and Warren also cite the critic Richard Chase, who restates the allegory that death "is apparently a successful citizen who has amorous but genteel intentions. He is also God."

Reviewing the criticism written during the decades of Dickinson's canonization in *Becoming Canonical in American Poetry*, Timothy Morris claims that male academic critics inserted themselves into the role of lover–God, certain that they would succeed in understanding Dickinson as Higginson did not. Morris argues that these critics heard Dickinson's voice "not as the distinctive idiom of a particular Victorian woman, but as the secret, unrepressed voice of Everywoman—a voice that was largely the creation of their own fantasies."

A disturbing fact surrounding Dickinson's canonization is that the works of other women writers disappeared from anthologies at the same time that her poems appeared; by midcentury she had become the token woman writer of nineteenth-century American literature. The 1950 *Oxford Book of American Verse*, edited by the influential scholar F. O. Matthiessen, is an important touchstone in this process. His selection of poets includes, together with forty-three men, the colonial poet Anne Bradstreet, Dickinson, and six modernist women poets. Black and working-class authors also disappeared from textbooks and reading lists during this period. White male academics homogenized the canon as they defined their role as defenders of cultural masterpieces rather than shapers and disseminators of literary culture (the role that Higginson, for example, had assumed). There were specific reasons for the elimination of women writers. Nineteenth-century women's literary culture was seen as promoting feminine values that could undermine the masculine toughness needed to fortify the culture of a modern world power.

Morris speculates that Dickinson posed no threat because she did not publish during her lifetime and was dead before her works entered the critical discourse. As early as 1896 critic Harry Lyman Koopman had celebrated Dickinson as a voice of feminine truth free of the "decorous support networks" of women's print culture. Dickinson seemed the exception to those nineteenth-century commonplaces that repelled these critics, from women's sexual unavailability to their prominence on the literary scene. Morris speculates that through her secret poems Dickinson seemed "to reach out to the virile male," who arrived in his carriage to rescue her from "immurement in the culture of ladylike gentility."

## FEMINIST LITERARY CRITICISM

Welcome as Johnson's editions were among Dickinson's readers in the 1950s and 1960s, his transcriptions and arrangements of the poems stirred controversy. Critics debated the significance of Dickinson's odd capitalization and punctuation, some claiming that she capitalized important words to indicate that she intended them as archetypes and that the dashes were actually a system of elocution marks showing how the poems should be recited aloud. R. W. Franklin, however, pointed out in *The Editing of Emily Dickinson* that Dickinson's handwritten texts were typical of the casual writing of her time, and that the same irregularities appeared in her household notes. Some scholars have claimed that Johnson overused the dash and that Dickinson herself would have used other punctuation if she had prepared the manuscripts for publication—something we will never know.

Working closely with Dickinson's writing, Franklin discovered an apparent contradiction in the tenets of New Criticism. Paradoxically, what the author intended to say was treated as irrelevant to the poem's meaning, whereas the author's text was considered sacred; the textual scholar's goal was to reproduce the poem exactly as the poet meant it to appear. Franklin observed that a scholar editing Dickinson's work faces an unresolvable problem since she provided no authoritative version of hundreds of her poems.

In the last quarter of the twentieth century, two developments revolutionized the reading of Dickinson's work: the advent of feminist literary criticism in the 1970s and the publication in 1981 of Franklin's facsimile edition of *The Manuscript Books of Emily Dickinson*. Both represented powerful challenges to earlier approaches to Dickinson's poems. Feminist critics challenged the New Critical view that poems could be evaluated and understood apart from their social settings, while the publication of the fascicles called into question whether individual poems could be treated as separate entities.

In the 1970s Dickinson's poems began to appear in anthologies of women's poetry intended to revive the reputations of forgotten women authors and to present canonical works in a new light, calling attention to how the writers resisted sexist oppression. "Because I could not stop for Death—" was included in the first of these feminist anthologies, *Women Poets in English* (1972) edited by Ann Stanford, as well as in several subsequent collections. Read in this new context, the focus shifts toward the speaker's experience and away from the formal and metaphysical tensions that Tate stressed in his reading. Another study exercise for this poem in Brooks and Warren's *Understanding Poetry* asks students to consider this leading question: Has the lady died, or is the poem about awareness? The expected answer, of course, is the latter: students are meant to subordinate the speaker's experience to an abstract interpretation concerning a state of mind. If one rejects the "right" answer and asks what the encounter means in material terms, the poem becomes a protest against the limited options in women's lives. The carriage ride may represent marriage or rape, but both signify moral and spiritual death.

Read in a more theoretical light, the poem protests women's roles in a centuries-long poetic tradition. In 1845 Edgar Allan Poe declared, "The death of a beautiful woman is, undoubtedly, the most poetical of topics," thereby underscoring an assumption that stretches from classical poetics to the modern lyric. In the Renaissance sonnet cycle, for example, a male courtier might worship an idealized dead woman or pursue a living but unattainable feminine ideal. In the Romantic lyric female figures are often interchangeable with inanimate nature. In this tradition male figures seek, create, and articulate knowledge, transcending physicality through a tragic understanding of the limits of human rationality. Female figures, silent and passive, serve as the medium through which male transformation takes place.

Because Dickinson was one of very few women writers whose works had not been forgotten when feminists began to write literary criticism in the early 1970s, revisionary readings of her poetry contributed to the formation of methods and articulation of tenets of feminist criticism. Her texts were often read as being distinctly feminine—sometimes even feminist—and many critics treated her as the very type of the woman poet struggling against patriarchal oppression. The most influential feminist essay on Dickinson, "Vesuvius at Home" by Adrienne Rich, brought to the fore a poem (P 754) that until then, had been little discussed:

> My Life had stood—a Loaded Gun—
> In Corners—till a Day
> The Owner passed—identified—
> And carried Me away—
>
> And now We roam in Sovereign Woods—
> And now We hunt the Doe—
> And every time I speak for Him—
> The Mountains straight reply—
>
> And do I smile, such cordial light
> Upon the Valley glow—
> It is as a Vesuvian face
> Had let its pleasure through—
>
> And when at Night—Our good Day done—
> I guard My Master's Head—
> 'Tis better than the Eider-Duck's
> Deep Pillow—to have shared—
>
> To foe of His—I'm deadly foe—
> None stir the second time—
> On whom I lay a Yellow Eye—
> Or an emphatic Thumb—
>
> Though I than He—may longer live
> He longer must—than I—
> For I have but the power to kill,
> Without—the power to die—

To Rich, writing in the 1970s, this poem seemed central to understanding not only Dickinson but also women of her own time and the condition of the female artist. "I think it is a poem about possession by the daemon," that is the "Genius of Poetry," Rich wrote. The poet is split between "an active, willing being" and "an object, condemned to remain inactive until the hunter—the *owner*—takes possession of it." Rich suggests that the "female consciousness" in this poem "exists in the ambivalence toward power, which is extreme." In defying the role of passive object, the poet risks being defined as "unwomanly" and "potentially lethal."

In their groundbreaking 1979 study of nineteenth-century women writers, *The Madwoman in the Attic,* Sandra Gilbert and Susan Gubar amplified Rich's view: they assert that Dickinson enacted anger at female subordination not only in her poetry but also in her reclusive life, through which she recovered a powerful, creative, autonomous self. As scholars read the works of forgotten nineteenth-century women writers, however, it became clear that Dickinson could not be treated as an exemplary case of resistance to sexist oppression. In *Dickinson and the Strategies of Reticence*, Joanne Dobson shows that nineteenth-century women writers had a multitude of strategies available to them in opposing conventional gender roles and that many took great risks in their lives and in their writing. In contrast, Dickinson's life appears almost fanatically conventional. In *Emily Dickinson: Woman Poet* Paula Bennett takes a different view of Dickinson's apparent conformity to gender norms, seeing it as a parodic shield for her strong challenge to "phallocentrism," the cultural centrality of male desire. Emphasizing the homoeroticism in Dickinson's poetry, Bennett rejects the supposition that her roles as a woman and a poet were in conflict.

Reading Dickinson's works in the context of class history also undermines the exemplary position early feminist critics accorded her. The pursuit of an autonomous self is common to Romantic poetry and is most accessible to writers like Dickinson, who had no need to earn money. Betsy Erkkila in "Emily Dickinson and Class" has argued that Dickinson's very resistance to patriarchy was grounded in class privilege. Her methods reinforced her elite status. In stitching together her manuscripts, she engaged in "a precapitalist mode of manuscript production" similar to those modes practiced in royal courts during earlier eras. "Publishing" her poems in letters to friends was also an aristocratic form of circulation. For Erkkila, Dickinson's resistance to the values of the marketplace had an ironic effect: "She, like other Romantic poets, ended by enforcing the separation of art and society and the corresponding feminization, trivialization, and marginalization of art."

### THE CONTEXT OF THE FAST CIRCLES

In contrast to Erkkila, Martha Nell Smith views Dickinson's resistance to the marketplace positively, stating that her self-made "books"—her fascicles and correspondence—present a "radical alternative" to commercial publishing. Smith advocates reading Dickinson's poems in their contexts in the letters and fascicles. Franklin did not see any deliberate order to the poems within a fascicle, but Smith and other scholars have shown that reading a familiar poem within its fascicle can undermine long-held assumptions about its meaning. For example, Sharon Cameron, in her 1992 study of Dickinson's fascicles, *Choosing Not Choosing,* discovered that other poems in the fascicle that contains "Because I could not stop for Death—" raise questions about who has died; it may not be the speaker—as nearly every critic has assumed—but her lover.

Susan Howe, an early advocate of reading the poetry within the context of the manuscripts, provides a start in contextualizing "My Life had stood—a Loaded Gun—" in *My Emily Dickinson* (1985). Like Rich, she reads it as a poem about gender and power, but her reading sets the poem within the context of history and literary texts. She interlaces Renaissance and colonial history and narratives of the frontier and the Civil War with citations from Dickinson's favorite authors: Shakespeare, Emily Brontë, Robert Browning, and Elizabeth Barrett Browning. She also links the poem to Dickinson's "Master" letters and other correspondence, as well as to poems within and beyond the fascicle that holds it.

To read "My Life had stood—a loaded Gun—" within its fascicle (numbered 34 by Franklin) places it in contiguity with poems from which it had been separated throughout its publication history. The eighteen poems comprising the fascicle first appeared dispersed among seven books that were published between 1890 and 1945. Johnson, too, separated them; their numbers in his editions range from 478 to 993. Franklin found that three sheets of the fascicle had long been kept with a group of poems with which they did not belong. "My Life had stood—a loaded Gun—" falls in the middle of the restored fascicle.

Martha Nell Smith argues that what binds the poems in a fascicle together is not formal unity, thematic progression, or an underlying story. She proposes that by responding to the movement of images and themes throughout the fascicle, the reader becomes aware of an overall texture of resonance and meaning. Read as Smith suggests, fascicle 34 is remarkably coherent. Scenes and tones shift, but the whole works as a poem cycle exploring connections between death and aesthetic value. Sharon Cameron points out that the first and last poems of this fascicle both concern death, but the subject in the first one ("Bereavement in their death to feel" [P 645]) finds no compensation, while that of the last one ("Essential Oils—are wrung" [P 675]) does. Furthermore, the first poem describes the situation of a reader (Howe associates this poem with Dickinson's reading of Emily Brontë), while the last poem explores the craft of the poet. For William Shurr this fascicle is one of several whose subjects include Dickinson's status as a poet and the presence-through-absence of a beloved. These are central themes in the tradition of the love lyric, particularly the sonnet cycle: the poet exercises his skill by laboring to transcend his frustrated desire for a dead or unattainable lady. Fascicle 34 blurs the gendered roles of the male-authored lyric tradition: it abounds in dead women, but the gender of the speaker—whether the voice of Dickinson herself or of a female or male persona—is never made clear.

The poems following "Bereavement in their death to feel" begin to explore various ways of transcending the problem that the "vital kinsmanship" one feels with "immortal friends" concerns mortality. The speaker posits opposite modes of imagining, one vast and the other small ("I think to live—May be a Bliss" [P 646] and "A little Road—not made of Man—" [P 647]) and dismisses both as inaccessible means of transcendence. The next poem ("Her Sweet turn to leave the Homestead" [P 649]) imagines a journey that, like "Because I could not stop for Death—," conflates a wedding and a funeral. This poem becomes a romance about a princess whose suitors must pursue quests through impossible landscapes if they wish to win her:

Of Her Father—Whoso ask Her—
He shall seek as high
As the Palm—that serve the Desert—
To obtain the Sky—

Distance—be Her only Motion—
If 'tis Nay—or Yes—
Acquiescence—or Demurral—
Whosoever guess—

He—must pass the Crystal Angle
That obscure Her face—
He—must have achieved in person
Equal Paradise—

The lady may be dead, accessible only to those who die, or the "Crystal Angle" may represent an upper window obscuring her face. By giving the lady's home the same name as her own Dickinson suggests self-referentiality implying the inaccessibility of her own hermetic verse.

"Pain—has an Element of Blank—" (P 650) describes the ground zero of trauma: there is no transcendence other than insight into the nature of pain. "So much Summer" (P 651) fits into both the fairy-tale and love-lyric traditions if it is read as an interaction between a suitor and an inaccessible lady. A feeling of illegitimacy is associated with the vast mode, while the small mode represents sufficiency. "Promise This—When You be Dying—" (P 648) casts the theme of unattainable love as a first-person plea without specifying the gender of either the speaker or the beloved. The speaker pleads to possess the beloved's body after his or her death. The following stanza takes up the common theme of sonneteers, namely, that poetry will immortalize the beloved by creating her likeness:

Poured like this—My Whole Libation—
Just that You should see
Bliss of Death—Life's Bliss extol thro'
Imitating You—

The lover imagines not that the beloved's soul will go to heaven, as in popular mourning verse, but that the lover will have the power to manipulate natural events surrounding the beloved's corpse—a selfish, possessive wish:

Mine—to guard Your Narrow Precinct—
To seduce the Sun
Longest on Your South, to linger,
Largest Dews of Morn

To demand, in Your low favor
Lest the Jealous Grass
Greener lean—Or fonder cluster
Round some other face—

In the next poem the speaker claims, "I had no time to Hate—" (P 478), adding,

Nor had I time to Love—
But since
Some Industry must be—
The little Toil of Love—
I thought—
Be large enough for Me—

This might be the frustrated lover of the previous poem explaining his or her morbid labors, but its humility reflects ironically on the inflation of those toils.

In "My Life had stood—a Loaded Gun—" (P 754), which follows, the dialectical tension of hate and love unabated in the previous poem is sustained as ammunition. Utilizing the metaphor of a gun and a hunter, Dickinson seems to solve problems that remained unresolved in the first half of the fascicle. The Owner who appears in the poem provides transport into the previously inaccessible scenery of the sublime, where the speaker's agency surpasses that imagined by the lover pleading to tend the beloved's corpse. Gone are the smallness, illegitimacy, and contortion associated with self-expression in "So much Summer"; the speaker's smile itself is sublime, drawing a vast response from the landscape. The "Toil of love" is hunting the doe and killing the foe, causing death rather than tending to the dead. The sexual consummation missed by failed suitors is dismissed as inferior to protecting the Owner. The speaker delights in the mastery achieved through evasions of the gendered polarity of male subject and female object. The hunted doe or foe would represent the elusive ladylove in an Elizabethan sonnet, but here the speaker joins the "master" on the hunt, as if he were the courtly poet and the speaker, if human, a devoted page, cross-gendered like a disguised Shakespearean heroine, if female. Speaking as a metaphorical weapon that acts only through the master's agency, Dickinson speaks as the voice of craft itself.

The last stanza presents another twist on the theme of art's immortality and human mortality:

Though I than He—may longer live
He longer must—than I—
For I have but the power to kill,
Without—the power to die—

No poet boasts of his ability to immortalize the beloved. The instrument must preserve its user if it is to be of use, but nature and the feminine are merely the means for this dyad's (gun and hunter) interdependent, destructive action.

Viewed within the context of the fascicle, "My Life had stood—a Loaded Gun—" looks transitional—perhaps a pivotal but not a final statement. Dickinson goes on to reinvent the vast and the small, exploring both from the point of view of experience rather than inaccessibility. Feminine nature returns as an agent of reconciliation rather than a scene of destruction, joining an unspecified pair through domestic "Toils of love" administered on a cosmic scale ("The Sunrise runs for Both—" [P 710]). The small world is not complete in itself and suffers from the loss of the sublime, a loss compensated for by brave singing ("No Bobolink—reverse His Singing" [P 755]). "One Blessing had I than the rest" (P 756) describes an experience of the sublime. The "good Day" in "My Life had stood—a Loaded Gun—" resonates in this experience, which is so fulfilling that it resembles its opposite, despair or pain. It stupefies the speaker, who claims it stifled her questioning:

Why Bliss so scantily disburse—
Why Paradise defer—
Why Floods be served to Us—in Bowls—
I speculate no more—

But the questioning immediately resumes ("Victory comes late—" [P 690]). As in "No Bobolink—reverse His Singing," it is small creatures who suffer in the meeting of large and small: "Cherries—suit Robins— / The Eagle's Golden Breakfast strangles—Them—." The last two lines link this poem to the theme of unfulfilled love and give a plaintive edge to the dutiful voice in "I had no time to Hate—": "God keep His Oath to Sparrows— / Who of little Love—know how to starve—." The fascicle turns again to the vast in a poem that transforms the master–gun scene into a harmonious landscape ("The Mountains—grow unnoticed—" [P 757]), where the mountains, needing no audience, reflect the sun's colors back to him when he seeks "fellowship—at night—."

Dickinson next returns to the problem of death and compensation, first separating the death of a woman from the masculine lyric tradition and then experimenting with compensations related to the sublime. "These—saw Visions—" (P 758) cryptically imitates popular funeral verse, closing with a reference to paradise, as if Dickinson discarded the imaginary elements of the earlier poems of death to fashion a simple memorial. The poem avoids idealizing the dead girl, highlighting her agency in life (she saw visions, spoke, and ran) and a very material "Toil of Love," the traditionally female task of preparing a corpse for burial. The speaker in "Strong Draughts of Their Refreshing Minds" (P 711) is again a reader (like the speaker in the fascicle's first poem) who comments on the power of texts, figured as a liquor distilled from "an Hermetic Mind—," to sustain one through vast landscapes, the settings of sublime agency. "We miss Her, not because We see—" (P 993) links the loss of a woman to the theme of union through the sublime by scrambling a common sentiment of the funeral-verse tradition: Our missing her is mitigated by the knowledge that she watches us from her place among heavenly beings:

> We miss Her, not because We see—
> The Absence of an Eye—
> Except its Mind accompany
> Abridge Society
>
> As slightly as the Routes of Stars—
> Ourselves—asleep below—
> We know that their superior Eyes
> Include Us—as they go—

"Essential Oils—are wrung—" (P 675) returns to the theme of art's immortality, much altered since it first appears in "Promise this—when you be dying" and "My Life had stood—a Loaded Gun—." The "Sealed Wine" extracted from the "Hermetic Mind" reappears here as the perfume extracted from a rose. The sublime alone is insufficient:

> The Attar from the Rose
> Be not expressed by Suns—alone—
> It is the gift of Screws—

A tool is needed to extract essence. As instruments, the screws are kindred to the gun, but their destructive work is feminized. They create a sachet reproducing the vast ("Summer") in an enclosed feminine space ("Lady's Drawer"). Dickinson separates the rose, a standard lyric symbol for the beloved, from the lady whose body lies in rosemary, an herb symbolizing remembrance. The closing lines suggest collaboration between the two scents (rose and rosemary) in keeping the dead woman's memory alive.

Beyond reading the poems within their fascicles, Martha Nell Smith recommends that the correspondence also be read within context for the poems. To pursue the threads of fascicle 34, following Smith's guidelines, one should note that Dickinson sent "Victory—comes late" to Bowles and "We miss Her, not because we see" and "Essential Oils—are wrung—" to Susan Dickinson. Susan's version of "Essential Oils—are wrung—" separates the craft of poetry from the lyric object, the beautiful dead woman. It ends with the lady lying in "spiceless Sepulchre," implicitly decaying. No essence assists in keeping her memory alive; the art of extracting essence condenses the dialectic of the vast and the small, but it does not memorialize. The compensation for death in this conclusion comes not from artfully preserving the memory of the dead but from the inner workings of a made object, its reproduction of the sublime in an enclosed, private space.

"READING" DICKINSON

A new variorum edition of Dickinson's poetry, with typographical reproductions of the manuscripts edited by R. W. Franklin, was scheduled to appear in 1998. Yet in some scholarly circles this long-awaited project was already considered obsolete. Jerome McGann has asserted that typography fundamentally misrepresents Dickinson's work. He points out that Dickinson treated her "textual medium" as an end in itself, "as part of the aesthetic field of writing."

> In an age of print publication, manuscripts of writers tend to stand in medias res, for they anticipate a final translation into that "better world" conceived as the printed word. In Dickinson's case, however, the genres that determine the aspirations of her work are scriptural rather than bibliographical: commonplace book writing, on one hand, and letter writing on the other.

McGann argues that in order to edit Dickinson's work adequately "one needs to integrate the mechanisms of critical editing into a facsimile edition." Such a project is under way. Headed by Martha Nell Smith, the Emily Dickinson Editorial Collective is preparing a CD-ROM edition that not only reproduces the visual qualities of Dickinson's pages but also allows the reader to explore the many linkages between Dickinson's poems and letters.

If, indeed, Dickinson's individual works should each be treated as contextually interconnected, then hypertext would seem her perfect medium. One is tempted to theorize that if she had owned a computer, she would not have needed to stitch fascicles; interlinked electronic files would have been far superior for her purposes. But will the hypertext edition give readers a more authentic experience of Dickinson? Her "intentions" for the posthumous publication of her work—if she had any such intentions—remain as obscure today as ever. Hypertext will not provide access to the lady beyond the Homestead's "Crystal Angle." The movement way from typeset books into hypertexted facsimiles does, however, once again indicate her poetry's resistance to any single standardized form of presentation and its adaptability to new ways of reading.

What is suggested about the reader if the "right" way to read Dickinson's work is in an intricate contextual web? Each experience of reading her, whether as a specialist or an amateur, becomes an editorial performance. When the facsimile edition was published, Susan Howe noted: "The Franklin edition is huge, Dickinson's handwriting is often difficult to decipher, and the book is extremely expensive. Few readers will have a chance to use it for reference, which is a pity, because it is necessary for a clearer understanding of her writing process." If this was the right way to read the poems, it was inaccessible to most readers, and a CD-ROM will be even less accessible than a printed edition of her collected works in a paperback selection.

For readers without access to Dickinson's "context," Rich's reading of "My Life had stood—a Loaded Gun—" remains exemplary. She does not claim to have arrived at the ultimate meaning; instead, through the poem she gains insight into her own situation. Rich writes: "More than any other poet, Emily Dickinson seemed to tell me that the intense inner event, the personal and psychological, was inseparable from the universal; that there was a range for psychological poetry beyond mere self-expression." For Rich, writing in the 1970s, this unprecedented validation had a political dimension: she was creating art within a movement whose theme was that power relations pervade the personal sphere, where middle-class women spent most of their lives. In 1891 Mabel Todd saw a different manifestation of the "intense inner event" in readers' sensitivity to Dickinson's poetry. Despite the shallowness of their era, Todd noted, they responded to fundamental themes.

Perhaps one key to the fascination of Dickinson's writing is that it may not represent a structure of intended connections at all but rather something informal that has been preserved. Suppose that the formal and conceptual experimentation in her verse represents not an open rebellion against public cultural forms but a private casualness, a determined amateurism—or suppose that private casualness *is* the rebellion. The little poems would then be crafted correlates to our everyday thoughts, few of which we speak or act upon. The passion with which Dickinson's readers have carried her poems away for over a century like lovers rescuing them from the narrow privacy of the Homestead, may be a disguised desire to have our own haunted, hermetic inner lives transported and their significance validated—even (improbably) canonized. To consider this possibility is to enter into a cyberspace where the vast and the small morph into one another, and virtual love and virtual death travel together toward virtual immortality.

# Selected Bibliography

## WORKS OF EMILY DICKINSON

POETRY

*Poems by Emily Dickinson.* Edited by Mabel Loomis Todd and T. W. Higginson. Boston: Roberts Brothers, 1890. Reprinted, Boston: Little, Brown, 1922.
*Poems by Emily Dickinson, Second Series.* Edited by Mabel Loomis Todd and T. W. Higginson. Boston: Roberts Brothers, 1891.
*Poems by Emily Dickinson, Third Series.* Edited by Mabel Loomis Todd. Boston: Roberts Brothers, 1896.
*The Single Hound: Poems of a Lifetime.* Edited by Martha Dickinson Bianchi. Boston: Little, Brown, 1914.
*The Complete Poems of Emily Dickinson.* Edited by Martha Dickinson Bianchi and Alfred Leete Hampson. Boston: Little, Brown, 1924.

*Further Poems of Emily Dickinson.* Edited by Martha Dickinson Bianchi and Alfred Leete Hampson. Boston: Little, Brown, 1929.
*The Poems of Emily Dickinson.* Edited by Martha Dickinson Bianchi and Alfred Leete Hampson. Boston: Little, Brown, 1930.
*Unpublished Poems of Emily Dickinson.* Edited by Martha Dickinson Bianchi and Alfred Leete Hampson. Boston: Little, Brown, 1935.
*The Poems of Emily Dickinson.* Edited by Martha Dickinson Bianchi and Alfred Leete Hampson. Boston: Little, Brown, 1937.
*Bolts of Melody: New Poems of Emily Dickinson.* Edited by Mabel Loomis Todd and Millicent Todd Bingham. New York: Harper, 1945.
*The Poems of Emily Dickinson.* Edited by Thomas H. Johnson. 3 vols. Cambridge, Mass.: Belknap Press of Harvard University Press, 1955.
*The Complete Poems of Emily Dickinson.* Edited by Thomas H. Johnson. Boston: Little, Brown, 1960.
*The Manuscript Books of Emily Dickinson.* Edited by R. W. Franklin. 2 vols. Cambridge: Belknap Press of Harvard University Press, 1981.

CORRESPONDENCE

*The Letters of Emily Dickinson.* Edited by Mabel Loomis Todd. 2 vols. Boston: Roberts Brothers, 1894.
*The Life and Letters of Emily Dickinson.* Edited by Martha Dickinson Bianchi. Boston: Houghton Mifflin, 1924.
*Letters of Emily Dickinson.* Edited by Mabel Loomis Todd. New York: Harper, 1931.
*Emily Dickinson Face to Face: Unpublished Letters, with Notes and Reminiscences.* Edited by Martha Dickinson Bianchi. Boston: Houghton Mifflin, 1932.
*Emily Dickinson's Letters to Dr. and Mrs. Josiah Gilbert Holland.* Edited by Theodora Van Wagenen Ward. Cambridge, Mass.: Harvard University Press, 1951.
*The Letters of Emily Dickinson.* Edited by Thomas H. Johnson and Theodora Ward. 3 vols. Cambridge, Mass: Harvard University Press, 1958.
*The Years and Hours of Emily Dickinson.* Edited by Jay Leyda. 2 vols. New Haven, Conn.: Yale University Press, 1960.

*Emily Dickinson: Selected Letters.* Edited by Thomas H. Johnson. Cambridge, Mass.: Belknap Press of Harvard University Press, 1986.

MANUSCRIPT PAPERS

The Dickinson Papers manuscript collection is housed in the Houghton Library of Harvard University, Cambridge, Mass.

## *CRITICAL AND BIOGRAPHICAL STUDIES*

Bennett, Paula. *Emily Dickinson: Woman Poet.* New York: Harvester Wheatsheaf, 1990.

———. *My Life, a Loaded Gun: Dickinson, Plath, Rich, and Female Creativity.* Urbana: University of Illinois Press, 1990.

Bingham, Millicent Todd. *Emily Dickinson: A Revelation.* New York: Harper, 1954.

Bogan, Louise. "A Mystical Poet." In *Emily Dickinson: Three Views* by Archibald MacLeish, Louise Bogan, and Richard Wilbur. Amherst, Mass.: Amherst College Press, 1960. Pp. 27–34.

Cameron, Sharon. *Lyric Time: Dickinson and the Limits of Genre.* Baltimore, Md.: Johns Hopkins University Press, 1979.

———. *Choosing Not Choosing: Dickinson's Fascicles.* Chicago: University of Chicago Press, 1992.

Capps, Jack L. *Emily Dickinson's Reading, 1836–1886.* Cambridge, Mass.: Harvard University Press, 1966.

Chase, Richard. *Emily Dickinson.* New York: William Sloane Associates, 1951.

Dandurand, Karen. "New Dickinson Civil War Publications." *American Literature* 56: 17–27 (March 1984).

———. *Dickinson Scholarship: An Annotated Bibliography, 1969–1985.* New York: Garland, 1988.

Diehl, Joanne Feit. *Dickinson and the Romantic Imagination.* Princeton, N.J.: Princeton University Press, 1981.

Dobson, Joanne. *Dickinson and the Strategies of Reticence: The Woman Writer in Nineteenth-Century America.* Bloomington: Indiana University Press, 1989.

*Emily Dickinson Journal*, vols. 1–5. Niwot: University of Colorado Press, 1992–1997.

Erkkila, Betsy. "Emily Dickinson and Class." In *The American Literary History Reader.* Edited by Gordon Hutner. New York: Oxford University Press, 1995. Pp. 291–317.

Farr, Judith. *The Passion of Emily Dickinson.* Cambridge, Mass.: Harvard University Press, 1992.

Fisher, Phillip. "American Literature and Cultural Studies since the Civil War." In *Redrawing the Boundaries.* Edited by Stephen Greenblatt and Giles Gunn, eds. New York: Modern Language Association, 1992. Pp. 232–250.

Franklin, R. W. *The Editing of Emily Dickinson: A Reconsideration.* Madison: University of Wisconsin Press, 1967.

Gilbert, Sandra M., and Susan Gubar. *The Madwoman in the Attic: The Woman Writer and the Nineteenth-Century Literary Imagination.* New Haven, Conn.: Yale University Press, 1979.

Holland, Jeanne. "Scraps, Stamps, and Cutouts: Emily Dickinson's Domestic Technologies of Publication." In *Cultural Artifacts and the Production of Meaning: The Page, the Image, and the Body*, edited by Margaret J. M. Ezell and Katherine O'Brien O'Keeffe. Princeton, N.J.: Princeton University Press, 1993. Pp. 139–181.

Homans, Margaret. *Women Writers and Poetic Identity: Dorothy Wordsworth, Emily Brontë, and Emily Dickinson.* Princeton, N.J.: Princeton University Press, 1980.

Howe, Susan. *My Emily Dickinson.* Berkeley, Calif.: North Atlantic Books, 1985.

———. "These Flames and Generosities of the Heart: Emily Dickinson and the Illogic of Sumptuary Values." *Sulfur* 28: 134–155 (Spring 1991).

Loeffelholz, Mary. *Dickinson and the Boundaries of Feminist Theory.* Urbana: University of Illinois Press, 1991.

McGann, Jerome. "The Rationale of Hypertext." Institute for Advanced Technology in the Humanities, University of Virginia. http://jefferson.village.virginia.edu/public/jjmzf/rationale.htm/

Morris, Timothy. "Dickinson: Reading the 'Supposed Person.' " In his *Becoming Canonical in American Poetry.* Urbana: University of Illinois Press, 1995. Pp. 54–80.

Oberhaus, Dorothy Huff. *Emily Dickinson's Fascicles: Method and Meaning.* University Park: Pennsylvania State University Press, 1995.

Reynolds, David S. "The American Women's Renaissance and Emily Dickinson." In his *Beneath the American Renaissance: The Subversive Imagination in the Age of Emerson and Melville*. Cambridge, Mass.: Harvard University Press, 1988. Pp. 387–437.

Rich, Adrienne. "Vesuvius at Home: The Power of Emily Dickinson." In her *On Lies, Secrets, and Silence: Selected Prose, 1966–1978*. New York: Norton, 1979. Pp. 157–183.

Sewall, Richard B. *The Life of Emily Dickinson*. 2 vols. New York: Farrar, Straus and Giroux, 1974.

Sewall, Richard B., ed. *Emily Dickinson: A Collection of Critical Essays*. Englewood Cliffs, N.J.: Prentice-Hall, 1963.

Shurr, William H. *The Marriage of Emily Dickinson: A Study of the Fascicles*. Lexington: University of Kentucky Press, 1983.

Smith, Martha Nell. *Rowing on Eden: Rereading Emily Dickinson*. Austin: University of Texas Press, 1992.

Smith, Robert McClure. *The Seductions of Emily Dickinson*. Tuscaloosa: University of Alabama Press, 1996.

Tate, Allen. *On the Limits of Poetry*. New York: Swallow Press, 1948.

Wilson, R. Jackson. *Figures of Speech: American Writers and the Literary Marketplace, from Benjamin Franklin to Emily Dickinson*. New York: Knopf, 1989.

Wolff, Cynthia Griffin. *Emily Dickinson*. New York: Knopf, 1986. Reprinted, Reading, Mass.: Addison-Wesley, 1988.

—*JANET GRAY*

# T. S. Eliot
## 1888–1965

*I*N THE 1920s, T. S. Eliot's densely allusive style gained him an international reputation on the order of Albert Einstein's, but his fondness for European models and subjects prompted some of his compatriots to regard him as a turncoat to his country and to the artistic tradition of the new it had come to represent. Yet Eliot's allusiveness recalls a distinctively native tradition of self-consciousness that precedes the idea of America his critics invoked. Perhaps the most useful way to characterize Eliot, in fact, is as a New England writer burdened by religious questioning and riven by conflicts about internal and external authority. That he managed to transform this struggle into the mark of a modern sensibility says something both about the power of his writing and about the complexities of what we mean when we talk about modernist literature.

The first and probably the definitive questioning of Eliot's American qualities took place in the 1910s and 1920s and involved a dialogue between William Carlos Williams and Ezra Pound. Williams, a passionate admirer of Thoreau's concentration on the local and the here and now, was particularly offended by *The Waste Land* and the poems that preceded it, and lamented in his *Autobiography* that the publication of *The Waste Land* "wiped out our world. . . . Eliot returned us to the classroom just at the moment when I felt that we were on the point of an escape to matters much closer to the essence of a new art form" rooted in "locality. . . . To me especially it struck like a sardonic bullet. I felt at once that it had set me back twenty years."

But Williams' notion of American poetry did not go unchallenged even then. Ezra Pound replied to an earlier expression of Williams's sentiments in no uncertain terms:

BALLS! My dear William. At what date did you join the ranks of the old ladies? . . . You can idealize [America] all you like but . . . . you have the advantage of arriving in the milieu with a fresh flood of Europe in your veins, Spanish, French, English, Danish. You had not the thin milk of New York and New England from the pap, and you can therefore keep the environment outside you, and decently objective.

### AN AMERICAN POET

Pound's perception was acute. Whether we regard Eliot's literary self-consciousness, still unsettling, as the expression of an empowering tradition or a debilitating disease, it remains the distinctive trace of a New England sensibility, not a departure from it. Eliot himself recognized as much early on and caricatured himself in self-portraits in which he appears as a New Englander more comfortable in literature than in life—in his memorable phrase, a "Burbank with a Baedeker" on a permanent grand tour.

At the end of the twentieth century, Eliot's relationship with the past looked much more remarkable than his self-caricature or Pound's defense, and uncannily like that of Williams' principal American predecessor, Walt Whitman. Writing on contemporary poetry in July 1919 in the *Egoist,* for example, Eliot spoke of the way poetry affected him in erotic and occult terms that unmistakably recall the following from one of Whitman's "Calamus" poems, "Whoever You Are Holding Me Now in Hand":

Whoever you are holding me now in hand,
Without one thing all will be useless,
I give you fair warning before you attempt me
    further,
I am not what you supposed, but far different.

Who is he that would become my follower?
Who would sign himself a candidate for my
    affections?

The way is suspicious, the result uncertain, perhaps
    destructive,
You would have to give up all else, I alone would
    expect to be your sole and exclusive standard

"There is a close analogy," Eliot writes in the *Egoist,* "between the sort of experience which develops a man and the sort of experience that develops a writer." To write is to be touched by a relation

of profound kinship, or rather of a peculiar personal intimacy, with another, probably a dead author. It may overcome us suddenly, on first or after long acquaintance; it is certainly a crisis; and when a young writer is seized with his first passion of this sort he may be changed, metamorphosed almost, within a few weeks even, from a bundle of second-hand sentiments into a person. The imperative inti-

macy arouses for the first time a real, an unshakable confidence. That you possess this secret knowledge, this intimacy, with the dead man, that after few or many years or centuries you should have appeared, with this indubitable claim to distinction; who can penetrate at once the thick and dusty circumlocutions about his reputation, can call yourself alone his friend: it is something more than *encouragement* to you. It is a cause of development, like personal relations in life. Like personal intimacies in life, it may and probably will pass, but it will be ineffaceable. . . . The usefulness of such a passion . . . [is] various. For one thing it secures us against forced admiration. . . . We may not be great lovers; but if we had a genuine affair with a real poet of any degree we have acquired a monitor to avert us when we are not in love. . . . [For another] our friendship gives us an introduction to the society in which our friend moved; we learn its origins and its endings; we are broadened. We do not imitate, we are changed, and our work is the work of the changed man; we have not borrowed, we have been quickened, and we become bearers of a tradition.

It is as if, finally, "dead voices speak through the living voice"—a real "incarnation."

Eliot's account suggests something fundamental about the way his poetry compounds exquisite sensitivity to verbal nuance with uncommonly direct access to unconscious power. This was what Randall Jarrell had in mind in an essay entitled "Fifty Years of American Poetry" when he wrote that, far from being an over-intellectualized poet, Eliot managed to convey raw unconscious power. "From a psychoanalytic point of view," he suggested, Eliot was "far and away the most interesting poet of [the] century" and perhaps "one of the most subjective and daemonic poets who ever lived, the victim and helpless beneficiary of his own inexorable compulsions [and] obsessions."

Nor is the psychological power that Jarrell describes the only quality that safeguards Eliot's allusiveness from the whiff of the classroom Williams ascribed. If Eliot's verse (especially his early verse) is saturated with earlier poetry, it is also instinctively and programmatically suspicious of the claims of the writing it invokes. In part this is because from the time he was very young Eliot temperamentally questioned everything about himself. Indeed his truest sense of himself, like that of Lord Claverton, his alter ego in his 1959 play, *The Elder Statesman*, seems to have included the feeling that

> Some dissatisfaction
> With myself, I suspect, very deep within myself
> Has impelled me all my life to find justification
> Not so much to the world—first of all to myself.
> What is this self inside us, this silent observer,
> Severe and speechless critic, who can terrorise us
> And urge us on to futile activity,
> And in the end, judge us still more severely
> For the errors into which his own reproaches
>    drove us?

This self-distrust forms Eliot's literary style, generating a characteristic self-reflexive irony that his philosophical studies deepened into a principled and radical resistance to positives of many kinds—propositional, stylistic, and emotional. Early in the century the force of this irony helped define writing in English and, more generally, the sensibility of the modern mind. For it is related to fundamental twentieth-century paradigms of thought. (As in the work of Ludwig Wittgenstein, for instance, for whom, as Richard Shusterman reminds us, "doctrines of the radical indeterminacy of aesthetic concepts and the logical plurality and essential historicity of aesthetic judgment . . . work to undermine the charm and credibility of both deductive and inductive models of critical reasoning.") Eliot's irony conditions not only his characteristic tone but also the structural procedures of his narrative verse, producing the jumps and fragmentation that caused so many of his first readers to associate his work with jazz.

Eliot himself articulated his intellectual skepticism in specifically American terms. Reviewing Henry Adams' autobiography, *The Education of Henry Adams*, in the 1919 *Athenaeum*, he spoke of "the Boston doubt: a scepticism which is difficult to explain to those who are not born to it"—"a product, or a cause, or a concomitant, of Unitarianism" that "is not destructive, but it is dissolvent." And in examining Eliot's early life and writing, recent commentators (particularly Eric Sigg and Manju Jain) have pointed to peculiarly American contexts of his skepticism and of its poetic and intellectual products. Eliot's ironic attitudes were early associated with his membership in an American social elite in decline, and with the disdain of that elite for the forces of immigration and tolerance that were transforming the nation. From another perspective, both Eliot's religious leanings and his tendency to reformulate them in poetic terms derive, as his remarks about "the Boston doubt" suggest, from his family's Unitarian roots, and from the Unitarians' struggle to universalize traditional authority.

And yet Unitarian universalism, from the perspective of traditional New England Calvinism, seems inadequate, and behind Eliot's questioning of Unitarian universalism stands a substantial literary history that includes the critiques of Ralph Waldo Emerson in the fiction of Nathaniel Hawthorne and Henry James. Some if not all these issues played themselves out in the development of pragmatist philosophy at Harvard in what has been called the golden age of American philosophy, and as a graduate student in the discipline trained there at that moment, Eliot honed his skepticism in a climate that both encouraged radical thinking and disapproved of it when it overstepped the bounds of humanitarian meliorism.

## BACKGROUND AND YOUTH

But such matters are better considered in relation to the particulars of Eliot's life. Thomas Stearns Eliot was born in Saint Louis, Missouri, the youngest member of a family that took pains to impress on him the importance of its history and achievement. His paternal grandfather, William Greenleaf Eliot, was distantly related to Henry Wadsworth Longfellow, John Greenleaf Whittier, and Herman Melville, and had been a protégé of William Ellery Channing, the dean of American Unitarianism. William Eliot graduated from Harvard Divinity School, then moved toward the frontier. He founded the Unitarian church in Saint Louis and soon became a pillar of the midwestern city's religious and civic life. He helped start the Academy of Science and Washington University (where he taught metaphysics) as well as Smith Academy for boys and the Mary Institute for girls. Because of William's ties to these schools, the Eliot family chose to remain in their urban Locust Street home long after the area had run down and their peers had moved to suburbs.

William Greenleaf Eliot dearly wanted his son to enter the clergy, but Henry Ware Eliot resisted. In 1865 (after his father had alienated a substantial part of his congregation by his Unionist loyalties), Henry arranged for a commission as lieutenant in the Union army, but the war ended before his commission arrived. He thereafter made a life in business, starting in wholesale grocery and going bankrupt manufacturing acetic acid. By the time Thomas Eliot was born, however, Henry was the prosperous president of the Hydraulic-Press Brick Company. Eliot's mother, Charlotte Champe Stearns Eliot, was a former teacher, an energetic social work volunteer at the Humanity Club of Saint Louis, and an amateur poet with a taste for Emerson. She augmented her husband's sense of duty and industry with an idealism and humanitarianism that T. S. Eliot resisted all his life.

Eliot was by far the youngest of seven children, born when his parents were secure in their midforties and his siblings were half grown. Afflicted with a congenital double hernia, he was in the constant eye of his mother and five older sisters, when he was not left in the care of an Irish nurse, Annie Dunne. Dunne sometimes took him with her to Catholic mass. In his youth, Eliot passed through the city's muddy streets and its exclusive drawing rooms. He attended Smith Academy until he was sixteen. The year he graduated he visited the 1904 Saint Louis World's Fair and was so taken with the display of native villages from around the world that he wrote short stories about primitive life for the Smith Academy Record. In 1905 he departed for a preparatory year at Milton Academy outside of Boston, prior to following his older brother, Henry, to Harvard.

Eliot's attending Harvard seems to have been a foregone conclusion. His father and mother, jealously guarding their connection to Boston's Unitarian establishment, brought the family back to Boston's North Shore every summer and in 1896 built a substantial house at Eastern Point in Gloucester. As a boy, Eliot foraged for crabs and became an accomplished sailor, trading the Mississippi in the warm months for the rocky shoals of Cape Ann. This seasonal migration deprived him of regional identity and reinforced his social alienation. Looking back in 1928, he wrote his friend, the English critic Herbert Read, that he had always wanted to write

an essay about the point of view of an American who wasn't an American, because he was born in the South and went to school in New England as a small boy with a nigger drawl, but who wasn't a southerner in the South because his people were northerners in a border state and looked down on all southerners and Virginians, and who so was never anything anywhere and who therefore felt himself to be more a Frenchman than an American and more an Englishman than a Frenchman and yet felt that the U.S.A. up to a hundred years ago was a family extension.

Beginning Harvard in the fall of 1906, Eliot impressed many classmates with his archness and his cosmopolitan social ease. Like his brother Henry before him, Eliot lived freshman year in a fashionable private dormitory in a posh neighborhood around Mt. Auburn Street known as the "gold coast." He joined a number of clubs, including the literary Signet. And he began a romantic attachment to Emily Hale, a refined Bostonian who once played Mrs. Elton opposite his Mr. Woodhouse in an amateur production of Jane Austen's *Emma.* Among his teachers, Eliot was drawn to the forceful moralizing of the scholar of world literature Irving Babbitt and the stylish skepticism of the philosopher and critic George Santayana, both of whom reinforced his distaste for the reform-minded, progressive university shaped by his cousin, Charles William Eliot, who was then in the final years of his long, distinguished presidency. His attitudes, however, did not prevent him from taking advantage of the elective system that President Eliot had introduced. As a freshman, his courses were so eclectic he soon wound up on academic probation. He recovered his academic standing and persisted in his studies, attaining a B.A. in an elective program best described as comparative literature in three years, and an M.A. in English literature in the fourth.

In December 1908 a book that Eliot found in the Harvard Union library changed his life: Arthur Symons' *The Symbolist Movement in Literature* introduced him to the poetry of Jules Laforgue. Laforgue's combination of ironic elegance and psychological nuance effected the literary communion with the dead Eliot describes above, convincing Eliot that he was a poet and giving him a voice. By 1909–1910 his vocation had been confirmed: he joined the board and was briefly secretary of Harvard's literary magazine, the *Advocate,* and he could recommend to his classmate William Tinckom-Fernandez the last word in French sophistication—the *vers libre* of Paul Fort and Francis Jammes. (Tinckom-Fernandez returned the favor by introducing Eliot to Francis Thompson's "Hound of Heaven" and John Davidson's "Thirty Bob a Week," poems Eliot took to heart, and to the verse of Ezra Pound, which Eliot had no time for.) At the *Advocate,* Eliot started a lifelong friendship with Conrad Aiken.

In May 1910 a suspected case of scarlet fever almost prevented Eliot's graduation. By that fall, though, he was well enough to undertake a post-graduate year in Paris, where he felt as if he was alive for the first time. (Lyndall Gordon, in *Eliot's Early Years,* notes that his handwriting even changed its shape.) He lived at 151 bis rue St. Jacques, close to the Sorbonne, and struck up a warm friendship with a fellow lodger, Jean Verdenal, the medical student who died in the battle of the Dardanelles and to whom Eliot dedicated "The Love Song of J. Alfred Prufrock." With Verdenal he entered the intellectual life of France, which Eliot later recalled, was then swirling around the figures of Émile Durkheim, Pierre Janet, Rémy de Gourmont, Pablo Picasso, and Henri Bergson. Eliot attended Bergson's lectures at the College de France and was temporarily converted to Bergson's philosophical interest in the progressive evolution of consciousness. Characteristic of a lifetime of conflicting attitudes, though, Eliot also gravitated toward the politically conservative (indeed monarchistic), neoclassical, and Catholic writing of Charles Maurras. Warring opposites, these enthusiasms worked together to foster a professional interest in philosophy and propelled Eliot back to a doctoral program at Harvard the next year.

### INVENTIONS OF THE MARCH HARE

In 1910 and 1911 Eliot copied into a leather notebook he entitled "Inventions of the March Hare" the poems that would establish his reputation: "The Love Song of J. Alfred Prufrock," "Portrait of a Lady," "Preludes," and "Rhapsody on a Windy Night." Combining some of the robustness of Robert Browning's monologues with the incantatory elegance of symbolist verse, and compacting Laforgue's poetry of alienation with the moral earnestness of the "Boston doubt," these poems explore the subtleties of the unconscious with a caustic wit. Above all they express Henry James's lament that Americans living in the confines of their gentility and idealism never seem to live at all. Eliot's expression of this lament can be found in "The Love Song of J. Alfred Prufrock":

> There will be time, there will be time
> To prepare a face to meet the faces that you meet;
> There will be time to murder and create,
> And time for all the works and days of hands
> That lift and drop a question on your plate;
> Time for you and time for me,
> And time yet for a hundred indecisions,
> And for a hundred visions and revisions,
> Before the taking of a toast and tea.

What universalizes the upper-class angst of these poems is Eliot's ability (as in the following extract from "Portrait of a Lady") to translate social claustrophobia into images of life and death, vitality and asphyxiation, and most interestingly into a verbal struggle for existence between fleeting moments of authentic expression and a conventional and suffocating rhetoric.

> And I must borrow every changing shape
> To find expression . . . dance, dance
> Like a dancing bear,
> Cry like a parrot, chatter like an ape.
> Let us take the air, in a tobacco trance—

The combined effect of Eliot's early poems was unique and compelling and their assurance staggered contemporaries who were privileged to read them in manuscript. Conrad Aiken marvelled at "how sharp and complete and *sui generis* the whole thing was, from the outset. The *wholeness* is there, from the very beginning."

Eliot's youthful notebook, including some poems he never published, has recently been edited and annotated by Christopher Ricks. Ricks's annotations confirm Eliot's scattered remarks about his debt not only to Laforgue and Charles Baudelaire but also to the British poets of the 1890s who first began to explore the French sym-bolists—the group of writers including Stéphane Mallarmé, Paul Verlaine, and Arthur Rimbaud. To Ricks's account one must add Eliot's most interesting assessment of the situation in English letters at the time of his first composition. Writing in French in *La Nouvelle revue française* in May 1922, Eliot confessed that his generation of American poets owed its opportunity to an accident of literary history. The British poets of the 1890s, who had just succeeded in emancipating themselves from the worst insularities of Victorian poetry, died before they could fully exploit their French inheritance. Symbolism, with its appeal to the suggestive rather than to the explicit, its appeal to the unconscious, and its daring manipulation of syntax in the service of hermeticism was an untapped resource.

His own generation, he said, owed a special debt to Oscar Wilde, the most talented writer of that generation. For not only had Wilde showed them the way and then died, but the disgrace of his trial and subsequent imprisonment for homosexual offenses eliminated any influence his British friends had on English culture, and required their successors to disguise affiliations with aestheticism the public would probably never have accepted. Wilde's criticism, as collected in his book called *Intentions*, Eliot said, was the focus of a new movement, and the source of a genuine moral value—the indifference to worldly consequences—that might have revolutionized British literature in the 1890s, and would revolutionize it in the next generation. With Wilde's fall, the link of Eliot's generation to the tradition of fine writing in English represented by Ben Jonson, John Dryden, Samuel Johnson, Matthew Arnold, John Ruskin, and Walter Pater had been effaced, and remained to be reestablished by three literatures isolated by the break and rendered "provincial"— British, American, and Irish.

Though Eliot's notebook poems suggest only in part his involvement with British aestheticism, they do reveal crucial interests associated with the decadents (the group of late-nineteenth-century French and English writers) to which Eliot was unable himself to give poetic form in 1910–1911, but that would condition the poetic and intellectual preoccupations of the next part of his life. Among these was a fascination with insanity and unmoored perspective, like that in a suppressed section of "Prufrock" called "Prufrock's Perivigilium" (not published with the original edition of the poem but included in Ricks's edition):

And when the dawn at length had realized itself
And turned with a sense of nausea, to see what it
  had stirred:
The eyes and feet of men—
I fumbled to the window to experience the world
And to hear my Madness singing, sitting on the
  kerbstone
[A blind old drunken man who sings and mutters,
With broken boot heels stained in many gutters]
And as he sang the world began to fall apart . . .

GRADUATE STUDIES

In the fall of 1911 Eliot returned from France, and as part of his graduate studies in philosophy at Harvard began to examine border states of consciousness of many kinds, from insanity in Janet's studies of hysteria, to the "primitive mind" as it had been adumbrated by Durkheim and Lucien Lévy-Bruhl, to the literature of mystic vision, both Western and Eastern. (He took almost as many courses in Sanskrit and Hindu thought as he did in philosophy. He had, as Cleo McNelly Kearns points out, inherited this interest from Emerson, but he pursued it with a scholarly rigor that far surpassed the American poets of the previous century.)

Working in a faculty that included Santayana, William James, the visiting Bertrand Russell, and Josiah Royce, Eliot eventually undertook a dissertation on Bergson's neo-idealist critic F. H. Bradley and produced a searching philosophical critique of consciousness. Acute especially about the way interpretation constitutes and constructs mental objects and discourses, Eliot's philosophical work was highly critical of the platitudes of the nascent disciplines of pyschology and the social sciences. Using Bradley's skepticism to question vast areas of the contemporary intellectual landscape, he finally turned it even against its source, attacking especially Bradley's suggestion of the possibility of a synthesis or harmony of momentary perspectives.

It is hardly surprising, therefore, that much of his poetry from these years has to do with madness and disconnection. In a letter to Conrad Aiken in September 1914 he speaks of three years of worry and nothing good written since "Prufrock," but also shares this uncertainly hopeful thought: "It's interesting to cut yourself to pieces once in a while, and wait to see if the fragments will sprout." This is what he tried to do in a long fragmentary work ("the 'Descent from the Cross' or whatever I may call it"), part of which he sent to Aiken. This work was intended to include the sado-masochistic "Love Song of St. Sebastian":

You would love me because I should have stran-
  gled you
And because of my infamy.
And I should love you the more because I had
  mangled you
And because you were no longer beautiful
To anyone but me.

"Then," he wrote Aiken, "there will be an Insane Section, and another love song (of a happier sort) and a recurring piece quite in the French style. . . . Then a mystical section—and a Fool-House section beginning

Let us go to the masquerade and dance!
I am going as St. John among the Rocks
Attired in my underwear and socks . . ."

But Eliot was "disappointed" in the verses and wondered whether he "had better knock it off for a while." The stuff, he wrote Aiken in November 1914, seemed to him "strained and intellectual." "I know," he said, "the kind of verse I want, and I know that this isn't it, and I know why."

As John Mayer has pointed out in his 1989 work *T. S. Eliot's Silent Voices*, "The Descent from the Cross" with its associated poems (some of which were published in *Inventions of the March Hare* and some in *"The Waste Land": A Facsimile and Transcript*) represented an early staging of the great poems of the 1920s. Eliot's "descent" was a parody of the New Testament's, and the sequence described what Mayer calls "a parody hero engaged in a parody quest, his movement no longer physical and outward . . . but inward and psychic into the self and its nightmare world." For Eliot and for modern poetry, though, the important issue was not the subject but the treatment, with outrageous parody allowing Eliot to produce camp juxtapositions of wildly different tonalities. This was "cut[ting] yourself to pieces . . . and wait[ing] to see if the fragments will sprout" with a vengeance, but in 1914 it was, as Eliot said, still strained and intellectual. It lacked the disciplined representation of dramatic vignettes and ventriloquized voices that Eliot was soon to master. And beyond that it lacked a feeling for how to register and organize vision and voice as if extensions of a single sensibility.

ELIOT SETTLES IN ENGLAND

By 1914, when Eliot left on a traveling fellowship to Europe, he had persuaded a number of Harvard's philosophers to regard him as a potential colleague. However, as Manju Jain argues in *T. S. Eliot and American Philosophy*, his willingness to turn radical skepticism against the highminded humanitarianism of his colleagues alienated the department and would have cost him a position in it had he wanted one. Eliot spent the early summer of 1914 at a seminar in Marburg, Germany, with plans to study in the fall at Merton College, Oxford, with Harold Joachim, F. H. Bradley's colleague and successor. The outbreak of war quickened his departure from Germany. In August he was in London with Conrad Aiken, and by September Aiken had shown Eliot's manuscript poems to Ezra Pound, who, not easily impressed, was won over. Pound called on Eliot in late September and wrote to Harriet Monroe, the editor of the Chicago-based *Poetry* magazine, that Eliot had "actually trained himself *and* modernized himself *on his own*." Eliot and Pound initiated a collaboration that would change Anglo-American poetry, but not before Eliot put down deep English roots.

In early spring 1915 Eliot's old Milton Academy and Harvard friend Scofield Thayer (later editor of the *Dial),* also at Oxford (where Eliot had been since October 1914), introduced Eliot to Vivienne (also Vivien) Haigh-Wood, a dancer and a friend of Thayer's sister. Eliot was drawn instantly to Vivienne's exceptional frankness and charmed by her family's Hampstead polish. Abandoning twenty-five years of social tentativeness, on June 26, 1915, he married Vivienne on impulse at the Hampstead Register's Office. His parents were shocked, and then, when they learned of Vivienne's history of emotional and physical problems (and her associated history of taking opiates), profoundly disturbed. The marriage nearly caused a family break, but it also indelibly marked the beginning of Eliot's English life. Vivienne refused to cross the Atlantic in wartime, and Eliot took his place in literary London.

Eliot and his wife at first turned to Bertrand Russell, who shared with them both his London flat and his considerable social resources. Russell and Vivienne, however, became briefly involved, and the arrangement soured. Meanwhile Eliot tried desperately to support himself by secondary school teaching and with a heavy load of reviewing and extension lecturing. To placate his worried parents, he labored on with his Ph.D. thesis, "Experience and the Objects of Knowledge in the Philosophy of F. H. Bradley." (Eliot finished it in April 1916, but did not receive his degree because he was reluctant to undertake the trip to Massachusetts required for a thesis defense.) As yet one more stimulating but taxing activity, he became literary editor of the avant-garde magazine the *Egoist*. Then in spring 1917 he found steady employment; his knowledge of several languages qualified him for a job in the foreign section of Lloyds Bank, where he evaluated a broad range of continental documents. The job gave him the financial security he needed to turn back to poetry, and in 1917 he received an enormous boost from the publication of his first book, *Prufrock and Other Observations*, printed by the *Egoist* with the silent financial support of Ezra and Dorothy Pound.

For a struggling young American, Eliot soon acquired extraordinary access into British intellectual life. With Russell's help he was invited to country house weekends where visitors ranged from political figures like Herbert Henry Asquith to a constellation of writers, artists, and philosophers from the influential Bloomsbury group that included such figures as Virginia Woolf, Lytton Strachey, and E. M. Forster. At the same time Pound facilitated Eliot's entry into the international avant-garde, where Eliot mixed with the aging Irish poet William Butler Yeats, the English painter and novelist Wyndham Lewis, and the Italian futurist writer Tommaso Marinetti. More accomplished than Pound in the manners of the drawing-room, Eliot gained a reputation in the world of belles lettres as an observer who could shrewdly judge both accepted and experimental art from a platform of apparently enormous learning. It did not hurt that he calculated his interventions carefully, publishing only what was of first quality among his work and creating around himself an

aura of mystery. In 1920 he collected a second slim volume of verse (*Poems*) and a volume of criticism (*The Sacred Wood*). Both displayed a winning combination of erudition and jazzy bravura, and both built upon the understated discipline of a decade of philosophical seriousness. Eliot was meanwhile proofreading the *Egoist*'s serial publication of Joyce's *Ulysses* and, with Pound's urging, starting to think of himself as part of an international movement in experimental art and literature.

Especially in *The Sacred Wood*, Eliot took care to cover over his roots. The volume was originally conceived as a mixture of criticism and poetry under the title of "The Art of Poetry" and was intended as the expression of an American poet-critic aimed at an American audience. Eliot wrote in a July 1919 letter to the lawyer and patron John Quinn, who was attempting to place the book in New York, that he believed it "appropriate" to showcase the review of Henry Adams' *Education* and another article on American literature he had written for the *Athenaeum,* and offered that Adams was "a type that I *ought* to know better than any other." But the volume was rejected first by Knopf and then by Boni and Liveright and John Lane. In revising it for a British press Eliot chose to emphasize abstract literary categories like "The Perfect Critic" rather than the cultural and moral categories that had characterized his recent articles on Adams, Henry James, and Nathaniel Hawthorne. He also strategically placed himself in a context of European artistic endeavor. In "Tradition and the Individual Talent," for example, he famously admonishes the aspiring writer to develop a "historical sense" that will compel him to write "not merely with his own generation in his bones, but with a feeling that the whole of the literature of Europe from Homer and within it the whole of the literature of his own country has a simultaneous existence and composes a simultaneous order." The original, intended venue of Eliot's first collection of criticism would in contrast have sharply outlined his own social and intellectual setting and would have gone a long way toward clarifying the American background of his poetry from "Prufrock" to *The Waste Land* (1922).

Yet if Eliot was about to persuade the London literary world of his cosmopolitanism with the publication of *The Sacred Wood*, circumstances contrived to drive him inward and back as well. Eliot's father died in January 1919, producing a paroxysm of guilt in the son who had hoped he would have time to heal the bad feelings caused by his marriage and emigration. At the same time Vivienne's emotional and physical health deteriorated, and the financial and emotional strain of her condition took its toll. After an extended visit in the summer of 1921 from his mother and his sister Marion, Eliot suffered a nervous collapse and, on his physician's advice, took a three month's rest cure, first on the British seacoast at Margate and then at a sanatorium at Lausanne recommended by Bertrand Russell's friend Ottoline Morrell.

### THE WASTE LAND

Whether because of the breakdown or the long-needed rest it imposed, Eliot broke through the limitations he had felt since 1911 and completed the long poem that he had envisioned in 1914 and had begun in earnest in 1919. Assembled out of dramatic vignettes based on Eliot's London life, *The Waste Land*'s extraordinary intensity stems from a sudden fusing of diverse materials into a rhythmic whole of great skill and daring. Though from the 1930s onward it would be forced into the mold of an academic set-piece on the order of Milton's "Lycidas," *The Waste Land* was at first correctly perceived as a work of jazz-like syncopation. His friend Conrad Aiken insisted that Eliot's "allusive matter" was important primarily

for its private "emotional value" and described the whole as "a powerful, melancholy tone-poem"— a work like 1920s jazz that was essentially iconoclastic and provocative.

Aiken's intuition is confirmed by the opening of *The Waste Land*'s third section, "The Fire Sermon," which demonstrates how inappropriate it is to call Eliot's allusiveness imitative. Here it is clear that for Eliot literary borrowings represent sites at which eruptions of identification from below the level of one's own voice struggle for authenticity with the clichéd rhetoric of the quotidian self. In *The Waste Land*, Eliot's composite narrator is intensely aware of the literariness, the rhetorical quality, of his every utterance. Much of the poem's characteristic irony and punch comes from this self-consciousness. As in not only Eliot's own experience but also the fictional lives of Prufrock, Gerontion, and his other dramatic figures, one of the terrors of the narrator of *The Waste Land* is that he has forfeited life to books, and is trapped in ways of thinking and feeling acquired through convention. To use the bitter phrases of Eliot's essays contemporary with *The Waste Land*, his emotional life is a terminal victim of "the pathology of rhetoric" and the "pastness of the past." And so in the opening of "The Fire Sermon," the horrors of Eliot's vision are compounded by a self-consciousness that shadows every attempted escape from solipsism into the imaginative richness of poetry.

In the following passage, every allusion is set off by implied quotation marks and so renders a self-consciousness on the part of the speaker that poetry is only literature and that to quote poetry is less to express genuine feeling than to sink deeper into solipsism:

The river's tent is broken: the last fingers of leaf
Clutch and sink into the wet bank. The wind
Crosses the brown land, unheard. The nymphs are
   departed.
Sweet Thames, run softly, till I end my song.
The river bears no empty bottles, sandwich papers,

Silk handkerchiefs, cardboard boxes, cigarette ends
Or other testimony of summer nights. The nymphs
   are departed.
And their friends, the loitering heirs of city
   directors;
Departed, have left no addresses.
By the waters of Leman I sat down and wept . . .
Sweet Thames, run softly till I end my song,
Sweet Thames, run softly, for I speak not loud or
   long.
But at my back in a cold blast I hear
The rattle of the bones, and chuckle spread from
   ear to ear.
A rat crept softly through the vegetation
Dragging its slimy belly on the bank
While I was fishing in the dull canal
On a winter evening round behind the gashouse
Musing upon the king my brother's wreck
And on the king my father's death before him.
White bodies naked on the low damp ground
And bones cast in a little low dry garret,
Rattled by the rat's foot only, year to year.
But at my back from time to time I hear
The sound of horns and motors, which shall bring
Sweeney to Mrs. Porter in the spring.
O the moon shone bright on Mrs. Porter
And on her daughter
They wash their feet in soda water
*Et O ces voix d'enfants, chantant dans la coupole!*

These lines take their dominant tone from a series of surrealistic images in which subconscious anxiety, as in a bad dream or a psychotic delusion, is projected onto human and nonhuman objects. In them, emotional fantasies, sometimes of self-loathing, extend through a series of unconnected images in a medium where ego integration seems to be nonexistent. In synecdochic progression, a river, falling leaves, the brown land, bones, a rat, Ferdinand, his brother and his father (ll. 19–20 above, alluding to *The Tempest*), Mrs. Porter and her daughter all become extensions of a whole (but not continuous) state of anxiety. Eliot's narrator projects his feelings of isolation, vanished protection, and loss first onto the river, whose tent of leaves is "broken" (the inappropriately violent adjective emphasizes the feeling of grief behind

the loss), and then onto the falling leaves, which animistically have fingers that "clutch" for support as they sink into decomposition and oblivion. Then defenselessness becomes a shrinking from attack as the leaves fade into the brown land, "crossed" by the wind. (Ten lines hence the crossing wind will become a "cold blast" rattling sensitive bones, and, metamorphosed, the insubstantial malevolence of a "chuckle spread from ear to ear.") Still later, after an interlude of deep-seated loss, isolation turns into self-disgust as the narrator projects himself onto a rat whose belly creeps softly and loathsomely through the vegetation. (Both rat and vegetation are extensions of the decomposing leaves.) The rat's living body merges with a corpse's, and the narrator apprehends himself first as rotting and sodden flesh, feeling "naked on the low damp ground," and then as dry bones, rattled by the rat's foot as he was rattled before by the cold wind.

But the opening of "The Fire Sermon" is not simply an English version of the kind of French symbolist poetry that uses images to express the ambivalence of the subconscious mind. Eliot's poetry is self-dramatizing. In the way it echoes literature of the past and in its self-conscious use of elevated or colloquial language, it dramatizes a Prufrockian sensibility with a power and subtlety unavailable to the Eliot of 1911. In the passage we are considering, this sensibility is caught between two double binds: a yearning for the vitality of common life combined with a revulsion from its vulgarity, and an inclination toward poetry combined with a horror of literature. This vacillation, superimposed over the poetry's *progression d'effets*, brings the world of unconscious impulse into contact with the humanized world of language. In "The Fire Sermon," this drama begins as the literary word "nymphs" emerges from a series of more or less pure images. As it unfolds, the phrase "the nymphs are departed" suggests Eliot's desire to recuperate his lost sense of fullness in a world of pastoral poetry, and for a moment Eliot appropriates Edmund Spenser's voice: "Sweet Thames, run softly, till I end my song."

The immediate result is a disgust with modern life. Hence the following three lines, where that disgust can be heard in a series of jolting colloquialisms. But both Eliot's poetic nostalgia and his disgust with the quotidian soften in the ninth line: there is real sorrow in the speaker's statement that the "nymphs" and their vulgar friends have deserted him—a sorrow sounded in the repetition of "departed" twice in two lines. When the speaker reassumes the linguistic personae of the past in the glissando of the next three lines, therefore, it strikes us as a gesture taken faute de mieux. That is, we sense by this point that Eliot's speaker has some awareness that the great phrases of the past are as unreal as they are beautiful. As his reminiscence of Spenser's "Prothalamion" sounds, we detect a note of self-consciousness in the nostalgia, as if the voice inhabiting the lines were feeling its own inauthenticity. When yet a third quotation is added, to the Psalms and again to Spenser, this discomfort explodes in mid-flight. "But at my back," the speaker begins, and we expect to hear the rest of Andrew Marvell's immortal lines: "But at my back I always hear / Time's wingéd chariot hurrying near." Instead, the feeling of desolation that had called up the line swells out into bitterness: even the cherished texts of the past cannot charm away the bleak realities of life. This realization shatters Eliot's poetic continuity, and causes him to interrupt Marvell's lines with a sardonic assertion of the primacy of the here and now ("the rattle of the bones, and chuckle spread from ear to ear"). This tune, like Mrs. Porter's, is not Spenserian and its leering swell only mocks. At which point the last line, from Paul Verlaine, combines the highest reaches of eloquence with an icy rejection of eloquence itself.

If Williams is right and this is poetry of the classroom, it must also be said that the classroom belongs in the kind of American school in which student back talk abounds. No less than Emerson in *The American Scholar* or Thoreau in the opening of *Walden*, Eliot here seems only able to respect that part of the past that genuinely comes alive in the present. And when it does, as for example in passages in which Dante seems to speak through Eliot's voice ("I had not thought death had undone so many"), one feels an uncanny power that has more to do with relations with the dead than with imitations of previous masters.

## AMERICAN RESONANCES

Moreover, the situations of *The Waste Land* are no less American than Eliot's characteristic attitudes and procedures. The poem presents a number of circumstances in which an Emerson-like consciousness, savoring its own transcendental insight, blunders into the web of human relations and is then shocked awake by the evil produced by withdrawing from a relationship it had entered half aware. This situation Eliot once described (in an essay on Thomas Middleton's *Changeling*) as "the tragedy of the not naturally bad but . . . undeveloped nature . . . suddenly trapped in the inexorable toils of morality . . . and forced to take the consequences of an act which it had planned light-heartedly."

From "Portrait of a Lady" to the stage play *The Family Reunion* (1939) and beyond, Eliot makes such situations his subject. As his youthful letters to Conrad Aiken suggest, he considered himself aloof, a cold observer of others, but a man who by that very condition understood the secret heart of humanity. His stance in *Prufrock and Other Observations* recalls Hawthorne's comment early in his career (in "Sights from a Steeple") that "the most desirable mode of existence might be that of a spiritualized Paul Pry, hovering invisible round man and woman, witnessing their deeds, searching into their hearts, borrowing brightness from their felicity and shade from their sorrow, and retaining no emotion peculiar to himself." And the self-disgust that pervades Eliot's observer's voice—most striking perhaps in "La Figlia che Piange"—resonates with Hawthorne's own ambivalent identifications with Chillingworth in *The Scarlet Letter* or Holgrave in *The House of the Seven Gables* or Coverdale in *The Blithedale Romance* or Kenyon in *The Marble Faun.*

But Eliot's most important affinities with Hawthorne emerge in *The Waste Land,* where his representations of criminal-clairvoyant and observer-alien converge. The poem illustrates what Eliot meant when he said in a 1918 essay called "The Hawthorne Aspect [of Henry James]" that in Hawthorne character is always "the relation of two or more persons to each other." In the poem's different voices, we hear not solitaries but people striving for life's feast of relation, only to fall instead into ghoulish patterns of victim and victimizer. And the central observer, personified as Ovid's Tiresias, presents us with the archetype of these failed relations—a figure implicated in the situations he perceives and menaced by the truths they threaten to impart.

For the most part oblivious to the American resonances of these themes, postwar Britain claimed *The Waste Land* as its own. Pound, who helped pare and sharpen the poem when Eliot stopped in Paris on his way to and from Lausanne, praised it with a godparent's fervor not as an American but as a modern achievement. It did not hurt that 1922 also saw the long-heralded publication of *Ulysses,* or that Eliot in 1923 linked himself and Joyce with Einstein in the public mind in an essay entitled "*Ulysses,* Order and Myth." Meteorically, Eliot, Joyce, and to a lesser extent Pound were joined in a single glow—each nearly as notorious as Picasso.

## CLASSICIST, ROYALIST, ANGLO-CATHOLIC

The masterstroke of Eliot's career was to parlay the international success of *The Waste Land* by means of an equally ambitious (and equally international) publication of a different kind. With Jacques Rivière's *La Nouvelle revue française* in mind, in 1922 Eliot jumped at an offer from Lady Mary Rothermere, wife of the publisher of the *Daily Mail,* to edit a high-profile literary journal. The first number of the *Criterion* appeared in October 1922. Like *The Waste Land,* it took the whole of European culture in its sights. As the *Criterion*'s editorial voice Eliot was placed at the center of first the London and then the Continental literary scene.

In 1923 Eliot, however, was too consumed by domestic anxiety to appreciate his success. In 1923 Vivienne nearly died, and Eliot, in despair, came close to a second breakdown. The following two years were almost as bad, and Eliot, disabled by his desperation was prevented from further exploration of his psychological situation, writing his friend, the English poet and critic Richard Aldington, that "*The Waste Land* . . . is a thing of the past . . . and I am now feeling toward a new form and style." One result was "The Hollow Men" (1925), concerned, as Eliot said about Dante, with "the salvation of the soul" rather than for human beings "as 'personalities'":

> Those who have crossed
> With direct eyes, to death's other Kingdom
> Remember us—if at all—not as lost
> Violent souls, but only
> As the hollow men
> The stuffed men.

In 1925, Eliot's material situation was relieved by a lucky chance that enabled him to at least escape from the demands of his job at the bank. Geoffrey Faber, of the new publishing firm of Faber and Gwyer (later Faber and Faber), saw the advantages of Eliot's dual expertise in business and letters and recruited him as literary editor.

At about the same time, Eliot reached out for religious support. Having long found his family's Unitarianism unsatisfying, he turned to the Anglican church. The seeds of his faith might have already been obvious in "The Hollow Men," but the poem was read as a sequel to *The Waste Land*'s philosophical despair when it first appeared in *Poems, 1909–1925* (1925). Thus few followers were prepared for Eliot's baptism into the Church of England in June 1927. And so, within five years of his avant-garde success, Eliot provoked a second storm. The furor grew in November 1927 when Eliot took British citizenship and again in 1928 when he collected a group of politically conservative essays under the title of *For Lancelot Andrewes* and prefaced them with a declaration that he considered himself "classicist in literature, royalist in politics, and Anglo-Catholic in religion."

Eliot's poetry now addressed explicitly religious situations. In the late 1920s he published a series of shorter poems in the Faber "Ariel" series—short pieces issued in pamphlet form within striking modern covers. These included "Journey of the Magi" (1927), "A Song for Simeon" (1928), "Animula" (1929), "Marina" (1930), and "Triumphal March" (1931). Steeped in Eliot's study of Dante and the late Shakespeare, all these meditate on spiritual growth and anticipate the longer and more celebrated *Ash-Wednesday* (1930), a dialogue of self and soul:

> Because I do not hope to turn again
> Because I do not hope
> Because I do not hope to turn
> Desiring this man's gift and that man's scope
> I no longer strive to strive towards such things
> (Why should the agèd eagle stretch its wings?)
> Why should I mourn
> The vanished power of the usual reign?

"Journey of the Magi" and "A Song for Simeon," Browningesque dramatic monologues, speak to Eliot's desire, pronounced since 1922, to exchange the symbolist fluidity of the psychological lyric for a more traditional dramatic form:

> 'A cold coming we had of it,
> Just the worst time of the year
> For a journey, and such a long journey:
> The ways deep and the weather sharp,
> The very dead of winter.'
> And the camels galled, sore-footed, refractory,
> Lying down in the melting snow.
>
> ("Journey of the Magi")

## KINDS OF DRAMA

Eliot spent much of the last half of his career attempting one kind of drama or another, with an idea of reaching (and bringing together) a large and varied audience. As early as 1923 he had written parts of an experimental and striking jazz play, *Sweeney Agonistes*, never finished but published in fragments in 1932 and performed by actors in masks by London's Group Theatre in 1934. The play contains some of Eliot's most striking lines, and perhaps his most explicit statement of the recurrent situations of *The Waste Land*:

> I knew a man once did a girl in
> Any man might do a girl in
> Any man has to, needs to, wants to
> Once in a lifetime, do a girl in
> . . . . . . . . . . . . . . .
> He didn't know if he was alive
>       and the girl was dead
> He didn't know if the girl was alive
>       and he was dead
> He didn't know if they both were alive
>       or both were dead
> If he was alive then the milkman wasn't
>       and the rent-collector wasn't
> And if they were alive then he was dead.
> . . . . . . . . . . . . . . .
> When you're alone like he was alone
> You're either or neither
> I tell you again it don't apply
> Death or life or life or death.

Some critics consider Eliot's decision to pursue West End drama rather than to follow up the jazz idiom of *Sweeney Agonistes* the biggest mistake of his career. To Eliot, however, the development was a natural and inevitable part of the public duties of his new spiritual life. In early 1934 he composed a church pageant with accompanying choruses entitled *The Rock*, performed in May and June 1934 at Sadler's Wells. Almost immediately following, Bishop Bell commissioned a church drama having to do with Canterbury Cathedral. The play, entitled *Murder in the Cathedral*, was performed in the Chapter House at Canterbury in June 1935 and was moved to the Mercury Theatre at Notting Hill Gate in November and eventually to the Old Vic. At its best, the dramatic poetry of *Murder in the Cathedral* incorporates the fraught tensions of self-examination in the rhythms of public speech:

> You know and do not know, what it is to act or
>     suffer.
> You know and do not know, that acting is suffer-
>     ing,
> And suffering action. Neither does the actor suffer
> Nor the patient act. But both are fixed
> In an eternal action, an eternal patience

In the plays that he wrote starting in the late 1930s, Eliot attempted to conflate a drama of spiritual crisis with a Noel Coward-inspired treatment of social manners. Though Eliot based *The Family Reunion* on the plot of Aeschylus' *Eumenides*, he designed it to tell a story of Christian redemption. The play opened in the West End in March 1939 and closed to mixed reviews five weeks later. Eliot was disheartened, but after World War II he fashioned more popular (though less powerful) combinations of the same elements to much greater success. *The Cocktail Party*, with a cast that included Alec Guinness, opened to a warm critical reception at the Edinburgh Festival in August 1949 and enjoyed a popular success starting on Broadway in January 1950. Eliot's last two plays were more labored and fared less well. *The*

*Confidential Clerk* had a respectable run at the Lyric Theatre in London in September 1953, and *The Elder Statesman* premiered at the Edinburgh Festival in August 1958 and closed after a lukewarm run in London in the fall.

## *FOUR QUARTETS*

Eliot's reputation as a poet and man of letters, increasing incrementally from the mid 1920s, advanced and far outstripped his theatrical success. As early as 1926 he had delivered the prestigious Clark Lectures at Cambridge University (published posthumously in 1993 as *The Varieties of Metaphysical Poetry*), followed in 1932–1933 by the Norton Lectures at Harvard (published in 1933 as *The Use of Poetry and the Use of Criticism*). Thereafter he won just about every honor the academy or the literary world had to offer. In 1948 Eliot received the Nobel Prize for literature during a fellowship stay at the Princeton Institute for Advanced Study. By 1950, his authority had reached a level that seemed comparable in English writing to figures like Samuel Johnson or Samuel Taylor Coleridge.

The lasting achievement of the second half of Eliot's career—a poetry of introspective self-accusation—contrasted, however with his swelling celebrity. After 1925 Eliot's marriage steadily deteriorated, making his public success hollow. During his Norton year at Harvard he separated from Vivienne, but would not consider divorce because of his Anglican beliefs. For most of the 1930s he secluded himself from Vivienne's often histrionic attempts to embarrass him into a reconciliation and made an anguished attempt to order his life upon his editorial duties at Faber and the *Criterion* and around work at his Kensington church. He also reestablished communication with Emily Hale, especially after 1934, when she began summering with relatives in the Cotswolds.

Out of an experience that inspired feelings of 'what might have been' associated with their visit to an abandoned great house, Eliot composed "Burnt Norton," which was published as the last poem in his *Collected Poems, 1909–1935*. With its combination of symbolist indirection and meditative gravity, "Burnt Norton" gave Eliot the model for another decade of major verse. In its first movement, the poem questioned the familiar through riddling negations and reaching for (and finally attaining) a hold on a mysterious reality by a semantic, syntactic, and prosodic mastery Eliot would never thereafter surpass:

> What might have been is an abstraction
> Remaining a perpetual possibility
> Only in a world of speculation.
> What might have been and what has been
> Point to one end, which is always present.
> Footfalls echo in the memory
> Down the passage which we did not take
> Towards the door we never opened
> Into the rose-garden. My words echo
> Thus, in your mind.

In 1938 Vivienne Eliot was committed to Northumberland House, a mental hospital north of London. In 1939, with World War II impending, the *Criterion*, which had occupied itself with the deepening political crisis of Europe, ceased publication. During the blitz Eliot served as an air raid warden, but spent long weekends as a guest with friends in the country near Guildford. In these circumstances he wrote three more poems, each more somber than the last, patterned on the voice and five-part structure of "Burnt Norton." "East Coker" was published at Easter 1940 and took its title from the village that Eliot's ancestor Andrew Eliot had departed from for America in the seventeenth century. (Eliot had visited East Coker in 1937.) "The Dry Salvages," published in 1941, reverted to Eliot's experience as a boy sailing on the Mississippi and on the Massachusetts coast. Its

title refers to a set of dangerously hidden rocks near Cape Ann. "Little Gidding" was published in 1942 and had a less private subject suitable to its larger ambitions. Little Gidding, near Cambridge, had been the site of an Anglican religious community that maintained a perilous existence for the first part of the English civil war. Paired with Eliot's experience walking the blazing streets of London during World War II, the community of Little Gidding inspired an extended meditation on the subject of the individual's duties in a world of human suffering. Its centerpiece was a sustained homage to Dante written in a form of terza rima dramatizing Eliot's meeting with a "familiar compound ghost" he associates with Yeats and with Swift.

Its effect is stunning, mesmerizing, and, unobserved by its first readers, it represents a culminating instance of the experience Eliot alludes to in the passage from the *Egoist* from more than twenty years previous, in which writing poetry approximates a submission of body and soul to the restless spirits of the dead:

> So I assumed a double part, and cried
> And heard another's voice cry: 'What! are *you*
>     here?'.
> Although we were not. I was still the same,
>     Knowing myself yet being someone other—
>     And he a face still forming; yet the words
>         sufficed
> To compel the recognition they preceded.
>     And so, compliant to the common wind,
>     Too strange to each other for misunderstanding,
> In concord at this intersection time
>     Of meeting nowhere, no before and after,
>     We trod the pavement in a dead patrol.

*Four Quartets* (1943), as the suite of four poems was entitled, for a period displaced *The Waste Land* as Eliot's most celebrated work. The British public especially responded to the topical references in the wartime poems and to the tone of Eliot's public meditation on a common disaster. Eliot's longtime readers, however, were more reticent. Some, notably F. R. Leavis, praised the philosophical suppleness of Eliot's syntax, but distrusted his swerve from a rigorously private voice.

## A SUMMING UP

Eliot wrote no more major poetry after the war, turning entirely to his plays and to literary essays, the most important of which revisited the French symbolists and the development of language in twentieth-century poetry. After Vivienne died in January 1947, Eliot led a protected life as a flatmate of the critic John Hayward. In January 1957 he married his secretary Valerie Fletcher and attained a degree of contentedness that had eluded him all his life. He died on January 4, 1965, and, following his instructions, his ashes were interred in the Church of Saint Michael in East Coker. A commemorative plaque on the church wall bears his chosen epitaph—lines chosen from *Four Quartets*: "In my beginning is my end." "In my end is my beginning."

At century's end, Eliot's reputation stood lower than at any time since 1922. Frequently criticized (as he himself—perhaps just as unfairly—had criticized Milton) for a deadening neoclassicism, Eliot in the eyes of post-structuralist critics is guilty of far worse. Suspicious of his conservative religious and political convictions, readers have reacted with increasing impatience to his assertions of authority—obvious in *Four Quartets* and implicit in the earlier poetry. The result, amplified by the intermittent rediscovery of Eliot's occasional anti-Semitic rhetoric, has been a progressive downward revision of his once towering reputation and an attack on his sophisticated irony from the position of a supposedly more sophisticated postmodernism. Thus Paul de Man (whose own wartime anti-Semitism, discovered after his criticism of Eliot, complicated the issue) in *Blindness and Insight* reduced Eliot's subject to a "nostalgia for immediate revelation." De Man's comments, reinforced by the influential judgments of Harold Bloom ("anyone adopting the profession of teaching literature in the early 1950s entered a discipline virtually enslaved . . . by the entire span of [Eliot's] preferences and prejudices") and of Terry Eagleton (who in *Criticism and Ideology* calls Eliot's modernist fragmentation simply a disguise for "totalising mythological forms"), have become staples of postmodernist criticism, and Eliot has acquired the status of a "bad eminence" (Bloom's term) on the contemporary scene.

However, multivarious tributes from practicing poets of many schools during the Eliot centenary year of 1988 indicate that at least some of the prevailing negative reaction has to do with the continuing intimidation of Eliot's poetic voice. In a period less engaged with politics and ideology than the 1980s and 1990s, the lasting strengths of his poetic technique will likely reassert themselves. Already the strong affinities of Eliot's post-symbolist style with such influential poets as Wallace Stevens (Eliot's contemporary at Harvard and a fellow student of George Santayana) have been reassessed, as has the tough philosophical skepticism of his prose. A master of poetic dissonance and poetic syntax, a poet who shuddered to repeat himself, a dramatist of the terrors of the inner life (and of the evasions of conscience), Eliot remains one of the twentieth century's major poets. And, as he himself affirmed at the end of his life, in a 1960 address entitled "The Influence of Landscape upon the Poet," his success cannot be dissociated from his New England origins. Acknowledging the Emerson-Thoreau Award and membership in the American Academy of Arts and Letters, Eliot said he had been forced to "as[k] myself whether I had any title to be a New England poet—as is my elder contemporary Robert Frost, and as is my junior contemporary Robert Lowell." And disarmingly—but firmly—he replied: "I think I have."

# Selected Bibliography

## WORKS OF T. S. ELIOT

POETRY AND PLAYS

*Prufrock and Other Observations.* London: The Egoist Ltd., 1917.

*Ara Vos Prec.* London: The Ovid Press, 1920; *Poems.* New York: Knopf, 1920.

*The Waste Land.* New York: Boni and Liveright, 1922; Richmond, Surrey: The Hogarth Press, 1923.

*Poems, 1909–1925.* London: Faber & Gwyer, 1925; New York: Harcourt, Brace, 1932. (Includes the first book publication of "The Hollow Men.")

*Journey of the Magi.* London: Faber & Gwyer, 1927; New York: William Edwin Rudge, 1927.

*A Song for Simeon.* London: Faber & Gwyer, 1928.

*Animula.* London: Faber & Faber, 1929.

*Ash-Wednesday.* London: Faber & Faber, 1930; New York: The Fountain Press, 1930.

*Anabasis: A Poem by St.-J. Perse with a Translation into English by T. S. Eliot.* London: Faber & Faber, 1930. (Eliot's free translation, supervised by Perse.)

*Marina.* London: Faber & Faber, 1930.

*Triumphal March.* London: Faber & Faber, 1931.

*Sweeney Agonistes: Fragments of an Aristophanic Melodrama.* London: Faber & Faber, 1932.

*The Rock: A Pageant Play.* London: Faber & Faber, 1934.

*Murder in the Cathedral.* London: Faber & Faber, 1935; New York: Harcourt, Brace, 1935.

*Collected Poems, 1909–1935.* London: Faber & Faber, 1936; New York: Harcourt Brace, 1936. (Includes the first publication of "Burnt Norton.")

*The Family Reunion.* London: Faber & Faber, 1939; New York: Harcourt, Brace, 1939.

*Old Possum's Book of Practical Cats.* London: Faber & Faber, 1939; New York: Harcourt Brace, 1939.

*East Coker.* London: Faber & Faber, 1940.

*The Dry Salvages.* London: Faber & Faber, 1941.

*Little Gidding.* London: Faber & Faber, 1942.

*Four Quartets.* New York: Harcourt, Brace, 1943; London: Faber & Faber, 1944.

*The Cocktail Party: A Comedy.* London: Faber & Faber, 1950; New York: Harcourt Brace, 1950.

*The Confidential Clerk.* London: Faber & Faber, 1954; New York: Harcourt, Brace, 1954.

*The Elder Statesman.* London: Faber & Faber, 1959; New York: Farrar, Straus and Cudahy, 1959.

*The Complete Poems and Plays, 1909–1950.* New York: Harcourt Brace, 1952. Reprint, 1971.

*Poems Written in Early Youth.* London: Faber & Faber, 1967; New York: Farrar, Straus and Giroux, 1967.

*Complete Plays.* New York: Harcourt, Brace, 1967; also published as *Collected Plays.* London: Faber & Faber, 1962.

*The Waste Land: A Facsimile and Transcript of the Original Drafts Including the Annotations of Ezra Pound.* Edited by Valerie Eliot. London: Faber & Faber, 1971; New York: Harcourt, Brace, Jovanovich, 1971.

*Inventions of the March Hare: Poems, 1909–1917.* Edited by Christopher Ricks. London: Faber & Faber, 1996; New York: Harcourt, Brace, Jovanovich, 1997. (Eliot's first poetic notebook and some early typescripts. Lavishly annotated.)

CRITICISM AND OTHER PROSE

"In Memory of Henry James." *Egoist* 5(1):1–2 (January 1918).

"The Hawthorne Aspect [of Henry James]." *Little Review* 5(4):47–53 (August 1918).

"A Sceptical Patrician." [Review of Henry Adams, *The Education of Henry Adams*] *Athenaeum* 4647:361–362 (May 23, 1919).

"Reflections on Contemporary Poetry, IV." *Egoist* 6(3):39–40 (July 1919).

*The Sacred Wood: Essays on Poetry and Criticism* (London: Methuen, 1920; New York: Knopf, 1921.

"Lettre D'Angleterre." *La Nouvelle Revue Française* 9(104):617–624 (May 1922).

*Homage to John Dryden: Three Essays on Poetry of the Seventeenth Century.* London: Hogarth Press, 1924.

*For Lancelot Andrewes.* London: Faber & Gwyer, 1928; New York: Doubleday, 1929.

*Dante.* London: Faber & Faber, 1929.

*Selected Essays, 1917–1932.* London: Faber & Faber, 1932; New York: Harcourt, Brace, 1932. Revised and amplified as *Selected Essays.* New York: Harcourt, Brace, 1950; London: Faber & Faber, 1951.

*The Use of Poetry and the Use of Criticism: Studies in the Relation of Criticism to Poetry in England.* London: Faber & Faber, 1933; Cambridge: Harvard University Press, 1933. (The Harvard Charles Eliot Norton Lectures for 1932–1933.)

*After Strange Gods: A Primer of Modern Heresy*. London: Faber & Faber, 1934; New York: Harcourt, Brace, 1934. (The Page-Barbour Lectures at the University of Virginia, 1933.)

*Elizabethan Essays*. London: Faber & Faber, 1934; reprinted as *Essays on Elizabethan Drama*. New York: Harcourt, Brace, 1956. (The London volume includes the first book publication of "John Marston.")

*Essays Ancient and Modern*. London: Faber & Faber, 1936; New York: Harcourt, Brace, 1936. (Revision of *For Lancelot Andrewes*.)

*The Idea of a Christian Society*. London: Faber & Faber, 1939; New York: Harcourt, Brace, 1940.

*A Sermon Preached in Magdalene College Chapel*. Cambridge: Cambridge University Press, 1948.

*Notes Towards the Definition of Culture*. London: Faber & Faber, 1948; New York: Harcourt, Brace, 1949.

*American Literature and the American Language*. Saint Louis, Mo.: Washington University, 1953. (An address delivered at Washington University, with an appendix on the Eliot Family and Saint Louis.)

*Of Poetry and Poets*. London: Faber & Faber, 1957; New York: Farrar, Straus, and Cudahy, 1957.

"The Influence of Landscape upon the Poet." *Daedalus* 89(2):420–422 (Spring 1960).

*George Herbert*. London: Longmans, 1962.

*Knowledge and Experience in the Philosophy of F. H. Bradley*. London: Faber & Faber, 1964; New York: Farrar, Straus, 1964. (Eliot's 1916 Harvard Ph.D. dissertation in philosophy.)

*To Criticize the Critic and Other Writings*. London: Faber & Faber, 1965; New York: Farrar, Straus & Giroux, 1965.

*The Varieties of Metaphysical Poetry*. Edited by Ronald Schuchard. London: Faber & Faber, 1993; New York: Harcourt, Brace, 1994. (Eliot's 1926 Cambridge University Clark Lectures and 1933 Johns Hopkins University Turnbull Lectures, extensively annotated.)

CORRESPONDENCE

*The Letters of T. S. Eliot: Volume I, 1898–1922*. Edited by Valerie Eliot. London: Faber & Faber, 1988; New York: Harcourt, Brace, 1988. (The first of a projected four-volume edition.)

INTERVIEWS

Hall, Donald. "The Art of Poetry, I: T. S. Eliot." *Paris Review* 21: 47–70 (Spring/Summer 1959). Reprinted in *Writers at Work: Interviews from "Paris Review."* Edited by Dick Kay. London: Penguin, 1972.

Lehmann, John. "T. S. Eliot Talks about Himself and the Drive to Create." *New York Times Book Review*, 20 November 1953.

Shahani, Ranjee. "T. S. Eliot Answers Questions." *John O'London's Weekly* 63(1369):497–498 (19 August 1949). Reprinted in *T. S. Eliot: Homage from India*. Edited by P. Lal. Calcutta: Writers Workshop, 1965. Pp. 120–34.

"T. S. Eliot: An Interview." *Granite Review*, 24(3): 16–20 (1962).

"T. S. Eliot Gives a Unique Photo-Interview." *Daily Express*, 20 September 1957.

MANUSCRIPT PAPERS

The most important collections of Eliot's manuscripts can be found at the Houghton Library, Harvard University, at the New York Public Library, and at the libraries of King's and Magdalene College, Cambridge. Smaller collections exist at the Bienecke Library, Yale, the Bodleian Library, Oxford, and (largely correspondence) the Humanities Research Center, Austin, Texas, the Huntington Library, San Marino, California, and the library of Princeton University, among others.

## BIBLIOGRAPHY

Gallup, Donald. *T. S. Eliot: A Bibliography. Revised edition*. New York: Harcourt, Brace, 1969.

## BIOGRAPHICAL AND CRITICAL STUDIES

Ackroyd, Peter, *T. S. Eliot: A Life*. New York: Simon and Schuster, 1984.

Aiken, Conrad. "An Anatomy of Melancholy." *New Republic*, 7 February 1923. Reproduced in *T. S. Eliot: The Waste Land: A Casebook*. Edited by C. B. Cox and Arnold Hinchliffe. London: Macmillan, 1969. Pp. 93–99.

Bloom, Harold. "Reflections on T. S. Eliot." *Raritan* 8(2): 70–87 (1988).

Browne, Martin. *The Making of T. S. Eliot's Plays.* Cambridge: Cambridge University Press, 1969.

Bush, Ronald. *T. S. Eliot: A Study in Character and Style.* New York: Oxford University Press, 1984.

————. *T. S. Eliot: The Modernist in History.* Cambridge: Cambridge University Press, 1991.

Cooper, John Xiros. *T. S. Eliot and the Ideology of "Four Quartets."* New York: Cambridge University Press, 1995.

Cox, C. B., and Arnold Hinchliffe, eds. *T. S. Eliot: The Waste Land: A Casebook.* London: Macmillan, 1969.

Crawford, Robert. *The Savage and the City in the Work of T. S. Eliot.* New York: Oxford University Press, 1987.

Davidson, Harriet. *T. S. Eliot and Hermeneutics: Absence and Interpretation in "The Waste Land."* Baton Rouge: Louisiana State University Press, 1985.

Eagleton, Terry. *Criticism and Ideology:* 1976. Reprint, London: Verso, 1985.

Ellis, Steve. *The English Eliot: Design, Language and Landscape in "Four Quartets."* New York: Routledge, 1991.

Gardner, Helen. *The Art of T. S. Eliot.* 1950. Reprint, New York: Dutton, 1959.

————. *The Composition of "Four Quartets."* London: Faber & Faber, 1978.

Gordon, Lyndall. *Eliot's Early Years.* New York: Oxford University Press, 1977.

————. *Eliot's New Life.* New York: Oxford University Press, 1988.

Grant, Michael, ed. *T. S. Eliot: The Critical Heritage.* 2 vols. London: Routledge & Kegan Paul, 1982.

Gray, Piers. *T. S. Eliot's Intellectual and Poetic Development, 1909–1922.* Brighton, Sussex: Harvester Press, 1982.

*The Harvard Advocate.* 125(3) (December 1938). (Special T. S. Eliot issue; contains an important memoir by W. G. Tinckom-Fernandez and essays by Conrad Aiken, Robert Lowell, Wallace Stevens, Robert Penn Warren, among others.)

Howarth, Herbert. *Notes on Some Figures behind T. S. Eliot.* London: Chatto and Windus, 1965.

Jain, Manju. *T. S. Eliot and American Philosophy: The Harvard Years.* Cambridge: Cambridge University Press, 1992.

Jarrell, Randall. *The Third Book of Criticism.* New York: Farrar, Straus & Giroux, 1969.

Julius, Anthony. *T. S. Eliot, Anti-Semitism, and Literary Form.* New York: Cambridge University Press, 1995.

Kearns, Cleo McNelly. *T. S. Eliot and Indic Traditions: A Study in Poetry and Belief.* New York: Cambridge University Press, 1987.

Kenner, Hugh. *The Invisible Poet: T. S. Eliot.* New York: McDowell, Obolensky, 1959.

————, ed. *T. S. Eliot: A Collection of Critical Essays.* Englewood Cliffs, N.J.: Prentice-Hall, 1962.

Kojecky, Roger. *T. S. Eliot's Social Criticism.* New York: Farrar, Straus & Giroux, 1971.

Leavis, F. R. *New Bearings in English Poetry.* London: Chatto and Windus, 1938.

————. *The Living Principle: English as a Discipline of Thought.* New York: Oxford University Press, 1975.

Litz, A. Walton, ed. *Eliot in His Time.* Princeton, N.J.: Princeton University Press, 1973.

Lobb, Edward, ed. *Words in Time: New Essays on Eliot's "Four Quartets."* London: Athlone, 1993.

Longenbach, James. *Modernist Poetics of History: Pound, Eliot, and the Sense of the Past.* Princeton, N.J.: Princeton University Press, 1987.

Menand, Louis. *Discovering Modernism: T. S. Eliot and His Context.* New York: Oxford University Press, 1987.

Matthiessen, F. O. *The Achievement of T. S. Eliot.* New York: Oxford University Press, 1935.

Mayer, John. *T. S. Eliot's Silent Voices.* New York: Oxford University Press, 1989.

Moody, A. D. *Thomas Stearns Eliot, Poet.* Cambridge: Cambridge University Press, 1979.

————, ed. *The Cambridge Companion to T. S. Eliot.* Cambridge: Cambridge University Press, 1994.

Olney, James, ed. *T. S. Eliot: Essays from the Southern Review.* New York: Oxford University Press, 1988. (Includes an important unpublished essay of Eliot's and valuable memoir material.)

Read, Herbert. "T.S.E.: A Memoir." In *T. S. Eliot: The Man and His Work.* Edited by Allen Tate. London: Chatto and Windus, 1967.

Ricks, Christopher. *T. S. Eliot and Prejudice.* London: Faber & Faber, 1988.

Sencourt, Robert. *T. S. Eliot: A Memoir.* New York: Dodd, Mead, 1971.

Shusterman, Richard. *T. S. Eliot and the Philosophy of Criticism.* London: Duckworth, 1988.

Sigg, Eric. *The American T. S. Eliot: A Study of the Early Writings.* New York: Cambridge University Press, 1989.

Skaff, William. *The Philosophy of T. S. Eliot: From Skepticism to a Surrealist Poetic, 1909–1927.* Philadelphia: University of Pennsylvania Press, 1986.

Smith, Carol H. *T. S. Eliot's Dramatic Theory and Practice.* Princeton, N.J.: Princeton University Press, 1963.

Smith, Grover. *T. S. Eliot's Poetry and Plays: A Study in Sources and Meaning.* Chicago: Chicago University Press, 1950. Enlarged ed., 1960.

———. *"The Waste Land."* London: Allen & Unwin, 1983.

Soldo, John. *The Tempering of T. S. Eliot.* Ann Arbor, Mich.: UMI Research Press, 1983.

Southam, B. C. *A Student's Guide to the Selected Poems of T. S. Eliot.* 1968. Revised ed., New York: Harcourt, Brace, 1996.

Tate, Allen, ed. *T. S. Eliot: The Man and His Work.* London: Chatto and Windus, 1967.

Williams, William Carlos. *Autobiography.* New York: New Directions, 1951.

Witemeyer, Hugh, ed. *Pound/Williams: Selected Letters of Ezra Pound and William Carlos Williams.* New York: New Directions, 1996.

—RONALD BUSH

# William Faulkner
## 1897–1962

*E*ARLY ON THE morning of November 10, 1950, William Faulkner received a telephone call at Rowan Oak, his home in Oxford, Mississippi, telling him that he had been selected to receive the Nobel Prize for literature for 1949. At the time, Faulkner knew that he had a small band of faithful supporters in the United States, including Saxe Commins, his editor at Random House; Evelyn Scott, a novelist from Tennessee who had been one of the first admirers of *The Sound and the Fury* (1929); and Malcolm Cowley, who had edited *The Portable Faulkner* (1946) hoping to lift Faulkner's work to new visibility. He also knew that in Europe—where Albert Camus, André Malraux, and Jean-Paul Sartre had praised his work— his reputation was higher than it was in the United States and that rumors linking his name to the Nobel Prize had been circulating for years. In August 1945, Cowley had written him, in a letter later included in *The Faulkner-Cowley File,* telling him that Sartre had said that "pour les jeunes en France, Faulkner c'est un dieu" (for young people in France, Faulkner is a god). In March 1946, Thorsten Jonsson, one of his Swedish translators, had publicly predicted that he would win the prize, and in 1949, when no prize was announced, rumors that Faulkner would be the next recipient had intensified.

## FAULKNER'S REPUTATION AND READERS

Yet, aside from the small tempest created by the publication of *Sanctuary* in 1931, none of Faulkner's novels sold well, and during the middle 1940s demand for his books virtually disappeared. Furthermore, although Cowley's book was already contributing to a reassessment, there were few signs of gains anywhere in the United States, including the South. Indeed, few people from his region praised his work, and many would spend years trying to decide whether to feel ashamed or proud of the role that the South played in providing the settings, history, and folkways on which his prize-winning fiction was based. Shortly after the announcement of the Nobel Prize, the *New York Times* responded in an editorial, quoted by Robert Penn Warren in his introduction to *Faulkner: A Collection of Critical Essays,* saying that, given "the enormous vogue of Faulkner's works" among foreigners, "Americans must fervently hope" that admirers of his works understood that most Americans thought them "too often vicious, depraved, decadent, corrupt." Rape and incest might be common pastimes in Faulkner's imaginary South, the *Times* added, but they were "not elsewhere in the United States."

Over the next decade, Faulkner's reputation

grew significantly. Publicity generated by the prize helped, as did Faulkner's decision to use his acceptance speech as a "pinnacle" from which to voice long-standing concerns and convictions: that people are too often consumed by fear and that fear is the basest of all human emotions; that only "problems of the human heart in conflict with itself" inspire good writing; and that stories written without "love and honor and pity and pride and compassion and sacrifice" are ephemeral and doomed. In fact, as many critics have noted, these ideas are related to Faulkner's great fiction in ways more complex, if not more tenuous, than some unwary readers have assumed. Yet, like the prize, these views helped gain him new readers and a second look, and soon his reputation began rising in Europe and the United States, including the South, as well as other parts of the world, especially Latin America and Japan and, later, even countries like China, where his fiction had once been banned.

During the 1930s and early 1940s, Faulkner spent considerable time as a screenwriter in Hollywood, trying to make money to compensate for the small returns from his novels. But when he returned early in 1951, it was for a shorter stint, on more favorable terms, a change attributable directly to his ascending reputation. Later that year, he returned to Europe, which he had first visited in 1925, as he did again in 1952 and 1953. In 1954, after *A Fable* was published, he visited Europe again and then traveled to Brazil and Peru on the first of several "goodwill" tours for the U.S. State Department. Back home he found himself caught up in escalating civil rights disputes, in which he took moderate positions that disappointed some people outside the South and offended or even enraged others inside it. But the controversy that left him feeling uncomfortable at home strengthened the State Department's interest in him, and in 1955 he left on a trip that took him to Japan for three weeks and then to Manila, Rome, Paris, England, and Iceland.

Gradually, however, Faulkner's restlessness began to abate. In 1957, he visited Greece for the State Department; in 1961, he went to Venezuela. But from 1957 to 1962, he spent most of his time working on his last three novels—*The Town* (1957), *The Mansion* (1959), and *The Reivers* (1962)—while dividing time between Oxford and Charlottesville, Virginia, where he was writer-in-residence at the University of Virginia. When he died of a coronary occlusion in 1962, on July 6, the birthday of his great-grandfather, the "Old Colonel," he was back home in Mississippi, and it is there, in St. Peter's cemetery in Oxford, that he is buried in the Falkner family plot.

## THE CHALLENGES OF FAULKNER'S FICTION

At least two questions lie waiting for us in Faulkner's belated rise to public and critical acclaim. First, why did recognition of his achievements lag so far behind that of such contemporaries as F. Scott Fitzgerald and Ernest Hemingway, to take two writers of fiction, or T. S. Eliot, to name another "difficult" modernist writer? And, second, why did his fiction—especially given its close ties to a region thought of as culturally backward and with its own reputation for being unusually demanding—continue to lay claim to our attention a hundred years after his birth? Yet, by promising to reward investigation while resisting final answers, these questions can help us identify qualities that make Faulkner's best fiction appealing as well as demanding—namely, his ways of remaining so resolutely interrogative in mood that he creates roles for his readers that are often more active than passive and that occasionally become virtually collaborative. "There is then creative reading as well as creating writing," Ralph Waldo Emerson writes in the nineteenth paragraph of "The American Scholar," where the mind of the reader is drawn into "labor and invention" and the pages of a book become "luminous with manifold allusion."

It is toward something like "creative reading" that Faulkner's best fiction leads us. Like their titles—"That Evening Sun" (1931; reprinted in *Collected Stories of William Faulkner*), *The Sound and the Fury, Absalom, Absalom!* (1936), and *Go Down, Moses* (1942)—his stories and novels often begin by evoking the presence of other songs, plays, or stories that we are challenged to recall. In addition, one work can evoke the presence of another—as *The Sound and the Fury* does of "That Evening Sun" and as *Absalom, Absalom!* does of *The Sound and the Fury,* to cite two examples—so that earlier stories are being rewritten and we, in reading one, are rereading the other. Although we know, especially from examining the manuscripts, that Faulkner characteristically worked on his novels and stories with great care, we also know that they are more likely to come to us as fractured or fragmented narratives than as conventional narratives. Some of them begin abruptly, as though caught in midstride, in a kind of interruption; others move unevenly toward a last line that resembles an ending and may even provide a sense of one, without providing a traditional sense of closure— as we see, for example, in the last lines of *As I Lay Dying* (1930) (" 'Meet Mrs Bundren,' he says.") and *Absalom, Absalom!* (". . . I dont. I dont! I dont hate it! I dont hate it!"). *As I Lay Dying* consists of fifty-nine sections told by fifteen narrators, and *The Sound and the Fury* comprises four different versions of one family's story, each very different from the others. In both novels the reader must try to compare, contrast, and reconcile different versions of the same scenes while also working to fill in gaps in one version with information or impressions gathered from another.

In short, we are drawn into roles that become investigative and even collaborative, where we must strive for total recall and yet must also actively try to figure things out. Sometimes our tasks resemble those of detectives, who search for clues in order to solve mysteries. Sometimes they parallel those of historians, who must search for facts in order to discover meaningful patterns among them. And occasionally, in works such as *Absalom, Absalom!* and *Go Down, Moses,* they resemble those we associate with creative artists, who enhance existing facts by reading them as if others still missing were present or who engage in imaginative amplifications and rearrangements of facts that refuse to yield meaning or closure to mere analysis, however thorough. In short, we must be willing to let Faulkner's stories and novels teach us about our role as readers. Emerson's pairing of creative reading with creative writing can help us understand this role, for hidden in that pairing is a reminder that the question of why a great work of art proves rewarding cannot finally be separated from the question of how it does what it does.

It is, of course, one thing to recognize that creative reading can be rewarding as well as challenging, and that a writer's willingness to engage his readers in such reading stems, at least in part, from a special kind of generosity. It is quite a different thing to understand why Faulkner gained reputation earlier in Europe than in the United States. One explanation of this lies in the fact that several of Faulkner's older contemporaries— writers like James Joyce, Marcel Proust, and Virginia Woolf—had already begun reeducating the reading public in Europe. A second lies in the squeamishness and defensiveness that lay behind the *New York Times* editorial and that was even more prevalent in the American South. In 1958 C. Vann Woodward, a distinguished historian, published an essay called "The Search for Southern Identity," reprinted as the first essay in *The Burden of Southern History* (1960), that addresses the several forces that worked to impede native recognition of Faulkner's achievement.

Faulkner's fiction, like Southern history, Woodward suggests, cuts against the grain of American culture by confronting three unpleasant as well as "un-American" experiences (p. 17). First, the South had a long, intense experience with poverty in a country blessed with unparalleled economic abundance. Second, several painful encounters with failure and defeat—including "not only an overwhelming military defeat but long decades of defeat in . . . economic, social, and political life" (p. 19)—set the South apart in a country accustomed to success and victory. Third, the South carried a heavy burden of guilt associated not only with its poverty and failure but also with its defense of the systematic subjugation and exploitation of other human beings for profit, through institutionalized slavery and segregation, while it continued to proclaim its devotion to human freedom as an inalienable right and to equality of opportunity as a corollary of that freedom. And, finally, the South did these things while living within a nation accustomed to thinking of itself as fundamentally good and innocent. Further complicating these un-American experiences, both for the South's sense of itself and for its relations with the rest of the United States, was the Southerners' un-American habit of acquiring a strong sense of place and a strong sense of being historically rooted. To live in the South, especially for the thoughtful young, meant becoming identified with terrible injustices and humiliating defeats in a country where most people came to consider themselves free from history and to think of history as something unpleasant that happened only to weaker, less fortunate, and probably less deserving people.

Woodward thus provides ways of rethinking the relationship between the regional thrust of Faulkner's fiction and its uneven progress in acquiring a broad readership. First, he helps us understand the resistance of Southern readers to be reminders of the failures, contradictions, and defeats that define their history and to the exposure of such things to the inspection of distant readers. Second, he suggests ways of accounting for the unwillingness of Northern readers to have

"foreigners" associate them and their exemplary nation with the poverty, backwardness, and hypocrisies of the South. And third, he helps us understand why international readers—unhampered by the guilt felt by Southern readers and by the illusions held to by most other Americans—might have come to Faulkner's fiction with fewer distractions, despite having to overcome language barriers. For most readers outside the United States have more in common with the negative historical experiences of Southerners than with the triumphant experiences of "typical" Americans, and yet they are less likely than Southerners to feel defensive when confronted with specifically "Southern" versions of them.

Finally, of course, Faulkner's fiction must appeal to us in and through its manner as well as its substance, as Emerson's formulation also suggests. It must make its way among us one reader at a time, by showing us that it can enlarge and enrich our lives by burdening and entangling us in worlds in which characters often come to feel burdened and entangled. Like many of Faulkner's characters, many of his readers tend to resist such engagements. But readers willing to put forth the effort have found that his novels and stories can teach them to perform the tasks that reading the works requires—including those tasks associated with becoming creative readers, or put another way, Faulkner's deputies and collaborators.

## EARLY LIFE AND WORK

William Faulkner, the first of four sons of Murry Cuthbert and Maud Butler Falkner, was born William Cuthbert Falkner on September 25, 1897, in the small town of New Albany, Mississippi. In 1898, when his father was appointed treasurer of a railroad built by his great-grandfather W. C. Falkner and controlled by his grandfather J. W. T. Falkner, the family moved to Ripley, another small northern Mississippi town. In 1902, to the disappointment of Faulkner's parents, J. W. T. Falkner decided to sell the family railroad, virtually forcing Murry's small family, which then included two younger sons, Murry C. Falkner Jr., born in 1899, and J. W. T. Falkner III, born in 1901, to move to Oxford, where the family's other operations and connections were centered.

There, sponsored by his father, Murry moved from job to job, looking unsuccessfully for something that could match the charm the railroad held for him. J. W. T. Falkner was a successful lawyer and banker and a prominent player in social and political affairs of the region. Traces of him can be found in several of Faulkner's novels, including *Sartoris* (1929). But he showed almost as little interest in sharing power with Murry as Murry did in the various positions he held after moving to Oxford. Finally, after nearly fifteen years of shifting around, Murry settled into a job as secretary and business manager at the University of Mississippi, a position he held for ten years, only to lose it in a political shuffle shortly before he died in August 1932.

By contrast, Faulkner's mother was very strong-willed, and with her equally strong-willed mother, Lelia Swift Butler, she became as much the center of Faulkner's immediate family as his grandfather—or the "Young Colonel," as he was called—was of the Faulkner clan. "Damuddy," as her grandsons called their maternal grandmother, and as the Compson children in *The Sound and the Fury* call theirs, visited the family frequently even before she moved in with them in 1902, where she remained until her death on June 1, 1907, just two and a half months before the birth of the fourth and last of the Falkner boys, Dean Swift. "Don't Complain—Don't Explain" was the message Maud Falkner hung above the stove in her kitchen, and it was a motto she lived by and sought to imprint on the minds of her sons. With their father, the boys explored a different world. They played baseball, flew kites, and rode horses; they visited places he associated with men, including

the livery stable, the train station, and the courthouse square; and they studied things their father loved, including the wildlife and vegetation found in the big woods and open fields around Oxford, which seemed almost impervious to time and change, less cluttered by the trappings of civilization, and made simpler by the absence of women. In 1954, long after he had begun using his knowledge of the history and prehistory of his native region in his fiction, Faulkner wrote an essay called "Mississippi," which was later reprinted by James B. Meriwether in *Essays, Speeches, and Public Letters by William Faulkner.* In it he places the region he had come to think of as his own under the aspect of slow time, as an almost limitless space:

> In the beginning it was virgin—to the west, along the Big River, the alluvial swamps threaded by black almost motionless bayous and impenetrable with cane and buckvine and cypress and ash and oak and gum; to the east, the hardwood ridges and the prairies where the Appalachian mountains died and buffalo grazed; to the south, the pine barrens and the moss-hung liveoaks and the greater swamps less of earth than water and lurking with alligators and water moccasins, where Louisiana in its time would begin.

But young Faulkner also spent time in his family home, in its attic and on its porches, being tutored by his mother and grandmother. Maud Falkner was an avid reader as well as a talented painter. Having taught all her sons to read before she entrusted them to the public school, she continued to direct their reading after they were in school, especially William's. Damuddy knew how to draw, paint, and sculpt, and she encouraged the boys to try all three. With her help they learned to design and build miniature villages. Like her daughter, Lelia Butler was as firm in the things she despised as in those she valued, and they included the profanity and whiskey that she and her daughter thought of as evil and associated with men, especially after Murry Falkner started drinking so much that he was at times taken to the Keeley

Institute near Memphis for "the cure," an ordeal Faulkner later repeated.

Though never an avid student, young Faulkner was for a time a successful one. But in the fifth grade his interest waned, his attendance dropped off, and his grades began to suffer. He stayed in school primarily to play sports and delay disappointing his mother. Finally, however, he cut short his second attempt at his senior year and left school without a diploma, to the considerable disappointment of his family, especially his mother. Looking back, one of his classmates remembered him standing around a great deal, watching and listening while his classmates played and talked. Indeed, the habit of presenting himself as an attentive observer became something he apparently carried with him everywhere he went—to the town square, the livery stable, and the depot, where he listened as friends of his family or even chance strangers told tales; to family gatherings, where relatives and servants swapped family stories about the "old times" and the legendary "Old Colonel," who had become a lawyer, soldier, planter, writer, politician, and railroad entrepreneur; and to campfires on hunting trips, where his father and his father's friends traded stories. Soon, it was almost as though stillness and silence had become his personal trademarks. Even at school parties he tended to watch while other students danced.

By 1916, when it became clear that his second attempt at finishing high school was going to fail, Faulkner had formed two important friendships. One was with Phil Stone. As a member of a prominent Oxford family who shared Faulkner's interests in literature, especially in poetry, and admired Faulkner's early writings, Stone proved especially valuable. He loaned Faulkner books and talked about writers he had begun reading at Yale, where he was a student; he encouraged Faulkner's efforts to write, and, by praising his work, he gave some legitimacy to Faulkner's efforts in a community disinclined to take such things seriously. The second was with Lida Estelle Oldham, a member of another prominent Oxford family with whom he had attended high school. But when Faulkner became a serious suitor rather than a friend of the family, the relationship became strained. (Years later, they were married.) But the years between Faulkner's final departure from high school and his emergence as a published writer were far too chaotic to suit his family or Estelle's, and Estelle's responded by opposing the courtship.

After quitting school, Faulkner worked briefly in his grandfather's bank and then began hanging around the University of Mississippi. In 1917, his first published work, a drawing, appeared in the yearbook *Ole Miss*. A year later—shortly after Estelle's family announced her engagement to Cornell Franklin, whose prospects at the time were far more promising than Faulkner's—Faulkner decided to leave Oxford. Having tried to enlist in the army only to be rejected as too short and slight, he caught a train to New Haven, where Stone had graduated from Yale College and entered Yale Law School. There, with Stone's help, he met interesting people, frequented the Brick Row Print and Book Shop, and found work at the Winchester Repeating Arms Company. But talk of World War I, which the United States entered in April 1917, was everywhere. Determined not to be left behind, he went to New York, changed the spelling of his name by adding a "u," forged documents to establish English citizenship, and enlisted in the Royal Air Force, only to see the war end during the third and final stage of his training.

In early December 1918, when Faulkner returned to Oxford, he wore the uniform not of a cadet but of a war hero, complete with wings and an overseas cap, and he was armed with stories that exaggerated everything about his military experience. In 1919–1920, he took courses at Ole Miss, which waived entrance requirements for veterans. But he soon dropped out and began taking odd jobs, primarily as a carpenter and painter, while continuing to participate in student groups interested in poetry, drama, and art. Both his drawings and his poems of this period show the deep influence of fin de siècle English and French aestheticism—associated with stylistic purity and precision, or more generally with "art-for-art's-sake," and with writers like Walter Pater, and novels and poems about novelists and poets. Such concerns continued to be a strong presence in his writings and drawings, sometimes in witty or ironic ways, even after he turned from poetry to fiction, as we see especially in an unfinished novel, "Elmer," which is about an aspiring artist, and *Mosquitoes* (1927), which is about a colony of artists and their followers. But during the early 1920s, when Phil Stone's influence remained strong, it was primarily English and French poetry of the late nineteenth and early twentieth centuries that he was reading and poetry that he was trying hardest to write. The first results of these efforts were individual poems, one of which was published in the *New Republic* in August 1919. In the early 1920s he turned decisively toward poem sequences, as we see in *Vision in Spring,* a handmade copy of which he gave to Estelle Oldham Franklin in 1921 (though it was not published until 1984), and in *The Marble Faun* (1924), his first published book. *Vision in Spring,* in particular, made it clear how much he thought of himself as a poet writing for Estelle.

> You are so young. And frankly you believe
> This world, this darkened street, this shadowed wall
> Are bright with beauty you passionately know
> Cannot fade nor cool nor die at all.
>
> Raise your hand, then, to your scarce-seen face
> And draw the opaque curtains from your eyes;
> Profoundly speak of life, of simple truths,
> The while your voice is clear with frank surprise.

### TOWARD THE GREAT DISCOVERY

Between Faulkner's first national publication in 1919 and his second, in the *Double Dealer* in June 1922, came rejections that were only partly offset by the books he was making and the frequency with which his poems, sketches, drawings, and reviews, as well as one short story, were appearing in university publications. During these years he also wrote a one-act play called *The Marionettes* (1977), for a drama group at the university that included several people he liked and trusted, notably Ben Wasson, who became a close friend and Faulkner's first literary agent. But feeling restless, he left for Greenwich Village, hoping to find interesting work and, with Stone's help, to make contact with a more varied audience. Once there, he took a job at the Doubleday, Doran Bookstore, which was managed by Elizabeth Prall, through whom he met her husband, Sherwood Anderson, the first major literary figure he had encountered. But within a few months, he was back in Oxford, ready to accept the most improbable job he ever held—as postmaster of the university post office.

With a regular paycheck and a job that, as he defined it, left him ample leisure time, he played golf and continued to read, write, and draw. Contributing poems, sketches, and reviews to university publications, he seemed for a time to have found a rhythm that worked for him. In fact, however, he was primarily turning out retread versions of older work, as though his conception of himself as a writer had somehow become fixed. Soon, as his restlessness mounted, the protests of post office patrons, which had once been largely humorous, began to change in tone. In 1924, three developments—official notification that charges of neglect of duty, indifference to patrons, and abuse of mail had been filed against him; his waning interest in the kinds of things he was writing and the publications in which they were appearing; and the publication of *The Marble Faun* in December 1924—spurred him to resign his position and leave Oxford again in 1925, this time for New Orleans.

In New Orleans, Faulkner renewed his friendship with Prall and Anderson and through them found a colony of writers and artists—William Spratling, Hamilton Basso, Lyle Saxon, John McClure, Julius Friend, and Roark Bradford, to name a few—among whom he felt comfortable. He still seems to have listened more than he talked when conversations turned from storytelling to discussions of Freud, the anthropologist James Frazer, and the philosopher Henri Bergson, or the writers T. S. Eliot, Joseph Conrad, and James Joyce. But he apparently found the conversations stimulating. Soon he was writing with renewed intensity both for the *Double Dealer* and for the *New Orleans Times-Picayune,* which actually paid him for his work. Two important collections of his writings from this period, *William Faulkner: Early Prose and Poetry* and especially *New Orleans Sketches,* which includes stories as well as sketches, provide a valuable sense of his rapid move toward prose fiction. But it was the example of Anderson as well as the experience of writing stories and sketches, coupled with his memories of the narrative traditions he had absorbed in his boyhood and youth that inclined him decisively toward fiction. And the result, his first novel, *Soldiers' Pay,* transformed his life as a writer both by turning him toward fiction and by renewing his hope that he could become a writer of consequence.

Writing with deepened intensity, first in New Orleans and then in Pascagoula, Mississippi, he finished *Soldiers' Pay* near the end of June, roughly six months after his arrival in New Orleans. In it he contrasts two figures that had become crucial to him: one a young cadet for whom the war ended before he had a chance to fight and the other a young pilot whose face is so disfigured by a "dreadful scar" that it leaves him longing to die and makes people who see him "sick at the stomach." If in the first of these figures we see something of the disappointment that Faulkner had personally experienced, in the second we recognize the horrors he had contemplated and heard about but had not experienced, and in their juxtaposition lies his first sustained effort to discover ties between his own experiences and those of the heroes and victims of his generation.

Assured that Anderson would recommend his manuscript to the publisher Horace Liveright, Faulkner sailed for Europe with William Spratling. Landing in Genoa, he started toward Paris, walking much of the way. Later, he visited England and took another long walking tour of France, seeing cathedrals and old ruins as well as battlefields made famous by World War I. Back in Paris, he worked on two stories about artists and writers—one called "Mosquito," which became his second novel, and the other called "Elmer," which was not published until after his death. He and Stone had talked about his staying in Europe for several years. But soon after he had begun working on his new projects, he learned that the publishers Boni and Liveright had accepted *Soldiers' Pay,* and he began feeling anxious to go home. By Christmas he was back in Oxford, looking like a typical bearded bohemian writer and trying to write fiction while awaiting the February publication of his first novel.

Although *Soldiers' Pay* is a minor performance, it had three important impacts on Faulkner's career. First, as the projects he had begun in Paris make clear, it permanently swayed him toward writing fiction. Second, though the reviews were mixed, they were favorable enough to get him a contract from Horace Liveright for a second book. Third, although its publication gave obvious credibility to his sense of himself as a writer in Oxford, rumors about its scandalous contents, inspired in part by echoes of James Branch Cabell's *Jurgen* (1914), soon surrounded him in controversy. For years people had been treating him as a ne'er-do-well; now they began treating him as a scandalmonger. He decided to leave Oxford, bound first for New Orleans and then for Pascagoula, hoping to resume his unsuccessful courtship of Helen Baird, a young woman he had met before his trip to Europe and for whom he had already made two handprinted books: an allegory called "Mayday," dated January 27, 1926, and first published in 1977; and a sonnet sequence called "Helen: A Courtship," dated June 1926 and first published in 1981.

*Mosquitoes,* Faulkner's second novel, grew out of one of the projects he had begun in Paris, and it is dedicated to Helen. Although it may have been written with his publisher, Horace Liveright, and reviewers in mind, *Mosquitoes* clearly was not meant to endear Faulkner to people back home. It is considerably more scandalous than *Soldiers' Pay,* in part because its cast includes an array of artists and pseudo-artists who talk about, contemplate, or engage in varied sexual activities and in part because one of its characters, a man named Fairchild, discusses art as a kind of perversion and ties it directly to sexual sublimation: "In art, a man can create without any assistance at all. . . . A perversion, I grant you, but a perversion that builds Chartres and invents Lear is a pretty good thing." In addition, it offended several friends and acquaintances in New Orleans, who found sometimes unflattering traces of themselves in it.

### THE GREAT DISCOVERY

Part roman à clef, part *Künstler Roman* (novel having an artist as the central character), part novel of ideas, and part satire, *Mosquitoes* falls well short of accomplishing everything it attempts. Yet despite its flaws, it remains interesting, especially in relation to Faulkner's efforts to define himself as an artist. Like *Mosquitoes,* several short pieces that date from the period just before and after *Soldiers' Pay*—notably, "Nympholepsy" and "Carcassonne"—also bear in interesting ways on Faulkner's efforts to find a style and a territory of his own. For the final stage of the imaginative move that redefined him as a writer, signaling what was to come—namely, fiction that would establish him as one of the major writers of the twentieth century—began in late 1926 and

early 1927, soon after he finished *Mosquitoes.* In one sense, that move consisted of his surrendering his earliest conception of himself as a writer, namely, as a poet, and the self-conscious fumbling for exactitude that he associated with writing poetry—a conception reflected in the highly "poetic," allusional, impressionistic style of his early sketches, which clearly remain the work of a poet. In another, it unfolded as an imaginative appropriation of what he later called "my own little postage stamp of native soil"—that is, the old tales and talking he had heard in his boyhood and youth; the scenes, the folkways, and folklore; the terrain, the vegetation, and the history of northern Mississippi.

Faulkner began with two interrelated projects—one called "Father Abraham," about a poor white family named Snopes, which was finally published in 1983, and one about an aristocratic family named Sartoris that was published in two different forms, as *Sartoris* (1929) and as *Flags in the Dust* (1973). Both of these works are set in an imaginary town named "Jefferson" and an imaginary kingdom called "Yoknapatawpha County" that are based on Oxford and the country surrounding it, as the map Faulkner drew for *Absalom, Absalom!,* where he describes his imaginary kingdom as consisting of 2,400 square miles and as having a population of 15,611—9,313 black and 6,298 white—makes clear.

Created as corollaries of Oxford, Mississippi, and Lafayette County, Jefferson and Yoknapatawpha gave Faulkner access to the full range of Mississippi social life that he had spent years observing and even studying—in towns, on farms, and around campfires, among women and men, rich and poor, black and white. They gave him access to the region's physical culture; its architecture and machinery; its typography and geography; its animals, wild and domesticated; and its vegetation, wild and cultivated. And they gave him access to the prehistory and to the still unfolding history, written and oral, of a region that extended back through the nineteenth century to a time before northern Mississippi had been rediscovered, explored, and settled. Eventually, he wrote many short stories and thirteen novels set either entirely or partially in Yoknapatawpha County, the last of them being *The Reivers,* published on June 4, 1962, almost exactly a month before his death. More immediately, the imaginative move that he came to think of as his "great discovery" enabled him to realize that he knew many things—including the rhythms and intonations, the words and the turns of phrase, the speech patterns and the voices of many people—without quite knowing how he knew them. Beyond that, he also discovered that he possessed a sense of form—a sense of life as narrative—that was yet another gift of the region he wrote about. "In a city," Ezra Pound wrote in 1921 in a review of Jean Cocteau's *Poésies 1917–1920,* where "visual impressions succeed each other, overlap, overcross" and often come as "a flood of nouns without verbal relations," people acquire a sense of life that is "cinematographic," but in a village, where people learn to think in terms of sequence and shared knowledge, by virtue of knowing who did what before, during, and after the last great war or revolution, and so forth, inhabitants acquire a sense of life as "narrative."

The American South of Faulkner's boyhood and youth still belonged to what Pound describes as a "village" world and associates with "narrative." But Faulkner realized that the life of traditional village worlds was moving rapidly toward what Pound calls a "cinematographic" world, and he also realized that, looked at carefully, villages such as the one he knew best—with a recent frontier past, aristocratic pretensions, and modern, materialistic ambitions—had always been too jumbled and helter-skelter, too broken and conflicted, too torn between looking back and racing forward to be caught and conveyed in traditional narrative forms, where continuity reigns. Over the next several decades—most notably in works like *The*

*Sound and the Fury, As I Lay Dying, Light in August* (1932), *Absalom, Absalom!,* and *Go Down, Moses,* but in scores of others as well—he became a specialist in constructing fragmented narratives in which the continuity and perfect form of traditional narratives exists only as an unattainable possibility and in which, as a result, the role of the reader would necessarily be enlarged and made more creative as well as more challenging.

"Father Abraham," one of the two projects with which Faulkner began exploring the imaginary county that was crucial to his great discovery, remains crude and unfinished. In it we meet the Snopes family who figured prominently in a wide range of stories as well as the novels, written over the next several decades, that form the core of the "Snopes trilogy"—*The Hamlet* (1940), *The Town,* and *The Mansion.* But *Flags in the Dust,* the project on which he chose concertedly to work in the winter of 1926–1927, focuses on the aristocratic Sartoris family that bears important resemblances to the Falkner clan. And in it the upstart Snopes clan plays a subordinate role, as does the middle-class Benbow family. Yet it is the combined presence of these three families that enables Faulkner to bring a wide part of Yoknapatawpha's rapidly changing social and cultural scene, as well as both great wars, the Civil War and World War I, into play, making it still one of the most inclusive of his Yoknapatawpha novels.

Faulkner's third novel helps make more comprehensible his emergence as a writer of stunning and demanding originality, for it introduces the geography and history, the races and social classes, the rises and falls, the victories and defeats that became central to his imagined world. Both the Civil War and World War I are introduced as national events that change the local community of Jefferson, accelerating the decline of the Sartoris family and the rise of the Snopes family. Early in both *Sartoris* and *Flags in the Dust,* we encounter the Old Colonel, John Sartoris, whose ties are to the Civil War, and his grandson, young Bayard

Sartoris, who has survived World War I. But the Old Colonel, even though he is by then dead, enters *Flags in the Dust* as "a far more definite presence" than the people who spend their days talking about him. And when our attention shifts toward young Bayard, we realize that we are moving toward a future that has no chance of matching the achievements of the past. We realize that Bayard is haunted not only by memories of the war and fear that no achievement of the future can match his family's glorious past but also by guilt for having survived a war in which his brother, Lieutenant John Sartoris, has died.

In 1927 Faulkner's third novel was rejected by Horace Liveright, who described Faulkner's first novel as stronger than his second and his third as so diffuse that it ought not to be offered to another publisher. Responding to Liveright, Faulkner tried to sound confident. But in fact he was so distressed that he began talking about giving up writing altogether. Having tried to revise the manuscript himself, he sent it, along with several stories he had been unable to place with magazines, to his old friend Ben Wasson, who was working in New York as an agent. After substantial cuts by Wasson, it was finally published as *Sartoris* by Harcourt, Brace. With cuts restored, it was published much later as *Flags in the Dust.* Flawed though both works are, taken together they make clear why Faulkner continued to think of them as marking his great discovery and as containing what he called, in a conference at the University of Virginia (May 23, 1958), "the germ of [his] apocrypha."

At the time, however, Faulkner's sense that he had discovered an inexhaustible kingdom served to make Liveright's emphatic rejection of it all the more difficult to handle. After sending the manuscript to Wasson, he began working his way through one of the darkest periods of his life. Helen had responded to his overtures by marrying someone else. But as Estelle's marriage began to fall apart, she became more and more dependent both on Faulkner and on the long-deferred marriage of

which neither of their families approved. Faulkner's response was to begin working alone, in virtual secrecy, on stories about some children named Compson, who clearly had ties to his own childhood. And from this move, which was in one sense clearly regressive, he resumed one of the most remarkable periods of innovative productivity in the history of American literature.

### THE SOUND AND THE FURY

Two stories—"That Evening Sun" and "A Justice"—came first, both involving children named Compson. Then, sometime in the early spring of 1928, he began working on a piece called "Twilight" that he later entitled *The Sound and the Fury.* It had been clear in some of his earlier fiction, as it is in "That Evening Sun" and "A Justice," that Faulkner's deepest sympathies often centered on vulnerable children, especially those burdened with flawed, self-involved parents who leave them to face loss and consternation alone. But both his secretive way of working on *The Sound and the Fury* and his way of talking about it in later years, in which he showed uncharacteristic consistency as well as deep feeling, suggest that it occupied a special place in his memory as well as his career. It began, he made clear, by his rejecting those who had rejected him. "One day," he said in an introduction to the book written later, "I seemed to shut a door between me and all publishers' addresses and book lists. I said to myself, Now I can write." And so he had no plan, saying to himself, "I wont have to worry about publishers liking or not liking this at all." Wasson had substantially cut and revised *Flags in the Dust* with Faulkner's acquiescence, and after some ten rejections, he finally found a publisher for it. But when Wasson made a few changes in *The Sound and the Fury,* Faulkner replied with a clear note, saying that he had "effaced" Wasson's changes and that he did not want him to do any more tampering with the "script."

It was the character Caddy, or more precisely his feelings for her, Faulkner reported, that turned a story called "Twilight" into the novel called *The Sound and the Fury:* "I loved her so much," he said. "I couldn't decide to give her life just for the duration of a short story." She was, he said, "the beautiful one," his "heart's darling." So what began as a short story became a longer story that insisted on being told four times. "And that's how that book grew. That is, I wrote that same story four times." Simple and moving in its basic action, *The Sound and the Fury* traces the stories of four children—three sons, Benjamin (called Benjy), Quentin, and Jason, and one daughter, Candace (called Caddy)—as they come of age during the last stages of the decay and dissolution of a once proud family, now represented by them and their cold, self-involved, manipulative parents. With no one to count on except each other and no one to shield and guide them except the family's black servants, especially Dilsey, Caddy and her brothers must make their ways through a world that seems simultaneously to be winding down and spinning out of control. But *The Sound and the Fury* is as innovative formally as it is bleak thematically.

In one sense it is a single story told four times—the first-person narratives of Benjy, then Quentin, then Jason, and finally in the third person; in another sense it is four different stories, as though to remind us that shared experiences—such as the death and funeral of a grandmother the children call "Damuddy"—can tear people apart rather than draw them together. As we see events from four different perspectives, *The Sound and the Fury* allows us, as collaborative readers, to discover that while the act of remembering has close ties to repetition, being and living do not, even when they are intended or appear to have such ties. In *The Sound and the Fury* we move first through two narratives that are intensely private and then through two

that are more familiar and public. But there is loss as well as gain in this movement, as we see especially in the third section of the novel, which is told by Jason, whose passionate intensity is allied not with the best that is in us, but with the worst: "Once a bitch always a bitch, what I say," he begins, in a voice that is filled with self-pity, rage, and bigotry.

For Faulkner, writing *The Sound and the Fury* became a process of release as well as discovery. The result was an experience and a novel that he continued to talk about with deep gratitude and tenderness for as long as he lived. Time and again when he spoke of the novel, it was in terms of how little he knew when he began it and how much he learned as he wrote it. But like many modern masterpieces, *The Sound and the Fury* took considerable time in gaining acceptance, in part at least because it requires that we become collaborative, if not creative, in comparing and contrasting different versions of the same scenes and in discerning and sorting out the spiritual motives as well as physical needs that lie hidden in what characters say and do.

REPETITION AS REVISION

With his sense of purpose as a writer restored, Faulkner began a period of astonishing productivity that was also astonishingly eventful. In the five years from 1928 to 1932, he completed more than forty stories and four novels—*The Sound and the Fury, As I Lay Dying, Sanctuary,* and *Light in August.* Over the next five years, he published *A Green Bough* (1933) and *Doctor Martino and Other Stories* (1934) and either finished or wrote *Pylon* (1935), the stories that became *The Unvanquished* (1938), and *Absalom, Absalom!* On June 20, 1929, he and Estelle Oldham Franklin, whose marriage to Cornell Franklin had ended in divorce, finally concluded their long off-and-on courtship by being married. But that event did not slow his productivity, though it increased his need to make money. A year later, while he was finishing *As I Lay Dying,* they bought an antebellum home on the edge of Oxford, which they named Rowan Oak and began restoring. In January 1931, their first child, Alabama Faulkner, died in infancy. In May 1932, Faulkner took the first of many jobs in Hollywood, primarily to make money. On August 7, 1932, his father died. On June 24, 1933, Jill Faulkner, their second daughter, was born. Later that year, Faulkner bought his first airplane and began flying avidly, an experience that contributed directly to his writing *Pylon.* Flying had provided the subject-matter of "Landing in Luck," his first published story. And he had continued to write stories about barn-storming pilots, the focus of *Pylon.* In 1935, while he was writing *Absalom, Absalom!,* his youngest brother, Dean, whose interest in flying he had encouraged, died in a crash. And in February 1938, he fulfilled his dream of becoming a "country farmer" by buying Greenfield Farm.

As early as age nine, Faulkner had begun saying, "I want to be a writer like my great-granddaddy"—a statement that is almost as remarkable for its simplification of W. C. Falkner's highly controversial, many-faceted life as it is for its bearing on Faulkner's career. Yet given the outpouring of work that followed his discovery of Yoknapatawpha, it seems clear that, whether consciously or not, he had begun preparing for his life as a writer at an early age by listening and observing as well as reading. We know from his library as well as from interviews and recorded conversations with students at the University of Virginia that he was much better read than he suggested when he described himself as a country man with meager formal education and no literary friends. In addition, we know that long before he began his literary career he had acquired, primarily from oral traditions, a textured, if exaggerated, sense of the role that his large, extended, and entangled family had played in the history of northern Mississippi, beginning with the Old Colonel's exploits in settling the region, fighting its wars, and building its first railroad. The Old Colonel, Faulkner said in an interview with Robert Cantwell in 1939, had ridden through northern Mississippi "like a living force." Given his family's entanglements in the state and region's brief, conflicted history, it seems almost inevitable that family stories would merge with regional stories, and that given the importance of the Civil War and World War I in the experiences of his family and the region, these stories would become entangled in the stories of the American South and the United States. There is a sense in which simply being as retentive as Faulkner meant becoming entangled in a web of people and events that began with family and extended beyond it to virtually endless associations.

The sights, sounds, and oral traditions—"the rag-tag and bob-ends of old tales and talking" and "old mouth-to-mouth tales," to borrow lines from *Absalom, Absalom!*—that Faulkner began gathering during his boyhood and youth stayed with him a lifetime. But the playfulness of mind that manifested itself in restless experimentation—in revisions and extensions of stories heard and remembered and even of stories he had already told and retold—is as much a trademark of his imagination and writings as this retentiveness of mind. Both of these principles—one associated with repetition, the other with revision—are present in virtually all his works. *As I Lay Dying* is a story of a family, and there is a sense in which it traces a single action centered around the burial of Addie Bundren, the mother. But because it is composed of many parts narrated by many narrators, the reader must sift through and sort out different versions of the crucial events in the family's story, trying to locate a putative whole in the broken narrative. In this effort, *As I Lay Dying* is typical of Faulkner's best work, for similarly creative tasks are required by works as varied in subject, setting, and style as *Light in August, The Wild Palms* (1939), *Absalom, Absalom!,* and *Go Down, Moses.*

Some of his novels, notably *Go Down, Moses,* comprise stories that he and his characters describe as having already been told and retold. Others, including *Absalom, Absalom!,* stage and restage the telling and retelling of different versions of the stories of which they are made up. As a result, beginning with *The Sound and the Fury* and *As I Lay Dying,* voices with different intonations and turns of phrase began to populate and define the world of Faulkner's fiction as trademarks of different characters. In short, two seemingly incompatible principles—respectful retentiveness and repetition, on one side, and creative, playful, and even irreverent revision, on the other—feed his stories and novels. Retentiveness and repetition provide the narrative material and revision engages his readers in creative retelling that is learned from and modeled on the activities of his characters. These two principles find expression in the action and the structure of stories and novels in which tellings lead to retellings, and retellings, however respectful, become revisions, and revisions, however radical, become at least in part retellings.

Faulkner's great discovery, which is properly associated with his discovery of Yoknapatawpha during the writing of *Flags in the Dust,* was dynamic rather than static, at least in part as a result of the creative tension that he discovered in the play between repetition and revision during the writing of *The Sound and the Fury.* In one way or another, this second aspect of his great discovery figured in virtually all the fiction that followed it, most powerfully as well as variously in *As I Lay Dying, Light in August, Absalom, Absalom!,* and *Go Down, Moses.*

### NOVELS OF THE 1930S

Like *The Sound and the Fury, As I Lay Dying* is the story of inadequate parents and their wounded children. In *As I Lay Dying,* however, it is a poor country family named Bundren with no aristocratic past or pretensions. The central figure is Addie, the mother, around whose death and burial the action of the novel revolves. There are five children—Cash, Darl, Dewey Dell, Jewel, and Vardaman—instead of four, and we hear directly from each of them as well as from a variety of neighbors, acquaintances, and passersby. Yet Addie, who remains central to the life of the family even after she is dead, is given only one of the novel's many sections, while even Anse, the feckless father who spends most of his time and virtually all his limited energy trying to get other people—his children, friends, neighbors, and even chance strangers—to do things for him, is given three. In short, with fragmentation dominating its form and isolation dominating the internal lives of its characters, *As I Lay Dying* becomes a novel about people who share things that do not unite them and are further separated by their hidden needs and desires and idiosyncratic modes of thought and perception. As a result, it imposes large tasks of balancing and reconciling on its reader.

*Sanctuary* is one of Faulkner's darkest indictments of Jefferson's social and political life. In it he uses devices made familiar in gangster and detective novels, which gained considerable popularity in the 1920s and even more in the 1930s, in order to depict both the urban underworld of Memphis, built of the profits from gambling, illegal sex, and whiskey, and the rural underworld of Yoknapatawpha, built on profits from illegal whiskey. However, neither of these underworlds matches either the ruthlessness or the shrewdness that the "respectable" world of Jefferson employs, both legally and illegally, in protecting the interests of a wealthy, powerful man named Judge Drake. Making a mockery of justice, the "respectable" people of Jefferson serve Judge Drake's interests. They bribe and intimidate public officials in order to convict an innocent man, and manipulate naive, lower-class people into lynching and burning the same innocent, underclass victim, a man named Lee Goodwin, whom they have wrongfully convicted. Ostensibly all this is done in the name of avenging the violation of Judge Drake's young daughter, Temple, though the deeper concern is clearly with reestablishing his power.

Like *Sanctuary, Light in August* reminds us of the several roles that illegal whiskey plays in rural Yoknapatawpha, and it casts a harsh eye on the legal justice system and on the cultural work of intimidation as well as revenge performed by illegal and brutal forms of punishment, including castration and lynching. Class and gender play dominant roles in *Sanctuary,* while race and gender take precedence in *Light in August.* And while the classism and misogyny we encounter in *Sanctuary* remain largely secular, the racism and misogyny in *Light in August* are heavily inflected by Christianity. Finally, although the sheriff and a woman who runs a boardinghouse try to speak for Jefferson society, more than any other of Faulkner's major novels, *Light in August* is about outcasts. Even longtime residents like Joanna Burden and Gail Hightower live alone in dark houses, estranged from the community. Byron Bunch lives in a boardinghouse and spends Saturdays working alone and Sundays in a rural church that no one in Jefferson knows anything about. Lucas Burch exploits the community but flees social obligations as well as personal commitments. Lena Grove, an unwed mother who refuses to feel shame or to settle down before she has seen more of the world, comes to Jefferson and then leaves it, taking Byron Bunch with her. And Joe Christmas, a fatherless and motherless child, arrives in Jefferson after having traveled a thousand savage and lonely streets and roads, looking for something he cannot completely name, only to die there without ever having found a place to call "home."

*Light in August* is built of several different narrative strands—one describing Lena Grove's search for a world unlike any she has ever known; another taking up Joanna Burden, whose family is from New England and who, though born in Yoknapatawpha, lives and dies there as an outsider; a third portraying Gail Hightower, a failed husband and defrocked minister who tries to make his life an extension of a glorious Southern past that never existed; and one characterizing Joe Christmas, a lonely child who becomes a conflicted, doomed man seeking something, whether love, home, or peace he is never quite sure, though he does believe that it "didn't seem to be a whole lot to ask in thirty years." Yet, except for the story of Lena, who is one of the few Faulkner characters to escape Yoknapatawpha, *Light in August* is an overwhelmingly bleak novel—grotesque, grim, and compelling.

In *Absalom, Absalom!,* perhaps his greatest novel, Faulkner presents different versions of several entangled tales, as he does in *Light in August.* This time, however, he relies more directly on characters whose remembering becomes talking and whose listening leads to more remembering and talking. He thus evokes the past and also conveys a sense of the constitutive role that narrative discussion, like narrative art, can play in bringing the past into the present. If, as Hannah Arendt suggests in *On Revolution,* all thought begins with remembrance and "no remembrance remains secure" until it finds expression in language, it may well follow that events tend to sink back into futility "unless they are talked about over and over again." The manner in which "incessant talk" can save events from futility by making them part of the living present, Arendt suggests, "may best be seen in the novels of William Faulkner," whose "literary procedure" is in this sense "highly 'political.'" For even if Faulkner is not "the only author to use" incessant talk in this way, Arendt adds, he is surely among those who have used it most relentlessly, especially in *Absalom, Absalom!,* where incessant talk reflects the role of the author and redefines the role of the reader.

The incessant talk of characters like Miss Rosa Coldfield, Mr. Compson, Quentin Compson, and

Shreve McCannon not only imposes itself on us, it also draws us into a process of articulation that makes *Absalom, Absalom!,* even more emphatically than *The Sound and the Fury, As I Lay Dying,* and *Go Down, Moses,* a work that calls for "creative reading." In it we encounter characters who come to realize that the privilege of reading and hearing imposes a burden—or opportunity—of interpreting and speaking. In *Flags in the Dust,* Faulkner juxtaposes the Civil War and World War I, challenging us to recognize that the South suffered in the first of these wars the kind of decimation, devastation, and disillusionment that Europe suffered in the second. More generally, by making his fiction an elaborate analogue of his inherited province, he not only took possession of it but also drew us into a process in which assessments lead to recognitions and recognitions lead to reassessments. In short, in the same motion in which he takes imaginative possession of the story of the rise and fall of the house of Sutpen, by tracing it from its origins in the early nineteenth century to its crumbling during and after the Civil War, he not only frames a story that involves racism, incest, and miscegenation, but also creates a narrative so intricate, that it re-forms us as readers, making us his deputies.

Indeed, in *Absalom, Absalom!,* he creates what we might think of as a process by which a reluctant listener-reader becomes a determined and even a compulsive teller of the tale. In the first scene, he describes Quentin Compson's "very body" as "an empty hall echoing with sonorous" names and as "a barracks filled with stubborn back-looking ghosts." "Why tell me about it?," Quentin thinks, as Miss Rosa goes on and on telling and retelling him the story of Thomas Sutpen. "What is it to me?" Later, after he begins telling and retelling the story to Shreve McCannon, and Shreve, in turn, begins telling the story to Quentin, we see Quentin and Shreve going back and forth: "Am I going to have to have to hear it all again . . . I am already hearing it all over again," Quentin thinks. Both

Quentin and Shreve thus become listeners of whom something like total recall is required, but surmise and speculation, or what they call "play," are also necessary. Even though they sometimes resist the burdens that such tasks impose on them, they go on repeating the names they have heard and pursuing the ghosts they have encountered. In some moments, different incidents present themselves as things they have somehow "absorbed." In others, they remain elusive, as things that just "dont explain." And both of these senses of things come back again and again to strike "the resonant strings of remembering" that trigger more telling and listening. One thing that holds Quentin and engages Shreve is a concern for the past as an action that they must try to understand—in part by examining the conflicted motives that informed the deeds that shaped and misshaped lives and in part by studying the unexpected as well as the expected consequences that flowed from them. But they are also challenged by their sense of the complexity and the human significance of narrative recounting, whether it unfolds as a process of speaking and hearing or as one of writing and reading.

From one perspective, Faulkner's fiction may be said to consist of remembering that becomes writing. Certainly, one part of what he wanted to preserve was his sense of the world that he saw fading around him. "All that I really desired was a touchstone," he wrote in an essay about the composition of *Sartoris,* edited for publication by Joseph Blotner in 1973; and nothing would serve "but that I try . . . to recreate between the covers of a book the world" that "I was already preparing to lose and regret." In short, he wanted to convey his own sense of his world; he wanted to "capture" and "preserve" the "feeling of it." But he also bequeathed this desire to his characters in something like the way that his ancestors had bequeathed it to him and thus made it so central a wellspring of his art, and so much a shaping force within it, that he also bequeathed it to his readers. Among several things that offend Miss Rosa is her fear that her story, and the story of her family, will be lost unless she or someone else finds words for them. By telling or having her story told, she hopes to preserve it, as Quentin recognizes shortly before he begins trying to tell the story, for himself as well as for her. Miss Rosa's motives, though personal, are in the end something more. In her incessant voice we recognize compulsive needs and pervasive ambivalences. Even as she discloses unrelenting resentment and anger, she also discloses something like unrelenting loyalty, if not love. Her voice goes on and on, "not ceasing but vanishing into and then out of the long intervals like a stream," because she cannot bear to have the story of her family and region go untold and be forgotten, lost. "*It's because she wants it told,*" Quentin says, in deepening recognition, "*so that people whom she will never see*" will know at last the story of "*the blood of our men and the tears of our women.*"

Although the burden of the past looms large in his fiction, Faulkner is not in the usual sense of the term a historical novelist. He seeks neither to recapture the past nor to invest it with motives of the present. As remembering leads to talking and talking leads to listening and to more remembering and talking, his fiction not only assimilates, preserves, and transmits the past but also openly and even aggressively transforms it. In novels like *Absalom, Absalom!*, narrative explorations of history lead to the creation of stories that escape the boundaries set by terms like history and myth. One part of the inclusive narrative process depicted in Faulkner's fiction consists of narrators engaged in acts of remembering, conserving, and repeating; another consists of narrators engaged in acts of hearing, sifting, and discarding; and yet another consists of narrators engaged in inventing or creating people and events that seem right because they are probably true enough even if they never existed anywhere except in stories. His characters thus create fiction in the same motion and for the same reasons that they explore history—in order to create meaning by bringing life and art, history and fiction, under the aspect of narrative.

As the boundaries between terms such as these begin to dissolve, however, so, too, do the boundaries that demarcate family relationships and establish distinctions based on gender, class, and race. We see some of the results of this dissolution in *The Sound and the Fury,* especially in the complex relationship between Caddy and Quentin, and in *As I Lay Dying,* especially in the varied relations between Addie and her children. We also find it in *Absalom, Absalom!,* in the relationships of Henry Sutpen, Judith Sutpen, and Charles Bon and between Quentin and Shreve. And we recognize it in *Light in August* in the relationship of Joe Christmas and Joanna Burden, in the story of Gail Hightower, and in the pairing of Lena Grove and Byron Bunch—to take a few examples. First in *Light in August* and *Absalom, Absalom!* and then more emphatically in *Go Down, Moses,* Faulkner began to sense that in order to make visible the deeper cultural and political implications of his work he would have to create stronger, even more deeply damaged and openly resistive voices than he had in his earlier works and then place them in a more deeply fractured narrative of the kind that *Go Down, Moses,* became as he revised, juxtaposed, extended, augmented, and partially integrated the fragments of which it is made.

## FAULKNER'S ACHIEVEMENT

Faulkner's emergence as a major writer is unusually complicated because of his strained relations both to the "modernist" or "formalist" literary tradition (which we associate with Proust, Joyce, Pound, Eliot, and Stevens, which sought to make of literature a secular equivalent of religion—that is, something in whose perfection one could believe) and to the "Southern Renaissance," as it is sometimes called (which sought to restore cultural respectability to the American South, an effort we associate with Cleanth Brooks, John Crowe Ransom, Allen Tate, and Robert Penn Warren). For, although Faulkner's presence looms large in both these movements, he played a smaller role in them than many lesser contemporaries. Beginning with *The Sound and the Fury,* he forged his own version of the high formalist or modernist mode; and he did so in part by giving his fiction a strong regional cast. His finest work is strongly regional, and yet it is marked by striking technical experimentation—by a wide range of narrative voices; by different modes of condensation, elaboration, substitution, and rearrangements; by versions and counter-versions of the same story. His art is one of discontinuity—of breaks and interruptions, deferrals and regressions, proliferating perspectives and sudden inversions. But it is also one in which the search for form looms large. At times he seems committed to saying everything at once and so uses as many formulations as he can find; at other times he seems determined to treat genuine mysteries as sacred both to art and to life. His characters must finally live in faith because they can never fully understand themselves or save their worlds. Yet they are not free to desist from trying to move beyond faith to certainty and beyond hope to assurance.

In short, Faulkner's fiction is a fiction of repetition and revision. In it he evokes, preserves, and transmits different senses of the past, displaying an overt commitment to his inherited stories or, more broadly perhaps, his traditions. Repetition is one of the principles that binds together both individual works and groups of works. Yet the minds and voices that Faulkner creates not only repeat and preserve, they also enact elaborate transformations of the stories they seek to tell, as though mindful that mere remembering and repeating represent a form of captivity or even of suicide: "Am I going to have to have to hear it all again?" Quentin asks. "I am going to have to hear it all over again I . . . I am listening to it all over again I shall have to never listen to anything else but this again

forever." Yet even in Quentin, who is on familiar terms with the story, the threat of being held tightly triggers a principle of resistance. Having listened and repeated, Quentin and later Shreve insist on condensing and elaborating, substituting and rearranging, surmising and speculating. Although they begin in recapitulation, they go on to discover and invent, as though to remind us that the search for origins can become a pathway to originality. It is by copying and repeating the stories they have heard or, put another way, by absorbing Miss Rosa's voice and Mr. Compson's and each other's, that they move through play and improvisation toward the creation of something that strikes us as probably true enough.

Faulkner is widely thought of as a difficult writer. In this, too, his mode is one we might think of as modernist. But the other side of the considerable demands that he makes is a remarkable generosity. No writer, ancient or modern, has shared more fully the tasks and even the prerogatives of the writer with his characters and his readers. In his method of creative transformation through remembering, talking, and listening we can locate both primitive and sophisticated versions of Faulkner's labors as a novelist and of our labors as readers. Especially in novels like *Absalom, Absalom!,* or in *Go Down, Moses,* his characters become models for his readers—in their willingness to listen and to attempt total recall, to arrange and rearrange, to sort and sift and discard, to surmise and speculate, or to work and play in the hope that somehow all "the rag-tag and bob-ends" of their lives and of those of their families and regions will finally fall into some telling pattern. Furthermore, though their hopes are never fully satisfied, they are never merely frustrated. Faulkner's novels and stories do not finally belong to what the French poet Charles Baudelaire called the "sublime literature" of despair and hopelessness in which the reader learns to long for goodness and hope only as remedies. However confusing and intimidating they may sometimes seem to us, his finest works exemplify and engage us in the process of creating meaning by teaching us the skills required for reading them.

Faulkner's fiction is full of wry, understated humor, and it is frequently playful as well—as we see in gentler works like *The Reivers,* in predominantly comic works like *The Hamlet,* and even in novels like *As I Lay Dying*, where comic and macabre elements mingle. But to measure, even tentatively, his achievement, we must recognize that the seemingly contradictory qualities that infuse his work—darkness and exuberance, a commitment to preserving the past and to radical improvisation and innovation—prove to be interdependent and interactive. Having discovered that the tensions between these contradictory impulses projected themselves endlessly for him, Faulkner realized that he wanted them to do just that. As much as any writer of his time, he found his imaginative task in exploring rather than resolving the divisions that drove him, between darkness and exuberance, between copying, following, and repeating, on one side, and improvising, innovating, and creating, on the other. So it was by going back and forth that he created his stories and novels. Having said early that he wanted to be a writer, he later began to equivocate. At times he implied that he was a writer only in addition to and after other things: "I'm a farmer," he said in an interview in 1951, included by James B. Meriwether and Michael Millgate in *Lion in the Garden,* "I ain't a writer. . . . Why, I don't even know any writers." Later, in an interview in 1955, also in *Lion in the Garden,* he acknowledged being a writer but denied being "a literary man": "I don't keep abreast of literature," he said, and "[don't read] for style . . . or method" but "about people." In fact, Faulkner's sense of himself centered not only on being a writer but also on being a particular kind of writer, which is to say, modern. In the same interviews in which he equivocated about his vocation, he mentions classical literature, the Bible, Shakespeare, Keats, and Cervantes, as well

as the fiction writers of many countries, including Honoré de Balzac, Leo Tolstoy, Nathaniel Hawthorne, Charles Dickens, and Herman Melville. In addition, he speaks frequently of several late nineteenth- and early twentieth-century figures, including Joseph Conrad, James Joyce, and T. S. Eliot.

Early in his life, in a letter written from Paris to his Aunt Bama, Mrs. Walter B. MacLean, Faulkner described one of his stories as being "so beautiful that when I finished it I went to look at myself in a mirror" and thought, "Did that ugly ratty-looking face, that mixture of childishness and unreliability and sublime vanity, imagine that?" In 1953, nearly thirty years later, with most of his work behind him, he wrote to Joan Williams expressing a similar yet even more telling sense of disassociation between the man he was and the work he had done.

> And now, at last, I have some perspective on all I have done. I mean, the work apart from me, the work which I did, apart from what I am. . . . And now I realise for the first time what an amazing gift I had: uneducated in every formal sense, without even very literate, let alone literary, companions, yet to have made the things I made. I dont know where it came from. I dont know why God or gods or whoever it was, selected me to be the vessel. Believe me, this is not humility, false modesty: it is simply amazement. I wonder if you have ever had that thought about the work and the country man whom you know as Bill Faulkner—what little connection there seems to be between them.

Although we shall never know exactly how he did it, we can be fairly certain that he managed to devise a sense of the artist that was consonant with his deepest sense of himself. Earlier, looking back on the writing of *The Sound and the Fury,* in the introduction to it that was published in 1973, Faulkner had anticipated the moment "when not only the ecstasy of writing would be gone, but the unreluctance and the something worth saying too." In 1950, in a letter to Malcolm Cowley written shortly after he had received the Nobel Prize, and later included in the *Faulkner-Cowley File,* he anticipated "the moment, instant, night: dark: sleep: when I would put it all away forever that I anguished and sweated over, and it would never trouble me anymore." Between his earliest anticipations of that moment and his final confrontation with it, however, he created a series of masterpieces—*The Sound and the Fury, As I Lay Dying, Light in August, Absalom, Absalom!, The Hamlet,* and *Go Down, Moses,* to name six—that together accomplish three large tasks. First, they epitomize modern fiction's radical insistence on its own inventiveness, in part by making the process of imaginative creation one of their subjects and in part by sharing it widely with a cast of characters we would not ordinarily associate with inventiveness. Second, they present the problems of human creativity or inventiveness, of human meaning, and of the meaningfulness of human existence each as a version of the other. And third, they place each of these dilemmas under the aspect of things discovered and rediscovered and under the aspect of things fabricated and invented. Of few writers of this century can so much be said.

## Selected Bibliography

### WORKS OF WILLIAM FAULKNER

NOVELS AND SHORT STORIES

*Soldiers' Pay.* New York: Boni and Liveright, 1926.
*Mosquitoes.* New York: Boni and Liveright, 1927.
*Sartoris.* New York: Harcourt, Brace, 1929.
*The Sound and the Fury.* New York: Cape and Smith, 1929.
*As I Lay Dying.* New York: Cape and Smith, 1930.
*Sanctuary.* New York: Cape and Smith, 1931.
*These 13.* New York: Cape and Smith, 1931.
*Idyll in the Desert.* New York: Random House, 1931.
*Miss Zilphia Gant.* Dallas: Book Club of Texas, 1932.
*Light in August.* New York: Smith and Haas, 1932.
*Doctor Martino and Other Stories.* New York: Smith and Haas, 1934.

*Pylon.* New York: Smith and Haas, 1935.
*Absalom, Absalom!* New York: Random House, 1936.
*The Unvanquished.* New York: Random House, 1938.
*The Wild Palms.* New York: Random House, 1939.
*The Hamlet.* New York: Random House, 1940.
*Go Down, Moses and Other Stories.* New York: Random House, 1942. (In subsequent printings and other editions, "and Other Stories" was omitted from the title in order to stress the unity of the work.)
*Intruder in the Dust.* New York: Random House, 1948.
*Knight's Gambit.* New York: Random House, 1949.
*Collected Stories of William Faulkner.* New York: Random House, 1950. (Includes "That Evening Sun," "A Justice," and "Carcassone.")
*Notes on a Horsethief.* Greenville, Miss.: Levee Press, 1951.
*Requiem for a Nun.* New York: Random House, 1951.
*A Fable.* New York: Random House, 1954.
*Big Woods.* New York: Random House, 1955.
*The Town.* New York: Random House, 1957.
*The Mansion.* New York: Random House, 1959.
*The Reivers: A Reminiscence.* New York: Random House, 1962.
*The Wishing Tree.* Illustrated by Don Bolognese. New York: Random House, 1967.
*Flags in the Dust.* Edited by Douglas Day. New York: Random House, 1973.
*Mayday.* Edited by Carvel Collins. Notre Dame, Ind.: University of Notre Dame Press, 1977.
*Father Abraham.* Edited by James B. Meriwether. With wood engravings by John DePol. New York: Random House, 1983.
"Elmer." Edited by Dianne L. Cox. *Mississippi Quarterly* 36:337–460 (summer 1983). Also in Joseph Blotner et al., eds. *William Faulkner Manuscripts.* Vol. 1. Edited by Thomas L. McHaney. New York: 1987.

POETRY AND DRAMA

*The Marble Faun.* Boston: Four Seas, 1924.
*A Green Bough.* New York: Smith and Haas, 1933.
*Requiem for a Nun: A Play.* New York: Random House, 1959.
*The Marionettes.* With an introduction and textual apparatus by Noel Polk. Charlottesville: University Press of Virginia, 1977.
*Helen: A Courtship and Mississippi Poems.* With introductory essays by Carvel Collins and Joseph Blotner. New Orleans, La.: Tulane University; Oxford, Miss.: Yoknapatawpha Press, 1981.

*Vision in Spring.* With an introduction by Judith L. Sensibar. Austin: University of Texas Press, 1984.

COLLECTED WORKS, ESSAYS, AND INTRODUCTIONS

*The Portable Faulkner.* Edited by Malcolm Cowley. New York: Viking, 1946, 1967.

*William Faulkner: Early Prose and Poetry.* Edited by Carvel Collins. Boston: Little, Brown, 1962.

*Essays, Speeches, and Public Letters by William Faulkner.* Edited by James B. Meriwether. New York: Random House, 1965 (contains the text of his Nobel Prize acceptance speech).

*The Faulkner-Cowley File: Letters and Memories 1944–1962.* Edited by Malcolm Cowley. New York: Viking, 1966.

*New Orleans Sketches.* Edited by Carvel Collins. New York: Random House, 1968.

"An Introduction for *The Sound and the Fury.*" Edited by James B. Meriwether. *Southern Review* 8:705–710 (autumn 1972).

"An Introduction to *The Sound and the Fury.*" Edited by James B. Meriwether. *Mississippi Quarterly* 26:410–415 (summer 1973).

*Selected Letters of William Faulkner.* Edited by Joseph Blotner. New York: Random House, 1977.

*Uncollected Stories of William Faulkner.* Edited by Joseph Blotner. New York: Random House, 1979.

*Faulkner's MGM Screenplays.* Edited by Bruce F. Kawin. Knoxville: University of Tennessee Press, 1982.

*Country Lawyer and Other Stories for the Screen.* Edited by Louis D. Brodsky and Robert W. Hamlin. Jackson: University Press of Mississippi, 1987.

*Thinking of Home: William Faulkner's Letters to His Mother and Father, 1918–1925.* Edited by James G. Watson. New York: Norton, 1992.

SCREENPLAYS

*The Road to Glory.* Screenplay by Faulkner and Joel Sayre. Directed by Howard Hawks. Twentieth Century-Fox, 1936.

*To Have and Have Not.* Screenplay by Faulkner and Jules Furthman from the novel by Ernest Hemingway. Directed by Howard Hawks. Warner Brothers, 1944.

*The Big Sleep.* Screenplay by Faulkner, Jules Furthman, and Leigh Brackett from the novel by Raymond Chandler. Directed by Howard Hawks. Warner Brothers, 1946.

*Land of the Pharaohs.* Screenplay by Faulkner, Harry Kurnitz, and Harold Jack Bloom. Directed by Howard Hawks. Warner Brothers/Continental Company, 1955.

INTERVIEWS

*Faulkner at Nagano.* Edited by Robert A. Jelliffe. Tokyo: Kenkyusha, 1956.

*Faulkner in the University: Class Conferences at the University of Virginia 1957–1958.* Edited by Frederick L. Gwynn and Joseph L. Blotner. Charlottesville: University Press of Virginia, 1959.

*Faulkner at West Point.* Edited by Joseph L. Fant and Robert P. Ashley. New York: Random House, 1964.

*Lion in the Garden: Interviews with William Faulkner, 1926–1962.* Edited by James B. Meriwether and Michael Millgate. New York: Random House, 1968.

*Talking About William Faulkner: Interviews with Jimmy Faulkner and Others.* Edited by Sally Wolff and Floyd Watkins. Baton Rouge: Louisiana State University Press, 1996.

MANUSCRIPT COLLECTIONS

Collections of Faulkner's manuscripts and papers are housed at the following libraries: Beinecke Rare Books and Manuscript Library, Yale University; Berg Collection, New York Public Library; Humanities Research Center, University of Texas; Louis Daniel Brodsky Collection, Kent Library, Southeastern Missouri State University; Princeton University Library; Rowan Oak Papers, Special Collections, University of Mississippi; William Faulkner Foundation Collection, Special Collections, Alderman Library, University of Virginia; and William B. Wisdom Collection, Howard-Tilton Memorial Library, Tulane University.

*BIBLIOGRAPHIES*

Blotner, Joseph. *William Faulkner's Library: A Catalogue.* Charlottesville: University Press of Virginia, 1964.

Brodsky, Louis D., and Robert W. Hamblin, eds. *Faulkner: A Comprehensive Guide to the Brodsky Collection.* (5 vols.) Jackson: University Press of Mississippi, 1982–1988.

Butterworth, Keen. "A Census of Manuscripts and Typescripts of William Faulkner's Poetry." *Mississippi Quarterly* 26:333–359 (summer 1973).

Hayhoe, George F. "Faulkner in Hollywood: A Checklist of His Film Scripts at the University of Virginia." *Mississippi Quarterly* 31:407–419 (summer 1978).

Massey, Linton R. *"Man Working" 1919–1962. William Faulkner: A Catalogue of the William Faulkner Collection at the University of Virginia.* Charlottesville, University Press of Virginia, 1968.

Meriwether, James B. "William Faulkner: A Checklist." *Princeton University Library Chronicle* 18:136–158 (spring 1957).

————. *William Faulkner: An Exhibit of Manuscripts.* Austin: University of Texas Press, 1959.

————. *The Literary Career of William Faulkner: A Bibliographical Study.* Princeton: Princeton University Press, 1961.

————. "The Short Fiction of William Faulkner: A Bibliography." *Proof* 1:293–329.

## CRITICAL AND BIOGRAPHICAL STUDIES

Abadie, Ann, ed. *William Faulkner: A Life on Paper.* Jackson: University Press of Mississippi, 1980.

Arendt, Hannah. *On Revolution.* New York: Viking, 1963.

Beck, Warren. *Faulkner.* Madison: University of Wisconsin Press, 1976.

Bleikasten, André. *The Ink of Melancholy: Faulkner's Novels from "The Sound and the Fury" to "Light in August."* Bloomington: Indiana University Press, 1990.

Blotner, Joseph. *Faulkner: A Biography.* New York: Random House, 1974.

————, ed., "William Faulkner's Essay on the Composition of *Sartoris.*" *Yale University Library Gazette,* 47 (Jan. 1973), 123–24.

Brodhead, Richard, ed. *Faulkner: New Perspectives.* Englewood Cliffs, N.J.: Prentice Hall, 1983.

————. *William Faulkner: The Yoknapatawpha Country.* New Haven, Conn.: Yale University Press, 1963.

Brooks, Cleanth. *William Faulkner: Toward Yoknapatawpha and Beyond.* New Haven, Conn.: Yale University Press, 1978.

Carpenter, Meta, and Orin Borsten. *A Loving Gentleman: The Love Story of William Faulkner and Meta Carpenter.* New York: Simon and Schuster, 1976.

Cullen, John B., with Floyd C. Watkins. *Old Times in the Faulkner Country.* Chapel Hill: University of North Carolina Press, 1961.

Davis, Thadious M. *Faulkner's "Negro": Art and the Southern Context.* Baton Rouge: Louisiana State University Press, 1983.

Duvall, John N. *Faulkner's Marginal Couple: Invisible, Outlaw, and Unspeakable Communities.* Austin: University of Texas Press, 1990.

Falkner, Murry C. *The Falkners of Mississippi: A Memoir.* Baton Rouge: Louisiana State University Press, 1967.

Faulkner, John. *My Brother Bill: An Affectionate Reminiscence.* New York: Trident, 1963.

————. *Faulkner and the Southern Renaissance.* Jackson: University Press of Mississippi, 1982.

————. *New Directions in Faulkner Studies.* Jackson: University Press of Mississippi, 1984.

————. *Faulkner and Women.* Jackson: University Press of Mississippi, 1986.

Fowler, Doreen, and Ann Abadie, eds. *Faulkner and Race.* Jackson: University Press of Mississippi, 1988.

Franklin, Malcolm. *Bitterweeds: Life with William Faulkner at Rowan Oak.* Irving, Tex.: Society for the Study of Traditional Culture, 1977.

Gray, Richard. *The Life of William Faulkner: A Critical Biography.* Oxford, England, and Cambridge, Mass.: Blackwell Publishers, 1994.

Gresset, Michel. *Fascination: Faulkner's Fiction, 1919–1936.* Adapted from the French by Thomas West. Durham, N.C.: Duke University Press, 1989.

Grimwood, Michael. *Heart in Conflict: Faulkner's Struggles with Vocation.* Athens: University of Georgia Press, 1987.

Harrington, Evans, and Ann Abadie, eds. *Faulkner, Modernism, and Film: Faulkner and Yoknapatawpha, 1978.* Jackson: University Press of Mississippi, 1979.

Hoffman, Frederick J., and Olga Vickery. *William Faulkner: Three Decades of Criticism.* East Lansing: Michigan State University Press, 1960. (Includes "Time in Faulkner: *The Sound and the Fury*" by Jean-Paul Sartre. Also: Interview with Robert Coutwell.)

Irwin, John T. *Doubling and Incest/Repetition and Revenge: A Speculative Reading of Faulkner.* Baltimore: Johns Hopkins University Press, 1975.

Jenkins, Lee. *Faulkner and Black-White Relations: A Psychoanalytic Approach.* New York: Columbia University Press, 1981.

Karl, Frederick R. *William Faulkner, American Writer: A Biography.* New York: Weidenfeld and Nicolson, 1989.

Kawin, Bruce F. *Faulkner and Film.* New York: Ungar, 1977.

Kinney, Arthur F. *Faulkner's Narrative Poetics: Style As Vision.* Amherst: University of Massachusetts Press, 1978.

Magny, Claude-Edmonde. *The Age of the American Novel: The Film Aesthetic of Fiction between the Two Wars.* New York: Ungar, 1972. Translated by Eleanor Hochman from *L'Age de roman américain.* Paris: Seuil, 1948.

Matthews, John T. *The Play of Faulkner's Language.* Ithaca, N.Y.: Cornell University Press, 1982.

McHaney, Thomas L. *William Faulkner's "The Wild Palms."* Jackson: University Press of Mississippi, 1975.

Millgate, Michael. *The Achievement of William Faulkner.* New York: Random House, 1966.

Minter, David. *William Faulkner: His Life and Work.* Baltimore: Johns Hopkins University Press, 1980.

Moreland, Richard C. *Faulkner and Modernism: Rereading and Rewriting.* Madison: University of Wisconsin Press, 1990.

Morris, Wesley, and Barbara Alverson Morris. *Reading Faulkner.* Madison: University of Wisconsin Press, 1989.

Mortimer, Gail L. *Faulkner's Rhetoric of Loss: A Study of Perception and Meaning.* Austin: University of Texas Press, 1983.

Page, Sally R. *Faulkner's Women: Characterization and Meaning.* De Land, Fla.: Everett/Edwards, 1972.

Parker, Robert Dale. *Faulkner and the Novelistic Imagination.* Urbana: University of Illinois Press, 1985.

Porter, Carolyn. *Seeing and Being: The Plight of the Participant Observer in Emerson, James, Adams, and Faulkner.* Middletown, Conn.: Wesleyan University Press, 1981.

Pound, Ezra. Review, Jean Cocteau, *Poésies, 1917–1920. Dial* 70:110 (January 1921).

Reed, Joseph W. *Faulkner's Narrative.* New Haven, Conn.: Yale University Press, 1973.

Ross, Stephen M. *Fiction's Inexhaustible Voice: Speech and Writing in Faulkner.* Athens: University of Georgia Press, 1989.

Sensibar, Judith L. *The Origins of Faulkner's Art.* Austin: University of Texas Press, 1984.

Skei, Hans H. *William Faulkner: The Novelist As Short Story Writer. A Study of William Faulkner's Short Fiction.* Oslo: Universitetsforlaget, 1985.

Sundquist, Eric J. *Faulkner: The House Divided.* Baltimore: Johns Hopkins University Press, 1983.

Vickery, Olga. *The Novels of William Faulkner.* Baton Rouge: Louisiana State University Press, 1959.

Wadlington, Warwick. *Reading Faulknerian Tragedy.* Ithaca, N.Y.: Cornell University Press, 1987.

Wagner, Linda, ed. *Faulkner: Four Decades of Criticism.* East Lansing: Michigan State University Press, 1973.

Warren, Robert Penn, ed. *Faulkner: A Collection of Critical Essays.* Englewood Cliffs, N.J.: Prentice-Hall, Inc., 1966.

Wasson, Ben. *Count No 'Count: Flashbacks to Faulkner.* Jackson: University Press of Mississippi, 1983.

Watson, James G. *Letters and Fictions.* Austin: University of Texas Press, 1987.

Webb, James W., and A. Wigfall Green, eds. *William Faulkner of Oxford.* Baton Rouge: Louisiana State University Press: 1965.

Weinstein, Philip M. *Faulkner's Subject: A Cosmos No One Owns.* New York and Cambridge, Cambridge University Press, 1992.

Wells, Dean Faulkner, and Lawrence Wells. "The Trains Belonged to Everybody: Faulkner As Ghost Writer." *Southern Review* 12:864–871 (autumn 1976).

Williamson, Joel. *William Faulkner and Southern History.* New York: Oxford University Press, 1993.

Wittenberg, Judith Bryant. *Faulkner: The Transfiguration of Biography.* Lincoln: University of Nebraska Press, 1979.

Woodward, C. Vann. *The Burden of Southern History.* Baton Rouge: Louisiana State University Press, 1960.

Wyatt, David M. *Prodigal Sons: A Study in Authorship and Authority.* Baltimore: Johns Hopkins University Press, 1980.

*—DAVID MINTER*

# F. Scott Fitzgerald
## 1896–1940

$I$N DECEMBER 1940, after years of declining health and failing literary prospects, F. Scott Fitzgerald collapsed and died in the Hollywood apartment of Sheilah Graham, the gossip columnist he once, in a fit of pique, called his paramour. Graham had afforded more than companionship during Fitzgerald's final years of dislocation and estrangement in California: she had lavishly dispensed insider gossip about the movie industry that was assimilated by him into his last stories and novel. Their relationship sustained Fitzgerald during a final astonishing period of productivity that contradicts the popular depiction of a profligate author who squandered his talent. Journalists reporting Fitzgerald's death mourned the passing of youthful promise, stagnated genius, and unfulfilled talent. They reduced Fitzgerald to a cultural artifact, a symbol of the "lost generation." With his literary reputation conspicuously suspended in the 1920s, Fitzgerald represented the excesses and decadence of his generation. And yet, by the centennial of his birth, the novelist E. L. Doctorow reflected in "F. S. F., 1896–1996, R.I.P": "Of that triumvirate of hero-novelists who came of age in the twenties, we may salute the big two-hearted pugilist, and stand in awe of the mesmerist from Mississippi, but it's the third one we mourn, the Jazz Age kid, our own Fitzgerald."

Anticipating Doctorow's heroic projection of

sorrowful kinship, Malcolm Cowley long contemplated this "exile's return." As he wrote to Kenneth Burke on October 26, 1950:

> Fitzgerald . . . is a perfect example of your theory of social analogy. In all his early work the hero represents the rising middle class, the heroine represents inherited money, they kiss as if he were embracing a pile of stock certificates—and then, since Fitzgerald distrusts the leisure class and thinks they are mysterious, her relatives kill the hero.

Cowley, busy editing his selection of twenty-eight of Fitzgerald's stories for Scribners, had discovered a signature tension in Fitzgerald's life and work: the often antithetical relationship between happiness and money.

Fitzgerald, as Lionel Trilling proposed in *The Liberal Imagination* (1953), was "perhaps the last notable writer to affirm the Romantic fantasy, descended from the Renaissance, of personal ambition and heroism, of life committed to, or thrown away for, some ideal of self." Edmund Wilson, reflecting upon the "semi-excluded background" of America's Irish Catholics, noted in his journal that neither Scott nor his friend Gerald Murphy, no matter what their financial reserves, would ever be "'out of the top drawer' in New York." And so, alienated from his Midwestern, middle-class origins and ceaselessly striving for the unattainable security of wealth and class, Fitzgerald lived a morality play in which money and happiness were at odds.

Although most of Fitzgerald's best-known work exploits this opposition, "The Rich Boy," written during the spring and summer of 1925 (just after the publication of *The Great Gatsby*), attempts to ameliorate it. Seen by the biographer Matthew Bruccoli as central to understanding Fitzgerald's complex attitude toward wealth and class, the story owes its special celebrity to its opening confidence:

> Let me tell you about the very rich. They are different from you and me. They possess and enjoy early, and it does something to them, makes them soft where we are hard, and cynical where we are trustful, in a way that, unless you were born rich, it is very difficult to understand. They think, deep in their hearts, that they are better than we are because we had to discover the compensations and refuges of life for ourselves. . . . The only way I can describe young Anson Hunter is to approach him as if he were a foreigner and cling stubbornly to my point of view. If I accept his for a moment I am lost—I have nothing to show but a preposterous movie.

Anson Hunter embodies the unattainable "centeredness" that the extremely rich represented for Fitzgerald, a "natural state of things" that preserved the remove and glamour of their habits and circumstance. He distinguishes as well the feudal self-sufficiency, the "clan-forming" nature of money in the East from the "snobbish West [where] money separates families to form 'sets.' " Unhappy at Yale, young Anson "began to shift the centre of his life to New York" in search of "the irreproachable shadow he would some day marry" and accepting "without reservation the world of high finance and high extravagance, of divorce and dissipation, of snobbery and of privilege."

Ernest Hemingway, Fitzgerald's most celebrated contemporary, read "The Rich Boy" as a projection of Fitzgerald's life among the idle rich. In "The Snows of Kilimanjaro" (first published in *Esquire* in August 1936), Hemingway's narrator subordinates "Fitzgerald" to the needs of his own character and design:

> He remembered poor Scott Fitzgerald and his romantic awe of them and how he had started a story that once began, 'The very rich are different from you and me.' And how someone had said to Scott, Yes they have more money. But that was not humorous to Scott.

Hemingway remained for many readers Fitzgerald's essential debunker. And yet Fitzgerald himself (whether in response to the Depression or to Hemingway's literary betrayal), on March 4, 1938, emphasized his estrangement from the rich as he depicted the psychological estrangement of his relatively impoverished circumstance: "That was always my experience—a poor boy in a rich town; a poor boy in a rich boy's school; a poor boy in a rich man's club at Princeton. . . . I have never been able to forgive the rich for being rich, and it has colored my entire life and works." The sheer ordinariness of Fitzgerald's birth and childhood does little to explain the "preposterous movie" that became his life.

## EARLY LIFE AND EDUCATION

Francis Scott Key Fitzgerald was born in St. Paul, Minnesota, on September 24, 1896, the third child and only son of Edward Fitzgerald and Mary (Mollie) McQuillan. As Fitzgerald recalled in "Author's House" (*Esquire,* July 1936): "Well, three months before I was born my mother lost her other two children and I think that came first of all though I don't know how it worked exactly. I think I started then to be a writer." His father, son of Michael Fitzgerald (a dry goods merchant from Maryland) and Cecilia Ashton Scott (descendent of the Scotts and Keys of colonial Maryland), first cousin to Mary Surratt (hanged as a co-conspirator in the Lincoln assassination case), was like his son a migrant. After attending Georgetown University, Edward sought opportunity in the West, establishing the American Rattan and Willow Works of St. Paul, Minnesota. Edward was president of the company, but he never achieved the financial security that would bring his family peace. Driven ill by fear that she would be unable to provide the proper upbringing for her surviving child, Mollie supplemented the family income with a modest stipend from the McQuillans. When the Willow Works failed in 1898, Edward moved the family to Buffalo, New York, so that he could accept a position at Procter and Gamble as a wholesaler.

Little in the family's economic circumstances improved as a fourth child died shortly after birth in 1900; Edward was transferred to the company's branch office in Syracuse, where a daughter, Annabel, was born in July 1901. In September 1902, Fitzgerald began his schooling at Miss Goodyear's School, where he became a voracious reader, especially fond of Scribners' children's magazine, *St. Nicholas.* After his father's transfer back to Buffalo in 1905, Fitzgerald entered Miss Narden's School, where he formalized his early educational and spiritual relationship with the Catholic Church. An erratic student, Fitzgerald nonetheless committed early to the narrative potential of history. Whether inspired by his father's Civil War stories or simply anxious to create a place for himself as storyteller, he quickly merged his identities as reader and writer. The boy who loved the heady historical romances of Sir Walter Scott was soon writing a history of America and a biography of George Washington.

In 1908, when Edward was fired by Procter and Gamble, the family returned to St. Paul. Fitzgerald and his sister lived with their maternal grandmother, while their parents lived just blocks away. Resigned to her husband's lack of business acumen, Mollie, who like Mrs. Buckner in "The Scandal Detectives" was a "woman of character, a member of Society in a large Middle-Western city," assumed the role of family financial adviser

and secured for her children the middle-class life. Although McQuillan funds enabled the family to eventually assume the comfort and dignity of St. Paul's posh Summit Avenue, they did little to assuage Fitzgerald's growing sense of disadvantage as a parvenu. Fitzgerald in midlife conceded to John O'Hara that the puzzle of his adolescence was a typically American crisis between ancestry and circumstance. As he patiently explained in a letter of July 18, 1933: "I am half black Irish and half old American stock with the usual exaggerated ancestral pretension. . . . So being born in that atmosphere of crack, wisecrack and countercrack I developed a two cylinder inferiority complex." A latter-day Huck Finn, Fitzgerald found his studies at St. Paul Academy, which he had entered in 1908 upon his family's return to St. Paul, increasingly boring, preferring a self-charted territory to the assigned world of mathematics and Latin declensions. Fixated upon his destiny as a writer, he had by late 1910 prepared an "outline chart of my life" and the *Thoughtbook of Francis Scott Key Fitzgerald* (1965). His historical narratives, which began to appear with some frequency in the school's *Now and Then,* were often revisions of his father's Civil War tales.

Frustrated by his lingering academic deficiencies at St. Paul's, the family enrolled Fitzgerald at the Newman School in Hackensack, New Jersey, where he began his "discipline" training in the fall of 1911. He continued to be an unreliable student even in his preferred disciplines of history and English. Although writing remained his passion (his stories appearing regularly in the *Newman News*), football increasingly competed for his remaining time and energy. By the end of his second year, Fitzgerald excelled in football, lingered behind in academics, and aspired to continue his education at Princeton University. It was also during this year that he met Father Sigourney Webster Fay, the mentor who was immortalized in *This Side of Paradise* as Monsignor Darcy and forever exemplifies the spirit of intellectual adventure and romance in the Irish Catholic. In the spring of 1913, Fitzgerald set his sights on Princeton (distinguished in *This Side of Paradise* by "its atmosphere of bright colors and its alluring reputation as the pleasantest country club in America"), taking the entrance examinations that he hoped would, with his inheritance from Grandmother McQuillan, secure his destiny.

Though less-than-distinguished results on these exams necessitated an interview and supplementary testing, Fitzgerald prevailed, persuading the university to conditionally admit him. Prewar Princeton, a place of "country club" amenities and lingering Presbyterian expectations, challenged Scott's social discernment with its rigidly defined class structures. Unable to distinguish himself through social standing or academics, he sought acceptance through writing and membership in the Triangle Club (a performance organization founded by Booth Tarkington) and football. Classwork remained tedious, with literature in the hands of a "surprisingly pallid English department, top-heavy, undistinguished and with an uncanny knack of making literature distasteful to young men" (*Afternoon of an Author,* p. 75). Fitzgerald's fellow students John Peale Bishop, the model for the poet Thomas d'Invilliers in *This Side of Paradise,* and Edmund Wilson, Fitzgerald's "intellectual conscience," formed the core of his literary circle, shaping his early reading and thinking. Reading widely in what he called "quest books," he grew beyond the fiction of Tarkington, H. G. Wells, and Compton Mackenzie to the naturalism of Frank Norris and his brother, Charles.

During his second year, academic disqualification from his extracurricular activities, the Triangle Club and football, failed to lessen the pleasure Fitzgerald took from the performance of "Fie! Fie! Fi-Fi!" (his book and lyrics won first place in the Triangle Club annual competition). Reviewers of the club's touring Christmas show were taken by the wit and panache of the lyricist responsible for

The place for you is way out West,
From manicuring take a rest,
Far too long you've tarried,
Fie! Fie! Fi-Fi!

A trip home to St. Paul complicated his already tenuous grip on his studies by introducing a "top girl" into his life. The beautiful and wealthy Ginevra King, object of nearly daily correspondence over the spring, lingered in Fitzgerald's imagination as the first of his top girls.

So compromised had his academic standing become in 1915–1916 that Fitzgerald had to repeat his junior year. His success in the Triangle Club and the *Nassau Literary Magazine* did little to compensate for his intellectual remove from his studies. Vexed by his lack of academic progress and inspired by Edmund Wilson's New York literary life, he readied himself for a world beyond Princeton, one redefined by America's entry into the Great War. When Fitzgerald enlisted in 1917, he carried with him into training, though not into battle, his deepening passion for "the literary" as defined by Alfred, Lord Tennyson, Algernon Charles Swinburne, Wells, and George Bernard Shaw, a passion that drew *This Side of Paradise* from the draft of "The Romantic Egotist," a novel from his final undergraduate days at Princeton. In the fall of 1917, Second Lieutenant Fitzgerald reported to Fort Leavenworth, Kansas, where he found military training as irksome as academic discipline, since both interfered with writing. In early 1918, after a period of undistinguished service, Fitzgerald requested leave so that he might return to Princeton to complete his novel, which was published as *This Side of Paradise.* In late spring, after a sojourn at the Cottage Club, he forwarded the manuscript to Scribners and turned his attention once again to the army. He served briefly at posts in Kentucky and Georgia before transferring to Camp Sheridan, near Montgomery, Alabama, where he oversaw a platoon preparing for overseas service. He never graduated from Princeton.

Without his novel to distract him, Fitzgerald committed to his duties as well as to his leisure. And that July, at the Country Club of Montgomery, he met the top girl who became his wife. Zelda Sayre, first glimpsed by Fitzgerald as she performed the "Dance of the Hours," was the popular daughter of Alabama Supreme Court Justice Anthony D. Sayre. Beautiful, willful, resistant to the intellect, Zelda exerted an emotional and aesthetic power that became inextricable from Fitzgerald's work. His Princeton preoccupation with quest literature informed his literary and romantic pursuits. Even his courtship of Zelda rested upon his publishing success. On August 19, 1918, in a lengthy expression of encouragement and rejection, Scribners notified Fitzgerald that in spite of his novel's "originality," it failed "to work up to a conclusion."

The war ended before Captain Fitzgerald shipped out. Upon discharge, he moved to New York City to work in the advertising business and join Wilson's literary world. Zelda, uninterested in marrying an unsuccessful author, cagily resisted Fitzgerald's long-distance courtship. Financial anxieties and emotional traumas characterized the winter and spring of 1919. His repeated trips to Montgomery prompted Zelda's dismissal of him. Fitzgerald found himself unable to prosper on the combined income from his advertising job and the occasional story in H. L. Mencken's *Smart Set.* Finding himself stymied in publishing and thwarted in love, he returned in the summer of 1919 to St. Paul to write.

Without Zelda's correspondence, Fitzgerald found writing all consuming. Neither his parents' offer of work, as an advertising manager at a local wholesale house, nor his financial extremity distracted him from his quest to revise his novel. In September, the editor Maxwell Perkins accepted *This Side of Paradise* for publication by Scribners. Anxious to secure money *and* happiness, Fitzgerald committed to the former in the hope that the latter would follow. Stories, many gleaned from his Princeton years, published in *Smart Set, Scribner's Magazine,* and *Saturday Evening Post* supplemented his income until the publication of *This Side of Paradise* the following spring. "Head and Shoulders," published on February 21, 1920, in George Horace Lorimer's *Saturday Evening Post,* marked the beginning of Fitzgerald's income from the "slicks." These high-paying, mass-circulation magazines, in particular, the *Post,* provided his widest audience and most reliable income. With the support of Perkins and Harold Ober, his agent, Fitzgerald confidently returned to Montgomery to fulfill his romantic quest. Plying Zelda with orchids, platinum-and-diamond trinkets, and a steady stream of cocktails, he won her promise to marry, but only upon the publication of *This Side of Paradise.*

### THIS SIDE OF PARADISE

*This Side of Paradise,* published in March 1920, is a spirited novel of prewar college life, romance and virtue, initiation and quest. Its stylistic uncertainties are experimental (influenced by the sequential aesthetic of movies) and naive (troubled by the recalcitrance of the narrative form). Scribners' editorial quarrel with the novel's earlier ending inspired Fitzgerald's advance in narrative form as he converted his "Romance and a Reading List" into a novel of self-education and preparation, preliminaries for a life yet lived. A textured romance, it tells the story of Amory Blaine's educational and amorous quests—from a childhood shaped by his mother to his education at Princeton, from the Catholic teachings of Monsignor Darcy to the heart lessons of his lovers—and their apparent irresolution. The work is divided into two major sections, bridged by a war "interlude."

The first section, "The Romantic Egotist" grounds Amory's life in the obsessive and quirky love of Beatrice, his mother, a woman "critical about American women, especially the floating population of ex-Westerners." Companion, confidant, and son, Amory travels the world with this mother of means. "Attached to no city," the "Blaines of Lake Geneva" epitomize for Fitzgerald the suburban world of the mannered middle class. This world of ritual, chivalric codes, and social hierarchy inevitably leads Amory to decide "definitely on Princeton." Sometimes as farcical as Oscar Wilde, sometimes as languidly earnest as Compton Mackenzie, Fitzgerald captures the heartbreaking vulnerability of the undergraduate ritual. Thinly veiled autobiography—in which, for example, "Fie! Fie! Fi-Fi!" becomes "Ha-Ha Hortense!"—underwrites the broader, experiential fabric in which popular song and current events conspire to contemporize the novel. Amory's "quests of adventure" challenge his honor, tempt his virtue, and prepare him for a life of duty. Monsignor Darcy, modeled on Monsignor Fay, embodies the religiosity of discipline and romance for Amory. Although the eighteen-year-old Amory "lacked somehow that intense animal magnetism that so often accompanies beauty in men or women," he was ready for love. Ginevra King, Fitzgerald's former top girl, serves as the model for Isabelle, Amory's unsuccessful love. Neither "brazen" nor "innocent," these "babes in the woods" strive without flourishing and their romance wanes.

Following the war-centered epistolary exchange that constitutes the "Interlude," "The Education of a Personage," the second section, develops through Amory's distinction between a personality and a personage. Amory, learning that fortune can be fate, suffers the collapse of his family's wealth and compromises in love. Debutantes, reckless romantics, and prostitutes test Amory's virtue. And still love remains elusive: Rosalind, the focus of the opening drama "The Débutante," rejects Amory's narrow atmosphere and romantic visions, and Eleanor, the quintessence of beauty, solidifies Amory's individualized Catholic insight of sexualized evil. The

corner turned at the end of the novel, as Amory contemplates Monsignor Darcy's teachings, marks the "direction and momentum of this new start."

It is given to few novels to define a generation. What *On the Road* and *The Catcher in the Rye* did for Jack Kerouac and J. D. Salinger in the 1950s, creating authorial celebrities out of generational defiance, this "novel about flappers written for philosophers" did for Fitzgerald in the 1920s. For, as Matthew Bruccoli emphasizes, "it was received in 1920 as an iconoclastic social document—even as a testament of revolt." As an idealized and popularized portrait of America's youth culture, *This Side of Paradise* met with immediate success. Reviewers throughout the country, even those far from metropolitan centers, found the work daring, favorably self-conscious, and presumptuous. While most reviewers celebrated its modernity and originality, the reviewer for the *Sun* and the New York *Herald* saw beyond mere stylistic disconnection and innovation to the work's deeper generational focus and spiritual core, identifying *This Side of Paradise* as a "self-conscious and self-critical offering" of those "whom 1917 overtook in college."

## SCOTT AND ZELDA

On April 3, 1920, Scott and Zelda were married at St. Patrick's Cathedral in New York City, and, for a time, money and happiness were theirs. But when, in July 1932, Scott reflected upon this moment of newborn celebrity in "My Lost City," he could but remember "riding in a taxi one afternoon between very tall buildings under a mauve and rosy sky; I began to bawl because I had everything I wanted and knew I would never be so happy again." Already justly famous for their financial and social indulgences and weary of the city, the couple escaped New York for the serenity of Westport, Connecticut, where Scott finished his story "May Day." But the pastoral setting did little to quiet the parties that turned from quarrels into hangovers and betrayals. After visiting Zelda's family in Montgomery, the couple returned to New York, securing an apartment on Fifty-ninth Street near the Plaza Hotel. Scott, perhaps reflecting upon the wretched excesses of his marriage, began work on "The Flight of the Rocket," a working title for his next novel, *The Beautiful and the Damned* (1922). This novel chronicles the "life of one Anthony Patch between his 25th and 33rd years. . . . He is one of those many with the tastes and weaknesses of an artist but with no actual creative inspiration. How he and his beautiful young wife are wrecked on the shoals of dissipation is told."

*Flappers and Philosophers,* a collection of stories published by Scribners in September 1920, brought mixed reviews but welcome income to the young couple. Few reviews sounded the dour note of *The Nation,* which complained that the stories "have a rather ghastly rattle of movement that apes energy and a hectic straining after emotion that apes intensity." Most singled out "The Ice Palace" and "Bernice Bobs Her Hair" for special recognition for their startlingly original flappers.

Work on *The Beautiful and the Damned,* the dramatization of *This Side of Paradise,* and a scenario for Dorothy Gish at D. W. Griffith's production company preoccupied Fitzgerald throughout an otherwise uneventful autumn. In February 1921, when Zelda became pregnant, the Fitzgeralds decided upon a trip to Europe. In late April, Scott sent Ober the manuscript for *The Beautiful and the Damned;* in May the couple sailed upon a Cunard liner for Europe. Europe disappointed Scott, bringing to the surface a familiar provincialism and xenophobia. Mid-journey, in July, he wrote to Edmund Wilson:

> [Europe] is of merely antiquarian interest. Rome is only a few years behind Tyre + Babylon. The negroid streak creeps northward to defile the nordic race. Already the Italians have the souls of blackamoors. Raise the bars of immigration and permit only Scandinavians, Teutons, Anglo Saxons + Celts to enter.

By late July the Fitzgeralds had returned to Montgomery to await the birth of their child. But in late August, unhappy with the southern insistence upon confinement during pregnancy, they relocated to St. Paul in the hope that Zelda might relax in her "delicate condition." Justly celebrated in his hometown, Fitzgerald went about a confident and productive routine as he revised for publication the serialized *Beautiful and the Damned,* which *Metropolitan* had edited from a draft.

## THE BEAUTIFUL AND THE DAMNED

Published in *Metropolitan Magazine* from September 1921 to March 1922, *The Beautiful and the Damned* turns the fluid world of Amory Blaine's romance into the fixed determinism of Anthony Patch's degradation. Although he is born into privilege and educated at Harvard, Anthony, unlike Amory, has no ideal vision of himself. He drifts into a life of idleness, intellectual speculation, and debauchery that draws destructive energy from the "siren," Gloria Gilbert. In its depiction of a couple's descent into ruin, the novel, though not essentially autobiographical, does reflect Fitzgerald's increasing apprehension about his relationship with Zelda. By the summer of 1930, the novel itself became a mediational force between them; as Scott explained in a letter intended for (but perhaps not sent to) Zelda: "I wish the Beautiful and Damned had been a maturely written book because it was all true. We ruined ourselves—I have never honestly thought that we ruined each other."

The first section introduces the reader to the carefully groomed Patch, "a distinct and dynamic personality, opinionated, contemptuous, functioning from within outward." In 1913, this twenty-five-year-old Harvard graduate "drew as much consciousness of social security from being the grandson of Adam J. Patch as he would have had from tracing his line over the sea to the crusaders." Anthony's world of bonded security surrenders to the eighteen-year-old siren, Gloria. She inspires him "to pose": "He wanted to appear suddenly to her in novel and heroic colors"; she challenges him to defend his "do nothing" ethic (a worldview that resurfaced in Philip Barry's *Holiday* [1928]): "His words gathered conviction—'it astonishes me. It—it—I don't understand why people think that every young man ought to go down-town and work ten hours a day for the best twenty years of his life at dull, unimaginative work, certainly not altruistic work.' " Anthony's romantic quest, though troubled, is not thwarted: he has, by the end of the section, "knocked and, at a word, entered."

The second section assesses "the breathless idyll of their engagement" and moves quickly to the "intense romance of the more passionate relationship," which dissipates: "The breathless idyll left them, fled on to other lovers; they looked around one day and it was gone, how they scarcely knew. . . . The idyll passed, bearing with it its extortion of youth." From its midpoint, the novel commits to the misplaced and misspent, turning maudlin in its celebration of youth: "It is in the twenties that the actual momentum of life begins to slacken, and it is a simple soul indeed to whom as many things are significant and meaningful at thirty as at ten years before." Indolence and inebriation become their solace and justification. The section closes as the war begins, Gloria contemplating a future in the movies, Anthony preparing for officers' training camp.

The final section opens with Anthony's affair with Dot. Consummated at the Bijou Moving Picture Theatre, the liaison seems itself a cinematic projection. Dorothy Raycroft is Gloria's opposite: "the girl promised rest." Absence from Gloria emphasizes his cowardice; he has become "com-

pletely the slave of a hundred disordered and prowling thoughts which were released by the collapse of the authentic devotion to Gloria that had been the chief jailer of his insufficiency." However tranquil the southern respite, Anthony has grown too cowardly for its complications, necessitating the abandonment of Dot. Return to Gloria simply brings to the fore their earlier frustrations. The long anticipated inheritance slips away and with it the Patches' hope for their aristocratic lives. Facing compromised fortune, Anthony accedes to his middle-class status, noting when challenged, "Why pretend we're not? I hate people who claim to be great aristocrats when they can't even keep up the appearances of it." Such admissions seem to hasten their decline into stuporous middle age, contracting the once "enormous panorama of life." In the end, the disillusioned and dissipated Anthony gets his money too late to save his soul.

Reviews of Anthony's slow-tempo descent revealed discomfort with what the Philadelphia *Public Ledger* called the "reckless . . . life" of the "jazz-vampire period." While some reviews took issue with style, complaining about the author's "puppet" or "dummy" characters, others took the course of disavowal, sharing the Detroit *Saturday Night*'s grim hope that "future generations" would realize the fictive nature of Fitzgerald's world, for if everyone were like this, "the race would perish of cirrhosis of the liver, delirium tremens, locomotor ataxia, paresis, dementia praecox and other pleasant ailments." In an unsigned piece in *Bookman,* Wilson troubled over Fitzgerald's midwestern and Irish influences. In "Friend Husband's Latest" (New York *Tribune,* April 2, 1922), Zelda Sayre (for which she was paid $15.00) recommends *The Beautiful and the Damned* "as a manual of etiquette" and for its "dietary suggestion," and its "interior decorating department."

Frances Scott (Scottie) Fitzgerald was born October 26, 1921, in St. Paul. Book reviews, playwriting, and ideas for a travel project occupied the new father's time. The New York party for Scribners' publication of *The Beautiful and the Damned* on March 4, 1922, coincided with Zelda's second, unexpected pregnancy and subsequent abortion. Spring and summer were devoted to his play, *The Vegetable* (a viable publication [1923] that failed in production), attempts to work with David O. Selznick (writing movie treatments), and preparation of his second story collection, *Tales of the Jazz Age* (1922). In the fall of 1922, restless in Minnesota, the Fitzgeralds left Scottie in St. Paul and sought housing in New York. Traveling with John Dos Passos, the Fitzgeralds met Ring Lardner at Great Neck, Long Island. That "riotous island," the setting for *Gatsby,* encouraged the couple to resume their former lives of debauchery. At the height of the prohibition era, the Fitzgeralds descended into the depths of alcoholic intemperance Scott had so grimly depicted in *The Beautiful and the Damned.*

While stories for the "slicks" and advances from Perkins and Ober funded the work on *The Great Gatsby,* they failed to provide the needed income for the Fitzgeralds' lavish lifestyle. Scott and Zelda never knew where their money went; they were, as Bruccoli concludes, "collaborators in extravagance." Needing to explain his finances to himself and his readers, Fitzgerald submitted to the *Post* a wry essay entitled "How to Live on $36,000 a Year." He earned $1,000 for the essay. By spring 1924, Fitzgerald was able to write Perkins about his plans for his next novel, "the sustained imagination of a sincere and yet radiant world." In May, the Fitzgeralds sailed for Europe and, after a brief stay in Paris, ventured to the Riviera, where Scott worked feverishly on *Gatsby* while Zelda flirted with a French pilot, Edouard Jozan. That summer they met Gerald and Sara Murphy, American expatriates of considerable means who inspired the model expatriates of *Tender Is the Night.* Gerald, whom Dick Diver more than casually resembles, had panache and affluence, the "power of arousing a fascinated and

uncritical love." But as Wilson cautioned, "Gerald . . . was also a somewhat eccentric and an independent figure who could hardly be assigned to any 'life style' or group."

### THE GREAT GATSBY

The Fitzgeralds wintered in Rome, where Scott finished *Gatsby* and sent it off to Perkins. In April of 1925 they arrived in Paris, shortly before *The Great Gatsby* was published. Drained by persistent financial and marital woes, Fitzgerald greeted Perkins' news of slow sales and encouraging reviews with characteristic defeatism. He was convinced that his title ("only fair, rather bad than good") and lack of a compelling female character ("women controll [sic] the fiction market at present") had hurt sales. Hack writing, he decided, would have to underwrite the next novel, and if it failed to do so, then, said Fitzgerald, "I'm going to quit, come home, go to Hollywood and learn the movie business." His frustration was palpable, yet he knew the significance of his achievement. In a letter postmarked May 15, 1925 (written in response to a young writer's admiration), he emphasized his accomplishments and his goals:

> *Gatsby* was far from perfect in many ways but all in all it contains such prose as has never been written in America before. From that I take heart. From that I take heart and hope that some day I can combine the verve of *Paradise,* the unity of the *Beautiful + Damned* and the lyric quality of *Gatsby,* its aesthetic soundness, into something worthy of the admiration of those few.

Readers familiar with Fitzgerald's work were surprised by the compactness (nine brief chapters) and conventional appearance of *The Great Gatsby.* Gone were the placard devices of the earlier novels, the poetic and dramatic disruptions of narrative, the mid-chapter titles and mid-novel divisions. At first glance, only the epigraph from

Thomas d'Invilliers in *This Side of Paradise* signals a continuity with the author's earlier work. Intensely atmospheric, minimally though finely detailed and chromatically enhanced settings replace the promptbook interiors and back-lot exteriors of the first two novels. The intermittently spontaneous and apt dialogue of the earlier novels has become the perfect and intense exchanges of *Gatsby*. And though all such refinements contribute to the success of *Gatsby*, they do not explain a brilliance that resides in the plot-unifying force of the narrator. Unlike the progressive worlds of *This Side of Paradise* and *The Beautiful and the Damned*, *Gatsby* requires a narrator capable of integrating the romance of a self-revising past into the taut narrative of an ongoing novel. A character in the novel but not intimately part of the plot, Nick Carraway survives its daunting circularity and perhaps even thrives in it by absenting himself from it. Embarrassed by Tom Buchanan's tawdry tryst with Myrtle Wilson, Nick, at once a participant and "casual watcher" of the affair, explains: "I was within and without, simultaneously enchanted and repelled by the inexhaustible variety of life."

Nick Carraway is more than a narrator: he is the reader's access to Gatsby. He is innocent of the rumors concerning Gatsby, new to the spectacles of the place, and skeptical of the unfolding dramas. With an ordinariness Fitzgerald says he learned from Joseph Conrad (crediting, in particular, the preface to *The Nigger of the Narcissus*), Nick becomes the ideal spectator-narrator for this man who "represented everything for which [he had] an unaffected scorn." *The Great Gatsby* intertwines several narratives: the external story of Nick's summer with Gatsby on Long Island, the internal history of Jimmy Gatz's self-fashioning into Jay Gatsby, the enduring obsession of Gatsby for Daisy, and the fatal plot progression that integrates these resisting narratives of love and money. In the beginning and the end, *The Great Gatsby* belongs to Nick.

Nick Carraway, third-generation midwesterner and Yale man, moves to West Egg, Long Island, for a summer of fresh air and undisturbed reading of "a dozen volumes on banking and credit and investment securities" and unwittingly rents "a house in one of the strangest communities in North America . . . on that slender riotous island which extends itself due east of New York." From the "small eyesore" that was his home, Carraway had the "consoling proximity of millionaires—all for eighty dollars a month." He moved in part to be near his second cousin, Daisy, wife of a former Yale football star, the independently wealthy Tom Buchanan. Buchanan, a "sturdy straw-haired man of thirty with a rather hard mouth . . . a cruel body," seems violently preoccupied by the collapse of civilization. As he chides Nick, "The idea is if we don't look out the white race will be . . . utterly submerged. It's all scientific stuff; it's been proved." Visiting the Buchanans is a friend from Daisy's adolescence, the "incurably dishonest" professional golfer Jordan Baker. During their first meeting, Nick learns that Tom has "some woman in New York" and that he "has been depressed by a book." Somewhat perplexed by his first social outing, Nick returns home to see the dim shadow of his neighbor, the man he presumes to be Gatsby, reaching toward a point distinguished by "nothing except a single green light, minute and far away, that might have been the end of a dock." Within this opening chapter, Fitzgerald has established or alluded to *Gatsby*'s primary characters and its dominant setting.

The next two chapters enhance Nick's narrative credibility, displaying his ability to orchestrate the subplots supportive of, but not vital to, the Gatsby narrative. Fitzgerald exploits his contrasting settings, rendering them essential to the plot: the dreary Wilson family filling station and the pitiful New York walk-up apartment accent the tawdriness of Tom's liaison with Myrtle Wilson as well as the grandeur of Gatsby's mansion. While these fastidiously detailed interiors and social exteriors are critical for plot and character enhancement, they pale beside Fitzgerald's celebrated depiction of the necessary crossing, the threshold world between New York and West Egg, where "the motor road hastily joins the railroad and runs beside it for a quarter of a mile":

> This is a valley of ashes—a fantastic farm where ashes grow like wheat into ridges and hills and grotesque gardens; where ashes take the forms of houses and chimneys and rising smoke and, finally, with a transcendent effort, of ash-gray men who move dimly and already crumbling through the powdery air.

And as if this industrial wasteland were insufficient, it is presided over by the surreal "eyes of Doctor T. J. Eckleburg . . . blue and gigantic," which "look out of no face, but, instead, from a pair of enormous yellow spectacles which pass over a non-existent nose." Gatsby's "World's Fair" mansion with its blue manicured lawns, a product of the very industrial fortune that underwrites its grotesque twin, the valley of ashes, gestures first with its prodigality, not its society. Seemingly unattended by the host, Gatsby's party liberates haphazard speculation, rumors by random guests. Such conjecture assumes a literal force as Gatsby becomes as "absolutely real" as his "Merton College Library" of books with uncut pages. A succession of counterfeit identities—"Oxford man," "German spy," murderer—adumbrates Gatsby's own serial projections of himself, complementing the mystery that he himself sustains.

Gatsby physically and spiritually dominates the second stage of Nick's narrative, in which it is confirmed, as Gatsby knew, that he and Nick were in "ecstatic cahoots" all along. His reputation must be cleared, or at least stabilized, before the love story can progress. Nick accompanies Gatsby to a dingy cellar on Forty-second Street to meet his "business gonnegtion," Meyer Wolfsheim. The intimacy of their association levels the social register catalogued earlier of "folks who come to Gatsby's parties." To Gatsby, Wolfsheim, the man who "fixed the World's Series back in 1919" is a gambler who seized opportunity, but for Nick he is a criminal who has done the previously unthinkable: "play[ed] with the faith of fifty million people—with the single-mindedness of a burglar blowing a safe." A complementary biographical narrative, supplied by the dishonest Jordan Baker, depicts Gatsby as Daisy's lost suitor. What Nick reads as "coincidence," Jordan corrects into plan: "Gatsby bought that house so that Daisy would be just across the bay." At that moment, Gatsby "came alive" for his narrator, "delivered suddenly from the womb of his purposeless splendor."

Nick's cottage becomes the site of Gatsby's reunion with Daisy. The material world seems to recede as Gatsby "revalued everything in his house according to the measure of response it drew from her well-loved eyes." The once cavernous mansion, familiar only when filled with strangers, grows curiously intimate as the lovers wander through its rooms. And yet, in the very heart of this novel, there is an absence that persists despite the fulfillment of its dream. As Nick, whose "presence made them feel more satisfactorily alone," concludes, "There must have been moments even that afternoon when Daisy tumbled short of his dreams—not through her own fault, but because of the colossal vitality of his illusion."

A reporter's query occasions Nick's aside concerning Gatsby's origins, placed "here with the idea of exploding those first wild rumors about his antecedents." Jay Gatsby reverts to James Gatz of North Dakota, a young man with a "Platonic conception of himself" who reinvents himself at the moment he sees Dan Cody's yacht dock. In a quintessentially American projection, Gatsby becomes what he sees: "vast, vulgar, and meretricious beauty." Although he, like so many other of Fitzgerald's protagonists, expects an inheritance that doesn't come, Gatsby makes his way.

Daisy, while flattered by Gatsby's renewed attentions, refuses to disavow Tom. Gatsby, as if responding to a challenge, not a warning, cries, "Can't repeat the past? . . . Why of course you can! . . . I'm going to fix everything just the way it was before." His attempts to reconstitute an unlived past prove his undoing. Gatsby's final revaluation of Daisy begins with his lamentable assertion: "Her voice is full of money." The couples form and reform. At Gatsby's party, Tom and Daisy join with Nick and Jordan, isolating Gatsby; on the road through the valley of ashes, Gatsby and Daisy occupy one car, Tom and Jordan and Nick the other, abandoning Myrtle as they drive "on toward death through the cooling twilight." Myrtle dies under the wheels of a car driven by Daisy; Gatsby dies at the hands of Myrtle's husband, who believes that Gatsby was driving. Wilson, after shooting Gatsby, kills himself: "The holocaust was complete." Even in death, Gatsby demands further elaboration. Nick elicits complementary portraits from Wolfsheim and Henry C. Gatz, Gatsby's father, who read of his son's death in a Chicago newspaper.

For many reviewers, *The Great Gatsby* dramatized the grating sensibilities of the aging New Youth, rendering it simultaneously avant-garde and passé. Commentators recognized Fitzgerald's maturity of style and structure, some even noting the sophisticating influence of Henry James and Edith Wharton on this novel of manners. No other contemporary reviewer was as unreserved as Gilbert Seldes, who, in the *New Criterion*, noted that *The Great Gatsby* "is a brilliant work, and it is also a sound one; it is carefully written, and vivid; it has structure, and it has life. To all the talents, discipline has been added."

THE CRASH: ZELDA AND AMERICA

In late April 1925, shortly after settling in Paris, Fitzgerald met Ernest Hemingway. In awe of Hemingway's robust reputation, Fitzgerald pre-sented himself as timid and uncertain about art and sex. These episodes are painfully and unreliably commemorated in Hemingway's *A Moveable Feast* (1964). His meeting with Wharton, after her somewhat cautious praise of *Gatsby*, went little better—his compliments and brothel jokes did little to engage the grande dame. By June, Fitzgerald had revised the stories to appear in *All the Sad Young Men*, including "The Rich Boy," "Winter Dreams," and "Absolution." The collection was published on February 26, 1926, to enthusiastic reviews. In "Art's Bread and Butter," William Rose Benét suggests the dangers of such productivity when he notes Fitzgerald's "almost uncanny facility for magazine writing" and senses "the pressure of living conditions rather than the demand of the spirit" in many of the stories.

In the remaining months of 1926, the Fitzgeralds toured and drank among the moneyed of the world. He had written little, despite the fact that months had passed since he had explained his "new novel" to Maxwell Perkins: "It is something really NEW in form, idea, structure—the model for the age that Joyce and Stien [sic] are searching for, that Conrad didn't find." Early ideas about an "intellectual murder on the Leopold-Loeb idea" succumbed to an obsessive interest in World War I and its battlefield sites (research that eventually surfaced in *Tender Is the Night*).

Throughout 1926, the Fitzgeralds drifted between Paris and the Riviera in the hope of capturing some of the magic of their earlier stay. Finances were reasonably good: collateral income from *Gatsby* and revenue from stories should have enabled Fitzgerald to write in leisure. It was, however, a year of monumental distractions and excess. Hemingway's influence on Fitzgerald, who yearned to assume Hemingway's bravado and profanity, was destabilizing. Zelda and Scott grew socially so unpredictable and hazardous that even the Murphys shied away from their extreme misbehavior. As Gerald Murphy later explained to Calvin Tomkins, "Their idea was that they never depended upon parties. I don't think they cared very much for parties, so called, and I don't think they stayed at them very long. They were all out, always searching for some kind of adventure *outside* of the party." By September, a somber Fitzgerald recorded in his *Ledger:* "Futile, shameful useless but the $30,000 rewards of 1924 work. Self disgust. Health gone."

Early in 1927, Fitzgerald accepted an offer from United Artists to script a "flapper comedy." This brief two-month stint was unremarkable except for two encounters: one with the ingenue Lois Moran, who inspired the character of Rosemary Hoyt in *Tender Is the Night,* and one with Irving Thalberg, the Metro-Goldwyn-Mayer producer who inspired the character of Monroe Stahr, in *The Last Tycoon.* After two months on the West Coast, Scott and Zelda relocated to Ellerslie, a mansion near Wilmington, Delaware. There Scott, in spite of his increasing addictions to alcohol and smoking, settled into a work routine that produced several stories, though little progress on his novel. He did, however, complete the Basil stories, a series drawn from his St. Paul adolescence and published in the *Post* from March 1928 to February 1929. Zelda, bored with rural life, began ballet lessons, believing that she had made a professional commitment.

In April 1929, weary with Wilmington and flush with income from a batch of *Post* stories, the Fitzgeralds returned to Paris for the spring and summer. Increasingly manic, Zelda became committed to her ballet lessons, while Scott, perpetually distracted, drifted through a literary society that included James Joyce, Sylvia Beach, John Peale Bishop, and Thornton Wilder. The Fitzgeralds returned to Delaware in October, with Scott able to show little more than promises to Maxwell Perkins. From the spring of 1929 to the early summer of 1930, the Fitzgeralds knew no peace. Restlessly drifting through France, nearly destroyed by Scott's alcoholism and Zelda's increasing madness, Scott confided in his *Ledger:* "Thirty

two years old (And sore as hell about it) OMINOUS No Real Progress in ANY way + *wrecked myself with dozens of people.*" On April 23, 1930, Zelda was admitted to the Malmaison clinic near Paris "in a state of acute anxiety, restlessness, continually repeating: 'This is dreadful, this is horrible, what is going to become of me?' " She discharged herself three weeks later and attempted to return to ballet, only to collapse in late May and enter Valmont clinic in Switzerland. By early June, she was diagnosed as schizophrenic and committed to Les Rives de Prangins clinic on Lake Geneva.

Although his *Ledger* summary suggested disaster—" *'The Crash! Zelda + America'* "—Fitzgerald continued to work steadily on the stories that paid the bills. The five Josephine stories, a complementary series to the Basil stories, began appearing in the *Post* in April 1930, eventually earning $32,000. He became a slave to the "slicks" as he abandoned all work on his novel and wrote stories to pay for Zelda's hospitalization as well as his own upkeep. Although economic pressures forced Fitzgerald to write quickly and publish, they did not prevent him from writing some memorable work. "Babylon Revisited" remains the most celebrated of his stories. Charlie Wales, Fitzgerald's alter ego, discusses the ruins of his life with the Ritz barman: " 'I heard that you lost a lot in the crash.' 'I did,' and he added grimly, 'but I lost everything I wanted in the boom.' 'Selling short.' 'Something like that.' " Christmas 1930, in spite of Scottie's visit to Zelda at Prangins, was a grim and hopeless affair that was followed by the death of Fitzgerald's father in January. While in the States, Scott visited Zelda's family in Alabama to apprise them of her condition.

In the summer of 1931, while Zelda was being treated as an outpatient at Prangins, the family traveled a bit, even visiting the Murphys in Austria. In September, after Zelda's discharge, they sailed for America in the hope of relocating to Montgomery. Later that fall Scott, somewhat weary of relying upon story income, accepted an offer from Thalberg at Metro-Goldwyn-Mayer to write a screenplay for Jean Harlow, *Red-headed Woman.* Upon his return from Hollywood in January 1932, Zelda suffered another breakdown and was taken by Scott to the Phipps Psychiatric Clinic at the Johns Hopkins University Hospital in Baltimore. In May, Scott rented a house on the Turnbull estate in suburban Maryland. While Zelda's condition deteriorated and her expenses spiraled, Scott's per-story income from the *Post* dropped to below his rate in 1925. Fitzgerald himself was hospitalized in August 1932 at the Johns Hopkins University Hospital for typhoid fever and fatigue. He was readmitted several times over the next few years for treatment of the ravages of alcoholism as well as transient fevers related to a chronic lung ailment. In October 1932, Zelda's *Save Me the Waltz,* her autobiographical novel, was published by Scribners. Poorly edited and riddled with errors, the novel sold less than half of its printing of 3,010 copies.

### TENDER IS THE NIGHT

In the summer of 1932, more than seven years after the publication of *The Great Gatsby,* Fitzgerald began work in earnest on *Tender Is the Night.* Although he had sent endless favorable reports to Perkins and Ober over the years, he had not begun substantial plotting until late that summer. At last, he recognized the course:

> The novel should do this. Show a man who is a natural idealist, a spoiled priest, giving in for various causes to the ideas of the haute Burgeoise [sic], and in his rise to the top of the social world losing his idealism, his talent and turning to drink and dissipation.

His year-end *Ledger* exclaimed: "Novel intensive begins."

Published serially in *Scribner's Magazine* from January to April 1934 (Scribners published the novel on April 12, 1934), *Tender Is the Night* extends Amory's chivalric codes from *This Side of Paradise* and Gatsby's acquisitive passion to the middle-aged world of Dr. Dick Diver's "intricate destiny." The novel rewards intense consideration as a metanarrative on the art of fiction. For within its discussion of Diver's professional and intellectual disintegration, manifested early in the novel in his inability to revise his many pamphlets into a significant medical treatise, lies Fitzgerald's self-incriminating tale of the hack story-writer who took nearly a decade to write a novel. It is also a continuation of an earlier disquisition into American national identity, jotted in his *Notebooks* and included in "The Swimmers," in which he mused:

> France was a land, England was a people, but America, having about it still that quality of the idea, was harder to utter—it was the graves at Shiloh and the tired, drawn, nervous faces of its great men, and the country boys dying in the Argonne for a phrase that was empty before their bodies withered. It was a willingness of the heart.

*Tender Is the Night* places the postmortem world of ever-dying ideals that Fitzgerald had long associated with America into a new context. Analytically dispassionate and less theatrical than *The Beautiful and the Damned, Tender Is the Night* suffers from many of the earlier novel's structural flaws and burdensome length. Anxiously and hastily revised from the serial publication in progress, the novel declares Fitzgerald's adept psychologically intense characterization even as it casts those characters adrift, unmoored in the pastel indolence of the Riviera.

The first section draws the reader into a society of the "notable and fashionable," the Riviera of 1925. Located in France at the time of the Fitzgeralds' first visit, at the moment of Scott's greatest productivity, *Tender Is the Night* recasts the drama of a threatened, depleted love into one of intellectual and professional compromise. As with the earlier novels, peripheral characters abound, serving primarily to extend the emotional circumstance and history of Dick and Nicole Diver. Rosemary Hoyt (a "ripping swimmer") is filming on the Riviera. Palpably an ingenue, treated with kindly condescension by the Divers and their intimates (Abe North, the "entirely liquid" composer who suggests Fitzgerald, and Tommy Barban, the volatile mercenary who resembles Hemingway), Rosemary advances the narrative by challenging the very origins of the Divers' relationship. "From the middle of the middle class, catapulted by her mother onto the uncharted heights of Hollywood," Rosemary derives her security from her social contentment, stardom, and youth. Such average securities breed the confidence necessary for Rosemary's seduction of Dick.

Dick suffers from the opposite affliction: he is, or was, used to thinking about himself as exceptional. While lacking the meteoric brilliance of Gatsby and the predictable grooming of Anthony Patch, he betrays an intellectual distinction. Even Diver's society is rarefied: "To be included in Dick Diver's world for a while was a remarkable experience: people believed he made special reservations about them, recognizing the proud uniqueness of their destinies, buried under the compromises of how many years." His was a world of "exquisite consideration and politeness."

The story of Rosemary's crush, with peripheral entanglements of duels and chivalric interventions, articulate the mysteries of Shiloh and Argonne earlier invoked in "The Swimmers." Rosemary enters giddily into the "expensive simplicity of the Divers": first by attending parties with Nicole and Dick, then by shopping and lunching with Nicole, and finally by seducing Dick. "Extraordinary innocence" marks this affair that Dick distinguishes from the "active love" he feels for Nicole. Rosemary acquiesces to these terms because she believes in the "inner intensity" of passion, that which has cooled between Dick and Nicole and seems vital between them. The

Great War haunts this careless world of denial, becoming at once inescapable reality and generational metaphor for the couple's perceptual dilemma. A tour of a battlefield generates excitement in Dick and longing in Rosemary:

> They came out of the neat restored trench, and faced a memorial to the Newfoundland dead. Reading the inscription Rosemary burst into sudden tears. Like most women she liked to be told how she should feel, and she liked Dick's telling her which things were ludicrous, and which things were sad. But most of all she wanted him to know how she loved him, now that the fact was upsetting everything, now that she was walking over the battle-field in a thrilling dream.

Throughout the opening book, Dick intellectualizes and socializes his ethereal presence. Other characters, resigned to life's confusions and threats, can be spared only by his intervention. The chivalric code, so essential to Amory's self-conception in *This Side of Paradise,* echoes with a loyalty to the history and literature of the South here as Dick "perceived all the maturity of an older America . . . and sat again on his father's knee, riding with Moseby while the old loyalties and devotions fought on around him."

The second section explores Dick's early years in Zurich as psychiatric resident in the spring of 1917, his moment "of intricate destiny" and the place where he met Nicole Warren, the patient who becomes his wife. Nicole, brilliant and beautiful, but schizophrenic, persuades Dick, then serving in the army, to tend to her professionally and emotionally. In literary letters distinguished by "helpless caesuras and darker rhythms," she makes her appeal to Captain Diver "because there is no one else." She violates the very logic of his life, threatens his professional remove, and saps the energy necessary to his research. Upon marrying Nicole in 1919, he accedes to a complex world of wealth, incest, and illness that threatens his very existence. Nicole had long ago been raped by her father. As if in compensation, she becomes the beneficiary of the family fortune, which underwrites Dick's practice in Switzerland, and inherits the means and miseries of the American nouveaux riches. Her schizophrenia embodies the pathological relationship between happiness and money, and through it Dick must confront his own doubts concerning the costs and profits of his relationship with Nicole and with his practice. His partnership suffers, undermined by his progressive ambivalence toward his practice and by his chronic drinking.

Failure liberates Dick to wander about Europe on journeys that bypass the story line of the book's first section. He surfaces in Rome in 1929, where a much-matured Rosemary is filming her latest movie. Dick and Rosemary, like extras from a story by Henry James, lunch at the "Castelli dei Caesari, a splendid restaurant in a high-terraced villa overlooking the ruined forum of an undetermined period of the decadence." Attempts to revive their affair fail, as sketched in Fitzgerald's "General Plan": "He is in Rome with the actress having a disappointing love affair too late he is beaten up by the police."

The third section begins by declaring Nicole "less sick than any one thinks—she only cherishes her illness as an instrument of power." Unable to stabilize his relationship with Nicole or the finances of the Warren-funded clinic, Dick relinquishes his partnership in the clinic—and is "relieved": "Now without desperation he had long felt the ethics of his profession dissolving into a lifeless mass." The Divers return to the Riviera, "which was home," and seem "unified" again. Soon, tired of "Dick's growing indifference, at present personified by too much drink," Nicole leaves him for Tommy Barban: "She did not want any vague spiritual romance—she wanted an 'affair'; she wanted a change." This change leaves Dick "at liberty" to leave Europe, return to the States, and establish a general practice in upstate New York.

Reviews for Fitzgerald's much-anticipated novel were mixed. The decade it had taken Fitzgerald to complete the work had witnessed a transformation from the prodigality of the 1920s to the economic collapse and austerity of the 1930s. Few commentaries actually noted the disjunction between the times and the novel, but John O'Hara saw that as a problem central to its reception, claiming that it "came out at precisely the wrong time in the national history." Fitzgerald's drunken decadence had, by the Depression, become a cliché. And yet, Philip Rahv, in an unlikely reading for the *Daily Worker,* pronounced the work a "fearful indictment of the moneyed aristocracy." Fitzgerald continued to anguish over the novel's structure (even proposing a revised edition for the Modern Library in which the plot is developed chronologically), but reviewers ignored the author's reservations and troubled instead over theme and characters. Style, for many readers, no longer compensated: as the unsigned *Time* review complained: "Though he often writes like an angel, he can still think like a parrot."

The extraliterary judgments were often the most compelling in their approval. *The Journal of Nervous and Mental Disease,* in one of Fitzgerald's favorite reviews, concluded that *Tender Is the Night* constituted "an achievement which no student of the psychobiological sources of human behavior, and of its particular social correlates extant today, can afford not to read." Unable to await Hemingway's judgment, Scott wrote in May, hoping to reap the much-needed encouragement of a master reading. Hemingway responded with a three-page personal assault on Fitzgerald's talent and manhood, laced with self-aggrandizing counsel:

Forget your personal tragedy.... You see Bo, you're not a tragic character. Neither am I. All we are is writers and what we should do is write. Of all people on earth you needed discipline in your work and instead you marry someone who is jealous of your work, wants to compete with you and ruins you.

*THE CRACK-UP*

Throughout the remainder of 1934, Zelda's madness and his own alcoholism enslaved Fitzgerald. The anxiously anticipated income from *Tender Is the Night* was never realized, and a historical novel was never written. His withered life became the stuff of the self-accusatory essays of *The Crack-Up.* With the death of the *Post*'s Lorimer, Fitzgerald lost his most reliable and generous market. Arnold Gingrich's support at the new men's magazine *Esquire* never provided more than a subsistence income. Dean Gauss neglected Fitzgerald's proposal to lecture at Princeton on the art of fiction; Perkins and Ober refused additional loans. Only the Modern Library *Gatsby* and *Taps at Reveille,* a collection of stories published in March 1935, kept Fitzgerald in public view. Suicidal mania kept Zelda in the privacy of Baltimore's Sheppard-Pratt Hospital. Writing in June 1935, she saw with anguished clarity the circumstance of their marriage:

Now that there isn't any more happiness and home is gone and there isn't even any past and no emotions but those that were yours where there could be any comfort—it is a shame that we should have met in harshness and coldness where there was once so much tenderness and so many dreams. Your song.

Scott, unable to distinguish between his love and art, concluded: "The voices fainter and fainter— How is Zelda, how is Zelda—tell us—how is Zelda."

In late 1935, dissipated and riddled with doubt, Fitzgerald sought the seclusion of the North Carolina mountains to write "The Crack-Up." (By April 1936, Zelda was admitted to a clinic in nearby Asheville, where she was cared for on a residential and outpatient basis; she perished there in a fire in 1948.) These autobiographical essays, written for Gingrich at *Esquire,* appeared in February, March, and April of 1936, to the amazement of his readers and the disgust of his intimates.

Perkins and Hemingway were scornfully embarrassed by Fitzgerald's sputtering humanity; Dos Passos was contemptuous of Fitzgerald's self-absorption in what he called in a letter of October 1936 "the middle of the general conflagration."

In the summer of 1937, overwhelmed by debt, Fitzgerald accepted a six-month contract from Metro-Goldwyn-Mayer and moved to the Garden of Allah on Sunset Boulevard. His accomplishments as a novelist worked against him as a screenwriter, most painfully in his attempt to script Erich Maria Remarque's *Three Comrades* for the producer Joseph Mankiewicz. Working steadily from August 1937 to February 1938, Fitzgerald was unable to submit a screenplay acceptable to Mankiewicz. Mankiewicz's revisions "disillusioned" Fitzgerald, who complained in a letter of January 20, 1938:

For nineteen years, with two years out for sickness, I've written best-selling entertainment, and my dialogue is supposedly right up at the top. But I learn from the script that you've suddenly decided that it isn't good dialogue and you can take a few hours off and do much better.

During the one-year contract renewal period, which brought work on *Marie Antoinette, The Women,* and *Madame Curie,* Fitzgerald lived with Sheilah Graham in the beach colony of Malibu. Shortly before his contract expired, they moved again, this time to the warmth of the upper San Fernando Valley, a cottage at Belly Acres on the Encino estate of the actor Edward Everett Horton. After eighteen months at Metro-Goldwyn-Mayer, Fitzgerald sought work at a number of smaller studios. In January 1939, he worked briefly on David O. Selznick's production of *Gone with the Wind,* then joined Budd Schulberg on *Winter Carnival* (the Dartmouth College debacle celebrated in Schulberg's novel *The Disenchanted*).

Fitzgerald's relationship with Graham sustained and confused his remaining years. At once captivated and appalled by this woman who reminded him of Zelda, Fitzgerald intellectually tutored the woman who emotionally tended to him. Most of the time, his daughter, Scottie, studying at Vassar College, and Sheilah prompted unexpectedly responsible behavior from Fitzgerald, who was anxious to share the wisdom of his life. His correspondence with Scottie, especially during his final years, while she was a student at Vassar, reflects the patient urgency of a dying man. As he wrote on July 7, 1938:

> When I was your age I lived with a great dream. The dream grew and I learned how to speak of it and make people listen. Then the dream divided one day when I decided to marry your mother after all, even though I knew she was spoiled and meant no good to me. . . .
>
> I never wanted to see again in this world women who were brought up as idlers. . . . When you began to show disturbing signs at about fourteen, I comforted myself with the idea that you were too precocious socially and a strict school would fix things. . . .
>
> But I don't want to be upset by idlers inside my family or out. I want my energies and my earnings for people who talk my language.
>
> I have begun to fear that you don't. You don't realize that what I am doing here is the last tired effort of a man who once did something finer and better.

As Fitzgerald reinscribed his life for his daughter, he initiated the reordering of his reputation for subsequent generations of readers.

In the fall of 1939, Fitzgerald began work on *The Last Tycoon.* He wrote to Kenneth Littauer at *Collier's* on September 29, 1939, to explain his story of Metro's "boy wonder" (the producer Irving Thalberg), in which *no single fact is actually true.*" Financial miseries, however, necessitated another series for *Esquire:* the Pat Hobby stories, tales of a hack screenwriter who has not been hot since the silents. Fitzgerald's life assumed the lineaments of Pat Hobby's as one by one his connections failed: *Collier's* and the *Post* refusing serial rights to the planned novel, Littauer at *Col-*

*lier's* and Perkins at Scribners declining his request for an advance.

## THE LAST TYCOON

*The Last Tycoon* survives as a literary fragment, an intricately planned episodic structure with fully realized characters and a tenuous plot. Whether two thirds "finished," as originally thought, or "half-way" considered, as Matthew Bruccoli believes, the novel reveals Fitzgerald's culminating brilliance in his deft handling of character, dialogue, and setting. Anxious to avoid the structural inconsistencies of *Tender Is the Night,* he adhered to the nine-chapter compression and participant-narrator of *The Great Gatsby.* Obsessive outlines and plot revisions into episodes resembled his screenwriting routine. As he had suggested in "Handle with Care" (the March 1936 "Crack-Up" essay):

> As long past as 1930, I had a hunch that the talkies would make even the best selling novelist as archaic as silent pictures. . . . But there was a rankling indignity, that to me had become almost an obsession, in seeing the power of the written word subordinated to another power, a more glittering, a grosser power.

Cecelia Brady, daughter of Monroe Stahr's partner (who Fitzgerald describes as "a shrewd man, a gentile, and a scoundrel of the lowest variety"), narrates the loves and life of Stahr. Cecelia (recalling *Gatsby*'s Nick Carraway) "is *of* the movies but not *in* them," rendering her acutely observant and passionately uninvolved. Stahr, as Fitzgerald confided in his synopsis, "is Irving Thalberg" and he reenacts the tragedy of Thalberg's "great adventure."

Unfinished at his death, although it was published as a memorial gesture by Scribners in 1941 as *The Last Tycoon: An Unfinished Novel, The Love of the Last Tycoon: A Western* has been restored to a work in progress by Bruccoli for the

*Cambridge Edition of the Works of F. Scott Fitzgerald.* Working from Fitzgerald's series of five typescript outlines, Bruccoli, guided by the correspondence of Graham and Frances Kroll (Fitzgerald's secretary) as well as by Edmund Wilson's earlier synopsis, has recast Fitzgerald's "western" into its unfinished form of an opening chapter (which introduces Cecelia and Hollywood, "a mining town in lotus land," as essential characters) and several related Stahr "episodes" (at the studio, on the set, in love, at Malibu). Some critics suggest that the novel's persistent fragmentation suggests Fitzgerald's failing capacities to retain his work in progress; Bruccoli vehemently rejects this reading, asserting that "the drafts indicate that Fitzgerald was proceeding carefully without concern for a deadline." Writing to Zelda on December 13, 1940, Fitzgerald suggested the tentative nature of work in his condition:

> The novel is about three-quarters through and I think I can go on till January 12 without doing any stories or going back to the studio. I couldn't go back to the studio anyhow in my present condition as I have to spend most of the time in bed where I write on a wooden desk.

By late 1940, Fitzgerald was confronting a rapidly deteriorating physical condition and a failing literary reputation. The popularity of Hemingway's *For Whom the Bell Tolls,* a novel that Scott deemed "thoroughly superficial . . . [with] all the profundity of Rebecca," deepened his depression as he considered their relative success as writers. In late November, he suffered chest pain so debilitating that he moved into Graham's first-floor apartment to avoid unnecessary exertion. On December 21, 1940, Fitzgerald collapsed and died of a massive coronary occlusion. After a viewing service in the Wordsworth Room at the Pierce Brothers Mortuary in West Los Angeles, Fitzgerald's body was sent, at Zelda's request, to be buried at Rockville Union Cemetery in Maryland. Neither Zelda nor Sheilah attended the service.

*The Last Tycoon* assured Fitzgerald an ongoing readership. Published on October 27, 1941, the Scribner edition, edited by Wilson, reprinted a selection of stories as well as *The Great Gatsby.* The reviews were tentative, though unusually enthusiastic: *Time* reflected that *The Last Tycoon* contained "scenes of beauty and power. Completed, it might or might not have been a *Citizen Kane* about the movie industry." *The Crack-Up* (1945), Wilson's New Directions compilation of the *Esquire* essays and uncollected letters, notebook entries, and essays, found a new audience. Fitzgerald's autobiographical tracts, notes, and letters were liberated by his death. Reviews celebrated his heroism and tragedy, Mark Schorer's "Fitzgerald's Tragic Sense" proclaiming *The Crack-Up* "a classic of literary self-revelation . . . [that] transcends mere pathos." *The Stories of F. Scott Fitzgerald* (1951), Cowley's selection of familiar and previously unpublished work, initiated a popular and scholarly reevaluation of Fitzgerald's work.

The continued interest in Fitzgerald's work, especially *The Great Gatsby,* has secured his academic and popular reputation. In the last two decades of the twentieth century, however, publication of the correspondence and several biographies, especially Bruccoli's monumental *Some Sort of Epic Grandeur,* has complicated the critical picture. The Fitzgerald centennial celebrations at Princeton University and St. Paul, Minnesota, and the controversies over the Cambridge University Press critical edition of his work suggest both how vital Fitzgerald's work remains and how problematic it seems to some readers unable or unwilling to accept Fitzgerald's personal and generational indulgence in racist and anti-Semitic characterizations. While partisans like Matthew J. Bruccoli tend to overlook such qualifying factors in their appraisals of Fitzgerald's work, more skeptical readers, like Walter Benn Michaels, use such prejudices as a means of reading the author culturally. At the readings during St. Paul's centennial celebration, "unpleasant words" (that is, descriptions construed as racist and xenophobic) were "crossed out and translated into modernly acceptable vocabulary." Despite the understandable difficulties some readers have with such transgressions, writers as diverse as J. D. Salinger, John Cheever, Joan Didion, and John Updike have found Fitzgerald's parables of class, money, and the difficulty of happiness to be powerful models for their own work. Fitzgerald's occasional lapses in taste or judgment do not negate the force and elegance of his prose. Even the most thoughtful reader is likely to succumb to the heroic splendor of his writing.

## Selected Bibliography

### WORKS OF F. SCOTT FITZGERALD

NOVELS

*This Side of Paradise.* New York: Scribners, 1920.
*The Beautiful and the Damned.* New York: Scribners, 1922.
*The Great Gatsby.* New York: Scribners, 1925.
*Tender Is the Night.* New York: Scribners, 1934. Revised 1951. (Preface by Malcolm Cowley, with the author's final revisions.)
*The Last Tycoon: An Unfinished Novel.* New York: Scribners, 1941. (This first edition includes *The Great Gatsby* and selected short stories.)

SHORT STORIES

*Flappers and Philosophers.* New York: Scribners, 1920. (Eight stories, including "The Ice Palace" and "Bernice Bobs Her Hair.")
*Tales of the Jazz Age.* New York: Scribners, 1922. (Eleven stories, including "May Day; or, From President to Postman" and "The Diamond as Big as the Ritz.")
*Taps at Reveille.* New York: Scribners, 1935. (Eighteen stories, including "The Scandal Detectives," "The Freshest Boy," "The Night of Chancellorsville," "The Last of the Belles," and "Babylon Revisited.")

*The Stories of F. Scott Fitzgerald.* New York: Scribners, 1951. (Twenty-eight stories with an introduction by Malcolm Cowley, including "Absolution," "The Diamond as Big as the Ritz," "Bernice Bobs Her Hair," "The Ice Palace," "May Day," "Magnetism," "The Rich Boy," "The Scandal Detectives," "Crazy Sunday," and "Babylon Revisited.")
*Babylon Revisited and Other Stories.* New York: Scribners, 1960. (Ten stories, including "The Ice Palace," "The Diamond as Big as the Ritz," "Winter Dreams," "The Rich Boy," and "Crazy Sunday.")
*The Mystery of the Raymond Mortgage.* New York: Random House, 1960. (The first edition of F. Scott Fitzgerald's first story, written when he was thirteen years old.)
*The Pat Hobby Stories.* New York: Scribners, 1962. (Seventeen stories with an introduction by Arnold Gingrich, including "Boil Some Water—Lots of It," "Pat Hobby and Orson Welles," "Pat Hobby Putative Father," "The Homes of the Stars," and "Two Old-Timers.")
*The Basil and Josephine Stories.* Edited by Jackson Bryer and John Kuehl. New York: Scribners, 1973. (Fourteen stories.)
*Bits of Paradise.* Edited by Matthew J. Bruccoli and Scottie Fitzgerald Smith. New York: Scribners, 1974. (Eleven stories, including "The Swimmers" and " 'What a Handsome Pair!' " with ten stories by Zelda Fitzgerald.)
*The Price Was High: The Last Uncollected Stories of F. Scott Fitzgerald.* Edited by Matthew J. Bruccoli. New York: Harcourt Brace Jovanovich/Bruccoli Clark, 1979. (Fifty stories from mass-circulation magazines, primarily from the *Saturday Evening Post.*)
*The Short Stories of F. Scott Fitzgerald.* Edited by Matthew J. Bruccoli. New York: Scribners, 1989. (Forty-three stories, including "The Swimmers," "Bernice Bobs Her Hair," "The Ice Palace," "May Day," "The Diamond as Big as the Ritz," "The Rich Boy," and "Babylon Revisited.")

ESSAYS AND OTHER WORKS

*Fie! Fie! Fi-Fi.* New York: John Church, 1914.
*The Crack-Up.* Edited by Edmund Wilson. New York: New Directions, 1945. (With other uncollected pieces, notebooks, and unpublished letters; also contains letters to Fitzgerald from Gertrude Stein, Edith Wharton, T. S. Eliot, Thomas Wolfe, and John Dos

Passos and essays and poems by Paul Rosenfeld, Glenway Wescott, John Dos Passos, John Peale Bishop, and Edmund Wilson.)

*Afternoon of an Author.* Princeton, N.J.: Princeton University Library, 1957; New York: Scribners, 1958. (Stories and essays, with an introduction and notes by Arthur Mizener, including "Princeton," "Who's Who—and Why," "How to Live on $36,000 a Year," "Author's House," and "Afternoon of an Author.")

*The Apprentice Fiction of F. Scott Fitzgerald, 1907–1917.* Edited by John Kuehl. New Brunswick, N.J.: Rutgers University Press, 1965. (Twelve stories, including "The Mystery of the Raymond Mortgage.")

*Thoughtbook of Francis Scott Key Fitzgerald.* Edited by John Kuehl. Princeton, N.J.: Princeton University Library, 1965.

*F. Scott Fitzgerald in His Own Time: A Miscellany.* Edited by Matthew J. Bruccoli and Jackson R. Bryer. Kent, Ohio: Kent State University Press, 1971. (Poems and lyrics; student contributions to *Nassau Literary Magazine* and the *Princeton Tiger;* public letters and statements; interviews with, among others, Frederick James Smith and Harry Salpeter; reviews; essays; and editorials.)

*F. Scott Fitzgerald's Ledger: A Facsimile.* Edited by Matthew J. Bruccoli. Washington: NCR/Microcard Books, 1972. (With an annual accounting of Fitzgerald's earnings from 1919 through 1936.)

*F. Scott Fitzgerald's Screenplay for "The Three Comrades" by Erich Maria Remarque.* Edited by Matthew J. Bruccoli. Carbondale: Southern Illinois University Press, 1978.

*The Notebooks of F. Scott Fitzgerald.* Edited by Matthew J. Bruccoli. New York: Harcourt Brace Jovanovich/Bruccoli Clark, 1978.

*Poems, 1911–1940.* Edited by Matthew J. Bruccoli. Bloomfield Hills, Mich., and Columbia, S.C.: Bruccoli Clark, 1981.

*F. Scott Fitzgerald on Writing.* New York: Scribners, 1985.

*F. Scott Fitzgerald: Inscriptions.* Columbia, S.C.: Matthew J. Bruccoli, 1988.

*Babylon Revisited: The Screenplay.* New York: Carroll and Graf, 1993.

*F. Scott Fitzgerald on Authorship.* Edited by Matthew J. Bruccoli with Judith S. Baughman. Columbia: University of South Carolina Press, 1996. (Letters, articles, and notebook entries on the art of writing.)

CORRESPONDENCE

*The Letters of F. Scott Fitzgerald.* Edited by Andrew Turnbull. New York: Scribners, 1963.

*Scott Fitzgerald: Letters to His Daughter.* Edited by Andrew Turnbull with an introduction by Frances Fitzgerald Lanahan. New York: Scribners, 1963.

*Dear Scott/Dear Max: The Fitzgerald-Perkins Correspondence.* Edited by John Kuehl and Jackson R. Bryer. New York: Scribners, 1971.

*As Ever, Scott Fitz—.* Edited by Matthew J. Bruccoli and Jennifer McCabe Atkinson. Philadelphia: Lippincott, 1972. (The letters between Fitzgerald and his agent, Harold Ober.)

*Correspondence of F. Scott Fitzgerald.* Edited by Matthew J. Bruccoli and Margaret M. Duggan, with Susan Walker. New York: Random House, 1980.

*F. Scott Fitzgerald: A Life in Letters.* Edited by Matthew J. Bruccoli with Judith S. Baughman. New York: Scribners, 1994.

COLLECTED WORKS

*The Portable F. Scott Fitzgerald.* New York: Viking, 1945. (Selected by Dorothy Parker with an introduction by John O'Hara; includes *The Great Gatsby, Tender Is the Night,* "Absolution," "The Baby Party," "The Rich Boy," "May Day," "The Cut-Glass Bowl," "The Offshore Pirate," "The Freshest Boy," "Crazy Sunday," and "Babylon Revisited.")

*Borrowed Time.* London: Grey Walls Press, 1951. (Nine stories including "The Cut-Glass Bowl," "May Day," "The Camel's Back," "The Rich Boy," and "Babylon Revisited.")

*Three Novels of F. Scott Fitzgerald.* New York: Scribners, 1953. (Includes *The Great Gatsby,* with an introduction by Malcolm Cowley; *Tender Is the Night,* with the author's final revisions and edited by Malcolm Cowley; and *The Last Tycoon,* edited by Edmund Wilson.)

*The Bodley Head Scott Fitzgerald.* 6 vols. London: Bodley Head, 1958–1963. (Volume 1 [1958]: *The Great Gatsby, The Last Tycoon,* "May Day," "The Diamond as Big as the Ritz," "The Crack-Up," "Handle With Care," "Pasting It Together," and "Crazy Sunday"; Volume 2 [1959]: "Echoes of the Jazz Age," "My Lost City," "Ring," "Early Success," letters to Frances Scott Fitzgerald, *Tender Is the Night* [original version], "The Last of the Belles," "Pat Hobby Himself," "An Alcoholic Case," and "Financing Finnegan"; Volume 3 [1960]:

*This Side of Paradise, The Crack-Up,* "The Cut-Glass Bowl," "The Curious Case of Benjamin Button," "The Lees of Happiness," "The Rich Boy," "The Adjuster," and "Gretchen's Forty Winks"; Volume 4 [1961]: *The Beautiful and the Damned,* "The Rough Crossing," and "Babylon Revisited"; Volumes 5 and 6 [1963]: reprint of Malcolm Cowley's *The Stories of F. Scott Fitzgerald.*)

*The Fitzgerald Reader.* Edited by Arthur Mizener. New York: Scribners, 1963. (Includes *The Great Gatsby,* sections of *Tender Is the Night* and *The Last Tycoon,* a selection from *The Crack-Up,* and assorted stories.)

*The Cambridge Edition of the Works of F. Scott Fitzgerald.* Edited by Matthew J. Bruccoli. Cambridge, England, and New York: Cambridge University Press, 1991–. (Of the fifteen projected volumes, these have been published: *The Great Gatsby* [1991]; *The Love of the Last Tycoon: A Western* [1992]; *This Side of Paradise* [1995]).

MANUSCRIPTS

*F. Scott Fitzgerald Manuscripts.* 18 vols. Edited by Matthew J. Bruccoli with associate editor Alan Margolies and consulting editors Alexander P. Clark and Charles Scribner III. New York: Garland, 1990–1991. (Includes *This Side of Paradise, The Beautiful and the Damned, The Great Gatsby* galleys, *Tender Is the Night* [the Melarky and Kelley versions and the Diver version], *The Last Tycoon, The Vegetable,* stories and articles.)

The F. Scott Fitzgerald papers are held at the University of South Carolina and the Department of Rare Books and Special Collections, Princeton University Library.

## BIBLIOGRAPHIES AND CONCORDANCE

Bruccoli, Matthew J. *F. Scott Fitzgerald: A Descriptive Bibliography.* Pittsburgh: University of Pittsburgh Press, 1972. Revised, 1987.

———. *Supplement to F. Scott Fitzgerald: A Descriptive Bibliography.* Pittsburgh: University of Pittsburgh Press, 1980.

Bryer, Jackson R. *The Critical Reputation of F. Scott Fitzgerald: A Bibliographical Study.* Hamden, Conn.: Archon, 1967. Supplement, 1984.

Crosland, Andrew T. *A Concordance to F. Scott Fitzgerald's "The Great Gatsby."* Detroit, Mich.: Bruccoli Clark/Gale Research, 1975.

## BIOGRAPHICAL STUDIES

Berg, Scott. *Maxwell Perkins: Editor of Genius.* New York: Dutton, 1978.

Bruccoli, Matthew Joseph. *Scott and Ernest: The Authority of Failure and the Authority of Success.* New York: Random House, 1978.

———. *Some Sort of Epic Grandeur: The Life of F. Scott Fitzgerald.* Revised edition. New York: Carroll and Graf, 1991.

Buttitta, Tony. *After the Good Gay Times.* New York: Viking, 1974.

Graham, Sheilah. *College of One.* New York: Viking, 1967.

Latham, John Aaron. *Crazy Sundays: F. Scott Fitzgerald in Hollywood.* New York: Viking, 1971.

Le Vot, André. *F. Scott Fitzgerald: A Biography.* Translated by William Byron. Garden City, N.Y.: Doubleday, 1983.

Mellow, James R. *Invented Lives: F. Scott and Zelda Fitzgerald.* Boston: Houghton Mifflin, 1984.

Meyers, Jeffrey. *Scott Fitzgerald: A Biography.* New York: HarperCollins, 1994.

Miller, Linda Patterson, ed. *Letters from the Lost Generation: Gerald and Sara Murphy and Friends.* New Brunswick, N.J.: Rutgers University Press, 1991.

Mizener, Arthur. *The Far Side of Paradise: A Biography of F. Scott Fitzgerald.* Boston: Houghton, Mifflin 1965.

O'Hara, John. *Selected Letters of John O'Hara.* Edited by Matthew J. Bruccoli. New York: Random House, 1978.

Ring, Frances Kroll. *Against the Current: As I Remember F. Scott Fitzgerald.* San Francisco: Donald L. Ellis/Creative Arts, 1985.

Smith, Scottie Fitzgerald, Matthew J. Bruccoli, and Joan P. Kerr, eds. *The Romantic Egoists: A Pictorial Autobiography from the Scrapbooks and Albums of F. Scott Fitzgerald and Zelda Fitzgerald.* New York: Scribners, 1974.

Tomkins, Calvin. *Living Well Is the Best Revenge.* New York: Viking, 1971.

Turnbull, Andrew. *Scott Fitzgerald.* New York: Ballantine, 1971.

Wilson, Edmund. *The Twenties: From Notebooks and Diaries of the Period.* Edited by Leon Edel. New York: Farrar, Straus & Giroux, 1975.

## CRITICAL STUDIES

BOOKS

Allen, Joan. *Candles and Carnival Lights: The Catholic Sensibility of F. Scott Fitzgerald.* New York: New York University Press, 1978.

Berman, Ronald. *"The Great Gatsby" and Modern Times.* Urbana: University of Illinois Press, 1994.

Bruccoli, Matthew J. *The Composition of "Tender Is the Night": A Study of the Manuscripts.* Pittsburgh: University of Pittsburgh Press, 1963.

———. *"The Last of the Novelists": F. Scott Fitzgerald and "The Last Tycoon."* Carbondale: Southern Illinois University Press, 1977.

Callahan, John F. *The Illusions of a Nation: Myth and History in the Novels of F. Scott Fitzgerald.* Urbana: University of Illinois Press, 1972.

Chambers, John B. *The Novels of F. Scott Fitzgerald.* New York: St. Martin's, 1989.

Cross, K. G. *Scott Fitzgerald.* New York: Capricorn Books, 1964.

Eble, Kenneth. *F. Scott Fitzgerald.* New York: Twayne, 1963. Revised, 1977.

Higgins, John A. *F. Scott Fitzgerald: A Study of the Stories.* New York: St. John's University Press, 1971.

Miller, James E. Jr. *F. Scott Fitzgerald: His Art and His Technique.* New York: New York University Press, 1964.

Phillips, Gene D. *Fiction, Film, and F. Scott Fitzgerald.* Chicago: Loyola University Press, 1986.

Sklar, Robert. *F. Scott Fitzgerald: The Last Laocoön.* New York: Oxford University Press, 1967.

Stanley, Linda A. *The Foreign Critical Reputation of F. Scott Fitzgerald: An Analysis and Annotated Bibliography.* Westport, Conn.: Greenwood Press, 1980.

Stern, Milton R. *The Golden Moment: The Novels of F. Scott Fitzgerald.* Urbana: University of Illinois Press, 1970.

———. *"Tender Is the Night": The Broken Universe.* New York: Twayne, 1994.

Way, Brian. *F. Scott Fitzgerald and the Art of Social Fiction.* London: Arnold; New York, St. Martin's, 1980.

COLLECTIONS OF ESSAYS

Bloom, Harold, ed. *F. Scott Fitzgerald.* New York: Chelsea House, 1985.

———. *F. Scott Fitzgerald's "The Great Gatsby."* New Haven, Conn.: Chelsea House, 1986.

Bruccoli, Matthew J., ed. *New Essays on "The Great Gatsby."* Cambridge, England, and New York: Cambridge University Press, 1985.

Bryer, Jackson R., ed. *F. Scott Fitzgerald: The Critical Reception.* New York: Burt Franklin, 1978.

———. *The Short Stories of F. Scott Fitzgerald: New Approaches in Criticism.* Madison: University of Wisconsin Press, 1982.

Cowley, Malcolm, and Robert Cowley, eds. *Fitzgerald and the Jazz Age.* New York: Scribners, 1966.

Donaldson, Scott, ed. *Critical Essays on "The Great Gatsby."* Boston: G. K. Hall, 1984.

Eble, Kenneth, ed. *F. Scott Fitzgerald: A Collection of Criticism.* New York: McGraw-Hill, 1973.

Kazin, Alfred, ed. *F. Scott Fitzgerald: The Man and His Work.* Cleveland: World, 1951.

LaHood, Marvin J., ed. *"Tender Is the Night": Essays in Criticism.* Bloomington: Indiana University Press, 1969.

Lee, A. Robert, ed. *Scott Fitzgerald: The Promises of Life.* New York: St. Martin's, 1989.

Lockridge, Ernest, ed. *Twentieth Century Interpretations of "The Great Gatsby."* Englewood Cliffs, N.J.: Prentice-Hall, 1968.

Mizener, Arthur, ed. *F. Scott Fitzgerald: A Collection of Critical Essays.* Englewood Cliffs, N. J.: Prentice-Hall, 1963.

CRITICAL ARTICLES

Billy, Ted. "Acts of Madness or Despair: A Note on *The Secret Agent* and *The Great Gatsby.*" *Studies in American Fiction* 11, no. 1:101–106 (spring 1983).

Breitwieser, Mitchell. "*The Great Gatsby:* Grief, Jazz, and the Eye-Witness." *Arizona Quarterly* 47:17–70 (autumn 1991).

Cohen, Milton A. "Fitzgerald's Third Regret: Intellectual Pretense and the Ghost of Edmund Wilson." *Texas Studies in Literature and Language* 33:64–88 (spring 1991).

Dickstein, Morris. "Fitzgerald's Second Act." *South Atlantic Quarterly* 90, no. 3:555–578 (summer 1991).

Dillon, Andrew. "*The Great Gatsby:* The Vitality of Illusion." *Arizona Quarterly* 44:49–61 (spring 1988).

Doctorow, E. L. "F. S. F., 1896–1996, R.I.P." *The Nation* 263, no. 9:36 (September 30, 1996).

Edwards, Owen Dudley. "The Lost Teigueen: F. Scott Fitzgerald's Ethics and Ethnicity." In *Scott Fitzgerald: The Promises of Life.* Edited by A. Robert Lee. New York: St. Martin's Press, 1989. Pp. 181–214.

Epstein, Joseph. "F. Scott Fitzgerald's Third Act." *Commentary* 98, no. 5:52–57 (November 1994).

Fetterlly, Judith. "Who Killed Dick Diver? The Sexual Politics of *Tender Is the Night.*" *Mosaic* 17, no. 1: 111–128 (winter 1984).

Frase, Brigitte. "Censored Centennial?" *Hungry Mind Review.* Winter 1996–1997. Pp. 13, 55.

Fussell, Edwin S. "Fitzgerald's Brave New World." *ELH* 19, no. 4: 291–306 (December 1952).

Giddings, Robert. "*The Last Tycoon:* Fitzgerald as Projectionist." In *Scott Fitzgerald: The Promises of Life.* Edited by A. Robert Lee. New York: St. Martin's, 1989. Pp. 74–93.

Hearn, Charles R. "F. Scott Fitzgerald and the Popular Magazine Formula Story of the Twenties." *Journal of American Culture* 18, no. 3:33–40 (fall 1995).

Kuehl, John. "Scott Fitzgerald: Romantic and Realist." *Texas Studies in Literature and Language* 1:412–426 (autumn 1959).

Merrill, Robert. "*Tender Is the Night* as a Tragic Action." *Texas Studies in Literature and Language,* 25:597–615 (winter 1983).

Toles, George. "The Metaphysics of Style in *Tender Is the Night.*" *American Literature* 62, no. 3:423–444 (September 1990).

Trilling, Lionel. "F. Scott Fitzgerald." In *The Liberal Imagination: Essays on Literature and Society.* Garden City, N.Y.: Doubleday Anchor, 1953. Pp. 235–244.

Tuttleton, James W. "F. Scott Fitzgerald and the Magical Glory." *The New Criterion* 13, no. 3:24–31 (November 1994).

Wanlass, Susan. "An Easy Commerce: Specific Similarities between the Writings of T. S. Eliot and F. Scott Fitzgerald." *English Language Notes* 32, no. 3:58–69 (March 1995).

Whitley, John S. " 'A Touch of Disaster': Fitzgerald, Spengler and the Decline of the West." In *Scott Fitzgerald: The Promises of Life.* Edited by A. Robert Lee. New York: St. Martin's Press, 1989. Pp. 157–180.

*—C. K. DORESKI*

# Robert Frost
## 1874–1963

*I*N 1959 LIONEL Trilling, then one of America's most prominent literary critics, spoke at a banquet given by Henry Holt and Company on the occasion of Robert Frost's eighty-fifth birthday. After reviewing Frost's laudatory critical reception and nearly mythical status, Trilling startled some of his audience by commenting that he thought of Frost as "a terrifying poet." Trilling was referring to the dark side of Frost's poetic vision, which is skeptical, sometimes nihilistic, though more stoic than despairing, and nearly always leavened with irony, wit, or play. Frost most deliberately explores a somber view in poems like "The Most of It," "Desert Places," "Design," and "Neither Out Far nor In Deep." But his poetry cannot easily be divided into dark and light motifs. With a late couplet from *In the Clearing* (1962) he reminds us that "It takes all sorts of in and outdoor schooling / To get adapted to my kind of fooling." Fooling—play—underlies every emotional stance in the poems, and while the consequent ambiguity sometimes underscores Frost's skepticism it mainly serves to keep his language flexible and witty—and intense.

Several years before Trilling's speech, Randall Jarrell in "The Other Frost" and "To the Laodiceans"—both of which appear in Jarrell's *Poetry and the Age* (1953)—explored the grimmer and more challenging aspects of Frost's poetry.

Jarrell points out in "To the Laodiceans" that a great source of pleasure in Frost's work is the range from "the most awful and most nearly unbearable parts of the poem, to the most tender, subtle, and loving," which the poet treats with "so much humor and sadness and composure, with such plain truth" and "a joy strong enough to make us forget the limitations and excesses and baseness that these days seem unforgettable." Understanding and appreciating its full emotional, psychological, and aesthetic range remains the pleasure and critical challenge of Frost's work.

Most of Frost's best-known poetry is set in the landscapes of New Hampshire and Vermont, particularly around the Derry, New Hampshire, farm where he lived for several years attempting to support his family as a chicken farmer and a part-time teacher at Pinkerton Academy. The Derry farm families provided the voices Frost would inscribe in *North of Boston* (1914) in poems such as "Blueberries," "The Death of the Hired Man," "The Code," and "The Mountain." Frost was not by birth a New Englander but a Californian, and he wrote at least some of his quintessentially New England poems while living in England. These apparent anomalies should not come as a surprise: Frost approached rural New England with fresh eyes and ears. Moreover—as William Wordsworth's poem "I Wandered Lonely as a Cloud" reminds us—we must bear in mind the role that memory always plays not only in re-creating but in intensifying experience. One of Frost's favorite New Englanders was Henry David Thoreau who, although a native of Concord and sometimes social in his way, spent his brief life estranged by intellect and sensibility from ordinary New Englanders. Despite assuming the mask of the farmer, Frost also stood outside rural society not to criticize but to reinvent it in what in a letter to John Bartlett he called the "dramatic accent" of poetry.

Only a few poems return to Frost's California childhood, but two of them are revealing. "Auspex," a late poem (in *In the Clearing*), satirizes the same Frost myth Trilling noted seriously:

> Once in a California Sierra
> I was swooped down upon when I was small
> And measured, but not taken after all
> By a great eagle bird in all its terror.

The bird, the boy's parents claim, rejected him because he "would not make a Ganymede": that is, model himself on the Trojan boy who was carried off by an eagle because of his beauty to be Zeus's cupbearer. (During the Middle Ages Ganymede embodied homosexual love.) In "Auspex" Frost resists the presumption that there was something he could not become, and indeed his career demonstrated he could make a great deal of himself. But his parents were correct as far as the allegory in the poem goes: Frost could not be a cupbearer for Zeus or any other god; he distanced himself from homosexuality; and although unquestionably a handsome man he would never have claimed to possess great beauty. The wit in the poem exists in the protest "I have remained resentful to this day / When any but myself presumed to say / That there was anything I couldn't be." The lines suggest that though the choice of Ganymede as the metaphor for Frost's potential is inappropriate, his parents took the actual event involving an eagle literally and, based on a misapplication of the Ganymede myth, both they and Frost himself came to unlikely conclusions.

If "Auspex" deals humorously with a childhood memory, "Once by the Pacific"—in *A Witness Tree* (1942)—takes a harsh Old Testament view of the origin of life and the future of humanity. The title suggests that this poem, too, derives from Frost's childhood memories, but the prophecy the poem offers, as it ironically personifies a nature antithetical to the human, is based on the adult perception that God's creation is fundamentally hostile.

> The shattered water made a misty din.
> Great waves looked over others coming in,
> And thought of doing something to the shore
> That water never did to land before.
> The clouds were low and hairy in the skies,
> Like locks blown forward in the gleam of eyes.

The second-person voice resists identity and even responsibility for its perceptions by shrugging them off on the reader:

> You could not tell, and yet it looked as if
> The shore was lucky in being backed by cliff,
> The cliff in being backed by continent.

This skeptical "as if" rhetorical construct is typical of Frost in his darker moments. The skepticism is rooted in uncertainty, and even the perception that leads to this doubt is veiled in uncertainty or ambiguity ("You could not tell"). The second "as if" of the poem leads to a resounding if frightening closure, in which nature gives way to the rage of the Old Testament God at his harshest:

> It looked as if a night of dark intent
> Was coming, and not only a night, an age.
> Someone had better be prepared for rage.
> There would be more than ocean water broken
> Before God's last *Put out the Light* was spoken.

With grim humor Frost refrains from identifying the "someone" and explaining how that mortal could possibly prepare for such a cataclysm. To moderate his gloomy poem, Frost wields his sense of play, invoking and reworking the biblical phrase "And God said let there be light" to leaven the most terrible of prophecies.

### EARLY LIFE

Frost's complex mixture of humor and foreboding, his respect for knowledge, and his sometimes anti-intellectual approach to learning reflect his equally complex family background. Born in San Francisco on March 26, 1874, Robert Lee Frost was the first child of William Prescott Frost Jr. and Isabelle Moodie. Frost's father was a Harvard graduate, an extroverted journalist, editor, and politician, while his mother, who had been born in Scotland, was a teacher, a poet, and sometimes a visionary. His father's excessive drinking and gambling at one point caused the parents to separate, and Isabelle took Robert, then two years old, east to visit his Frost grandparents in Lawrence, Massachusetts. When in 1885 William Prescott Frost Jr. died of tuberculosis, leaving nothing to his family, Isabelle and her two children (Jeanie was born in 1876) went back to live in Lawrence. William Prescott Frost Sr., like his son, disciplined the children with sternness and severity and displayed no generosity toward the widowed Isabelle, whom he blamed for the death of William Prescott Frost Jr. Robert, despite his grandfather's various acts of generosity, never entirely forgave him.

To free herself from the oppression of the elder Frosts, Isabelle took her children to Salem Depot, New Hampshire, only a few miles from Lawrence, and taught in the district school. This was Frost's first experience with rural New England life, which brought with it his first extended period of formal schooling. Salem and Derry, where Robert and Elinor would later spend the early years of their marriage and where their children would be born, were similar farm towns, stony-soiled, mod-

erately hilly, neither prosperous nor impoverished. In 1888 Frost entered Lawrence High School, where while working his way to the head of his graduating class he developed an interest in astronomy, earning a telescope by selling subscriptions to the *Youth's Companion.* He later commemorated this interest in the poem "The Star-Splitter," in which he subjects his youthful pursuit to an ironic adult skepticism. He writes of "Brad McLaughlin's" telescope (obtained by burning down his house for insurance money): "It's a star-splitter if there ever was one / And ought to do some good if splitting stars / 'Sa thing to be compared with splitting wood." The narrator of this poem finds little use for a telescope himself. In "Desert Places" Frost reinforces the notion that we need not look to the stars to understand the extremities of the human condition:

> They cannot scare me with their empty spaces
> Between stars—on stars where no human race is.
> I have it in me so much nearer home
> To scare myself with my own desert places.

Frost's first published poem, "La Noche Triste," derived from William Prescott's *History of the Conquest of Mexico* (1843), is in a very different mode. The poem, which appeared in the *Lawrence High School Bulletin* in 1890, is a grim but uncritical celebration of a heroic conquest by "freemen" who "live, and rule, and die / Where they [the Aztecs] ruled alone." Frost would rarely again write so unskeptical or uncomplicated a poem, but in "La Noche Triste," a minor epic, he was already displaying considerable skill in the use of both full and half rhyme; he also showed a generally firm control (with a few lapses) of a rhythmic impetus reminiscent of Henry Wadsworth Longfellow.

Frost was an excellent student. He gained a solid grasp of Latin, Greek, and history, which enabled him to pass the entrance examinations for Harvard College. As editor of the *Bulletin* in his senior year he published several of his own editorials and articles, including the fanciful "Petra and Its Surroundings," describing in colorful detail a place he would never see. More important is "A Monument to After-Thought Unveiled," which presents a miniature program for himself: "Aggressive life is two-fold: theory, practice; thought, action: and concretely, poetry, statesmanship; philosophy, socialism—infinitely." Though Frost would later reject socialism he retained an interest in statesmanship, and in old age used a goodwill trip to the Soviet Union to test his skills. Poetry would later divide itself into theory and practice; in the course of what he called "barding around," in a letter to Louis Untermeyer, he would bring an aggressive energy to promoting and publicizing his work and himself that would almost equal the effort he expended on writing.

More important than this early attempt at theorizing his life's work was meeting and falling in love with Elinor Miriam White, his co-valedictorian, whom he would pursue and eventually marry. First, however, he had to establish himself as some sort of breadwinner. He began by entering Dartmouth College, which was cheaper than Harvard and approved by his grandfather, who thought Harvard had ruined Frost's father. The most important intellectual discovery Frost made at Dartmouth was Francis Turner Palgrave's *Golden Treasury of Best Songs and Lyrical Poems in the English Language* (1861), which exposed him to a wider variety of English poetry than he had previously experienced. Otherwise Dartmouth failed to interest him, and he dropped out (or may have been expelled, suggests his biographer Jeffrey Meyers) at the end of his first semester. After attempting a variety of teaching, factory, and newspaper jobs, he finally persuaded Elinor to marry him in 1895.

Before that, however, a curious episode took place. Frost had published his first poem in a professional journal, the *Independent,* in 1894. "My Butterfly," which would eventually appear in *A*

*Boy's Will* (1913), is a competent though stilted fin de siècle poem of longing, languor, and death written in an aloof and deliberately anachronistic style. Frost arranged to have it and four other poems published in a little book; he had only two copies of the book printed. In the fall he took one copy of the book to Elinor at St. Lawrence University and received a cool reception. Distraught, he threw away the second copy and wandered down to the Dismal Swamp on the Virginia–North Carolina border. His poem "Kitty Hawk," written and published late in life, tells one version of the adventures he had then among boatmen and hunters. He had gone off, he sometimes claimed, to lose himself in the swamp, but in the end he seems to have had an amusing trip and to have forgotten his thoughts of suicide, if he ever had any.

DERRY: 1901–1912

For the first seventeen years of his marriage, till he moved to England, Frost supported his growing family by a variety of efforts, mostly chicken farming and teaching. He made another attempt at college, attending Harvard for two years while teaching part-time. In 1901 his grandfather died and left Frost the farm in Derry on which he and his family were living. Many of Frost's most famous poems germinated during the Derry years; all four of his surviving children would remember the farm in Derry as their childhood home. The first child, Elliott, did not live beyond his fourth year. His death of cholera in 1900 and, in the same year, Frost's mother's death from cancer, was the cause of serious depression for both Frost and Elinor. The terrible strain between them at this trying time finds voice in "Home Burial," in which a mother who has recently lost her first child accuses her husband of indifference. He actually suffers not from indifference but from the inability to express emotion, a distinction she is in no mood to make. In the climax of the poem, frustrated by their mutual lack of communication, she finds herself driven to "cry out on life" (as Frost puts it in "The Most of It") for its general indifference, complaining that

> The nearest friends can go
> With anyone to death, comes so far short
> They might as well not try to go at all.
> No, from the time when one is sick to death,
> One is alone, and he dies more alone.
> Friends make pretense of following to the grave,
> But before one is in it, their minds are turned
> And making the best of their way back to life
> And living people, and things they understand.
> But the world's evil. I won't have grief so
> If I can change it. Oh, I won't, I won't!

Of course the woman's husband cannot adequately answer her great Shakespearean lament, no more than anyone could. The death of Elliott, and the later deaths of Elinor, his son Carol, and his daughter Marjorie, would haunt and scar Frost's life to the end. But though "Home Burial" offers no consolation, no hope for the flayed marriage, no poem has more fully and honestly responded to the terrible death of a child and the emotional turmoil that ensues.

Though one of his finest, "Home Burial" is only one of many blank verse narratives, dramatic poems, lyrics, and monologues Frost composed during the years in Derry and immediately after in England as he looked back on those years. In his small southern New Hampshire farm town Frost read a great deal of literature, but much of the impetus for the development of his poetics derived from listening to the speech of neighboring farmers, a pungent colloquial talk Ralph Waldo Emerson had also admired.

The plain-spoken voice Frost derived from this speech first found public expression in a series of articles he wrote for the *Poultryman, Farm-Poultry,* and the *Eastern Poultryman* in 1903–1905, but it soon began to appear in the poems he was occasionally publishing in magazines and newspapers.

Writing to his former student John Bartlett in 1914 while in England, Frost explained his notion of the sentence as a structural and sonic device: "A sentence is a sound in itself on which other sounds called words may be strung." To write without a sense of the "sentence-sounds" preceding the actual placement of the words courts failure, he explains in a letter published in *Selected Letters of Robert Frost* (1964). These sentence-sounds are

> apprehended by the ear. They are gathered by the ear from the vernacular and brought into books. . . . A man is all a writer if *all* his words are strung on definite recognizable sentence sounds. The voice of the imagination, the speaking voice must know certainly how to behave how to posture in every sentence he offers.
>
> A man is a marked writer if his words are largely strung on the more striking sentence sounds.

Or as Frost put it in a December 1914 letter to Sidney Cox, which also appears in *Selected Letters:*

> The sentence as a sound in itself apart from the word sounds is no mere figure of speech. . . . I shall show the sentence sound opposing the sense of the words as in irony. And so till I establish the distinction between the grammatical sentence and the vital sentence. The grammatical sentence is merely accessory to the other and chiefly valuable as furnishing a clue to the other.

The sentence-sound (an ironic opposition to grammar and a way of catching the vernacular of speech through its own sound and rhythm), rather than the sentence (an accumulation of sounds and senses of particular words), forms the basis of Frost's original and deceptively simple poetics. In poems like "A Servant to Servants" (in *North of Boston*) the sentence-sound imitates speech with precision but renders speech compatible with the strong traditional rhythm of blank verse:

> You take the lake. I look and look at it.
> I see it's a fair, pretty sheet of water.
> I stand and make myself repeat out loud

The advantages it has, so long and narrow,
Like a deep piece of some old running river
Cut short off at both ends. It lies five miles
Straight away through the mountain notch
From the sink window where I wash the plates,
And all our storms come up toward the house,
Drawing the slow waves whiter and whiter and
　　whiter.

The vernacular voice, the Shakespearean rhetorical effects (for example, the repetition of "whiter"), and the comfortable invocation of an unusual but clarifying simile mark this passage indelibly as being by Frost.

But the great flexibility of Frost's apparently casual voice shows up not only in his blank verse poems, where we would expect it, but also in more formally constructed poems, like his sometimes astonishing sonnets. In "Design," for example, at the close of a virtuoso performance, a sonnet rhymed *abbaabba acaacc,* Frost undermines the argument of his poem with a characteristic dropping of the voice, turning on the key word "if":

I found a dimpled spider, fat and white,
On a white heal-all, holding up a moth
Like a white piece of rigid satin cloth—
Assorted characters of death and blight
Mixed ready to begin the morning right,
Like the ingredients of a witches' broth—
A snow-drop spider, a flower like a froth,
And dead wings carried like a paper kite.

What had that flower to do with being white,
The wayside blue and innocent heal-all?
What brought the kindred spider to that height,
Then steered the white moth thither in the night?
What but design of darkness to appall?—
If design govern in a thing so small.

Several of Frost's poems have this skeptical type of closure. An argument about some large issue—here the presence or role of a plan or design in the universe—is carefully constructed, made seemingly persuasive, and then cast into doubt by the final lines. The satisfaction expressed by this poem's discovery of the minute scale on which cosmic questions may occur is subtly expressed but prevents the poem from seeming pointlessly ominous, though its view of the creation is undeniably a cruel one. "For Once, Then, Something," "In a Disused Graveyard," "An Old Man's Winter Night," and "After Apple-Picking" are among the other poems that use the freedom and flexibility of Frost's grasp of vernacular sentence-sound to introduce in their closures fresh notes of doubt, unexpected rationality, wit, or even cynicism.

"The Tuft of Flowers," published first in 1906 in the Derry *Enterprise* when Frost began teaching part-time at Pinkerton Academy, offers in graceful couplets an early example of Frost's grasp of the sentence-sound and his insistence that "all poetry is a reproduction of the tones of actual speech":

I went to turn the grass once after one
Who mowed it in the dew before the sun.

The dew was gone that made his blade so keen
Before I came to view the leveled scene.

Not every couplet constitutes a complete sentence, but this opening pair establishes the movement of the poem. The ease of the couplets enables the poem to embrace an internal dialogue, in which the speaker asserts that

I must be, as he had been,—alone,

"As all must be," I said within my heart,
"Whether they work together or apart."

However, the discovery of a tuft of unspecified flowers engenders a reversal by alerting the speaker to the bond of love that at least sometimes exists between humans and nature, and this insight becomes empathy:

And dreaming, as it were, held brotherly speech
With one whose thought I had not hoped to reach.

"Men work together," I told him from the heart,
"Whether they work together or apart."

With three daughters and a son to support—Lesley (born in 1899), Carol (a son, born in 1902), Irma (born in 1903), and Marjorie (born in 1905); a sixth child, Elinor (born in 1907) lived only two days—the Derry years, however productive for Frost's poetry, were trying. Frost's chicken farming came to nothing, and though his position at Pinkerton Academy (part-time for a term, then full-time) was rewarding, it was not the career he envisioned for himself. It did, however, offer the opportunity to refine his pedagogical ideas, which would serve him well later, and the pleasure of directing student productions of plays by Christopher Marlowe, John Milton, Richard Brinsley Sheridan, and William Butler Yeats, which he did with gusto. His revision of the Pinkerton English curriculum and the year he spent teaching at the State Normal School in Plymouth (subsequently renamed Plymouth State College) helped him develop the conversational and informal pedagogy for which later, at Amherst College and the University of Michigan, he became famous. Frost imagined that he could achieve personal success and also support his family as a poet, though he saw that it would require drastic action to make this happen.

ENGLAND: 1912–1915

The dramatic move to England, financed by selling the Derry farm, succeeded partly through luck and partly through Frost's tactful use of new and important acquaintances in the London literary world. Frost was lucky in that the widow of David Nutt decided to publish his first book, *A Boy's Will,* in 1913 and his second, *North of Boston,* in 1914. He was tactful in his dealings with a wide variety of literary people, some of whom he genuinely liked and some of whom he found less congenial. In various ways F. S. Flint, Harold Monro, Ezra Pound, Lascelles Abercrombie, and Edward Thomas stimulated or encouraged Frost. Pound reviewed *A Boy's Will* and introduced Frost to Richard Aldington, Ford Madox Ford (then Hueffer), and William Butler Yeats, who told him that his book was "the best poetry written in America for a long time." Frost formed his closest friendship with Edward Thomas, whom he encouraged to turn from travel writing (at which Thomas excelled) to poetry. Thomas' death in World War I in 1917 grieved Frost perhaps only slightly less than the deaths in his own family.

Frost entered the literary world as a mature artist: *A Boy's Will* is a carefully ordered sequence of lyric poems. Somewhat like James Joyce's *A Portrait of the Artist as a Young Man* (1914–1915) it traces the development of a young man's sensibility from boyhood to early maturity. To help guide the reader along this progression, Frost originally added glosses in the table of contents but later dropped them. The intended development is reasonably clear without the glosses; their primary effect, as Frost may have come to realize, was to add an air of dreaminess at odds with the sharply drawn effects of the strongest poems. Poems such as "Into My Own," "A Late Walk," "Storm Fear," "Rose Pogonias," "The Tuft of Flowers," and "A Line-Storm Song" display a command of the established conventions of lyric poetry and Frost's well-developed ear for sentence-sounds. They justify Yeats's praise. But one of the best and now most famous poems in the volume is "Mowing"; this sonnet, written in hexameters, introduces a plain grace and colloquial movement that carries the reader in a new direction, toward the eclogues and dramatic poems of *North of Boston.* "Mowing" echoes the mower poems of Andrew Marvell; and Mark Scott has claimed in a 1991 essay that Andrew Lang's

"Scythe Song" was Frost's source. But the voice in "Mowing" is distinctly Frost's, illustrating the perfection of his colloquial, sentence-based rhetoric:

> There was never a sound beside the wood but one,
> And that was my long scythe whispering to the
>     ground.
> What was it it whispered? I knew not well myself;
> Perhaps it was something about the heat of the sun,
> Something, perhaps, about the lack of sound—
> And that was why it whispered and did not speak.
> It was no dream of the gift of idle hours,
> Or easy gold at the hand of fay or elf:
> Anything more than the truth would have seemed
>     too weak
> To the earnest love that laid the swale in rows,
> Not without feeble-pointed spikes of flowers
> (Pale orchises), and scared a bright green snake.
> The fact is the sweetest dream that labor knows.
> My long scythe whispered and left the hay to make.

Rejecting the fairies and elves and dreaminess common to much of the poetry written in the years before World War I, Frost demonstrates how graceful the voice of actual experience can be. The world of work, in which so much of his poetry centers, contains in its actuality all the dreams available, desirable, or necessary. Frost insists not only on the material beauty and grace of the world but also on its adequacy for the poet. Although Frost's poems offer some genuinely transcendent moments, they suggest that transcendence typically comes through accepting the material actuality and adequacy of this world.

*North of Boston,* Frost's second book, perhaps the most important of his long career, appeared in May 1914 while he was living near Dymock, Gloucestershire. (He had moved his family there in order to be closer to the poets Wilfrid W. Gibson and Lascelles Abercrombie.) *North of Boston* contains many of Frost's most famous poems, including "Mending Wall," "The Death of the Hired Man," "Home Burial," "After Apple-Picking," and "The Wood-Pile." Unlike the lyrics of *A Boy's Will,* most of these poems are blank verse dramatic poems or monologues (or eclogues or pastorals, as some critics have called them). They most fully demonstrate how Frost's use of sentence-sound, his ear for colloquial syntax, and his powerful sense of irony can empower a poem that lacks or avoids the rhymes and other sonic devices of the lyric.

Thematically the poems in *North of Boston* cover a wide range, including the isolation of the individual and the difficulty of communication ("Home Burial," "The Fear," "A Servant to Servants," "The Code"); the weight and oppression of the past ("Mending Wall"); the relationship between nature and culture ("The Wood-Pile"); the possibilities of human communion ("The Death of the Hired Man," "Blueberries," "A Hundred Collars," "The Generations of Men," "The Black Cottage"); and death and transcendence ("After Apple-Picking"). The subject matter derives mostly from Frost's observations of his fellow farmers in Derry; the poems catch not only the rhythms of the farmers' speech but also a sense of their relationship to the land. Frost is far from being a merely regional poet, but the stony northern New England landscape embodies a physical isolation that corresponds to the mental isolation that plays so large a role in these poems. Frost's vision is not necessarily bleak: some of the poems in *North of Boston* are about successfully overcoming isolation, and others, especially "The Wood-Pile," illustrate the opportunities for self-discovery created by isolation.

"The Wood-Pile" opens with an echo of Dante's picture of the traveler lost in the wilderness of life:

> Out walking in the frozen swamp one gray day,
> I paused and said, "I will turn back from here.
> No, I will go on farther—and we shall see."

The brief indecision, the abrupt resolve, and the Emersonian insistence on *seeing* characterize Frost's poems about entering or envisioning the wilderness, including such famous ones as "Stopping by Woods on a Snowy Evening" and "Desert Places." Here the swamp with its frozen and featureless landscape resists naming or definition and reminds Frost that he is in the world of nature, not of human culture:

> The hard snow held me, save where now and then
> One foot went through. The view was all in lines
> Straight up and down of tall slim trees
> Too much alike to mark or name a place by
> So as to say for certain I was here
> Or somewhere else: I was just far from home.

A small unidentified bird attracts Frost's eye and he imagines it suspects him of trying to steal a feather. But after watching for a few moments Frost discovers a woodpile neatly cut and stacked, and this sign of human life returns him to human concerns. Impressed and comforted by this mark of civilization in the wilderness, he places a positive construction on its being abandoned, assuring himself that the woodcutter, instead of having died, has busied himself with other projects:

> only
> Someone who lived in turning to fresh tasks
> Could so forget his handiwork on which
> He spent himself, the labor of his ax,
> And leave it there far from a useful fireplace
> To warm the frozen swamp as best it could
> With the slow smokeless burning of decay.

Yet the sheer uselessness of the woodpile decaying where it stands provokes an ironic closure that returns the poem to the picture of wild desolation suggested at the beginning by the view of "tall slim trees," an inimical, featureless landscape indifferent to human needs and concerns.

Several of Frost's poems present the natural world as a grim, desolate landscape indifferent or hostile to his presence, but usually, as in "Desert Places," "The Census-Taker," and "The Most of It," the mind of the poet compensates by offering

refuge, an ironic retort, or an assertion of selfhood. In some of the dramatic poems, however, the discovery of comparable indifference, hostility, or sheer otherness in another person generates a terrifying scenario. "Home Burial" dramatizes the cruel disaffection in an uncommunicative marriage. The death of the couple's first child brings about the crisis. The husband sees the wife standing on the stairway looking out through a small window and brusquely questions her:

>                "What is it you see
> From up there always—for I want to know."
> She turned and sank upon her skirts at that,
> And her face changed from terrified to dull.
> He said to gain time: "What is it you see,"
> Mounting until she cowered under him.
> "I will find out now—you must tell me, dear."

Finally he realizes that she is looking out upon the tiny family plot in which he recently buried their child. As the poem develops, it becomes increasingly clear that the sexual hierarchy suggested by the phrase "Mounting until she cowered under him" defines a key aspect of the agonizing relationship in which husband and wife are unable to apprehend each other's emotional needs. The husband, habitually silent about his emotions, expresses himself so indirectly the wife believes him to be without feeling, while she expresses herself as vehemently as a Shakespearean heroine, befuddling her husband with rhetorical absolutes. They cannot agree upon the mutuality of their grief because they differ too much in how they express it. The wife reproaches the man for having dug the child's grave and, moments later, spoken with seeming indifference about farm matters, she quotes him: "Three foggy mornings and one rainy day / Will rot the best birch fence a man can build." She is unable to read her husband's indirection; if she had actually understood the birch fence metaphor, she would have found it cruel. Her husband, on the other hand, finds her grief excessive, self-defeating, and inimical to their relationship:

> "What was it brought you up to think it the thing
> To take your mother-loss of a first child
> So inconsolably—in the face of love.
> You'd think his memory might be satisfied—"

There can be no reconciliation. The wife, after expanding her grief to indict the world, threatens to take her emotional needs elsewhere, and the husband responds by threatening force. The death of the child has brought out the worst or the weakest in each of them, and the poem closes without hope.

Though "Home Burial" surely draws upon the emotional circumstances of the death of Elliott, which deeply grieved both Frost and his wife, it is not an autobiographical poem. Frost did not suffer from emotional inarticulateness; if anything, he may have sometimes expressed himself all too volubly. Nonetheless, great suffering is as likely to drive people apart as to bring them together. The death of Elliott and later of Marjorie surely generated enormous pain for both Frosts. By 1938 when Elinor died, inflicting the worst of all losses on her husband, the couple had suffered enough for several lifetimes, though Frost would have to suffer more, alone, with the insanity of Irma and the suicide of his only son, Carol.

Most of *North of Boston* is concerned with less dramatic aspects of human interaction than those represented in "Home Burial." Perhaps the most frequently quoted and misquoted poem in the volume is "Mending Wall." The opening poem, "Mending Wall" in perfectly colloquial blank verse delineates the important theme of drawing and understanding the boundaries between people. The poem mixes foreboding and tolerance and depicts the mystery of otherness by blurring the distinctions between the natural and the human world. What is the "something . . . that doesn't love a wall"? Is it a human or a natural force, or a combination of both?

> Something there is that doesn't love a wall,
> That sends the frozen-ground-swell under it,
> And spills the upper boulders in the sun;
> And makes gaps even two can pass abreast;

Frost heaves and hunters, nature and culture, and something left unnamed combine to topple parts of the wall that the first-person narrator, whom we might take to be Frost, and his neighbor agree on a certain day to repair. But why do they need a wall between them, asks Frost. The neighbor responds, "Good fences make good neighbors," but with the "mischief of spring" in him, Frost refuses to accept this answer and probes for more:

> "*Why* do they make good neighbors? Is it
> Where there are cows? But here there are no cows.
> Before I built a wall I'd ask to know
> What I was walling in or walling out,
> And to whom I was like to give offense.
> Something there is that doesn't love a wall,
> That wants it down."

That something, perhaps, is the need for human companionship and communication, the something that should have breached the barrier between the protagonists of "Home Burial," for instance. The neighbor, however, cannot share Frost's interrogative mood. "Like an old-stone savage armed," the neighbor moves in the "darkness" of his refusal to question received values. Rather than enter into a discussion, he adheres to what Frost realizes is "his father's saying"; he "likes having thought of it so well / He says again, 'Good fences make good neighbors.' " Frost does not endorse this saying but questions it. The poem advocates knowledge against the blind ignorance of tradition ("I'd ask to know / What I was walling in or walling out"), and it does so for the sake of human communication. Like most of the other dramatic poems in *North of Boston*, "Mending Wall" stands for dialogue against silence, for breaching (if not wholly breaking down) the barriers of history, ego, and tradition.

RETURN TO AMERICA: THE ESTABLISHED POET

At the close of 1914 Henry Holt and Company had agreed to publish Frost's books in the United States, and he was on the verge of the greatest success any twentieth-century American poet would enjoy. When World War I broke out, Frost borrowed money to return to America with his family, taking along Edward Thomas' fifteen-year-old son Merfyn, who was to visit friends in New Hampshire. In February 1915 the Frosts and Merfyn arrived in New York where Frost met with his editor at Holt, Alfred Harcourt, who would become a close friend. American journals were now enthusiastically publishing Frost's work; *North of Boston,* just published, garnered excellent reviews including an especially enthusiastic one by Amy Lowell; and *A Boy's Will* would appear in April and also receive favorable notices.

In June, Frost moved to Franconia, New Hampshire, and began to become accustomed to giving the readings and lectures that would occupy much of his time and energy for the rest of his life. In 1916 he accepted a teaching position at Amherst College, to begin in the winter of 1917; after a three-year hiatus (1920–1923) caused by disagreements between him and President Alexander Meiklejohn about the curriculum, Frost taught at least occasionally at Amherst for much of the rest of his life (sometimes spending part of the school year also teaching at the University of Michigan). Frost enjoyed literary celebrity, and as his shyness dissipated he became popular on the lecture circuit. Lecture and reading fees would soon become his largest source of income, though the royalties from his books, especially from collected editions, were substantial.

*Mountain Interval,* which appeared in November 1916, was not as enthusiastically received as his two earlier books. The reviews were favorable, but critics seemed to have nothing new to say about Frost, and the comments have a perfunctory quality, which might indicate that Frost's achievement was already being taken for granted. W. S. Braithewaite, for example, refers to "that indescribable magic which Mr. Frost evokes from the plain and severe quality of New England life and character"; Harriet Monroe in *Poetry* links him to Edgar Lee Masters; and Sidney Cox in the *New Republic* finds "sincerity" the "fundamental and embracing quality" of Frost's new book. Braithewaite and Monroe see Frost as a regional poet, Cox finds him a moralist, and no one has anything substantive to say about the aesthetic qualities of the poems.

*Mountain Interval,* unlike *A Boy's Will,* a collection of lyrics, and *North of Boston,* a group of narrative poems, mixes Frost's two predominant genres. Perhaps, as William H. Pritchard has suggested, Frost no longer wished to be read as a "merely lyric or merely narrative writer." In any case all Frost's future books, except for the verse dramas *A Masque of Reason* (1945) and *A Masque of Mercy* (1947) would mix various kinds of poems. *Mountain Interval* contains some of Frost's best poems, including "An Old Man's Winter Night," "The Oven Bird," "The Cow in Apple Time," "Range-Finding," and "The Hill Wife." Two of his most anthologized poems embody the bemused lyric meditation and stark, tragic vision central to Frost's poetics. "The Road Not Taken," written with Edward Thomas in mind, is often misread as a poem advocating nonconformity, but it is really a meditation on the difficulty—perhaps the impossibility—of making an intelligent choice when faced with the unknown. " 'Out, Out—' " takes its title from Lady Macbeth's harsh self-reproach, and in a way it too is "a tale / Told by an idiot, full of sound and fury, / Signifying nothing": Frost's poem—about the death of a boy injured by a saw—seems to be spoken by a moral idiot who draws no conclusions but merely notes that the spectators of the incident, "since they / Were not the one dead, turned to their affairs." The indifference of the speaker and the other witnesses seems unspeakably cruel, but it simply reiterates what the wife in "Home Burial" means when she notes that "The nearest friends can go / With anyone to death, comes so far short / They might as well not try to go at all."

The best-known poem in *Mountain Interval* is "Birches," the last line of which—"One could do worse than be a swinger of birches"—has come to define Frost. (One biography of Frost is even entitled *Robert Frost: A Swinger of Birches.*) If we read "Birches" as an allegory of the playful and heaven-aspiring activity of poetry writing it does indeed define Frost very well. The swinger of birches is a farm boy, far from town, with no other boys to play baseball with. His swinging from the tops of the trees bends them but doesn't bow them the way ice storms do:

> Often you must have seen them
> Loaded with ice a sunny winter morning
> After a rain. They click upon themselves
> As the breeze rises, and turn many-colored
> As the stir cracks and crazes their enamel.
> Soon the sun's warmth makes them shed crystal
>   shells
> Shattering and avalanching on the snow-crust—
> Such heaps of broken glass to sweep away
> You'd think the inner dome of heaven had fallen.
> They are dragged to the withered bracken by the
>   load,
> And they seem not to break; though once they are
>   bowed
> So low for long, they never right themselves:
> You may see their trunks arching in the woods
> Years afterwards, trailing their leaves on the
>   ground
> Like girls on hands and knees that throw their hair
> Before them over their heads to dry in the sun.

Rather than having the ice storm (which Frost identifies with "Truth," a kind of literary naturalism) bend them, however, he prefers to envision the farm boy doing it, so that the adult Frost can imagine adopting the role himself when responsibilities and sorrows press too heavily upon him:

> So was I once myself a swinger of birches,
> And so I dream of going back to be.
> It's when I'm weary of considerations,
> And life is too much like a pathless wood
> Where your face burns and tickles with the
>   cobwebs
> Broken across it, and one eye is weeping
> From a twig's having lashed across it open.
> I'd like to get away from earth awhile
> And then come back to it and begin over.

He must return to earth because "Earth's the right place for love," but the climb "*Toward heaven*" (Frost's emphasis) refreshes, enlightens, and cheers.

In 1917 Edward Thomas was killed by shell fire at the battle of Arras, adding to Frost's sorrows. Frost had been successful in getting Thomas' poetry published in America, which was some consolation, but Thomas was a close friend and Frost never forgot him. In *New Hampshire: A Poem with Notes and Grace Notes* (1923) he would eulogize Thomas in a poem plainly entitled "To E. T.," addressed to its subject and sounding as much like one of Thomas' own poems as Frost's. But the most memorable poem Frost would write of his friend is "Iris by Night" (in *A Further Range,* 1936), which describes an evening walk when "came a moment of confusing lights" as a dazzling spectrum embraced Frost and Thomas. A moonbow, a rare meteorological phenomenon, seemed to consecrate their friendship:

> Then a small rainbow like a trellis gate,
> A very small moon-made prismatic bow,
> Stood closely over us through which to go.
> And then we were vouchsafed the miracle
> That never yet to other two befell
> And I alone of us have lived to tell.
> A wonder! Bow and rainbow as it bent,
> Instead of moving with us as we went,
> (To keep the pots of gold from being found)
> It lifted from its dewy pediment
> Its two mote-swimming many-colored ends,
> And gathered them together in a ring.

And we stood in it softly circled round
From all division time or foe can bring
In a relation of elected friends.

The union depicted here is as permanent as memory itself and yet as fragile as the atmospheric event. Though Frost survives his friend, the ring, like a wedding ring, attests to the mystical solemnity, emotional depth, and duration of the epiphanic moment. As Brad Leithauser remarks in reviewing the Library of America edition of Frost's work in the *New York Review of Books* "Iris by Night" "must be one of the most moving poems ever dedicated to friendship . . . the work of . . . a true friend and a great heart."

Despite the relatively modest success of *Mountain Interval,* Frost's reputation continued to grow during and after the war years. The National Institute of Arts and Letters elected him a member. His play *A Way Out* was published in *The Seven Arts* in 1917 and performed two years later by Amherst students. *Poetry* magazine awarded him a one-hundred-dollar prize for "Snow." He met the other well-known American poets—Sara Teasdale, Vachel Lindsay, Carl Sandburg, Louis Untermeyer, and Amy Lowell—as an equal. Of these, Untermeyer would become an essential friend, correspondent, and promoter of Frost's work, while the others, especially Lowell and Sandburg, would come to seem rivals, though in Sandburg's case a friendly one. But with the publication of only three small collections of poems, some of them written many years before, Frost had already assumed a preeminent role among contemporary American writers, a position he would never lose.

### THE 1920S: *NEW HAMPSHIRE*

In 1920 a dispute that began with Frost's distaste for Stark Young, a popular teacher at Amherst College who was homosexual and particularly opinionated about aesthetics, led to an open dispute with President Meiklejohn. Frost resigned his post at Amherst, sold his farm in Franconia, and bought property in South Shaftsbury, Vermont. Meanwhile his sister Jeanie, who had grown paranoid over the years, was arrested in Portland, Maine, for disturbing the peace. Frost went to Portland and had Jeanie committed to the state mental hospital in Augusta. More encouragingly, to provide him with the financial security to write poetry, Henry Holt began paying Frost one hundred dollars a month as a consulting editor. Meanwhile his fame as a speaker and reader grew, and he made visits to various colleges, including, in 1921, the University of Michigan, where he was offered a one-year fellowship. In October he moved his family to Ann Arbor, where he would live and work for part of the year for some time to come. Ann Arbor would prove to be an especially congenial setting. Frost arranged a lecture series there featuring his favorite colleagues, or rivals, including Amy Lowell, Louis Untermeyer, Carl Sandburg, Vachel Lindsay, and prose writers such as Hamlin Garland and Dorothy Canfield Fisher. The university awarded Frost an honorary M.A. in 1922.

Frost published two books in 1923. *Selected Poems* appeared in March, and *New Hampshire* in November. *New Hampshire,* which brought Frost his first of four Pulitzer Prizes, contains many of his most frequently anthologized poems, including "The Star-Splitter," "The Ax-Helve," "Fire and Ice," "In a Disused Graveyard," "Nothing Gold Can Stay," "The Aim Was Song," "Stopping by Woods on a Snowy Evening," "For Once, Then, Something," "Evening in a Sugar Orchard," "A Hillside Thaw," and "The Need of Being Versed in Country Things." In fact, almost every poem is memorable except the title poem, a long, rambling, self-conscious mock-Horatian eclogue about the state in which Frost had until recently resided and the state of American material well-being.

"For Once, Then, Something" offers a teasing glimpse of the possibilities of transcendence and the likelihood of being self-deluded in searching for the ineffable. Frost at first asserts his right to kneel at well-curbs (the stone rims around the mouths of wells) in such a way as to see himself "in the summer heaven godlike / Looking out of a wreath of fern and cloud puffs." He admits, however, that *"Once"* he saw something "beyond the picture, / Through the picture, a something white, uncertain." He cannot identify this something, only attest to its momentary presence. A drip from a fern, a touch of naturalism, obliterates the vision. He toys with the possibilities (and the reader) by asking "What was that whiteness? / Truth? A pebble of quartz?" but can assert, at last, only that "For once" he saw "something" other than himself. Whether this poem indicts or endorses the Romantic notion that empathic observation of nature can lead to a glimpse of the spiritual ineffable is hard to say.

The playful humor of "For Once, Then, Something" does not negate the serious issue of transcendence. Nor does the more serious tone of "Stopping by Woods on a Snowy Evening" conceal Frost's wit in playing off a jaunty meter and rhyme scheme against a situation of dark intent, one that seems to bring him face to face with oblivion. The emphatic rhyme scheme—*aaba bbcb ccdc dddd*—imposes a stuttering hesitancy on the opening of the poem, a mood of doubt and irresolution in keeping with the situation.

> Whose woods these are I think I know.
> His house is in the village though;
> He will not see me stopping here
> To watch his woods fill up with snow.
>
> My little horse must think it queer
> To stop without a farmhouse near
> Between the woods and frozen lake
> The darkest evening of the year.

Yet with the personification of the horse a self-awareness enters the poem, and the mood shifts as the narrator recognizes the loneliness, loveliness, and dark depth before him:

> He gives his harness bells a shake
> To ask if there is some mistake.
> The only other sound's the sweep
> Of easy wind and downy flake.

The domestic woodlot, the possession of a neighbor, gives way to a beautiful otherness inimical to the human. To enter the woods, or even to stay very long looking into them, would undo the life the narrator still has before him, and he isn't ready for that:

> The woods are lovely, dark and deep,
> But I have promises to keep,
> And miles to go before I sleep,
> And miles to go before I sleep.

The critic Richard Poirier has pointed out that this poem is about ownership—the first line alerts us to this—and the difficulties of self-possession. The ownership of land is a business matter, and the narrator of this poem has business to carry on. But he also needs to be reminded, or to remind himself, that if he does not claim himself fully through consciousness, if he drifts off to sleep in the snowfall, he will lose himself forever to a hypnotic beauty he can never possess.

Another poem that depicts the need to assert our humanity against nature, "On a Tree Fallen across the Road," a Shakespearean sonnet in the first person plural, avoids the seriousness of "Stopping by Woods" by personifying a storm in playful tones and arguing for the inconsequence of natural violence:

> The tree the tempest with a crash of wood
> Throws down in front of us is not to bar
> Our passage to our journey's end for good,
> But just to ask us who we think we are.

A fallen tree does not represent a serious challenge to human progress, but in "The Need of Being Versed in Country Things" the burning of a house means an absolute end to human presence in the location. Even so, the natural presence that is there echoes the lost humanity, the "murmur" of birds—phoebes—"more like the sigh we sigh / From too much dwelling on what has been." In the context of the muted apocalyptic vision of the poem, to be "versed in country things" means to avoid imposing human emotions on the natural world. Speaking of the birds, Frost observes:

> For them there was really nothing sad.
> But though they rejoiced in the nest they kept,
> One had to be versed in country things
> Not to believe the phoebes wept.

And yet, to retain their human sympathies, the poet and the reader with him have to believe the phoebes wept. The sheer impossibility of avoiding anthropomorphism defines us in the face of an intractable otherness.

"Good-by and Keep Cold" deals with the problem of defining an apt relationship between human beings and nature: specifically, between the poet and his recently planted orchard. Written in anapestic tetrameter (the first foot of each line being a trochee), a difficult and showy meter, "Good-by and Keep Cold" seems at first to be a practical exposition, like one of Virgil's *Georgics,* on the difficulties faced by orchards in winter, when deep steady cold is better than alternating cold and thaw. But it is really about the narrator's need to go about his business, as in "Stopping by Woods," and the need to detach himself from what he can never be part of: "My business awhile is with different trees, / Less carefully nurtured, less fruitful than these. . . ."

Not every poem in *New Hampshire* deals with the difficulty of understanding the relationship between the human and the natural worlds, however. One of the finest poems Frost ever wrote, "The Witch of Coös," the first part of "Two Witches," is a dramatic dialogue in which a narrator visiting a backwoods farm listens to a woman and her son discuss her supernatural abilities and visions. The story the woman tells is of a deep winter night when she heard a skeleton rise from its grave in the cellar, creep up the stairs and confront her, then continue up to the attic, where presumably it still resides. The narrator of the poem reveals that the woman's lover had been murdered by her now deceased husband, and he refuses to either treat the ambulatory skeleton as a fact or to entirely reject the woman's story. Though the story seems impossible, the woman's manner of telling it is too coherent and playful to suggest insanity. When she admits, over her son's interjected obfuscations, that the skeleton was her lover, killed by her husband, the stark truth seems to complete rather than to contrast with her otherwise improbable story. Though some critics, refusing to take the ghostly narrative seriously, have read this poem as a tale of psychological evasion, it is possible to read it quite the other way around, as a tale honed through many retellings to eventually help the woman face the ugly truth she now confesses. The only fact the narrator, in the concluding lines, can confirm is the name of the dead husband. The stark naming—"Toffile Lajway"—represents everything left unknown. Randall Jarrell in "The Other Robert Frost" claims that " 'The Witch of Coös' is the best thing of its kind since Chaucer," and most readers of Frost would probably agree.

## FAMILIAL TRAGEDIES

The title poem of *New Hampshire* meanders. Nevertheless the book as a whole solidified Frost's reputation. Much of the story of the remainder of his life is of countless honors received, dinners attended, readings and lectures given. Still, his domestic life and the need to make money shaped his routine. When Frost began teaching at Ann Arbor, Elinor worried about their being distant from their children, who were now on their own. When Marjorie became seriously ill both Frost and Elinor returned to Pittsfield, where Marjorie and Lesley had started a bookshop, to look after her. Frost successfully concluded his year at Michigan (the first of several), found time to return to Amherst for a lecture, gave talks at Bryn Mawr and Union College, and accepted a new arrangement with Amherst in which he assumed no formal teaching responsibilities. In January 1927 he moved back to Amherst, where five years later he bought a fine house and seemed to settle permanently. He continued to divide his teaching efforts between Amherst and Michigan, traveled and lectured widely, and signed a new contract with Holt that included a royalty increase and monthly payments of two hundred and fifty dollars for a five-year period.

In the late 1920s Frost's children grew up and married, but they did not achieve the stability their parents had. Frost's daughter Irma married John Cone and produced a grandson, Jack, in 1927, but her mental state gradually became unbalanced. Marjorie developed tuberculosis and a heart condition. In 1929 Lesley, married to Dwight Francis, gave birth to her first child, but she divorced her husband in 1931, soon after their daughter Lesley Lee Francis was born. Carol's future wife Lillian, a close friend of Marjorie, also developed tuberculosis and moved to Monrovia, California, for her health. Marjorie, attempting to make a normal life for herself, despite her poor health, met Willard Fraser, an archaeologist, and became engaged to him. The personal and financial difficulties of Frost's children meant he had considerable expenses for travel and for their medical treatment, and he intensified his lecture schedule to raise the needed funds.

The ominous series of difficulties that began in the late 1920s culminated in one of the major tragedies of Frost's life. In 1934 Marjorie, married the year before, gave birth to a daughter and contracted puerperal fever. Frost had her flown to the Mayo Clinic, where despite intensive treatment she died on May 2. After Marjorie's burial in Billings, Montana, Frost brought her husband and baby back to Amherst with him and Elinor. He wrote to Louis Untermeyer, "The noblest of us all is dead and has taken our hearts out of the world with her" (*Selected Letters*). In 1936 Frost privately published *Franconia,* a small volume of Marjorie's poems.

Through these difficult years Frost remained productive as a poet and published three important volumes. In November 1928 *West-Running Brook* appeared, along with a revised *Selected Poems;* in 1930 *Collected Poems* earned him his second Pulitzer Prize; and in 1936 *A Further Range,* his most controversial book, won him his third. Reviews of *West-Running Brook* were favorable, even flattering, but some such as Frederick Pierce's piece in the *Yale Review* (December 1928) struck a note of concern expressing disappointment with "the smallness, limitation, almost barrenness of the theme itself." The "theme," which disturbed some other reviewers too, and would bother more when *A Further Range* appeared, involved Frost's insistent (and to some, socially irresponsible) individualism. Individualism was embodied in the metaphor of the brook too stubborn to flow east as all the nearby brooks did or, even worse, in the figure of "A Lone Striker," who appears in the first poem in *A Further Range:* his idiosyncratic disregard for the necessities of work seemed to mock the labor movement that had become so central to the struggle against the Great Depression.

Certainly Frost is not a poet with a social program; in fact he went out of his way to mock social reformers, claiming to prefer the world exactly as it was, warts and all. In a letter to Kimball Flaccus he wrote, "I wouldnt give a cent to see the world, the United States or even New York made better. I want them just as they are for me to make poetical on paper. I dont ask anything done to them that I dont do to them myself. I'm a mere selfish artist most of the time." But Frost denied himself the role of the reformer because he had a proper sense of his role as an artist. He inadvertently proved the wisdom of this choice when in his later work, after 1940 or so, he assumed the voice of the sage and of the cracker-barrel philosopher, substituting a kind of political folk wisdom for imagery and metaphor and abandoning much of his previous artistry.

In *West-Running Brook, A Further Range,* and most of *A Witness Tree* Frost's artistry generally remains at its mature peak. *West-Running Brook,* besides its satirical title poem, a dialogue in which a husband and wife discuss with some acrimony the nature of contraries and beginnings, contains some memorable lyrics, including "Acquainted with the Night," "Once by the Pacific," "Spring Pools," "A Winter Eden," "Sand Dunes," and "Canis Major." The tone of much of the collection, particularly the section originally entitled "Fiat Nox," is grimmer than most of Frost's previous work. "Acquainted with the Night," an unusual sonnet in terza rima except for a final couplet, illustrates the lonely necessity of individualism by dramatizing the singularity of existence:

I have been one acquainted with the night.
I have walked out in rain—and back in rain.
I have outwalked the furthest city light.

I have looked down the saddest city lane.
I have passed by the watchman on his beat
And dropped my eyes, unwilling to explain.

I have stood still and stopped the sound of feet
When far away an interrupted cry
Came over houses from another street,

But not to call me back or say good-by;
And further still at an unearthly height,
One luminary clock against the sky

Proclaimed the time was neither wrong nor right.
I have been one acquainted with the night.

In this dark little drama only the clock that with grim humor proclaims "the time . . . neither wrong nor right" even faintly speaks for Frost's sense of play. As Frank Lentricchia has pointed out: "The terror of loneliness experienced by the self [in this poem]. . . . flows from a fully aware and mature consciousness," and is all the more terrible for it. "Acquainted with the Night" is not merely about the philosophical awareness of individuality but is a genuinely existential confrontation with nothingness.

Yet the social, not the philosophical, stance of Frost's poetry disturbed some critics in the 1930s. When eight years after *West-Running Brook, A Further Range* appeared, reviewers still treated Frost's work with respect, even adulation; but some of the most prominent critics dissented on the important issue of the book's political, economic, and social content. Rolfe Humphries, for example, writing in the *New Masses* deplored Frost's "excursion into the field of the political didactic." *News-Week* entitled a review "Frost: He Is Sometimes a Poet and Sometimes a Stump-Speaker" and found the book "disappointing." Newton Arvin, writing in *Partisan Review,* declared Frost a minor poet "on the sandy and melancholy fringes of our actual life."

Politically self-conscious reviewers were disturbed not only by "A Lone Striker" but also by the now famous poem "Two Tramps in Mud Time," which distinguishes between working for necessity and working for pleasure and concludes by arguing that Frost the individualist would not recognize such a distinction. Thus, in the reading of some, the poem declares Frost to be indifferent to social necessities. Referring to the two ways of working the poem concludes:

But yield who will to their separation,
My object in living is to unite
My avocation and my vocation
As my two eyes make one in sight.
Only where love and need are one,
And the work is play for mortal stakes,

Is the deed ever really done
For Heaven and the future's sakes.

Critics might reasonably have objected to so didactic an ending to a poem that contains such images as

A bluebird comes tenderly up to alight
And turns to the wind to unruffle a plume
His song so pitched as not to excite
A single flower as yet to bloom.

The didactic note troubles other poems, too, like "The White-Tailed Hornet," "A Blue Ribbon at Amesbury," "Build Soil," and "A Drumlin Woodchuck." Deeper into the volume, however, appear strong poems like "The Old Barn at the Bottom of the Fogs," "Desert Places," "Design," "Neither Out Far nor In Deep," and "The Figure in the Doorway," all of which further develop the themes of confronting nothingness, the isolation of the individual, and the uncertainty of the relationship between the human and the natural worlds. *A Further Range* is Frost's darkest and most demanding collection, and though some of its grimmer notes may derive from the poet's personal tragedies the book does seem, despite its critics' complaints, a serious—though oblique—response to the economic and social difficulties of the Great Depression, rather than a reflection on merely personal difficulties.

*A Further Range* won Frost his third Pulitzer Prize in 1937, but his personal troubles continued. That year Elinor underwent surgery for breast cancer; the Frosts traveled to Gainesville, Florida, to spend the winter with Lesley and her children and allow Elinor to recover her strength. However, after a devastating series of heart attacks in March 1938, Elinor died. Frost, stricken with guilt, collapsed and was unable to attend Elinor's cremation. Lesley blamed her father for hastening Elinor's death by forcing her to climb stairs (though living on the second floor was Elinor's idea) and told him he should never have had chil-

dren. Elinor had been diagnosed many years before with a heart condition that perhaps should have precluded childbirth, so to that extent Lesley was right. The deaths of Elliott and Marjorie, the marital difficulties of Lesley and Irma, and finally the death of Elinor seemed more than either Lesley or her father could bear. Lesley's accusations, whether justified or not, greatly added to his private sufferings.

## "THE FIGURE A POEM MAKES"

That June a disheartened and lonely Frost resigned from Amherst College once again, sold his house, and moved back to South Shaftsbury. Kathleen Morrison, known as Kay, whom Frost had known for several years, invited him to visit friends in West Dover, Vermont, with her. Frost became infatuated and asked Morrison to leave her husband, Theodore Morrison, a lecturer at Harvard, and marry him. Though she refused, she agreed to become his secretary and arrange his lectures and readings. She performed this service for the rest of his life. With the publication of Jeffrey Meyers' biography *Robert Frost* (1996), this relationship, which had been described by most of Frost's previous biographers as platonic, came under fuller scrutiny. Meyers graphically explored the sexual relationship between Frost and Morrison, which had remained entirely secret until partly exposed by the publication of Robert Spangler Newdick's biography *Newdick's Season of Frost* (1976). The secrecy, maintained through Morrison's lifetime, came about largely because Lawrance Roger Thompson, Frost's major biographer, also had an affair with Morrison, and the ensuing complications seemed to him best concealed, though he detailed the evidence in his unpublished notes.

Yet the nature of the relationship between Frost and Morrison seems, in retrospect, plainly delineated in Frost's poetry. "The Silken Tent," a love poem Frost wrote for Morrison, is vividly sensual and suggests how she balanced her love obligations. A seamless one-sentence sonnet, the poem embodies Morrison "as in a field a silken tent," which is stirred by a summer breeze and sways, bound not by a "single cord" but "loosely bound / By countless silken ties of love and thought / To everything on earth the compass round." Only when one tie goes "slightly taut" does she feel at all confined. Though the poem may simply signify Morrison's generally rich engagement with the world, it may also represent her embroilment in numerous love affairs; the "capriciousness of summer air," her cheerful promiscuity; the "slightest bondage," her apparently unconfining marriage.

Despite the stress of their relationship, Morrison's presence made the rest of Frost's life less lonely and depressing than it might have been. Carol Frost committed suicide in the house in South Shaftsbury in 1940, shooting himself with a hunting rifle while his son Prescott slept upstairs. Irma by 1947 had deteriorated so badly that Frost had her committed to the New Hampshire State mental hospital. Writing and teaching and lecturing through these difficult years of declining health, Frost required both practical assistance and emotional support, and Morrison offered both.

"The Silken Tent" was the first poem, after two epigraphs, in *A Witness Tree,* which appeared in 1942 and won Frost his fourth Pulitzer Prize. The first fourteen poems form a sequence working backward in time and level of experience from the ecstasy of "The Silken Tent" through the dark natural sublimities of "Come In" and "The Most of It" to the willful sexual cruelty of "The Subverted Flower" and the allegorical narrative (about a "stolen lady") of "The Discovery of the Madeiras." Some of these poems are among Frost's very best lyrics, but despite the celebratory "Silken Tent" the vision of the universe they project, like that of "Design," is a difficult and challenging one.

In 1939 Frost published "The Figure a Poem Makes," his most famous prose statement, as a preface to a new edition of his collected poems. In the essay he argues that a poem begins in delight and ends in wisdom. But "delight" and "wisdom" seem inadequate terms to frame poems like "Come In" and "The Most of It." These poems find the natural world inimical to human needs and desires, but they offer in their graceful unfolding a compensatory beauty. For example, a stanza from "Come In" reads:

> Far in the pillared dark
> Thrush music went—
> Almost like a call to come in
> To the dark and lament.

Like "Stopping by Woods," "Come In" tempts the speaker with a beguiling darkness that he refuses on the grounds that he has not been asked and would not "come in . . . even if asked." In "The Most of It" someone finding himself alone in the universe calls across the landscape—across a lake—hears only the echo of his voice, and receives no "original response," except once, when an "embodiment" crashes through a rockfall, splashes through the lake, and in swimming toward him reveals itself "as a great buck . . . / Pushing the crumpled water up ahead." This indifferent though beautiful creature, the poem concludes, "was all"—meaning it was either utterly inadequate or wonderfully, totally adequate but unacceptable to the lone person who wants "counter-love," which the natural world will never give him.

None of the poems in *A Witness Tree* are as garrulous and clumsy as "Build Soil," the "Political Pastoral" in *A Further Range* that justifiably irritated some reviewers. But except for "Trespass" the poems following "The Quest of the Purple-Fringed" display a serious diminution of Frost's powers. A lack of subtlety, a reduced technique—heavy-handed rhymes and clumsy rhythms—and a didactic certainty, already present in the weaker poems of *A Further Range,* spoil much of Frost's late work. Though he would publish two more collections, as well as his two "masques," only one major poem remained to be written. This was the masterpiece "Directive," which appeared in *Steeple Bush* (1947) and redeemed an otherwise unprepossessing book. Jarrell, in reviewing it in the *New York Times* remarked that "most of the poems in [*Steeple Bush*] merely remind you, by their persistence in the mannerisms of what was genius, that they are productions of somebody who once, and somewhere else, was a great poet." Nonetheless he remarks of "Directive" that "there are weak places in the poem, but they are nothing beside so much longing, tenderness, and passive sadness." Later in his revised version of the review, the essay "To the Laodiceans," Jarrell quotes "Directive" in its entirety and comments that "it shows the coalescence of three of Frost's obsessive themes, those of isolation, of extinction, and of the final limitations of man."

"Directive" invites the reader to withdraw from "all this now too much for us" and follow a "guide . . . / Who only has at heart your getting lost" into a region of abandoned villages and rutted stony roads to find a site (perhaps where Frost and his family once lived) where lie the shattered dishes of a children's playhouse and a cellar hole "Now slowly closing like a dent in dough." Here the guide offers a drink from "A broken drinking goblet like the Grail," and a toast, "Drink and be whole again beyond confusion." This poem of redemption in memory both mocks and honors the rituals through which salvation traditionally comes. Robert Lowell calls "Directive" a journey "to the destroyed homestead of [Frost's] early marriage." It is a sad and beautiful poem and the truest ending to Frost's poetic life.

## LAST WRITINGS

*A Masque of Reason* (1945) and *A Masque of Mercy* (1947) are not Jonsonian masques but resemble the radio plays popular at the time that they were written. Both masques received some very severe reviews (and some favorable ones); both are talky, marred by unsuccessful humor and unconvincing profundities. In *Reason* a couple who turn out to be Job and his wife carry on a rather arch discussion with God in which the role of the wife seems to be to represent the underlying mystery of the universe, while in *Mercy* Jonah appears as a refugee (a "poor, poor swallowable little man," one character calls him) whose fear of God, reflected in the other characters, reveals the paradoxical nature of our conceptions of divinity. The first masque enlarges upon the Old Testament story; the second pits the Old Testament notion of harsh divinity against the New Testament's emphasis on mercy (a key character in *Mercy* is named Paul). Both masques suffer from self-consciously metaphysical dialogue and lack of drama, but in dealing with issues of religious concern (Frost was skeptical about faith) they serve as somewhat interesting afterwords to the long career in poetry that precedes them.

The last decades of Frost's life were eventful. Continuing to teach at Dartmouth, Harvard, and Amherst again (this time with a lifetime appointment), Frost traveled extensively, even on a U.S. State Department visit to Brazil, where Elizabeth Bishop was impressed by his lecture. In 1957 he made his third trip to England and received honorary degrees from both Oxford and Cambridge universities. On his return, although he had objected to the award of the 1948 Bollingen Prize to Ezra Pound for *The Pisan Cantos,* Frost materially participated in freeing Pound from his confinement at St. Elizabeths Hospital where Pound had been sent when found unfit to stand trial for treason. Frost's involvement in Pound's situation led to his playing a larger public role. In 1961 he read a poem at the presidential inauguration of John F. Kennedy. In 1962 Frost traveled to Russia at the invitation of the State Department and met with Premier Nikita Khrushchev, with whom he talked for an hour and a half. Unfortunately he spoke unguardedly (and not entirely honestly) to the press on his return, and this strained his friendship with Kennedy.

*In the Clearing* (1962), Frost's last book, contains a few sharp epigrams and the long autobiographical poem "Kitty Hawk," which is written in a clumsy meter varying from dimeter to trimeter. "The Draft Horse" is a terse and frightening mystery, "Pod of the Milkweed" a witty meditation, and "Questioning Faces" a single startling and dramatic image:

> The winter owl banked just in time to pass
> And save herself from breaking window glass.
> And her wings straining suddenly aspread
> Caught color from the last of evening red
> In a display of underdown and quill
> To glassed-in children at the window sill.

The "evening red," suggesting the crimson of disaster that would have occurred if the owl had not "banked in time," enriches this picture with Frost's characteristic sense of the doubleness of metaphor. Beyond a few strong poems, however, *In the Clearing* only faintly echoes the poet's former voice. The reviews were generally respectful, but the most honest one may have been in the *Wisconsin Library Bulletin,* which noted that Frost's new poems were "closer to jingles than to the memorable poetry we associate with his name." In December Frost learned he had prostate and bladder cancer. After a series of pulmonary embolisms he died in his eighty-ninth year on January 29, 1963. Following a private memorial service in Appleton Chapel at Harvard and a public one at Johnson Chapel, Amherst College, Frost's ashes were buried beside Elinor's in the Frost family plot in Old Bennington, Vermont.

Since Frost's death, dozens of books and hundreds of articles on his work and life have appeared, most notably Lawrance Roger Thompson's three-volume biography, which almost ruined Frost's reputation by portraying him as a petty, malevolent man obsessed with personal ambitions. Since then, other biographical and critical studies, especially William H. Pritchard's 1984 biography, have greatly modified that picture, and Frost's reputation as a poet has grown large enough to outweigh concern with his personal shortcomings. Frost the man was surely imperfect, but along with William Butler Yeats and Thomas Hardy he is one of the greatest twentieth-century poets to write in traditional prosodic forms. His best poems are as well-known and widely admired as any in the English language. Critical interest in Frost's work continues to grow.

## Selected Bibliography

### WORKS OF ROBERT FROST

POETRY

*A Boy's Will.* London: David Nutt, 1913; New York: Henry Holt, 1915.

*North of Boston.* London: David Nutt, 1914; New York: Henry Holt, 1914.

*Mountain Interval.* New York: Henry Holt, 1916.

*New Hampshire: A Poem with Notes and Grace Notes.* New York: Henry Holt, 1923.

*West-Running Brook.* New York: Henry Holt, 1928.

*A Further Range.* New York: Henry Holt, 1936.

*A Witness Tree.* New York: Henry Holt, 1942.

*A Masque of Reason.* New York: Henry Holt, 1945.

*Steeple Bush.* New York: Henry Holt, 1947

*A Masque of Mercy.* New York: Henry Holt, 1947.

*In the Clearing.* New York: Holt, Rinehart, and Winston, 1962.

COLLECTIONS

*Selected Poems.* New York: Henry Holt, 1923. Revised, 1928. Again revised, 1934.

*Collected Poems.* New York: Holt, 1930. Revised 1939.

*Selected Poems.* London: Jonathan Cape, 1936. (Contains introductory essays by W. H. Auden, C. Day Lewis, Paul Engle, and Edwin Muir.)

*Complete Poems of Robert Frost.* New York: Henry Holt, 1949.

*Aforesaid.* New York: Henry Holt, 1951.

*Selected Poems.* Harmondsworth, England: Penguin Books, 1955.

*Selected Poems.* New York: Holt, Rinehart, and Winston, 1963. (Includes an introduction by Robert Graves.)

*The Poetry of Robert Frost: The Collected Poems, Complete and Unabridged.* Edited by Edward Connery Lathem. New York: Holt, Rinehart, and Winston, 1969.

*Robert Frost: Poetry and Prose.* Edited by Edward Connery Lathem and Lawrance Thompson. New York: Holt, Rinehart, and Winston, 1972.

*Collected Poems, Prose & Plays.* Edited by Richard Poirier and Mark Richardson. New York: Library of America, 1995.

CORRESPONDENCE AND OTHER PROSE WRITINGS

*The Letters of Robert Frost to Louis Untermeyer.* Edited by Louis Untermeyer. New York: Holt, Rinehart, and Winston, 1963.

*Robert Frost and John Bartlett: The Record of a Friendship.* Edited by Margaret Bartlett Anderson. New York: Holt, Rinehart, and Winston, 1963.

*Robert Frost: Farm-Poultryman.* Edited by Edward Connery Lathem and Lawrance Thompson. Hanover, N. H.: Dartmouth Publications, 1963.

*Selected Letters of Robert Frost.* Edited by Lawrance Thompson. New York: Holt, Rinehart, and Winston, 1964.

*Interviews with Robert Frost.* Edited by Edward Connery Lathem. New York: Holt, Rinehart, and Winston, 1966.

*Selected Prose of Robert Frost.* Edited by Hyde Cox and Edward Connery Lathem. New York: Holt, Rinehart, and Winston, 1966.

*Family Letters of Robert and Elinor Frost.* Edited by Arnold E. Grade. Albany: State University of New York Press, 1972. Foreword by Lesley Frost.

*Robert Frost on Writing.* Edited by Elaine Barry. New Brunswick, N. J.: Rutgers University Press, 1973.

*Prose Jottings of Robert Frost: Selections from his Notebooks and Miscellaneous Manuscripts.* Edited by Edward Connery Lathem and Hyde Cox. Lunenberg, Vt.: Stinehour, 1982.

*Stories for Lesley.* Edited by Roger D. Sell. Charlottesville: University Press of Virginia, 1984. (Illustrated by Warren Chappell.)

BIBLIOGRAPHIES AND CONCORDANCES

Greiner, Donald J. *The Merrill Checklist of Robert Frost.* Columbus, Ohio: C. E. Merrill, 1969.

Lathem, Edward Connery. *A Concordance to the Poetry of Robert Frost.* New York: Holt Information Systems, 1971.

————. *Robert Frost 100.* Boston: Godine, 1974.

Lentricchia, Frank, and Melissa Christensen Lentricchia. *Robert Frost: A Bibliography, 1913–1974.* Metuchen, N. J.: Scarecrow, 1976.

Van Egmond, Peter. *The Critical Reception of Robert Frost.* Boston: G. K. Hall, 1974.

————. *Robert Frost: A Reference Guide, 1974–1990.* Boston: G. K. Hall, 1991.

BIOGRAPHICAL STUDIES

Cox, Sidney. *A Swinger of Birches: A Portrait of Robert Frost.* New York: New York University Press, 1957.

Evans, William R. *Robert Frost and Sidney Cox: Forty Years of Friendship.* Hanover, N. H.: University Press of New England, 1981.

Francis, Lesley Lee. *The Frost Family's Adventure in Poetry: Sheer Morning Gladness at the Brim.* Columbia: University of Missouri Press, 1994.

Frost, Lesley. *New Hampshire's Child: The Derry Journals of Lesley Frost.* Albany: State University of New York Press, 1969.

Gould, Jean. *Robert Frost: The Aim Was Song.* New York: Dodd, Mead, 1964.

Lathem, Edward Connery, and Lawrance Thompson. *Robert Frost and the Lawrence, Massachusetts, High School Bulletin: The Beginning of a Literary Career.* New York: Grolier Club, 1966.

Mertins, Louis. *Robert Frost: Life and Talks—Walking.* Norman: University of Oklahoma Press, 1965.

Meyers, Jeffrey. *Robert Frost.* Boston: Houghton Mifflin, 1996.

Newdick, Robert Spangler. *Newdick's Season of Frost: An Interrupted Biography of Robert Frost.* Albany: State University of New York Press, 1976.

Pritchard, William H. *Frost: A Literary Life Reconsidered.* New York: Oxford University Press, 1984.

Sergeant, Elizabeth Shepley. *Robert Frost: The Trial by Existence.* New York: Holt, Rinehart, and Winston, 1960.

Thompson, Lawrance. *Robert Frost: The Early Years, 1874–1915.* New York: Holt, Rinehart, and Winston, 1966.

———. *Robert Frost: The Years of Triumph, 1915–1938.* New York: Holt, Rinehart, and Winston, 1970.

Thompson, Lawrance, and R. H. Winnick. *Robert Frost: The Later Years, 1938–1963.* New York: Holt, Rinehart, and Winston, 1976.

Walsh, John Evangelist. *Into My Own: The English Years of Robert Frost, 1912–1915.* New York: Grove Press, 1988.

## CRITICAL STUDIES

### BOOKS

Bagby, George F. *Frost and the Book of Nature.* Knoxville: University of Tennessee Press, 1993.

Bromwich, David. *A Choice of Inheritance: Self and Community from Edmund Burke to Robert Frost.* Cambridge: Harvard University Press, 1989.

Brower, Reuben. *The Poetry of Robert Frost: Constellations of Intention.* New York: Oxford University Press, 1963.

Burnshaw, Stanley. *Robert Frost Himself.* New York: Braziller, 1986.

Cady, Edwin Harrison, and Louis J. Budd, eds. *On Frost: The Best from American Literature.* Durham, N. C.: Duke University Press, 1991.

Committee on the Frost Centennial of the University of Southern Mississippi, ed. *Frost: Centennial Essays.* Jackson: University Press of Mississippi, 1974.

Cook, Reginald Lansing. *Robert Frost: A Living Voice.* Amherst: University of Massachusetts Press, 1974.

Cox, James M. ed. *Robert Frost: A Collection of Critical Essays.* Englewood Cliffs, N.J.: Prentice-Hall, 1962.

Cramer, Jeffrey S. *Robert Frost among His Poems: A Literary Companion to the Poet's Own Biographical Contexts and Associations.* Jefferson, N. C.: McFarland, 1996.

D'Avanzo, Mario L. *A Cloud of Other Poets: Robert Frost and the Romantics.* Lanham, Md.: University Press of America, 1991.

Gerber, Philip L., ed. *Critical Essays on Robert Frost.* Boston: G. K. Hall, 1982.

———. *Robert Frost.* Boston: Twayne, 1982.

Greiner, Donald J. *Robert Frost: The Poet and His Critics.* Chicago: American Library Association, 1974.

Hadas, Rachel. *Form, Cycle, Infinity: Landscape Imagery in the Poetry of Robert Frost.* Lewisburg, Pa.: Bucknell University Press, 1985.

Holland, Norman Norwood. *The Brain of Robert Frost: A Cognitive Approach to Literature.* New York: Routledge, 1988.

Kearns, Katherine. *Robert Frost and a Poetics of Appetite.* New York: Cambridge University Press, 1994.

Kemp, John C. *Robert Frost and New England: The Poet as Regionalist.* Princeton: Princeton University Press, 1979.

Lentricchia, Frank. *Robert Frost: Modern Poetics and the Landscapes of Self.* Durham, N.C.: Duke University Press, 1975.

Monteiro, George. *Robert Frost and the New England Renaissance.* Lexington: University Press of Kentucky, 1988.

Morrison, Kathleen. *Robert Frost: A Pictorial Chronicle.* New York: Holt, Rinehart, and Winston, 1974.

Munson, Gorham Bert. *Robert Frost: A Study in Sensibility and Good Sense.* New York: George H. Doran, 1927.

Oster, Judith. *Toward Robert Frost: The Reader and the Poet.* Athens: University of Georgia Press, 1991.

Poirier, Richard. *Robert Frost: The Work of Knowing.* New York: Oxford University Press, 1977.

Squires, Radcliffe. *The Major Themes of Robert Frost.* Ann Arbor: University of Michigan Press, 1963.

Tharpe, Jac, ed. *Frost: Centennial Essays II.* Jackson: University Press of Mississippi, 1976.

———, ed. *Frost: Centennial Essays III.* Jackson: University Press of Mississippi, 1978.

Thompson, Lawrance. *Fire and Ice: The Art and Thought of Robert Frost.* New York: Henry Holt, 1942.

Thornton, Richard, ed. *Recognition of Robert Frost: Twenty-Fifth Anniversary.* New York: Henry Holt, 1937.

Wilcox, Earl J., ed. *Robert Frost: The Man and the Poet.* Rock Hill, S.C.: Winthrop College, 1981.

### ESSAYS AND REVIEWS

Anonymous. "Frost: He Is Sometimes a Poet and Sometimes a Stump-Speaker." *News-Week,* May 30, 1936, p. 40.

Anonymous. Review of *In the Clearing. Wisconsin Library Bulletin* 58:240 (July–August 1962).

Arvin, Newton. "A Minor Strain." *Partisan Review* 3:27–28 (June 1936).

Bagby, George F. "The Promethean Frost." *Twentieth-Century Literature* 38, no. 1:1–19 (Spring 1992).

Bell, Vereen. "Robert Frost and the Nature of Narrative." *New England Review and Bread Loaf Quarterly* 8, no. 1:70–78 (Autumn 1985).

Benoit, Raymond. "An American Hierophany: The Wood-Pile in Hawthorne and Frost." *Arizona Quarterly* 44, no. 2:22–27 (Summer 1988).

Boroff, Marie. "Sound Symbolism as Drama in the Poetry of Robert Frost." *PMLA* 107, no. 1:131–144 (January 1992).

Braithewaite, W. S. "Fifteen Important Volumes of Poems Published in 1916," in his *Anthology of Magazine Verse for 1916 and Year Book of American Poetry.* New York: Laurence J. Gomme, 1916. P. 247.

Brodsky, Joseph. "On Grief and Reason." *New Yorker,* September 26, 1994, pp. 70–78.

Cornett, Michael E. "Robert Frost on Listen America: The Poet's Message to America in 1956." *Papers on Language and Literature* 29, no. 4:417–435 (fall 1993).

Cox, Sidney. "The Sincerity of Robert Frost." *New Republic* 12 (August 25, 1917), 109–111.

Dawes, James R. "Masculinity and Transgression in Robert Frost." *American Literature* 65, no. 2:297–312 (June 1993).

Doreski, William. "Meta-Meditation in Robert Frost's 'The Woodpile,' 'After Apple-Picking,' and 'Directive.' " *Ariel* 23, no. 4:35–49 (October 1992).

———. "Robert Frost's 'The Census-Taker' and the Problem of Wilderness." *Twentieth Century Literature* 34, no. 1:30–39 (Spring 1988).

Evans, Oliver H. "'Deeds That Count': Robert Frost's Sonnets." *Texas Studies in Literature and Language* 23, no. 1:123–137. (Spring 1981).

Francis, Lesley Lee. "Robert Frost and the Majesty of Stones upon Stones." *Journal of Modern Literature* 9, no. 1:3–26 (winter 1981–1982).

Heaney, Seamus. "Above the Brim: On Robert Frost." *Salmagundi* nos. 88–89:275–294 (fall/winter 1990–1991).

Hoffman, Daniel. "Robert Frost: The Symbols a Poem Makes." *Gettysburg Review* 7, no. 1:101–112 (winter 1994).

Humphries, Rolfe. "A Further Shrinking." *New Masses,* August 1, 1936, pp. 41–42.

Jarrell, Randall. "Tenderness and Passive Sadness." *New York Times Book Review,* June 1, 1947, p. 4. Reprinted in his *Kipling, Auden & Co: Essays and Reviews 1935–1964.* New York: Farrar, Straus, 1980, pp. 140–142.

———. "The Other Frost" and "To the Laodiceans." In his *Poetry and the Age.* New York: Knopf, 1953, pp. 28–36, 37–69.

———. "Robert Frost's 'Home Burial.'" In his *The Third Book of Criticism.* New York: Farrar, Straus, 1969, pp. 191–234.

Leithauser, Brad. "Great Old Modern." *New York Review of Books,* August 8, 1996, pp. 40–43.

Lowell, Robert. "New England and Further." In his *Collected Prose,* edited by Robert Giroux. New York: Farrar, Straus & Giroux, 1987, pp. 179–212.

Monroe, Harriet. "Frost and Masters," *Poetry* 9 (January 1917), 202.

Pierce, Frederick. "Three Poets Against Philists." *Yale Review* 18:364–366 (December 1928).

Richardson, Mark. "Robert Frost and the Motives of Poetry." *Essays in Literature* 20, no. 2:273–291 (fall 1993).

Scott, Mark. "Andrew Lang's 'Scythe Song' Becomes Robert Frost's 'Mowing': Frost's Practice of Poetry." *Robert Frost Review* 30–38 (fall 1991).

Sheehy, Donald G. "(Re)Figuring Love: Robert Frost in Crisis, 1938–1942." *New England Quarterly* 63, no. 2:179–231 (June 1990).

Special Robert Frost Sections. *South Carolina Review* no. 19 (summer 1987); no. 21 (fall 1988).

Trilling, Lionel. "A Speech on Robert Frost: A Cultural Episode." In James M. Cox, *Robert Frost: A Collection of Critical Essays.* Englewood Cliffs, N.J.: Prentice-Hall, 1962. Pp. 151–158.

*—WILLIAM DORESKI*

# Nathaniel Hawthorne
## *1804–1864*

*E*XACTLY AT THE center of *The Scarlet Letter,* the book that made Nathaniel Hawthorne central to the history of the American novel, Arthur Dimmesdale beholds an immense red *A* lighting up the midnight sky. As Reverend Dimmesdale stares in horror at this cosmic exposure of his unconfessed sin, the calm, rational voice of Hawthorne's narrator intervenes to say that the minister is deluded: Dimmesdale may have seen a meteor flashing through the sky, "but with no such shape as his guilty imagination gave it." Yet, two pages after being assured that this *A* was a private fantasy, the reader learns that the same shape was seen by the Puritan public at large, although the community understands the heavenly letter to signify not that Reverend Dimmesdale is a secret adulterer but that Governor Winthrop, who died on the night it appeared, is now an angel.

This dramatic and curious scene raises a series of questions that Hawthorne's stories and novels repeatedly ask and that we must ask as well in assessing the relationship between Hawthorne's actual life and times and the life of his imagination. What is the relationship, the episode of the midnight letter implicitly queries, between the actual and the imagined, between public reality and private fantasy? Is there any authoritative means of judging human perceptions and interpretations, any source or principle of certainty by which we can know truth from falsehood, good from evil, whether the *A* means adulterer or angel, or whether any such sign has appeared at all? To what degree do the dominant values and assumptions of a society or of a historical moment shape the character and the perspective of every inhabitant of that society or moment, even those who may imagine themselves to be outcasts and rebels? Is imagination itself unhealthy, guilty, self-indulgent?

These are some of the questions about his own art and about the bases of the individual's and society's knowledge, motivation, and morality that fascinated and sometimes terrified Nathaniel Hawthorne. He explored such questions through a form and style of writing that he called "romance" and that he famously (but misleadingly) defined as "a neutral territory, somewhere between the real world and fairy-land, where the Actual and the Imaginary may meet, and each imbue itself with the nature of the other." Romance was an old and familiar literary label when Hawthorne took it up; a term that recalled the genre of medieval quest narratives in which a hero pursues an exalted or sacred object through enchanted landscapes and perilous trials. The quest motif is prominent in Hawthorne's fiction. However, Hawthorne adapted the genre to his own nineteenth-century American preoccupation more thoroughly and skillfully than any of his contemporaries who also appropriated the term romance.

Hawthorne's questers tend not to reach their objects. Or the objects, once reached, are found to be different from what the quester imagined or intended. Or the obsessiveness of the quest itself turns out to destroy the object or to unfit the quester to possess it. In Hawthorne's realm of romance, enchantment is never safe from exposure as delusion or deception. A character's outward quest through an alien landscape veils or mirrors an inward journey to an estranged self. A community's or a nation's forward quest toward a utopian future somehow leads it backward to the unburied remains of a less-than-ideal past. And through all these variations on the quest motif, Hawthorne pursues the question of the relationship between the "Actual" and the "Imaginary"—the questions of whether the two categories can be defined or differentiated and of how they interact to produce our visions of the past, of others, and of ourselves. I called Hawthorne's famous definition of romance misleading because it implies that these capitalized categories are simple and settled and that their meeting is peaceful. But as we will see, Hawthorne's life and art were highly charged, not neutral, territories that interpenetrated each other in complicated and unsettling ways.

## HAWTHORNE'S ANCESTRAL FAMILY

It is commonly said that the most important presence in a boy's life is his father. Some psychologists, in fact, have suggested that a young child sees his or her father as the embodiment of the actual. Hawthorne's father was, indeed, an important presence for his son, but Hawthorne knew him only in imagination. Nathaniel Hathorne Sr. (his son, whom we know as Nathaniel Hawthorne, inserted the *w* in the family name) was a sailor, a ship captain from the seaport town of Salem, Massachusetts. In August of 1801, he married Elizabeth Clarke Manning, one of nine children of a successful Salem merchant. Seven months later, while Hathorne was voyaging in the East Indies, his wife gave birth to a daughter, Elizabeth. (Contrary to our contemporary myth, premarital sex in America did not begin in the 1960s and was, in fact, not that exceptional an occurrence in the early national period.) The Hathornes' second child, Nathaniel, was born on July 4, 1804. A third child, Maria Louisa, arrived in January of 1808, but her father never saw her. At the time of her birth, Captain Hathorne was sailing off the South American coast near Surinam, where, a few weeks later, he contracted yellow fever and died. In nearly seven years of marriage, he had spent a total of seven months at home—perhaps only a few weeks during the lifetime of his three-and-a-half-year-old son.

After her husband's death, Elizabeth Manning Hathorne moved out of the Hathorne family home, where her short married life had been spent with her mother-in-law and her husband's sisters. The venerable and once-prominent Hathornes of Salem had long been a family in decline, and Mrs. Hathorne viewed her continued dependence on them as a ticket to a grim social and economic future. So she returned to her father's house, where her three young children grew up among their Manning relations and without connection, except in name, to the Hathornes. But the Hathorne connection remained powerful in her son's imagination. In his youth, Hawthorne pored over the ship's logbooks, written in his father's hand, that recorded the details and routes of Captain Hathorne's voyages. He supplemented the images of his father's nautical life that he gleaned from the logbooks by reading travel narratives, histories, and adventure stories about the exotic regions in which Nathaniel Hathorne had sailed. And as he imaginatively recharted his father's geographic movements, so Hawthorne studied local history and lore to retrace the temporal course of his paternal family line, from esteemed leaders and defenders of the seventeenth-century Puritan colony at Massachusetts to himself.

Hawthorne's imaginative link to his paternal family history was one of the essential springs of his literary career. Yet when he began to sign his stories, after at first publishing anonymously, Hawthorne changed the family name, adding the *w*. The gesture is an interesting and characteristically ambivalent one that both marks Hawthorne's psychological embrace of his Hathorne heritage and signifies his deviation from it. Hawthorne intended the new spelling to augur the change in family fortunes that he hoped his success as a writer would bring about. But changing ancestral family fortunes also involved changing—or at least questioning—ancestral family values. This is the bargain with the memory of his forebears that Hawthorne strikes in "The Custom-House," his long introductory essay to *The Scarlet Letter: A Romance* (1850). Taking upon himself the role of family "representative," Hawthorne proposes to reverse "the dreary and unprosperous condition of the race, for many a long year back" by expiating in his work the sins his ancestors had committed in theirs.

The particular ancestors Hawthorne has in mind in "The Custom-House" are the first two American Hathornes, William and his son, John. William Hathorne came to Massachusetts from England in 1630, the year Massachusetts Bay Colony was founded, and served as a colonial legislator and a major in the Salem militia. But despite many better deeds, Hawthorne writes, "this grave, bearded, sable-cloaked and steeple-crowned progenitor,—who came so early, with his Bible and his sword," was most famous for his bitter suppression of heretics, "as witness the Quakers, who have remembered him in their histories, and relate an incident of his hard severity towards a woman of their sect." As for John Hathorne, when the people of Salem village convinced themselves in 1692 that witchcraft was the cause of their economic and spiritual troubles, he was one of the

judges who presided over the trials that sent twenty accused witches—all but two of them women—to their deaths. Thus, in his introduction to *The Scarlet Letter,* a historical novel about the branding and persecution of a woman who deviates from Puritan custom and law, Hawthorne identifies the shared sin of his Puritan ancestors as the branding and persecution of deviant women.

It is consistent with Hawthorne's ambivalent identification with and disavowal of these ancestors that for almost a hundred and fifty years readers and critics of *The Scarlet Letter* have debated whether his treatment of Hester Prynne repents the sin of the Puritan Hathornes or repeats it. Most have felt that Hester's story, not Dimmesdale's, is the emotional core of the novel and that Hester commands the author's deepest imaginative sympathies. Indeed, Hawthorne affiliates himself with Hester in his introduction when, claiming to have found the remnant of her actual letter among some old documents in the customhouse attic, he holds the scarlet cloth to his own breast and feels himself branded by its "burning heat." Both the novel's plot and Hawthorne's authorial commentary, however, ultimately refuse to allow Hester to reject Puritan moral authority or even to escape Puritan jurisdiction; on the contrary, Hester is shown at the end to humbly accept her punishment and to wear its symbol to her grave, years longer than "the sternest magistrate of that iron period would have imposed it."

Hawthorne's attitudes toward women, in his fiction and in his life, proceed from his intense concern with the issue of male and female gender roles—a concern that derived partly from the circumstances of his childhood, partly from his vocational choice, and partly from mid-nineteenth-century American society's pervasive preoccupation with, and contestation over, the relative characters, rights, and spheres of women and men. Understanding Hawthorne requires that this issue be addressed. In his communion with his ancestors in "The Custom-House," however, Hawthorne sees his own deviation from the patriarchal Hathorne norm to be a matter not of feminist impulses but of literary ones. Through the imagined voices of these ancestors, Hawthorne, in a famous and important passage, ventriloquizes his own lifelong uncertainty of the usefulness—and of the masculinity—of writing stories.

Doubtless, however, either of these stern and black-browed Puritans would have thought it quite a sufficient retribution for his sins, that, after so long a lapse of years, the old trunk of the family tree, with so much venerable moss upon it, should have borne, as its topmost bough, an idler like myself. No aim, that I have ever cherished, would they recognize as laudable; no success of mine—if my life, beyond its domestic scope, had ever been brightened by success—would they deem otherwise than worthless, if not positively disgraceful. "What is he?" murmurs one gray shadow of my forefathers to the other. "A writer of story-books! What kind of business in life,—what mode of glorifying God, or being serviceable to mankind in his day and generation,—may that be? Why, the degenerate fellow might as well have been a fiddler!" Such are the compliments bandied between my great-grandsires and myself, across the gulf of time! And yet, let them scorn me as they will, strong traits of their nature have intertwined themselves with mine.

### THE MANNINGS AND MANHOOD

I have argued to this point that Hawthorne's literary vocation grew out of his quest for connection with his father and with the eventful, if morally ambiguous, past of his Hathorne ancestry. But Hawthorne's "home-feeling with the past," as he describes it in "The Custom-House," must not obscure the fact (as critics have sometimes allowed it to do) that he lived not with Hathornes in a seventeenth-century Puritan theocracy but with Mannings in a nineteenth-century capitalist democracy and that his imaginative life, as well as his actual one, was shaped by these circumstances. In the passage just quoted, for example, the anxiety

Hawthorne expresses about the manliness of literary endeavor is produced in him not, in the first place, by the attitudes of his dead relatives but by those of his living ones and of his own American generation.

Hawthorne came of age as the United States was first establishing itself as an aggressive commercial society devoted to rapid economic and territorial expansion. Marketplace considerations and competitive individualism increasingly defined the dominant American ethos, replacing—or at least reducing the influence of—earlier religious and agrarian values and communal structures. In this society, energetic activity, practical pursuits, and material achievements were the approved measures of masculinity. The psychological pressure on American males of the early nineteenth century to prove their manhood was heightened by another aspect of their historical situation. This generation's fathers and grandfathers had been America's founding fathers, the men who had conceived, liberated, and established the nation. They were officially worshipped by the younger generation, but with a tinge of filial resentment. What could the sons ever do to acquire for themselves the stature of these mythic forebears?

For the sons of old New England families, this question was especially acute. Boston and its surrounding towns had been the hub of colonial affairs and the birthplace of the Revolution, but the geography of economic opportunity and political power in the burgeoning republic was shifting southward and westward. After the War of 1812, for example, Hawthorne's native Salem ceased to be a major port, even as American shipping and trade expanded and prospered. Moreover, the New England ministry—that traditional route to masculine prestige and social influence for young men who, like Hawthorne, were more intellectually and imaginatively than practically inclined—was also losing its centrality in the new commercial culture. Ralph Waldo Emerson, after resigning from his Boston pulpit, put it bluntly in a famous speech ("The American Scholar") to the Phi Beta Kappa Society at Harvard (1837): "Speculative men," he reported, are commonly scorned by "so-called 'practical men'" who address the clergy as women and effectively disenfranchise them from men's affairs.

This emerging American ideology of practical manhood and of a distinct separation between male and female spheres of endeavor was etched not only into the culture but also into the household in which Hawthorne grew up. As he approached adolescence, Hawthorne's mother and sisters effectively ceded authority and responsibility for his upbringing to his uncle, Robert Manning. Uncle Robert was an energetic and capable man who put scientific business and agricultural principles to work in establishing himself as a successful land broker, a stagecoach-line manager, and an eminent horticulturalist. After his father's death in 1813, Robert took over the direction of the Manning family businesses and lands in Massachusetts and Maine. By this time, he had already assumed control over the affairs of his siblings—who depended on and deferred to his judgment but sometimes resented his dictatorial manner—and over the education of his nephew.

Robert Manning sought to instill in his charge the manly virtues of discipline, industry, practicality, and order. Hawthorne took refuge in idleness, imagination, and reading. A curious event in his young life among the Mannings suggests the depth of his psychological resistance to familial and societal expectations. When he was nine, Hawthorne hurt his foot playing outdoors. The injury seemed minor, and a procession of doctors were mystified by the young boy's apparent inability to walk on the foot for more than a year, during which time Hawthorne escaped regular school attendance and amused himself by reading, playing, and dreaming at home. In the fiction that he later produced, one of Hawthorne's most frequent character types is the misfit male dreamer,

a man of highly developed intellectual, spiritual, or artistic sensitivity who seeks to evade conventional male responsibilities or to resist the dominant paradigm of manliness that he often finds embodied in a hypermasculine counterpart. Examples of such character pairs include Fanshawe and Butler in *Fanshawe* (1828), Owen Warland and Robert Danforth in "The Artist of the Beautiful" (1844), Clifford and Jaffrey Pyncheon in *The House of the Seven Gables* (1851), Coverdale and Hollingsworth in *The Blithedale Romance* (1852), and Donatello and Kenyon in *The Marble Faun* (1860). Typically, Hawthorne treats his male romantics with a mixture of wistful affection and ironic condescension.

Like the dreamers he later created, the young Hawthorne could not long inhabit an unencumbered imaginative realm. Shortly after his return to school, his mother took up residence on Manning family lands in Raymond, Maine. The children stayed with her during the summers, and throughout his adolescence this frontier village represented to Hawthorne the domain of wilderness, of women, and of freedom. During the school terms, however, Hawthorne and his sisters returned to Salem, the domain of Uncle Robert. Then, beginning in 1818, Elizabeth and Louisa were allowed to stay with their mother year-round, and Hawthorne alone was sent back. Gender division was now geographically enforced in Hawthorne's family. Hawthorne's letters from Salem to his mother and sisters in Maine expressed his longing to be there with them and, on one occasion, his wish to have been born a girl. And the act of writing—whether to them or for himself—became a way to challenge or escape, at least in imagination, the world in which he found himself, the world of Robert Manning. Still, what he wrote of his Hathorne ancestors was also true of his Manning guardian: "Strong traits of their nature have intertwined themselves with mine."

Hawthorne's internalization of strong traits of his uncle's nature is strikingly evident in the self-reflective early tale "Passages from a Relinquished Work" (1834). The title of this work exemplifies its central dilemma and the central dilemma in the life of its author at the time it was written: the tension between the impulse to pursue a literary vocation and the impulse to abandon that desire. In the tale, Hawthorne's first-person narrator defies the authority of his guardian, the suggestively named Parson Thumpcushion, by remaining resolutely "aloof from the regular business of life" and at last leaving home to become a wandering storyteller. But the narrator approaches this objective with hesitation, even shame, and several times defers his debut. At last, on a cheap tavern stage, he recites a story he has written to an audience that rolls on the floor with delight, but his success is instantly transformed to horror and remorse. Upon leaving the platform he is handed a letter from his guardian, uncannily addressed to him at the tavern under his assumed name. He cannot bear to read this letter, but he does not have to, for its mere presence evokes for him "the puritanic figure of my guardian, standing among the fripperies of the theatre, and pointing to the players,—the fantastic and effeminate men, the painted women, the giddy girl in boy's clothes, merrier than modest,—pointing to these with solemn ridicule, and eyeing me with stern rebuke." Literary pursuits, in this passage and others in the tale, are associated not only with insubstantiality and immorality but also with gender confusion; at the end, the narrator flees the scene, unable to return home, yet oppressed with "the guilt and madness of my life."

Hawthorne wrote "Passages from a Relinquished Work" in the middle of his famous twelve-year period of reclusive literary labor. For four years he had attended Bowdoin College in Brunswick, Maine, where he established friendships with two young men—Henry Wadsworth Longfellow and Franklin Pierce—who used their subsequent fame and influence on his behalf later in life. At Bowdoin, too, he had committed himself to becoming a writer and had bet another friend at graduation in 1825 that he would not marry for at least twelve years while he devoted himself to his art. Hawthorne's mothers and sisters had moved back to Salem, where they had the family home to themselves. Uncle Robert, who still supported his sister and her children, had married in 1824 and moved with his wife into a new house, and the rest of Hawthorne's aunts and uncles had either died or had also left the Manning home. From ages twenty-one to thirty-three, Hawthorne wrote and read in the attic study of his mother's house in Salem. His only regular companions were the women of his family, particularly his sister Elizabeth, whom he sent to the Salem Athenaeum to borrow the histories and documentary literature of early New England that he meticulously consumed. Toward the end of this period, hoping to generate some income, Hawthorne also collaborated with his sister in editing a magazine and in writing a volume for a children's history series.

For the most part, however, Hawthorne worked alone at his story-writing. Often, he questioned the legitimacy, sometimes the sanity, of this life. Often, the results of his literary efforts dissatisfied him, and he apparently destroyed a number of early stories. But, as in his tale "The Devil in Manuscript" (1835), even the destruction of some of his work fueled his ambition rather than marked its relinquishment. There, a young writer called Oberon (a college nickname of Hawthorne's) decides to burn his unpublished stories. As he explains to a friend before consigning his manuscripts to the flames:

> You cannot conceive what an effect the composition of these tales has had on me. I have become ambitious of a bubble, and careless of a solid reputation. I am surrounding myself with shadows, which bewilder me, by aping the realities of life. They have drawn me aside from the beaten path of the world, and led me into a strange sort of solitude,—a solitude in the midst of men,—where nobody wishes for

what I do, nor thinks nor feels as I do. The tales have done all this. When they are ashes, perhaps I shall be as I was before they had existence. Moreover, the sacrifice is less than you may suppose, since nobody will publish them.

However sound these reasons may be, Oberon must get drunk before carrying out his intention. And when the intense heat of his burning creations ignites the chimney and the roof of the apartment house, eliciting fire bells and a general panic in the street, Oberon exults that his work has finally "set the town on fire" and cannot wait to write a story about it.

At least in part, Hawthorne was temperamentally inclined to Oberon's "strange sort of solitude," and he experienced this sense of psychic isolation both before and after the years of his self-directed literary apprenticeship. It is the defining quality of Fanshawe, the title character of the short novel that Hawthorne began while he was an undergraduate at Bowdoin. A young man who feels "unconnected with the world," Fanshawe is fashioned as an observer of the desires and struggles of others. When, through a series of lucky accidents, he finds himself in a position to marry a vivacious young woman and to inherit her father's commercial fortune, he declines both and instead dies at age twenty. Hawthorne paid to have *Fanshawe* published anonymously in 1828, but he soon came to dislike this juvenile work and never publicly acknowledged having written it. Perhaps this rapid disaffection was the result of his awareness that by the early 1830s he had begun to produce some truly mature and powerful tales— tales that still tended to feature solitary or psychically isolated heroes (or anti-heroes) but that were not in the least "unconnected with the world."

## THE PROBLEM OF SELF-KNOWLEDGE

In his readings of colonial history, his observations of the society bustling around him, and his reflections on his own character and life, Hawthorne came to see that the imaginary and the actual could never be neatly separated. The activities and products of the imagination—beliefs, values, fears, desires—shaped both individual and collective understandings of reality. Oberon's cry—"My brain has set the town on fire!"—was not a mere play on words; private imaginings and fantasies could and did ignite communities, even nations, and make history. For proof of this proposition, Hawthorne needed only to recall the most notorious event in the history of his own native town and paternal ancestry: the Salem witch trials. This he did in his great story "Young Goodman Brown" (1835).

"Young Goodman Brown" does not directly represent the witch trials but draws several characters' names and even some phrases from actual accounts of them. Brown lives in Salem Village, which in 1692 was the poorer sister community of Salem Town and the place where the accusations began. The key to a historical reading of this tale, however, is the nature of the evidence that, in Goodman Brown's judgment, convicts many of his most respected neighbors and, finally, his own wife of communion with the devil. For Brown's verdict is rendered on the same basis as the verdicts of John Hathorne and the other judges at the Salem trials. That basis is "spectral evidence"— the appearance to a "victim" of witchcraft of the disembodied image or specter of a witch doing or saying something evil. The Salem judges ruled this evidence legally admissible on the theological premise that only the devil could summon such a specter to appear and that only the specter of a person in league with the devil could be so summoned. In Hawthorne's story, Brown sees and hears the specters of his townspeople in the forest, and when a single piece of physical evidence—the pink ribbon from his wife's bonnet that Brown seizes from the branch of a tree—confirms his suspicions, Hawthorne's language is careful not to ratify the factual presence of the ribbon but merely to say that this is what Brown "beheld." Brown may be projecting onto others not only the images he thinks he sees but also his own guilt for having journeyed into the forest himself.

Brown is not alone in his susceptibility to self-deception, nor is his error or sin representative solely of the accusers of 1692. By keeping his tale's reference to the witch trials implicit and indirect, Hawthorne is able to broaden the scope of its inquiry into the relationship between perception and reality and the ability to distinguish good from evil. Was the entire Puritan errand to transform the heathen wilderness into a Christian "city upon a hill" a grand self-delusion, an imagined righteousness that actually facilitated evil? This radical possibility is raised by a key passage early in the tale in which Brown tells the figure of the devil that his family heritage prevents him from going any farther into the forest. But upon Brown's assertion that his forefathers have been "a race of honest men and good Christians since the days of the martyrs" and that he would be "the first of the name of Brown that ever took this path," his companion smiles and replies:

> I have been as well acquainted with your family as with ever a one among the Puritans; and that's no trifle to say. I helped your grandfather, the constable, when he lashed the Quaker woman so smartly through the streets of Salem; and it was I that brought your father a pitch-pine knot, kindled at my own hearth, to set fire to an Indian village, in King Philip's war. They were my good friends, both.

To study history, Hawthorne wryly suggests here, is to encounter diabolical deeds that those who did them believed to be godly. And to recognize this irony is necessarily to wonder whether the same may be true of the deeds and attitudes of the present.

In some respects, the fact that the Calvinist theology of the early New England colonists had given way to liberal Unitarian thought by Hawthorne's time only made the skeptical questions of "Young Goodman Brown" more relevant to post-Puritan America. With this liberalization of religion had come a general de-emphasis on original sin and the drama of salvation in New England churches and an increased emphasis on moral activism and social reform. The 1830s and 1840s, in particular, were decades marked by an explosion of reform societies and movements that were often millennial in their ambition and enthusiasm. Appealing to the dictates of Christian conscience, reformers organized to effect the abolition of the moral and social ills that kept the real America from fulfilling the promise of the ideal America: adultery, alcoholism, discrimination against women, exploitation of labor, prostitution, seduction, and slavery. Hawthorne typically doubted the benefits of social reform and distrusted the motives and the intensity of reformers; these sentiments are clearly conveyed in such stories of the 1840s as "The Birth-mark" (1843), "The Celestial Rail-road" (1843), and "Earth's Holocaust" (1844), and in the novel *The Blithedale Romance*. Hawthorne's suspicion of reform and reformers reflected, in part, a political conservatism that deepened as he aged. A sentence he wrote about Hester Prynne aptly described the rift between his own political imagination and his practical politics: "It is remarkable, that persons who speculate the most boldly often conform with the most perfect quietude to the external regulations of society." Hawthorne's conservatism also derives partly from the radical skepticism expressed in "Young Goodman Brown" about the capacity of individuals or communities to reliably distinguish good deeds from evil ones, let alone to act them out.

The depth of this skepticism set Hawthorne apart from the group of New England literary intellectuals who, in the late 1830s and early 1840s, gravitated around Emerson to form the transcendental movement. Mingling the humanistic theology of Unitarianism with the naturalistic paratheology of Romanticism, the transcendentalists held that divinity suffused the natural creation and inhabited every person. Transcendentalists argued that people must—and could—break through the crust of convention and artifice that blocked their access to the lessons of nature and to the fount of godliness in themselves. By means of such a breakthrough, an individual could achieve immediate instinctive access to truth and goodness. Emerson epitomizes this faith, in the Harvard oration cited earlier, when he says of the transcendental quester that "the deeper he dives into his privatest, secretest presentiment, to his wonder he finds this is the most acceptable, most public, and universally true." But for Hawthorne, an individual's "privatest, secretest presentiment" is more likely to be a Freudian than an Emersonian one: not a recognition of universal truth, that is, but an unrecognizable tangle of aggressive and libidinal urges, a riot of unconscious personal desires and fears. This is another implication of the multilayered "Young Goodman Brown." For many details of the story support the view that what prompts the newlywed Brown's visit to the forest, and drives the mental orgy of secret sin that he stages there, is his inability to reconcile his idealized image of his pointedly named wife, Faith, with the fact of their sexual life together and, particularly, with her evident sexuality—symbolized by the pink ribbon.

Hawthorne surely anticipates Freud in his two earliest important tales, "Roger Malvin's Burial," and "My Kinsman, Major Molineux," both first published in 1832. "Roger Malvin's Burial" depicts the mysterious workings of a psychological repetition compulsion in the life of Reuben Bourne, who, in his youth, saved himself by abandoning his dying comrade and mentor, Roger Malvin, after both had been wounded in an Indian fight, and who, years later, accidentally shoots—on the very spot of his friend's non-burial—the son that his wife, Malvin's daughter, has borne him. "My Kinsman, Major Molineux" also reveals Hawthorne's intuitive comprehension of what Freud later theorized as the oedipal relationship between

sons and fathers or father figures. In this tale, as in "Young Goodman Brown," the meaning of a seemingly righteous public and historical event is unsettled by the suggestion that it may be motivated by irrational private fantasies and desires. Yet, here, the event in question is not the long-discredited Salem witch trials but the sacrosanct American Revolution.

The scene is not the Revolution itself but one of the earlier political skirmishes between the representatives of patriarchal British authority and the representatives of young America that prefigured the eventual war. A country lad, young Robin (his surname is never given but is likely Molineux) has made his way to the city to entrust his future to his powerful kinsman, the British colonial administrator Major Molineux. Robin does not know his kinsman's exact address; however, swelling with pride in his lofty connection and full of expectation at the wealth and influence it will bring him, he assumes that the first person he meets will worshipfully lead him to the Major's house. But the simple intention to join with his kinsman seems to propel Robin into a dream, or a nightmare, landscape in which no one he meets will give him directions and everyone seems conscious of a secret joke or irony about his situation that he cannot fathom. Robin carries a small club and contemplates doing violence with it to many of the people along his way whom he feels belittle him and block his path, but they are adults and usually carry larger weapons, so he refrains. At last, the rage and frustration that have been building within Robin are released, and the ominous secret that has permeated the dreamlike environment is revealed, when Major Molineux appears, tarred and feathered and in the process of being run out of town by a wild procession. The colonists all roar in glee at the overthrow of this foreign authority, but Robin's joyful shout is loudest of all.

This story can be read—but not read well—as a patriotic allegory. Robin, representative of young America, in his youth seeks the patronage and protection of his powerful older kinsman, representative of England. But coming of age demands independence, which is achieved when Robin recognizes that his true desire all along was not to serve this master but to revolt against him and, as he is advised to do in the tale's final words, "rise in the world without the help of your kinsman, Major Molineux." This interpretation, however, represses the troubling implication of Hawthorne's tone and imagery that the demand for independence is not so much founded on rational and righteous principles as it is rooted in violent and anarchic impulses. Major Molineux is described not as a tyrant but as "an elderly man, of large and majestic person, and strong, square features, betokening a steady soul." On the other hand, "as if a dream had broken forth from some feverish brain," the revolutionaries prance "like fiends that throng in mockery around some dead potentate . . . in senseless uproar, in frenzied merriment, trampling all on an old man's heart."

If one's conscious intentions may conceal contradictory unconscious fantasies, and if one cannot reliably determine the moral status of one's acts, then it may be asked whether one can know oneself at all. Many of Hawthorne's early tales ask this question, but perhaps none goes so far in suggesting the fragility, the inexplicability, and—anticipating a twentieth-century literary development—even the Kafkaesque absurdity of the self as the brief tale "Wakefield" (1835). Set in London, the prototype of the disorienting modern city that was only beginning to develop in the United States, "Wakefield" may be counted (along with Edgar Allan Poe's "The Man of the Crowd," written a few years later) among the earliest narratives of urban anonymity and alienation. But the alienation of the title character is more psychological than environmental. Wakefield is an ordinary, even dull, middle-aged man living a quiet, conventional life. On a perverse whim, he

rents rooms a block from his home and, one evening, tells his wife he has business in the country. He sneaks to his rented flat, curious how it will feel to drop out of his life for a day or two and observe his familiar environment from a short distance. But the day passes into a week, then into a year, and it is not until twenty years later that Wakefield, happening to get caught in a shower as he peeks in the window of his forsaken residence at his forsaken wife, returns. The story leaves him in the foyer, and Hawthorne points to this moral: "Amid the seeming confusion of our mysterious world, individuals are so nicely adjusted to a system, and systems to one another and to a whole, that, by stepping aside for a moment, a man exposes himself to a fearful risk of losing his place forever."

### ESTABLISHING HIMSELF

Between 1825 and 1837, the anonymous storywriter Nathaniel Hawthorne often felt that, like Wakefield, he had stepped aside from the world. But he was about to gain his place in it. In 1837, *Twice-Told Tales,* a collection of eighteen of Hawthorne's previously published stories, appeared under the author's own name. Five years later, Hawthorne printed a revised and expanded edition. While these volumes did not sell large numbers of copies, they captured the attention of influential people within northeastern literary and political circles. Various qualities of Hawthorne's writing contributed to the critical praise he began to win: its deft counterbalancing of elegant, elevated diction against unsettling, sometimes sensationalistic subject matter; its simultaneous moralism and openness to interpretation; the appeal of its American historical settings and modern psychological themes to a reading community very much concerned both with American roots and with the inner life of the individual. But personal and political circumstances, as well as literary qualities, also played a role in the establishment of Hawthorne's reputation.

Hawthorne's Bowdoin classmate Longfellow, who had become a prominent poet and translator, wrote two laudatory reviews of *Twice-Told Tales* for the respected *North American Review,* and an energetic young critic, Evert Duyckinck, in a series of articles that he authored or solicited for magazines he edited, took Hawthorne up as the exemplar of American literary genius. "Of the American writers destined to live," Duyckinck wrote, "he is the most original, the one least indebted to foreign models or literary precedents of any kind." In fact, Hawthorne, like most great writers, was indebted to many models—including Edmund Spenser, John Bunyan, Gothic romance, and the historical, travel, and adventure narratives that he consumed in his youth—although he combined and adapted them in distinctive ways. But American critics of the 1830s and 1840s were particularly anxious to find a literary representative of the United States: a writer who incorporated and rivaled the best in British literature yet could be viewed as quintessentially American. Hawthorne was an attractive nominee.

Party politics was another factor in Hawthorne's passage from literary obscurity to literary repute. Indeed, from the late 1830s, Hawthorne's association with the Democratic Party significantly shaped the course of his life. Before the creation of the antislavery Republican Party, the Democrats and the Whigs vied for national power. The Whig Party, favored by men of commerce and much of the cultural elite, emphasized the need for stable political and economic institutions; the Democrats, marked by the legacy of the commoner president Andrew Jackson, spoke for the authority invested in the popular will. In truth, as time passed, the two parties differed in policy less than they resembled each other in their shared commitment to the political spoils system. But to the extent that the Whigs billed themselves as the party of tradition, social distinction, and national

heritage, it was valuable for the Democrats to be able to claim the allegiance of a writer who possessed the literary grace and American pedigree of Nathaniel Hawthorne.

Hawthorne's political impulses were divided between the conservative's deep skepticism of radical change and the radical's desire to unsettle arbitrary, complacent, and unimaginative elites. His historical tales thus tended at once to link the present to an illustrious colonial past and to subject leading figures, episodes, and institutions of that past to a kind of democratic or popular critique. Both of these tendencies suited the image that the Democratic Party wished to project. So Hawthorne became its favored writer and, between 1838 and 1845, most of the new stories he wrote were printed in a party-affiliated publication, the *United States Magazine and Democratic Review.* In 1839, Democratic friends also secured for Hawthorne a paying administrative position as weigher and gauger at the Boston Custom House. Hawthorne needed more money than he could make writing stories because, in addition to his emergence on the literary and political scenes, he had also emerged on the social scene and (having won his college bet) wished to marry.

Among those who took note of the publication of *Twice-Told Tales* was Hawthorne's fellow Salemite, Elizabeth Peabody. The eldest daughter of a distinguished New England family, Peabody was a teacher, essayist, and social activist, a champion of educational reform and of rights for women. The bookshop that she opened in Boston in 1840 became a center for literary and philosophical conversation and housed the series of public seminars given by the transcendentalist and early American feminist Margaret Fuller. In 1837, Peabody sought out her reclusive neighbor and introduced him to her intellectual and family circle. At the Peabody home, Hawthorne met Elizabeth's younger sister, Sophia, with whom he quickly formed an intense mutual attachment. Sophia Peabody was also an intellectually accomplished young woman, but delicate physical and emotional health had conspired with Peabody family dynamics to define her, since girlhood, as someone whose talents would grace the domestic sphere rather than be used to escape or challenge its confines.

One year after Sophia Peabody married Nathaniel Hawthorne in 1842, Margaret Fuller published the long essay "The Great Lawsuit: Man *versus* Men: Woman *versus* Women," which she soon expanded into the book *Woman in the Nineteenth Century* (1845). There, Fuller argued that—sadly, for women and men—American society simply prohibited an educated modern woman (like Fuller herself) from attaining both a loving heterosexual union and intellectual or professional autonomy. Elizabeth Peabody and Sophia Peabody Hawthorne each sacrificed one aspect of this oppositional equation. Sophia took on the pleasures and frustrations of the Angel of the House, assuming the role of cult object in the middle-class Cult of True Womanhood. This wifely and motherly role called upon a woman not to abandon the hope of public significance but to achieve it through private influence, and not necessarily to sacrifice personal ambition but to satisfy it vicariously.

At the time of their engagement in 1839, thirty-five-year-old Nathaniel Hawthorne and thirty-year-old Sophia Peabody viewed themselves as destined mates. For Sophia, the newly recognized author was her shining knight, come in the nick of time to free her from perpetual childhood in her parents' house and to offer her a home of her own. Moreover, he was a knight whose manly armor concealed a delicate aestheticism, akin to her own, and who needed her as much as she did him. As for Hawthorne, marriage gave him the stake and place in the world that he had feared he would never have. And Sophia's conventional femininity and wifely devotion helped define and secure his image of himself as a man. In his marriage,

Hawthorne reproduced and reinforced the sharp gender divisions that he had challenged in his youth. But the conventionality of the relationship, with its eventual tensions, enabled him to explore the complexities of sex roles and relations in his novels more freely and deeply than he would have done had he and Sophia never married.

Hawthorne's engagement lasted three years, during which time he tried to determine how he would support a wife. The job in the Boston Custom House was tedious and distant from Sophia in Salem, and Hawthorne resigned it at the end of 1840. A few months later, he invested in and joined a commune that transcendentalist reformers were starting at Brook Farm in West Roxbury, Massachusetts. Utopian socialist communes and other experiments in collective living had sprung up regularly in the United States since 1837, when mismanagement, bad speculative investments, and financial overextension in the banking industry triggered a national economic crisis that dragged on through seven years of depression and widespread unemployment. The Brook Farm organizers imagined a community in which shared agricultural labor and cooperative teaching in the school they established on the premises would both provide for the members' material needs and afford everyone leisure time for intellectual and artistic pursuits.

Hawthorne was less interested in demonstrating the viability of utopian socialist principles than he was in finding a viable situation for himself and his future wife—one that would both sustain them economically and enable him to write. He lived at Brook Farm from April to October of 1841, at first enjoying the physical labor, the fellowship, and the beauty of the environment and writing to Sophia about their future home there. But his experience and his hope soon soured. Hawthorne needed privacy, and he found that farmwork deadened his literary imagination rather than stimulated it. As his narrator, Miles Coverdale, puts it in *The Blithedale Romance,* the novel based on his

Brook Farm experience that Hawthorne wrote eleven years later: "The clods of earth, which we so constantly belabored and turned over and over, were never etherealized into thought. Our thoughts, on the contrary, were fast becoming cloddish." Worse, communal living inhibited that "farther withdrawal towards the inner circle of self-communion" without which, Coverdale, who can be understood as Hawthorne, reports, "I lost the better part of my individuality."

Still without a workable life plan, Hawthorne married Sophia Peabody on July 9, 1842. The couple had been offered the inexpensive rental of a historic parsonage, the Old Manse, owned by the Emerson family in Concord. They lived there for three years, during which time Hawthorne wrote and published the nineteen new stories and sketches that he collected, along with some older ones, in the volume *Mosses from an Old Manse* (1846). At the Old Manse as well, the Hawthornes' first child, Una—named after the allegorical heroine of Spenser's *The Faerie Queene*—was born in 1844. Despite his rising literary status, Hawthorne could not support his family on his earnings, and when the Emersons required the return of the Old Manse, poverty forced Sophia and Una to live for a few months with the Peabodys (who had moved to Boston) while Hawthorne returned to his mother's house in Salem. In April 1846, two months before the birth of his son, Julian, friends in the Democratic Party helped Hawthorne obtain another government appointment: surveyor of the Salem Custom House. The family was reunited in Salem, and for the next three years Hawthorne became a full-time civil servant. In his mid-forties, Hawthorne was a bureaucrat whose former literary career, as he saw it, had not produced a single work of substance—that is, a novel. But, in the words of the dramatic sentence on which both Hawthorne's essay "The Custom-House" and the future of American literature turned, "the past was not dead."

## THE SCARLET LETTER

Many dimensions of the actual contribute to a great work of the imagination. Hawthorne's desire to define his connection to his Puritan ancestors was one circumstance of his creation of *The Scarlet Letter,* but other, more immediate circumstances also shaped the book he wrote. The election of the Whig candidate for president, Zachary Taylor, in 1848 led to Hawthorne's firing from the Salem Custom House the following June. Hawthorne's allies mounted a public protest, claiming that this estimable American writer had always held himself above partisan politics and should not be treated by the new administration like some party hack. The Whigs responded publicly that Hawthorne was a Democratic party hack who during his tenure in office had overlooked, if not benefited personally by, political corruption in the collection of customs. Hawthorne turned from this controversy immediately to the writing of *The Scarlet Letter,* galvanized to prove that the real Nathaniel Hawthorne was and would be an artist, not a sacked government bureaucrat. Yet the novel itself is linked to Hawthorne's political experience by one of its chief concerns: the trauma to a sensitive, private person of being publicly branded an evildoer.

This link between Hester Prynne and her author is one source of her empathetic portrayal. But a larger contemporary political context also informed Hawthorne's imagination of Hester and checked his affection toward her. In 1848, a wave of revolutionary activity shook many established European governments and toppled a few. Americans followed these events closely and took sides, some celebrating the spirit of democracy they discerned in these revolts, others lamenting the violence and the potential for anarchy intrinsic to acts of revolution. Hawthorne's use of the image of the guillotine to describe his own political "axing" and his choice of the word "scaffold" rather than "stocks" to designate the Puritan place of punishment suggest his consciousness of European revolutionary violence as he wrote *The Scarlet Letter*. And, as he had shown in "My Kinsman, Major Molineux" and other tales, Hawthorne suspected and feared even the most justifiable revolutionary fervor.

Accordingly, in the chapter entitled "Another View of Hester," Hester Prynne is reimagined as a woman whose social ostracism has produced not a repentant—or even an unrepentant—American sinner but a European-style revolutionary, dangerously ready to reject "the whole system of ancient prejudice, wherewith was linked much of ancient principle." We can learn much about the stylistic and thematic design of *The Scarlet Letter* simply by taking note of the rhythmic and conceptual balancing of "ancient prejudice" and "ancient principle" in this phrase. Hawthorne repeatedly builds such tensions into the syntax, characters, and events of the novel and allows no revelation or resolution to dissipate them entirely. Hester, in this case, exposes the deep flaws and prejudices of the ancien régime, but, Hawthorne asks, might not this same flawed order sustain necessary social structures and principles that egalitarian, individualist, and, especially, feminist passions would swamp?

As he wrote *The Scarlet Letter,* Hawthorne was both invigorated and disturbed by the sense that conventional structures of support were collapsing all around him. Psychologically nearer to home than either the European revolutions or the loss of his government job and regular paycheck was the death of his mother, one month after he was fired from the custom house and one month before he began his novel. Hawthorne's journal testifies to the event's powerful emotional effect on him and suggests that it reactivated the repressed and still unresolved insecurities and psychosexual conflicts of his adolescence. In one journal entry, Hawthorne describes himself standing at his mother's deathbed, seeing through the window his five-year-old daughter, Una, frolicking in the yard below and feeling the three of them to be joined and frozen in a tableau representing "the whole of human existence at once." Una was a precocious, high-spirited, and mercurial child in whom Hawthorne perceived (with mingled wonder and fear) the reflection of his own unruly, fanciful, and "feminine" qualities. She was also the model for *The Scarlet Letter*'s Pearl, who is characterized in terms drawn from Hawthorne's journal observations of his daughter. Indeed, the intense, complex, guilty, and often secret family drama played out by all the principal characters in *The Scarlet Letter* may be seen as Hawthorne's brilliant imaginative adaptation and deflection of his own psychic familial entanglements—entanglements that his mother's recent death made current and vivid for him as he wrote.

In this context, the tableau of Hawthorne, his mother, and Una is suggestively re-created by Dimmesdale, Hester, and Pearl in the novel's central scaffold scene. Literally, of course, Dimmesdale's never-named sin is adultery, not incest, but many aspects of his crime and character are consistent with that of an oedipal figure. His forbidden sex act, for instance, is not dramatically enacted but predates the novel's time frame, is figured mainly as guilty consciousness, and strikes many readers as practically unimaginable. And in relation both to Hester and to Chillingworth, Hester's original husband and a vengeful father figure who appears out of nowhere to torture the transgressing young man with whom he shares a home and whom he pretends to nurture, Dimmesdale often seems more a son than a lover or peer.

Thus, national and international politics, psychic and genealogical family relations, and vocational circumstances, among other influences, all went into the making of *The Scarlet Letter*. In this respect, the novel bears out Hawthorne's introductory description of how romance works: "Whatever, in a word, has been used or played with, during the day, is now invested with a quality of strangeness and remoteness, though still almost as vividly present as by daylight." But *The Scarlet Letter* is only a neutral territory in the sense that its varied and powerful ideological and emotional charges, like its characters, are arrayed against one another to produce a tense equilibrium that none of Hawthorne's later three novels so effectively achieved. This tension is sustained and extended by the narrative's syntactic patterns. Sentences that propose to summarize or clarify events and their meanings are models of equivocation. Hester's public deportment bespeaks either humility or pride; Dimmesdale's veiled confessions are both heartfelt and hypocritical; Chillingworth's terrible vengeance is performed through deeds of mercy. Or Hawthorne employs the device of multiple choice, enumerating for his readers a range of possible interpretations of the same phenomenon but authorizing none.

Structurally, *The Scarlet Letter* is similarly poised. An introduction and a conclusion frame twenty-three chapters, of which the first, the twelfth (or middle chapter), and the last take place on the scaffold in Puritan Boston's public square. The scaffold literally and figuratively stands for public revelation, but in each of the three scaffold scenes more is concealed than revealed, more questions are begged than answered. In the first, Hester's letter and infant reveal her adultery, but she conceals her relationship with Dimmesdale and her recognition of Chillingworth from the authorities, who would know all. In the middle scene, Dimmesdale stands with Hester and Pearl, but this is a mock confession, more masochistic theatrics than moral and familial acknowledgment on Dimmesdale's part, and since it is midnight, it is witnessed by no one but Chillingworth.

In the last scene, beneath the chapter title "The Revelation of the Scarlet Letter," little is revealed. It is not clear whether Dimmesdale's ultimate upstaging of Hester is an act of conscience and self-sacrifice or the height of egotistical self-absorption ("behold me here, the one sinner of the world!"), whether the minister has taken the road to redemption or simply the easy way out. And neither his verbal confession nor the exposure of the mark on his chest is unambiguously interpreted—or even acknowledged—by all. Accordingly, the moral that Hawthorne's narrator offers at the conclusion of these events is admitted in advance to be only one of many possible morals. And when it is pronounced, this moral turns out to be not only inadequate or even irrelevant to the action of the novel but almost self-canceling in its articulation: "Be true! Be true! Be true! Show freely to the world, if not your worst, yet some trait whereby the worst may be inferred!"

Hawthorne reported to a friend that when he read the concluding chapters of *The Scarlet Letter* to Sophia, she found them so disturbing that she went straight to bed "with a grievous headache." Like Wakefield, in his perverse impulse to unnerve his wife, Hawthorne was delighted. He felt he had written a "hell-fired" story—every rebellious Romantic artist's dream. But Hawthorne was only in part a rebellious Romantic artist; in at least equal measure, he embraced an older, classical model of the writer as representative, not scourge, of established community values. And *The Scarlet Letter,* as we have seen, was only in part a rebellious book. Emerson could proclaim in his essay "Self-Reliance" that "whoso would be a man, must be a nonconformist" and boast, in the same famous paragraph, that "I shun father and mother and wife and brother when my genius calls me." Hawthorne neither shared this attitude politically nor could afford it emotionally or financially.

## LATER NOVELS

*The Scarlet Letter* was brought out in March of 1850 by Ticknor, Reed, and Fields, a new and aggressive firm that remained Hawthorne's publisher for the rest of his life and well after his death. The novel secured Hawthorne's literary reputation and created a market for a new printing of *Twice-Told Tales* in 1851 (the publication date is 1852), and a new volume of stories, *The Snow-Image, and Other Twice-Told Tales,* early the next year. Supplementing his income from these works by writing an occasional children's storybook, Hawthorne finally managed to live as a professional writer, despite the growth of his family by the birth of a third child, Rose, in 1851. In 1850, the family had moved to a house in the Berkshires, in western Massachusetts, where Hawthorne met Herman Melville. Melville was working on his magnum opus, *Moby-Dick* (1851), a novel whose formal complexity and manic, blasphemous energy completely alienated the readership that Melville had achieved with his earlier, more conventional narratives of adventure at sea and exotic travel. Meanwhile, Hawthorne—to whom Melville dedicated *Moby-Dick*—was trying to complete a second novel that he hoped would increase his own readership by correcting the only fault that reviewers of *The Scarlet Letter* had generally agreed upon: the book's darkness. Mid-nineteenth-century American readers of fiction, the majority of whom were women, did not mind sensation and sin but wanted some brightness along the way and some uplift at the end; unrelieved gloom sent too many to bed with headaches, which might afford an author some malicious fun but was not very good for business.

In *The House of the Seven Gables,* Hawthorne was determined to dispel some of the gloom. Indeed, the name of the character that he invented for the job means "sunlight." Phoebe Pyncheon—a simple, cheerful, and pure young girl who resembles "a prayer, offered up in the homeliest beauty of one's mother-tongue"—is modeled after Hawthorne's idealized image of his wife as redemptive domestic angel.

> Phoebe's presence made a home about her—that very sphere which the outcast, the prisoner, the po-tentate, the wretch beneath mankind, the wretch aside from it, or the wretch above it, instinctively pines after—a home! She was real! Holding her hand, you felt something; a tender something; a substance, and a warm one; and so long as you should feel its grasp, soft as it was, you might be certain that your place was good in the whole sympathetic chain of human nature. The world was no longer a delusion.

*The Scarlet Letter* presents a fallen woman and lacks healthy and safe domestic spaces or relations. Its successor invokes the presence of the virginal Phoebe to turn a very unpromising house—inhabited by embodiments or ghosts of "the outcast, the prisoner, the potentate" and the wretch beneath, beside, and above mankind—into a home.

The project of converting the seven-gabled ancestral Pyncheon house into a tender domestic haven is beset by two formidable problems. First, the structure is historically and metaphorically founded on an ancient crime. In the seventeenth century, the original Pyncheon, claiming dubious title to land that had been cultivated by a farmer named Matthew Maule, finally acquired the property on which both his mansion and the aristocratic House of Pyncheon came to be built by arranging for Maule to be executed as a witch. Thus, the house stands as, and stands for, the triumph of injustice, false social distinction, and inherited wealth, extending itself across generations. Moreover, as a consequence of the original Pyncheon sin, Pyncheon heirs have tended to suffer mysterious deaths on their property, apparent victims of Matthew Maule's deathbed curse upon them. And if the house itself has not been haunted by Maule's vengeful spirit, at moments in its history its inhabitants have been assailed and beguiled by Maule's actual descendants.

While the house of the seven gables has been the site of an ancient curse, it has become the site of modern commercialism. As the novel opens in the present day, the current proprietor—the impoverished, unworldly spinster Hepzibah Pyncheon—finds herself "reduced now, in that very house, to be the hucksteress of a cent-shop." This is the second obstacle to any effort to establish in this place a domain of harmony, virtue, and affection. For if these domestic virtues are incompatible with the legacy of the aristocratic past, they are scarcely better accommodated by the economy of the republican present. The hard-heartedness, snobbery, and guilty consciences of unrightful owners have been replaced by the insecurity, isolation, and empty materialism of competitive traders.

The plot of *The House of the Seven Gables,* like that of "My Kinsman, Major Molineux," traces the decline of age and the triumph of youth, the passage from an old order to a new one, the exchange of families and economies defined by birth for families and economies created by choice and effort. Like the early story, the novel may be read as a celebration of this "progress" only if one ignores its acid critique of the emerging democratic order and its various indications that, despite appearances, the new may not cleanly break or clearly differ from the old. Hawthorne writes, in a suggestive passage:

> In this republican country, amid the fluctuating waves of our social life, somebody is always at the drowning-point. The tragedy is enacted with as continual a repetition as that of a popular drama on a holiday, and, nevertheless, is felt as deeply, perhaps, as when an hereditary noble sinks below his order. More deeply; since, with us, rank is the grosser substance of wealth and a splendid establishment, and has no spiritual existence after the death of these, but dies hopelessly along with them.

Many of the symbolic motifs of *The House of the Seven Gables* may be observed here. Figures of inevitable repetition alternate with figures of unpredictable fluctuation; images of gross materiality mingle with images of sheer evanescence. But all these figures and images seem to point toward decline and death. The aristocrat "sinks" under the weight and corruption of his heritage; the republican drowns without a trace in the anonymity and fluidity of the marketplace. Only Phoebe can unburden this past and anchor this present. Or can she?

A country cousin, Phoebe Pyncheon bears the family name but not the family guilt. Her arrival brings sunlight, tidiness, and bustling energy to the old house and its exhausted occupants—Hepzibah and her helpless brother, Clifford, whose nerves have been ruined by his long false imprisonment for the murder of the wealthy former head of the Pyncheon family. Phoebe puts Hepzibah's store in order and keeps it from failing, soothes Clifford and draws him out into the air of the garden, and begins to win the affection of the tenant who occupies one remote gable of the house. A model of the modern individual, the tenant Holgrave is a restless and intelligent young man with little purpose or stake in life until Phoebe begins to ground him. But Phoebe cannot transform the man who owns and embodies the House of Pyncheon and who combines inherited with commercial wealth, and criminality with legal authority, in his formidable person. Judge Pyncheon is introduced in a chapter called "The Pyncheon of To-day." But he also seems to be the Pyncheon of yesterday and tomorrow, for we learn that he is both the incarnation of his earliest ancestor and the man whose business and political cronies have arranged to have him elected the next governor of Massachusetts.

If Phoebe's domain is to be believed in, Judge Pyncheon must be a delusion. So Hawthorne exorcises him. In the most forced of happy endings, laced with tones of frustration and despair, the Judge sits down in his ancestral chair and dies there of apoplexy. Holgrave discovers the corpse a day later and leaves it sitting in the next room while he confesses to Phoebe that he loves and needs her and that his real name is Maule. The young lovers (still ignoring the corpse) exchange vows. "They were conscious of nothing sad nor old," Hawthorne writes. "They transfigured the earth, and made it Eden again, and themselves the two first dwellers in it." But if Phoebe Pyncheon Maule and her spouse are the new Eve and Adam, Judge Pyncheon remains the unseen Ruler of their Universe, for it is the late judge's inherited fortune that furnishes their domestic paradise and his "elegant country-seat" that houses it.

*The Blithedale Romance,* published a year after *The House of the Seven Gables,* also concerns an attempt to transfigure the earth and make it Eden again. But while the ending of its predecessor pretends that transfiguration is a proposition about to be realized, the beginning of *The Blithedale Romance* admits it to be a dream already abandoned. Miles Coverdale, the only first-person narrator of a Hawthorne novel, recalls his brief participation in a failed utopian community like Brook Farm in a tone of mingled nostalgia and scorn—a tone epitomized in his fanciful depiction of the most suitable setting for the telling of this tale: "Around such chill mockery of a fire some few of us might sit on the withered leaves, spreading out each a palm towards the imaginary warmth, and talk over our exploded scheme for beginning the life of Paradise anew."

Coverdale is a brilliant example of a figure rare in literature before the twentieth century—the self-reflective first-person narrator who interrogates the makeup of his own consciousness and the grounds or groundlessness of his perceptions as he presents what he thinks and sees. In this character Hawthorne represents and diagnoses his own, with painful honesty, and through the story that Coverdale tells, Hawthorne plays intricate variations on some of his leading themes: the interpersonal and psychological bonds of the past; the difficulty of distinguishing altruism from egotism and communion with others from manipulation of them; and the troubling interconnectedness of sexual, literary, criminal, and spiritual energies, which all share the impulse to transgress and reform the world as it exists. Such interconnected-

ness is implied by the multiple associations of the word "romance" in the novel's title. The romance is, first, the actual Blithedale experiment in social and spiritual reform, the "exploded scheme for beginning the life of Paradise anew." Second, it is the imaginative representation of that experiment, the literary work itself. Finally, both the Blithedale romance and *The Blithedale Romance* are bound up with "romance" in the sense of sexual affection and intrigue. Coverdale, like Hawthorne, is at once enthralled by the transformative possibilities of all these species of romance and distrustful of them.

The Blithedale reformers propose to create a new volitional kind of familial and social structure in which individuality is enhanced and bolstered by group support while competitiveness gives way to cooperation. Instead, what emerges—at least in Miles Coverdale's view—is the paradoxical deepening of personal isolation in an environment of smothering interdependency. Each of the main characters carries unrevealed secrets and old, private purposes into the new collective space. Beneath a veil of sympathy and commonality, the characters seek to mold others to their wills, and what disturbs Coverdale more than this imperialism itself is to see how easily molded, how readily re-formed, human beings are. The veil is an important motif in *The Blithedale Romance,* an image of the inviting yet forbidding barrier between one soul and another, a sheer fabric that partly conceals and partly exposes the person behind it. The master of the veil is the novel's chief villain, Professor Westervelt, a mesmerist whose traveling exhibitions display his psychic power over his subject and medium, the Veiled Lady. In horror, Coverdale reports: "Human character was but soft wax in his hands; and guilt, or virtue, only the forms into which he should see fit to mould it." But Westervelt cannot be escaped or overcome in this novel about reform because, as the quoted description implies, his profane sport with human clay is precisely the same as the novelist's and the reformer's.

Professor Westervelt (whose name seems to encompass the western world) exhibits what Hawthorne's stories often teach: the instability of human identity and the fragility of the individual self's autonomy and self-knowledge. Ultimately, however, Hawthorne cannot accept this lesson, whether it proceeds from mesmerism, reform, or his own art. In particular, he cannot accept his insight that traditional male and female sexual identities and relations may be arbitrary and unstable social forms. In *The Blithedale Romance,* as he did in *The Scarlet Letter* and in his last novel, *The Marble Faun; or, The Romance of Monte Beni* (1860), Hawthorne creates a freethinking, powerfully attractive, sexually experienced woman who resists the normative posture of female submissiveness, who drives the plot, and who challenges figures of masculine authority. In each case, Hawthorne delights in his heroine's vitality and rebellion, confirms her critique of patriarchy, and then punishes her for it. Here, perhaps as a function of the first-person narration, the woman's seductiveness and critical stance are most overt, and her punishment is most brutal. Zenobia, named after an Amazon queen and partly modeled on Margaret Fuller, is a noted writer and speaker on the rights of women whose vision of gender equality is integral to the Blithedale reforms and whose magnetism draws all three of the principal male characters to her. But by the end she has been abandoned by all three in favor of her passive, infantile half-sister; has been made to adore the self-centered, chauvinistic Hollingsworth, renounce her feminism in abjection to him, and commit suicide when he rejects her anyway; and, for good measure, has been fished by a hooked dredging pole through the breast from the bottom of the pond into which she's thrown herself. Coverdale's, and Hawthorne's, inadmissible psychic affinity with Ze-

nobia is marked only by the frenzy of her repudiation and by the self-lacerating tone of the novel's ending.

## FINAL YEARS

In 1852, the Hawthornes moved into a house in Concord called the Wayside. Ironically, given Hawthorne's lifelong personal and literary struggle to create for himself a habitable home in the world, the name of his last American residence connoted impermanence, motion. Hawthorne was by then an established literary eminence, but his financial position was hardly secure. An opportunity to secure it arose when his college friend Franklin Pierce, a prominent politician, became the Democratic presidential nominee and commissioned Hawthorne to write a biography for use in the campaign. In *Life of Franklin Pierce* (1852), Hawthorne articulated Pierce's accommodationist position (which accorded with his own fear of radical reform) that African slavery in the southern and southwestern states was to be tolerated in the interest of preserving the Union. The original sin of slavery that divided America would be eradicated, apparently, much as the embodiment of ancestral crime had been in *The House of the Seven Gables.* For slavery, like Judge Pyncheon, was "one of those evils which Divine Providence does not leave to be remedied by human contrivances, but which, in its own good time, by some means impossible to be anticipated, but of the simplest and easiest operation, when all its uses shall have been fulfilled, it causes to vanish like a dream." When Pierce was elected, Hawthorne received the plum diplomatic post of U.S. consul at Liverpool, and in the summer of 1853 he and his family sailed to the country that his last published book, a collection of essays on England, affectionately designated *Our Old Home: A Series of English Sketches* (1863).

The Hawthornes lived in England for four years, and when Pierce was not reelected, they embarked on a European tour before their return to the United States, settling for stays of some months amid the monuments of Renaissance art in Rome and Florence. In 1858, when he began to write *The Marble Faun* in Italy, Hawthorne was once again experiencing one of the recurrent crises of identity, value, and confidence that had plagued and inspired him since childhood. Five years absent from a changed United States that was ominously drifting toward civil war, and no longer an official man of affairs, Hawthorne also felt alienated from the imaginative pole of his identity, having written no fiction since 1852. Europe, meanwhile, bombarded him in his middle age with difference, otherness—not only different sights, sounds, and customs, but people (Catholics, Jews, the urban poor) whose lives suggested different orders of experience and different understandings of the workings of history and culture. Characteristically, Hawthorne's attraction to environments, ideas, and cultural practices that challenged his familiar norms was attended by guilt, resistance, and apprehension of danger. Catholic, art-laden Italy was such an environment. In fact, it seemed to Hawthorne the worldly incarnation of the territory of romance that before his visit had existed for him only in imagination: a fascinating, multilayered, yet vaguely sinister and corrupting, realm in which one wandered at the risk of losing one's way home. And, hauntingly, this psychological danger was physiologically realized for the Hawthorne family, when fourteen-year-old Una contracted a near-fatal case of malaria—or "Roman fever," as it was colloquially termed—while sketching at night in the Roman Coliseum.

Hawthorne built *The Marble Faun* out of this riot of sensory and intellectual stimuli, psychological and vocational insecurities, and paternal guilt and fear. Fearing for Una's life, Hawthorne experienced strong feelings of guilt during the months of her delirium while he was writing: guilt for having brought her to this treacherous "home of art" and for having emotionally withdrawn from her when she reached adolescence, just as he had forsaken the rebellious, imaginative side of himself that he had always seen in his oldest daughter. *The Marble Faun* is both an attempt to recover this creative vitality and a record of Hawthorne's final self-protective repudiation of its demands. "Roman fever" functions for Hawthorne as a metaphor for the allure of the foreign, an attraction that is paradoxically enlivening yet deadly. And "the foreign," as represented in this novel, encompasses Europe, Catholicism, female sexuality, moral relativism, and, finally, art itself.

The plot of *The Marble Faun* concerns the European apprenticeship of two young American artists, Hilda and Kenyon, who in many ways resemble Phoebe and Holgrave in *The House of the Seven Gables*. In Rome, these two chaste Americans are befriended and partially initiated into the world of art, history, and sexual and moral complexity by two fascinating, mixed-race Europeans with family secrets: Miriam, a dynamic and troubled Jewish painter; and Donatello, a man-child who seems to marry human and animal traits and who strikingly resembles an ancient marble statue of a faun. Eventually, the Americans discover that their artistic vocation and their European friends can be embraced only if they are prepared to abandon their rigid ideal of religious, aesthetic, and moral absolutism. Since they are not prepared to do so, they regretfully renounce Miriam and Donatello and everything they stand for and prepare to sail home, comforted by the bond of affection that has formed between them in their mutual rejection of the adulterated realm of the "Imaginary." Or is what they reject the "Actual"?

In the preface to *The Marble Faun*, Hawthorne characterized his "dear native land" as "a country where there is no shadow, no antiquity, no mystery, no picturesque and gloomy wrong, nor anything but a commonplace prosperity, in broad and simple daylight." Written at a moment when the shadow of slavery's "gloomy wrong" had eclipsed every aspect of national life, and published one year before the outbreak of the Civil War, these remarks testify to the desperation for stability and simplicity that Hawthorne shared in 1859 with his last American characters, Hilda and Kenyon. In 1860, the Hawthornes returned not to a nation of sunny, guiltless, and common prosperity but, as Hawthorne put it in an essay, "Chiefly about War Matters. By a Peaceable Man," that he published in the *Atlantic Monthly* two years later, to "a social system thoroughly disturbed." Neither in his "dear native land" nor in the realm of his imagination could Hawthorne find a home. One symptom of this double alienation was that between 1860 and 1864, Hawthorne tried and failed to write three novels, all versions of a story in which an American attempts to regain a lost ancestral estate in England. Another symptom was that Hawthorne's physical and emotional energy unaccountably began to wane. His hair turned white suddenly, and, without seeming to suffer from any recognizable disease, he became lethargic and frail. On May 19, 1864, while on a trip to New Hampshire with Franklin Pierce, Hawthorne died in his sleep. He was buried four days later at Sleepy Hollow cemetery in Concord.

It is tempting to read the manner of Hawthorne's death as an allegory of the interpenetration of the actual and the imaginary that produced his work and troubled his life. Hawthorne's work has lived beyond his time largely because the writing communicates—in spite of and through its denials, and those of its author—how mysterious and multiform, and how inextricable, these two categories are, whether in the making of a novel, a person, a marriage, a history, or a country. Illusion, even self-deception, Hawthorne's fiction suggests, is a part of all these realities. As a man and as a writer, Hawthorne harbored and exposed many of the abiding illusions and self-deceptions of his culture and of ours. In doing both, he may be said to have fulfilled the ambiguous commandment of *The Scarlet Letter* and to have been true.

# Selected Bibliography

## WORKS OF NATHANIEL HAWTHORNE

*Fanshawe.* Boston: Marsh and Capen, 1828.

*Twice-Told Tales.* Boston: American Stationers, 1837. Expanded two-volume edition, Boston: James Monroe, 1852. (Includes "Wakefield.")

*Grandfather's Chair: A History for Youth.* Boston: E. P. Peabody; New York: Wiley & Putnam, 1841.

*Biographical Stories for Children.* Boston: Tappan & Dennet, 1842.

*Mosses from an Old Manse.* New York: Wiley & Putnam, 1846. Revised, Boston: Ticknor & Fields, 1854. (Includes "The Birth-Mark," "The Celestial Rail-road," "Earth's Holocaust," "Passages from a Relinquished Work," "Roger Malvin's Burial," and "Young Goodman Brown.")

*The Scarlet Letter: A Romance.* Boston: Ticknor, Reed & Fields, 1850.

*The House of the Seven Gables.* Boston: Ticknor, Reed & Fields, 1851.

*A Wonder-Book for Girls and Boys.* Boston: Ticknor, Reed & Fields, 1851.

*The Snow-Image, and Other Twice-Told Tales.* Boston: Ticknor, Reed & Fields, 1852. (Includes "My Kinsman, Major Molineux" and "The Devil in Manuscript.")

*The Blithedale Romance.* Boston: Ticknor, Reed & Fields, 1852.

*Life of Franklin Pierce.* Boston: Ticknor, Reed & Fields, 1852.

*Tanglewood Tales for Girls and Boys.* Boston: Ticknor, Reed & Fields, 1853.

*The Marble Faun; or, The Romance of Monte Beni.* Boston: Ticknor & Fields, 1860.

*Our Old Home: A Series of English Sketches.* Boston: Ticknor & Fields, 1863.

Twenty-three volumes of *The Centenary Edition of the Works of Nathaniel Hawthorne,* edited by William Charvat, Roy Harvey Pearce, Claude M. Simpson, and Thomas Woodson (Columbus: Ohio State University Press, 1962–) have appeared to date. These volumes contain all the tales, novels, sketches, and children's writings; drafts of the late unfinished novels; the American, French, and Italian notebooks; the letters; and miscellaneous poetry and prose. The imminent publication of Hawthorne's English notebooks will complete the edition.

## BIBLIOGRAPHIES

Blair, Walter. "Hawthorne." In *Eight American Authors: A Review of Research and Criticism.* Edited by Floyd Stovall. New York: Norton, 1963. Pp. 100–152.

Boswell, Jeanetta. *Nathaniel Hawthorne and the Critics: A Checklist of Criticism, 1900–1978.* Metuchen, N.J.: Scarecrow, 1982.

Clark, C. E. Frazer. *Nathaniel Hawthorne: A Descriptive Bibliography.* Pittsburgh: University of Pittsburgh Press, 1978.

Gale, Robert L. *A Nathaniel Hawthorne Encyclopedia.* New York: Greenwood, 1991.

Newman, L. B. V. *A Reader's Guide to the Short Stories of Nathaniel Hawthorne.* Boston: G. K. Hall, 1979.

## CRITICAL AND BIOGRAPHICAL STUDIES

Anderson, Quentin. "Hawthorne's Boston." In his *The Imperial Self: An Essay in American Literary and Cultural History.* New York: Knopf, 1971.

Arvin, Newton. *Hawthorne.* Boston: Little, Brown, 1929.

Baym, Nina. *The Shape of Hawthorne's Career.* Ithaca, N.Y.: Cornell University Press, 1976.

———. "Nathaniel Hawthorne and His Mother: A Biographical Speculation." *American Literature* 54, no. 1:1–27 (March 1982).

Bell, Michael Davitt. *Hawthorne and the Historical Romance of New England.* Princeton, N.J.: Princeton University Press, 1971.

Bercovitch, Sacvan. *The Office of "The Scarlet Letter."* Baltimore: Johns Hopkins University Press, 1991.

Brodhead, Richard. *The School of Hawthorne.* New York: Oxford University Press, 1986.

Buell, Lawrence. *New England Literary Culture: From Revolution through Renaissance.* Cambridge: Cambridge University Press, 1986.

Carton, Evan. *The Rhetoric of American Romance: Dialectic and Identity in Emerson, Dickinson, Poe, and Hawthorne.* Baltimore: Johns Hopkins University Press, 1985.

———. " 'A Daughter of the Puritans' and Her Old Master: Hawthorne, Una, and the Sexuality of Romance." In *Daughters and Fathers.* Edited by Lynda E. Boose and Betty S. Flowers. Baltimore: Johns Hopkins University Press, 1989. Pp. 208–232.

———. *"The Marble Faun": Hawthorne's Transformations.* New York: Twayne Publishers, 1992.

Cohen, B. Bernard, ed. *The Recognition of Nathaniel Hawthorne: Selected Criticism since 1828.* Ann Arbor: University of Michigan Press, 1969. (Evert Duyckinck's remarks quoted in the text are to be found in the chapter entitled "Nathaniel Hawthorne.")

Colacurcio, Michael J. "Footsteps of Ann Hutchinson: The Context of *The Scarlet Letter.*" *English Literary History* 39, no. 3:466–489 (1972).

———. *The Province of Piety: Moral History in Hawthorne's Early Tales.* Cambridge, Mass.: Harvard University Press, 1984.

Crews, Frederick. *The Sins of the Fathers: Hawthorne's Psychological Themes.* New York: Oxford University Press, 1966.

Erlich, Gloria. *Family Themes and Hawthorne's Fiction: The Tenacious Web.* New Brunswick, N.J.: Rutgers University Press, 1984.

Feidelson, Charles Jr. *Symbolism and American Literature.* Chicago: University of Chicago Press, 1953.

Gilmore, Michael T. *American Romanticism and the Marketplace.* Chicago: University of Chicago Press, 1985.

Hawthorne, Julian. *Nathaniel Hawthorne and His Wife: A Biography.* 2 vols. Boston: Houghton Mifflin, 1884 and 1885.

———. *Hawthorne and His Circle.* New York: Harper and Brothers, 1903.

Herbert, T. Walter. *Dearest Beloved: The Hawthornes and the Making of the Middle-Class Family.* Berkeley: University of California Press, 1993.

James, Henry. *Hawthorne.* London: Macmillan, 1879.

Lathrop, Rose Hawthorne. *Memories of Hawthorne.* Boston: Houghton Mifflin, 1897.

Luedtke, Luther S. *Nathaniel Hawthorne and the Romance of the Orient.* Bloomington: Indiana University Press, 1989.

Matthiesson, F. O. *American Renaissance: Art and Expression in the Age of Emerson and Whitman.* New York: Oxford University Press, 1941.

Mellow, James R. *Nathaniel Hawthorne in His Times.* Boston: Houghton Mifflin, 1980.

Melville, Herman. "Hawthorne and His Mosses." *Literary World* (August 1850). Reprinted in *The Shock of Recognition: The Development of Literature in the United States, Recorded by the Men Who Made It.* Edited by Edmund Wilson. Garden City: Doubleday, 1943. Pp. 187–204.

Newberry, Frederick. *Hawthorne's Divided Loyalties: England and America in His Works.* Ruther-ford, N.J.: Fairleigh Dickinson University Press, 1987.

Pearce, Roy Harvey, ed. *Hawthorne Centenary Essays.* Columbus: Ohio State University Press, 1964.

Reynolds, David S. *Beneath the American Renaissance: The Subversive Imagination in the Age of Emerson and Melville.* New York: Knopf, 1988.

Reynolds, Larry J. "*The Scarlet Letter* and Revolutions Abroad." In his *European Revolutions and the American Literary Renaissance.* New Haven, Conn.: Yale University Press, 1988.

Tompkins, Jane P. *Sensational Designs: The Cultural Work of American Fiction, 1790–1860.* New York: Oxford University Press, 1985.

*—EVAN CARTON*

# Ernest Hemingway
## 1899–1961

$E$RNEST HEMINGWAY RANKS as the most famous of twentieth-century American writers: like Mark Twain, Hemingway is one of those rare authors most people know about, whether they have read him or not. The difference is that Twain, with his white suit, ubiquitous cigar, and easy wit, survives in the public imagination as a basically lovable figure, while the deeply imprinted image of Hemingway as rugged and macho has been much less universally admired. For all his fame, Hemingway has been regarded less as a writer dedicated to his craft than as a man of action who happened to be afflicted with genius. When he won the Nobel Prize in 1954, *Time* magazine reported the news under *Heroes* rather than *Books* and went on to describe the author as "a globe-trotting expert on bullfights, booze, women, wars, big game hunting, deep sea fishing, and courage." Hemingway did in fact address all those subjects in his books, and he acquired his expertise through well-reported acts of participation as well as of observation: by going to all the wars of his time, hunting and fishing for great beasts, marrying four times, occasionally getting into fistfights, drinking too much, and becoming, in the end, a worldwide celebrity recognizable for his signature beard and challenging physical pursuits.

## PAPA HEMINGWAY

To a considerable degree, Hemingway was complicit in the formation of his public persona. As a young man living in Chicago and bored by pretentious drawing room talk about art and artists, he rejected out of hand the role of the epicene indoor aesthete. If he were to become a writer, it was going to be at the opposite pole from Proust and his cork-lined room. Hemingway had grown up in close touch with the outdoors, and throughout his life he pursued the sports afield and astream that he had learned from his father. In doing so, Hemingway undoubtedly took some pleasure in confounding public expectations about how a writer should look and behave. The Papa Hemingway persona actually served him as a defense, protecting the more complicated person behind that mask. But once the persona took hold, it did not let go, and as a consequence Hemingway dwindled into a celebrity, which is to say a person who is famous for being famous, whose personality has been narrowed down to a few instantly recognizable trademarks. The process had the unfortunate effect of confusing Hemingway's work with his life, or rather with those parts of his life that were lived in open view; it subordinated his literary accomplishment to his personal renown.

Many readers, or would-be readers, think they dislike Hemingway before they have read a word he's written, simply because of his personal reputation. These people include those opposed to killing, whether on the battlefield or in the Gulf Stream or in the bullring. They include many women who mistrust masculine bravado. Although Hemingway is "unquestionably an artist of the first rank," Kurt Vonnegut remarked in 1990, he is also "a little hard to read *nowadays,*" following the ascendancy of the conservation and feminist movements. Yet there is nothing new about the tendency to disparage Hemingway on the grounds of his subject matter and his style. The tendency has been there from the beginning.

Virginia Woolf, in her 1927 review of Hemingway's early work, found fault with the "self-conscious virility" of his fiction and with what struck her as his excessive use of dialogue. Wyndham Lewis, another British writer, took Woolf's reservations further in a 1934 diatribe called "The Dumb Ox," in which he accused Hemingway of creating stupid and insensitive characters and of presenting them in a kind of baby talk borrowed from Gertrude Stein. Both Woolf and Lewis acknowledged Hemingway's considerable skill, but both also assumed that in writing about such violent topics as war, boxing, and bullfighting—and doing so in the most basic English—Hemingway was adopting an unrealistically muscular pose. Woolf, in particular, objected to the title of *Men Without Women* (1927) and to the remark included in the jacket copy that "the softening feminine influence [was] almost wholly absent" from the book. When you warned a reader that this was a man's book or a woman's book, she argued, you "brought into play sympathies and antipathies" that had nothing to do with art. Actually, Hemingway's title was a misnomer, for although most of the stories in *Men Without Women* concentrate on death and brutality, four of the thirteen deal directly or indirectly with love and marriage gone wrong, including "A Canary for One," about the

breakup of Hemingway's first marriage, and the brilliant "Hills Like White Elephants," in which the narrator's sentiments manifestly lie with a woman being coerced by her male companion into having an abortion.

In fact, in several of his stories about men and women Hemingway comes down on the side of the woman. Perhaps the most notable exception is his presentation of the difficult and demanding mother of Hemingway's character Nick Adams, a boy who grows into manhood through a series of psychic shocks recounted in *In Our Time* (1925), *Men Without Women,* and *Winner Take Nothing* (1933). But to assume that Hemingway's fiction is hostile to women generally is to misread his work on the basis of preconceptions about the author and the way his fiction was construed by his earliest interpreters.

As for his supposedly narrow and limited prose style, here again Hemingway's reputation has suffered from false comparisons between the hairy-chested celebrity and the virtually anonymous writer-craftsman laboring in solitude at his desk. Something of that confusion pervades the declaration, on the cover of a 1995 edition of his collected stories, that "Hemingway wrote in short, declarative sentences and was known for his tough, terse prose." Well, yes and no. Here is Nick Adams after setting up camp during his solitary fishing trip in "Big Two-Hearted River," the long concluding story of *In Our Time:*

> Now things were done. There had been this to do. Now it was done. It had been a hard trip. He was very tired. That was done. He had made his camp. He was settled. Nothing could touch him. It was a good place to camp. He was there, in the good place. He was in his home where he had made it. Now he was hungry.

This could hardly be said more simply, or in Lewis' terms, in a more dull-witted and infantile way. All day long Nick has been occupied in reaching his destination and preparing for the next day's fishing. The meticulous process of doing one thing after another has kept him from thinking about whatever it is in his past that has been troubling him—the trauma of World War I, Hemingway told us in a 1959 essay. The radical plainness of the language of "Big Two-Hearted River" precisely suits the first-this, then-that ritual Nick has been going through to shut down "the need for thinking," just as the staccato sentences reflect the jumpiness of Nick's mind.

But neither Nick Adams nor his creator is a simpleton incapable of lyrical description. At the beginning of the story, Nick gets off the train to begin his hike, and from a bridge he watches some "very satisfactory" trout in the river below, as a kingfisher flies overhead:

> As the shadow of the kingfisher moved up the stream, a big trout shot upstream in a long angle, only his shadow marking the angle, then lost his shadow as he came through the surface of the water, caught the sun, and then, as he went back into the stream under the surface, his shadow seemed to float down the stream with the current, unresisting, to his post under the bridge where he tightened facing up into the current.

This passage and the one previously quoted could hardly be more different in sentence structure or length. In the first, there are thirteen sentences averaging just over five words per sentence. In the second, one sentence meanders for seventy-nine words. Moreover, in the camp passage, Hemingway relies on the verb "to be" almost exclusively, so that when a verb with some suggestive value appears (as in the sentence "Nothing could touch him"), it takes on extraordinary significance. The trout passage is far more sophisticated, full of active verbs—"moved," "shot," "marking," "lost," "caught," "float," "tightened"—that dramatize the upstream progress of the trout. But both passages employ common adjectives and both are full of repetition: the unashamed reiteration of such nouns as "stream" and "shadow" in the second passage is particularly striking. And the verb "tightened"

is powerfully echoed in the brief paragraph that follows that passage:

> Nick's heart tightened as the trout moved. He felt all the old feeling.

Watching the trout evokes real happiness in Nick. He shares a certain kinship with the fish: to keep his mind straight, he too must hold against the current.

When critics write about a monolithic Hemingway style, they usually have his early fiction in mind—the first three books of stories and the novels *The Sun Also Rises* (1926) and *A Farewell to Arms* (1929). Yet even within "Big Two-Hearted River," written during his most experimental period (the Paris years from 1921 through 1924), Hemingway hardly wrote in one discrete fashion. What he wanted to convey dictated the way he wrote: style and content had to work together. Then, his prose changed as he grew older. Sentences in *A Moveable Feast,* written in the late 1950s and published posthumously in 1964, average twice as long as those in "Big Two-Hearted River," and many more of them are complex in form. What remained constant throughout his career was a predilection for everyday language. In both "Big Two-Hearted River" and *A Moveable Feast,* nearly three out of four nouns are monosyllabic.

Hemingway's limited diction represented a rebellion against the high-minded but essentially empty rhetoric he had been brought up on. His reaction was very much like that of other modernist writers such as T. S. Eliot, advocate of "the objective correlative" (Eliot believed that emotion could be expressed in art only by letting "a set of objects, a situation, a chain of events" stand for the unnamed emotion), and Ezra Pound, who deprecated emotional "slither" and advised one to avoid all abstractions. In a famous passage in *A Farewell to Arms,* the protagonist, Frederic Henry, reflects on the grandiloquence of patriotic speech:

I was always embarrassed by the words sacred, glorious, and sacrifice and the expression in vain. We had heard them, sometimes standing in the rain almost out of earshot, so that only the shouted words came through, and had read them, on proclamations that were slapped up by billposters over other proclamations, now for a long time, and I had seen nothing sacred, and the things that were glorious had no glory and the sacrifices were like the stockyards at Chicago if nothing was done with the meat except to bury it. There were many words that you could not stand to hear. . . . Abstract words such as glory, honor, courage, or hallow were obscene beside the concrete names of villages, the numbers of roads, the names of rivers, the numbers of regiments and the dates.

Hemingway's Frederic Henry repudiates chauvinistic catchphrases as false to experience: only words of concrete specification will serve.

### THE MAKING OF A WRITER

Lieutenant Henry comes by his disillusionment naturally enough, for like his creator, he is badly wounded in World War I. Hemingway went to Italy as a Red Cross ambulance driver in the summer of 1918, and a few weeks later, in order to get closer to the front, volunteered to serve in a canteen at Fossalta on the Piave River. He was passing out cigarettes and chocolates to the troops in a forward trench when, shortly after midnight on July 8, an Austrian Minenwerfer canister exploded, lodging 237 metal fragments in his feet and legs, and a heavy machine-gun bullet ripped through his right knee. The effects of the wounding were traumatic to the young Hemingway, who was two weeks shy of his nineteenth birthday. "I died then," he was later to write, and for a long time he found it difficult to sleep without a light against the darkness. He was to revisit the site at least once himself, in 1923, and oftener, the memory of it, in his fiction. Colonel Richard Cantwell, in *Across the River and into the Trees* (1950), defecates on the spot where he was wounded.

In 1966, in what became an extremely influential critical interpretation, Philip Young argued that Hemingway's near fatal injury on the Italian front was a traumatic event that lay at the source of most of Hemingway's writing. According to this psychoanalytical "wound theory," Hemingway's frequent fictional accounts of confrontation with death and danger were manifestations of a "repetition compulsion" to confront and eventually master the trauma he went through at Fossalta. The same compulsion, Young believed, accounted for Hemingway's repeatedly testing his courage by climbing into bullrings, hunting wild game, and facing enemy fire during subsequent wars. He put himself at risk and paid the consequences, suffering an astounding series of blows to the head and limbs.

The wound theory provided a persuasive way of reading Hemingway, but like all single-cause theories it oversimplified the case and over time has proved too limited to encompass his wide-ranging body of work. Drawing lines of cause and effect between a writer's life and his art is an inherently risky proposition, yet even if that critical privilege be granted, it would be more accurate to see Hemingway the writer as formed through a *series* of injuries inflicted before and after, as well as during, the night of July 8, 1918. To recuperate from that wound, for example, the young Hemingway was sent to a Red Cross hospital in Milan. There he fell in love with a Red Cross nurse named Agnes von Kurowsky, seven years his senior. When he came back to the United States early in 1919, it was understood that she would follow and they would marry. Instead, she became romantically entangled with an Italian officer and broke off the relationship with a "Dear Ernest" letter to the effect that she expected much of him in the future but that really he was just "a kid," too young for her. This jilting, one of the strongest emotional blows of his life, plunged Hemingway into the depths of depression. Two years later he married Hadley Richardson, who was—probably not accidentally—slightly older than Agnes. It would be four years, however, before he could work off the pain in "A Very Short Story," which appeared in *In Our Times,* where Agnes is portrayed as the faithless Luz. The rejection had its long-term impact, too, as shown in Hemingway's practice of breaking off friendships—sometimes brutally—before he could be hurt, and in his serial marriages: invariably he had a new wife in the wings as the final act in an existing union played out.

Unquestionably the most important woman in Ernest Hemingway's life was his mother, Grace Hall Hemingway. The parents of almost all major male American writers run to a strikingly consistent pattern: a dominant mother and a relatively weak (or absent or dead) father, and this was true of Hemingway's parents as well. Grace Hall had begun a career as an opera singer before coming home to Oak Park, Illinois, to marry Clarence Edmonds Hemingway, a young general practitioner. Ernest Miller Hemingway, the second of their six children, was born July 21, 1899, about eighteen months after the arrival of his older sister Marcelline. Like most people in Oak Park—a suburb of Chicago at the borders of which the saloons stopped and the churches began—the Hemingways were pious Christians. They assembled for family prayers daily after breakfast and on Sundays attended the First Congregational Church. During the summers they traveled to Windemere, their cabin at Walloon Lake in northern Michigan, where Dr. Hemingway instructed his children in nature lore and taught them to fish and hunt. The marriage seemed wholesome enough, but there was trouble beneath the facade. A strong person sure of herself and her opinions, Grace Hemingway was unusual among women of her time in that she took no interest in the domestic arts. Instead of cooking and cleaning, she devoted much of her time to giving music lessons, which supplemented the family income and paid for household help. She was also used to getting her own way. In the spring of 1919 she undertook to build a cottage of her own up in Michigan at some distance from Windemere, where she could rest and be by herself.

Clarence opposed this project and went so far as to write to the builder announcing that he would not be responsible for any debts incurred during the construction, but to no effect. Grace had made up her mind and the cottage was built.

A more important problem, carefully concealed from public view, was Dr. Hemingway's mental illness. Both in 1903 and 1908 he took trips away from home to ameliorate his "nervous condition." "Just make a business of eating and sleeping and forgetting," Grace advised him on the second occasion—advice much like that Nick Adams attempts to follow on his solitary fishing trip. In 1909 Dr. Hemingway wrote his wife a letter itemizing his several life insurance policies and advising her in the event of his passing not to tell all she knew "should there be any doubt at all as to the cause of death." The letter apparently signaled a contemplated suicide: nineteen years later, in December 1928, he killed himself with a bullet to his right temple. The family attributed the suicide to financial reversals and to the onset of diabetes and angina, with no mention of depression. Ernest himself did not acknowledge Clarence Hemingway's mental problems as a contributing cause. He blamed his father's death on his mother: as he saw it, she had emasculated his father and driven him to suicide. After his father's death Ernest provided some financial support to his mother, but he rarely spoke of her thereafter except in the most derogatory terms. Late in life he insisted that he hated her.

From boyhood on, there had been a measure of discord between the forceful mother and the headstrong son. The disaffection reached its worst stage during the summer of 1920, shortly after Ernest's twenty-first birthday. It had been eighteen months since he had come back from Italy, yet he had not taken a full-time job, and both his parents were worried about his future. He and a friend were staying at Walloon Lake, and Grace believed they were not pulling their weight in terms of performing the necessary chores around the place. Worse yet, Ernest was openly rebellious when Grace tried to tell him what to do. Matters boiled over when

Ernest and his friend took his younger sisters Ursula and Sunny, along with two thirteen-year-old girlfriends of theirs, on a clandestine postmidnight picnic. The escapade might have gone undiscovered had not the mother of one of the thirteen-year-olds knocked on the door of the Hemingway cabin at three in the morning, demanding to know the whereabouts of her daughter.

The next day Grace banished her son from Windemere with a scathing letter. In sending Ernest away, she had the full support of her husband, who had been at the lake and observed his son's disobedient ways. Even before the picnic episode Dr. Hemingway had twice written Ernest advising him to leave the cabin, to find a job that paid decent wages, and to stay away until invited back. Nonetheless Ernest focused his resentment on his mother, who in her letter of dismissal suggested that emotional and economic debts were interchangeable. Her children were born, she began, "with a large and prosperous Bank Account, seemingly inexhaustible." But the persistent and unavoidable withdrawals made during childhood and adolescence made the balance of her mother-love account "perilously low." Now it was time for Ernest to repay her with gratitude and appreciation and small gestures of recognition, not with open defiance. She concluded her letter with a passage that, in effect, accused her son of intentionally immoral behavior:

> Unless you, my son Ernest, come to yourself, cease your lazy loafing, and pleasure seeking,—borrowing with no thought of returning;—Stop trying to graft a living off anybody and everybody, spending all your earnings lavishly and wastefully on luxuries for yourself. Stop trading on your handsome face, to fool gullable [sic] little girls, and neglecting your duties to God and your Saviour Jesus Christ, unless, in other words, you come into your manhood,—there is nothing before you but bankruptcy.
> *You have overdrawn.*

For Ernest Hemingway, who like his parents was brought up on the principles of the Protestant ethic, it was a message he could neither forgive nor forget.

## NICK ADAMS

An unhappy childhood was the best possible training for a writer, Hemingway once commented, and he obviously felt that he qualified as well-trained on those grounds, to which were added the adult traumas of his wartime wound, his jilting by Agnes, his mother's rejection, and his father's suicide. The character in his fiction who most closely resembles him is Nick Adams, the protagonist of fifteen stories published in his lifetime, and of still others published posthumously, all of which are collected in *The Nick Adams Stories* (1972). In the stories Nick progresses from a young boy growing up on a lake in the north country to an adolescent vagabond on the road to a soldier victimized by a terrifying wound. In the manuscript versions of the stories about Nick, Hemingway sometimes substituted his own name, or his nickname, Wemedge, for that of Nick, and the temptation is to regard the fictional character as a thinly disguised version of his creator. But Nick Adams goes through a number of experiences that Hemingway did not, and in contradiction both to Hemingway's public image and the critical stereotype of his heroes, Nick is distinctly not someone who seeks out challenges to his courage. It is true that he is, to employ another phrase often applied to Hemingway protagonists, very much a youth whom *things happen to,* but he neither invites nor welcomes the blows that life delivers. Instead he does his best to shy away from trouble.

In "Indian Camp" and "The Doctor and the Doctor's Wife"—the first two stories of *In Our Time*—Nick goes through a process of disillusionment with both of his parents, especially his father. At the beginning of "Indian Camp," Nick's father answers a late-night emergency call to the Indian settlement down at the lake, and since father and son have been camping out together, he takes Nick along. An Indian woman has been in labor for two days, while her husband—immobilized by an accident—lies confined in the bunk overhead listening to her agonized cries. Working without anesthetic or his usual instruments, Dr. Adams delivers the baby by cesarean section while keeping up a running commentary for the benefit of his son. He does not hear the woman's screams, he tells the boy, because the screams "are not important." But Nick cannot ignore them, and neither can the woman's husband. With the baby successfully delivered, Nick's father feels as "exalted and talkative as football players . . . after a game." "Ought to have a look at the proud father," he remarks expansively. "They're usually the worst sufferers in these little affairs." But when he pulls back the blanket, he discovers that the Indian has cut his throat. Nick, who has wished to be somewhere else for a long time, is standing a good distance away but has a good view of the upper bunk when Dr. Adams, lamp in one hand, tips the dead Indian's head back with the other.

The story presents Nick's father in ambivalent terms. Although skillful in performing his obstetrical duties, he betrays an unattractive egotism. Other stories demonstrate other shortcomings. In "The Doctor and the Doctor's Wife," Nick's father backs down from a fight with an Indian bully who openly provokes him, then suffers the further indignity of a lecture from his wife on controlling his anger. In "Now I Lay Me," Nick's mother burns her husband's prized collection of arrowheads while he is away hunting. When the doctor returns, he utters no word of remonstrance to her. Instead, in an attempt to restore his authority, he issues a series of commands to Nick: to fetch a rake, to take his gun and game bags into the house, to bring a newspaper on which he can lay out any arrowheads that have not broken into pieces in the fire.

The most thorough portrait of Nick's father comes in "Fathers and Sons," written after Dr.

Hemingway's suicide and printed as the concluding story of *Winner Take Nothing.* "Nicholas Adams," now a father himself, is on a driving trip with his son when the landscape brings back memories of hunting with his father. He recalls among other things his father's extraordinary eyesight and his wonderful shooting ability. But he also remembers his father's prudery where sex was concerned, summed up in the advice "that the things to do was to keep your hands off of people." And he remembers, too, the day his father aroused him into a murderous rage. Presumably to save money, Nick was required to wear a hand-me-down suit of his father's underwear. "Nick loved his father but hated the smell of him," and even though freshly washed, the underwear still carried the smell. To avoid having to wear it, Nick goes fishing and conveniently "loses" the underwear. Whipped for lying when he comes home, Nick sits inside the woodshed with his shotgun loaded looking across at his father on the screen porch and thinking, "I can blow him to hell," before the anger passes. That Nick's father later committed suicide is implied but not stated in the story. Nick thinks about his father's death, about the handsome job the undertaker did on his father's face; Nick's son wonders why he has never been taken to see his grandfather's "tomb."

Considered as a group, the stories about Nick Adams and his parents clearly come from autobiographical sources, but this is not to say that Hemingway's fiction simply recounts what happened in his life. There is no evidence, for example, that Dr. Hemingway took young Ernest to watch him perform a cesarean or that Ernest ever ran away from home, rode the rails, and got beaten up, as Nick does in "The Battler." Hemingway wrote *out of* his experience, not *about* it. At the same time, however, the similarities between the doctors Adams and Hemingway are very close indeed. Clarence Hemingway, like his fictional counterpart, had the eyes of an eagle, taught his son how to fish and shoot, held puritanical views about sex, was strict with money, was dominated by his wife, and, finally, killed himself. In that respect, the end of "Indian Camp" has more to do with Nick's introduction to death—and its disturbingly close relationship to birth—than with the character of Nick's father. In the rowboat going home, the boy seeks his father's counsel on the subject. Why did the Indian husband kill himself? "He couldn't stand things, I guess." Do many people kill themselves? "Not very many, Nick." Was dying hard? "No, I think it's pretty easy, Nick. It all depends."

### A FASCINATION WITH DEATH

From boyhood on, Hemingway was fascinated by death and particularly by suicide. Five of his seven completed novels end with the death of a male protagonist; a sixth ends with the death of the heroine. A number of his stories take a macabre approach to the subject. In "An Alpine Idyll," published in *Men Without Women,* an Austrian peasant whose wife has died props up his wife's frozen corpse and hangs a lantern from her jaw all one winter. "A Natural History of the Dead," published in *Winner Take Nothing,* reports in detail the disconcerting changes unburied corpses undergo when exposed to the weather. At bullfights, when a *torero* fails to kill a bull properly, the bull is dispatched with a short knife, or *puntillo.* Hemingway liked to see the *puntillo* do its swift work, "exactly like turning off an electric light bulb." The very first story he published in high school ends with a suicide, and so does another take he sketched out in a boyhood notebook but never wrote: "Mancelona. Rainy night. Tough looking lumberjack. Young Indian girl. Kills self and girl." His adolescent preoccupation with suicide was brought close to home during the 1920s, when he began to be victimized by attacks of depression, or "black ass," as he called it. He could imagine how a man could be so weighed down by obligations as to commit suicide, he wrote Gertrude Stein in

1923. When he broke off his marriage to Hadley in 1926 in order to marry Pauline Pfeiffer, he and Pauline agreed to stay apart for a hundred days as a test of their resolve. During this separation the black ass descended; he did not recover from what he called "the general bumping-off phase" until he and Pauline were reunited.

Yet two years later, when his father killed himself, Ernest chose to reject melancholia as a precipitating cause. "We are the generation whose fathers shot themselves," one of his manuscript fragments reads. "It is a very American thing to do and it is done, usually, when they lose their money, although their wives are almost always a contributing cause." Much as he was disposed to blame his mother, though, Hemingway could not condone what his father had done. According to Freud, the death of a father is the most important event in a man's life, and the suicide of a father a still more troubling experience. In taking his own life, Dr. Hemingway had granted his son tacit permission to do the same thing, but in his writing thereafter Ernest repeatedly distanced himself from that inheritance. He even considered writing a novel based on his father "killing himself and why," and though he never did so—too many people were still alive, he said—he had Robert Jordan in *For Whom the Bell Tolls* (1940) explicitly repudiate the example of his own father's suicide.

An American professor who fights for the Loyalists during the Spanish Civil War, Jordan lies painfully wounded at the end of the novel but refuses to take the easy way out. To steel himself against self-destruction, he thinks of his father and grandfather, who closely parallel Hemingway's own. Jordan's grandfather, like Anson T. Hemingway, was a Civil War veteran who distinguished himself under fire. His father, like Clarence Edmonds Hemingway, shot himself with a Smith and Wesson revolver because he was a coward and would not stand up to his wife's bullying. Jordan "understood his father and he forgave him everything and he pitied him but he was ashamed of him." His father's contrary example keeps Jordan from killing himself as the pain becomes excruciating and the fascist troops approach. Let them come, he thinks: "I don't want to do that business my father did."

That Nick's confrontation with death is the principal theme of "Indian Camp" would have been more obvious—perhaps too obvious—if Hemingway had not decided to discard the original beginning of that story. In the omitted fragment Nick, his father, and his Uncle George are camping out together. When the two men decide to do some night fishing, they leave Nick behind in his tent, with instructions to fire three shots if there is an emergency. The boy, who is perhaps ten years old, has only recently become aware of his own mortality. Lying alone in the dark, he is overcome by a fear of dying, and so he fires the three shots. When his father and uncle hurry back, Nick invents a yarn about a fox or a wolf nosing around the tent. Uncle George is annoyed about having his fishing interrupted by such foolishness, but Nick's father is more understanding. "I know he's an awful coward," he says of his son, "but we're all yellow at that age." At that point the original beginning breaks off, to give way to the story as we know it with its curiously abrupt opening paragraph: "At the lake shore there was another rowboat drawn up. The two Indians stood waiting."

In deciding to delete the original opening passage, Hemingway was putting into practice his famous "iceberg principle." According to that principle, the dignity of a work of fiction depends on keeping seven-eighths of its base beneath the surface. If a writer leaves something out because he does not know it, there will be a hole in the story. But "anything you know you can eliminate and it will only strengthen your iceberg." Careful reading of Hemingway manuscripts shows that he did not invariably follow this procedure, but there are several notable deletions of beginnings, in addition to the three shots episode of "Indian Camp." Two beginnings—of "Fifty Grand" and of

*The Sun Also Rises*—he lopped off at the behest of F. Scott Fitzgerald.

### THE SUN ALSO RISES

Fitzgerald and Hemingway met in Paris late in April 1925 and immediately formed a friendship that did not begin to unravel until Fitzgerald went back to the United States at the end of the following year. At the time they met, Fitzgerald was a well-established writer who had published half a dozen books, while Hemingway, three years his junior, was only beginning to make a literary reputation. Hemingway brought to the relationship his considerable talent, the experience he had accumulated during the war and several subsequent years in Europe, and his remarkable charisma. He and Hadley had come to Paris in the fall of 1921 and lived there inexpensively on the proceeds of her trust fund and the money Ernest earned as a foreign correspondent. His real vocation, though, was fiction, and he was struggling to write, first, "one true sentence" and then the early stories and, in time, a novel. In those years on the Left Bank, as Hadley recalled, men loved him, and so did women, children, and dogs. "It was something."

Hemingway arrived with an almost embarrassingly laudatory letter of introduction from Sherwood Anderson, whom he had befriended in Chicago. This introduction brought him into contact with major figures in the Parisian artistic community, and almost everyone Hemingway met became his enthusiastic supporter. Gertrude Stein advised him to get out of journalism and to write with greater discipline. "Begin over again and concentrate," she instructed him after reading one overly descriptive work. She also became a family friend, serving as godmother to the Hemingways' son Bumby. (Bumby's real name was John; Hemingway had two other sons, Patrick and Gregory, with his second wife, Pauline.) Ezra Pound sang Hemingway's praises to Ford Madox Ford, who took him on as an associate editor of the *Transatlantic Review.* Hemingway was "the finest prose stylist in the world," Pound maintained of the twenty-four-year-old writer. Hemingway's sentences struck the reader, Ford said, like pebbles fetched fresh from a brook.

Hemingway did not lack for supporters in Paris then, but he wanted to reach a wider audience than that of the little magazines and limited editions and, if possible, make a living into the bargain. Fitzgerald, a successful popular writer, was ideally situated to serve as a mentor in this regard. He encouraged Hemingway to leave the firm of Boni & Liveright, which published *In Our Time,* in order to join him at Scribners under the editorship of Maxwell Perkins. Fitzgerald wrote a laudatory review of *In Our Time* when it came out in the fall of 1925 and acted as Hemingway's agent in sending out stories to magazines. He loaned his friend money and offered sympathy and support as Hemingway's marriage to Hadley collapsed. Perhaps most important of all, Fitzgerald advised Hemingway to scrap the beginning of *The Sun Also Rises.*

The manuscript as Fitzgerald read it in the summer of 1926 started with a self-conscious and chatty introduction containing inside information on the Left Bank and its habitués. The opening paragraph read:

> This is a novel about a lady. Her name is Lady Ashley and when the story begins she is living in Paris and it is Spring. That should be a good setting for a romantic but highly moral story. As every one knows, Paris is a very romantic place. Spring in Paris is a very happy and romantic time. Autumn in Paris, although very beautiful, might give a note of sadness or melancholy that we shall try to keep out of this story.

Fitzgerald, who had more or less delivered Hemingway to Scribners on the basis of the promise of his first novel, was appalled. His written critique called attention to "about 24 sneers, superiorities,

and nose-thumbings-at-nothing" in the opening chapters, accused Hemingway of "elephantine facetiousness," and recommended that he cut twenty-five hundred words. This was harsh criticism, but Hemingway was too dedicated a craftsman not to learn from it. He not only took Fitzgerald's advice but also went one step further. Instead of reducing the original section in length, he severed the first four thousand words entirely and began with "Robert Cohn was once middleweight boxing champion of Princeton."

In so doing, Hemingway was operating on the iceberg principle, since if *The Sun Also Rises* is not strictly speaking a novel about Lady Ashley, nonetheless Brett Ashley is the central figure in the book, the one around whom all the principal male characters revolve. Brett is sexually promiscuous, but she has reasons. Like Catherine Barkley in *A Farewell to Arms* and Maria in *For Whom the Bell Tolls,* Brett is a victim of the war. Her "true love" died of dysentery at the front. The man she married on the rebound—and acquired her title from— came back from the war so disturbed that he slept with a loaded revolver and threatened to kill her. During wartime service as a volunteer she met and fell in love with Jake Barnes, but *his* war injury left him incapable of sexual intercourse. When the novel begins, she is engaged to Mike Campbell, a charming ne'er-do-well with a history of not paying his debts. She spends a weekend at San Sebastian with Robert Cohn, thinking it will be "good for him," but it has the opposite effect. Jake, Mike, and Robert are all on the scene at the fiesta in Pamplona, interacting in various stages of jealousy and anger when Brett further complicates the situation by becoming enraptured by the nineteen-year-old bullfighter Pedro Romero. She calls on Jake, who can refuse her nothing, to introduce her to Romero. At the end of the novel she summons Jake to Madrid: "AM RATHER IN TROUBLE," her telegram reads, but what Brett really wants is someone to talk to about her affair with Romero. He had wanted to marry her, she tells

ERNEST HEMINGWAY / 179

Jake, but she could not do that; at thirty-four, she will not be "one of these bitches that ruins children." Jake says nothing to encourage these revelations. When they go out to dinner afterwards, he eats an enormous dinner and drinks enough to stun an ox.

Excessive drinking is commonplace among the expatriates depicted in *The Sun Also Rises*. The world of this novel, generally immersed in alcohol as well as promiscuity, prostitution, and homosexuality, strikes many readers as one of self-indulgent immorality. Yet Hemingway insisted that it was a "very moral" book. That Brett has certain standards, for example, is reflected in her decision to send Romero away. She will not take money from him, just as she will not accept Count Mippipopolous' offer of ten thousand dollars to accompany him to Biarritz. This financial scrupulousness, along with her observation that she is "paying" for the hell she has "put chaps through," fits into a morality of compensation that runs through the novel and is explicitly articulated by Jake Barnes. Lying awake in Pamplona, he thinks that in having Brett for a friend, he "had been getting something for nothing" and that sooner or later the bill will arrive.

> I thought I had paid for everything. Not like the woman pays and pays and pays. No idea of retribution or punishment. Just exchange of values. You gave up something and got something else. Or you worked for something. You paid some way for everything that was any good. . . . Either you paid by learning about them, or by experience, or by taking chances, or by money.

This axiom resonates closely with the sermons about "clean money" and the sanctity of work that the Rev. William E. Barton—the brother of the founder of the Red Cross, Clara Barton, and the father of the adman Bruce Barton, whose best-selling book *The Man Nobody Knows* celebrated Jesus Christ as a capitalist in disguise—used to preach to the Hemingways back in Oak Park.

Despite his participation in the revels of the fiesta, Jake Barnes possesses a basically religious sensibility. "Some people have God. . . . Quite a lot," he tells Brett during their final confrontation, and though he refers to himself as "a rotten Catholic" he is repeatedly drawn to cathedrals. Once, in church, Jake prays to "make a lot of money," but the operative word is the verb. He does not pray to *have* a lot of money, or simply to have it descend upon him without effort. According to Jake's ethical system, you have to earn your way.

Jake Barnes is hardly a paragon of virtue, of course. His narration throughout is colored by his jealousy of Cohn, and he substantially demeans himself by procuring Pedro Romero for Lady Ashley. He does not insist on the universal applicability of his "exchange of values" principle. In five years time, he thinks, it might seem "just as silly as all the other fine philosophies" he has had. But, he immediately adds, perhaps that is not true. "Perhaps as you went along you did learn something." In fact, as applied to the novel, Jake's philosophy provides an accurate standard for measuring character. *The Sun Also Rises* is full of examples of the financially corrupt, among them greedy French waiters, bike riders who fix races, and even "pilgrims" from Dayton, Ohio, who use bribery to commandeer all the seats in a train dining car.

Jake is differentiated from his immediate companions, Robert Cohn and Mike Campbell, by virtue of being a working newsman; Cohn and Campbell have both been damaged by inherited wealth, or the promise of it. Cohn uses money from home to buy his way into the editorship of a literary magazine and out of romantic entanglements with women. He also persistently misunderstands people and situations. Turning a deaf ear to the world around him, he foolishly imagines himself a kind of chivalric knight defending the honor of his lady fair. He does not even get Brett's name right, persistently calling her "Lady Brett" in spite of Jake's pointed remark that "her name's

Lady Ashley." Mike Campbell, unlike Cohn, can be genuinely funny in a self-deprecatory way. He will inherit a great deal of money one day, which brings him hell's own amount of credit, but Mike is not to be trusted in financial matters. Back in England he is "an undischarged bankrupt"; he typically sponges off the other characters. Jake more closely resembles his friend Bill Gorton, who is sometimes inebriated but is a successful practicing writer. But whereas both Jake and Bill work to pay for the good things in life, neither achieves the moral stature of the bullfighter Romero, who puts himself at great risk through the meticulous performance of his craft.

Much critical attention has been paid to the distinctions between characters like Jake Barnes and Pedro Romero. According to the stereotypical view, Barnes is an example of the "Hemingway hero," who remains basically the same from book to book. Supposedly Hemingway's protagonists—including Nick Adams, Jake Barnes, Frederic Henry, Robert Jordan, and Richard Cantwell—resemble each other so much that they can be lumped into one generic category. Moreover, the so-called Hemingway hero is modeled closely upon the author himself. He is an outdoorsman but no primitive. He is extremely sensitive to the disordered world he inhabits and the pain it inflicts. He wishes he were more courageous or more principled in the conduct of his life, but he does the best he can under stress. If one accepts this construct, as many interpreters of Hemingway have done, virtually all his fiction can be read as one ongoing work.

Standing in contrast to the Hemingway hero, according to this critical theory, is the "code hero," so-called because he is able to live up to standards beyond the reach of ordinary humans. He is honorable and courageous and will fight to the bitter end against overwhelming odds. He exhibits, in short, that quality of "grace under pressure" Hemingway first apotheosized in a letter to Fitzgerald. Often the code hero is of Hispanic origins, like

Romero or the equally brave but less skillful Spanish bullfighter in "The Undefeated," published in *In Our Time,* or Santiago in *The Old Man and the Sea* (1952). Characteristically the code hero cannot overcome the forces he confronts, but by facing death or terrible danger directly and with dignity he provides an example for the rest of us of how to behave. As a way of looking at much of Hemingway's fiction, the antithesis between Hemingway hero and code hero has a certain usefulness. Yet it does not take adequate notice of Hemingway's accomplishment in creating sharply differentiated characters. His protagonists do not really resemble each other, or Hemingway himself, that closely. Frederic Henry, in *A Farewell to Arms,* provides a case in point.

## A FAREWELL TO ARMS

The title of this 1929 book, which with *The Sun Also Rises* constitutes Hemingway's finest work as a novelist, has a double meaning. It tells the story of both the war, with which Frederic makes his separate peace, and of a love affair between Frederic and Catherine Barkley, which ends tragically with Catherine's death. There are certain unmistakable parallels between Frederic Henry's experience and that of his creator. Frederic Henry, like Ernest Hemingway, is severely wounded during World War I, and he falls in love with a woman who helps nurse him back to health. As a consequence many readers have assumed that Frederic's experience more or less mirrors Hemingway's. Yet *A Farewell to Arms* is very much an invented novel, and Hemingway goes to considerable lengths to distinguish his protagonist from himself. For one thing, Frederic, who had been a student of architecture in Italy when World War I broke out, is considerably older and more knowledgeable than Hemingway was. He serves on the Austro-Italian front from 1915 to 1917, when Ernest Hemingway was still in high school. Catherine

Barkley dies in the spring of 1918, when Hemingway was working as a cub reporter at the *Kansas City Star.* Hemingway did not see any of the action he writes about in the novel, yet through books and maps and the power of his imagination, he makes it seem, as he put it in a 1935 article, "that the things he relates all really happened and that he is just reporting" them.

Hemingway further separates himself from his protagonist by making Frederic a less than admirable character, at least at the beginning of the novel. When he and Catherine meet, it is clear that she has been rendered emotionally vulnerable because of the death of her fiancé. Nonetheless Frederic takes advantage of the situation, pretending to emotions he does not feel in order to win the game of courtship. Even after they become lovers, he does not give much of himself to the relationship. "When you love," the priest in the officers' mess tells Frederic, "you wish to do things for. You wish to sacrifice for. You wish to serve." Both Catherine and Frederic fail to live up to this ideal, but for different reasons. Catherine goes too far: she lets Frederic become her "religion" and she seeks to obliterate her own personality by merging with him. (In her selfless devotion, she stands at the opposite extreme from the real-life nurse Agnes von Kurowsky.) Frederic does not go far enough, at least until near the end. He is called "boy" or "baby" by practically everyone who knows him, and it takes him a long time to grow up.

That Frederic does finally learn to love gives the novel its poignancy. As Catherine suffers through the agony of her labor, he wants to be of service; he feels grateful when the doctor lets him administer the anesthetic. He realizes at last what he stands to lose should the loving, humorous, and intelligent Catherine die. In his confusion he thrashes about for explanations: they had broken the rules by sinning against conventional morality, or it was simply bad luck, or it was "just nature giving her hell." In a desperate prayer he offers to

"do anything" if God will only please make her not die. Finally, as in "Indian Camp," there is a cesarean, but this time both baby and mother die, and there is nothing to be done about it.

Hemingway maintained that he wrote thirty-nine different versions of the ending of *A Farewell to Arms,* and scholars who have followed the trail of his manuscripts confirm that figure, or something close to it. The variant endings fall into a number of different categories. In the original ending for the *Scribner's Magazine* serial, for instance, Frederic proceeds to relate what has happened to him and to his wartime companions since the night in April 1918 when Catherine Barkley died. But all the versions are alike in leaving behind the bitter aftertaste of negation. *A Farewell to Arms* is a novel about love irredeemably lost, and it is fitting that it should close with an emphasis on the "nada" that confronts Frederic as it does the bereft old man in Hemingway's "A Clean, Well-Lighted Place," which appeared in *Winner Take Nothing.* After the hemorrhaging kills Catherine, the doctor tries to reassure Frederic that they had done the right thing to operate, but he will not respond. There is "nothing to do," "nothing to say," he does "not want to talk about it." It is not "any good" trying to say good-bye to Catherine either. Nothing is left but to walk back to the hotel in the rain.

*A Farewell to Arms* stimulated considerable controversy when it was first published, offending patriotic Italian-Americans, disturbing the queasy for its graphic and detailed portrayal of Catherine's passing, angering the fastidious for its barracks language, and earning banishment in Boston for its frank treatment of the extramarital affair between Frederic and Catherine. Despite such objections, most readers then as now were genuinely moved by the book. The beauty and power of its prose placed the thirty-year-old Hemingway in the front rank of American writers. The consensus is that Hemingway peaked early, and that after *The Sun Also Rises* and *A Farewell to Arms* he never again produced a novel that measured up to his capabilities. This emphatically does not mean that his subsequent work can or should be dismissed out of hand. Even very great writers cannot produce an unbroken string of masterpieces. Whatever they publish merits attention.

### WRITINGS OF THE 1930S

In Hemingway's case, while the decade of the 1930s did not result in any one book that stands among his best, it was still a period of substantial productivity and development. In *Death in the Afternoon* (1932) and *Green Hills of Africa* (1935), he converted his interest in bullfighting and big-game hunting into book-length studies. Many aficionados consider *Death in the Afternoon* the best book in English on the subject of bullfighting. Hemingway presents the world of *toreo* sympathetically, subordinating its brutality by treating it as a necessary part of a basically cathartic ritual. He also candidly evaluates the performance of various bullfighters, criticizing those who demean their craft by faking danger or playing to the crowd. Assuming the mantle of the expert, Hemingway goes on to comment about such apparently extraneous matters as painting, writing, and sexuality in a series of hypothetical dialogues with an inquisitive and irreverent "Old Lady."

*Green Hills of Africa* is essentially an account of Hemingway's 1935 safari to Africa. As he expressed it in the foreword, his intention was "to write an absolutely true book to see whether the shape of a country and the pattern of a month's action [could,] if truly presented, compete with a work of the imagination." The answer, for most readers, is no. The African setting is effectively evoked, but the story line—which depends on a rivalry between Hemingway and his friend Charles Thompson over who can bag the bull kudu with the largest horns—remains very thin. To his credit, though, Hemingway not only records what happened (he was bested by Thompson) but also ad-

mits to his own foolish compulsion to turn the safari into an adversarial contest. "It's impossible not to be competitive," as white hunter Philip Percival told him at the end of the actual trip. "Spoils everything, though."

In *Green Hills of Africa,* as in *Death in the Afternoon,* Hemingway introduces an otherwise inessential character—a veteran Africa hand called Kandisky—who asks questions on several far-ranging topics. Among other things, he tells Kandisky why good writers go wrong. One problem is their perceived if not real need for enough money to lead conventional lives. "They have to write to keep up their establishments, their wives, and so on, and they write slop." Another was the danger of compromising their art by conforming to the political fashions of the day. Hemingway advocated instead a thoroughgoing individualism. "A writer if he is good should be against the state no matter what it is. There will always be plenty of bad writers who will work for the state. A good writer has something that is not for sale." These principles, and the African trip, were very much on his mind as he turned to write his two wonderful long stories of 1936, "The Snows of Kilimanjaro" and "The Short Happy Life of Francis Macomber," and his 1937 novel, *To Have and Have Not.*

The marriages depicted in the stories have both been deeply compromised by the financial inequality of the partners. Margot Macomber may be regularly unfaithful to her husband Francis, but as the narrator sarcastically observes, "They had a sound basis of union. Margot was too beautiful for Macomber to divorce her and Macomber had too much money for Margot ever to leave him." The situation is transposed in the more autobiographical "Snows of Kilimanjaro," where the writer Harry is married to a rich woman and engaged in a life of idleness that "dull[s] his ability and soften[s] his will to work." As he lies dying of gangrene in Africa, Harry thinks of all the stories he has never written; he is inclined to blame his wife Helen for what he has left undone. But he knows that he himself has "destroyed his talent by not using it, by betrayals of himself and what he believed in, by drinking so much that he blunted the edge of his perceptions, by laziness, by sloth, and by snobbery, by pride and by prejudice, by hook and by crook." And it "was strange, too, wasn't it," he goes on in his continuing self-excoriation, "that when he fell in love with another woman, that woman should always have more money than the last one?" In Hemingway's own case, his second wife, Pauline Pfeiffer, was a wealthy woman, and it was through her generosity—and that of her doting Uncle Gus—that he was able to buy a house in Key West, go on safari in Africa, and otherwise indulge his enthusiasm for hunting and fishing.

Like many American writers, Hemingway felt the pull to the left as the Depression worsened. "Country is all busted," he wrote a friend in October 1932, ". . . 200,000 guys on the road like the wild kids in Russia." Something had gone wrong at the heart of the system, but Hemingway was distrustful of programmatic solutions. Through the mid-1930s Hemingway maintained his position that a writer was or at least should be "an outlyer like a gypsy" and stay independent of partisan politics. Thus the most contemptible figure in *To Have and Have Not* is the fellow-traveling novelist Richard Gordon, who corrupts his talent in order to gain cachet with the fashionable left. But Hemingway's doctrine of radical individualism also begins to give way in this poorly constructed novel. The hero is Harry Morgan, a boat captain who, in order to make a living, is forced to rent out his boat and himself for a series of illegal and dangerous activities. Morgan is Hemingway's most proletarian character, and in a politically charged section of the book, Hemingway contrasts Morgan's situation and that of the other have-not working stiffs with the bourgeois haves idling away their time on yachts off Key West. Among the haves is Henry Carpenter, an unemployed, unmarried thirty-six-year-old homosexual who com-

mits suicide when his monthly income shrinks to two hundred dollars a month on account of imprudent investments. "The money on which it was not worth while for him to live," the novelist comments, "was one hundred and seventy dollars more a month than the fisherman Albert Tracy had been supporting his family on at the time of his death three days before."

Economic injustice is an important theme in *To Have and Have Not,* and it was welcomed by the communist establishment as evidence that Hemingway, like other leading writers, was "waking up to the historic necessity of joining the fight for a better life." At best, however, the novel makes only a qualified statement of that kind. It ends, to be sure, with the mortally wounded Harry Morgan making what seems to be a plea for collective action. "One man alone ain't got. . . . No matter how a man alone ain't got no bloody fucking chance." To which the narrator adds, "It had taken him a long time to get it out and it had taken him all of his life to learn it." But this apparent embrace of collectivism is accompanied by a forceful disparagement of any governmental solutions. When Morgan is driven to rum-running to support his family, for example, "one bunch of Cuban government bastards" costs him an arm, and "another bunch of U.S. ones" takes away his only means of livelihood, his boat. The New Deal can only offer him a job at less pay than would feed his kids. Morgan is reduced to stealing his own boat back and hiring himself out on one last job for firebreathing Cuban revolutionaries who manage to get him killed. To the extent that *To Have and Have Not* carries a message, it is that big government oppresses, revolution brutalizes, and politics and art do not mix.

WRITINGS OF THE 1940S AND 1950S

Not until the outbreak of the Spanish Civil War did Hemingway find a cause he could believe in, and then—characteristically—it was what he was *against* that aroused him. He became an ardent antifascist, who campaigned against Franco's forces in almost every possible way. He contributed money for ambulances. He reported on the war as a foreign correspondent with a decided bias in favor of the Loyalists. In collaboration with director Joris Ivens, a Dutch communist, he wrote and narrated the 1938 propaganda film *The Spanish Earth,* and showed it at fund-raising events in the United States. In his 1938 play, *The Fifth Column,* the protagonist Philip Rawlings is a counterespionage agent in Madrid who gives up his comfortable way of life and his romance with the attractive Dorothy Bridges (a character modeled after Hemingway's then-companion and wife-to-be Martha Gellhorn), to devote himself totally to the cause. Rawlings remarks at the end, "Where I go now I go alone, or with others who go there for the same reason I go": to make sure that people will be able to live and work with dignity, not as slaves.

Hemingway's most overtly leftist work, *The Fifth Column* is little read or remembered. In the more important *For Whom the Bell Tolls* (1940), Hemingway's major novel about the Spanish war, the dedication of avowed communist Philip Rawlings is replaced by the more reasoned judgment of Robert Jordan. Jordan comes to Spain to fight for the Republic, but what he learns at the Hotel Gaylord about the attempt of Russian communists to appropriate the Spanish cause for their own ends tempers his idealism. In the novel Hemingway shows both sides as guilty of crimes of inhumanity; the most vicious figure of all is André Marty, commander of the International Brigades. Still, Jordan resists a descent into cynicism. Disillusioned as he may be by the machinations of the communists, he remains a devout antifascist and fights to the end under that banner. He blows up a bridge and stays behind, wounded, so that the others in his guerrilla band may escape.

Jordan is motivated in this final act of self-sacrifice less by politics than by his love for the Spanish woman Maria and fellow feeling for the members of the guerrilla band he has joined. Much of the power of the novel derives from his relationships and from the depiction of two very different female figures. Pilar is the strongest woman Hemingway ever conceived. Physically powerful and sexually earthy, wise in the ways of the world yet mystically gifted, Pilar becomes the de facto leader of the guerrillas when her husband Pablo reveals his self-centered cowardice. She also promotes and supervises the love affair between Jordan and Maria. Another of the vulnerable war-wounded women Hemingway invented in his novels, Maria has been repeatedly raped by the fascists. She is called "rabbit" for her closely cropped hair and understandably fearful manner, yet is nursed back to wholeness through the power of love.

To many critics, Maria is the embodiment of a male fantasy: a young, beautiful, compliant creature who—in a famous scene—acknowledges that the "earth moved" when she and Robert were making love. More justifiably criticized on feminist grounds is the heroine of *Across the River and into the Trees,* Hemingway's next novel. There was a ten-year gap between this novel and the previous one, much of it due to Hemingway's activities during World War II. From the Finca Vigía, his home in Cuba, he was involved initially in searching for German submarines aboard his yacht the *Pilar.* Later, attached as a correspondent to the 22d Infantry Regiment, he witnessed some of the fiercest fighting of the war in the battle of the Hurtgenwald and—contrary to his code as a journalist—formed his own group of irregulars to do reconnaissance work and participate in the liberation of Paris. During the war years, Hemingway and Martha Gellhorn went their separate ways. In spring 1944, Hemingway met and established a liaison with his fourth wife-to-be, Mary Welsh.

In any event, after so long an interim, much was expected of *Across the River and into the Trees.* The expectations were not realized. The book takes place over a span of three days in Venice, where Richard Cantwell, a fifty-year-old American colonel, eats, drinks, makes love to a nineteen-year-old Italian countess named Renata, and dies of a heart attack. Renata's name means "reborn," of course, and suggests how Hemingway intended the novel to function on a symbolic level. But whatever rebirth his protagonist may go through is imperfectly communicated. On the surface level not much happens. Cantwell holds forth to his adoring young lover on a variety of subjects, including his own long love affair with Venice, the lamentable decline of the military, and—more broadly—how to live and die. In earlier books Hemingway occasionally plays the expert, but in no other work of fiction does he let a protagonist make pronouncements on so extensive a scale. Based to some degree on Hemingway's infatuation with a real young Italian countess, the novel struck many readers as an unfortunate self-parody.

If *Across the River and into the Trees* was a disappointment, the triumph of *The Old Man and the Sea* (1952) more than made up for it. The simple and strangely moving saga of the fisherman Santiago and his battle with a giant marlin had been gestating in Hemingway's mind for fifteen years, and he produced the twenty-six-thousand-word book in but six weeks at the beginning of 1951. Published first as the entire contents of a single issue of *Life* that sold more than 5 million copies and adopted, over a period of time, as standard reading in many schools, *The Old Man and the Sea* has undoubtedly attracted a wider readership than anything else Hemingway wrote. The theme of the novel is a common one in his work. The old fisherman demonstrates tremendous determination and endurance in capturing the marlin, but sharks consume his catch before he can reach shore. Santiago has not won, for in Hemingway's universe it is not possible to conquer the forces working against humankind. But Santiago *is* undefeated and can go happily to his rest, dreaming of lions on the beach. Hemingway had been telling versions of this story for a long time, but never before had he evoked its primal power so effectively. Something of the potency of *The Old Man and the Sea* undoubtedly derived from the book's distinct Christian overtones and from the mythic quality of the mentor-disciple relationship between Santiago and his young apprentice, Manolin.

*The Old Man and the Sea* struck a chord that resounded throughout the world, and it was instrumental in winning Hemingway the Nobel Prize in 1954. Earlier that year, in the course of another journey to Africa, Hemingway barely survived two plane crashes in two days. Accounts of his demise ran in the newspapers, but he was so badly hurt he could take little pleasure in reading these premature obituaries. Among his injuries were a severe concussion; damage to his liver, spleen, and kidney; temporary loss of vision in the left eye and hearing in the left ear; a crushed vertebra; sprains of the right arm and shoulder and left leg; paralysis of the sphincter; and first degree burns on his face, arms, and head. He never entirely recovered from these injuries, and as the decade of the 1950s wore on his physical deterioration was exacerbated by menacing spells of depression and of paranoia. After undergoing a series of shock treatments in the winter and spring of 1961, he persuaded his doctors to send him home to Ketchum, Idaho, where he killed himself with a shotgun blast to the forehead early on the morning of July 2.

## POSTHUMOUS PUBLICATIONS

Far more than the images of most writers, Hemingway's has undergone drastic reconfiguration in the wake of posthumous publications. It is probably an exaggeration to assert, as did two recent critics, that "the Hemingway you were taught about in high school is dead." Yet it is true that the author of the apparently simple morality tale *The Old Man and the Sea* is in the process of being supplanted by someone far more complicated and far less clearly defined. The most important of the Hemingway books that have emerged since his death are *A Moveable Feast, Islands in the Stream* (1970), and *The Garden of Eden* (1986). In addition, about one-fourth of an as yet unpublished "African book," which draws on Hemingway's safari of 1953–1954, appeared in *Sports Illustrated* (1971–1972). All of the posthumously published material was written during the last fifteen years of Hemingway's life. Though he was unable to complete any of his final manuscripts to his entire satisfaction, they were put into publishable form, with some alterations, by his widow, Mary Hemingway, and his editors. Considered as a group, Hemingway's last works reveal two preoccupations: first, Hemingway's difficulty in practicing his craft amid the distractions and difficulties that threatened to overwhelm him; second, an obsession with sexual androgyny, lesbianism, and homosexuality.

Of all the final writings, *Islands in the Stream* was composed earliest. Hemingway worked on it periodically from 1945 to 1952, as his "sea novel" in three parts, with *The Old Man and the Sea* originally intended to constitute the fourth. Episodic and rambling, *Islands in the Stream* is disappointing as a work of art, yet highly revealing as documentation of Hemingway's sense of professional conflict. The protagonist is Thomas Hudson, a painter living in the Caribbean who has severed nearly all human ties in order to devote himself completely to his art. During the course of the novel, he loses all three of his sons—two in an automobile accident, one in World War II—bids farewell to his first wife, who is the one true love of his life, and is himself gunned down by a German U-boat. Serving as a kind of artistic double to the ascetic painter is the writer Roger Davis, a far more likable fellow who shows real affection for Hudson's sons. But Davis has let his emotions get

the better of him—he is quick to anger and to love—and his career has suffered as a result.

The way an artist should conduct his life was obviously very much on Hemingway's mind as he created these two contrasting figures. He pursued the subject further in the unpublished sections of the "African book" he next embarked upon. Unlike *Green Hills of Africa*, the typescript of this book is no mere report on the quotidian details of a safari. Instead, Hemingway traces the attempt of an aging writer, his creativity in decline, to construct an existence for himself exclusive of the art that has always functioned as a measure of his self-worth.

From the subject of what is to become of a writer past his prime, it was more or less natural that Hemingway's attention should shift back to the Paris years when, as a young man full of energy and ambition, he first mastered his craft. The writing of *A Moveable Feast* was also provoked by Hemingway's unexpected recovery, sometime in late 1956 or early 1957, of his manuscripts from the 1920s about the people he had known in Paris. Several of those people come off very badly in *A Moveable Feast*. Hemingway's benefactor, Fitzgerald, is excoriated for wasting his talent and for letting domination by his wife and by alcohol get the better of him. Hemingway's mentor, Gertrude Stein, is cruelly portrayed as a hysterical lesbian, and Ford Madox Ford as a wheezing, foul-smelling egotist. Organized as a series of vignettes, *A Moveable Feast* is basically a memoir, but in his prefatory remarks Hemingway suggests that it may "be regarded" as a work of fiction. Actually it reads like a parable about how the good artist—a totally dedicated, hardworking, happily married young man named Ernest Hemingway—managed to overcome the sorry examples of such unprofessional artists as, especially, F. Scott Fitzgerald. If Hemingway, struggling with his sharpened pencils at a café or in an unheated room, going hungry and learning from the Cézannes in the Luxembourg Museum, is the hero of this parable, the heroine is his wife Hadley, kind and loving and understanding. The villains—in addition to the bad writers, who include the "pilot fish" (a vicious veiled reference to onetime friend John Dos Passos)—are the rich (particularly Gerald and Sara Murphy) and the best friend (Pauline Pfeiffer), who together undermine and drain the vitality of the Hemingways' ideal marriage. Despite its scathing portrayals, the brilliantly written *A Moveable Feast* manages to cast a glow on those glorious years in the 1920s when Hemingway was making himself into a writer. As he writes in the final paragraph, "This is how Paris was in the early days when we were very poor and very happy."

Standing in contrast to *A Moveable Feast* and easily the most startling of Hemingway's posthumous publications is *The Garden of Eden,* a novel of 250 pages fashioned from an unfinished manuscript three times that length. Just like the memoir, *The Garden of Eden* has a young writer for a protagonist. Moreover, in each book the writer suffers the trauma of irrevocably losing hard-won work: in *A Moveable Feast* Hemingway recounts the story of how Hadley left a valise containing all his early stories at a Paris train depot; in *The Garden of Eden* Hemingway has the wife of the writer David Bourne burn his notebooks. Otherwise, though, and particularly in the area of sexuality, the two books could hardly be more different. Throughout *A Moveable Feast,* the idealized Hemingway is aggressively heterosexual, deeply scornful of homosexual and lesbian arrangements, and, in that respect, resembles most of his fictional heroes. David Bourne in *The Garden of Eden,* on the other hand, is drawn into playing cross-sexual roles by his erotically experimental wife, Catherine. In bed, for example, she mounts him and calls herself "Peter" and him "my girl Catherine." Later, both David and Catherine become involved with the bisexual Marita, forming an uneasy ménage à trois. As the plot unfolds, the dominating and mentally disturbed Catherine becomes jealous of

David's absorption in his writing and torches his manuscripts. One of these, the story of how David, on an elephant hunt in Africa, had reluctantly led his father to the kill, is reconstructed as evidence that his talent has survived the destructive (and at the same time oddly invigorating) effects of Catherine's experiments in androgyny. At the end David is working and living with the submissive Marita.

This rather unlikely happy ending was not, in all probability, what Hemingway intended. In fact, he left behind a provisional ending in which David is reunited with Catherine, who has undergone treatment at a clinic in Switzerland; she elicits from David a promise to join her in suicide should her madness recur. Also omitted from the published novel is a long parallel plot involving Nick and Barbara Sheldon. Barbara Sheldon is sexually attracted to Catherine, which prefigures the later Catherine-Marita relationship. Nick, a painter, wears his hair the same length as his wife's, a detail that anticipates the moment when Catherine cuts her hair and David dyes his blond so that they will look the same. A hair fetish had surfaced in several of Hemingway's earlier novels, including *A Farewell to Arms, To Have and Have Not,* and *For Whom the Bell Tolls.* In fact, most of the themes explored in *The Garden of Eden,* including male androgyny, female madness, unconventional sexual behavior, and the relationships between all of these and creative capability, were present in Hemingway's earlier books. But until the 1986 appearance of *The Garden of Eden* they were largely ignored. The effect of the posthumous novel, where these themes were treated with absolute candor, was to send readers back to Hemingway with a far more open attitude. Here was a writer, it became clear, who was troubled by an almost obsessive concern with issues of sexuality. No longer could he be easily dismissed as a practitioner of machismo, or confidently pigeonholed as a misogynist whose fictional women exist solely for the use and benefit of his male characters. The most interesting, powerful, and complex character in *The Garden of Eden* is Catherine Bourne.

Biographers and critics have assisted in producing a radical reassessment of Hemingway. Using psychoanalytic and historical approaches, they have interpreted the author and his work as formed by mixed gender signals he received during his childhood. His mother decided to "twin" Ernest and his older sister Marcelline, dressing and grooming them alike until they were of school age. Ernest's hair was cut in a Dutch bob to resemble his sister's. During most of the year, spent in Oak Park, the two youngsters wore identical dresses, while during the summers they spent in Michigan both were decked out in boyish outdoor costumes. Ernest was brought up to conform to the model of the Victorian gentleman, as portrayed in the popular fiction most honored in the Hemingway household: a figure at once courteous and forceful, sensitive and manly, a combination—to draw from two best-sellers of the late nineteenth century—of Little Lord Fauntleroy and Huckleberry Finn. This knowledge of Hemingway's childhood has formed the basis for a theory about Hemingway and androgyny that while useful as a guide nonetheless tends to become as reductively inaccurate when sweepingly applied to Hemingway's writing as the earlier wound theory. Hemingway is too complicated to fit into any one niche.

THE WRITER'S CRAFT

Another vital factor in revising the macho image of Hemingway was the opening of nearly twenty thousand pages of his manuscripts in 1975 and their installation at the John F. Kennedy Library in Boston in 1980. There scholars from around the world could see the evidence, if any were needed, of a master craftsman. Hemingway's revisions are painstaking in the extreme, and the multiple drafts of his stories and novels reveal an extraordinary sensitivity to language and its nuances. Contrary to what Hemingway's iceberg principle had led scholars to expect, Hemingway's successive drafts show that he typically made significant additions as well as subtractions as he worked toward final copy.

Sometimes overlooked in the emphasis on his understated prose style is the point that Hemingway's characteristic method resembles drama more than narrative. Often there is very little action in his fiction. He is less interested in telling what happened than in revealing what his characters are like, but he does not allow an authorial voice to instruct the reader or point the way. Instead, character is revealed through dialogue and through descriptive passages that either function like stage directions or evoke a mood. "The Killers" (1927), one of Hemingway's most often anthologized stories, provides a case in point. In this underworld tale, the two hit men Al and Max, who in their double-breasted suits, tight overcoats, and derby hats look like "a vaudeville team," come to a diner in Summit, Illinois, to murder-for-hire a boxer named Ole Andreson. To amuse themselves while they wait, the killers terrorize the counterman George and gag with towels the two others on duty, Nick Adams and Sam the Negro cook. When Ole Andreson does not show up for dinner, the killers leave. It is made clear, however, that they will eventually carry out their contract, and once they are gone Nick goes to the boxer's room to warn him. Andreson thanks Nick, but he is tired of running and certain he cannot escape his fate. Back at the diner, George suggests that Andreson must have double-crossed somebody and tells Nick not to think about it. This is advice Nick cannot take; in the end, he resolves to get out of town.

This bare-bones plot summary does little to convey the strength of the story, which is principally concerned with the shock to Nick's system of encountering, first, two banal murderers who might be comic figures but for their submachine guns, and second, a polite and dispirited victim who has no interest in running to avoid his own death. What he left out of "The Killers," Hemingway observed in 1959, was "all Chicago, which is hard to do in 2,951 words," but he also left out a great deal more. For example, a substantial majority of those 2,951 words are spoken in conversation. Hemingway relies principally on dialogue, moves his dramatis personae around with brief stage directions, and leaves it up to the reader to take the point. Only in a couple of places does he allow himself the luxury of commentary. One comes after Al and Max have gone and George has untied Nick and the cook. Instead of writing that Nick Adams had been frightened or terrified or humiliated by the killers who tied up the cook and himself, Hemingway wryly reduces Nick's abasement to the bare observation that "he had never had a towel in his mouth before." And then he permits himself to gloss a line of dialogue. When Sam says not once but twice, "I don't want any more of that," Nick reacts differently, or so it would seem. "Say," he says, "What the hell?" Then Hemingway adds, "He was trying to swagger it off."

In addition, there is one short scene that does not seem to fit in with the rest of the story. This comes when Nick encounters Ole Andreson's landlady immediately after the fighter has sent him away with the repeated observation that there isn't "anything to do" about his impending murder. The landlady is good-hearted and chatty and totally ignorant of the situation, while Nick has nothing much to say. She had told "Mr. Andreson" he ought to take a walk on a fine fall day like this one, she says, but he "didn't feel like it." He has been "in the ring, you know," she tells Nick, who knows. But you would never suspect he had been a fighter, she adds, "except from the way his face is. . . . He's just as gentle." Nick responds only, "Well, good-night, Mrs. Hirsch," but it turns out that he is speaking to Mrs. Bell, who is taking care of the rooming house for Mrs. Hirsch. This last confusion is one of several discrepancies in the story. The counterman George is in charge of Henry's lunchroom, for instance, and the clock on the wall is twenty minutes fast. In the universe of "The Killers," things are not what they seem.

But otherwise, what is the purpose of the conversation with Mrs. Bell? Or, as British playwright Tom Stoppard, an admirer of Hemingway, has asked, "What on earth is this about?" Coming from a dramatist of Stoppard's skill, the question may be taken as a rhetorical one that simply calls attention to Hemingway's genius in inventing this scene. But the question may be answered too: what is going on is that Mrs. Bell, in her benign fashion, represents those ordinary folk who do not and will not encounter the absolute evil that has just confronted Nick Adams. Nick will never again feel comfortable in her world, any more than Krebs in "Soldier's Home," after his experience in the war, is able to imagine a place for himself in his mother's placid and predictable way of life. None of this is actually uttered in "The Killers," but the point is there, between the lines.

In much of Hemingway's fiction, as in "The Killers," violence impinges on everyday existence and leaves everything altered. Yet death and danger have nothing to do with those excellent narratives in which Hemingway explores with sensitivity the difficult relationships between men and women. In this fiction it is striking how often Hemingway uses silence or monosyllabic responses to convey emotion. Like all accomplished dramatists, he understood that in dialogue what is not said can be fully as important as what is. Consider for example Jake's uncomfortable near-silence when Brett cannot stop telling him about her affair with Pedro Romero or Frederic's insensitively monosyllabic reaction to Catherine's announcement that she is pregnant or, in "A Canary for One," the husband's quiet concentration on a fallow landscape as he and his wife return to Paris to establish separate residences. In these and similar works, conversational evasions combine with descriptions of landscape to communicate feelings that Hemingway must leave unarticulated in order to avoid the sentimental and superficial.

Hemingway's influence on those who came after him has been pervasive. His supposedly tight-lipped style and ferocious subject matter are highly susceptible to parody, not all of it intentional. Tough-guy heroes who strut across the literary landscape derive from Hemingway, and so does a great deal of not particularly effective writing using a self-consciously limited vocabulary. Another legacy is his famous image, which continues to provoke young dreamers at their word processors into thinking that the writer's life is one of romance rather than drudgery. The talented storyteller Tobias Wolff, for one, grew up worshipping Hemingway for "a lot of the wrong reasons, although," he notes, "I loved his work, too." Inaccurate though it may be, the legend of Ernest Hemingway is slow to die and has not lost its capacity to attract admirers. Still it is the work that matters and will last.

## Selected Bibliography

### WORKS OF ERNEST HEMINGWAY

BOOKS

*In Our Time.* New York: Boni & Liveright, 1925.
*The Torrents of Spring.* New York: Scribners, 1926.
*The Sun Also Rises.* New York: Scribners, 1926.
*Men Without Women.* New York: Scribners, 1927.
*A Farewell to Arms.* New York: Scribners, 1929.
*Death in the Afternoon.* New York: Scribners, 1932.
*Winner Take Nothing.* New York: Scribners, 1933.
*Green Hills of Africa.* New York: Scribners, 1935.
*To Have and Have Not.* New York: Scribners, 1937.
*The Fifth Column and the First Forty-Nine Stories.* New York: Scribners, 1938. Republished as *The Short Stories of Ernest Hemingway.* New York: Scribners, 1953.
*For Whom the Bell Tolls.* New York: Scribners, 1940.
*Across the River and into the Trees.* New York: Scribners, 1950.
*The Old Man and the Sea.* New York: Scribners, 1952.
*A Moveable Feast.* New York: Scribners, 1964.
*Byline: Ernest Hemingway.* Edited by William White. New York: Scribners, 1967.
*Islands in the Stream.* New York: Scribners, 1970.
*The Nick Adams Stories.* New York: Scribners, 1972.
*The Garden of Eden.* New York: Scribners, 1986.
*The Complete Short Stories of Ernest Hemingway.* New York: Scribners, 1987.

CORRESPONDENCE

*Ernest Hemingway: Selected Letters, 1917–1961.* Edited by Carlos Baker. New York: Scribners, 1981.
*Hemingway in Love and War: The Lost Diary of Agnes von Kurowsky, Her Letters, and Correspondence of Ernest Hemingway.* Edited by Henry Serrano Villard and James Nagel. Boston: Northeastern University Press, 1989.
*The Only Thing That Counts: The Ernest Hemingway–Maxwell Perkins Correspondence, 1925–1947.* Edited by Matthew J. Bruccoli with Robert W. Trogdon. New York: Scribners, 1996.

### BIBLIOGRAPHIES

August, Jo. *Catalog of the Ernest Hemingway Collection at the John F. Kennedy Library.* 2 vols. Boston: G. K. Hall, 1982.
Hanneman, Audre. *Ernest Hemingway: A Comprehensive Bibliography.* Princeton, N.J.: Princeton University Press, 1967.
———. *Supplement to Ernest Hemingway: A Comprehensive Bibliography.* Princeton, N.J.: Princeton University Press, 1975.
Larson, Kelli A. *Ernest Hemingway: A Reference Guide, 1974–1989.* Boston: G. K. Hall, 1990.

### BIOGRAPHIES

Baker, Carlos. *Ernest Hemingway: A Life Story.* New York: Scribners, 1969.
Donaldson, Scott. *By Force of Will: The Life and Art of Ernest Hemingway.* New York: Viking, 1977.

Griffin, Peter. *Along with Youth: Hemingway, the Early Years*. New York: Oxford University Press, 1985.

———. *Less Than a Treason: Hemingway in Paris*. New York: Oxford University Press, 1990.

Kert, Bernice. *The Hemingway Women*. New York: Norton, 1983.

Lynn, Kenneth S. *Hemingway*. New York: Simon & Schuster, 1987.

Mellow, James R. *Hemingway: A Life Without Consequences*. Boston: Houghton Mifflin, 1992.

Reynolds, Michael S. *The Young Hemingway*. Oxford: Basil Blackwell, 1986.

———. *Hemingway: The Paris Years*. Oxford: Basil Blackwell, 1989.

———. *Hemingway: The American Homecoming*. Cambridge, Mass.: Basil Blackwell, 1992.

———. *Hemingway: The 1930s*. New York: Norton, 1997.

Reynolds, Michael S. *Hemingway's First War: The Making of "A Farewell to Arms."* Princeton, N.J.: Princeton University Press, 1976.

Rovit, Earl, and Gerry Brenner. *Ernest Hemingway*. Revised edition. Boston: Twayne, 1986.

Smith, Paul. *A Reader's Guide to the Short Stories of Ernest Hemingway*. Boston: G. K. Hall, 1989.

Spilka, Mark. *Hemingway's Quarrel with Androgyny*. Lincoln: University of Nebraska Press, 1990.

Stephens, Robert O. *Hemingway's Nonfiction: The Public Voice*. Chapel Hill: University of North Carolina Press, 1968.

Svoboda, Frederic Joseph. *Hemingway & "The Sun Also Rises": The Crafting of a Style*. Lawrence: University Press of Kansas, 1983.

Waldhorn, Arthur. *A Reader's Guide to Ernest Hemingway*. New York: Farrar, Straus & Giroux, 1972.

Young, Philip. *Ernest Hemingway: A Reconsideration*. University Park: Pennsylvania State University Press, 1966.

## *CRITICAL STUDIES*

Baker, Carlos. *Hemingway: The Writer as Artist*. Revised edition. Princeton, N.J.: Princeton University Press, 1972.

Beegel, Susan F. *Hemingway's Craft of Omission: Four Manuscript Examples*. Ann Arbor: UMI Research Press, 1988.

Brenner, Gerry. *Concealments in Hemingway's Works*. Columbus: Ohio State University Press, 1983.

Burwell, Rose Marie. *Hemingway: The Postwar Years and the Posthumous Novels*. Cambridge: Cambridge University Press, 1996.

Conley, Nancy R., and Robert Scholes. *Hemingway's Genders: Rereading the Hemingway Text*. New Haven, Conn.: Yale University Press, 1994.

Fenton, Charles A. *The Apprenticeship of Ernest Hemingway: The Early Years*. New York: Farrar, Straus & Young, 1954.

Flora, Joseph M. *Hemingway's Nick Adams*. Baton Rouge: Louisiana State University Press, 1982.

Grebstein, Sheldon Norman. *Hemingway's Craft*. Carbondale: Southern Illinois University Press, 1973.

Oldsey, Bernard Stanley. *Hemingway's Hidden Craft: The Writing of "A Farewell to Arms."* University Park: Pennsylvania State University Press, 1979.

Raeburn, John. *Fame Became of Him: Hemingway as Public Writer*. Bloomington: Indiana University Press, 1984.

## *COLLECTIONS OF CRITICISM*

Baker, Carlos, ed. *Ernest Hemingway: Critiques of Four Major Novels*. New York: Scribners, 1962.

Benson, Jackson J., ed. *The Short Stories of Ernest Hemingway: Critical Essays*. Durham, N.C.: Duke University Press, 1975.

———. *New Critical Approaches to the Short Stories of Ernest Hemingway*. Durham, N.C.: Duke University Press, 1990.

Donaldson, Scott, ed. *The Cambridge Companion to Hemingway*. Cambridge: Cambridge University Press, 1996.

Meyers, Jeffrey, ed. *Hemingway: The Critical Heritage*. London: Routledge & Kegan Paul, 1982.

Nagel, James, ed. *Hemingway: The Writer in Context*. Madison: University of Wisconsin Press, 1984.

Stephens, Robert O., ed. *Ernest Hemingway: The Critical Reception*. New York: Burt Franklin, 1977.

Wagner-Martin, Linda, ed. *Ernest Hemingway: Six Decades of Criticism*. East Lansing: Michigan State University Press, 1987.

Weeks, Robert P., ed. *Hemingway: A Collection of Critical Essays*. Englewood Cliffs, N.J.: Prentice Hall, 1962.

*—SCOTT DONALDSON*

# Langston Hughes
## 1902–1967

*I*N 1924, WHEN at the age of twenty-two Langston Hughes found himself broke in the Italian city of Genoa, he composed one of the most famous poetic statements in twentieth-century American literature, "I, Too":

> I, too, sing America.
>
> I am the darker brother.
> They send me to eat in the kitchen
> When company comes,
> But I laugh,
> And eat well,
> And grow strong.
>
> Tomorrow,
> I'll be at the table
> When company comes.
> Nobody'll dare
> Say to me,
> "Eat in the kitchen,"
> Then.
>
> Besides,
> They'll see how beautiful I am
> And be ashamed—
>
> I, too, am America.

The poem stands as both a social and poetic credo, a public and private declaration. And just as from the public perspective, speaking for all African Americans, Hughes's "I" is still waiting to sit equally at the American table, so Langston Hughes is still waiting to be fully acknowledged as one of America's great poets.

Many critics, both white and black, would not disagree with Harold Bloom's comment, in an introduction to a volume of essays on Hughes. Bloom all but apologizes to the reader for editing such an enterprise, saying that "social and political considerations . . . will provide something of an audience for Hughes's poetry." Such social and political considerations—a kind of reverse discrimination—we can assume, were what caused Bloom to include Hughes in the series *Modern Critical Views*. Hughes is at Bloom's literary table because an African American poet is needed, despite deep reservations about whether he belongs. Hughes may have had a larger popular audience since the 1930s, that "something of an audience" as Bloom dismissively terms it, than Bloom's own favorite modern American author, Wallace Stevens, but the scholars and critics who pass judgment on writers have, like Bloom, usually not seen how beautiful Hughes is, nor have they been ashamed of their assessments.

Why is there such resistance to Hughes? One reason is that Hughes is viewed as a folk poet who found his material in the lives of the people around him and simply transferred that world to the page. Hughes, in this view, functions as something of a journalist; his poetry serves as a good barometer of African American social and political opinions, but rarely transmutes these views into "art." Hughes's forthright expression of the frustration of African Americans in a segregated world violated the New Critical maxim that a poem should not mean but be. Many of Hughes's most famous poems "mean," like "Merry-Go-Round" (collected in *Shakespeare in Harlem*, 1942), which opens:

> Where is the Jim Crow section
> On this merry-go-round,
> Mister, cause I want to ride?

or the well-known "Harlem" section of *Montage of a Dream Deferred* (1951):

> What happens to a dream deferred?
>
> Does it dry up
> like a raisin in the sun?
> Or fester like a sore—
> And then run?
> Does it stink like rotten meat?
> Or crust and sugar over—
> like a syrupy sweet?
>
> Maybe it just sags
> like a heavy load.
>
> *Or does it explode?*

In an essay fittingly called "My Adventures as a Social Poet" (collected in *Good Morning Revolution*, 1973), Hughes spoke of how some people thought that poets should meditate about things beyond the mundane and worldly. "Try as I might to float off into the clouds," Hughes said, "poverty and Jim Crow would grab me by the heels, and right back on earth I would land." At the end of the essay, Hughes explained why he could not look at "roses" or "moonlight" as vehicles for reveries beyond the actual, present world: "For sometimes in the moonlight my brothers see a fiery cross and a circle of Klansmen's hoods. Sometimes in the moonlight a dark body swings from a lynching tree—but for his funeral there are no roses." After World War II, the critical consensus in universities looked upon social poetry with disdain; it was considered too direct, too didactic, too simple. Hughes responded on more than one occasion that it was also too true.

In fact, as Donna Harper has noted in *Not So Simple: The "Simple" Stories by Langston Hughes*, "the words *Simple* and *Simplicity* recur in analyses of Langston Hughes's work. A disturbing consequence of this trend has been an exclusion of Hughes's works as texts of modern criticism, a dismissal of Hughes as being too simple to merit literary analysis." Such neglect was most obvious in the area of textual scholarship. Before 1990, the only notable works on primary sources were Faith Berry's pioneering collection of uncollected writings, *Good Morning Revolution: Uncollected Writings of Social Protest* (1973) and the edition of the letters of Hughes and Arna Bontemps selected by Charles Nichols (1980). With the appearance in the 1990s of an expanded edition of Berry's volume, new editions of the Simple stories and the short fiction collected by Harper, the collection of *Chicago Defender* columns by Christopher De Santis, the publication of Hughes and Zora Neale Hurston's *Mule Bone* (1991) by Henry Louis Gates, and *The Collected Poems of Langston Hughes* (1994), the situation improved. But the need remains for a critical edition of Hughes's major works.

Hughes was probably already aware of his "simple" reputation when he gave one of his most enduring creations, the Harlem everyman Jesse B. Semple, the nickname "Simple" in 1943. Hughes certainly learned from the examples of Walt Whitman and Carl Sandburg, but the white author who probably had the most influence on Hughes was Mark Twain. All three used what Harper has called the "illusion of simplicity" to make profound statements, and all three laced much of their writings with ironic humor. But only with studies like those of R. Baxter Miller and Steven Tracy on the poems, Hans Ostrom on the short fiction, and Harper on the Simple stories have scholars begun to seriously investigate how, to use the words of Baxter Miller, Hughes's subtle use of language and "complex use of metaphor belied his seemingly transparent treatment of folk life."

Like Twain, Hughes himself contributed to, or even created, his reputation as a careless and simple writer. When discussing how he composed his poems, Hughes says in his autobiography *The Big Sea* (1940) that

> there are seldom many changes in my poems. Generally, the first two or three lines come to me from something I'm thinking about, or looking at, or doing, and the rest of the poem (if there is to be a poem) flows from those first few lines, usually right away. If there is a chance to put the poem down then, I write it down. If not, I try to remember it until I get to a pencil and paper: for poems are like rainbows: they escape you quickly.

Hughes's self-presentation as a finder rather than a maker of poems went against the prevalent critical attitude favoring poetic craftsmen. Scholars have routinely taken this passage at face value. But evidence clearly shows that this was not how Hughes always worked. "When Sue Wears Red" (from *The Weary Blues*), one of his best-known poems, reads:

When Susanna Jones wears red
Her face is like an ancient cameo
Turned brown by the ages.

Come with a blast of trumpets,
Jesus!

When Susanna Jones wears red
A queen from some time-dead Egyptian night
Walks once again.

Blow trumpets, Jesus!

And the beauty of Susanna Jones in red
Burns in my heart a love-fire sharp like pain.

Sweet silver trumpets,
Jesus!

The version of this poem published in *Crisis* magazine in 1923 had only the three stanzas without the "trumpet" refrains. The refrains were not added until the poem was reprinted in Hughes's first volume of poetry, *The Weary Blues*. In his first autobiography, however, Hughes obscures the real textual history of the work by suggesting that he wrote the poem, complete with the "trumpets," while he was a high school student in Cleveland. Clearly, then, the account that Hughes offers of his method of composition in *The Big Sea* is less than accurate. Hughes may have thought that many critics, especially white critics, were not ready to accept a black craftsman, and so he cultivated a "folk poet" persona. It also allowed Hughes, in the tradition of the trickster figure in African American culture best known through the stories about Br'er Rabbit, which Henry Louis Gates has described in *The Signifying Monkey,* to employ a pose of simplicity to make fun of "literal" readers.

For example, in *The Big Sea,* Hughes tells a story of how he was elected class poet in grammar school, which required him to read an original piece at commencement.

> There were two Negro children in the class, myself and a girl. In America most white people think, of course, that *all* Negroes can sing and dance, and have a sense of rhythm. So my classmates, knowing that a poem had to have rhythm, elected me unanimously—thinking, no doubt, that I had some, being a Negro. . . . That was the way I began to write poetry. It had never occurred to me to be a poet before, or indeed a writer of any kind.

This is vintage Hughes, since, as in much of Twain, the passage deconstructs itself at various levels. White people did, of course, think that African

Americans could sing and dance, but that certainly did not mean that they thought that blacks could, or should, read a poem at graduation. And Hughes certainly did not decide to become a writer because a group of white children thought that he would be good at it. He is clearly subverting the idea that a black author needs such valorization from the white world with his tale of unanimous "election" by white sixth-graders. But some critics, amazingly, have taken this story seriously. Some still do.

One of the most puzzling elements in current discussions of Hughes is the failure to read Hughes's deflection of attention away from himself as an individual creator as a sign that he wanted to hide or obscure something about himself. Arnold Rampersad says of the first of Hughes's autobiographies, "In a genre defined by confession, Hughes appears to give nothing away of a personal nature." Certainly in one important area, his sexuality, Hughes, who never married or had children, gave almost nothing away.

Was Hughes gay? Some evidence suggests that he might have been. Would that change how we should read Hughes? Inevitably, it must. But we have not had a good examination of certain aspects of Hughes, such as his tendency to speak with a strong female voice in his blues poems, in the light of recent gay, or queer, criticism. Would such an investigation undermine Hughes's position as a "social poet" concerned about the African American condition in America? Absolutely not. But it would add a layer of meaning to our understanding of the poet.

Some of Hughes's writing strikes one as unsophisticated, childish, even simple by adult standard—and for a very good reason: Hughes often directed his work toward young people. Dianne Johnson, in her study of African American children's literature, states that "during the thirties and forties, Langston Hughes and Arna Bontemps are the most notable contributors" to this field. As Johnson puts it, Hughes and his friend Bontemps

were attempting to fill a great need. Critics often ignore Hughes's lifelong commitment to the project of creating black children's literature; no other major American poet of the century was as engaged in such an enterprise. But, of course, white poets grew up reading stories about children with their racial identity. Hughes had not, and tried to ensure that coming generations of African American children would have books about kids like themselves. Every Christmas, cities around the country stage annual productions of *The Nutcracker, A Christmas Carol,* and, in recent years, *Black Nativity,* with lyrics by Langston Hughes. In that work, as he did so often, he once again inserted an African American voice where it had not been before.

Still, as Rampersad observed in the preface to *The Collected Poems of Langston Hughes,* the "truth indeed is that Hughes published many poems that are doggerel. To reach his primary audience—the black masses—he was prepared to write 'down' to them." In fact, Hughes often reached such audiences through public appearances; for periods of his life he lived primarily on earnings received from recitations to African American audiences. In this arena, Hughes was after a different reaction from the kind that came from critics in academic posts. In the second of his autobiographies, *I Wonder As I Wander: An Autobiographical Journey* (1956), he wrote of how he had "worked out a public routine of reading my poetry that almost never failed to provoke, after each poem, some sort of audible audience response—laughter, applause, a grunt, a sigh, or an 'Amen!'" Hughes has sometimes been compared to the poet William Wordsworth in drawing upon common language and the lives of ordinary people. But the similarity ends there. Hughes's goal was not just to make poetry from the people, but also to give, to use the title of a chapter of his second autobiography, "poetry to the people." Many modern American writers have sounded those words, only to draw back from the consequences of what communicating to a mass, semieducated audience meant to one's work. Hughes never drew back from an attempt to engage his people. Speaking of African Americans in the south in 1931, Mary McLeod Bethune, the renowned black educator, told Hughes simply, "They need poetry." Throughout his life, Hughes tried to bring poetry to his people.

### EARLY LIFE

And the dark-faced child, listening,
Knows that Aunt Sue's stories are real stories,
He knows that Aunt Sue never got her stories
Out of any book at all,
But they come
Right out of her own life.
          ("Aunt Sue's Stories," from *The Weary Blues*)

Hughes was born James Langston Hughes in Joplin, Missouri, on February 1, 1902. His parents were not well matched, and Hughes's father, an engineer, soon left to seek employment opportunities first in Cuba and then, after 1903, in Mexico. For much of his childhood, Hughes lived with his maternal grandmother in Lawrence, Kansas, while his mother worked in various places throughout the Midwest. In *The Big Sofa* Hughes reported that he "had been very lonesome growing up by myself, the only child, with no father or mother around." He found solace in books and listening to his grandmother's stories. "Through my grandmother's stories life always moved, moved heroically toward an end. Nobody ever cried in my grandmother's stories. They worked, or schemed, or fought, But no crying." It is not surprising that Mary Langston's stories moved heroically toward an end. The family was poor after the death of her husband, Charles Langston, in 1892, but it had a proud tradition. Hughes's grandmother had attended Oberlin College, where she met both her first husband, Lewis Leary, who died with John Brown at Harpers Ferry in 1859, and her second husband, Charles Howard Langston. Langston

was a mulatto, the son of a rich white Virginia farmer and a freed slave, and Hughes would draw on that family history in a number of works, notably his play *Mulatto* (in *Five Plays,* 1963). Charles Langston was a leader in the abolitionist movement and later active in Republican politics in Lawrence. From Mary Langston and her two husbands, Hughes inherited a strong mission of service to the race, embodied in one of his prize possessions, the shawl that had covered Lewis Leary's body at Harpers Ferry.

Hughes learned different lessons from his parents, neither of whom encouraged his poetic aspirations. His mother, Carrie Langston, often made financial demands of her son. In his novel *Not without Laughter* (1930), Hughes drew on his own experience when he has the protagonist's mother say that since her teenage son is "big enough to hold a job," he "ought to be wanting to help me. . . . Instead of that, he's determined to go back to school." Hughes's relationship with his father was even more difficult. Hughes had only spent a few months with James Hughes before he was seventeen, when he was invited to spend the summer with his father in Mexico. Yet his father had occupied a special place in the boy's imagination. As Hughes put it in *The Big Sea,* "My father, permanently in Mexico during those turbulent years, represented for me the one stable factor in my life." Yet, when reunited, father and son soon clashed on a major issue. "My father hated Negroes. I think he hated himself, too, for being a Negro." Many of Hughes's best early poems explored the nature of, and the beauty in, the African element of African American identity. To a degree, these poems are Hughes's answer to his father's attitude to his own race, such as "My People" (in *Weary Blues*):

The night is beautiful,
So are the faces of my people.

The stars are beautiful,
So are the eyes of my people.

Beautiful, also, is the sun.
Beautiful, also, are the souls of my people.

And "Dream Variations" (in *Weary Blues*), which ends:

To fling my arms wide
In the face of the sun,
Dance! Whirl! Whirl!
Till the quick day is done.
Rest at pale evening . . .
A tall, slim tree . . .
Night coming tenderly
Black like me.

It was during the painful year that he spent with his father in Mexico after his high school graduation, when he was nineteen, that Hughes published his first mature poems in *Crisis,* the magazine of the National Association for the Advancement of Colored People (NAACP). The importance of *Crisis* to Hughes cannot be overestimated. It was not simply that it became a major outlet for his work throughout his life. It was also that the young Hughes, like the protagonist, Sandy, in his novel *Not Without Laughter,* read the journal and knew that an African American poet had a significant African American medium to reach an African American audience. The generation of the Harlem Renaissance, Hughes's generation, might well be described as the children of *Crisis.* Because they read it as teenagers, they could conceive of a new kind of literary career.

### HARLEM RENAISSANCE YEARS

The rhythm of life,
Is a jazz rhythm,
Honey.
The Gods are laughing at us.
("Lenox Avenue: Midnight," from *The Weary Blues*)

Hughes first saw Harlem in 1921, when he went to New York to enroll at Columbia University.

He left after his freshman year and, before entering Lincoln University in January 1926, he worked, among other things, as a messman on a ship sailing to Africa, in the kitchen of a Paris nightclub, and at a number of menial jobs in Washington, D.C. But Harlem remained central in his life during this time. It held the African American journals, *Crisis, Opportunity,* and the *Messenger*—in which most of his poems appeared—his literary friends, and the allure of being the largest grouping of African Americans anywhere. Other members of the Harlem Renaissance, like Sterling Brown and Zora Neale Hurston, wrote about African American life in the rural South. Hughes drew heavily on the urban experience resulting from the African American northern migration, of which Harlem was the largest and most vibrant example.

In 1922, with the composition of the poem "The Weary Blues" (collected in *The Weary Blues*), Hughes began to experiment with how to incorporate African American musical motifs from the blues, jazz, and spirituals into his verse. In the last stanza of "The Weary Blues," Hughes has the piano player sing an actual blues song he had heard as a child in Kansas City, imitating and yet at the same time modifying the technique of "literary quotations" made famous by such poets as Ezra Pound and T. S. Eliot:

Thump, thump, thump went his foot on the floor.
He played a few chords then he sang some more—
    "I got the Weary Blues
    And I can't be satisfied
    Got the Weary Blues
    And can't be satisfied
    I ain't happy no mo'
    And I wish that I had died."
And far into the night he crooned that tune.
The stars went out and so did the moon.
The singer stopped playing and went to bed
While the Weary Blues echoed through his head.
He slept like a rock or a man that's dead.

By the end of 1925, Hughes had published more than seventy poems, had written for the

March 1925 special African American issue of *Survey Graphic* and the anthology *The New Negro,* and had won first prize in a poetry contest sponsored by *Opportunity* magazine. The young poet had arrived, a fact further signaled by the appearance the next year of his first volume of verse, *The Weary Blues,* which was published by Knopf at the urging of the author and critic Carl Van Vechten. Hughes achieved a strong poetic voice early, and the book contains a number of poems that have had a secure place in Hughes's canon ever since, like "The Negro Speaks of Rivers," "I, Too," "Aunt Sue's Stories," and "The Weary Blues." In addition to poems that celebrated the beauty of African Americans and their heritage, Hughes included poems about their struggle for a better existence in a racially divided contemporary America, as in "Mother to Son":

Well, son, I'll tell you:
Life for me ain't been no crystal stair.
It's had tacks in it,
And splinters,
And boards torn up,
And places with no carpet on the floor—
Bare.
But all the time
I'se been a-climbin' on,
And reachin' landin's,
And turnin' corners,
And sometimes goin' in the dark
Where there ain't been no light.
So boy, don't you turn back.
Don't you set down on the steps
'Cause you finds it's kinder hard.
Don't you fall now—
For I'se still goin', honey,
I'se still climbin',
And life for me ain't been no crystal stair.

From the beginning of his career, Hughes saw the position of African Americans as analogous to the fate of people of color around the world, and he has had a significant international reputation from the 1920s until the present. The pessimistic "Lament for Dark Peoples" appeared in *The Weary Blues*:

I was a red man one time,
But the white men came.
I was a black man, too,
But the white men came.

They drove me out of the forest.
They took me away from the jungles.
I lost my trees.
I lost my silver moons.

Now they've caged me
In the circus of civilization.
Now I herd with the many—
Caged in the circus of civilization.

There were also poems about Harlem, celebrating the vibrant nightlife Hughes experienced when, as he put it (in a chapter heading in *The Big Sky*), "the Negro was in vogue." In poems like "Negro Dancers":

Me an' my baby's
Got two mo' ways
Two mo' ways to de Charleston!
and "Jazzonia"
In a Harlem cabaret
Six long-headed jazzers play.
A dancing girl whose eyes are bold
Lifts high a dress of silken gold.
Oh, singing tree!
Oh, shining rivers of the soul!

Hughes suggests that in song and dance African Americans can not only escape present woes but can also enter an ecstatic world closed to whites. Mixed in with these poems about black identity and race were others about personal despair and suicide, such as "Suicide's Note" ("The calm, / Cool face of the river / Asked me for a kiss."), and short lyrics about ships and seamen (as in "Port Town," "Sea Calm," and "Death of an Old Seaman"). *The Weary Blues* was an impressive first volume, but it lacked consistent quality and a unifying aesthetic perspective. It announced Hughes's arrival as a poet, without clearly indicating where he was headed next.

In 1926, with the financial help of Amy Spingarn, the wife of NAACP leader Joel Spingarn, Hughes enrolled at Lincoln University in Pennsylvania, from which he graduated in 1929. At about the same time, Hughes began to develop a coherent aesthetics through discussions with other young African American writers, especially Hurston, Wallace Thurman, Bruce Nugent, and Rudolph Fisher. Hughes announced their literary declaration of independence from both white and what he called "the Nordicized Negro intelligentsia" in his famous essay, "The Negro Artist and the Racial Mountain."

> We younger Negro artists who create now intend to express our dark-skinned selves without fear or shame. If white people are pleased we are glad. If they are not, it doesn't matter. We know we are beautiful. And ugly too. The tom-tom cries and the tom-tom laughs. If colored people are pleased we are glad. If they are not, their displeasure does not matter either. We build our temples for tomorrow, strong as we know how, and we stand on the top of the mountain, free within ourselves.

Early in the essay he states that

> jazz to me is the one inherent expression of Negro life in America; the eternal tom-tom beating in the Negro soul—the tom-tom of revolt against weariness in a white world.... Yet the Philadelphia clubwoman is ashamed to say that her race created it and she does not like me to write about it.

In his second book of poems, *Fine Clothes to the Jew* (1927), Hughes consistently attempted to follow his own advice and "to grasp and hold some of the meanings and rhythms of jazz." Rampersad noted that "as a measure of his deeper penetration of the culture and his increased confidence as a poet, three kinds of poems are barely present in *Fine Clothes to the Jew*—those that directly praise black people and culture, those that directly protest their condition, and those that reflect his own personal sense of desolation." The "I," or narrative voice, in the poems of *The Weary Blues* often seemed to be Hughes. The "I" in the poems of *Fine Clothes to the Jew* is nearly always a character, often a woman, taken from the blues tradition, as in "Hard Daddy," which opens:

> I went to ma daddy,
> Says Daddy I have got the blues.
> Went to ma daddy,
> Says Daddy I have got the blues.
> Ma daddy says, Honey,
> Can't you bring no better news?

Hughes had employed some black dialect in *The Weary Blues,* but dialect predominates in *Fine Clothes to the Jew.* In the place of jazz dancers who seem, at moments, to escape the world of poverty and prejudice, Hughes presents a harder reality, as in "Elevator Boy," which begins:

> I got a job now
> Runnin' an elevator
> In the Dennison Hotel in Jersey.
> Job ain't good though.
> No money around.
> Jobs are just chances
> Like everything else.
> Maybe a little luck now,
> Maybe not.

And a sharper irony appears in "Red Silk Stockings," which opens:

> Put on yo' red silk stockings,
> Black gal,
> Go out an' let de white boys
> Look at yo' legs.

These poems can be read as a more powerful indictment of the treatment of African Americans in a white world than the more conventional, direct laments on that subject in his first volume. But this was not how they were interpreted upon their publication. Many African American newspapers attacked the book for presenting the race in a bad light, and Hughes later became embarrassed by the seemingly anti-Semitic title. On the heels of the disastrous reception of *Fire!!,* an avant-garde magazine brought out in 1927 by Hughes and his young literary friends to be a small journal like the kinds that white writers had, the attack on his second volume caused Hughes to rethink his aesthetics and his literary declaration of independence. His next volume from Knopf, *The Dream Keeper and Other Poems* (1932), was directed at young people and was full of conventional poems of the kind that were absent from *Fine Clothes to the Jew.*

Another reason that Hughes did not build on the aesthetic of *Fine Clothes to the Jew* was that he had begun to care whether white people, or rather one white person, was pleased. In 1927, a wealthy white patron, Mrs. Charlotte Osgood Mason, provided Hughes, and Hurston, with a regular salary. Mrs. Mason had definite ideas about what her artists should write. She wanted "the primitive," as Hughes says in *The Big Sea.* She also wanted a novel. According to Rampersad, Hughes was not initially keen to undertake such an endeavor, but the prospect of $150 a week brought him around. Yet *Not without Laughter,* his semiautobiographical account of a boyhood in a working-class black family in the Midwest, is a welcome addition to African American fiction. Maryemma Graham has said that the novel is "unique in that it carries over some of the popular characterization" of blacks found in other fiction of the Harlem Renaissance "into what is clearly a realistic depiction of black life." The book also lends more insight into Hughes's character than perhaps any other work that he wrote, including his autobiographies.

The way in which Hughes invents for his fictional persona, Sandy, a guitar-playing father and an aunt who promises to support him through high school and provide book money, is an intriguing construction of the boyhood that Hughes wished he had had. The novel shows the strains of Hughes's attempting to balance Mrs. Mason's desire for "the primitive" with Hughes's own views.

Near the end of the book, Sandy imagines his race as "a band of dancers. . . . Black dancers—captured in a white world. . . . Dancers of the spirit, too. Each black dreamer a captured dancer of the spirit." But Sandy, unlike Mrs. Mason, rejects the notion that blacks are "dancers" by virtue of their genetics. "The other way round seemed better: dancers because of their poverty, singing because they suffered, laughing all the time because of the need to forget. . . . It was more like that, Sandy thought." So did Hughes, who found himself too restricted by Mrs. Mason's desire for African primitiveness. As Hughes later wrote in *The Big Sea,* "I was not Africa. I was Chicago and Kansas City and Broadway and Harlem." But, as Faith Berry points out, Hughes was just as restricted by the social and political implications of Mrs. Mason's love of the primitive. If African Americans were dancers, singers, and laughers because of their situation, then Hughes wanted to get on with the business of changing their lot.

## A TURN TO THE LEFT

Good morning, Revolution:
You're the very best friend
I ever had.
We gonna pal around together from now on.
("Good Morning, Revolution," from *Good Morning, Revolution*)

Hughes's celebrated turn to the political left in the 1930s was not a very hard turn. As Berry points out, Hughes had published poems in the *Workers Monthly* as early as 1925. Hughes, like many African Americans, was attracted by the fact that the Communists were the only white party that called for the complete end of segregation, and he appreciated their efforts in the defense of the Scottsboro defendants, nine young African Americans who had been convicted on suspect evidence of raping two white women in Alabama in 1931. Well into the 1940s, Hughes reminded readers of the *Chicago Defender* that Moscow was a city where there was no color bar—a fact to which he could personally attest from his stay in the Soviet Union in 1933–1934. Hughes was never a member of the Communist Party, but the radicalism expressed in such poems as "Black Workers" was not a passing fancy.

> The bees work.
> Their work is taken from them.
> We are like the bees—
> But it won't last
> Forever.

As Richard Barksdale observes in *Langston Hughes: The Poet and His Critics*, Hughes's move "from folk poet to 'indignant proletarian reformer'" was widely held to be "unfortunate" for his artistic career.

One poem, "Goodbye Christ" (in *Good Morning, Revolution*), written in the early 1930s, came back to haunt Hughes. It begins:

> Listen, Christ,
> You did alright in your day, I reckon—
> But that day's gone now

Later in the decade, religious and conservative groups picketed readings by Hughes, which caused cancellations of engagements. Hughes was forced to publicly repudiate the sentiments in the poem, a discouraging action that brought further criticism from the left. From 1940 until his death in 1967, Hughes was cautious in his public dealings with the Communists, but continued to contribute radical poems to the *New Masses* and *People's World* as late as 1946.

Hughes found the mainstream literary marketplace a bad medium for radical verse. Knopf, which had already brought out three books of verse by Hughes, turned down a collection of political poems, which came out as *A New Song* (1938) from the International Workers Order. Between *The Dream Keeper* in 1932 and *Shakespeare in Harlem* in 1941, this was the only volume of poetry Hughes published. Few of these songs ever reappeared in later poetic books, not even the powerful "Let America Be America Again," which opens:

> Let America be America again.
> Let it be the dream it used to be.
> Let it be the pioneer on the plain
> Seeking a home where he himself is free.

> (America never was America to me.)

When Hughes chose the texts for *The Langston Hughes Reader* (1958) and *Selected Poems* (1959), both published by mainstream New York houses, he attempted to erase most of the poetry of the 1930s from the record.

Hughes's turn to the left was also a turn to the world outside the predominantly African American community within which he had made his literary career in the 1920s. In 1930, he traveled to Cuba, where he was met by a delegation including the poet Nicolás Guillén, and then to Haiti, where he met with the Haitian writer Jacques Roumain. Hughes later translated works of Guillén, Roumain, and other Caribbean authors into English. In 1932–1933, he traveled to the Soviet Union in order to work on a film about race relations in the American South, *Black and White*. The movie project was soon abandoned, but Hughes finally returned to San Francisco in 1934 via Siberia, China, Japan, and Hawaii. Upon his return, he lived at the home of Noël Sullivan in Carmel, where his neighbors included the poet Robinson Jeffers and the muckraker Lincoln Steffens. In 1937, he went to Madrid to report on the Spanish Civil War. In no other decade did Hughes so often offer the hope that blacks and whites working together could overcome the problems of racism and poverty, and in no other decade did he meet so many whites who were equally sincere in that goal. Many of them, like Hughes himself, later paid for that hope by being hauled before the House Un-American Activities Committee and Senator Joseph McCarthy.

Hughes certainly never turned away from the African American journals that had carried his work in the 1920s. He published nearly as many poems in *Opportunity* from 1931 to 1940 as in the *New Masses,* for example, and many of these poems had more in common with the contents of *The Weary Blues* than with "Good Morning, Revolution" or "Goodbye, Christ." "Genius Child" (with its grim ending: "*Nobody loves a genius child. / Kill him*—and let his soul run wild!*") reprises the personal despair sounded in a number of poems of the 1920s, many of which were collected in the small, privately printed *Dear Lovely Death* (1931). And the often reprinted "Florida Road Workers" borrowed the ironic voice heard in *Fine Clothes to the Jew:*

Hey, Buddy!
Look at me!

I'm makin' a road
For the cars to fly by on,
Makin' a road
Through the palmetto thicket
For light and civilization
To travel on.

I'm makin' a road
For the rich to sweep over
In their big cars
And leave me standin' here.

Sure,
A road helps everybody.
Rich folks ride—
And I get to see 'em ride.
I ain't never seen nobody
Ride so fine before.

Hey, Buddy, look!
*I'm makin' a road!*

Many of Hughes's poems, like "Mother to Son" and the contents of *The Negro Mother and Other Dramatic Recitations* (1931), are dramatic monologues, so it is not surprising that Hughes harbored thoughts about becoming a playwright. He made several attempts in the late 1920s, notably the tragedy *Mulatto,* which in 1935 became the first play by an African American to appear on Broadway, and the comedy *Mule Bone,* written in cooperation with Hurston. The two authors had a falling out just before the play was to open in Cleveland. The text has been published by Henry Louis Gates, and the drama had its first performance in 1991 in New York. Hughes returned to drama after the break with Mrs. Mason, and during the 1930s he wrote more than nine plays, some of them racial in theme, like *Little Ham, When the Jack Hollers,* and *Soul Gone Home,* and some which reflected his radical politics, like *Scottsboro Limited* (1932), *Don't You Want to Be Free?,* and *Angelo Herndon Jones.* Hughes also collaborated on an opera, *Troubled Island* (1949), with the composer William Grant Still. On the whole, however, Hughes was not able to bring the sustained dramatic tension found in many of his monologues to the stage.

Two of his most significant publications in these years were the classic children's book, *Popo and Fifina* (1932), written with Arna Bontemps, and a collection of short stories, *The Ways of White Folks* (1934). In a typically "simple," yet subtle chapter title in his second autobiography, *I Wonder As I Wander,* "D. H. Lawrence between Us," Hughes relates how his desire to read Lawrence angered a lover. But the title also places Lawrence between Hughes and the reader, for Hughes says that the inspiration for the first stories of *The Ways of White Folks* came from reading the stories in Lawrence's *The Lovely Lady.* "If D. H. Lawrence can write such psychologically powerful accounts of folks in England, that send shivers up and down my spine, maybe I could write stories like his about folks in America." Hughes was particularly drawn to Lawrence's tales of "possessive people." In many of the stories in *The Ways of White Folks,* Hughes investigates how, fifty years after the end of slavery, whites still look upon African Americans as "possessions." As Maryemma Graham says, in this volume Hughes depicts "the cultural legacy of racism and its inherent features, interracial hypocrisy, sexual exploitation, and psychological repression" with a dry, ironic voice.

In "The Blues I'm Playing," a white patron, like Hughes's own Mrs. Mason, tries to dissuade her young black protégé from both marriage and the blues. Hughes contrasts Oceola's deep emotional life with the sterile, loveless, unappealing white world of her patron. In "Poor Black Fellow," a white couple cannot understand why the son of their maid, who they raised as their "own" after her death, refuses to accept their view of his place in the world. The word "own" recurs throughout the book; in "A Good Job Gone," a woman of the evening complains of her white client: "Just because they pay you, they always think they own you. No white man's gonna own me." Much of the tension in the stories comes from the confrontation between blacks who have put "slavery days" behind them and whites who have not. The book ends with the story "Father and Son," in which a white father views his mulatto offspring as "Cora's children" and insists, "I don't have trouble with my colored folks. They do what I say or what Talbot says, and that's all there is to it." The one son who asserts his birthright kills his father in a confrontation and then shoots himself to avoid a lynch mob.

In 1940, Hughes published his first autobiography, *The Big Sea.* New attention to the nature of African American autobiography as a genre helps us understand why Hughes seems reluctant to "confess." Hughes stands throughout the book both as an individual and a representative of his race. The poverty and racial exclusion that he encountered was experienced by nearly all African Americans, a fact that Hughes wants to keep before us. Further, Hughes's personal successes are not simply a sign of his innate talent, but also evidence that many African Americans have the ability to be poets and artists if given the opportunity. Like the characters in *The Ways of White Folks,* Hughes depicts himself involved in struggles against others who view him as a "possession" and who see his race as inferior. The first major challenge comes from his self-hating father, who offers the young Hughes wealth if he gives up his idea to be a poet among blacks. And the next challenge comes from his white patron, Mrs. Mason, who promises financial security if Hughes abdicates his artistic freedom. As Hughes shows in the stories of *The Ways of White Folks,* slavery might have been abolished, but the attitudes remained. *The Big Sea* is a tale of Hughes's escape to freedom, so that at the end he can begin anew as a full-time writer. Rampersad says that "the powerful ability of the text to convince its readers derives most from its astonishingly simple, water-clear prose, which certifies the integrity of Hughes's narrative." Yet, as we have seen, the simple style does not actually certify the integrity of the narrative, for Hughes did not, for example, write the version of "When Sue Wears Red" when he was in high school as the text suggests.

### THE RETURN TO HARLEM

So we stand here
On the edge of hell
In Harlem
And look out on the world
And wonder
What we're gonna do
In the face of what
We remember.
("Harlem," from *The Panther and the Lash: Poems of Our Times,* 1967)

The publication of *Shakespeare in Harlem,* says Barksdale, announced to the literary world that Hughes had returned poetically to Harlem. And not just poetically, for in 1941 Hughes moved to Harlem and made it his home for the rest of his life. Barksdale says of *Shakespeare in Harlem* that after "the somewhat frenetic international traveling of the 1930s and after the years of outspoken commitment to radical political and social causes, his literary homecoming was rather quiet. In fact the poems in this volume reflect a return to the folk poet" of *The Weary Blues* and *Fine Clothes to the Jew*. Hughes's picture of the life of African Americans in this volume lacks the exuberance of many of his poems which were written during the Harlem Renaissance, a difference that might stem partly from the fact that things were, in fact, grimmer after years of the Depression and also from the fact that a man at forty has less natural optimism, and less interest in doing the Charleston, than a man of twenty-four. With *Shakespeare in Harlem*, Hughes again writes extensively in the blues form he had utilized extensively in *Fine Clothes to the Jew,* but almost abandoned in the 1930s. "Evenin' Air Blues" ends:

> But if you was to ask me:
> How de blues they come to be,
> Says if you was to ask me
> How de blues they come to be—
> You wouldn't need to ask me:
> Just look at me and see!

Hughes also included a number of "ballads," poems with a similar tone and theme to his blues poems but that had four-line instead of six-line stanzas, like "Ballad of the Girl Whose Name Is Mud."

> A girl with all that raising,
> Its hard to understand
> How she could get in trouble
> With a no-good man.

The most powerful pieces in the volume are those that deal with race and segregation, like "Merry-Go-Round" and "Ku Klux" (which opens: "They took me out / To some lonesome place. / They said, 'Do you believe / In the great white race?'").

Hughes became a major voice for equal treatment for African Americans in the armed forces after the beginning of World War II, and a group of poems on this theme, entitled *Jim Crow's Last Stand,* was published by the Negro Publication Society of America in 1943. One poem, "Red Cross," dealt with the segregation of blood donations:

> The Angel of Mercy's
> Got her wings in the mud,
> And all because of
> Negro blood.

That year also saw the appearance of two of Hughes's most enduring creations. In his "Here to Yonder" column in the *Chicago Defender,* which he began writing in November 1942, Hughes introduced the character of Simple, or Jesse B. Semple, a Harlem everyman who converses about life with a more educated companion in the confines of Paddy's Bar. In the first columns, the subject was naturally about the war and segregation in the army. But Hughes then branched out to examine Simple's relations with his wife, from whom he is separated; his "good" girlfriend, Joyce; his "bad" girlfriend, Zarita; and his landlady. Hughes, with his uncanny ear, captured the speech of Harlem, and readers wrote in saying that they knew someone like Simple. But the truth is that no one in a bar had conversations like those that Simple had with his companion. For at the heart of the Simple stories is the question, as put by Simple himself, "What do you mean by all that language?"

> "If you hadn't quit your wife, you wouldn't need a divorce," I said. "If I had a wife *I* would stay with her," said Simple.

"You have never been married, pal, so you do not know how hard it is sometimes to stay with a wife."

"Elucidate," I said, "while we go into the bar for a beer."

"A wife you have to take with a grain of salt," Simple explained, "but sometimes the salt runs out."

"What do you mean by that parable?"

"Don't take seriously everything a wife says."

This is not the sort of conversation one might hear in a bar, in Harlem or elsewhere, largely because Simple's first comment, which ends the part of the dialogue one might hear in a bar, needs no further analysis. At this point one might expect commiseration, teasing, expressions of relief from the unmarried, but not "elucidation." Instead of elucidation, Simple "explains," and in turn is asked what he "means by that parable," which leads to a discussion of how to interpret what a wife "says." Simple's comments are filled with wordplay, as when he says: "In this life, I been underfed, underpaid, undernourished and everything but undertaken . . . and that ain't all, I been abused, confused, misused an' accused." Simple often puns on the larger vocabulary of his companion, as when Simple's girlfriend Joyce tells him, "Don't insinuate." "Before *you* sin, you better wait," Simple responds. And in many of the stories, as Donald Dickinson in his *American Writers* essay in 1979 noted, "Simple has the final word in a brief flash of wit." It is surprising that in the 1970s and 1980s, when deconstructionist and structuralist criticism were in vogue, scholars did not examine the Simple stories at the metatextual level to assess what all this language about language means.

It is said that after Samuel Beckett wrote *Krapp's Last Tape,* a male monologue, he then felt the need to compose *Happy Days,* a female counterpart. Something similar seems to have happened with Hughes, for soon after the appearance of Simple, Hughes created Madam Alberta K. Johnson, "Madam to you." Her similarity to Simple can be seen from "Madam's Calling Cards":

I had some cards printed
The other day.
They cost me more
Than I wanted to pay.

I told the man
I wasn't no mint,
But I hankered to see
My name in print.

MADAM JOHNSON,
ALBERTA K.
He said, Your name looks good
Madam'd that way.

Shall I use Old English
Or a Roman letter?
I said, Use American.
American's better.

There's nothing foreign
To my pedigree:
Alberta K. Johnson—
*American* that's me.

The irregular stanzas are much more effective than the four-line ballads in *Shakespeare in Harlem* because Madam has a stronger personality than the other speakers, and the irregularity of the line lengths can be attributed to the fact that she is semiliterate. And, like Simple, Madam often gets the upper hand by a semantic twist in the last line. If Madam proved less durable than Simple, it was largely because the dialogue form of the stories was more malleable than the monologues of the Madam poems. Still, the volume *One-Way Ticket* (1949) opens with twelve poems in which "Madam" offers her view of the world.

Hughes published one other volume of verse in the 1940s, *Fields of Wonder* (1947). It contains new poems along with pieces that date from the early 1920s but were left out of his earlier books. And thematically Hughes thought of it as his lyrical volume, with "lyrical" also encompassing nonracial or nature poems. Two sections of the book, "Stars over Harlem" and "Words Like Freedom," carry racial and political overtones, but the bulk of the volume contains works like "Distance Nowhere":

> I used to wonder
> About living and dying—
> I think the difference lies
> Between tears and crying.
>
> I used to wonder
> About here and there—
> I think the distance
> Is nowhere.

Hughes had chastised Countee Cullen in "The Negro Artist and the Racial Mountain" for desiring to "be a poet—not a Negro poet," which Hughes had interpreted as a desire to write like a white poet and, in essence, a desire to be white. Hughes may not have wanted to be white in 1947, but he wanted to have a volume of poetry, which, like volumes the white poets published, was not centered primarily on race. *Fields of Wonder* has received less attention from critics than Hughes's other work, in part for its very lack of attention to race. R. Baxter Miller has tried to recuperate the lyric voice of *Fields of Wonder* by showing how the poems, like "Desert," exhibit "a real concern with community." Still, Hughes ironically had predicted in his essay "My Adventures as a Social Poet" what the result would be, when he said: "Try as I might to float off into the clouds, poverty and Jim Crow would grab me by the heels." Hughes was rarely able to accomplish such a flight.

*One-Way Ticket* includes the racial and political poems written since *Shakespeare in Harlem* along with a few earlier pieces that had not been reprinted. The book starts out with twelve poems featuring Madam Alberta K. Johnson, and includes the strong "Note on Commercial Theatre":

> You've taken my blues and gone—
> You sing 'em on Broadway

> And you sing 'em in Hollywood Bowl,
> And you mixed 'em up with symphonies
> And you fixed 'em so they don't sound like me.
> Yep, you've done taken my blues and gone.
>
> You also took my spirituals and gone.
> You put me in *MacBeth* and *Carmen Jones*
> And all kinds of *Swing Mikados*
> And in everything but what's about me—
> But someday somebody'll
> Stand up and talk about me,
> And write about me—
> Black and beautiful—
> And sing about me,
> And put on plays about me!
> I reckon it'll be
> Me myself!
>
> Yes, it'll be me.

and "Visitors to the Black Belt":

> You can talk about
> *Across* the railroad tracks—
> To me it's *here*
> On this side of the tracks.
>
> You can talk about
> *Up* in Harlem—
> To me it's *here*
> In Harlem.
>
> You can say
> Jazz on the South Side—
> To me it's hell
> On the South Side:
>     Kitchenettes
>     with no heat
>     And garbage
>     In the halls.
>
> Who're you outsider?
>
> Ask me who I am?

The blues poems seem old; indeed, one of them, "Too Blue," with its echo of Hughes's early famous poem, seems to suggest that he has reached his limit in the genre. It opens:

I got those sad old weary blues
And I don't know where to turn.
I don't know where to go.
Nobody cares about you
When you sink so low.

In many respects, the poems of *One-Way Ticket* suggest that Hughes did not know where to turn. He could still turn out moving poems about race in America, but he had not seemed to grow between *Shakespeare in Harlem* and *One-Way Ticket* and certainly did not seem to be looking for ambitious new fields to till. In retrospect, however, some of the short poems of *One-Way Ticket*, like "Raid," "Deceased," and "Blues on a Box" suggested what Hughes would try next. But they hardly prepared readers for the "long" poem *Montage of a Dream Deferred* (1951).

### THE VOICE OF A DREAM DEFERRED

Lulu said to Leonard,
I want a diamond ring.
Leonard said to Lulu,
You won't get a goddamn thing!

> *A certain*
> *amount of nothing*
> *in a dream deferred.*
> ("Same in Blues," in *Montage of a Dream Deferred*)

*Montage of a Dream Deferred* certainly owes a debt to Gwendolyn Brooks's *A Street in Bronzeville,* another poetic sequence that attempts to offer a picture of life in the African American section of a major city. The opening section of *A Street in Bronzeville,* "Kitchenette," asks:

But could a dream send up through onion fumes
Its white and violet, fight with fried potatoes
And yesterdays' garbage ripening in the hall
Flutter, or sing an aria down these rooms

Even if we were willing to let it in,
Had time to warm it, keep it very clean
Anticipate a message, let it begin?

Hughes's long poem, like Brooks's, would also examine the state of "the dream" among urban African Americans. But in virtuosity of form and linguistic invention, *Montage of a Dream Deferred* surpasses both *A Street in Bronzeville* as well as Melvin Tolson's *Harlem Gallery* (1965) as the "epic" of African American poetry. The contrast between Brooks's opening, which fits an African American viewpoint into a modernist form, and Hughes's first section could not be more striking.

"Dream Boogie"

Good morning, daddy!
Ain't you heard
The boogie-woogie rumble
Of a dream deferred?

Listen closely:
You'll hear their feet
Beating out and beating out a—

> *You think*
> *It's a happy beat?*

Listen to it closely:
Ain't you heard
Something underneath
Like a—

> *What did I say?*

Sure,
I'm happy!
Take it away!

> *Hey, pop!*
> *Re-bop!*
> *Mop!*

> *Y-e-a-h*

In short segments, Hughes illustrates how the economics of poverty perverts dreams. In "Sister," the mother tells her son:

> *Did it ever occur to you, son,*
> *the reason Marie runs around with trash*
> *is she wants some cash?*

Amidst such poems, Hughes places "Juke Box Love Song," which reads like a Hughes poem about the vibrant Harlem of the 1920s, and, if the text is read as the love song on the juke box, can be seen as an oldie that plays among relationships centered on money.

> Take Harlem's heartbeat,
> Make a drumbeat,
> Put it on a record, let it whirl,
> And while we listen to it play,
> Dance with you till day—
> Dance with you, my sweet brown Harlem girl.

In a preface Hughes said that "this poem on contemporary Harlem, like be-bop, is marked by conflicting changes, sudden nuances, sharp and impudent interjections, broken rhythms, and passages sometimes in the manner of a jam session." Critics have tended to view the poem as if it *were* a jam session, to discuss whether the fusion of jazz and poetry works, and to compare it to the songs or recordings of famous blues artists. That is missing the point, for jazz is simply one element in the creation of the poem. For example, the title of the poem, *Montage of a Dream Deferred* clearly points to another art form marked by conflicting changes, sudden nuances, and sharp and impudent interjections, and suggests that the whole is meant to be a collage in the style of Romare Bearden as much as a jam session.

*Montage of a Dream Deferred* is the African American epic because its disparate parts do in fact present a forceful picture of Harlem that combines the language and forms of the place within the artistic framework used in the modern American epic poem of place, like William Carlos Williams' *Paterson,* Charles Olson's *The Maximus Poems,* and Melvin Tolson's *Harlem Gallery.* If Hughes's long poem has not always been granted that status, it is because criticism has yet to deal with the poem as a whole, rather than in pieces, and because many critics have not recognized, let alone fully treated, Hughes's achievement of building a poetic sequence on the forms and language of a pop culture which was beyond the knowledge of the intellectual establishment. Now that ethnic culture has become mainstream, and hip-hop has extended beyond its African American origins, we should finally be able to catch up to Hughes.

Hughes continued to publish poems in the 1950s, but his focus was elsewhere and it was his least productive decade poetically. Hughes himself had said that he was a "social poet," and in the early part of the decade, before his appearance in Washington before the House Un-American Activities Committee, he was keeping anything controversial at arm's length. He was able to survive the ordeal only slightly singed. He repudiated some of his radical verse as the youthful zeal of a young man, but he was not required to speak about friends and associates. It is worth noting that, both before and after acting "simple" before the committee, Hughes was engaged in transforming his Simple columns into books.

The first volume of Simple stories, *Simple Speaks His Mind,* appeared in 1950, followed by *Simple Takes a Wife* (1953), *Simple Stakes a Claim* (1958), and *Simple's Uncle Sam* (1965); there was also a play, *Simply Heavenly* (collected in *Five Plays*), which premiered in 1957. Harper, in her book *Not So Simple,* has investigated how Hughes altered the newspaper columns for book publication in order to form a coherent whole and to reach a multiracial audience. Audience was crucial to Hughes; he often altered a poem which he had published in an African American journal before he presented it to a white audience. Harper's study is the first to analyze this process in depth.

Hughes continued to oppose segregation at home as well as speaking out against colonialism abroad. He contributed "Memo to Non-White Peoples" to the South African journal *Africa South* (collected in *Good Morning, Revolution*).

They will let you have dope
Because they are quite willing
To drug you or kill you.

They will let you have babies
Because they are quite willing
To pauperize you—
Or use your kids as labor boys
For army, air force, or uranium mine.

They will let you have alcohol
To make you sodden and drunk
And foolish.

They will gleefully let you
Kill your damn self any way you choose
With liquor, drugs, or whatever.

It's the same from Cairo to Chicago,
Cape Town to the Caribbean,
Do you travel the Stork Club circuit
To dear Old Shepherd's Hotel?
(Somebody burnt Shepherd's up.)
I'm sorry but it is
The same from Cairo to Chicago,
Cape Town to the Carib Hilton,
Exactly the same.

Hughes's next volume of verse, however, was another long poem, *Ask Your Mama: 12 Moods for Jazz* (1961). In this work, Hughes attempts to fuse words and music, providing musical notations and instructions for accompaniment. The basic theme was again the deferred dream of civil rights in America and the world at large. The first section opens:

IN THE
IN THE QUARTER
IN THE QUARTER OF THE NEGROES

WHERE THE DOORS ARE DOORS OF PAPER
DUST OF DINGY ATOMS
BLOWS A SCRATCHY SOUND.
AMORPHOUS JACK-O'-LANTERNS CAPER
AND THE WIND WON'T WAIT FOR MID-
    NIGHT
FOR FUN TO BLOW DOORS DOWN.

Hughes recognized that his new work was difficult and so provided "Liner Notes for the Poetically Unhep," which give brief prose summaries of the issues engaged with in the sections of the poem. For the opening lines of the poem, Hughes wrote, "In Negro sections of the South where doors have no resistance to violence, danger always whispers harshly. Klansmen cavort, and havoc may come at any time." This hardly seems to be necessary information. At other times, the notes are only two or three sentences, which note the overall theme but fail to elucidate thorny passages. It is possible that Hughes was poking fun at the use made of notes by T. S. Eliot in *The Waste Land* and Melvin Tolson in *Harlem Gallery,* which many white critics hailed as the first truly African American modernist poem. At times the text seems to descend into a list of names.

Hughes's anger in this work was couched in the form of an insult, for both the title and some of the contents alluded to "the Dozens," a game of verbal abuse among African Americans in which derogatory comments are made about an opponent's female relatives. In *Ask Your Mama,* Hughes takes the Dozens outside the intra-ethnic environment in which it is usually played and puts it into the context of inter-ethnic situations, as, for example, in the section "Cultural Exchange":

AND THEY ASKED ME RIGHT AT CHRIST-
    MAS
IF MY BLACKNESS, WOULD IT RUB OFF?
I SAID, ASK YOUR MAMA.

THEY ASKED ME AT THE PTA
IS IT TRUE THAT NEGROES——?
I SAID, ASK YOUR MAMA

Or when Hughes speaks in "Horn of Plenty" of the experience of "the only Negroes on the block":

THEY RUNG MY BELL TO ASK ME
COULD I RECOMMEND A MAID.
I SAID, YES, YOUR MAMA.

Although Hughes says in an introductory note that the "Hesitation Blues" provide "the leitmotif for this poem" neither in that note nor elsewhere in his remarks does he call attention to the importance of the Dozens for *Ask Your Mama*. So the poem has several metatextual significations depending on audience. Certainly white readers would know that, in the passages quoted, the "Ask Your Mama" answers to questions were supposed to be insults. But most would have to process those answers without the context of the tradition of the Dozens, in which the insults are a shared verbal game. In *Ask Your Mama,* the structure of the African American game appears to provide a cover for Hughes to offer insults that are not meant in fun. As with Simple, we are forced to come to grips with the problem of what is meant by all that language.

### "STILL HERE"

I've been scarred and battered
My hopes the wind done scattered.
Snow has friz me, sun has baked me.
 Looks like between 'em
 They done tried to make me
Stop laughin', stop lovin', stop livin',
 But I don't care!
 I'm still here!

("Still Here")

Hughes's last collection, *The Panther and the Lash,* which came out shortly after his death in 1967, is dedicated to Rosa Parks, whose refusal to give up her seat on the bus sparked the Montgomery bus boycott in 1955. This dedication signals the collection's concern with social issues, with the civil rights movement at home, and with the struggle to end colonialism abroad. The volume has been criticized for offering contradictory political perspectives, sometimes expressing an anger approaching militancy in "Black Panther" and at other times offering a less assertive desire for integration. Part of the reason was that *The Panther*

*and the Lash* was a mixture of old and new poems. "Daybreak in Alabama," the last poem in the book, with its vision of unity ("And I'm gonna put white hands / And black hands and brown and yellow hands / And red clay earth hands in it") was written in 1940. Hughes's tone in his later poems on race and civil rights was more impatient and angry.

"Sweet Words on Race" captures Hughes's growing impatience with lack of progress toward the goal of real equality:

Sweet words that take
Their own sweet time to flower
And then so quickly wilt
Within the inner ear,
Belie the budding promise
Of their pristine hour
To wither in the
Sultry air of fear.

Hughes never lost his belief that the struggle was worth it. In another poem with a title that draws attention to language, "Question and Answer," he wrote:

Durban, Birmingham,
Cape Town, Atlanta,
Johannesburg, Watts,
The earth around
Struggling, fighting,
Dying—for what?

*A world to gain.*

Groping, hoping,
Waiting—for what?

*A world to gain.*

Dreams kicked asunder,
Why not go under?

*There's a world to gain.*

But suppose I don't want it,
Why take it?

*To remake it.*

Most of Hughes's enormous output was written to assist the remaking of the world. For Hughes, the poet was not just a dreamer, but also a dream keeper, a position that by its very definition had a social and political dimension. Donald Dickinson noted in his *American Writers* essay the irony in the fact that Hughes's reputation is stronger abroad than at home. One reason that Hughes looms large in the third world is that poets in those regions function as the dream keepers for their people living under the rule of colonial governments or military juntas. Hughes matters in places, that is, where poets and poetry still matter in the larger world. Hughes's writing is, according to Dickinson, "an illuminating and realistic portrait of the American black." But it is more than that. To a degree not yet completely recognized, it was an insightful investigation into the racial, social, and political meanings of the American language and an attempt to remake it. And he had amazing success. As Henry Taylor stated in his review of *The Collected Poems* in the *New York Times Book Review,*

It is the rare poet whose words enter the culture with the apparent durability of, say, "a dream deferred." Lorraine Hansberry's play "A Raisin in the Sun," Sara Lawrence-Lightfoot's book "I've Known Rivers"— the titles are phrases taken from the pen of Langston Hughes, and so is "black like me." To lodge such fragments so broadly and so deeply requires not only a gift for poetry but also an unusual affinity with the language of popular speech and song.

Hughes not only had the gift and the affinity to lodge such fragments so broadly and deeply, he also had the intention.

# Selected Bibliography

## WORKS OF LANGSTON HUGHES

### POETRY
*The Weary Blues.* New York: Knopf, 1926.

*Fine Clothes to the Jew.* New York: Knopf, 1927.
*Dear Lovely Death.* Amenia, N.Y.: Troutbeck Press, 1931.
*The Negro Mother and Other Dramatic Recitations.* New York: Golden Stair, 1931.
*The Dream Keeper and Other Poems.* New York: Knopf, 1932.
*A New Song.* New York: International Workers Order, 1938.
*Shakespeare in Harlem.* New York: Knopf, 1942.
*Jim Crow's Last Stand.* Atlanta: Negro Publication Society, 1943.
*Fields of Wonder.* New York: Knopf, 1947.
*One-Way Ticket.* New York: Knopf, 1949.
*Montage of a Dream Deferred.* New York: Holt, 1951.
*Selected Poems.* New York: Knopf, 1959.
*Ask Your Mama: 12 Moods for Jazz.* New York: Knopf, 1961.
*The Panther and the Lash: Poems of Our Times.* New York: Knopf, 1967.
*Don't You Turn Back.* New York: Knopf, 1969.
*The Collected Poems of Langston Hughes.* Edited by Arnold Rampersad and David Roessel. New York: Knopf, 1994.

### NOVELS AND SHORT STORIES
*Not without Laughter.* New York: Knopf, 1930.
*The Ways of White Folks.* New York: Knopf, 1934.
*Simple Speaks His Mind.* New York: Simon & Schuster, 1950.
*Laughing to Keep from Crying.* New York: Holt, 1952.
*Simple Takes a Wife.* New York: Simon & Schuster, 1953.
*Simple Stakes a Claim.* New York: Rinehart, 1958.
*Tambourines to Glory.* New York: Day, 1958.
*Something in Common and Other Stories.* New York: Hill and Wang, 1963.
*Simple's Uncle Sam.* New York: Hill and Wang, 1965.
*The Return of Simple.* Edited by Donna Sullivan Harper. New York: Hill and Wang, 1994.
*Short Stories.* Edited by Akiba Sullivan Harper. New York: Hill and Wang, 1996.

### PLAYS AND OPERAS
*Scottsboro Limited.* New York: Golden Stair, 1932.
*Troubled Island.* With William Grant Still. New York: Leeds Music, 1949. (Opera in three acts. First production: New York City Opera, 1949.)

*Five Plays*. Bloomington: Indiana University Press, 1963. (Includes *Mulatto, Little Ham, Soul Gone Home,* and *Simply Heaven*.)

*Mule Bone*. With Zora Neale Hurston. Edited by Henry Louis Gates. New York: Vintage, 1991.

### ESSAYS

*The Sweet Flypaper of Life*. New York: Simon & Schuster, 1955. (With photographs by Roy DeCarava.)

*Black Misery*. New York: Eriksson, 1969.

*Langston Hughes and the "Chicago Defender": Essays on Race, Politics, and Culture*. Edited by Christopher De Santis. Urbana: University of Illinois Press, 1995.

### NONFICTION

*Famous American Negroes*. New York: Dodd, Mead, 1954.

*Famous Negro Music Makers*. New York: Dodd, Mead, 1955.

*A Pictorial History of the Negro in America*. With Milton Meltzer. New York: Crown, 1956.

*Famous Negro Heroes of America*. New York: Dodd, Mead, 1958.

*Fight for Freedom: The Story of the NAACP*. New York: Norton, 1962.

*Black Magic: A Pictorial History of the Negro in American Entertainment*. With Milton Meltzer. Englewood Cliffs, N.J.: Prentice Hall, 1967.

### CHILDREN'S BOOKS

*Popo and Fifina*. With Arna Bontemps. New York: Macmillan, 1932. Reprinted, New York: Oxford University Press, 1993.

*The First Book of Negroes*. New York: Watts, 1952.

*The First Book of Rhythms*. New York: Watts, 1954.

*The First Book of Jazz*. New York: Watts, 1955.

*The First Book of the West Indies*. New York: Watts, 1956.

*The First Book of Africa*. New York: Watts, 1960.

### CORRESPONDENCE AND PAPERS

*Arna Bontemps–Langston Hughes: Letters 1925–1967*. Selected and edited by Charles Nichols. New York: Dodd Mead, 1980.

Hughes's papers are held by the James Weldon Johnson Collection, Beinecke Rare Book and Manuscript Library, Yale University.

### COLLECTED WORKS

*The Langston Hughes Reader*. New York: Braziller, 1958.

*Good Morning Revolution: Uncollected Writings of Social Protest*. Edited by Faith Berry. 2d ed. New York: Citadel Press, 1992. (Includes "Good Morning, Revolution," "Goodbye, Christ," "My Adventures as a Social Poet," and "Memo to Non-white Peoples.")

### AUTOBIOGRAPHIES

*The Big Sea*. New York: Knopf, 1940.

*I Wonder As I Wander*. New York: Rinehart, 1956.

### TRANSLATIONS

Roumain, Jacques. *Masters of the Dew*. New York: Reynal and Hitchcock, 1947. (Translated with Mercer Cook.)

Guillén, Nicolás. *Cuba Libre*. Los Angeles: Anderson and Ritchie, 1948. (Translated with Benjamin Carruthers.)

García Lorca, Federico. *Gypsy Ballads*. Beloit, Wis.: Beloit College, 1951.

Mistral, Gabriela. *Selected Poems*. Bloomington: Indiana University Press, 1957.

### WORKS EDITED BY LANGSTON HUGHES

*The Poetry of the Negro 1746–1949*. With Arna Bontemps. New York: Doubleday, 1949. Revised edition, 1970.

*The Book of Negro Folklore*. With Arna Bontemps. New,York: Dodd, Mead, 1958.

*An African Treasury: Articles, Essays, Stories, Poems*. New York: Crown, 1960.

*Poems from Black Africa*. Bloomington: Indiana University Press, 1963.

*New Negro Poets U.S.A.* Bloomington: Indiana University Press, 1964.

*The Book of Negro Humor*. New York: Dodd, Mead 1966.

*The Best Short Stories by Negro Writers: An Anthology from 1899 to the Present*. Boston: Little, Brown, 1967.

## BIBLIOGRAPHIES

Dickinson, Donald. *A Bio-Bibliography of Langston Hughes, 1902–1967*. 2d ed. Hamden, Conn.: Archon, 1972.

Mikolyzk, Thomas. *Langston Hughes: A Bio-Bibliography*. New York: Greenwood, 1990.

Miller, R. Baxter. *Langston Hughes and Gwendolyn Brooks: A Reference Guide*. New York: Garland, 1978.

O'Daniel, Therman. "A Selected Classified Bibliography." *CLA Journal* 11, no. 4:439–466 (June 1968).


*CRITICAL AND BIOGRAPHICAL STUDIES*


Barksdale, Richard. *Langston Hughes: The Poet and His Critics*. Chicago: American Library Association, 1977

Berry, Faith. *Langston Hughes: Before and Beyond Harlem*. 2d ed. New York: Citadel Press, 1992.

Bloom, Harold, ed. *Langston Hughes: Modern Critical Views*. New York: Chelsea House, 1989.

Emmanuel, James A. *Langston Hughes*. Boston: Twayne, 1967.

Gates, Henry Louis, and Anthony Appiah, eds. *Langston Hughes: Critical Perspectives Past and Present*. New York: Amistead, 1993.

Gibson, Donald. *Five Black Writers: Essays on Wright, Ellison, Baldwin, Hughes, and Le Roi Jones*. New York: New York University Press, 1970.

Harper, Akiba Sullivan. *Not So Simple: The "Simple" Stories of Langston Hughes*. Columbia: University of Missouri Press, 1995.

Jemie, Onwuchekwa. *Langston Hughes: An Introduction to His Poetry*. New York: Columbia University Press, 1976.

Johnson, Dianne. *Telling Tales: The Pedagogy and Promise of African American Literature for Youth*. New York: Greenwood, 1990.

Miller, R. M. Baxter. *The Art and Imagination of Langston Hughes*. Lexington: University of Kentucky Press, 1989.

Mullen, Edward J., ed. *Critical Essay on Langston Hughes*. Boston: G. K. Hall, 1986.

———. *Langston Hughes in the Hispanic World*. Hamden, Conn: Archon Books, 1977.

O'Daniel, Therman. *Langston Hughes, Black Genius: A Critical Evaluation*. New York: Morrow, 1971.

Ostrom, Hans. *Langston Hughes: A Study of the Short Fiction*. New York: Twayne, 1993.

Rampersad, Arnold. *The Life of Langston Hughes*. 2 vols. New York: Oxford University Press, 1986 and 1988.

Rollins, Charlemae. *Black Troubador: Langston Hughes*. Chicago: Rand McNally, 1970. (For young readers.)

Tracy, Stephen. *Langston Hughes and the Blues*. Urbana: University of Illinois Press, 1988.

Trotman, James C., ed. *Langston Hughes: The Man, His Art, and His Continuing Influence*. New York: Garland, 1995.

Wagner, Jean. *Black Poets of the United States from Paul Lawrence Dunbar to Langston Hughes*. Urbana: University of Illinois Press, 1973.

Individual articles are too numerous to provide, but special mention must be made of *The Langston Hughes Review,* a journal dedicated to the study of the poet.

—*DAVID ROESSEL*

# Henry James
## 1843–1916

HENRY JAMES PUBLISHED his first tales in the closing years of the Civil War and had produced by the time of his death, nearly midway through World War I, some twenty novels; 113 short stories and novellas; a vast body of literary, art, and cultural criticism; more than a dozen plays; and a series of travel books, not to mention three volumes of his personal memoirs, a biography, and perhaps as many as fifteen thousand letters. His status as one of the handful of American writers to occupy an important position in world literature rests on his great novels, from *Washington Square* and *The Portrait of a Lady* in the late 1870s and early 1880s, to *The Golden Bowl, The Ambassadors,* and *The Wings of the Dove* in the early years of the twentieth century. Moving from realism in his earlier fiction to an intense fusion of realism and symbolism in his later novels and tales, James brought fiction in English to the level of high art established by such European contemporaries and elders as Gustave Flaubert and Ivan Turgenev. He bridged the literary cultures of the Romantics and the late Victorians, on the one hand, and of the Victorians and modernists, on the other hand. He has had greater influence on the practice of other novelists and on critical approaches to the art of fiction than any other American writer.

As Graham Greene remarked, Henry James is "as solitary in the history of the novel as Shakespeare in the history of poetry."

James has never occupied in the popular imagination of American literature the central position he has long held in the eyes of fellow novelists and of specialized literary scholars. In the late 1990s, Nathaniel Hawthorne, William Faulkner, Herman Melville, Ernest Hemingway, and F. Scott Fitzgerald—or, for that matter, Kate Chopin and Alice Walker—are more likely to be taught in secondary schools and even in undergraduate surveys of literature. James's comparative neglect owes much to his reputation for writing difficult, ornate stories about the nuances of manners in a small, wealthy, elite class. Even tributes to James at times suggest that his work is stuffy. For example, acknowledging James as the transitional figure in the development of the modern novel, Virginia Woolf wrote,

These huge tight-stuffed rather airless books of henry james are in truth the bridge upon which we cross from the classic novel which is perfect of its kind to that other form of literature which if names have any importance should someday be christened anew—the modern novel, the novel of the twentieth century.

"Tight-stuffed" and "rather airless" or, in the language of John Carlos Rowe (in "Henry James and the Art of Teaching"), open to charges of "narrowness" and "irrelevance," James's fiction is read in American schools and colleges in remarkably low disproportion to his huge reputation and influence. Beyond the specialized circles of creative writers and literary scholars, Henry James's principal presence in contemporary culture has been through the translation of his works to other media, including, in the 1970s, 1980s, and 1990s, films of *Daisy Miller, The Europeans, The Bostonians, The Portrait of a Lady,* and *The Wings of the Dove.*

Henry James's fiction has been easily adaptable to stage and screen for many reasons: among others, his strong, often melodramatic plots; his memorable characters; and his focus on such enduring concerns as love, death, betrayal, and deception—and some of these reasons belie the idea that James is a writer who will increasingly be seen as narrow and irrelevant. There have always been, moreover, readers who have seen James as a passionately engaged political novelist. Ezra Pound extolled Henry James for his passionate advocacy of individual liberty. In the 1930s, when the leftward ideology of many intellectuals led to the discounting of "genteel" fiction in favor of "proletarian" literature, Stephen Spender made James the paradigm for the modern writer engaged in an analysis of the ills of the modern age. James's characters, Spender wrote (in *The Destructive Element*), "have a kind of awareness which is deeper than his own consciousness; they knew what the years were all the while *meaning.*" Spender was echoing an eloquent letter James wrote as World War I began:

> The plunge of civilization into this abyss of blood and darkness . . . is a thing that so gives away the whole long age during which we have supposed the world to be, with whatever abatement, gradually bettering, that to have to take it all now for what the treacherous years were all the while really making for and *meaning* is too tragic for any words.

Similarly, in the late 1940s, Lionel Trilling focused in *The Liberal Imagination* on the Henry James of *The Princess Casamassima,* an explicitly political novel whose major characters belong to the working and artisan classes not customarily associated with James. In the 1960s, Laurence Bedwell Holland, in *The Expense of Vision,* depicted a Henry James who exposed, in novels such as *The Golden Bowl,* the terrible destructive power of American innocence and American capital. And the last three decades have seen a multiplication of views of James as a key figure in exploring problems and contradictions in modern culture in such areas as gender, sexuality, class, race, colonialism, and power, thus changing what John Carlos Rowe characterized as "the stereotype of him as a difficult writer with little to say to the contemporary age."

## EARLY LIFE

Henry James was born on April 15, 1843, at 21 Washington Place, in New York City's Greenwich Village, the second child of an eccentric religious philosopher, Henry James Sr., and of his wife, Mary Robertson Walsh James. The future novelist was fifteen months junior to the James's first child, William, who became the leading philosopher and psychologist of turn-of-the-century America. Three other children followed in the next five years: Garth Wilkinson James (known as Wilky), Robertson James (known as Bob or Rob), and Alice. Henry James Sr. lived on an inheritance from his father, William James, of Albany, New York, who had immigrated from Ireland shortly after the American Revolution and had amassed one of the largest fortunes in the state as a timber magnate.

Thus enabled to devote himself to his own spiritual development and religious writings, the elder Henry James bestowed upon his children an unconventional, highly peripatetic education. Based alternately in New York City and in Albany—

though the Jameses are often considered New Englanders, Henry James's parents did not settle in Newport, Rhode Island, until 1858 and then moved to Boston, Massachusetts, in 1864—Henry James Sr. took his family on three extended European excursions during Henry James's first seventeen years (1843–1845, 1855–1858, and 1859–1860). Writing his autobiographies more than half a century later, James was so embarrassed by his father's bohemian unsettledness that he reduced the three excursions to two.

James's early fame was associated in the public mind with his invention of the "international theme," his creation of fictions in which conflict and drama were generated by the encounter of fresh, innocent Americans with sophisticated, often corrupt Europeans (or with Europeanized Americans). James's cosmopolitan grasp of English and Continental societies originates in his childhood saturation in life abroad. His earliest memory was of the Napoleonic column in the Place Vendôme in Paris, glimpsed from a carriage when he was two years old. His sense, however, that his family's transatlantic migrations represented a perhaps disreputable unconventionality was expressed in his fiction in the account of Isabel Archer's scandal-haunted childhood in Europe in *The Portrait of a Lady*. More poignantly, in his short story "The Pupil," James describes the bohemian irregularities of an American family in Europe, whose mode of life amounts to nothing less than child abuse for their sensitive son, the title character of the tale.

In America, Henry James Sr. introduced his son Henry to many of the leading writers and religious figures of the mid-nineteenth century. Such persons as William Cullen Bryant, Bronson Alcott, and Ralph Waldo Emerson were visitors in the James family parlor. The father encouraged in his children both a devotion to freedom and an aversion to materialism. He urged them to focus their energies on the life of the mind and of the spirit. His constant injunction to his children was to "Convert! Convert! Convert!"—meaning that they should convert their inherited wealth and material goods to spiritual goods. And yet students of the James family, such as F. O. Matthieson, have argued that the father who aimed to surround his children "as far as possible with an atmosphere of freedom" carried on a covert, lifelong campaign of psychological manipulation and coercion and espoused reactionary and repressive ideas about the role of women in particular. It must be said, nevertheless, that Henry Sr. appears to have been the major formative influence on two of the most brilliant and productive figures of their generation, William and Henry James. "Oh," he said on his deathbed in 1882, "I have such good boys—*such good boys!*"

The James family lived in Newport from 1858 to 1864, except for the year abroad in 1859–1860. In Newport, Henry James sketched and took long walks with William's art instructor, the painter John La Farge, who introduced him to the works of Robert Browning and to several leading French authors, most important, as a model and inspiration for James's own writing, Honoré de Balzac. There, too, he formed an important friendship with his intense cousin Mary (Minnie) Temple, who died of tuberculosis in 1870. James's later invention of "the American girl" as a distinctive type of fictional character owed much to Minnie. This debt is evident especially in his characters Isabel Archer in *The Portrait of a Lady* and Millie Theale (whose first name echoes Minnie's) in *The Wings of the Dove*.

### A LITERARY VOCATION

In 1861, William James gave up art to enter the Lawrence Scientific School at Harvard University. Henry followed him, enrolling in the Harvard Law School in 1862. These years saw the outbreak of the Civil War and the enrollment in the Union army of the two younger James boys. Neither of the older James brothers served in the war. Henry James's failure to do so, despite patriotic enthusiasm for the Union, is tied to an enduring mystery in American biography, his "obscure hurt" (the term he used in his memoirs). Fighting a blaze in a Newport stable as a volunteer fireman, James became jammed between the pumping equipment and the angle of a fence, producing back pain that persisted for many years. A specialist in Boston who examined James was unable to diagnose his symptoms. James seems to date the obscure hurt to the spring of 1861, coincident with the beginning of the Civil War. Leon Edel established, however, that the stable fire occurred in the fall of that year. More recently, we have learned that James was in fact drafted in 1863 but was then granted an exemption for "various complaints," suggesting that physical disability, in all probability the obscure hurt, was the basis for his deferment. In these years of trial for the Republic, James was rapidly embracing his literary vocation. After a year at Harvard, he withdrew to devote himself to writing. His first short story, "A Tragedy of Error," was anonymously published in 1864. From his very early twenties until his old age, James wrote for hours a day virtually every day, usually in the morning, establishing an extraordinarily sustained record of literary productivity.

Throughout the first dozen years of his literary life, James produced art and literary criticism for the leading American journals. He reviewed novels by popular American writers. He also reviewed leading British and French authors, including Charles Dickens, William Makepeace Thackeray, George Eliot, Balzac, and Flaubert. In these essays and reviews, James was intent on defining the terms on which he would vie for literary mastery. He was also establishing a cosmopolitan view of literary art, surveying British and Continental fiction as well as the American scene. His essays on the French writers introduced into the current of Anglo-American criticism serious consideration of the advanced French fiction of the day, of special interest to James because Flaubert and others took the writing of novels seriously as the practice of an art in a way that was atypical for their American and English contemporaries.

Of greatest interest during these years of James's literary apprenticeship are his works of fiction. Between 1864 and 1875, he published thirty-eight short stories, or "tales" as he preferred to call them, and a single novel, *Watch and Ward,* serialized in the *Atlantic Monthly* in 1871 and later ignored by James in accounts of his career. Several of his early tales show the influence of his great American predecessor, Hawthorne. In such tales as "The Romance of Certain Old Clothes" (1868), James drew on the Hawthornian tradition of the supernatural, used as a vehicle to convey psychological themes. Many of the early stories were laboratories for the development of the themes and character types favored by the mature writer. In "The Story of a Year" (1865) and "A Most Extraordinary Case" (1868), for example, James showed how loss of love could sap characters of their vitality, leading eventually to their deaths. Both "A Passionate Pilgrim" (1871) and "Madame de Mauves" (1874) are prototypes for James's famous "international theme," with American protagonists who make journeys from innocence to experience (and, often, to a higher innocence) through an encounter with the culture and people of the Old World. Longmore, the protagonist in "Madame de Mauves," moreover, is an early version of a character type that appears frequently in James's later fiction, the sensitive bachelor who fails to seize the main chance and thus fails really "to live," often by missing an opportunity to love and to be loved. Lambert Strether in *The Ambassadors* (1903) is cut from the same cloth as Longmore.

Other tales of particular interest written during this period include "The Last of the Valerii" (1874), which combines the supernatural and international themes and which seems to foreshadow very closely the marriage between an American heiress and an Italian aristocrat in *The Golden*

*Bowl* (1904); "A Landscape Painter" (1866) and "The Madonna of the Future" (1873), early examples of James's frequent tales of art and artists; and "A Light Man" (1869), which looks forward to James's unreliable narrators in such tales as "The Aspern Papers" (1888) and *The Turn of the Screw* (1898) and also may be interpreted as introducing the homosexual themes some recent commentators have emphasized in readings of tales and novels as diverse as "The Pupil" (1891), *The Sacred Fount* (1901), and *The Ambassadors.*

Travel, like art and literature, was an occasion for writing. James produced travel sketches and essays, not only abroad but also back in the States. Thus, returning to America from a European tour (1869–1870), he went from Cambridge (where his parents had moved in 1866), to Rhode Island, Vermont, and New York to write travel sketches for the *Nation*. Abroad again for more than two years (May 1872 to September 1874), James produced travel sketches for the *Nation* that were later collected, with other travel writings, in *Transatlantic Sketches* (1875). James's writing was bringing in a steady income, and from this point forward he earned enough as a writer to support himself.

In 1871, *Watch and Ward* was published serially in the *Atlantic Monthly*. James had high hopes for this flawed yet portentous performance; it would be, he wrote the *Atlantic,* "one of the greatest works of 'this or any age.'" The story centers on the relationship between Roger Lawrence and his ward: at age twenty-nine, Roger adopts an orphaned twelve-year-old girl, Nora Lambert. A latter-day Pygmalion, Roger attempts to mold Nora into his ideal bride. His eventually successful scheme is complicated and delayed by the emergence of other suitors for Nora. In the 1990s criticism of the novel, following the lead of Alfred Habegger, focused on James's appropriation of elements of contemporary "women's fiction," notably the motif of an orphaned girl or young woman whose destiny is resolved in a marriage with an older man. Often such fictional relationships are tinged with the suggestion of incest; the older man is a father figure or even a long-lost or hitherto unknown half brother or stepbrother. This pattern is evident not only in the relationship between Nora and Roger in *Watch and Ward* but also, more subtly and disturbingly, in the relationship between Isabel Archer and Gilbert Osmond in *The Portrait of a Lady* (1881).

After a decade as a writer, James was not yet a celebrity or a widely acknowledged master of the art of fiction. He had become, however, a self-supporting writer in a wide range of genres, among them art criticism, literary criticism, travel writing—very broadly conceived, since James's travel pieces were not merely Baedeker guides to places but also searching commentaries on the manners and morals, culture and politics, art and architecture of European and American society—and, of course, short stories, novellas, and the novel. He had developed, moreover, many of the themes of his later fiction: the social and moral fabric of American and European civilization; the ethical drama and social comedy generated through encounters between denizens of the Old World and the New; and the struggle of the free spirit, increasingly embodied in young American women, to escape being ground in what he called, in *The Portrait of a Lady* and in his notebook, "the very mill of the conventional." James's writing combined from the first moral seriousness, sophistication, and a highly polished style, marked by felicitous phrasing, urbane wit, and a high density of figurative language. James's tales, the novelist and *Atlantic Monthly* editor William Dean Howells said, "had characteristics which forbad any editor to refuse them."

The year 1875 was a watershed for James. He published his first three books: *A Passionate Pilgrim* (collected stories), *Transatlantic Sketches,* and *Roderick Hudson,* which he came to speak of as his first novel. Returning to America in September of 1874, he tried living and writing in New York City for much of 1875. Late that year, he embarked on his lifelong residence abroad. Although he always considered himself an American (despite his later renunciation of his American citizenship), he chose to live in Europe for reasons at least partly suggested at the end of the decade in his enumeration of the features of European society lacking in the thin soil on which Hawthorne was obliged to draw as an American novelist. To his notebooks he confided, "I have made my choice. . . . My choice is the old world—my choice, my need, my life." Arriving in London en route to Paris in 1875, he wrote to his family back home in Massachusetts: "I take possession of the old world—I inhale it—I appropriate it!"

### A MATURING STYLE

The years 1875 to 1883 mark a distinctive phase of James's career, following the apprenticeship of 1863–1874. James attained his mature power as a literary artist (though not by any means the final, complex evolution of his prose style). James followed *Roderick Hudson,* a far more fully achieved novel than *Watch and Ward,* with the highly successful novel *The American* (1877) and with two shorter novels that are gems of their kind, *The Europeans* (1878) and *Washington Square* (1880). He produced an impressive stream of tales and novellas as well, including *Daisy Miller* (1878), a transatlantic sensation that made him an international celebrity. He continued to produce challenging literary criticism, including *French Poets and Novelists* (1878) and *Hawthorne* (1879), the first book-length study of an American author, and more than seventy contributions to periodicals, including art and literary criticism, travel essays and cultural commentaries, and numerous stories. Nothing in this phase of James's career, however, even remotely rivals the achievement of *The Portrait of a Lady,* a novel that in thematic complexity, vivid and memorable characteriza-

tion, linguistic richness, dramatic structure and power, and philosophical depth at least equaled (or, in the view of many readers then and now, surpassed) any other masterpieces of American fiction created to date, including such novels as Hawthorne's *Scarlet Letter* and Herman Melville's *Moby-Dick.* In his 1882 essay "Henry James, Jr.," James's longtime friend William Dean Howells placed James virtually alone atop the pantheon of current practitioners of fiction in English, rivaled only by George Eliot. The following year, the English publisher Macmillan brought out the first collected edition of Henry James's novels and tales, in fourteen volumes.

The serialization of *Roderick Hudson* began in January 1875. Around the title character, a promising American sculptor, James organizes critiques of the provincialism of Roderick's native New England, particularly its inhospitality to artistic passion and genius; of the limitations of the expatriate colony in Rome, where Roderick goes to study art; and of the Romantic conception of artistic genius, characterized by egotism and a high capacity for self-destruction, embodied in Roderick himself. Roderick travels to Rome from Northampton, Massachusetts, under the patronage of Rowland Mallet, who serves as James's "center of consciousness" in the novel. Mallett is one of James's sensitive observers, a descendant of Longmore in "Madame de Mauves" and a precursor of Lambert Strether in *The Ambassadors.* The novel may be read as Rowland Mallett's story as much as Roderick's. While keeping his feelings to himself, Rowland falls in love with Roderick's fiancée, Mary Garland. Rowland does not tell Roderick he loves Mary until Roderick, who has disintegrated artistically and morally, provokes Rowland by asking for money to sustain his pursuit of a Europeanized American femme fatale, Christina Light, whose beauty, her mother hopes, will snare a rich, titled husband. After a dramatic confrontation between Roderick and Rowland, who lashes out at last at Roderick for his callous betrayal of Mary, Roderick wanders into an alpine storm and falls to his death, probably a suicide.

Both *Roderick Hudson* and James's next novel, *The American,* represent serious and in many respects successful attempts to master the demands of extended narrative. In *Roderick Hudson,* James created the only two characters to whom he returned in later works: Christina Light reappears as the title character in *The Princess Casamassima* (1886), and Gloriani, an artist who represents European sophistication and calculation, in contrast to Roderick's impetuous, "natural" genius, reappears to challenge the expanding sensibility of Lambert Strether in *The Ambassadors.*

Only six months elapsed between the end of the serialization of *Roderick Hudson* and the beginning of the serialization of *The American* in June 1876 (the work was published as a book in May 1877). In *The American* James carried to a higher pitch, and with greater technical success, his international theme. The American of the title, Christopher Newman, is the *new man* of America, a Christopher who reverses the voyage of his namesake Columbus in traveling to the Old World. Newman is a self-confident, rangy, big-hearted, acquisitive, wealthy American businessman, a westerner through and through, but also one of nature's noblemen, as noble in his own way as the haughtily aristocratic French family into which he aspires to marry. *The American* combines satiric humor with a romance that veers toward gothic melodrama. After the aristocratic Bellegardes, unable to stomach alliance by marriage with a commercial person, withdraw the approval they had apparently given for Newman's marriage to the widowed Claire de Cintré (née Bellegarde), Newman discovers evidence that Claire's mother and the older of her two brothers, Urbain de Bellegarde, murdered her long-dead father. As the novel moves toward its close, Claire is immured within a Carmelite convent, where she has taken vows of silence, and Newman briefly contemplates the revenge his knowledge of the Bellegardes' crime

puts within his grasp. Then, in a gesture characteristic of James's protagonists, he renounces revenge, by burning the incriminating letter.

Humor develops around a constellation of minor characters: a fortune-seeking young Frenchwoman, Noémie Nioche, and her father; the American couple, the Tristrams; a deadly earnest American clergyman, who becomes Newman's companion for a while as Newman tours Europe; and Valentin de Bellegarde, Claire's younger brother, the only member of the family (other than Claire herself) disposed to admit Newman into the family. Especially comic are Newman's misapprehensions of the Bellegardes and the aristocrats in their circle, who are often laughing at him when he believes they are laughing with him. Contemporary readers were disappointed in the failure of the relationship between Newman and Claire; they expected the conventional comedic-romantic resolution, marriage. James argued that his commitment to realism necessitated the unhappy ending:

> We are each the product of circumstances and there are tall stone walls which fatally divide us. I have written my story from Newman's side of the wall, and I understand so well how Mme de Cintré couldn't really scramble over from *her* side! If I had represented her as doing so . . . I should have felt as if I were throwing a rather vulgar sop to readers who don't really know the world and who don't measure the merit of a novel by its correspondence to the same.

In his 1907 preface to the novel, James conceded that he himself had succumbed to a romantic falsification: the Bellegardes would in reality have embraced a marriage that brought Newman's fortune into their hands. Equally in 1876 and in 1907, James was committed to realism, but his idea of what would have been truest to his characters and their situation had changed.

James lived in Paris from November 1875 until late 1876. *The American* reflects his relation to French society during that year. Like Newman, James was an outsider. He had no entrée to the aristocratic world of the Bellegardes or even to upper-middle-class French society. There were, nevertheless, associations in Paris from which James profited greatly, especially his friendship with the great Russian novelist Turgenev and his introduction, through Turgenev, to the literary circle surrounding Flaubert.

In December 1876, Henry James took lodgings at 3 Bolton Street, London, where he resided for the next decade. While there he took notable trips abroad—to America in the early 1880s and again in 1904–1905, and to the Continent on numerous occasions—England was henceforth his primary residence. In France he had seen "that I should be an eternal outsider." In England, though he was always marked as an American, as an "observant stranger," he quickly gained admission to a varied social circle, ranging from the aristocracy through the middle classes and including a wide acquaintance with leading editors, intellectuals, artists, writers, and political figures. The winter of 1878–1879, basking in the celebrity that *Daisy Miller* brought him, he dined out 107 times. He took possession of London, saturating himself in everything a restless walker of the city could observe of the multitudes who lived and died outside his own social sphere, the world of the lower middle classes and of the urban poor, the London of Dickens represented with surprising grittiness in *The Princess Casamassima*. Assimilating the strict proprieties and hierarchies of Victorian England, he could refine his international contrasts, comparing Paris with London, and England with America.

SOCIAL CONTRASTS: EUROPE AND AMERICA

Both *The Europeans* and *Washington Square* are set in America in the 1840s, the era of the novelist's early childhood. *The Europeans* is a concise ironic comedy about the encounter of a New England family, the Wentworths, with two cousins who import into their austere, Puritanical world the sophistication, bohemianism, joie de vivre, and mastery of appearances acquired through long immersion in Europe. The Europeans—Eugenia, Baroness Münster, and her brother Felix Young—come seeking their fortunes in the bosom of their wealthy New England cousins. In its serenely good-humored tone, the novel is reminiscent of Shakespearian romance, and in good Shakespearian fashion James deploys several sets of couples and concludes the novel with a pair of marriages. Two couples are particularly important. Gertrude, the one Wentworth daughter who yearns to escape the dry propriety of New England, marries Felix. Robert Acton, the most genial and least parochial member of the New England circle, cannot act on his feelings and propose to Eugenia because he concludes that she is not honest: she has fibbed to his mother, telling Mrs. Acton that Acton has "talked to me immensely of you," though Acton himself knows "that he had barely mentioned his mother to their brilliant guest."

Similar to *The Europeans* in its deft control of social comedy, *Washington Square* is a more powerful performance, a study of the destructive effect a brilliant, overbearing, and emotionally chilly widower has on his daughter. Although she will be an heiress (hence the title of the successful stage and film adaptations of this work, *The Heiress*), Catherine Sloper is so plain and dull she has not attracted suitors until Morris Townsend appears on the scene. Catherine falls hard for Morris, but her father, the acutely analytical Dr. Sloper, detects what has escaped poor Catherine, that Morris' motive is not love but the fortune Catherine will inherit from her father, greatly augmenting the ample funds she inherited from her mother. Dr. Sloper withholds approval of Townsend's suit, telling Catherine, in a terrible scene, to inform Morris that "if you marry without my consent, I don't leave you a farthing of money. That will interest him," Dr. Sloper adds, "more than anything else you can tell him." Catherine, courageously breaking from her inveterate role as the obedient daughter, arranges to elope with Morris, confident that he truly loves her. Townsend, however, proves Dr. Sloper right. Aware that Sloper will disinherit Catherine, Townsend fails to show up for the planned elopement. Catherine thereafter descends into confirmed old maidhood, dedicated to good works. Years later, after her father has died and she has inherited everything, Townsend returns to renew his suit, and Catherine definitively dismisses him. We last see her working on her embroidery, seated in her parlor, alone "for life, as it were."

James's portraits of the father and daughter make this simple tale vivid and poignant. The father, gifted with a caustic intelligence, is haunted by the loss of a brilliant wife, who died shortly after giving birth to Catherine. Dr. Sloper is irritated "at having produced a commonplace child . . . [though] it must not be supposed that Dr. Sloper visited his disappointment upon the poor girl, or ever let her suspect that she had played him a trick." As for "poor" Catherine, "her deepest desire was to please him, and her conception of happiness was to know that she had succeeded in pleasing him"; we learn, moreover, that "she was perfectly aware" that "she had never succeeded beyond a certain point." And yet, when she is finally ready to break with him—for love of Morris Townsend—and when he thwarts her by exposing, through his threat of disinheritance, Townsend's mercenary motive, the irony of the situation, as he deprives his daughter of the only chance of happiness she will ever have, is that he is right. She is not loved for her poor, plain self, and as she shows in her final renunciation of Townsend, she has too much self-respect and integrity to build a life with him on false grounds. In that last act of rejecting Townsend, she shows herself, the "poor girl," bereft "for life, as it were," to have her own kind of greatness.

Two other publications of the late 1870s bear special mention. First, in the summer of 1878, the novella *Daisy Miller* appeared in *Cornhill Magazine* and, almost simultaneously, was pirated as a slim book in New York. *Daisy Miller* charmed readers with its urbane wit, sharp portraiture, and taut, dramatic construction. Daisy is wholly unaware of the stir she creates by flaunting, in the tightly chaperoned colonies of Europeanized Americans in Switzerland and Italy, a freedom to consort with young men that was quite natural in provincial America. She dies, literally, of malaria, but symbolically she dies of the ostracism she suffers at the hands of compatriots who misread her innocent insouciance as immorality. Especially wounding is her rejection by a young man, Frederick Winterbourne, the center of consciousness in the tale, which may be read as the drama of his vacillating between two poles of belief: Is Daisy or is she not "a nice girl"? Only after her death does he realize that she was truly innocent and that he has missed, from having "lived too long in foreign parts," the chance for love with the young woman, who "would have appreciated one's esteem." The tale was a sensational best-seller, James became a celebrity, and "Daisy Miller" passed into popular culture. In Daisy, James created the paradigm of an enduring character-type in his own fiction and in American literature more generally: the American girl, possessed of spontaneity, freedom, and an eagerness to embrace life that the world, hardened, jaded, cynical, and treacherous in a variety of ways, almost invariably rebuffs. Daisy, like the much more complex and self-aware heroine of *The Portrait of a Lady,* is "ground in the very mill of the conventional."

In *Hawthorne,* James pays a peculiar tribute to his greatest American predecessor, the master whom he had emulated in his early tales. James's *Hawthorne* is not so much about Nathaniel Hawthorne as it is about James's attempt to define his own literary mastery in opposition to his precursor. This effort is evident in James's denigration of Hawthornian allegory and in his famous, almost self-parodying recital of the elements lacking in Hawthorne's world, elements whose absence, James suggests, would impoverish any novelist:

> No State, in the European sense of the word, and indeed barely a specific national name. No sovereign, no court, no personal loyalty, no aristocracy, no church, no clergy, no army, no diplomatic service, no country gentlemen, no palaces, no castles, nor manors, nor old country-houses, nor parsonages, nor thatched cottages nor ivied ruins; no cathedrals, nor abbeys, nor little Norman churches; no great Universities nor public schools—no Oxford, nor Eton, nor Harrow; no literature, no novels, no museums, no pictures, no political society, no sporting class—no Epsom nor Ascot!"

The Bolton Street flat remained James's home base until 1886, when he moved to 34 De Vere Gardens, Kensington. James traveled considerably during the 1880s. In the spring of 1880, he was in Florence, working on *The Portrait of a Lady*. There he met the American writer Constance Fenimore Woolson, whose relationship with James has been a subject of considerable dispute (see Leon Edel's *Life of Henry James* and Cheryl Torsney's *Artistry of Grief*). He spent most of the first half of 1881 in France and Italy. Late that year he returned to America for the first time in six years. In January 1882 James's mother died. He returned to England in May, only to rush back in December, hoping—and failing—to reach his father's bedside before he died. In September 1883 he returned to London, not to revisit his native country for twenty-one years. In November 1883, his brother Wilky died.

James's later forays out of England in the 1880s included several trips to France, Italy, and Switzerland. In England he led a rich social life, complicated by the arrival in England in 1884 of his sister, Alice, and her companion, Katharine Loring. Alice stayed in England until her death of breast cancer on March 6, 1892. During this time James developed important literary friendships with Robert Louis Stevenson and with the French novelist Paul Bourget (with whom James broke years later in response to Bourget's right-wing, anti-Semitic politics).

### THE PORTRAIT OF A LADY

Isabel Archer, the heroine of *The Portrait of a Lady,* is both beautiful and intellectual. (She has slogged through much heavy reading, including a history of German philosophy.) Orphaned and taken under the wing of Mrs. Touchett, her wealthy aunt, Isabel arrives in England, en route to the Continent, pursued by an American suitor, the industrial magnate Caspar Goodwood. She wins the hearts of her Anglicized American cousin, Ralph Touchett, who eschews courtship and marriage because he is stricken with tuberculosis, and of Lord Warburton, Ralph's friend, almost a fairy-tale English aristocrat, rich, politically powerful, robust, handsome, and animated by progressive ideas. Sensing that marriage would thwart her desire for infinite self-expansion, a kind of Emersonian aspiration to embrace the world as fully as possible, Isabel rejects proposals from Goodwood and Warburton. Yet Isabel falls prey to a pair of Europeanized Americans who set their claws into her after Ralph persuades his dying father to leave her a fortune.

Madame Merle, the first in a great line of truly affecting female villains in James's novels, had long ago been the mistress of the dilettante Gilbert Osmond and, unbeknownst to anyone but Osmond and Osmond's sister, had borne him a child, Pansy, whom Osmond raises as the child of his deceased wife. Madame Merle sets Osmond up to marry Isabel in order to secure Isabel's fortune for their daughter. James lets the reader in on the plot against Isabel, yet dramatizes Osmond's courtship of Isabel in a way that makes her falling in love with him thoroughly credible. The stupendous turning point of the novel (chapter 42) is a late-night solitary vigil in which Isabel, in a long passage prophetic of modernist stream-of-consciousness narration, meditates on her marriage and thinks through her own shortcomings and the character of her husband. Recognizing that Osmond is in some sense "the finest individual she had ever known," with a "mind more ingenious, more subtle, more cultivated, more trained to admirable exercises" than any she had ever encountered, Isabel also realizes that "he hated her" and that "as he led her into the mansion of his own habitation, then, then she had seen where she really was. . . . It was the house of darkness, the house of dumbness, the house of suffocation."

Most readers are troubled by the ending of *The Portrait of a Lady.* Defying Osmond's express wish, Isabel returns to England because Ralph is dying there. The last deathbed conversation between Isabel and Ralph is the great love scene of the novel. Offered a refuge from Osmond by Caspar Goodwood, Isabel sets off to return to her husband in Rome, whether constrained by propriety, or compelled to flee Goodwood's passionate embrace by her own fear of sexuality, or inspired by her promise to help Pansy, in love with a young man whose suit Osmond rejects. James observed in his notebook,

> The obvious criticism of course will be that it is not finished—that I have not seen the heroine to the end of her situation—that I have left her *en l'air.*—This is both true and false. The *whole* of anything is never told; you can only take what groups together.

The indeterminate conclusion, along with the complex interiority with which James invests his heroine, is part of the incipient modernism of *The Portrait of a Lady,* while the magisterial felicity of its prose, its thematic complexity and philosophical depth, and the vivid roundness of its many characters make it one of the great novels of the nineteenth century, fully at home on a shelf reserved for such works as George Eliot's *Middlemarch,* Leo Tolstoy's *Anna Karenina,* and Flaubert's *Madame Bovary.*

## POLITICAL NOVELS OF THE 1880S

The major novels of the 1880s that follow *Portrait* are all in some sense political works. Serialization of *The Bostonians* and *The Princess Casamassima* ran from 1885 into 1886, and in 1886 both came out, like the English first edition of *The Portrait of a Lady,* as triple-deckers, long novels issued in three volumes. In *The Bostonians,* James pits a passionate feminist scion of the New England reform tradition, Olive Chancellor, against an equally passionate traditionalist scion of the defeated but unbowed Southern aristocracy, Basil Ransom. Olive is probably a lesbian (though James treats the subject of sexuality with great tact), whereas Basil is aggressively heterosexual. They lock horns over Verena Tarrant, a beautiful young woman who dedicates her extraordinary oratorical gifts to the woman's movement, though her own commitment to the cause is of questionable depth. James deploys a fascinating array of secondary characters, including Selah Tarrant, Verena's father, a charlatan associated with radical reform movements, who literally sells his daughter to Olive; Dr. Prance, a masculinized professional woman; and Miss Birdseye, the matriarch of the Boston reformers, whose depiction scandalized Boston because it was believed—despite James's disavowals—to be a disrespectful portrait of Elizabeth Peabody, a beloved leader of progressive causes (and Hawthorne's sister-in-law). The tone of *The Bostonians* is generally satirical, but James powerfully conveys Olive Chancellor's radicalism and angst and Basil Ransom's reactionary views and the pain of the Southerner's dispossession. James's sympathies appear to be generously distributed, and the conclusion of the tale is at once ironic and sardonic. Carried off at last by the putative Prince Charming, Verena leaves Olive for Basil, but we last see Verena in tears, and James concludes that "It is to be feared that with the union, so far from brilliant, into which she was about to enter, these were not the last she was destined to shed."

In 1884, James had published, in *Longman's Magazine,* a defense of literary realism, freedom of imagination, and bold artistic experimentation. The "Art of Fiction" contains some of his most memorable formulations on imagination and the novel:

> Experience is never limited, and it is never complete; it is an immense sensibility, a kind of huge spider-web of the finest silken threads suspended in the chamber of consciousness . . . it is the very atmosphere of the mind; and when the mind is imaginative—much more when it happens to be that of a man of genius—it takes to itself the faintest hints of life, it converts the very pulses of the air into revelations. . . . I should certainly say to a novice, . . . Try to be one of the people on whom nothing is lost! . . . What is character but the determination of incident? What is incident but the illustration of character? . . . No good novel will ever proceed from a superficial mind; that seems to me an axiom which, for the artist in fiction, will cover all needful moral ground.

James's arguments in "The Art of Fiction" in favor of a quasi-naturalist realism ("He [the novelist] cannot possibly take too many [notes], he cannot possibly take enough") and of the freedom of an artist to range in imagination beyond his or her own experience ("The young lady living in a village has only to be a damsel upon whom nothing is lost to make it quite unfair . . . to declare to her that she shall have nothing to say about the military") read like a rationale for his own method and choice of subject in his second novel of 1886, *The Princess Casamassima.* For in this work he ventured far beyond the typical (or perhaps, rather, stereotypical) Jamesian milieu, setting his scenes among militant socialists of the artisan and working classes. He built the first section of his story around a grittily vivid, almost Dickensian, prison scene for which he took extensive notes in the style of French novelists such as Émile Zola and Edmond de Goncourt: as he wrote to a boyhood friend, "I have been all the morning at Millbank prison (horrible place) collecting notes for a fiction scene. You see, I am quite the Naturalist."

James's protagonist in *The Princess Casamassima,* "little Hyacinth Robinson," is indeed "one of the people on whom nothing is lost," as finely aware "as Hamlet and Lear, say, are finely aware." A child of working-class London, raised by a seamstress foster mother in a tenement, he is the progeny of a French maid and the English aristocrat she killed. She was given a life sentence for this murder (hence the prison scene, Hyacinth's sole encounter with his mother). Very much like Henry James in sensibility ("I had only to conceive his watching the same public show," James wrote in his preface, "the same innumerable appearances, I had watched myself, and of his watching very much as I had watched," Hyacinth nevertheless lacks James's entrée to the world of "freedom and ease, knowledge and power, money, opportunity and satiety" all too apparent, in the capital of the British Empire, to the dispossessed. By virtue of his social class Hyacinth finds "every door of approach shut in his face."

He falls "in love with the beauty of the world, actual order and all, at the moment of his most feeling and most hating the famous 'iniquity of its social arrangements.'" Unable to resolve this conflict as he wends his way through a fascinating set of characters—among many others: Christina Light, the Princess Casamassima, reappearing from *Roderick Hudson* as an aristocratic dabbler in radical politics; Millicent Henning, a robust working-class girl who has been very fond of Hyacinth and whom he, perhaps, loves; and Paul Muniment, a charismatic leader of the radical movement that Hyacinth joins—Hyacinth shoots himself through the heart with the pistol with which he had pledged to carry out the assassination of a nobleman fingered by the shadowy master-revolutionary Hoffendahl. Readers have not generally accorded this powerful, rich novel a high place among James's masterpieces, though Trilling and Mark Seltzer are notable exceptions.

The fourth major novel of the 1880s is *The Tragic Muse,* serialized from January 1889 through May 1890 and published in book form in June 1890. Despite many virtues, *The Tragic Muse* is the least successful of the big novels Henry James produced as a mature writer. The thematic unity of the novel, revolving around parallel conflicts between art and society and art and politics, is diffused among three central characters, none of whom commands interest with anything like the intensity of Isabel Archer, Olive Chancellor and Basil Ransom, and Hyacinth Robinson. James's vision of the novel grew around the character of the half-Jewish actress Miriam Rooth, whose theatrical career recalls those of Rachel (Elisa Félix) and of Sarah Bernhardt. Miriam drives hard for success, subordinating every other element of her life to her profession. The focus of the novel wavers, however, as attention moves from Miriam to Nick Dormer, who struggles to reconcile the demands of a promising parliamentary career (fiercely espoused by his fiancée, Julia Dallow, and financed by a wealthy backer, Mr. Carteret) with his aspiration to pursue the art of painting. The third central character is Peter Sherringham, a young diplomat and aficionado of the theater, who struggles between infatuation with Miriam Rooth and engagement to Nick's sister, Biddy Dormer, a thoroughly suitable consort for a rising star in the Foreign Office.

Miriam solves Peter's dilemma for him by making a practical marriage to a theatrical agent, freeing Peter to marry Biddy. Miriam's star as an actress is ascendant as the novel closes. Nick Dormer's fate is unresolved: with Julia's sanction and goaded on by the inspiring, disturbing provocations of his friend Gabriel Nash (an aesthete and

wit in the style of Oscar Wilde), Nick has pursued for some time the art of portraiture. Nash has sat for him, but his portrait gradually disappears, as does Nash himself. Nick finds himself "imagining in the portrait he had begun an odd tendency to fade gradually from the canvas" and the "disappearance 'without a trace'"of Nash himself is "that of a personage in a fairy-tale." Miriam, too, has sat for Nick. So has Julia. Nick successfully exhibits his portrait of Julia, and we are unsure in the end whether they will marry and whether Nick will remain a devotee of art or resume his political career. In a letter to William James, Henry James wrote, "I can only thank you tenderly for seeing so much good in the clumsy thing." *The Tragic Muse* is likely to remain unchallenged among James's major novels as the least often read for pleasure and the least often taught to boot.

In a decidedly minor novel, *The Reverberator* (1888), James treats the intrusiveness into private life of the modern media. Francie Dosson, a naive American girl, violates a confidence, nearly scuttling her marriage, by giving a newspaper columnist sensitive information about the family of her fiancé, Gaston Probert, a member of a highly Europeanized Franco-American family. Gaston resolves to marry Francie despite the rift this union will create between him and many members of his own affronted clan. Although perhaps underrated, *The Reverberator* has been overshadowed not only by James's other, more substantial novels of the 1880s, but also by several stellar tales and novellas among the nearly twenty James published during this fecund decade, notably "The Siege of London" (1883), "The Author of 'Beltraffio'" and "Lady Barberina" (both 1884), and "The Lesson of the Master" and "The Aspern Papers" (both 1888). The latter is one of James's comparatively rare first-person narratives. James deplored what he called in *Art of the Novel* "the terrible *fluidity* of self-revelation" of first-person narration. He preferred to narrate in the third person, predominantly from the viewpoint of one character, the "center of consciousness" or "central intelligence" of his story. Like *The Sacred Fount* and "The Turn of the Screw," "The Aspern Papers," with its "publishing scoundrel" narrator who trifles unconscionably with the heart of a lonely middle-aged woman in an attempt to gain possession of love letters penned by a mythical great poet of the early years of the nineteenth century, is a brilliant exception to James's general rule.

### THE 1890S: DRAMAS

In the first half of the 1890s, James experienced both personal and professional losses, only to recuperate powerfully in the last half of the decade. While he continued to produce notable short stories—including such masterpieces as "The Pupil" (1891), "The Real Thing" (1892), "The Middle Years" (1893), "The Coxon Fund" (1894), and "The Figure in the Carpet" (1896)—he concentrated from 1889 through early 1895 on the pursuit of popular success as a playwright. During these years, he undertook no new novels. Personal losses included the deaths of Catherine Walsh (Aunt Kate) in 1889, of James's friends Wolcott Balestier and James Russell Lowell (1891), of Alice James (March 1892), of the English actress Fanny Kemble (1893), of Constance Fenimore Woolson (January 1893, of a fall from a window in Venice, probably a suicide), and of Robert Louis Stevenson (1894).

James had long aspired to conquer the theater. In 1882, he had rendered *Daisy Miller* for the stage—with a happy ending! Although the prospective producers rejected the script, James published it in the *Atlantic Monthly*. To succeed in the theater, one had to please producers concerned, above all, with the box office bottom line. That James gave the stage *Daisy Miller* a happy ending, just as he did later to his moderately successful stage version of *The American*, suggests how much he felt compelled to pander to theatrical audiences. James's dream of conquering the stage, garlanded with celebrity and commercial success, marks his one great failure of self-knowledge as an artist. Devoted to his own high standards of realism and artistic integrity, James faced too great a stretch in seeking to accommodate himself to a form of entertainment that, like the movies, requires extensive collaboration rather than solitary artistic labor and exacts compromise in the interest of sales.

We will never know how many scenarios for plays James produced and circulated to theater managers between 1890 and 1895. Of eight extant plays from this period, only two were produced, *The American* and *Guy Domville*. The former was performed on a provincial tour throughout the winter and spring of 1891 before opening in London in late September, where it had a respectable run, closing in early December. Four plays written in the early 1890s but never produced were published in the two volumes titled *Theatricals* (1894 and 1895). Then, on January 5, 1895, *Guy Domville* opened to critical praise from the reviewers, including George Bernard Shaw, H. G. Wells, and William Archer (Henrik Ibsen's translator), but to catcalls and boos from a portion of the audience that competed with the applause of James's supporters in a cacophony prolonged for fifteen minutes while James stood before them. For "a nervous, sensitive, exhausted author," as James wrote to his brother William, public exposure to derision was searingly painful, filling James "with horror for the abysmal vulgarity and brutality of the theatre and its regular public" and demolishing in a moment "the dream and delusion of my having made a successful appeal to the cosy, childlike, naïf, domestic British imagination."

From this potentially crushing humiliation James rebounded with a spirited rededication to fiction. Some two weeks after the ghastly *Guy Domville* opening, he penned this exhortation to himself:

I take up my *own* old pen again—the pen of all my old unforgettable efforts and sacred struggles. To myself—today—I need say no more. Large and full and high the future still opens. It is now indeed that I may do the work of my life. And I will.

He soon converted his theatrical experience to fictional purposes, drawing a redemptive lesson from the preceding half decade:

Has a *part* of all this wasted passion and squandered time (of the last 5 years) been simply the precious lesson, taught me in that roundabout and devious, that cruelly expensive, way, *of the singular value for a narrative plan too* of the (I don't know *what* adequately to call it) the divine principle of the Scenario? . . . a key that, working in the same *general* way fits the complicated chambers of *both* the dramatic and the narrative lock.

James henceforth prepared scenarios for all his major fictions, tightly laying out their architecture through the alternation of picture and scene: picture denoting the passages in which the Jamesian narrator explores the nuances and permutations of thought and feeling at work beneath the surfaces of the genteel world of his fiction, and scene denoting the dramatic encounters between characters that economically and powerfully advance, define, and resolve their situations. In his notebooks, for instance, he elaborately worked out, through the "scenario" method, the design of *The Spoils of Poynton* and *What Maisie Knew*. Only one complete scenario, however, survives. James's "Project for *The Ambassadors*," escaped, in the Scribner archives, the fire to which he consigned most of his working papers and a great deal of correspondence late in 1909.

EXPERIMENTALISM IN THE NOVELS OF THE 1890S

James's tremendous period of productivity in the last half of the 1890s included, in order of publication, the novels *The Spoils of Poynton* (1897;

serialized as "The Old Things" in the *Atlantic Monthly* in 1896), *The Other House* (1896), *What Maisie Knew* (1897), and *The Awkward Age* (1899); two great novellas, *In the Cage* and "The Turn of the Screw" (both 1898); and several volumes of short fiction, including such major tales as "The Altar of the Dead" (1895) and "The Figure in the Carpet." These titles, and the titles of the short-story collections as well (*Terminations* [1895], *Embarrassments* [1896], and *The Soft Side* [1900]), suggest the densely symbolic accretions James was building up around his fundamentally realistic narratives. His syntax became more elaborate, and his diction became more slangy, developments perhaps related to a change in his method of composition. In 1897, probably midway through the composition of *What Maisie Knew*, the pain in his wrist he had intermittently experienced while writing in longhand became so severe he hired someone to take dictation, first by stenography and then on a typewriter. From then on, he composed by dictating.

*The Spoils of Poynton* is a stunning compact masterpiece anatomizing and satirizing the legal and quasi-tribal rituals of the British upper classes with respect to inheritance, marriage, and property. The "spoils" are the "old things," precious furnishings, art works, and objets d'art, that the widowed Mrs. Gereth stands to lose when her only son marries, displacing her, in favor of his bride, from the home she had shared with his father, for the entire property has accrued to him on Mr. Gereth's death. The center of consciousness is Fleda Vetch, a young woman who shares Mrs. Gereth's appreciation of the "spoils"—their inestimable distinction and value—as Owen Gereth does not, and as his fiancée Mona Brigstock, a rank Philistine in the dullest upper-middle-class mold, never could.

The struggle for the spoils, many of the finest pieces of which are removed by Mrs. Gereth to a lesser family home, Ricks, becomes also a drama within Fleda. Fleda loves Owen. He in turn eventually comes to love her; even he cannot blink away the contrast between her fineness and Mona's crassness. When he at last declares his love, however, Fleda urges him to stick honorably to his engagement to Mona until Mona herself breaks it. Mrs. Gereth, believing (as Mrs. Brigstock has given her to understand) that Mona feels she has lost Owen to Fleda, returns the spoils to Poynton, whereupon Mona and Owen in fact marry. From his honeymoon, Owen writes to Fleda, inviting her to take any one of the precious objets from Poynton. This short novel, some sixty-five thousand words long, ends as Fleda, arriving at the Poynton station to secure her memento, finds Poynton in flames, burning to the ground. Mrs. Gereth is a powerful, manipulative figure. She seeks to place Fleda in Owen's way in the hope that Fleda will redeem him from Mona and his own inadequately developed taste. Mona is a brute vulgarian. Owen, an amiable fellow, lacks Fleda's intensity and conviction. Although James had wished to focus on Mrs. Gereth and "on that most modern of our current passions, the fierce appetite for the upholsterer's and joiner's and brazier's work, the chairs and tables, the cabinets and presses, the material odds and ends, of the more labouring ages," this subtle narrative becomes above all the drama of Fleda's consciousness. Fleda's very Jamesian renunciation of Owen has teased readers; it is hard to know if she really loves Owen or, if she loves him, if she does not love her own perhaps fussy scruples more.

Subtler yet, deeper, richer, and more powerful than *The Spoils of Poynton*, *What Maisie Knew* displays James's intrepid experimentalism along with his ongoing exploration of the mores of the British upper classes. The challenge James set himself in this novel was to depict through the eyes of a little girl, Maisie Farange, who grows from age seven to about age twelve in the course of the story, the aftermath of her parents' bitter divorce and the series of relations into which the parents, Ida and Beale, subsequently enter, culminating in the elopement of the mother's new husband, Sir Claude (whom Ida Farange has long since abandoned for a rather sordid series of lovers) with the new wife of Beale Farange (Mrs. Beale, as she is called, having formerly been Maisie's nurse, Miss Overmore). Maisie herself is precociously in love with Sir Claude, but recoils in the end from accepting his invitation to join the eloping pair on a jaunt to the south of France, for what she has developed—under the tutelage of the stolid nurse, Mrs. Wix, who succeeded Miss Overmore, but far surpassing her mentor in the fineness of her ethical discrimination—is the moral sense, which is, after all, "what Maisie knew."

James delighted in the technical challenge of showing the whole of adult situations through the eyes of a child who "either wouldn't understand at all or would quite misunderstand," noting that "small children have many more perceptions than they have terms to translate them" and that "their vision is at any moment much richer, their apprehension even constantly stronger, than their prompt, their at all producible, vocabulary." The comedy that develops through James's satire of modern marriage, divorce, and adultery in a very fast set of late Victorians is erected upon a drama with tragic undertones arising from the cruelty and abuse to which Maisie is subjected—and which she, "our little wonder-working agent," in the words of James's preface, transcends "by drawing some stray fragrance of an ideal across the scent of selfishness, by sowing on barren strands, through the mere fact of presence, the seed of the moral life."

Equally but very differently experimental, *The Awkward Age* explores much of the same social and thematic terrain as *What Maisie Knew*. Here, however, rather than establishing a center of consciousness, like Maisie, James largely restricts the novel to dialogue. In form, *The Awkward Age*, far more than any of his other novels, resembles the scripts of his dramatic years. This experiment entailed, as he remarks in his preface, "the imposed absence of 'going behind.'" The dramatic situation was the effect on what James calls a "free circle" of adult sophisticates of introducing into the drawing rooms where they gather a young unmarried woman—a person whose very presence, according to the strict customs that precluded exposing unmarried girls to adult topics, should have brought an end to "'good' talk."

The central characters are Mrs. Brook (Mrs. Edward Brookenham), her daughter Nanda, Gustavus ("Van") Vanderbank, and Mr. Longdon. Mrs. Brook is a charming, roguish manipulator, one of James's greatest characters. Despite her conventional marriage to a colorless husband, she enjoys a relationship of mutual admiration and flirtation with Vanderbank, a highly eligible bachelor. Vanderbank proves too conventional to pursue a long contemplated engagement to Nanda because Nanda has been unacceptably exposed to the adult topics of her mother's social circle. Nanda is so compromised as to be rendered ineligible, in Vanderbank's eyes, for marriage. This outcome has been covertly engineered by Mrs. Brook, who ruthlessly secures her own relation with Vanderbank at her daughter's expense. Nanda, who loves Vanderbank, rusticates herself in the end, repairing to the eighteenth-century country house of an elderly protector, Mr. Longdon, an admirer, in an earlier generation, of Nanda's grandmother, Lady Julia, and an embodiment of the old proprieties and ideals of which Mrs. Brook is the antithesis. The novel unfolds in ten "books," each a dramatic occasion in the history of Mrs. Brook's circle, and each named for a character whose perspective supplies the keynote for the occasion. Ironically, Nanda Brookenham, like Maisie, is incorruptible; her fine moral sense is never tainted by the exposure that constitutes, in Vanderbank's eyes, her compromised and unmarriageable state.

The ghostly tale "The Turn of the Screw" was James's greatest popular success since *Daisy Miller*. Although James tended to denigrate "The Turn of the Screw" (calling it, in his preface, "a piece of ingenuity pure and simple, of cold artistic calculation, an *amusette* to catch those not easily caught," it is perhaps the greatest tale of the supernatural in English, enriched by the conundrum of whether it deals with the supernatural or, rather, with the psychosis of the unnamed principal narrator, whose struggle with two real or imagined ghosts for the souls of two children she serves as governess results in the boy's death and his sister's temporary derangement. "The Turn of the Screw" has become the text par excellence for critical commentary on the uncanny and on ambiguity in literature. There is nothing supernatural about "In the Cage," which also centers on a nameless young woman of the lower middle class, a telegraphist who attempts to decode the cryptic telegrams of her aristocratic clientele, which may concern affairs of the heart. In the 1990s, "In the Cage" became a focal point for critical consideration of James's treatment of gender and class politics.

THE LATE NOVELS: EARLY THEMES REVISITED

By the turn of the century, James had moved out of London to Lamb House in Rye, Sussex. There he enjoyed visits from relatives and friends, including his literary neighbors Joseph Conrad (whose important friendship with James had begun in 1896), Stephen Crane, H. G. Wells, and Ford Madox Ford. He still traveled frequently to London, where, from 1901 on, he had a permanent room at the Reform Club. In 1899, James B. Pinker became his literary agent. That year, he met the American-Norwegian sculptor Hendrik Andersen, the first of the younger men whose friendship warmed the last decade and a half of James's life (others with whom the elderly James had what Leon Edel termed "homoerotic" relationships and that later critics simply termed "homosexual" were Dudley Jocelyn Persse and the novelist Hugh Walpole. In 1900, he shaved off the beard he had worn since the mid-1860s.

The years 1900 to 1905 marked the climax of James's career. He published four novels, including three crowning masterpieces rivaled only, among his novels, by *The Portrait of a Lady*. He returned to the United States after twenty years' absence, staying for nearly a year (from August 1904 to July 1905), lecturing throughout the country and producing the essays published in *The American Scene* (1907). In 1905, he began revising selected stories and novels and writing prefaces for the New York Edition of *The Novels and Tales of Henry James* (1907–1909). And he kept up an active social life, including the beginning, in late 1903, of his important friendship with Edith Wharton.

*The Sacred Fount* groups easily with the works of the latter half of the 1890s in treating only English characters and society. Like "The Turn of the Screw," it is irresolubly ambiguous. The unnamed narrator develops, during a country house party at Newmarch, a theory of "sacred founts": he believes he can detect characters becoming younger and cleverer by draining the sacred founts of their spouses and lovers, who in turn become older and duller. The narrator seeks to read the affairs of the men and women gathered at Newmarch in the visible signs of the sacred fount transferences. Are the patterns he sees really there? Is he demented or clairvoyant? These questions cannot be answered. *The Sacred Fount* has been read by Adeline Tintner as James's joke on the narrator (and the reader) for focusing on "opposite sex" relationships, for failing to see that the lover to be sought for in the case of a key character, Gilbert Long, is male and that the novel is "homoerotic, homosexual."

The three great masterpieces that followed *The Sacred Fount* return to the paradigm of an earlier stage of James's career. All three are dramas about naive Americans whose lives are transformed through their relations with Europeans and Europeanized Americans. First in order of composition, *The Ambassadors* (1903) was the second to be published, following *The Wings of the Dove* (1902)

and preceding *The Golden Bowl* (1904). In these novels, James magisterially combines his inveterate psychological realism with a highly poetic literary symbolism.

In the preface to *The Ambassadors,* James calls the novel "quite the best, 'all round,' of my productions." An exquisitely well-made novel, with the "hour-glass symmetry" that E. M. Forster recognized in *Aspects of the Novel* (1927), it is also a kind of middle-aged bildungsroman, with its mid-fiftyish hero perhaps closer in predilections and sensibility to Henry James than any of his other characters. Lambert Strether, however, is an artist manqué rather than a tremendously productive writer like James; Strether merely edits a literary journal for which his fiancée, the wealthy widow Mrs. Newsome, is the patron. Strether's spiritual odyssey, moreover, is a function of his capacity to be duped and only gradually to see things as they really are.

The novel revolves around the contrast between the morality and culture of Strether's starting point, Woollett, Massachusetts, and Paris, to which Strether journeys on the "ambassadorial" mission of retrieving Mrs. Newsome's son Chad from the toils of a reputedly immoral woman so that Chad can come home to take up the advertising end of the family's manufacturing concern. Woollett is provincial, puritanical, and commercial. Paris is cosmopolitan, permissive, and aesthetic. Not only is the formerly callow Chad Newsome greatly improved, to Strether's initial view, by his Parisian experience, but he is also in a relationship—a "virtuous" one, Chad's friend Little Bilham assures Strether—with an extraordinarily beautiful and deeply charming woman, Madame de Vionnet. Strether accepts Little Bilham's assurance and quickly falls under the spell of Madame de Vionnet. He therefore defers pressuring Chad to return to Woollett, provoking Mrs. Newsome to send out additional ambassadors—her daughter, Sarah Pocock, Sarah's husband, Jim, and Jim's sister, Mamie, whom Chad is supposed to marry.

The novel hinges on two great scenes. The first is a Parisian garden party given by the sculptor Gloriani. There Strether meets Madame de Vionnet. There, too, he makes a tremendous speech, telling Little Bilham that he himself has missed the main chances of life. He enjoins the younger man to spurn his example: "Live all you can; it's a mistake not to." The second is the dramatic epiphany when Strether, on a country excursion by himself, happens upon Chad and Madame de Vionnet. At first, across an expanse of river on which the two are boating, he does not recognize them, and then he makes out that their initial impulse is to pretend not to recognize him. Strether realizes they have spent the night together at the inn where Strether then lunches with them. Now he knows the relationship is not in any technical sense "virtuous." Meeting afterward with Madame de Vionnet, Strether sees that she is abysmally in love with Chad and understands that she has maneuvered to detain Strether in Paris in a desperate struggle to keep Chad. Despite Chad's denials, they both know that however improved Chad may be, he is after all just Chad: in the end he will go back to the New England business and to Mamie Pocock. As the novel closes, Strether is poised to return to America. His conduct of his ambassadorial assignment has ended his engagement with Mrs. Newsome. Maria Gostrey, an American confidante, offers herself to Strether, but he rejects Maria for two reasons, one that is spoken—a fastidious determination not to have gotten anything for himself out of the whole business—and one that is implicit: he cannot love Miss Gostrey because he is really, now, in love with Madame de Vionnet.

In the far darker novel *The Wings of the Dove,* James returned to a character type absent from his novels since *The Portrait of a Lady,* the American girl who seeks her destiny through a transatlantic excursion. Milly Theale, young, beautiful, fabulously wealthy—"the heiress of all the ages"— embarks on a trip to England and then the Continent, seeking to experience life and love before

she dies, for she has a mysterious (and not readily apparent) disease. James opens the novel with two long sections that lay, for the great innocence to come, a trap constituted by the predicament of Kate Croy and Merton Densher. Kate, daughter of the financially ruined and disgraced Lionel Croy, lives with her wealthy aunt, Maud Lowder, "Britannia of the Market Place," who aims to parlay her niece's personal brilliance into an aristocratic connection by marrying Kate to the politically ambitious Lord Mark, who wants, in turn, to tap into Maud's fortune. Merton Densher, a dimly intellectual journalist booked by character and fate never to have money, loves Kate, she loves him in turn, and James effectively portrays their love as fresh and genuine. Kate plays for time, hoping "to square" Aunt Maud, with several motives: to retrieve her family's honor; to sustain the social position and power and the personal splendor of which she would be bereft without the only fortune in her grasp, Aunt Maud's; and eventually to marry Densher, whose courtship Aunt Maud interdicts— though Maud personally likes Merton—because of her very different marital design for Kate.

Milly Theale enters Aunt Maud's social circle in London under the tutelage of her traveling companion, Susan Shepherd Stringham (generally called Susan Shepherd), an old friend of Aunt Maud. Milly and Kate become friends. Milly learns that Densher is in love with Kate, but Kate allows Milly to believe that she does not love Densher. Milly, who had earlier met Densher in New York, is drawn to him. Lord Mark is drawn to Milly, who would make him far richer than Aunt Maud would were he to marry Kate. After accompanying Milly to an appointment with an eminent surgeon, Kate guesses that her friend is dying. Now she conceives a plot: Densher will marry Milly, Milly will die, leaving him her fortune, and at last Kate and Densher will marry, endowed with Milly's wealth.

The action moves from London to Venice, where Milly brilliantly and bravely holds court in a magnificent palazzo. Densher has followed her there and calls on her frequently. Slow to grasp what Kate has been up to, he at last realizes: "Since she's to die I'm to marry her?" In return for his co-operation, he gets Kate to sleep with him at last. Milly, falling under Densher's spell, rejects a proposal from Lord Mark. Lord Mark, embittered, reveals to Milly that Kate and Densher have all along been intimately allied. Milly then turns her face to the wall, her health declining thereafter toward death—but not before a final, undramatized meeting with Densher in which he finds himself "forgiven, dedicated, blessed." Later, in London on Christmas Day, he learns of Milly's death in Venice. He receives a letter in her hand, takes it unopened to Kate, and they burn it, unread. Densher is now in love with the dead girl. When legal papers bequeathing her fortune to him and Kate arrive, he says he will marry Kate without the money but not with it. Kate, seeing how things stand and grasping the emotional and fiscal realities more quickly than Densher, takes the money, replying to Densher's offer, "I'll marry you, mind you, in an hour . . . as we were" with the decisive last line of this powerful drama: "We shall never be again as we were!"

Maggie Verver in *The Golden Bowl,* like Milly Theale, is a naive American heiress. Maggie's old school friend Charlotte Stant, like Kate Croy, is dependent on wealthy friends to provide the social and material contexts her personal brilliance requires. Many readers of both novels have preferred the putative villains, Kate and Charlotte, to the putative heroines, Milly and Maggie. Thematically and ethically more complex than *The Wings of the Dove, The Golden Bowl* is nevertheless simpler in plot. Maggie has been her father Adam's sole companion since her mother's death in childbirth. Father and daughter remain very close after Maggie marries the Italian prince Amerigo, whom Maggie jokes she has acquired the way her tycoon-turned-connoisseur father acquires art for a museum he plans to erect in the American West. To

console Maggie for having "abandoned" him, Adam marries Charlotte. Both couples shuttle among their London mansions and a magnificent English country estate Adam has rented.

Maggie and Adam do not know, however, about an earlier love affair between Charlotte and Amerigo, from which the lovers had withdrawn because neither could bring to the match the fortune that each required. The Ververs' spouses, frequently left to their own devices while father and daughter consort together, resume their affair. The first half of the novel, "The Prince," develops this situation. The second half, "The Princess," chronicles Maggie's actions after she realizes what has happened. Without accusations or scenes—without ever revealing to the others what she knows—Maggie outmaneuvers Charlotte, arrives at a tacit understanding with her father, resulting in his determination to take Charlotte back to the United States (a fate Charlotte hyperbolically thinks of as her doom), and subjugates the awe-struck prince to her will.

*The Golden Bowl* has become a site of spirited contestation among commentators on James's fiction. Who are the real villains? Does the novel expose above all the quasi-incestuous perversion of father and daughter? In the Ververs' acquisition of spouses, so like their acquisition of artistic treasures, and in Maggie Verver's triumph, are we to see the terrible destructive power of American wealth and innocence, whereby human beings are reduced to the status of property? Or are we to take Maggie's victory to be a drama of love triumphant, with the chief evil in the novel being the duplicity of the adulterous pair, Charlotte and Amerigo? Are love, power, and art inseparably entangled with each other in this novel? Does Amerigo love his wife in the end, or is he simply in her thrall?

It is clear, amid these and many other similar questions, that James's novelistic art is operating at its very highest pitch in this novel, as shown, for instance, in his masterful depiction of Maggie's evolution from victim of duplicity to mistress of her fate, of Charlotte's passion for Prince Amerigo and her abysmal pain as Maggie successfully works to isolate the lovers from each other, and of Amerigo's character as an Italian noble, a *galantuomo* who is not so much in love with Charlotte at the time their affair resumes as he is indignant that anyone might think that a man such as he could be left alone with a woman as magnificent as Charlotte without making love to her. The complex strains of triumph and tragedy mingle in the closing phrases of the novel, as Charlotte and Adam take their leave for America, and Maggie and Amerigo, left alone, embrace:

> It kept him before her therefore, taking in—or trying to—what she so wonderfully gave. He tried, too clearly, to please her—to meet her in her own way; but with the result only that, close to her, her face kept before him, his hands holding her shoulders, his whole act enclosing her, he presently echoed: "'See'? I see nothing but *you*." And the truth of it had with this force after a moment so strangely lighted his eyes that as for pity and dread of them she buried her own in his breast.

The ambiguities do not detract from, but rather deepen the power of this grand finale to James's career as a novelist.

### LAST YEARS

James's other major works of the twentieth century include some of his greatest tales, notably "The Beast in the Jungle" (1903) and "The Jolly Corner" (1908); *The American Scene* (1907), perhaps after Alexis de Tocqueville's *Democracy in America* the greatest single commentary on American culture and civilization; three volumes of memoirs, *A Small Boy and Others* (1913), *Notes of a Son and Brother* (1914), and *The Middle Years* (unfinished and published posthumously in 1917); *Notes on Novelists* (1914), essays on Balzac, Flaubert, Zola, Sand, and others; a novelization of

his own unproduced play, *The Outcry* (1911), which concerns the morality of selling English art treasures to foreign buyers; two volumes of travel writing in the broadly conceived Jamesian vein, *English Hours* (1905) and *Italian Hours* (1909); and a two-volume biography of an expatriate American sculptor, *William Wetmore Story and His Friends* (1903).

Despite his continuing productivity, the last decade of James's life was darkened by the financial failure of the New York Edition, though its prefaces brought him enduring fame as the most influential theorist of fiction in English; by a severe nervous breakdown in 1910; and by personal losses, including the deaths of both Robertson and William James in 1910. Henry was with William's family when his beloved older brother died, having traveled to America with them in August; he spent nearly a year in the States, his last visit to his native land, returning to England in July 1911. In 1915, discovering that he was considered an alien and thus subject to wartime restrictions on internal travel (he had to report to the police to go back and forth between the London flat he had taken in 1913 and Lamb House, in Rye), James became a British citizen under the sponsorship of Prime Minister Herbert Asquith.

James was horrified by the outbreak of World War I. He threw himself into relief work, became chairman of the American Volunteer Motor Ambulance Corps in France in 1914, participated in Belgian relief, and visited the wounded in hospitals. On December 2, 1915, at his flat at Cheyne Walk, London, he suffered a stroke, followed by a second stroke two days later. On New Year's Day, 1916, King George V conferred upon him the Order of Merit. Henry James died on February 28, 1916. He was cremated in Golders Green, London, and his ashes were smuggled home by William's widow, Alice, to be buried beside the graves of his parents, his brother William, and his sister Alice in the family plot in Cambridge Cemetery.

# Selected Bibliography

## WORKS OF HENRY JAMES

### NOVELS

*Roderick Hudson.* Boston: Osgood, 1875.
*The American.* Boston: Osgood, 1877.
*Watch and Ward.* Boston: Houghton, Osgood, 1878.
*The Europeans.* London: Macmillan, 1878.
*Confidence.* London: Chatto and Windus, 1880.
*Washington Square.* New York: Harper and Brothers, 1880.
*The Portrait of a Lady.* London: Macmillan, 1881.
Collective Edition of 1883. 14 vols. (each separately titled). London: Macmillan, 1883.
*The Bostonians.* London: Macmillan, 1886.
*The Princess Casamassima.* London: Macmillan, 1886.
*The Reverberator.* London: Macmillan, 1888.
*The Tragic Muse.* Boston: Houghton, Mifflin, 1890.
*The Other House.* London: Heinemann, 1896.
*The Spoils of Poynton.* London: Heinemann, 1897.
*What Maisie Knew.* London: Heinemann, 1897.
*The Awkward Age.* London: Heinemann, 1899.
*The Sacred Fount.* New York: Scribners, 1901.
*The Wings of the Dove.* New York: Scribners, 1902.
*The Ambassadors.* London: Methuen, 1903.
*The Golden Bowl.* New York: Scribners, 1904.
*The Novels and Tales of Henry James* (New York Edition). 26 vols. New York: Scribners, 1907–1917. (Vols. 25 and 26, *The Ivory Tower* and *The Sense of the Past,* were added posthumously.)
*The Outcry.* London: Methuen, 1911.
*The Ivory Tower.* London: Collins, 1917. (Uncompleted.)
*The Sense of the Past.* London. Collins, 1917. (Uncompleted.)

### TALES

Titles marked with an asterisk are special titles assigned by James to books containing his tales. All other titles are actual tale titles, often used as the title of the book.

*A Passionate Pilgrim and Other Tales.* Boston: Osgood, 1875.
*Daisy Miller.* New York: Harper, 1879 [1878].
*An International Episode.* New York: Harper, 1879.
*The Madonna of the Future and Other Tales.* London: Macmillan, 1879.

*The Diary of a Man of Fifty and a Bundle of Letters.* New York: Harper, 1880.
*The Siege of London, The Pension Beaurepas, and the Point of View.* Boston: Osgood, 1883.
*Tales of Three Cities.* Boston: Osgood, 1884.
*The Author of "Beltraffio," Pandora, Georgina's Reasons, the Path of Duty, Four Meetings.* Boston: Osgood, 1885.
*Stories Revived.* 3 vols. London: Macmillan, 1885.
*The Aspern Papers, Louisa Pallant.* 2 vols. London: Macmillan, 1888.
*A London Life.* London: Macmillan, 1889.
*The Lesson of the Master.* New York: Macmillan, 1892.
*The Real Thing and Other Tales.* New York: Macmillan, 1893.
*The Private Life.* London: Osgood, McIlvaine, 1893.
*The Wheel of Time.* New York: Harper Brothers, 1893.
*\*Terminations.* London: Heinemann, 1895.
*\*Embarrassments.* London: Heinemann, 1896.
*In the Cage.* London: Duckworth, 1898.
*\*The Two Magics.* London: Heinemann, 1898.
*The Soft Side.* London: Methuen, 1900.
*The Better Sort.* London: Methuen, 1903.
*Julia Bride.* New York: Harper, 1909.
*\*The Finer Grain.* New York: Scribners, 1910.

### BIOGRAPHY AND AUTOBIOGRAPHY

*William Wetmore Story and His Friends: From Letters, Diaries, and Recollections.* 2 vols. Edinburgh: Blackwood, 1903.
*A Small Boy and Others.* New York: Scribners, 1913.
*Notes of a Son and Brother.* New York: Scribners, 1914.
*The Middle Years.* London: Collins, 1917. (Posthumous, uncompleted.)

### DRAMA

*Daisy Miller: A Comedy in Three Acts.* Boston: Osgood, 1883.
*Theatricals.* London: Osgood, McIlvaine, 1894.
*Theatricals: Second Series.* London: Osgood, McIlvaine, 1895.

### ESSAYS AND CRITICISM

*French Poets and Novelists.* London: Macmillan, 1878.
*Hawthorne.* London: Macmillan, 1879.
*Partial Portraits.* London: Macmillan, 1888.
*Essays in London and Elsewhere.* London: Osgood, McIlvaine, 1893.
*Picture and Text.* New York: Harper and Brothers, 1893.

*The Question of Our Speech.* Boston: Houghton, Mifflin, 1905.

*Notes on Novelists.* London: Dent, 1914.

TRAVEL WRITING

*Transatlantic Sketches.* Boston: Osgood, 1875.
*Portraits of Places.* London: Macmillan, 1883.
*A Little Tour in France.* Boston: Osgood, 1884.
*English Hours.* London: Heinemann, 1905.
*The American Scene.* London: Chapman and Hall, 1907.
*Italian Hours.* London: Heinemann, 1909.

CORRESPONDENCE

*The Letters of Henry James.* 2 vols. Edited by Percy Lubbock. London: Macmillan, 1920.

*Letters to A. C. Benson and Auguste Monod.* New York: Scribners, 1930.

*Theatre and Friendship: Some Henry James Letters.* London: Cape, 1932. (Letters of James to Elizabeth Robins.)

*Henry James and Robert Louis Stevenson: A Record of Friendship and Criticism.* Edited by Janet A. Smith. London: Hart-Davis, 1948.

*The Selected Letters of Henry James.* Edited by Leon Edel. New York: Farrar, Straus, 1995.

*Henry James and H. G. Wells.* Edited by Leon Edel and Gordon N. Ray. London: Hart-Davis, 1958.

*Henry James Letters.* 4 vols. Edited by Leon Edel. Cambridge, Mass.: Harvard University Press, 1975–1984.

*Selected Letters of Henry James to Edmund Gosse, 1882–1915: A Literary Friendship.* Edited by Rayburn S. Moore. Baton Rouge: Louisiana State University Press, 1988.

*Henry James and Edith Wharton: Letters, 1900–1915.* Edited by Lyall H. Powers. New York: Scribners, 1990.

*The Correspondence of Henry James and Henry Adams, 1877–1914.* Edited by George Monteiro. Baton Rouge: Louisiana State University Press, 1992.

*The Correspondence of William James.* Vols. 1–3: *William and Henry.* Edited by Ignas K. Skrupskelis and Elizabeth M. Berkeley. Charlottesville: University Press of Virginia, 1992–1994.

*The Correspondence of Henry James and the House of Macmillan, 1877–1914.* Edited by Rayburn S. Moore. Baton Rouge: Louisiana State University Press, 1993.

COLLECTED WORKS

Listed here are the most important collections of James's work by hands other than his own, both contemporary and posthumous.

*Within the Rim and Other Essays, 1914–15.* London: Collins, 1919. (James's essays on World War I.)

*The Novels and Stories of Henry James.* 35 vols. Edited by Percy Lubbock. London: Macmillan, 1921–1923.

*The Art of the Novel: Critical Prefaces by Henry James.* Edited by Richard P. Blackmur. New York: Scribners, 1934. (James's New York Edition prefaces, with an introduction by Blackmur.)

*The James Family, Including Selections from the Writings of Henry James, Senior, William, Henry, and Alice James.* Edited by F. O. Matthiessen. New York: Knopf, 1947.

*The Notebooks of Henry James.* Edited by F. O. Matthiessen and Kenneth B. Murdock. New York: Oxford University Press, 1947.

*The Scenic Art: Notes on Acting and the Drama, 1872–1901.* Edited by Allan Wade. New Brunswick, N.J.: Rutgers University Press, 1948.

*The Complete Plays of Henry James.* Edited by Leon Edel. Philadelphia: Lippincott, 1949.

*Henry James: The Painter's Eye: Notes and Essays on the Pictorial Arts.* Edited by John L. Sweeney. London: Hart-Davis, 1956.

*The Complete Tales of Henry James.* 12 vols. Edited by Leon Edel. Philadelphia: Lippincott, 1962–1965.

*Novels, 1871–1880: Watch and Ward, Roderick Hudson, The American, The Europeans, Confidence.* Edited by William T. Stafford. New York: Library of America, 1983.

*Literary Criticism: Essays on Literature, American Writers, English Writers.* Edited by Leon Edel. New York: Library of America, 1984.

*Literary Criticism: French Writers, Other European Writers, the Prefaces to the New York Edition.* Edited by Leon Edel. New York: Library of America, 1984.

*Novels 1881–1886: Washington Square, The Portrait of a Lady, The Bostonians.* Edited by William T. Stafford. New York: Library of America, 1985.

*The Complete Notebooks of Henry James.* Edited by Leon Edel and Lyall H. Powers. New York: Oxford University Press, 1987.

*Novels 1886–1890: The Princess Casamassima, The Reverberator, The Tragic Muse.* Edited by Daniel Mark Fogel. New York: Library of America, 1989.

*Collected Travel Writings: The Continent.* Edited by Richard Howard. New York: Library of America, 1993.

*Collected Travel Writings: Great Britain and America.* Edited by Richard Howard. New York: Library of America, 1993.

## BIBLIOGRAPHIES AND CONCORDANCES

Bradbury, Nicola. *An Annotated Critical Bibliography of Henry James.* New York: St. Martin's Press, 1987.

Bender, Claire E., and Todd K. Bender. *A Concordance to Henry James's "The Turn of the Screw."* New York: Garland, 1988.

Bender, Todd K. *A Concordance to Henry James's "Daisy Miller."* New York: Garland, 1987.

———. *A Concordance to Henry James's "The Awkward Age."* New York: Garland, 1989.

Bender, Todd K., and D. Leon Higden. *A Concordance to Henry James's "The Spoils of Poynton."* New York: Garland, 1988.

Budd, John Henry. *Henry James: A Bibliography of Criticism, 1975–1981.* Westport, Conn.: Greenwood Press, 1983.

Edel, Leon, and Dan H. Laurence. *A Bibliography of Henry James,* 3d ed. New York: Oxford University Press, 1982. (A complete listing of James's writings.)

Funston, Judith. *Henry James: A Reference Guide, 1975–1987.* Boston: G. K. Hall, 1991.

Hulpke, Erika. *A Concordance to Henry James's "What Maisie Knew."* New York: Garland, 1989.

Ricks, Beatrice. *Henry James: A Bibliography of Secondary Works.* Metuchen, N.J.: Scarecrow Press, 1975.

Scura, Dorothy. *Henry James, 1960–1974: A Reference Guide.* Boston: G. K. Hall, 1979.

Taylor, Linda J. *Henry James, 1866–1916: A Reference Guide.* Boston: G. K. Hall, 1982.

## FILMS, TELEVISION DRAMAS, PLAYS, AND OPERAS BASED ON THE WORKS OF HENRY JAMES

*The Ambassadors.* Television adaptation. Script by Denis Constanduros. Directed by James Cellan Jones. Three episodes. BBC, 1977.

*The Aspern Papers.* Opera by Dominick Argento. Libretto by Dominick Argento. First production: Dallas, 1988.

*Berkeley Square.* Film based on *The Sense of the Past.* Screenplay by Sonya Levien. Directed by Frank Lloyd. Twentieth Century–Fox, 1933.

*The Bostonians.* Film. Screenplay by Ruth Prawer Jhabvala. Directed by James Ivory. Merchant Ivory Productions, 1984.

*Daisy Miller.* Film. Screenplay by Frederic Raphael. Directed by Peter Bogdanovich. Paramount, 1974.

*The Europeans.* Film. Screenplay by Ruth Prawer Jhabvala. Directed by James Ivory. Merchant Ivory Productions, 1979.

*The Golden Bowl.* Television adaptation. Script by Jack Pulman. Directed by James Cellan Jones. Six episodes. BBC, 1972.

*The Heiress.* Film based on *Washington Square.* Screenplay by Ruth and Augustus Goetz. Directed by William Wyler. Paramount, 1949. (Adapted from the 1948 Broadway play by the Goetzes; revived on Broadway, 1995; also presented in numerous television productions.)

*The Innocents.* Film based on *The Turn of the Screw.* Screenplay by William Archibald and Truman Capote. Directed by Jack Clayton. Twentieth Century–Fox, 1961.

*The Lost Moment.* Film based on *The Aspern Papers.* Screenplay by Leonardo Bercovici. Directed by Martin Gabel. Universal-International, 1947.

*Owen Wingrave.* Opera by Benjamin Britten. Libretto by Myfanwy Piper. First production: London, 1971.

*The Portrait of a Lady.* Television drama. Script by Jack Pulman. Directed by James Cellan Jones. Six episodes. BBC, 1966.

*The Portrait of a Lady.* Film. Screenplay by Laura Jones; Directed by Jane Campion. Gramercy Pictures, 1996.

*The Spoils of Poynton.* Television drama. Script by Denis Constanduros. Directed by Peter Sasdy. Four episodes. BBC, 1970.

*The Turn of the Screw.* Opera by Benjamin Britten. Libretto by Myfanwy Piper. First production: Venice, 1954.

*The Turn of the Screw.* Television drama. Script by James Costigan. Directed by John Frankenheimer. NBC, 1959.

*The Wings of the Dove.* Opera by Douglas Moore. Libretto by Ethan Ayer. First production: New York City Opera, 1961.

*The Wings of the Dove.* Screenplay by Hossein Amani. Directed by Iain Softley. Miramax, 1997.

## BIOGRAPHICAL AND CRITICAL STUDIES

Allen, Elizabeth. *A Woman's Place in the Novels of Henry James.* London: Macmillan, 1984.

Anesko, Michael. *"Friction with the Market": Henry James and the Profession of Authorship.* New York: Oxford University Press, 1986.

Armstrong, Paul B. *The Challenge of Bewilderment: Understanding and Representation in James, Conrad, and Ford.* Ithaca: Cornell University Press, 1987.

———. *The Phenomenology of Henry James.* Chapel Hill: University of North Carolina Press, 1983.

Ash, Beth Sharon. "Frail Vessels and Vast Designs: A Psychoanalytic Portrait of Isabel Archer." *New Essays on "The Portrait of a Lady."* Edited by Joel Porte. New York: Cambridge University Press, 1990. Pp. 123-162.

———. "Narcissism and the Gilded Image: A Psychoanalytic Reading of *The Golden Bowl.*" *Henry James Review* 15:55–90 (Winter 1994).

Auchard, John. *Silence in Henry James: The Heritage of Symbolism and Decadence.* University Park: Pennsylvania State University Press, 1986.

Beach, Joseph Warren. *The Method of Henry James.* New Haven, Conn.: Yale University Press, 1918. Reprinted with corrections. Philadelphia: A. Saifer, 1954.

Beidler, Paul G. *Frames in James: "The Tragic Muse," "The Turn of the Screw," "What Maisie Knew," and "The Ambassadors."* Victoria, B.C.: English Literary Studies, University of Victoria, 1993.

Bell, Ian F. A. *Henry James and the Past: Readings into Time.* New York: St. Martin's Press, 1991.

Bell, Millicent. *Meaning in Henry James.* Cambridge, Mass.: Harvard University Press, 1991.

Bentley, Nancy. *The Ethnography of Manners: Hawthorne, James, Wharton.* Cambridge: Cambridge University Press, 1995.

———. "James and the Tribal Discipline of English Kinship." *Henry James Review* 15: 237–256 (Spring 1994).

Berland, Alwyn. *Culture and Conduct in the Novels of Henry James.* Cambridge: Cambridge University Press, 1981.

Blackall, Jean Frantz. *Jamesian Ambiguity and* The Sacred Fount. Ithaca, N.Y.: Cornell University Press, 1965.

Blair, Sara. *Henry James and the Writing of Race and Nation.* Cambridge: Cambridge University Press, 1996.

Booth, Wayne C. *The Rhetoric of Fiction.* Chicago: University of Chicago Press, 1961. Rev. ed. 1983.

Brodhead, Richard. *The School of Hawthorne.* New York: Oxford University Press, 1986.

Cameron, Sharon. *Thinking in Henry James.* Chicago: University of Chicago Press, 1989.

Cannon, Kelly. *Henry James and Masculinity: The Man at the Margins.* New York: St. Martin's Press, 1994.

Caramello, Charles. *Henry James, Gertrude Stein, and the Biographical Act.* Chapel Hill: University of North Carolina Press, 1996.

Carlson, Susan. *Women of Grace: James's Plays and the Comedy of Manners.* Ann Arbor: UMI Research Press, 1985.

Chatman, Seymour. *The Later Style of Henry James.* Oxford: Blackwell, 1972. Reprinted: Westport, Conn.: Greenwood, 1986.

Cox, James M. "The Memoirs of Henry James: Self-Interest as Autobiography." *Southern Review,* n.s. 22, no. 2:231–251 (April 1986).

Dawidoff, Robert. *The Genteel Tradition and the Sacred Rage: High Culture vs. Democracy in Adams, James, and Santayana.* Chapel Hill: University of North Carolina Press, 1992.

Donadio, Stephen. *Nietzsche, Henry James, and the Artistic Will.* New York: Oxford University Press, 1978.

Dupee, F. W. *Henry James.* New York: William Sloane, 1951.

Edel, Leon. *Henry James: A Life.* New York: Harper and Row, 1985.

———. *The Life of Henry James.* 5 vols. Philadelphia: J. B. Lippincott, 1953–1972.

Edel, Leon, and Adeline Tintner. *The Library of Henry James.* Ann Arbor: UMI Research Press, 1987.

Eliot, T. S. "In Memory" and "The Hawthorne Aspect." *Little Review* 5:44–53 (August 1918).

Feinstein, Howard. *Becoming William James.* Ithaca, N.Y.: Cornell University Press, 1984.

Felman, Shoshana. "Turning the Screw of Interpretation." *Yale French Studies* 55/56:94-207 (1977).

Fogel, Daniel Mark. *A Companion to Henry James Studies.* Westport: Greenwood Press, 1993. (See especially chapters by Charles Caramello, Richard A. Hocks, Carol Molly, Thomas M. Leitch, John Carlos Rowe, and Philip M. Weinstein.)

————. *Covert Relations: James Joyce, Virginia Woolf, and Henry James.* Charlottesville: University Press of Virginia, 1990.

————. *"Daisy Miller": A Dark Comedy of Manners.* Boston: Twayne, 1990.

————. *Henry James and the Structure of the Romantic Imagination.* Baton Rouge: Louisiana State University Press, 1981.

Fowler, Virginia C. *Henry James's American Girl: The Embroidery on the Canvas.* Madison: University of Wisconsin Press, 1984.

Freedman, Jonathan. *Professions of Taste: Henry James, British Aestheticism, and Commodity Culture.* Stanford: Stanford University Press, 1990.

————. "Trilling, James, and the Uses of Cultural Criticism." *Henry James Review* 14:141–150 (Spring 1993).

Fussell, Edwin Sill. *The Catholic Side of Henry James.* Cambridge: Cambridge University Press, 1993.

————. *The French Side of Henry James.* New York: Columbia University Press, 1990.

Gale, Robert L. *A Henry James Encyclopedia.* Westport, Conn.: Greenwood Press, 1989.

Graham, Kenneth. *Henry James: A Literary Life.* New York: St. Martin's Press, 1995.

Greene, Graham. *The Lost Childhood and Other Essays.* New York: Viking Press, 1951.

Greenwald, Elissa. *Realism and Romance: Nathaniel Hawthorne, Henry James, and American Fiction.* Ann Arbor: UMI Research Press, 1989.

Griffin, Susan M. *The Historical Eye: The Texture of the Visual in Late James.* Boston: Northeastern University Press, 1991.

Habegger, Alfred. *The Father: A Life of Henry James, Sr.* New York: Farrar, Straus & Giroux, 1994.

————. *Gender, Fantasy, and Realism in American Literature: The Rise of American Literary Realism in W. D. Howells and Henry James.* New York: Columbia University Press, 1982.

————. *Henry James and the "Woman Business."* New York: Cambridge University Press, 1989.

Hagberg, Garry. *Meaning and Interpretation: Wittgenstein, Henry James, and Literary Knowledge.* Ithaca, N.Y.: Cornell University Press, 1994.

Hall, Richard. "An Obscure Hurt: The Sexuality of Henry James." *New Republic,* April 28, 1979, pp. 25–31; May 5, 1979, pp. 25–29.

Heller, Terry. *The Turn of the Screw: Bewildered Vision.* Boston: Twayne, 1989.

————, and Priscilla Gibson Hicks. "A Turn in the Formation of James's New York Edition: Criticism, the Historical Record, and the Siting of *The Awkward Age.*" *Henry James Review* 16:195–221 (Spring 1995).

Hoffman, Charles, and Tess Hoffman. "Henry James and the Civil War." *New England Quarterly* 62:529–552 (1989).

Hocks, Richard A. *Henry James and Pragmatistic Thought: A Study in the Relationship Between the Philosophy of William James and the Literary Art of Henry James.* Chapel Hill: University of North Carolina Press, 1974.

Holland, Laurence Bedwell. *The Expense of Vision: Essays on the Craft of Henry James.* Princeton, N.J.: Princeton University Press, 1964.

Holly, Carol. *Intensely Family: The Inheritance of Family Shame and the Autobiographies of Henry James.* Madison: University of Wisconsin Press, 1995.

Horne, Philip. *Henry James and Revision: The New York Edition.* New York: Oxford University Press, 1990.

Howells, William Dean. "Henry James, Jr." In *William Dean Howells: Representative Selection.* Edited by Clara Marburg Kirk and Rudolph Kirk. New York: Hill and Wang, 1950. Pp. 345–355.

Jacobson, Marcia. *Henry James and the Mass Market.* University: University of Alabama Press, 1983.

Jobe, Stephen H. "A Calendar of the Published Letters of Henry James." Parts 1 and 2. *Henry James Review* 11:1–29, 77–100 (Winter and Spring 1990).

Jolly, Roslyn. *Henry James: History, Narrative, Fiction.* Oxford: Clarendon Press, 1993.

Kaplan, Fred. *Henry James: The Imagination of Genius.* New York: William Morrow, 1992.

Kaston, Carren Osna. *Imagination and Desire in the Novels of Henry James.* New Brunswick, N.J.: Rutgers University Press, 1984.

Kirschke, James. *Henry James and Impressionism.* Troy, N.Y.: Whitston Press, 1981.

Krook, Dorothea. *The Ordeal of Consciousness in Henry James.* New York: Cambridge University Press, 1962.

Lewis, R. W. B. *The Jameses: A Family Narrative.* New York: Farrar, Straus & Giroux, 1991.

Long, Robert Emmet. *The Great Succession: Henry James and the Legacy of Hawthorne.* Pittsburgh: University of Pittsburgh Press, 1979.

Margolis, Anne T. *Henry James and the Problem of Audience: An International Act.* Ann Arbor, Mich.: UMI Research Press, 1985.

Matthiessen, F. O. *Henry James: The Major Phase.* New York: Oxford University Press, 1944.

McWhirter, David B., ed. *Henry James's New York Edition: The Construction of Authorship.* Stanford, Calif.: Stanford University Press, 1995. (See foreword by John Carlos Rowe.)

Miller, J. Hillis. *The Ethics of Reading: Kant, de Man, Eliot, Trollope, James, and Benjamin.* New York: Columbia University Press, 1987.

Mizruchi, Susan L. *The Power of Historical Knowledge: Narrating the Past in Hawthorne, James, and Dreiser.* Princeton, N.J.: Princeton University Press, 1988.

Moon, Michael. "A Small Boy and Others: Sexual Disorientation in Henry James, Kenneth Anger, and David Lynch." In *Comparative American Identities: Race, Sex, and Nationality in the Modern Text.* Edited by Hortense Spillers. New York: Routledge, 1991. Pp. 151–156.

Naiburg, Suzi. "Archaic Depths in Henry James's 'The Last of the Valerii.'" *Henry James Review* 14:151–165 (Spring 1993).

Norrman, Ralf. *The Insecure World of Henry James's Fiction: Intensity and Ambiguity.* London: Macmillan, 1982.

Novick, Sheldon. "Henry James's First Published Work: Miss Maggie Mitchell in 'Fanchon the Cricket.'" *Henry James Review* 17:300–302 (Fall 1996).

———. *Henry James: The Young Master.* New York: Random House, 1996.

Parker, Hershel. "Deconstructing *The Art of the Novel* and Liberating James's Prefaces." *Henry James Review* 14:284–307 (Fall 1993).

———. "Henry James 'In the Wood': Sequence and Significance of His Literary Labors, 1905–1907." *Nineteenth-Century Fiction* 38:429–513 (1984).

Perosa, Sergio. *Henry James and the Experimental Novel.* Charlottesville: University Press of Virginia, 1978.

Person, Leland S., Jr. "Henry James, George Sand, and the Suspense of Masculinity." *PMLA* 106:515–528 (1991).

———. "James's Homo-Aesthetics: Deploying Desire in the Tales of Writers and Artists." *Henry James Review* 14:188–203 (Spring 1993).

Poirier, Richard. *The Comic Sense of Henry James: A Study of the Early Novels.* New York: Oxford University Press, 1960.

Posnock, Ross. *Henry James and the Problem of Robert Browning.* Athens: University of Georgia Press, 1985.

———. *The Trial of Curiosity: Henry James, William James, and the Challenge of Modernity.* New York: Oxford University Press, 1991.

Porte, Joel, ed. *New Essays on "The Portrait of a Lady."* Cambridge: Cambridge University Press, 1990.

Pound, Ezra. "Brief Note." *Little Review* 5:6–9 (August 1918).

———. "Henry James." In *The Literary Essays of Ezra Pound.* Edited by T. S. Eliot. New York: New Directions, 1968. Pp. 295–338.

Przybylowicz, Donna. *Desire and Repression: The Dialectic of Self and Other in the Late Works of Henry James.* University, Ala.: University of Alabama Press, 1986.

Purdy, Strother B. *The Hole in the Fabric: Science, Contemporary Literature, and Henry James.* Pittsburgh: University of Pittsburgh Press, 1977.

Rimmon-Kenan, Shlomith. *The Concept of Ambiguity: The Example of James.* Chicago: University of Chicago Press, 1977.

Rosenzweig, Saul. "The Ghost of Henry James." *Partisan Review* 11:436–455 (1944).

Rowe, John Carlos. *Henry Adams and Henry James: The Emergence of a Modern Consciousness.* Ithaca, N.Y.: Cornell University Press, 1976.

———. "Henry James and the Art of Teaching." *Henry James Review* 17:213–224 (Fall 1996).

———. *The Theoretical Dimensions of Henry James.* Madison: University of Wisconsin Press, 1984.

Seltzer, Mark. *Henry James and the Art of Power.* Ithaca, N.Y.: Cornell University Press, 1984.

Smit, David. *The Language of the Master: Theories of Style and the Late Writing of Henry James.* Carbondale: Southern Illinois University Press, 1988.

Spender, Stephen. *The Destructive Element: A Study of Modern Writers and Beliefs.* London: Jonathan Cape, 1935.

Springer, Mary Doyle. *A Rhetoric of Literary Character: Some Women of Henry James.* Chicago: University of Chicago Press, 1978.

Stevens, Hugh. "Sexuality and the Aesthetic in *The Golden Bowl.*" *Henry James Review* 14:55–71 (Winter 1993).

Stowe, William W. *Balzac, James, and the Realistic Novel.* Princeton, N.J.: Princeton University Press, 1983.

Stowell, H. Peter. *Literary Impressionism: James and Chekhov*. Athens: University of Georgia Press, 1980.

Teahan, Sheila. *The Rhetorical Logic of Henry James*. Baton Rouge: Louisiana State University Press, 1995.

Tintner, Adeline R. *The Book World of Henry James: Appropriating the Classics*. Ann Arbor, Mich.: UMI Research Press, 1987.

———. *The Cosmopolitan World of Henry James: An Intertextual Study*. Baton Rouge: Louisiana State University Press, 1991.

———. "A Gay *Sacred Fount*: The Reader As Detective." *Twentieth Century Literature* 41:224–240 (Summer 1995).

———. *Henry James and The Lust of the Eyes: Thirteen Artists in His Work*. Baton Rouge: Louisiana State University Press, 1993.

———. *The Museum World of Henry James*. Ann Arbor, Mich.: UMI Research Press, 1986.

———. *The Pop World of Henry James: From Fairy Tales to Science Fiction*. Ann Arbor, Mich.: UMI Research Press, 1989.

Torsney, Cheryl B. *Constance Fennimore Woolson: The Grief of Artistry*. Athens: University of Georgia Press, 1989.

———. "Henry James, Charles Sanders Pierce, and the Fat Capon: Homoerotic Desire in *The American*." *Henry James Review* 14:166–178 (Spring 1993).

Trilling, Lionel. *The Liberal Imagination: Essays on Literature and Society*. New York: Macmillan, 1948.

Veeder, William. "The Feminine Orphan and the Emergent Master: Self-Realization in Henry James." *Henry James Review* 12:20–54 (Winter 1991).

———. *Henry James—The Lessons of the Master: Popular Fiction and Personal Style in the Nineteenth Century*. Chicago: University of Chicago Press, 1975.

———. "The Portrait of a Lack." In *New Essays on "The Portrait of a Lady."* Edited by Joel Porte. New York: Cambridge University Press, 1990. Pp. 95–121.

———. "Toxic Mothers, Cultural Criticism: 'In the Cage' and Elsewhere." *Henry James Review* 14: 264–272 (Fall 1993).

Walker, Pierre A. *Reading Henry James in French Cultural Contexts*. DeKalb: Northern Illinois University Press, 1995.

Walton, Priscilla. *The Disruption of the Feminine in Henry James*. Toronto: University of Toronto Press, 1992.

Ward, J. A. *The Search for Form: Studies in the Structure of James's Fiction*. Chapel Hill: University of North Carolina Press, 1967.

Washington, Bryan R. *The Politics of Exile: Ideology in Henry James, F. Scott Fitzgerald, and James Baldwin*. Boston: Northeastern University Press, 1995.

Williams, Merle A. *Henry James and the Philosophical Novel: Being and Seeing*. New York: Cambridge University Press, 1993.

Wilson, Edmund. "The Ambiguity of Henry James." *Hound and Horn* 7:385–406 (1934). Reprinted in *Homage to Henry James 1843–1916*. Mamaroneck, N.Y.: Paul Appel, 1971.

Wilson, Michael. "Lessons of the Master: The Artist and Sexual Deployment in Henry James." *Henry James Review* 14:257–263 (Fall 1993).

Winnett, Susan. *Terrible Sociability: The Text of Manners in Laclos, Goethe, and James*. Stanford, Calif.: Stanford University Press, 1993.

Yeazell, Ruth Bernard. "Henry James." In *Columbia Literary History of the United States*. Edited by Emory Elliott et al. New York: Columbia University Press, 1988. Pp. 668–689.

———. *Language and Knowledge in the Late Novels of Henry James*. Chicago: University of Chicago Press, 1976.

—*DANIEL MARK FOGEL*

# Herman Melville
## 1819–1891

MELVILLE'S CAREER AS a literary artist began on a whaleship, a scene of appalling industrial exploitation and filth. Hunting down and killing whales with handheld weapons posed extreme dangers, and then came the butchering of the huge carcasses and boiling down the blubber. The reek of boiling whale oil and the smoke from the fire permeated clothing, sails, rigging, and beards, as did the odor from rotting remnants of blood and flesh. As the months went by, whaleships developed a powerful stench, discernible miles downwind. Whaling sailors were trapped aboard a floating slaughterhouse, ruled over by a captain empowered to kick them and beat them or to have them jailed at the next port. The captain was also empowered to keep the voyage going for years on end without regard to the desires or needs of the crew.

A man with a knack for telling stories was good to have on board, to help pass the time between spells of slaughter; there were many such men in the whale fishery, literate and illiterate, who sharpened their yarn-spinning skills through months of practice before experienced and critical audiences. Melville possessed the most prodigious gift for literary creation to surface in the official culture of nineteenth-century America, and when he appeared at age twenty-three on board the *Lucy Ann* bound from the Marquesas Islands to Tahiti,

he had just acquired a stock of marvelous new material. He had jumped ship in the Marquesas, to escape harsh treatment on the whaler *Acushnet,* and his experiences among the Marquesan cannibals were sexy, lurid, and fraught with adventure. He recounted them with hypnotic power.

Years later, while he was writing *Moby-Dick,* Melville spent an evening with Nathaniel and Sophia Hawthorne spinning his South Sea yarns. After he had departed it dawned on Sophia that Melville hadn't taken home his club, so she looked about the house to see where he had left it. Only after a search did she realize that the club had existed only in her imagination, conjured up by Melville's spellbinding stories of savage combat and disturbing exotic beauty.

### MELVILLE'S ERA

Melville lived a long life spanning an era that witnessed profound upheaval and change in American life. During his youth, whaling was one of many powerful new industries and a harbinger of the industrial development that resulted in the bureaucratic monopolies that were ascendant at the time of his death. Like the competitive new economy at large, whaling took place in a "man's world." Under market capitalism, the factory system destroyed household manufactures, and men were compelled to leave home in order to make a living. The home then became a "woman's sphere" of domestic pursuits—principally child-rearing—where loving solicitude offset the harshness of male competition. This new system of family life ushered in conventions of gender and sexuality that remain current today, including new relations of men with men.

The cutthroat competition of the whaling industry was an arena of individualist striving among owners and captains, and it produced a merciless working environment for sailors. In the all-male world of the whaler, as in prison life today, there was a substantial threat of sexual assault; yet there was also the opportunity for the cultivation of cherished friendships, a tender brotherhood offering solace for the harshness of their economic plight, and models of masculinity that provided alternatives to the cold isolation of warrior individualism. Men like Melville, who were sexually attracted to men, found the opportunity to fulfill that attraction and developed new conceptions of the moral and emotional complexities such attraction entailed.

Melville also lived through the century in which the government of the United States extended its authority across the continent as a whole. After quelling the rebellion of the Confederacy, the Union sponsored a swift expansion of the nation westward to the Pacific. The Civil War brought an end to slavery of blacks in the South, but the new continental empire governed from Washington was nonetheless pervasively racist and was established at the expense of peoples of color from sea to shining sea and to the islands beyond. The whaleship carried Melville to the Polynesian frontier, where native peoples suffered the crushing impact of the rising Anglo-European culture in the United States.

Melville was spiritually shaken by the profound changes taking place in America during his lifetime. He had absorbed a fundamental framework of thought that assumed God had created the world and had given it a moral structure. Human beings inhabit, so the theory ran, a unified and permanent edifice of divinely created reality that conforms to principles of universal truth. Yet Melville came to feel that he had known multiple worlds: the whaler was a world to itself, profoundly alien to the world of his upbringing; Polynesian society was another world of its own; and the America where he came to maturity was strange to the America into which he had been born. Confronting such dislocations, Melville conceived an epic ambition, that of seeking a new truth capable of binding the fragmentary realities of his life into a whole; his greatest literary achievements embody this quest and the discoveries he made as it failed. Melville's program of spiritual conquest was propelled by what he learned in the whaling industry, he declares in *Moby-Dick,* "for a whale-ship was my Yale College and my Harvard."

## MELVILLE'S YOUTH

Born Herman Melvill on August 1, 1819, he did not inherit a life of dangerous, degrading, and ill-paid labor, but one of exceptional privilege and social prominence. His father, Allan Melvill, was a wealthy businessman in New York City, an importer of fine textiles whose enterprises required European travel and whose personal library included a substantial holding in French literature. Allan's father was a hero of the American Revolution, Major Thomas Melvill, who had taken part in the Boston Tea Party. Herman's mother, Maria Gansevoort Melvill, boasted an even more distinguished ancestry. Her father, General Peter Gansevoort, was famous for his defense of Fort Stanwix; his success prevented British and Indian troops from reinforcing General John Burgoyne and his men before the Battle of Saratoga. Maria's brother, Peter Gansevoort, was a banker in Albany, New York, with all the dignity and responsibilities of a wealthy Dutch patroon.

The mercantile aristocracy of the Eastern seaboard that had supported the American Revolution found its economic and social position undermined in the turbulent economy of the early nineteenth century. Men who were born to upper-class privilege, like Allan Melvill, were forced to contend with a surging multitude of fierce new competitors who entered the economic fray with only their energy, wit, and hard work to sustain them. This rising middle class of "self-made men" remade the social landscape of America and established the "rags to riches story" as an abiding myth of American manhood.

Herman Melville lived out the reverse story, that of riches to rags. His father closed the New York business in 1830, when Herman was eleven, and retreated to Albany, where he frantically sought to regain his footing. But he became mentally deranged in 1832 and died soon after, leaving his wife with eight children. Peter Gansevoort sought to assist the family, which changed the spelling of its name to Melville so as to avoid Allan's creditors, but the Panic of 1837 cancelled all efforts at recovery. Herman tried to sustain himself working in a bank. He studied engineering briefly, taught school for a while, and then shipped on a relatively short voyage to Liverpool before he signed on the whaler *Acushnet* as a common sailor in 1840, bound for the South Seas.

Melville's sudden descent from patrician ease to working-class victimization would by itself have left psychological scars, but there is reason to believe that the young man also carried onto the whaleship a legacy of psychic trauma having more intimate origins. Allan's mental instability echoes the bizarre conduct of his own father, Thomas, and is reflected in the spells of manic excitement that seized Melville's older brother, Gansevoort, who, like his father, died relatively young beset by severe psychological disturbance. The family code, as Melville sketches it in his fiction, main-

tained an image of Allan as a moral paragon. It is hard to doubt Melville when he indicates that he virtually worshipped his father and suffered acute grief at losing him. Yet there is reason to believe that this idealized image was maintained in order to dispel the awareness of his father's shortcomings and to repress the resentment they aroused, so that Melville's abiding grief was complicated by rage and guilt. "I must not think of those delightful days," Melville comments in *Redburn,* "before my father became a bankrupt, and died, and we removed from the city; for when I think of those days, something rises up in my throat and almost strangles me."

Following Allan's death it appears that Maria retreated into an emotional fortress, coldly defending the patrician dignity that her husband's failure had so spectacularly failed to maintain; she may have looked to her sons for successes to recapture her former station. Such speculations probe mysteries that can never be fully untangled; Melville himself probed them in his fiction, with uncertain conclusions. Yet it is clear that he was relatively subdued as a boy and that looking back upon his young manhood he declared that his intellectual and emotional development had been stalled. "Until I was twenty-five," he said, "I had no development at all. . . . Three weeks have scarcely passed, at any time between then and now, that I have not unfolded within myself."

LITERARY BEGINNINGS

When Melville returned from his whaling voyage, he faced the penury that had sent him to sea in the first place. Yet as he visited his family and friends, he told his well-practiced tales of South Sea adventures, and it was suggested to him that these stories might make a book. The writing of *Typee: A Peep at Polynesian Life* (1846)—in Melville's twenty-fifth year—inaugurated his rapid and astonishing inner development.

*Typee* appears on the surface a curious hybrid. Published in England as part of John Murray's *Home and Colonial Library,* the work proposes to offer a reliable account of the weather, geography, history, political circumstances, and folkways of the Marquesas Islands—a "narrative of facts" for use by subsequent voyagers. But the book is also a high-spirited tale of exotic adventure, whose scenes are charged with narrative excitement and described with astonishing pictorial vividness. British reviewers of the work, unfamiliar with the economic realities that had sent the author whaling, found it impossible to believe that so intelligent and skilled a writer could ever have been a common sailor.

Beneath its engaging surface features, however, *Typee* reveals Melville's sharp resentment of the mercantile civilization invading the South Pacific. He declares that white Europeans and Americans do not possess the moral superiority that their claim to "civilization" asserts and concludes that the missionary program of bringing moral enlightenment to the "savages" is entirely misconceived. "I am inclined to think that so far as the relative wickedness of the parties is concerned, four or five Marquesan Islanders sent to the United States as Missionaries might be quite as useful as an equal number of Americans despatched to the Islands in a similar capacity."

Melville recognized that the missionary enterprise was a form of cultural imperialism that seconded and supported more tangible forms of subjugation. The destruction of native customs and the effort to instill "habits of industry" in island peoples had the effect of reducing them to a labor force for exploitative western business ventures. The indigenous peoples of the Pacific, he concluded, had been "civilized into draught horses, and evangelized into beasts of burden."

Melville was aware that his own inherited traditions prevented him from attaining an accurate comprehension of Marquesan life, and he organizes his narrative as a psychosocial drama in which imperfect interpretive frameworks successively assert themselves and then collapse. At the moments of encounter—on the boundary where familiar knowledge disintegrates in the presence of a deeply strange and potentially dangerous new reality—Melville's aesthetic response is most deeply awakened and his literary gift most powerfully displayed. He did not know what to make of the sexual customs of the Marquesans, yet their erotic vivacity struck him as a revelation of breathtaking and tender beauty.

When Melville entered the profession of writer, it was changing rapidly in America. Traditionally conceived as the avocation of leisured aristocrats, after the fashion of Washington Irving and James Fenimore Cooper, writing fiction was becoming responsive to the opportunities for profit offered by mass-market publishing. This commercialization and democratization of literature opened professional writing to women: Maria McIntosh, E. D. E. N. Southworth, and Harriet Beecher Stowe were all active in the mid 1840s, when Melville got his start; Sara Parton ("Fanny Fern") and Susan Warner followed as successful writers in the 1850s. The prime market for fiction was women, in their roles as wives and mothers, who were approached through carefully crafted advertising campaigns.

Robert Bonner, a pioneer of the new promotional techniques, insisted that his titles were "meant for the family . . . neither sectarian or political" and boasted of shunning works "that might offend the most pious old lady in a Presbyterian church." These popular works that celebrated fireside virtues are not as simpleminded as once supposed, and they often convey a shrewd analysis of the oppression women suffered both as homemakers and writers. Yet Melville's impulse to mock the pieties of middle-class culture, and to attack the economic injustices that sponsored it, set him at odds with the most powerful opinion makers of his time. American reviewers criticized his lighthearted treatment of erotic themes and his attack on the missionaries in *Typee,* and Melville was pressured by his American publisher into making an extensive expurgation of the work, which remained the standard American version throughout his lifetime.

Yet *Typee* was nonetheless a famous success and allowed Melville to reclaim his place in the patrician society of his birth. He dedicated the book to Lemuel Shaw, then chief justice of the Massachusetts Supreme Court, who had been among his father's closest friends. In 1847 he married the judge's daughter, Elizabeth Shaw, and settled down to continue his career as a writer of rollicking South Sea adventure stories. In *Omoo: A Narrative of Adventures in the South Seas* (1847), he resumed his attack on missions and confirmed his literary identity as a figure who was both an aristocrat and a ne'er-do-well and somehow adrift in the world. The Polynesian word "Omoo" means wanderer, and this term became Melville's nickname among his enlarging circle of literary associates in New York.

Among these new friends was Evert Duyckinck, a wealthy gentleman who was eager to promote the literary interests of America, believing that American literature should not be written in conformity with British models but should arise from distinctively American experiences. Duyckinck offered Melville access to his large personal library, and Melville plunged into an energetic project of self-directed reading, even as he turned to writing a third book in the style of *Typee* and *Omoo.* But after forty-five chapters of lighthearted Polynesian adventure, Melville transformed the tale into a prodigious allegory, entitled *Mardi and a Voyage Thither* (1849), in which Polynesian islands and archipelagoes represent philosophical systems, religious institutions, poetic theories, and political traditions. Melville explains that he was blown off course by a "blast resistless," the overpowering impulse to pursue social and religious issues that now convulsed his mind.

*Mardi*'s allegorical extravaganza marks the emergence of Melville's epic ambition, the impulse to gather all knowledge of self and world into one story of transcendent truth. The book forms a critical moment in the unfolding of his genius. Melville was exhilarated at discovering the amazing power of his intellect—beyond his knack for yarn-spinning—but the prophetic inspiration that drove him also revealed the warfare at his emotional and psychological center. He speaks of the great writers he is absorbing as independent presences within his own mind and indicates that the process of composition itself entails a terrifying loss of psychic control.

> I list to St. Paul who argues the doubts of Montaigne; Julian the Apostate cross-questions Augustine; and Thomas-a-Kempis unrolls his old black letters for all to decipher. Zeno murmurs maxims beneath the hoarse shout of Democritus, and though Democritus laugh loud and long, and the sneer of Phyrrho be seen; yet, divine Plato, and Proclus, and Verulam are of my counsel. . . . My cheek blanches white while I write; I start at the scratch of my pen; my own mad brood of eagles devours me; fain would I unsay this audacity; but an iron-mailed hand clenches mine in a vice, and prints down every letter in my spite.

Elizabeth Shaw Melville assisted with the production of the manuscript through May and June of 1848, making fair copy from Melville's rough draft. The two were living in a house in New York that Melville had purchased jointly with his brother Allan, where they lived with Melville's mother, Allan's wife, and four of Melville's unmarried sisters. Melville had paid his share of the cost—and was meeting household expenses—with a loan from Lemuel Shaw. When the reviewers scorned *Mardi* and the reading public shunned it, Melville forced himself to produce works that would sell.

Melville quickly composed a marketable account of his youthful voyage to Liverpool, entitled *Redburn: His First Voyage* (1849). He later condemned this work as the product of hack labor; nonetheless it traces out his reflections on the social transformation that had swept away the elite culture of his birth and forced him to scramble for a living. Like many other young men growing up in the 1830s, Redburn discovers that he is compelled to find his way in a world his father never imagined. Traveling to Liverpool as a common sailor was profoundly different from the journey taken by a wealthy businessman, and the city of Liverpool itself was not the same city. When Redburn tries to find his way through the streets using his father's guidebook, he is forced to conclude that "the thing that had guided the father, could not guide the son." What engages his consciousness at Liverpool most deeply is not business opportunity or impressive architecture, but the horrors of urban poverty.

Melville advanced these meditations in *White-Jacket; or, The World in a Man-of-War* (1850), his effort to write a moneymaking novel about his experiences aboard a United States Navy warship, the USS *United States,* that had carried him home from his whaling adventures in the Pacific. Melville had been appalled by the enforcement of military hierarchy aboard ship through torture: the aim of flogging was not simply to punish a man's disobedience, but to "break" him, as in the slave-holding South, to instill the subservient and tractable disposition necessary for his place in the hierarchy. Melville denounced flogging as "opposed to the essential dignity of man . . . [and] utterly repugnant to the spirit of our democratic institutions." And he declared that America must fulfill its role as a "political Messiah" to remove such injustices from human existence altogether: "We Americans are the peculiar, chosen people— the Israel of our time; we bear the ark of the liberties of the world." Yet as he explored the meanings of the "man-of-war-world" in *White-Jacket,* Melville continued to ponder the meaning of evils that political reform cannot correct, evils that appear native to human experience itself and that threatened to break his own spirit.

## MELVILLE AND HAWTHORNE

In the summer of 1850, Melville's career as a writer appeared to be under control: he was at work on what he called "a romance of adventure, founded upon certain wild legends in the Southern Sperm Whale Fisheries," and expected to finish late in the fall, in October or perhaps November. This plan was demolished, like the plan for *Mardi,* by the "blast resistless" of Melville's prophetic inspiration. He undertook a massive revision and enlargement of the whaling book, through nine months of furious labor, which resulted in the transcendent achievement of *Moby-Dick; or, The Whale* (1851). The sudden maturing of Melville's creative power has been explained in various ways. He himself credited the inspiration he derived from reading the works of Shakespeare, and his marginal notations in *King Lear* make clear that this tragedy entered deeply into his philosophical and religious meditations. Also significant is his move from New York City to a farm near Pittsfield, Massachusetts, close to a farmhouse where Nathaniel Hawthorne was living at the time, resulting in the two mens' friendship.

Melville already knew about Hawthorne and his work, but the appearance of *The Scarlet Letter* in the summer of 1850 was a momentous event, proving that an American writer could create literary art of the highest quality. Melville was moved to write a review for Evert Duyckinck's *Literary World* (August 17 and August 24, 1850) concerning Hawthorne's *Mosses from an Old Manse* that praised him for a philosophical profundity that superficial readers might well overlook, but appealing to those who possess a "Calvinistic sense of Innate Depravity and Original Sin." No true genius can exist, Melville declared, "without also possessing . . . a great, deep intellect, which drops down into the universe like a plummet." Shakespeare's "short, quick probings at the very axis of reality," are the key to his literary greatness, Melville asserted, and in attributing this power to Hawthorne, Melville sought to claim it for himself.

A personal intimacy sprang up between the two men that sustained Melville's spirit as he undertook the arduous and financially risky labor of transforming *Moby-Dick*. The letters from Melville to Hawthorne during this period speak of an "infinite fraternity of feeling," that involves a merging of souls, selves, and bodies. "When come you, Hawthorne?" Melville asks. "By what right do you drink from my flagon of life? And when I put it to my lips—lo, they are yours and not mine." Hawthorne was fifteen years older than Melville and answered Melville's yearning for the fatherly recognition and emotional support that he had lost in boyhood.

It is likely that Melville and Hawthorne were sexually attracted to each other, and it is possible that Melville sought to initiate an affair that Hawthorne declined. No evidence survives that conclusively substantiates this theory, yet the two men would have had good reason to keep this aspect of their relationship secret, if it existed. There was then no visible subculture validating and celebrating same-sex erotic relationships, capable of challenging the majority that considered homosexuality unnatural and depraved. Shipboard life was proverbially rife with "sodomy," as Melville sardonically notes when he jokes in *Typee* about a whaler tacking interminably around "Buggerry Island or the Devil's-Tail Peak," and his terror at the prospect of homosexual rape surfaces in *White-Jacket,* where he speaks of navy vessels as "wooden-walled Gomorrahs of the deep." Yet Melville also gives ample evidence of his attraction to physical beauty in men, as when he responds to the coquettish Marnoo in Typee Valley, and he also celebrated shipboard friendships that take on an atmosphere of intimacy and cherished meaning, as with Harry Bolton in *Redburn,* and Jack Chase in *White-Jacket.*

In the last years of his life, Melville kept a statue of Antinous—boy lover of the Emperor Hadrian—on his mantel, and in *Pierre* and *Billy Budd* he explores same-sex erotic issues with subtlety and care. For Hawthorne the issue of male-male sexuality was also an abiding literary preoccupation, though neither writer was exclusively homosexual, and both created powerful celebrations of heterosexual fulfillment. Introducing the radically unconventional meaning of life on the whaler in *Moby-Dick,* however, Melville gives same-sex desire and same-sex fulfillment a central place in the opening passages of the work.

## MOBY-DICK

*Moby-Dick* describes a spiritual quest that has reshaped the hero's soul. "Call me Ishmael," he declares at the outset, as though his given name has been swallowed up in the identity of an outcast and a wanderer. The name recalls the biblical Ishmael, the illegitimate son who was banished by his father, Abraham, when Abraham's wife bore Isaac, who was to bear God's blessing. Melville surrounds Ishmael's quest with other figures who are pariahs, excluded and persecuted by God's chosen people. Ishmael goes whaling aboard the *Pequod,* named for a tribe of Indians massacred by the Puritans; the *Pequod* is owned and operated by Quakers, who settled Nantucket after they were banished from Massachussetts Bay in the 1660s. The captain of the *Pequod* is Ahab, likewise named for an Old Testament pariah, King Ahab, who was destroyed by the God of Israel for sponsoring the worship of foreign gods.

At the beginning of the narrative, Ishmael recounts his initiation into the quest and makes fun of the greenhorn misgivings and confusions that he had to outgrow. Lacking the money to rent a single room, he is compelled to share his bed with a harpooner and is horrified to discover that his bedfellow is Polynesian. Queequeg is a splendid, muscular man covered with tattoos, who says his evening prayers by offering worship to a little ebony idol. Ishmael himself was "born and bred in the bosom of the infallible Presbyterian church," and in the course of his developing friendship with Queequeg, he attends a worship service where Father Mapple preaches a powerful Calvinist sermon on Jonah and the whale, proclaiming that the whale's attack on Jonah is a punishment for sin.

Calvinists taught that all men are innately depraved and deserve all the miseries and wretchedness than an unlucky life may bring them. A mark of such original sin is the human impulse to create idols, false gods constructed to fulfill human needs. Yet when Ishmael returns from Mapple's service to find Queequeg whittling away on his wooden god, he does not draw back in pious horror. On the contrary, he

> helped prop up the innocent little idol; offered him burnt biscuit with Queequeg . . . kissed his nose; and that done, we undressed and went to bed. . . . But we did not go to sleep without some little chat. . . . Thus, then, in our heart's honeymoon, lay I and Queequeg—a cozy, loving pair.

Homosexual intimacy and idolatry were conjoined in Calvinist teaching, twin emblems of innate depravity, yet at the outset of his quest, Ishmael accepts both. He seeks truth in a diversity of religious realities and sexual experiences, including those conventionally stigmatized and condemned.

Melville's spiritual quest in *Moby-Dick* seeks to transcend the limits imposed by partial and biased views that are misrepresented as universal truths. When Ishmael says that he wants to "sail about a little and see the watery part of the world," he means the two thirds of the earth's surface that most human beings never see, fraught with realities of shattering and potentially revelatory import. The oceans divulge clues to divine reality that remain invisible to those who never make the voyage, realities to be discovered through forbidden experiences in forbidden places. Thus Ishmael explains what allured him to the whaling voyage:

> Chief among these motives was the overwhelming idea of the great whale himself. Such a portentous and mysterious monster roused all my curiosity. Then the wild and distant seas where he rolled his island bulk; the undeliverable, nameless perils of the whale; these, with all the attending marvels of a thousand Patagonian sights and sounds, helped to sway me to my wish. With other men, perhaps, such things would not have been inducements; but as for me, I am tormented with an everlasting itch for things remote. I love to sail forbidden seas, and land on barbarous coasts. . . . By reason of these things, then, the whaling voyage was welcome; the great flood-gates of the wonder-world swung open, and in the wild conceits that swayed me to my purpose, two and two there floated into my inmost soul, endless processions of the whale, and midmost of them all, one grand hooded phantom, like a snow hill in the air.

Whaling bore the promise of insight into the ultimate order of reality for Ishmael because it was a voyage into God's creation. Genesis describes the world as the handiwork of a divine creator, and a tradition descending from Saint Paul teaches that the nature of God himself can be discerned in the characteristics of the world he made. A powerful version of this tradition in Melville's time was the trancendentalist program of symbolic meditation, classically outlined in Ralph Waldo Emerson's essay "Nature," which inspired an entire generation of American writers. Ishmael trusts that the visible world is charged with the meanings of an invisible and eternal order, so that nature provides an avenue to an understanding of eternal truth. He soon learns that the sailors on the *Pequod* share his mystical consciousness that the White Whale—that "hooded phantom"—reveals a divine reality and that Captain Ahab looks upon this reality with hatred. In fact, the Captain has dedicated the entire voyage to killing this one whale.

Captain Ahab seeks vengeance upon Moby Dick for having bitten off his leg; he sees this attack as an act of God but, unlike Jonah, does not believe he deserved it. "All visible objects, man, are but pasteboard masks," he explains, "but in each event—in the living act, the undoubted deed—there, some unknown but still reasoning thing puts forth the moulding of its features from behind the mask." Ahab's purpose in seeking the whale is to "strike through the mask," to strike back at the divine monster that has maimed him through Moby Dick. "All that most maddens and torments; all that stirs up the lees of things . . . all the subtle demonisms of life and thought; all evil, to crazy Ahab, were visibly personified, and made practically assailable in Moby Dick."

Ahab's announcement of his purpose strikes fire among his crew, and they frantically consecrate themselves to join in the quest, because in the depths of their minds they too have felt the supernatural hatred and the desire for revenge that Ahab makes explicit. Ishmael tells us that he was also prompted to join in Ahab's quest, for reasons that follow from the confusions and exasperations he has suffered in the effort to live out the promise of his transcendentalist faith.

Ishmael's rage against Moby Dick arises because he sees in the whale's whiteness an emblem of his own betrayal by the promise of symbolic meditation. In "The Whiteness of the Whale," Ishmael takes us through a blizzard of examples indicating the contradictory spiritual meanings found in whiteness: it represents the absolute purity of the Christian god but is also associated with such horrors as leprosy and the pale horse of death. That image of whiteness as double—both attractive and horrific—takes form in Ishmael's mind as a pattern of deceit, in which the beckoning wonderland reveals only "the heartless voids and immensities of the universe," a final emptiness that "stabs us from behind with the thought of annihilation." The world of nature is a whore, Ishmael concludes, whose appealing color is only an elaborate cosmetic, "whose allurements cover nothing but the charnel-house within." As the spiritual quester applies his symbolic sensitivities to the world of visible objects, he is spiritually destroyed: he "gazes himself blind at the monumental white shroud that wraps all the prospect around him. And of all these things the Albino whale was the symbol."

Ishmael eventually withdraws his allegiance to Ahab's quest, explaining in "The Try-Works" that he had been beguiled by the force of Ahab's monomania. Yet he does not arrive at a vision of divine goodness to countermand Ahab's vision of divine evil; Ishmael's religious consciousness survives, and his power of symbolic insight remains prodigious, but he no longer imagines that any unified vision of divine truth can be absolute.

The versatility of Ishmael's imagination—which is also Melville's imagination—has given rise to the abundance of meanings that have been found in *Moby-Dick* and to the intractable quarrels among those who want to believe that the work possesses a single dominant thesis. Chapter after chapter takes form as a poem of meditation that begins by describing some feature of whaling and then moves on to contemplate its possibilities of meaning. The process of weaving mats becomes an elucidation of freedom, fate, and chance. The whaleships encountered by the *Pequod* become emblems of diverse spiritualities. A great whale skeleton entangled in the jungle vines of a South Sea island becomes a figure of the interweaving of life and death, with flashes of divine sunlight darting through it. The insanity of a cabin boy is a divine madness, like that of Captain Ahab, the result of encountering God himself.

Ahab's insane quest has emerged in subsequent interpretation as a figure for the worldwide lust for domination and destruction embodied in western imperialism backed by western industrial might. The ideological processes that accompany political exploitation are dramatized by the way in which Moby Dick himself comes increasingly to resemble the fantasy of divine malignity that Ahab has projected into him, so that the quest becomes more and more self-justifying as it grows more dangerous and destructive. Ahab's cynical domination of the crew, which brings death to all but Ishmael, has been seen to prefigure totalitarian propaganda and the suicidal policies of modern nations gone mad in conquest. On the *Pequod* the captain and officers are white, and the harpooners are men of color—black, Native American, and Polynesian; the balance of the crew represents the rest of mankind, with all its variety of races and cultures. Melville sardonically observes that the whaling industry resembles American industry generally, as well as the military, in which the white American "provides the brains, the rest of the world as generously supplying the muscles." *Moby-Dick* is rich in passages that address the late-twentieth-century critical interest in signification, race, and class. The work also presents a world without women, where feminine qualities are attributed to the whales against which men direct their violence and where Ahab's one moment of willingness to give up the quest arises when he thinks of his wife and child at home.

Melville's central concern in *Moby-Dick* is religious; the work recurrently broods over ultimate meanings and mysteries. Environmentalists have elevated two symbols to religious significance, both of which are traceable to Melville. The photographs of the whole earth, in which national boundaries become invisible and insignificant in relation to the great loveliness of the blue oceans and the quiet shadings of brown on the continents, recapitulate Melville's impulse to include the "watery part of the world" in a comprehensive vision of our human home. The whale itself also has emerged as a figure of divine majesty in Nature, which is seriously threatened by an industry in which a single vessel can kill more whales than the entire New England fleet of Melville's time. Yet this religious fervor focuses on the baleen whales—right whales, gray whales, and the vast blue sulfur-bottom whales—because of their harmlessness to human beings. Melville saw divinity in the carnivorous sperm whale: his vision included the wantonly destructive realities of nature—tornadoes, great predators, and incurable maladies. These are mingled with nature's beauty in a finally inscrutable pattern that is symbolized by the sperm whale's battering-ram forehead.

> In the great Sperm Whale, this high and mighty godlike dignity inherent in the brow is so immensely amplified, that gazing on it, in that full front view, you feel the Deity and the dread powers more forcibly than in beholding any other object in living nature. For you see no one point precisely; not one distinct feature is revealed; no nose, eyes, ears, or mouth; no face; he has none, proper; nothing but that one broad firmament of a forehead, pleated with riddles; dumbly lowering with the doom of boats and ships, and men.

This awesome power invests a creature that is often playful and at peace, not a jealous solitary god, but preeminent in a happy pantheon. "If hereafter any highly cultured, poetical nation shall lure back to their birth-right, the merry May-day gods of old; and livingly enthrone them again in the now egotistical sky; on the now unhaunted hill; then be sure, exalted to Jove's high seat, the great Sperm Whale shall lord it."

Melville knew when he finished *Moby-Dick* that the book would not make money. "Dollars damn me," he wrote to Hawthorne. "What I feel most moved to write, that is banned,—it will not pay." *Typee* appeared a piece of childish trivia compared with the masterpiece just finished, and Melville wrote to Hawthorne how "horrible" it would be to go down in history as "a man who lived among the cannibals." Melville did not pause for rest before beginning another book, nor did he wait for the predictable negative reviews. He plunged into a new project that revealed the ferocity of his determination to pursue his radical intuitions and the ferocity of his rage against those who opposed and balked him.

From the outset of his career, Melville's phallic humor and ne'er-do-well adventures had annoyed the champions of the domestic ideal, who pictured the home as a redemptive haven in a heartless world. Stung by his financial failure, Melville resented the success of the literary domestics; he wrote sarcastically to his publisher that his new work would be "very much more calculated for popularity than anything you have yet published of mine." In fact, his rage took the form of a scathing and highly perceptive attack on the pathologies of intimate family relationships, particularly those between mothers and sons. *Pierre; or, The Ambiguities* (1852) begins with a sugary-sweet depiction of its young hero, Pierre Glendinning, worshipping his beautiful and reciprocally worshipful mother, in a scenario that portrays the intimacies of the domestic novel as incest.

Pierre and his mother, Mary, play out a "brother and sister" relationship whose erotic claims are apparent in Mary's determination to control Pierre's choice of a mate. When Pierre discovers that he has (or appears to have) an illegitimate half-sister, he falls passionately in love with her and claims her before the world as his wife. Melville archly observes that Pierre readily converted a sister into a wife because he had converted a mother into a sister, a cascade of pathologies framed in the rhetoric of heroic, selfless, intimate devotion.

The ideals of the middle class were not the only target of Melville's vengeful rage in *Pierre;* so also was his own patrician family. There is good reason to believe that Melville himself had an illegitimate half-sister, and he places such a scandal at the heart of his narrative. He traces out the family politics by which the truth is denied by Pierre's mother, is insinuated by a certain talkative

aunt, and is evidenced by an early portrait of his father that portrays him as a wealthy young rake. A multitude of details in *Pierre* are drawn from Melville's life: there was a portrait of his father like the one described, his mother was named Maria, and his maternal grandfather, General Peter Gansevoort, possessed trophies and achievements like those of "Grand Old Pierre" in the novel. No person sympathetic to the family's inner anguish could possibly have missed the point or failed to be wounded.

Melville portrayed Pierre's family tragedy not only as a personal difficulty but also as a dilemma of large cultural significance. Pierre's situation depicts shortcomings of the cult of domesticity that continue to plague American family life. He is brought up in a household from which his father is absent and his mother compensates for that absence—and for a feeling of betrayal by the father—by overinvolving herself in the life of her son. The fusion of rigid moralism and emotional self-indulgence in this relationship prepares the son for an explosion at the threshold of adulthood. This crisis reveals a split in the young man's emotional life, which is reflected in his dual response to women. He has a lofty affection for the pure and blue-eyed Lucy, but he is powerfully aroused—both sexually and artistically—by the dark-haired waif who bears the atmosphere of his father's secret life. Students of family history, as well as exponents of Freudian and Jungian psychoanalysis, have found in *Pierre* an astonishing insight into the unconscious realities of Melville's immediate culture, as well as a prophecy of social and intellectual developments far in the future.

Anticipating Freud, Melville dramatizes Pierre's faith in God as a mask for his adulation of his human father, who is all the more idealized because of his absence and the atmosphere of tacit suspicion surrounding him. Pierre maintains a shrine in his heart where "stood the perfect marble form of his departed father; without blemish, unclouded, snow-white, and serene. . . . Not to

God had Pierre ever gone in his heart, unless by ascending the steps of that shrine." The disclosure of his father's imperfection causes this "entire one-pillared temple of his moral life" to come crashing down and drives him forth upon a spiritual quest to reassemble the shattered fragments of his faith or to fashion a new one.

Pierre carries out his investigation of ultimate truth by writing a novel—as Melville had done in *Mardi* and *Moby-Dick*—but as he proceeds in the work of fashioning that novel, he is increasingly demoralized. In making a fiction about truth, he comes to suspect that truth itself is a fiction, merely a human creation. Yet Pierre's heroic spiritual ambition aims at envisioning a truth that is true, independent of the ways in which human beings conceive it. In the end, Pierre comes to despise his own heroic endeavor as fraudulent:

> Pierre saw the everlasting elusiveness of Truth; the universal lurking insincerity of even the greatest and purest written thoughts. Like knavish cards, the leaves of all great books were covertly packed. He was but packing one set the more. . . . So that there was nothing he more spurned than his own aspirations; nothing he more abhorred than the loftiest part of himself.

Supremely gifted at fashioning feelings and ideas into words, and uncannily attentive to the rhetorical schemes that his ancestral and surrounding culture supplied him, Melville came to see that all schemes of universal truth are ideological; driven by ulterior forces, they always imply more than they say explicitly.

Works of fiction may also attempt to say things that the writer must not say. In *White-Jacket,* Melville commented that "nature has not implanted any power in man that was not meant to be exercised"; yet if Melville was empowered to enjoy sexual relations with men, he faced a social consensus insisting that to exercise this capacity was unspeakably depraved. Homosexual writers in Melville's time, notably Walt Whitman, were com-

pelled to mask their sexual preference in their writing, to intimate their meanings for readers attuned to understand them in such a way that readers abhorring those meanings would not catch on. In "Hawthorne and His Mosses," Melville observed that a certain kind of writing is self-protective, "calculated to deceive—egregiously deceive—the superficial skimmer of pages." In his 1993 work *Closet Writing/Gay Reading: The Case of Melville's "Pierre,"* the critic James Creech, himself gay, has found in *Pierre* just such a pattern, in which the issue of incest—between Pierre and his mother and sister—functions as a cover for a homosexual passion that Pierre feels for his cousin, Glen Stanly, but more intensely for the fantasy object of his father's memory.

The ambiguities of writing are thus entangled with the ambiguities of reading, and for Melville the act of reading extended beyond books; it included the ongoing perception of the world, the process by which human beings discern reality. Such reading itself appeared unreliable, a method of investing the world with what the viewer wants to see. "Say what poets will," he observes, "Nature is not so much her own ever-sweet interpreter, as the mere supplier of that cunning alphabet, whereby selecting and combining as he pleases, each man reads his own peculiar lesson according to his own peculiar mind and mood."

## LATER WORKS

In *Pierre,* Melville investigates this process of selective interpretation as it unfolds in personal experience. His subsequent writings turn to consider it as a feature of social relations. The intellectual plateau Melville arrived at in *Pierre* would mark him as a great genius even if he had not been a writer of fiction: like Karl Marx and Charles Darwin he is a nineteenth-century figure whose ideas displayed their full intellectual power only in the twentieth century. Yet Melville was virtually alone with his ideas, and the yarn-spinning conviviality of his earlier writings now disappeared from his work. The bitter sarcasm of the opening of *Pierre* and the enormities of self-mockery at its center give way to a somber anguish at the end, in which Melville's voice—once so adept at stirring the reader to a sympathetic response—becomes unfathomably remote.

In 1853 "Bartleby the Scrivener: A Story of Wall Street" was published in *Putnam's Monthly.* Melville's title character scarcely speaks, in the midst of the voluble quarreling of the law office where he copies documents. Yet Bartleby's seemingly involutional silence slowly bores through the talk and reveals the social reality of the world he inhabits. The law office on Wall Street becomes an emblem for the impersonal bureaucracies that increasingly dominated urban America, with their crushing bleakness and relentless routine. Called into being by the requirements of a mass society, bureaucratic forms of organization took hold in the post office from whence Bartleby comes, the legal system where we meet him, and the prison where he dies.

In "Benito Cereno," which first appeared in 1855 in *Putnam's Monthly,* Melville likewise depicts the pervasive reality of racist oppression by describing a slave ship that has been taken over by the slaves. When the American captain, Amasa Delano, visits the vessel, the slaves compel their erstwhile masters to perform a charade making it appear that the whites are still in control. Delano is completely deceived by the charade and projects into it the conventional rhetoric justifying white oppression, just as Bartleby's associates project a belief in their personal dignity into the circumstances of their dehumanization. The result in both works is an eerie nightmarish reality, in which social injustices are seen to reside as much in the mentalities of individuals as in social arrangements.

Melville's withdrawal of his personal voice from engagement with the reader led to even more fascinating and radical explorations in *The Confidence-Man: His Masquerade* (1857), the last novel published in his lifetime. The narrative appears to concern the operations of a swindler—a confidence man—who is plying his trade aboard a riverboat, approaching various travelers with schemes designed to relieve them of their money. This confidence man first appears as a black cripple, who gives a list of persons who can vouch for him—a man with a weed, a man in a gray coat and white tie, a man with a big book, an herb doctor—and the subsequent appearances of the confidence man seem at first to correspond to the list. But it is not credible that the black cripple is the same person as the man with the weed or the other men, and the list he provides does not match the sequence of their appearances. The narrative is itself a con game on the reader, who expects a consistent protagonist and gets instead a series of discrepant incarnations. Moreover, as the avatars of the con man talk with their victims, their identities become confounded; it becomes impossible at points to tell who is talking, the con man or the victim.

Novels usually ride on the assumption that language describes the world; it seems obvious that reading the language of the novel will tell the reader what the world of the novel is like. *The Confidence-Man* turns this situation inside out: we are given descriptive passages and extended conversations that prompt us to conceive of a certain world. But as we place our confidence in that process—of deducing a world from the words—we are made to realize that it can't be done, that we are being tricked by Melville. But as our confidence is betrayed, it is also revealed to us. The novel prompts us to see that our confidence in the words—our trust in the language of the book—takes an active part; it participates in positively creating the world that the language appears only to describe. As confidence men gain the trust of their victims and lead them to believe in realities that are not there, so novelists exploit the trust of their readers to produce credible fictions. The creators of new forms of language create new forms of reading the experience we have outside literature and thus create real worlds. Instead of casting light on our experience, the most powerful literary artists call that experience into being.

The ordinary reality of the world, Melville discovers, is a fiction that is produced as human beings place confidence in patterns of language. Conventional characters in conventional novels become plausible as they correspond to these socially constructed fictions. But truly original characters have the opposite effect: they cast a light that re-creates the surrounding world, bringing visible things out of darkness. Melville likens the original character to a revolving light in a lighthouse, "raying away from itself all round it— everything is lit by it, everything starts up to it . . . so that, in certain minds, there follows upon the adequate conception of such a character, an effect, in its way, akin to that which in Genesis attends upon the beginning of things."

The multiple selves of the confidence man thus correspond to the multiple worlds that the imagination calls into being through language, both in novels and in the human experience outside novels. Without the confidence so solicited and so rewarded, there is no human world; yet such confidence can readily be betrayed. "Confidence is the indispensable basis of all sorts of business transactions," the confidence man declares. "Without it, commerce between man and man, as between country and country, would, like a watch, run down and stop."

The figures of Melville's story are adrift in a world where confidence is indispensable yet untrustworthy, where savage malcontents, embittered by betrayals, pour scorn upon all who ask for confidence and all who give it. These harshly critical and sarcastic jeremiahs cannot, however, get out of the game; they implicitly ask for confidence from their fellow travelers, and from the reader, and Melville equally suggests they do not deserve it.

The world Melville creates in *The Confidence-Man* is claustrophobic and baffling—seeming at times to be a paranoid fantasy—but it illuminates a social reality confronted by the generation of American men who came to maturity with Melville. The heroes of the new economic order were "self-made men," who rose in the world by their own industry and luck. Such men learned to operate in an impersonal and anonymous urban environment, where they inspired the trust necessary for business dealing through the cultivation of a trustworthy appearance, not through references to a network of prominent kinfolk and friends. The men who prospered in this new world were "confidence men," not that they were necessarily dishonest, but rather had learned perforce the art of securing the trust of strangers. They studied how to "win friends" in order to "influence people." Melville's *Confidence-Man* is a bitter satire on this world and on the casualties it produced, among them Melville himself.

*The Confidence-Man* was published in 1857, a bit more than a decade after *Typee,* and brought to a close Melville's lifetime career as a writer of prose fiction. It completed the development that had begun in *Mardi,* by which Melville lost readers as he matured in the literary genius that endowed *Moby-Dick, Pierre,* and *The Confidence-Man* with prophetic power. Without a college education, Melville had filled his work with an erudition that remains daunting to experts today; having begun his career as a convivial spinner of South Sea yarns, he composed *The Confidence-Man* in anguished solitude.

## LAST YEARS

Melville's granddaughter Frances Cuthbert Thomas was eight years old when Melville died in 1891, but she remembered girlhood visits to see her grandparents—how Melville had allowed her to build block houses with volumes of Schopenhauer on the floor of his study and how he had once taken her to play in the park. Her reminiscence, which appears in Merton M. Sealts Jr.'s 1974 work, *The Early Lives of Melville,* emphasizes that she "never felt the least bit afraid" of Melville, "was never the victim of his moods and occasional uncertain tempers." Thomas knew, even in girlhood, that among his victims were members of the family.

The domestic abuse that Melville dealt out has been a topic of intense controversy among scholars—like the illegitimate half-sister and his bisexuality—rendered more uncertain by the family's desire to keep such matters quiet. In May of 1867 Melville's wife was under pressure from her family to leave him, and members of Melville's own family agreed. Action was necessary, her brother stated, to cancel a problem that "has been a cause of anxiety to all of us for years past." Within the family, as later, attention focused on the question of whether Melville was "insane," but the true problem was that he abused his wife.

The rumors and hints that have penetrated the family's wall of silence suggest that Melville abused Lizzie, as Elizabeth was known, psychologically, badgered her harshly and unpredictably over her management of the household, and castigated her for failing to understand his ideas, perhaps taking out on her his failure to find public acclaim. It also appears that such episodes sometimes included physical abuse. They typically occurred when Melville was drunk but also took place when Melville was writing, or had exhausted himself by writing, and they prompted his wife's family to pay for trips abroad to improve Herman's "health," perhaps as early as 1849. These trips included a visit to the Holy Land in 1856–1857 after he completed *The Confidence-Man,* from which some members of the family apparently hoped he would never come back.

The family conclave seeking to separate Melville and his wife took place shortly after Melville published *Battle-Pieces and Aspects of the War*

(1866), a volume of Civil War poems, whereupon he accepted a post in the New York Custom House that allowed him for the first time since his marriage to gain a reliable income. His homes in New York and Pittsfield had been purchased on loans from his father-in-law, which he sought to repay from the earnings of his lecture tours and the writing of short fiction. Only in 1863 was he able to pay off his debt to his publisher, Harper and Brothers. Elizabeth Shaw Melville chose not to leave her husband in May of 1867, and the two of them grieved together in September of that year when their son Malcolm shot and killed himself, as they later worried and grieved over their second son, Stanwix, who took long voyages that put him out of touch with the family, and who died alone in San Francisco in 1886.

As he worked for his customhouse wages, Melville returned to the writing of poetry, publishing *John Marr and Other Sailors* (1888) and *Timoleon* (1891) in his remaining years. His major effort went into a poem of immense length, on the scale of *Moby-Dick,* eighteen thousand terse and allusive lines centering on the meditations of a doubt-ridden theological student visiting the Holy Land. *Clarel: A Poem and Pilgrimage in the Holy Land* (1876) revisits the religious issues that had occupied Melville earlier, enriched by extensive reading in biblical and theological controversy. Melville had no prospect of interesting a commercial publisher in this forbidding work and was overcome with gratitude when his uncle, Peter Gansevoort—who had aided the family so faithfully in the years since his father's death—agreed to bear the cost of publication.

At the time of his death on September 28, 1891, Melville retained enough of a reputation to merit obituary notices in New York City's newspapers, although *The New-York Times* ran the headline "The Late Hiram Melville." Alfred Pulitzer's *Morning Journal* wrote "He Was Held by Cannibals, but He Made It Lucrative," strangely fulfilling Melville's disgusted premonition, expressed to

Hawthorne forty years earlier, that he would be remembered as "a man who lived among the cannibals." Yet the loyalty of the proud and prominent family that had sustained Melville through his life aided in the restoration of his critical reputation that took place after World War I, when the collapse of high Victorian domestic pieties led readers to seek literary art possessing a disillusioned intellectual and moral integrity. Raymond Weaver, teaching at Columbia University in 1919, became excited about Melville's work and asked his students for help in learning as much as possible about him. One of those students was another Melville granddaughter, Eleanor Thomas (Mrs. Eleanor Melville Metcalf), who forthwith dug into the papers that the family had preserved and discovered another prose masterpiece, *Billy Budd, Foretopman* (1924).

### BILLY BUDD

The narrative of *Billy Budd* centers on an incident that Melville had known about intimately for many years, the execution of three men aboard the USS *Somers* in 1842. The *Somers* was on a training cruise, manned principally by apprentice boys, when Captain Alexander Mackenzie became persuaded that a mutiny was afoot and arrested three men as its leaders. Instead of placing the suspects in irons for trial ashore, Mackenzie concluded that a crisis existed that required immediate action: he ordered a drumhead court-martial, obtained a guilty verdict, and hanged the three. One of the hanged was an officer-in-training whose father was Secretary of War, who promptly concluded that his son had been murdered; his protests ignited a furious public controversy. Herman Melville's cousin Guert Gansevoort was an officer aboard the *Somers,* had served on the drumhead court-martial, and like Mackenzie was accused of murder in the subsequent furor.

From this drama, Melville fashioned a parable that is now the best loved and most widely read of his works. Like the *Somers* incident itself, the narrative of *Billy Budd* raises questions about the use of deadly force in maintaining civil order. The story takes place on a British warship that is legally empowered to "impress" sailors on merchant vessels, compelling them to serve on the warship irrespective of consent. Melville places the incident in an epoch when anxieties ran high about keeping discipline in the British navy. Because of the democratic ideals exalted by the French and American revolutions, Melville tells us, dangerous mutinies had broken out in the British fleet, so that all vessels were on guard against disorder.

Billy Budd is a merchant-sailor aboard the *Rights-of-Man,* who is impressed by Captain Vere of HMS *Bellipotent.* When Billy sings out "Goodbye to you . . . old *Rights-of-Man*" as he boards the naval vessel, the officers instantly reprimand and silence him, as though he were bidding farewell not only to his former shipmates but also to his democratic rights. Yet Melville declares Billy quite incapable of sarcastic double meanings; he was a "handsome sailor," gregarious, trusting, and good-natured. Billy's character is so winning, and his sense of fair play so deeply ingrained, that no external discipline appears necessary to govern his conduct. On the *Rights-of-Man* he was a "peacemaker," stopping quarrels among the men before they grew serious, and he is likewise popular among his new shipmates.

Some readers of the tale have held Billy to embody a primal innocence of a kind that renders social control unnecessary. If all men were as good-natured and ethically sensible as Billy, there would be no need for governments, for systems of law, or for the deadly force that backs them, including warships themselves and the officials who police shipboard order. Matching Billy's original goodness is the primal evil embodied in Claggart, the master-at-arms aboard the *Bellipotent,* who is precisely such a policeman. Seemingly because of an inward natural depravity, Claggart conceives a hatred for Billy and brings against him false charges of mutiny. Captain Vere orders the two men into his presence, where Claggart repeats the charge, whereupon Billy—stunned and baffled—strikes Claggart a single blow with his fist and kills him.

Captain Vere instantly sizes up the killing in the terms set forth here: he perceives Claggart as diabolically evil and Billy as angelically good. But Vere is not only a student of religious allegory, he is also a navy captain responsible for maintaining order in an era when it is threatening to collapse. "Struck dead by an angel of God!" he proclaims over the body of Claggart, "Yet the angel must hang!" Like Captain Mackenzie, Vere assembles a drumhead court-martial, obtains a guilty verdict, and has Billy hanged.

Is Vere a just and sober captain, realizing that earthly institutions can maintain only a proximate justice, not the subtle precision required in cases involving such exceptional persons as Claggart and Billy? Or is he a panic-stricken martinet who fails to recognize that the crew shares his instinctive dislike for Claggart and his love for Billy and will not see Claggart's death as a breakdown of authority if Billy is imprisoned for trial ashore? Or is Vere obsessed with the philosophical conundrums he has encountered in his long and solitary career of reading? Does he seize upon the emblematic features of the situation and insist upon taking the role of the decision maker faced with a tragic dilemma, when a more pragmatic soul would have found a way to finesse the dilemma and let Billy live?

What about Billy? Is his character so very harmless and innocent? Aboard the *Rights-of-Man,* on at least one occasion, he played out his role of peacemaker by beating up one of his shipmates. His striking of Claggart may be endearingly spontaneous, but it is also deadly. And it preempts the rights of the other parties: Billy acts

as prosecuting attorney, judge, and executioner in killing Claggart.

In recent years new questions have been raised about Claggart. It is agreed that he is malicious and concocts his charge against Billy out of hatred. But it now seems plausible that Melville saw this hatred as the outcome of a love that dare not speak its name. If Claggart is a man whose sexual desires are aroused by other men, he has lived a bitter life in which expressing such desires would invite loathing and contempt. Perhaps the hatred of same-sex passion controls his own conscience, so that admitting that passion to himself would trigger an agony of self-disgust. Melville tells us that Claggart could "even have loved Billy but for fate and ban," and the interplay between the two men suggests that Claggart means to convey, at least semideliberately, his erotic response. In Billy, Claggart confronts a blond young man of breathtaking physical beauty, who is aboundingly cheerful and free-spirited, never dreaming of the homophobic culture that ensnares Claggart or of the torture he occasions in the master-at-arms. It is not difficult to see how Claggart would envy and hate Billy because he loves him and would see him as an emblem of the evil that has made Claggart's life a living hell.

The conclusion of *Billy Budd* is a rendition of the core narrative around which the Christian tradition has organized its profoundest meditations regarding human sin, sorrow, and redemption, namely, the death and resurrection of Christ. As Billy is hanged, his body is sacramentally transfigured: it does not writhe and twist in the way common to death by hanging, and the rays of the rising sun in his blond hair make a radiant golden halo. "God bless Captain Vere!" Billy cries, as though forgiving the sin into which Vere has unwillingly fallen. This obscure incident aboard a peacetime warship becomes the stuff of an enduring legend in the fleet, the common sailors seeing in it an emblem of an anguish at the core of their own lives.

It is possible to argue that *Billy Budd* resolves the dilemmas that had convulsed Melville's mind from the outset of his career and forms what some critics have called "a testament of acceptance." Others have termed it a "testment of resistance." But it would be truer to say that the narrative—like Melville's greatest work generally—brings those issues unresolved into focus, in a consummate work of art that does not contain meanings so much as it produces new meanings for new generations of readers.

# Selected Bibliography

## WORKS OF HERMAN MELVILLE

ORIGINAL AMERICAN EDITIONS

*Typee: A Peep at Polynesian Life.* New York: Wiley and Putnam, 1846.

*Omoo: A Narrative of Adventures in the South Seas.* New York: Harper & Brothers, 1847.

*Mardi and a Voyage Thither.* New York: Harper & Brothers, 1849.

*Redburn: His First Voyage.* New York: Harper & Brothers, 1849.

*White-Jacket; or, The World in a Man-of-War.* New York: Harper & Brothers, 1850.

*Moby-Dick; or, The Whale.* New York: Harper & Brothers, 1851.

*Pierre; or, The Ambiguities.* New York: Harper & Brothers, 1852.

*Israel Potter: His Fifty Years of Exile.* New York: Putnam, 1855.

*The Piazza Tales.* New York: Dix and Edwards, 1856. (Contains "The Piazza," "Bartleby, the Scrivener," "Benito Cereno," "The Lightning-Rod Man," "The Encantadas, or Enchanted Isles," and "The Bell-Tower.")

*The Confidence-Man: His Masquerade.* New York: Dix and Edwards, 1857.

*Battle-Pieces and Aspects of the War.* New York: Harper & Brothers, 1866.

*Clarel: A Poem and Pilgrimage in the Holy Land.* New York: Putnam's Sons, 1876.

*John Marr and Other Sailors, with Some Sea-Pieces.* New York: De Vinne Press, 1888.

*Timoleon.* New York: Caxton Press, 1891.

*The Apple Tree Table and Other Sketches.* Princeton, N.J.: Princeton University Press, 1922.

*Shorter Novels of Herman Melville.* New York: Liveright, 1928. (Includes *Billy Budd,* first published in London as *Billy Budd and Other Prose Pieces* by Constable in 1924.)


CURRENT CRITICAL EDITIONS

*Clarel: A Poem and Pilgrimage in the Holy Land,* Edited by Walter Bezanson. New York: Hendrick House, 1960. (With an excellent critical introduction and notes.)

*Billy Budd, Sailor.* Edited by Harrison Hayford and Merton M. Sealts Jr. Chicago: University of Chicago Press, 1962. (Quotations of *Billy Budd* are taken from this edition, which contains the best available text.)

*Pierre; or, The Ambiguities.* Edited by Henry A. Murray. New York: Hendrix House, 1964. (The introduction offers a Jungian interpretation of Melville's artistic consciousness.)

*Typee: A Peep at Polynesian Life.* Edited by Harrison Hayford. New York: New American Library, 1965. (This Signet Classics Edition records the substantive differences between the first English and the first American editions and the expurgations made in the American Revised Edition.)

*The Confidence Man.* Edited by H. Bruce Franklin. New York: Bobbs Merrill, 1967. (The introduction and notes illuminate Melville's use of comparative religion and his radical literary strategies.)

*Moby-Dick; or, The Whale.* New York: 1967. (The Norton Critical Edition provides a comprehensive collection of critical and other supplementary material.)

*The Writings of Herman Melville.* Edited by Harrison Hayford, Hershel Parker, and G. Thomas Tanselle, 15 vols. Evanston, Ill.: Northwestern University Press, 1967–. (This Northwestern-Newberry edition provides critical text for Melville's complete works together with a complete textual history and a historical note on the composition and publication of each volume. *Typee* [1968], *Omoo* [1968], *Redburn* [1969], *Mardi* [1970], *White-Jacket,* [1970] *Pierre* [1971], *Clarel* [1991], *The Confidence-Man* [1984],

Correspondence [1993], *Israel Potter* [1982], *Journals* [1989], *Moby-Dick; or, The Whale* [1988], and *The Piazza Tales and Other Prose Pieces 1839–1860* [1987] have been completed. Each volume is also issued in an inexpensive paperback edition.)

*Billy Budd, Sailor and Other Stories.* Edited by Harold Beaver. New York: Viking Penguin, 1968. (Contains "Daniel Orme" and other late stories.)

*Poems of Herman Melville.* Edited by Douglas Robillard. Chapel Hill: University of North Carolina Press, 1976.

## CRITICAL AND BIOGRAPHICAL STUDIES

Berthoff, Warner. *The Example of Melville.* Princeton: Princeton University Press, 1972.

Bloom, Harold. *Modern Critical Interpretations: Herman Melville's "Billy Budd," "Benito Cereno," "Bartleby the Scrivener," and Other Tales.* New York, New Haven, Philadelphia: Chelsea House Publishers, 1987.

Bryant, John. *Melville and Repose: The Rhetoric of Humor in the American Renaissance.* New York and Oxford: Oxford University Press, 1993.

Creech, James. *Closet Writing/Gay Reading: The Case of Melville's "Pierre."* Chicago and London: University of Chicago Press, 1993.

Dimock, Wai-chee. *Empire for Liberty: Melville and The Poetics of Individualism.* Princeton: N.J.: Princeton University Press, 1989.

Franklin, H. Bruce. *The Wake of the Gods: Melville's Mythology.* Stanford, Calif.: Stanford University Press, 1963.

Garner, Stanton. *The Civil War World of Herman Melville.* Lawrence: University Press of Kansas, 1993.

Halttunen, Karen. *Confidence Men and Painted Women: A Study of Middle-Class Culture in America, 1830–1870.* New Haven, Conn.: Yale University Press, 1982. (Provides essential background for Melville's *Confidence-Man.*)

Hayford, Harrison. *The Somers Mutiny Affair.* Englewood Cliffs, N.J.: Prentice-Hall, 1959.

Herbert, T. Walter Jr. *Moby-Dick and Calvinism: A World Dismantled.* New Brunswick, N.J.: Rutgers University Press, 1977.

———. *Marquesan Encounters: Melville and the Meaning of Civilization.* Cambridge and London: Harvard University Press, 1980.

Jehlen, Myra, ed. *Herman Melville: A Collection of Critical Essays.* Englewood Cliffs, N.J.: Prentice Hall, 1994.

Kelley, Mary. *Private Woman, Public Stage: Literary Domesticity in Nineteenth-Century America.* New York: Oxford University Press, 1984. (An excellent discussion of the literary culture Melville found uncongenial and satirized in *Pierre.*)

Leverenz, David. "Ahab's Queenly Personality: A Man Is Being Beaten." In his *Manhood and the American Renaissance.* Ithaca, N.Y.: Cornell University Press, 1989.

Leyda, Jay. *The Melville Log: A Documentary Life of Herman Melville, 1819–1891,* 2 vols. New York: Harcourt, Brace, 1951. Reprinted, with supplementary entries, New York: Gordian Press, 1969.

Martin, Robert K. *Hero, Captain, and Stranger: Male Friendship, Social Critique, and Literary Form in the Sea Novels of Herman Melville.* Chapel Hill and London: University of North Carolina Press, 1986.

Metcalf, Eleanor M. *Herman Melville: Cycle and Epicycle.* Cambridge, Mass.: Harvard University Press, 1953. Reprinted Westport, Conn.: Greenwood Press, 1970.

Miller, Edwin Haviland. *Melville.* New York: George Braziller, 1975.

Olson, Charles. *Call Me Ishmael.* San Francisco: City Lights Books, 1947.

Parker, Hershel. *Herman Melville. A Biography.* Baltimore: Johns Hopkins University Press, 1996. (Volume 1 of a projected two volume biography.)

———. *Reading Billy Budd.* Evanston, Ill.: Northwestern University Press, 1990.

———, ed. *The Recognition of Herman Melville.* Ann Arbor: University of Michigan Press, 1967.

Reynolds, Larry J. "'Moby-Dick' and the Matter of France." In his *European Revolutions and the American Literary Renaissance.* New Haven, Conn.: Yale University Press, 1988. Pp. 97–124.

Robertson-Lorant, Laurie. *Melville: A Biography.* New York: Clarkson N. Potter, 1996.

Rogin, Michael Paul. *Subversive Genealogy: The Politics and Art of Herman Melville.* New York: Knopf, 1983.

Sealts, Merton M. Jr. *The Early Lives of Melville.* Madison: University of Wisconsin Press, 1974.

————. *Melville as Lecturer.* Cambridge, Mass.: Harvard University Press, 1957.

Sherrill, Rowland A. *The Prophetic Melville: Experience, Transcendence, and Tragedy.* Athens: University of Georgia Press, 1979.

Tolchin, Neal L. *Mourning, Gender, and Creativity in the Art of Herman Melville.* New Haven, Conn., and London: Yale University Press, 1988.

Wadlington, Warwick. *The Confidence Game in American Literature.* Princeton, N.J.: Princeton University Press, 1975.

Yanella, Donald, and Hershel Parker. *The Endless, Winding Way in Melville: New Charts by Kring and Carey.* Glassboro, N.J.: The Melville Society, 1981.

Young, Philip. *The Private Melville.* University Park: Pennsylvania State University Press, 1993.

## FILMS, PLAYS, AND MUSICAL WORKS BASED ON THE WRITINGS OF HERMAN MELVILLE

*Benito Cereno.* In Robert Lowell, *The Old Glory.* New York: Farrar, Straus & Giroux, 1965.

*Benito Cereno: Melville, Billy, and Mars: Moby-Dick.* In Joyce Sparer Adler, *Dramatization of Three Melville Novels: With an Introduction on Interpretation by Dramatization.* Lewiston, N.Y.: E. Mellen Press, 1992.

*Billy Budd.* Opera by Benjamin Britten; libretto by E. M. Forster and Eric Crozier. First production: London, Royal Opera, 1951.

*Billy Budd: A Play in Three Acts.* Play by Louis Osborne Coxe and Robert Harris Chapman. Princeton, N.J.: Princeton University Press, 1951.

*Billy Budd.* Screenplay by Peter Ustinov and DeWitt Bodeen, based on the play by Louis Osborne Coxe and Robert Chapman. Produced and directed by Peter Ustinov. Anglo-Allied Pictures, 1962.

[*Moby Dick*]. *The Sea Beast.* Directed by Warner Brothers, 1926. (A silent screen adaptation with a happy ending.)

*Moby Dick.* Screenplay by J. Grubb Alexander. Directed by Lloyd Bacon. Warner Brothers, 1930. (A sound remake of *The Sea Beast.*

*Moby Dick: A Play for Radio from Herman Melville's Novel.* Play by Henry Reed. 1947.

*Moby Dick.* Screenplay by Ray Bradbury and John Huston. Produced and directed by John Huston. With Gregory Peck, Richard Basehart, and Orson Welles. Moulin Productions, 1956.

[*Moby Dick*]. *Concertato, Moby Dick, for Orchestra.* Peter Mennin. New York: C. Fischer, 1956.

[*Moby Dick*]. *Moby Dick—rehearsed: A Drama in Two Acts.* Play by Orson Welles. New York: S. French, 1965.

*Moby Dick.* A radio play by Stewart Love and William O. Cumming, *Plays for Reading and Recording.* Boston: 1966.

*Moby Dick.* A cantata for male chorus, soloists, and orchestra. Text by W. Clark Harrington and music by Bernard Herrmann. The Aeolian Singers and The London Philharmonic Orchestra. HNH Records, 1967.

[*Moby Dick*]. *The Fiery Hunt, Experimental Drama with Dance.* In Charles Olsen, *The Fiery Hunt and Other Plays.* Bolinas, Calif: Four Seasons Foundation, 1977.

[*Moby Dick*]. *Concerto dell'Albatro.* A work for violin, violoncello, piano, chamber orchestra and reciting voice. Text based on *Moby Dick* (in Italian) with music by G. F. Ghedini. Suvini-Zerboni Recordings, 1987.

—*T. WALTER HERBERT*

# Vladimir Nabokov
## 1899–1977

"YOU CAN ALWAYS count on a murderer for a fancy prose style." This famous phrase from the opening of Humbert Humbert's narrative in *Lolita* (1955) takes us a long way into Vladimir Nabokov's world. Not because the claim is true, or even close to the truth. Many murderers, in and out of fiction, are merely brutal, entirely styleless, unless we choose to see brutality itself as a style. The claim is important for what it does rather than what it says. It offers its own pace and tone as an enactment of literary faith. Humbert is both boasting about his fancy style and apologizing for it, and Nabokov expects us to see that Humbert and his style are masks, devices in the service of a larger fiction. Humbert's flamboyance and Nabokov's discretion add up to Nabokov's own achievement in this novel, and many of his other novels are built in a similar way. We are both enticed and repelled by a performance visibly marked as a performance, and we wonder what is behind it.

### STYLE AND VIOLENCE

We can always count on Nabokov, we might say, to raise the question of style in relation to murder, either because his murderers see themselves as stylists, or because style is one of the few sustain-able human answers to the murderous idiocy and cruelty of chance. William Empson invited us, in a fine poem, to "learn a style from a despair." Nabokov invites us to see style as a denial of despair, and at the same time an acknowledgment of all the profuse reasons, historical and metaphysical, we have for despairing. "The history of man is the history of pain," a character says in *Pnin* (1957), and Nabokov's fiction is literally haunted by death, often violent, almost always sudden and absurd.

In March 1922 Nabokov's father, a liberal Russian politician in exile, was assassinated in Berlin by right-wing extremists. A grim irony complements the horror of this death, because the assassins were actually seeking to shoot someone else, Paul Miliukov, the leader of the party of the Constitutional Democrats. Nabokov senior, trying to defend Miliukov, was killed in his place. This event does not explain Nabokov's work—no event explains a work, as Nabokov himself would be the first to say. "The best part of a writer's biography," he insisted in *Strong Opinions*, "is not the record of his adventures but the story of his style." But I think we must see this bungled assassination not only as the dramatic incursion of arbitrary violence into the writer's life—the Russian Revolution had already amply represented

*263*

that—but as an image of the way history, for Nabokov, characteristically behaves. When he seeks to make sense of the world, to find patterns that contradict or reorder its random movements, it is this world he addresses, whether by miming murders or showing the destruction of the innocent: a world in which you are all too likely, alas, to step into a line of fire intended for someone else. A combination of evil intention and hapless error evokes, in miniature, Nabokov's whole philosophy of history and fate. Neither providence nor fortune rule this world, only human anger and incompetence, but the shapes of events often look as if they were drawn by a joking god, or a cartoonist with a taste for the bizarre. An appearance of design mocks and illuminates the failure of our designs. At times this appearance can even be a consolation.

A confused and dying man in *The Gift* (1938) has a moment of total lucidity. "There is nothing afterwards," he says. He listens to a "trickling and drumming" sound outside his window, and repeats, "There is nothing. It is as clear as the fact that it is raining." It is not raining. The sky is "dreamy and cloudless," and the impression of rain is created by a woman upstairs watering the flowers on her balcony. Later in the same novel the protagonist explains that he rented a room he disliked just because he saw in a neighboring room the blue dress of the girl he was to come to love: a sign of fate, he thinks. The girl says, "Only that wasn't my dress, it was my cousin Raissa's— she's very nice but a perfect fright. . . ."

It is important that the dying man is not wrong in his impression of the rain, only wrong about the source of the water. Similarly, when the poet John Shade, in *Pale Fire* (1962), says he is "reasonably sure" that he will wake tomorrow and that the day will be fine, his view is eminently sensible, but sadly disproved: how could he know he would be killed that evening by a person trying to kill someone else? These are stories not about delusion or the usefulness of doubt, but about the alarming, al-

most perverse, fragility of what look like certainties. Yet the discomfiture in these cases is accompanied by the hint of another order, the whisper of a witty and complicated plot. The young man in *The Gift* is not disappointed by the news about the wrong dress, and he doesn't think his theory of fate has been refuted by an untidy reality. He simply takes that reality itself as a mark of fate's deeper deviousness, evidence of an even more elaborate scheme. "Then it was still more ingenious," he says. "What resourcefulness! The most enchanting things in nature and art are based on deception." Humbert Humbert, in *Lolita*, calls fate a "synchronizing phantom." It is a phantom, and our accidents are accidents. But extravagant coincidences do occur, fragments of apparent design, that make the notion of a synchronizing agency all but irresistible: a metaphor that possesses the force of the literal, our only means of unfolding these fantastic structures, in history or in fiction.

"I confess I do not believe in time," Nabokov writes in his autobiography, *Speak, Memory* (1951, 1967). He is thinking of clocks, calendars, mortality, the death of loved ones. His resistance to time in this sense is both absurd and heroic, a desperate refusal of what cannot be refused. But it is also something else. We are time's victims, but not only its victims; and time itself has many modes. Time passes, but memory stays, and memory too is a form of time. Memory resurrects the past when it needs to, but it also keeps the past from dying, preserves it in everything but its material form. When Nabokov says he does not believe in time he means, among other things, that death and loss can only complete themselves in our minds, and that sequential time has no dominion there. We grieve for our dead, for our homeland, for the houses and countries to which we can never return. But then we resist their second dying, which occurs when we come to forget them, and even forget how much we cared for them.

I see again my schoolroom in Vyra, the blue roses of the wallpaper, the open window. Its reflection fills the oval mirror above the leathern couch where my uncle sits, gloating over a tattered book. A sense of security, of well-being, of summer warmth pervades my memory. . . . Everything is as it should be, nothing will ever change, nobody will die.

It is not, it will; they will—except in the memory. Nabokov's delight in style, his denial of despair and his absolute refusal of all pathos of loss, are often taken as aesthetic, escapist postures, flights from the reality of the world, and he himself quite often encouraged this view. In one of his most notorious mandarin announcements, made in a 1956 afterword to *Lolita,* he says, "For me a work of fiction exists only insofar as it affords me what I shall bluntly call aesthetic bliss, that is a sense of being somehow, somewhere, connected with other states of being where art (curiosity, tenderness, kindness, ecstasy) is the norm." He is stating what the work of fiction affords him, the writer of it, not what it may afford us; "exists" here must mean "comes alive as fiction," not merely "is available in the bookstore"; but even then that little spray of synonyms for art complicates most conventional conceptions of the aesthetic. There is a world, our world, where none of those things is the norm but where they can, nevertheless, fortunately be found. Art is not an evasion of this world but a redemption of what is best in it; it is where our curiosity, tenderness, kindness, ecstasy get to feel at home.

To see Nabokov's work as simply fleeing or refusing the harshness of the world is to miss the degree to which the violence of modern history and the fact of mortality are reflected there, as well as in his life. There are totalitarian states in *Invitation to a Beheading* (1938) and *Bend Sinister* (1947), extermination camps in *Lolita* and *Pnin,* and (on one level of the plot) a political assassination in *Pale Fire.* There are murders everywhere, often botched, but still lethal. There are

suicides, duels, and mysterious diseases. Almost none of Nabokov's characters lives to anything resembling old age—the startling exceptions are Van and Ada Veen in *Ada* (1969). It may well be that Nabokov is saying, through his style, that he does not believe in violence, as he does not believe in time. He would mean, not that violence does not happen—who could argue that?—but that violence, like linear time, is not all there is, and can be contested.

### LIFE

Nabokov was born in St. Petersburg, Russia, on April 23, 1899, into a well-to-do family—the Vyra mentioned above was their country estate. His grandfather was minister of justice under two tsars, and his father was a distinguished jurist who was jailed for his protests against the iniquities of the old regime, and who became, in 1917, a member of Alexander Kerensky's provisional government. After the Bolshevik coup and the start of civil war, Nabokov senior became minister of justice in the regional government of the Crimea, but then was forced, with his family, to flee from the advancing Red Army. They left the country on a Greek steamer from Sebastopol, and took up residence first in London then in Berlin. None of them was ever to see Russia again, although Nabokov's exile took him to Germany, France, the United States, and Switzerland, where he died in Lausanne, on July 2, 1977.

The boy learned English and French at home from governesses, attended the Tenishev School in St. Petersburg, and began to develop two of the man's enduring passions: playing chess and collecting butterflies. This early life is recorded in loving and startlingly precise detail in *Speak, Memory,* twelve of whose fifteen chapters are devoted to the years 1899 to 1919, that is, to Russia. The remaining chapters describe Nabokov's student years in Cambridge, England, his beginnings and success as an émigré writer in Germany, his move to France in 1937, and his departure for the United States in 1940.

In Berlin, Nabokov met and married Véra Slonim, his lifelong companion and collaborator, who survived him by almost fourteen years. Their one child, Dmitri, was born in 1934. Using the pseudonym Sirin, Nabokov published nine novels in Russian, and wrote another, *The Enchanter*, which he thought he had destroyed; it was discovered and translated by his son and published in 1989. "But the author that interested me most," Nabokov slyly says in *Speak, Memory*, thinking of Russian writers of the post-revolutionary emigration, "was naturally Sirin. He belonged to my generation." The second sentence, with its odd "he" and "my," suggests that Sirin is not only an old self, but another self, a writer who now lives only in the past tense. We do not need to exaggerate the difference, because there are considerable continuities linking Nabokov's Russian- and English-language works. Still, between the Russian Sirin and the American Nabokov there does fall the immense shadow of a change of language, a shadow that Nabokov experienced, before he managed to turn it into glittering light, as infinitely oppressive. The change, he said, was "like moving from one darkened house to another on a starless night during a strike of candlemakers and torchbearers," and to his wife he wrote that "I myself don't fully register all the grief and bitterness of my situation."

Nabokov also wrote short stories and plays in Russian in Berlin, and preparing for his stay in Paris wrote an essay and a story in French. The most striking incident here, though—eerily prophetic, even if he could not have known how spectacular the prophecy would turn out to be—is Nabokov's decision, while in Paris, to start writing fiction in English. He completed his subtle and mournfully funny novel, *The Real Life of Sebastian Knight*, in 1939, and after that wrote only shorter works in Russian. Soon after his arrival in the United States, he abandoned Russian altogether as a language for prose fiction. His collections *Nine Stories* (1947) and *Nabokov's Dozen* (1958) contain pieces written in English as well as older pieces written in Russian; and after "Lance" (1952), he wrote no more short stories at all in either language.

Nabokov and his family lived precariously in the United States at first, by his taking short-term teaching posts at Stanford University and Wellesley College, but he began to publish stories and pieces of his autobiography in the *New Yorker* and in 1948 he accepted a permanent post as professor of Russian literature at Cornell University. He gave his last lecture there early in 1959, and in 1961 he settled in Montreux, Switzerland. In the United States he had written *Bend Sinister, Lolita*, and *Pnin*, and had started work on *Pale Fire*. He had also written *Speak, Memory* and a short book on Gogol (*Nikolai Gogol*), and had completed a monumental translation of and commentary on Pushkin's *Eugene Onegin* (1964). In Switzerland, he finished *Pale Fire*; wrote his last three novels, *Ada, Transparent Things* (1972), and *Look at the Harlequins* (1974); and worked on another, unfinished novel called *The Original of Laura*. Between 1959 and 1971 virtually all his Russian novels were translated into English. After his death, three volumes of lectures were published, as well as a selection of letters. Nabokov's reputation at the close of the twentieth century is as secure as any literary reputation can be. *Lolita*, once an extraordinary object of scandal, is now routinely taken to be a masterpiece, and very large claims have persuasively been made for Nabokov's Russian fiction, particularly *The Defense* (1930) and *The Gift*. "I shall be remembered," Nabokov himself said in *Strong Opinions*, "by *Lolita* and my work on *Eugene Onegin*"— that "by" rather than "for" is one of his very rare slips in an English idiom, and has the effect of reminding us how extraordinary his English was. Or perhaps it is not even a slip, just a discreet figure of speech, a transfer of memory from readers to books. He may have been rating his *Onegin* too highly, but he was certainly rating the rest of his writing too low. He will be remembered, he is remembered, not just for a pair of works, but for a brilliant body of fiction in two languages, and for one of the most haunting and haunted of all autobiographies.

## FICTION AND MEMORY

Nabokov writes in *Speak, Memory*:

> I have often noticed that after I had bestowed on the characters of my novels some treasured item of my past, it would pine away in the artificial world where I had so abruptly placed it. Although it lingered on in my mind, its personal warmth, its retrospective appeal had gone. . . . The man in me revolts against the fictionist.

"The man" here is the autobiographer, and the picture is strongly tilted toward his view. Nabokov the novelist did not usually think of his fictional material as "pining away" in an "artificial world," and he did not place items there "abruptly." In his 1970 preface to the translation of *Mary* (1926), his first novel, the fictionist makes a curious peace with the man. "I had not consulted *Mashenka* [*Mary*] when writing . . . the autobiography a quarter of a century later; and now that I have, I am fascinated by the fact that . . . a headier extract of personal reality is contained in the romantization than in the autobiographer's scrupulously faithful account." Initially puzzled, because he "could not believe that a stylish imitation should be able to vie with plain truth," Nabokov decides the "explanation is really quite simple": he was younger then, the hero of *Mary* was "closer to his past" than the later Nabokov was to his own.

Given Nabokov's many declarations about the necessary artfulness of art and the sorry tricks of naturalism, it is a little odd to hear him speaking of the "plain truth," even in autobiography. The "true purpose of autobiography," Nabokov says in *Speak, Memory*, should be "the following of . . . thematic designs through one's life," and some of those designs are pretty fancy, far from plain, however truthful they may be. But he is not being ironic in his preface to *Mary*, only underplaying an interesting hand. The "simple" explanation is important, but not all there is. *Mary* is doubly a work of fiction: an invented world in which a character invents a world, makes the past his personal fiction. *Speak, Memory* is thoroughly orchestrated, meticulously shaped, but its premise is precisely that its world was not invented by the author and is not now lost. With these distinctions in mind, we can perhaps contemplate the dizzying crossover between the two works: where fiction catches more reality than memory, but memory knows more than fiction.

The setting of *Mary* is a boardinghouse in Berlin, peopled by Russian exiles. The house is so close to a railway line that trains literally shake it and seem to pass through. Metaphorically they do pass through it. For some of the boarders the place is a terminus: Podtyagin, the poet who wants to get to Paris but keeps being held up by paperwork and finally loses his passport, will die here, his slender immortality guaranteed by a few sentimental lines quoted on calendars; Klara, a typist of twenty-six, is waiting for love and will probably keep waiting. But for Ganin, the book's hero, the place is a junction, an end and a beginning. He learns that Mary, a girl he loved in Russia, now married to one of the oafs to be found everywhere in Nabokov's fiction, is about to arrive. Elated, he plans to meet her and take her away. But in the intervening days he remembers his affair with her so richly and completely that there is nothing left for the real Mary to do. She could only spoil her perfect reconstruction by being different—or even by being the same. As she comes into Berlin at one station, Ganin takes a train for France at another. We can assume that Mary does arrive, since she and her husband (not Ganin) reappear in Nabokov's later novel *The Defense,* also set in Berlin.

Details are everything for Nabokov, there are (almost) no allegories. Here he attends to the smell of sickness, the sound of a smile. Footfalls thump like a heartbeat, searchlights are sleeves in the sky, a shirt on a chair at night is like a man "struck rigid in the middle of a prayer." When Ganin learns that Mary is coming to Berlin the neon letters of a street advertisement seem to light up, like a famous sign in Robert Wiene's film *The Cabinet of Dr. Caligari,* and speak a private message. "Can-it-be-possible?" they say several times before they fade again into the darkness.

But if allegories are scarce, there are a number of figures that carry meanings well beyond that of their own named identity: individual Russians, for instance, who add up to an image of Russia; forms of metonymy. This is notably true of the remembered and imagined Mary, who is Russia for Ganin, while remaining her quite particular self. He thinks in a single, scarcely pausing sentence of "his future parting from Mary, his parting from Russia"; recognizes how far he is "from the warm mass of his own country and from Mary"; and finally does slip into allegory: "Tomorrow all his youth, his Russia, was coming back to him again." In *Speak, Memory,* Nabokov makes the same suggestion for Tamara, his other version of the girl who became Mary: "For several years . . . the loss of my country was equated for me with the loss of my love." But then it is important to understand exactly what Ganin and Nabokov are doing.

They are enacting a story of loss in variant forms. For Ganin, the past seems to be recoverable in two forms: in memory and in reality. His feat of memory, it turns out, is an extraordinary work of art, but it is an act of pure mind, and cannot alter reality; the past cannot return, what returns is never the past. "He had exhausted his memories, was sated by them, and the image of Mary . . . now remained in the house of ghosts, which itself was already a memory." The "house of ghosts" is the boardinghouse as Ganin has come to see it. "Other than that image no Mary existed, nor could exist." The later Nabokov would say there was an element of solipsism in such a claim. Ganin has no interest in any other Mary than his own; no interest in her interests. But his response to memory and the past is courageous and exhilarating. The fact that we cannot return to our country or our love is not contingent or remediable, and no train will bring them back to us—or no train except that of memory. *Speak, Memory* says the same, except that it lovingly prolongs the act of remembering that Ganin so intensely lives and so quickly abandons. We can, perhaps, meet our memories at the station if we meet them for their own sake, and do not mistake them for consolations in the present.

## THE OTHER SIDE

Nabokov's greatest work of memory and resurrection is *The Gift,* although it is also a work of leave-taking. The setting of this novel is again Berlin, and the shabby world of Russian émigrés. Fyodor Godunov-Cherdyntsev is a young poet about to become a novelist—to become the author of the book we are reading, and also of a "chess novel" that sounds like Nabokov's *The Defense.* He is a brilliant, self-admiring fellow, capable of intermittent affections and kindnesses, and also, by the end of the novel, of a lasting and enchanted love for an intelligent and lighthearted young woman. His arrogance is mitigated by the fact that the objects of his scorn, hearty vulgarians and petty scribblers, seem richly to merit his acrid comments on them, and by the fact that he is often very funny. He compares himself nervously to the one or two other writers he admires, and Nabokov, in his 1962 foreword to the translation, mischievously associates himself with them rather than with Fyodor. It is true that this is not a confessional novel, and that Nabokov is not and as he says, "never was," Fyodor. But he has lent Fyodor many of his gifts and passions and tastes, and in displaced form, one of the defining experiences of his life.

At the center of *The Gift* is an account of Fyodor's attempt to write a book about his lost father, an explorer and naturalist who, after many trips to the remotest parts of Asia, failed one day to return. He is presumed dead, and Fyodor keeps expecting to see his ghost. At other times Fyodor is sure his father is still alive. He recalls his father's language and habits, his departures. "It sometimes seemed to me then that I was unhappy," he writes, thinking of the length and frequency of his father's absences, "but now I know that I was always happy, that that unhappiness was one of the colors of happiness." He imagines his father's travels in extraordinary detail, as if he had taken part in every expedition, but alas these feats of the mind, these "mental visits to places which I have never seen," are similar to Ganin's memories of Mary, dreams capable of replacing reality but not of altering it. Fyodor gives up his book not because it is not beautiful or poetic, but because it is; because its "secondary poetization . . . keeps departing further and further" from the "real poetry" of what the naturalist actually saw. Fyodor's mother writes to him that she is "convinced that some day you shall yet write this book." The implication of the narrative is that he does not; and yet of course if he wrote *The Gift* he has written a book about his father, or part of a book, in telling his story of the attempt. In much the same way the projected biography of a writer in *The Real Life of Sebastian Knight* finally takes the form of the detailed, winding story of the biographer's researches.

The heroine of *The Gift*, Nabokov said, was "Russian Literature"; just as *Lolita,* he thought, could be seen as the record of his love affair with the "English language." These are playful phrases, but they are not casual. *Lolita* is not only about language, but language is perhaps its chief heroine. *The Gift* is not only about Russian literature, but that literature also shapes the book. In the first chapter Fyodor imagines reviews of his book of

poems, and revives and reports on the poems in the process. The second chapter associates the lost father with Pushkin, while the third chapter, Nabokov says, "shifts to Gogol." The fourth chapter reprints Fyodor's book on Nikolai Chernyshevsky, author of *What to Do?*, and regarded as the father of modern Russian intellectuals. This is a portrait of the artist as unhappy pedant, and is itself a masterpiece of capriciously used scholarship, rather like Nabokov's own book on Gogol (1944). Nabokov was writing an appreciation, though, and Fyodor is engaged in a demolition, allayed only by odd moments of tenderness for Chernyshevsky's solitude or unhappiness or stolid honesty or affection for his wife. Chernyshevsky is important not in his own right but because of what people have made of him. Fyodor wants his readers to see that a false idol compromises not the unfortunate object of adoration but the worshippers, in this case those who happily exchange art (which they fail to understand) for statistics and politics, and who indulge in what for Nabokov is one of the cardinal sins: "a contemptuous hatred of particularities." Fyodor's aim is "to keep everything as it were on the brink of parody." On the one hand there would be the "idiotic" popular biography, and "on the other hand an abyss of seriousness, and I must walk my way along this narrow ridge between my own truth and a caricature of it." In a later dialogue with himself, Fyodor thinks that he may not quite have stayed on the ridge, that his parodies of mannerisms perhaps themselves became a mannerism. The last chapter brings Fyodor together with the girl he loves (although they are locked out of their house, and we do not know how they get in, if they do), and delicately evokes a faith in the invisible harmonies of the world, which both Fyodor and his father have intuited but cannot express:

> as if the responsibility for his soul belonged not to him but to someone who knew what it all meant— he felt that all this skein of random thoughts, like everything else as well—the seams and sleaziness of

the spring day, the ruffle of the air, the coarse, variously intercrossing threads of confused sounds—was but the reverse side of a magnificent fabric, on the front of which there gradually formed and became alive images invisible to him.

This perception is enacted again and again in Nabokov's fiction, and hinted at in his interviews. It often takes the shape of a metaphor borrowed from the novelist's art, where the characters suddenly suspect they are figures in someone else's design. This happens, in variously discreet forms, at the end of *Invitation to a Beheading, The Real Life of Sebastian Knight, Bend Sinister,* and *Transparent Things.* John Shade, in *Pale Fire,* glimpses a mysterious order behind the very misprints of the world, a game of secret masters:

> It did not matter who they were. No sound,
> No furtive light came from their involute
> Abode, but there they were, aloof and mute,
> Playing a game of worlds. . . .

There they were. The characters in a novel undeniably have a creator who made them, but do we? Asked if he believed in God, Nabokov carefully said in *Strong Opinions,* "I know more than I can express in words, and the little I can express would not have been expressed, had I not known more."

Recent critical and biographical work, notably that of V. E. Alexandrov and Brian Boyd, has usefully stressed the importance of the "otherworld" in Nabokov's art—the word is Alexandrov's translation of *potustoronnost,* which Véra Nabokov said was her husband's "main theme," and "saturates everything he wrote." In *Look at the Harlequins,* Nabokov translates the word as "the hereafter." Nabokov is certainly not the determined disbeliever we often assume most modern writers are. The difficulty is to register his genuine interest in the "other side"—another way of translating the term—without literalizing all his scrupulously metaphorical ghosts or making him

into a turn-of-the-century spiritualist, a companion of the crankier friends of William Butler Yeats. If we put the hidden front of Fyodor's fabric together with John Shade's secret game we may be surprised either by the theological tilt of the thought or the extreme modesty of the intuitive claim: there is a pattern but we do not know who makes it or what it means. It is like saying we are in a novel, but we do not know the author or the plot. This would be an amazing consolation if we previously thought there was no novel at all; only slender comfort if we felt we needed to know more; and little better than atheism if we believed there was a God or a providence.

## CONSPIRACIES

There is a dark counterpart to these beneficent designs. A possible theology, in Nabokov, is almost always mirrored by a possible paranoia. Most of Nabokov's novels after *Mary* center on a malevolent scheme, a plot within the plot: a murder in *King, Queen, Knave* and *Despair;* an elaborate hoax in *Laughter in the Dark* and *Lolita;* a political conspiracy in *Invitation to a Beheading, Bend Sinister,* and *Pale Fire.* The exception is *Ada,* which looks back to *Mary* in a number of ways, but also portrays what we take to be the historical world as an alternative reality imagined only by the insane.

These questions are beautifully focused in Nabokov's "chess-novel," *The Defense.* Aleksandr Ivanovich Luzhin is a difficult child, morose, lonely, afraid of change, a sore trial to his parents, who would have preferred a son who resembled the sunny characters in the children's novels the father wrote. The boy loves magic, and Jules Verne and Conan Doyle—what he finds in their work is an "exact and relentlessly unfolding pattern"—but discovers his passion, a salvation that is also his nemesis, when he learns to play chess. By the age of fourteen he is a star, taking part in major tournaments. As an adult he is a master, but his game seems to freeze at a certain altitude. During an interval in a match, with the result still undecided, Luzhin has a breakdown, and begins to see life itself as a chess contest, a monstrous system of moves against him. He has married meanwhile, but his wife, a loving person driven by an intense pity for "helpless and unhappy" creatures, cannot help him except by surrounding him with care. A doctor dictates that he stay away from chess, a cure that may be worse than the disease, but that will at least keep Luzhin alive. Then chess creeps back into his life through a chance mention in a conversation he overhears, and Luzhin devises a last, desperate defense: "The only way out . . . I have to drop out of the game." Since the game is now literally his life, he means this literally too. He climbs through a bathroom window, and falls to his death. Even this move, Nabokov suggests, may not be enough to rescue Luzhin from his intolerable obsession. If there is a hereafter for Luzhin, chess will almost certainly be played there. Just before he lets go of the high ledge, he thinks he is "saved," but the narrator, in a language that curiously blends tenderness and cruelty, shows that the very ground Luzhin is about to hit has taken on for him the form of a chessboard: "The whole chasm was seen to divide into dark and pale squares, and at the instant when Luzhin unclenched his hand, at the instant when icy air gushed into his mouth, he saw exactly what kind of eternity was obligingly and inexorably spread out before him."

The horror here is that chess, even with all its "abysmal depths," is the only form of order and peace that Luzhin knows, his only chance of happiness, a sort of travesty of the order of that which Fyodor was later to put his faith in. Fyodor's insight, we could say, is the happy answer to Luzhin's insanity, but then this means that Luzhin's insanity is also a kind of twin to insight. One should not apply the term madness, John Shade says in *Pale Fire*, "to a person who delib-

erately peels off a drab and unhappy past and replaces it with a brilliant invention." The double mirror of insight and madness is a structure that haunts all of Nabokov's work, and I think is his final word, in fiction, on the question of transcendence. "That human life," he says in a lecture called "The Art of Literature and Commonsense," "is but the first installment of the serial soul and that one's individual secret is not lost in the process of earthly dissolution, becomes something more than an optimistic conjecture, and even more than a matter of religious faith . . ." This seems emphatic enough, although it is not entirely clear what "more" means here. But then the sentence ends, "when we remember that only commonsense rules immortality out." The argument for immortality rests on the humdrum nature of the case against it, and this, I think, is precisely the argument of Nabokov's fiction. Not that there is a hereafter, but that only pedestrian reason excludes it, and we have an obligation to imagine alternatives to our world, in whatever shape most closely meets our needs. This is not to conjecture or to have faith; it is, in a special sense, to invent, and in Nabokov's case to invent brilliantly and generously. It is a perilous enterprise, and among Nabokov's characters there are far more insane failures than even timid successes. For every Fyodor or John Shade glimpsing a figure in the fabric there are five or six Luzhins succumbing to terminal paranoia. But this is the point. We cannot know whether the secret orders we perceive are the products of our madness or of our best, most ideal sense. All we know is that the haphazard arrangements of the historical world do not reveal such patterns except to maniacs and artists. Possibly also to saints, but that would take us further than Nabokov wants to go openly.

Nabokov is often assumed to be thinking in *The Defense* more generally of the artist. Luzhin's wife sees chess as "a spectral art," and his father dreams of a son who would be a musical virtuoso. Luzhin's last chess game is described as if it were a complicated concert, with "muted violins," a singing chord and "a trace of melody," and it ends in "a kind of musical tempest . . . *agitato*." Luzhin, before this game, is compared to "a writer or composer" who fails to register change, in his art or in life, and "who has petrified in his art which was once new but has not advanced since then." In this light the novel becomes a fable that both confirms and refutes Henry James's story, "The Middle Years," with its elaboration of the "madness of art." All art runs the risk of madness, of succumbing to a tyranny of order. The art that escapes madness is the art that knows how to change and yet stay loyal to itself, how to appease and baffle the longing for pattern. In Nabokov's work the madness of art is often given to his characters, art's sanity being reserved for the text they inhabit. This is particularly the case in *Lolita* and *Pale Fire*. We might say it is Nabokov the artist who is sane, rather than the text, and critics regularly have. But to put it that way grants Nabokov an Olympian distance from his fictional figures, which dehumanizes the art, and I think the difference is more subtle than that. These madmen are monsters, no doubt about it, but trails of terrible possibility link them to us. Humbert, however much we disavow him, resembles everyone whose love is illicit (or who loves the illicit); Kinbote working on his commentary on John Shade's poem is a manic echo of Nabokov working on his commentary on *Eugene Onegin*. Nabokov is not Humbert or Kinbote, but he did not know them intimately, and did not see them as members of another species.

But there is an even deeper human fable in *The Defense*. Chess is not only an art, it is associated with love in its most alluring and forbidden forms. Luzhin learns how to play chess from an aunt who turns out to be his father's mistress—more precisely, his learning how to play is synchronized with his mother's first suspicion that his father has a mistress. Luzhin develops his game by playing with one of the youthful mistress's elderly ad-

mirers whom she has abandoned, and there are hints, through ellipsis and allusions to familiar clichés about the world of amorous rendezvous, that chess is sex for Luzhin, a descent into a kind of demimonde. It's not for nothing that Luzhin's father is such a fan of *La Traviata*, and Luzhin's chess mentor-manager Valentinov actually has "a peculiar theory" about love and chess: chess is for Luzhin "a special deflection" of the sexual urge. We need these hints to get at the mystery and potential scandal that chess represents in this book, but the hints are also mischievous and misleading. Chess is not a form of philandering for Luzhin, a gentleman's dalliance, it is his life and his death. It is his love, and love, even more than art, is the madness that besets Nabokov's heroes. When Valentinov, having disappeared, returns to Luzhin's life, his voice becomes "the music of the chessboard's evil lure," and "Luzhin recalled, with the exquisite, moist melancholy peculiar to recollections of love, a thousand games he had played in the past. . . . Everything was wonderful, all the shades of love, all the convolutions and mysterious paths it had chosen. And this love was fatal." The chessboard is not evil for everyone, of course, any more than adultery destroys everyone as thoroughly as it did Anna Karenina. Love is not itself madness, but it is madness for some, the point at which life and death intersect and become the same, a kind of conspiracy against the self.

This is precisely the situation Humbert Humbert meets in *Lolita*. The easiest way of thinking about his passion for little girls—certain girls, not all—between the ages of nine and fourteen is to see it as a monstrous deviance, not love at all. Every word in the novel invites us to see his passion as fully monstrous, in its cruelty, its self-absorption, its indifference to its effects on its object. But once the passion comes to concentrate on a particular young person, Dolores Haze, it is unmistakably a form of love, an exclusive, obsessive devotion to a single, endlessly desired object. Certainly Humbert's relation to the long tradition of famous unhappy lovers is one of burlesque and travesty, but that is because of his time and place and bad luck, rather than the quality of his feeling. And Nabokov expects us to see the truth in a travesty; this is one of the central secrets of his art.

Humbert is a transposed European, born on the French Riviera of an English mother and a father who was French-Austrian-Swiss, now occupying a room in the house of Charlotte Haze in the sunny New England town of Ramsdale. Humbert has been married and divorced, and has been hospitalized because of "a dreadful breakdown" that seems to have had to do with his unmanageable and unrealizable desires for young flesh. In Charlotte's daughter, Dolores, alias Lolita, he finds, he says, an exact replica of a girl he loved in childhood, "when I was a child and she was a child," as he puts it, quoting Edgar Allan Poe's "Annabel Lee." Humbert has various schemes for getting rid of Charlotte Haze, but ends up marrying her, and leaving the rest to fate, the "synchronizing phantom" we have already looked at. Fate obliges fulsomely: Charlotte discovers Humbert's diary, with its many offensive references to her, rushes out of the house in tears, and is killed by a car that she does not see, and that cannot avoid her because it is busy avoiding a dog that Humbert encountered the very first day of his spell in Ramsdale ("we almost ran over a meddlesome suburban dog"). Humbert becomes Lolita's protector, and effectively her father; and also, in a much more direct manner than his fiendish fantasies had anticipated, her lover. They travel across America, then return East to a town called Beardsley, where Lolita goes to school. "We had really seen nothing," Humbert writes.

> And I catch myself thinking today that our long journey had only defiled with a sinuous trail of slime the lovely, trustful, dreamy, enormous country that by then, in retrospect, was no more to us than a collection of dog-eared maps, ruined tour books, old tires, and her sobs in the night—every night, every night— the moment I feigned sleep.

Lolita takes part in a school play, written by the famous Clare Quilty, who is said to bear a strong resemblance to Humbert, but Humbert feels she is getting too involved in affairs that do not concern him, and they take off across America again. During this journey, Lolita disappears. Humbert only finds her three years later, married, pregnant, living in a place called Coalmont, "a small industrial community some eight hundred miles from New York City." He asks her to come away with him; she refuses. She reveals the name of the person who took her from him, and in a hopelessly unstylish murder scene, Humbert manages to kill him. Humbert is, as he writes, in a "psychopathic ward" awaiting trial for this crime. A foreword, by the ineffably pompous John Ray, Jr., Ph.D., tells us two things we cannot know, and could not predict, from Humbert's text. Humbert died of coronary thrombosis before his trial started, and Lolita died in childbirth a month and a half later. An imaginary French philosopher who appears both in *The Gift* and in *Invitation to a Beheading*, is said to have kept his hat on at funerals because he was waiting for death to show some respect first. Death is always a discourtesy in Nabokov, a form of murder even when its causes are, as we say, natural.

But the key moment in the conclusion of *Lolita*, even more important than Humbert's finding the loved girl again or killing her abductor, concerns his discovery of who that abductor was. It was Clare Quilty; who else could it be? The man who resembles Humbert, whose play took Lolita away even before the writer did, the drunk in the dark who happened to be at the hotel where Humbert spent his first night with Lolita. Humbert did not suspect this at the time, although of course Humbert the writer has organized his whole text around the meeting of his present knowledge and his old ignorance. What is extraordinary, though, is the language in which Humbert records his discovery, the horrible sense of order and peace in persecution, as if Humbert had somehow managed to marry Luzhin's torment to Fyodor's hope. Lolita speaks Quilty's name, and Humbert says:

> I, too, had known it, without knowing it, all along. There was no shock, no surprise. Quietly the fusion took place, and everything fell into order, into the pattern of branches that I have woven throughout this memoir with the express purpose of having the ripe fruit fall at the right moment; yes, with the express and perverse purpose of rendering—she was talking but I sat melting in my golden peace—of rendering that golden and monstrous peace through the satisfaction of logical recognition, which my most inimical reader should experience now.

This is the most extravagant instance of the author-god metaphor at work in Nabokov's fiction. Humbert, who is Quilty's victim the first time around, makes himself Quilty's author the second time—but then can only show himself falling, wanting to fall, into Quilty's plot. If there is a novel for Nabokov's Fyodor to be in, Fyodor is the hero of it. There is certainly a novel for Humbert to be in, but for all his mangled passion and his extraordinary literary gifts, Humbert can only be that novel's stooge, its fall guy. What is truly perverse is the delight he experiences at this thought. Better a plot that mocks us than no plot at all.

This perverse delight is precisely where the logic of transcendence all too often ends; and this conclusion is the reason for Nabokov's caution, his preference for travesty over confession in these important matters. John Shade's faith in a secret order is not canceled by his sudden, accidental death, and the meaning of Nabokov's father's life was not canceled by his murder. But Nabokov wants us to see such faith as precarious, threatened by life's blunt arguments as well as by random violence. Shade writes of "a feeling of fantastically planned / Richly rhymed life," and says he understands existence "only through my art, / In terms of combinational delight":

> And if my private universe scans right,
> So does the verse of galaxies divine

> Which I suspect is an iambic line.
> I'm reasonably sure that we survive
> And that my darling somewhere is alive,
> As I am reasonably sure that I
> Shall wake at six tomorrow, on July
> The twenty-second, nineteen fifty-nine,
> And that the day will probably be fine.

He does not wake the next day, but it is not his death that argues against his immortality, or against the chance of joining his dead daughter ("my darling") in the hereafter. It is the intricate relay of comparisons that calls all in doubt, as the reference to nonexistent rain qualifies the dying man's certainty in *The Gift*. Shade is as sure of his survival after death as he is of waking tomorrow, but he needs to be surer than that. Or rather he is trying to make a fabulous belief seem sensible, and has not quite understood that nothing is more treacherous, or more easily betrayed, than cautious optimism.

### INVENTING AMERICA

"*The Gift*," Nabokov said in 1962, "is the last novel I wrote, or ever shall write, in Russian." He did not know at that time that the unpublished *Enchanter* was still intact, and he worked on another Russian novel, fragments of which were published as the stories "Ultima Thule" and "Solus Rex," until he left Europe in 1940. But he did start preparing his linguistic move even earlier than his geographical shift. It is not only that he wrote *The Real Life of Sebastian Knight* in English, but he had translated his own *Despair* in 1935, that is, even before he started on *The Gift*. This fact makes that book's leave-taking from Russian literature all the more poignant. Nabokov's English became that of a master, but a master who resembled no one else. When he was compared to Joseph Conrad, that other great writer of English as a second (or third) language, Nabokov insisted to Edmund Wilson on the difference: "Conrad knew how to handle *readymade* English better than I; but I know better the other kind. He never sinks to the depths of my solecisms, but neither does he scale my verbal peaks."

Nabokov's verbal peaks have to do with his treating all English words and idioms as if he had just met them—in fact, he had been speaking English fluently since he was a small child—but also with his giving himself license to play with language, to let the words gang up and take tumbles, like children thoroughly enjoying themselves. Fyodor, in *The Gift*, says he is seeking "a final dictatorship over words," because in his book on Chernyshevsky "they are still trying to vote." Nabokov was too much of an autocrat to want any kind of universal suffrage for words, but Fyodor must be smiling at his own ambition. Language does not vote in Nabokov, but it does not submit either. It gets loose, gets up to mischief. Consider the idea, casually dropped into a list of criminals, of the "self-made widow," or of a movie "precariously based" on a novel; or the joke Nabokov repeatedly has his characters make about trains of thought. "Let me follow a train of thought." Humbert says. He thinks for a while, and Charlotte asks, "Was I on that train?" "You certainly were." Remember Humbert's casual, but transforming phrase: "countless motor courts proclaimed their vacancy in neon lights." No one who has read *Lolita,* I suspect, can drive past a sign saying "Vacancy," and take it to mean only that this is a place that has rooms. This is surely vacancy itself, sheer emptiness, an advertisement for the void.

Brian Boyd, in *Vladimir Nabokov: The American Years*, tells the story of Nabokov's taking the language test for American citizenship. The examiner asked the candidate to read a sentence in English, "The child is bold." Nabokov, either making a joke or adjusting to his new glasses, read, "The child is bald." Corrected, he said, "Yes, but you know, babies don't have much hair." Everyone dissolved in laughter. Nabokov later said, "I had a wonderful time becoming an American citizen." His capacity for irreverent, infectious, multifarious, linguistic invention seems infinite, and his "love affair" with the English language is one of the great (one of the few) happy love stories.

But there is another phrase in Nabokov's foreword to *The Gift* that looks forward even more dramatically and more lucidly to his American works. "In the days I worked on this book," he says, "I did not have the knack of recreating Berlin and its colony of expatriates as radically and ruthlessly as I have done in regard to certain environments in my later, English, fiction." This re-creation is what Nabokov comes to call "inventing." "It had taken me some forty years," he says in his afterword to *Lolita*, "to invent Russia and Western Europe, and now I was faced by the task of inventing America." So far so similar: both worlds are invented, and Nabokov reminds us that his "old worlds . . . are just as fantastic and personal as my new one is." But then what does it mean to say that the later inventions are more radical and ruthless?

It means several things. In *Lolita* it means that an elaborately perverse personality has been allowed to take over the whole text and have a field day, although there are numerous satirical echoes of a world we recognize all too well. "We insist you un-veto her non-participation in the dramatic group," a headmistress says to Humbert in his role of father. "I mean it is all part of the fun of being young and alive and beautiful." In *Pnin* the narrator is more discreetly radical and ruthless, since he seems at first just an old-fashioned storyteller. Gradually we learn not only that he is often condescending to his hero, a Russian professor on an American campus, but that he has slept with Pnin's former wife, and is about to take his job. The complication here is that the narrator is said to be a "prominent Anglo-Russian writer" who is interested in butterflies, and whose first names, like Nabokov's, are Vladimir Vladimirovich. Nabokov is not confessing his indiscretion or arrogance, but he is inviting us to think about the intersection of fictional and nonfictional worlds. The curious thing is that the seemingly foolish Pnin finds a source of strength in his very vulnerability, and leaves town rather than meet again the haughty narrator. The narrator is not always haughty, and does understand that Pnin "did not believe in an autocratic God. He did believe, dimly, in a democracy of ghosts." These are the ghosts of Russia and exile and of his dead loved ones, who return to haunt him as if they had never gone away: "murdered, forgotten, unrevenged, incorrupt, immortal."

In *Pale Fire* America itself is radically and ruthlessly made into an analogue for the world we know rather than a picture of it: a re-creation but in a curiously refracting mirror. This is a place where you dial 11111 in emergencies, and people drive cars called Kramlers and Pulexes. This America has states called Utana and Idoming; a man called Goldsworth who is associated with a college called Wordsmith. These names not only conflate and interchange Goldsmith and Wordsworth, they conjure up, as if in a mangled echo, the building where Nabokov's office was at Cornell: Goldwin Smith Hall. Is the "source" here the American academy or English poetry? Similarly, is New Wye, where Wordsmith is located, a memory of the Wye Valley, home of Tintern Abbey, or just a way of talking about New Y(ork)? There is a New York in *Pale Fire*, and a *New York Times*; and there is also plenty of unaltered historical detail. Robert Frost is mentioned; a famous poem of his is discussed.

The form of the book is itself radical: it is a novel in the form of a poem-and-commentary, complete with lunatic foreword and manic index. Charles Kinbote has made off with the manuscript of John Shade's poem *Pale Fire*, and this is his edition. Kinbote however claims to be King Charles the Beloved of Zembla, a man both in hiding and in exile. The person who kills Shade,

Kinbote insists, is a Zemblan assassin, sent to kill his king, who gets the wrong person. Another story lurks here too, though. Kinbote is not Charles the Beloved, he is not even Kinbote, not even a Zemblan, and maybe Zembla itself does not exist. Kinbote is Professor Botkin, a Russian, who has made up two new identities for himself, peeling off a no doubt "drab and unhappy past" and replacing it with "a brilliant invention." In this story, Shade is killed not by an assassin from Zembla but by an escapee from prison who mistakes Shade for the judge who put him away. These stories are clearly incompatible. Nabokov wants us to choose between them but also has made the choice pretty much impossible. The Botkin story looks like the "truth" in mundane terms, but since when were those terms so interesting? Kinbote is too fanciful and too desperate to be credible; Botkin too boring and too minor to be the only ground for these fantastic adventures. And in both versions of the story John Shade is killed by accident: no one is trying to kill him in either version. It is as if Nabokov were saying there is no satisfactory story we can tell about this death, perhaps about any death. The incredible story is richer, but it has the defect of its incredibility, and it often seems too simple, too blatant a compensation for unhappiness.

*Ada*, Nabokov said in *Strong Opinions*, "is mostly set in a dream America"; but that America is also a dream Russia, and a thoroughly realized alternative world, where electricity has been banned since a great disaster, and where water powers the telephones. In this world, called Demonia, or Antiterra, the British annexed France after the battle of Waterloo, the movies were invented in the 1880s, and the population of North America speaks both English and Russian. What we know as the former Soviet Union is, in the world of *Ada*, Tartary, a barbarous realm on the other side of the earth. Some towns and names are unchanged: Boston, Proust, California. Others are subtly deformed: the Hudson becomes the Goodson, Harvard becomes Aardvark, and Borges becomes Osberg, author of a book called *Lolita.*

*Ada* is more radical than ruthless in its re-creations; lingers fondly over the details of this imagined planet; becomes radical only when we are reminded that our world, the world of the readers, has been heard of on Antiterra; but is classified as a delusion of "deranged minds." Who are the doctors of this place to say that their patients are wrong when they imagine skyscrapers, refrigerators, elevators, gramophones, all of them absent from Antiterra but real enough, as we know, elsewhere? And who are we to say Antiterra does not exist? Have we not been living there for the duration of our reading of this (long) novel?

The hero and heroine of *Ada*, Nabokov's most lovingly cherished and only long-lived couple, are brother and sister, although it takes them some time to work this out, and the details are dizzying. Ada's acknowledged mother had an affair with Van's acknowledged father. There is a subtle and funny moment when all four, mother and father, daughter and son, have dinner together. The children are supposed to be cousins, and the adults are each married (or have been married) to someone else. Marina, Ada's mother, says to Ada "You know quite well that your father disapproves of your smoking at table." Dementiy, Van's father, says, "Oh, it's all right," and Marina has to remind him that she is thinking of her husband, Ada's nominal and legal father. At another point one of Ada's suitors (not Van) says of Marina's husband, "I guess it's your father under that oak, isn't it?" Ada says, "No, it's an elm."

Through this couple, who are pictured as now in their nineties, looking back on their childhood and long life, and writing this text, Nabokov radically revises his Russia and his America into a place entirely of the mind, a "dream America," and makes a love affair that in mood resembles the childhood relationships of *Mary* and *Speak, Mem-ory* into an extensive metaphor for the happiness of shared intelligence and the raptures of sexual contact. Incest is not a problem, at least not for the couple themselves, only "a confirmation of something both had forefelt in an obscure, amusing, bodily rather than moral way." Their father has different views, and separates them. Ada marries someone else, and the two get together again only after the death of her husband, when she is fifty and Van is fifty-two. Fortunately, they have an unusual amount of time left.

The ruthlessness in this novel belongs not to the re-creation or invention of a reality but to the "unique superimperial couple," as Ada calls them, who are the subject of the book. They are splendidly, amorally happy, but we can scarcely measure this fact unless there are morals they can ignore. This purpose is served by the incest taboo, but it is more lyrically and tragically met by the story of Ada's half-sister Lucette, a girl who has been in love with Van from childhood, and who is always kept out of their games and their presence—except on one occasion in later life, when the superimperial couple exploits her sexually. Her suicide, after a last rejection by Van, is one of the most desolate and delicate scenes in Nabokov's fiction, but her very existence is the shadow on the otherwise impeccable happiness of the lovers. "I cannot express," Ada says after Lucette's death, "how unhappy I am, the more so as we never learned . . . that such unhappiness could exist." Happiness is ruthless, exclusive, and cannot be otherwise. This is not a reason for rejecting it, only for remembering, as Nabokov does, that it has a price, even if one does not pay it oneself.

## AFTERLIFE

Transparency, in *Transparent Things*, is a quality of the world for those who know how to sink into history, particularly the history of small, neglected things—a pencil, for instance. The present surface fades, every moment of a former life comes back, the pencil is still graphite and a tree. "Transparent things, through which the past shines!" In human terms this means that a hotel room is full of its old inhabitants, from another century say; and also—if you happen to be trying to return to an old room, as the protagonist of this novel is—full of your previous self. Hugh Person, who has strangled his loved wife in his sleep, returns to Switzerland seeking not her ghost or his earlier happiness, but something like the pure, perceived past: "The desideratum was a moment of contact with her essential image in exactly remembered surroundings." Unfortunately the world is not transparent for the living—the novel is narrated by a figure who speaks for a group of dead persons—and so Hugh's death in a hotel fire at the end of the book is ambiguously hopeful. Human cries reach him in the midst of the flames, and "one of his last wrong ideas," we are told, "was that those were the shouts of people anxious to help him, and not the howls of fellow men." The mistake is similar to the assumption about the rain in *The Gift*, but is this one of Hugh's "last wrong ideas" because he will have no more ideas or because he will have no more wrong ideas? His end is described as "not the crude anguish of physical death but the incomparable pangs of the mysterious mental maneuver needed to pass from one state of being to another." If Hugh lives the difficulty will not be in finding the past, but in sifting it, learning to take it in small doses.

There is not much we can say about Nabokov's own afterlife as a person, but his literary legacy gets clearer and clearer. For many years he was not read in Russia at all, but his books, along with those of Alexandr Solzhenitsyn and Osip Mandelstam, began to circulate in samizdat in the 1970s, and as early as 1988 a number of his novels were publicly available. By the early 1990s, Aleksei Zverev tells us in *The Garland Companion,* "practically everything that Nabokov wrote in

Russian was brought out." His influence on Russian writers as different at Andrei Bitov, Iurii V. Trifonov, and Vasily P. Aksenev has been noted. The saddest thought in this region is that there may no longer be any native speakers of the Russian Nabokov wrote, not because no one speaks Russian or because most of the old émigrés have died, but because the resonances of a Russian unvisited by the Soviet experience are no longer native to anyone. This point is eloquently made by Gennady Barabtarlo, in his *Aerial View*, and has to be thought about. One would hope that with Nabokov, as with other writers of languages we have lost, the literary work actually teaches its readers the language they need.

Nabokov has a strong following of readers in France, Germany, Italy, and Spain, but his trace in these literatures is not highly noticeable. In England Martin Amis, author of *Money, Time's Arrow*, and *London Fields*, is a self-proclaimed admirer and imitator of Nabokov, and John Lanchester has written a recent, dazzling novel, *The Debt to Pleasure*, which is unimaginable without the antecedent of *Pale Fire*. But it is in America, in both Americas, that Nabokov's influence has flowered most fully. We find handsome acknowledgments of his attraction and importance in the works of the Argentinean Julio Cortázar and the Cuban Guillermo Cabrera Infante, and certain strands of North American fiction, especially those we associate with the novels of Thomas Pynchon and Don DeLillo, have fully absorbed what we might call the truth of paranoia—the chance of truth that hides among its terrible errors.

But it may be that Nabokov's most significant legacy is more diffuse and multiple, and more intimately linguistic and stylistic; something that affects writing itself, as well as individual writers. When he speaks of the "adventures" of a writer's style, Nabokov is reminding us not only how much language matters but also that language has its adventures—indeed, is an adventure. The breakthrough here is the realization that language is not opposed to anything we might call reality or history but a way of understanding them. After an art that turned away from the world in search of its own autonomy—and art has been doing this, in fits and starts, since the late nineteenth century—our most gifted writers seek an art that rediscovers the world through a radical and ruthless revision of it. High formalism and self-consciousness, in Nabokov's hands, prove that realism, the attempted imitation of the world as it seems to be, is often a long way from reality.

Ada as a child has a complex theory of the order of things. "Children of her type," Van says, forgetting for the moment that Ada is not a type at all, "contrive the purest philosophies." She divides her world into

> "real things" which were unfrequent and priceless, simply "things" which formed the routine stuff of life; and "ghost things," also called "fogs," such as fever, toothache, dreadful disappointments, and death.

Neither Ada nor Nabokov would argue that fever or death are unreal in the literal sense; their existence is not being denied. What is denied is their right to triumph over us. Reality, for Ada and Van and Nabokov and all his crazed and gifted heroes, is not just what there is or what resists us, it is the prize of a privileged moment. When reality, in Nabokov, loses the quotation marks it usually wears "like claws," we have not left the world behind, we have encountered one of its old, rare secrets.

## Selected Bibliography

### WORKS OF VLADIMIR NABOKOV

COLLECTED WORKS IN ENGLISH

*The Stories of Vladimir Nabokov*. New York: Knopf, 1995.

*Novels and Memoirs 1941–1951*. New York: Library of America, 1996.

*Novels 1955–1962*. New York: Library of America, 1996.

*Novels 1969–1974*. New York: Library of America, 1996.

NOVELS WRITTEN IN RUSSIAN

*Mary (Mashenka)*. Berlin: Slovo, 1926. English translation, New York: McGraw-Hill, 1970.

*King, Queen, Knave (Korol, dama, valet)*. Berlin: Slovo, 1928. English translation, New York: McGraw-Hill, 1968.

*The Defense (Zashchita Luzhina)*. Berlin: Slovo, 1930. English translation, New York: Putnam, 1964.

*The Eye (Soglyadatay)*. Paris: Sovremennye zapiski, 1930. English translation, New York: Phaedra, 1965.

*Glory (Podvig)*. Paris: Sovremennye zapiski, 1931. English translation, New York: McGraw-Hill, 1971.

*Laughter in the Dark (Kamera obskura)*. Paris: Sovremennye zapiski, 1933. English translation, published as *Camera Obscura*, London: John Long, 1936. New English language edition with author's alterations, Indianapolis: Bobbs-Merrill, 1938.

*Despair (Otchayanie)*. Berlin: Petropolis, 1936. English translation, New York: Putnam, 1966.

*The Gift (Dar)*. Paris: Sovremennye zapiski, 1938 (chapters 1, 2, 3, 5); New York: Chekhov Publishing House, 1952 (complete). English translation, New York: Putnam, 1963.

*Invitation to a Beheading (Priglashenye na kazn)*. Paris: Dom Knigi, 1938. English translation, New York: Putnam, 1959.

*The Enchanter (Volshebnik)*. English translation, New York: Putnam, 1986.

NOVELS WRITTEN IN ENGLISH

*The Real Life of Sebastian Knight*. Norfolk, Conn.: New Directions, 1941.

*Bend Sinister*. New York: Holt, 1947.

*Lolita*. Paris: Olympia Press, 1955; New York: Putnam, 1958. Russian translation by the author, New York: Phaedra, 1967.

*Pnin*. New York: Doubleday, 1957.

*Pale Fire*. New York: Putnam, 1962.

*Ada, or Ardor: A Family Chronicle*. New York: McGraw-Hill, 1969.

*Transparent Things*. New York: McGraw-Hill, 1972.

*Look at the Harlequins*. New York: McGraw-Hill, 1974.

SHORT STORIES

*The Return of Chorb (Vozvrashchenie Chorba).* Berlin: Slovo, 1929.

*Nine Stories.* Norfolk, Conn.: New Directions, 1947.

*Spring in Fialta (Vesna v Fial'te).* New York: Chekhov, 1956.

*Nabokov's Dozen.* Garden City, N.Y.: Doubleday, 1958.

*Nabokov's Quartet.* New York: Phaedra, 1966.

*A Russian Beauty and Other Stories.* New York: McGraw-Hill, 1974.

*Tyrants Destroyed and Other Stories.* New York: McGraw-Hill, 1975.

*Details of a Sunset and Other Stories.* New York: McGraw-Hill, 1976.


POEMS AND PLAYS

*Poems (Stikhi).* St. Petersburg: privately printed, 1916.

*The Empyrean Path (Gornii put').* Berlin: Grani, 1923.

*The Event (Sobytia).* Paris: Russkie zapiski, 1938.

*The Waltz Invention (Izobretenie Wal'sa).* Paris: Russkie zapiski, 1938.

*Poems.* Garden City, N.Y.: Doubleday, 1959.

*Poems and Problems.* New York: McGraw-Hill, 1971.

*Lolita: A Screenplay.* New York: McGraw-Hill, 1974.

*Poems (Stikhi).* Ann Arbor: Ardis, 1979.

*The Man from the USSR and Other Plays.* New York: Harcourt Brace Jovanovich/Bruccoli Clark, 1984.


MEMOIRS, INTERVIEWS, AND LETTERS

*Conclusive Evidence.* New York: Harper, 1951. Revised edition, as *Speak, Memory, An Autobiography Revisited.* New York: Putnam, 1967.

*Strong Opinions.* New York: McGraw-Hill, 1973.

*The Nabokov-Wilson Letters: Correspondence Between Vladimir Nabokov and Edmund Wilson, 1940–1971.* New York: Harper & Row, 1979.

*A Correspondence with His Sister (Perepiska s sestroi).* Ann Arbor: Ardis, 1985.

*Selected Letters, 1940–1977.* San Diego: Harcourt Brace Jovanovich/Bruccoli Clark, 1989.


CRITICISM AND TRANSLATIONS

*Nikolai Gogol.* Norfolk, Conn.: New Directions, 1944.

*Three Russian Poets: Selections from Pushkin, Lermontov, and Tyutchev in New Translations.* Norfolk, Conn.: New Directions, 1944.

*A Hero of Our Time.* Garden City, N.Y.: Doubleday, 1958.

*The Song of Igor's Campaign.* New York: Random House, 1960.

*Eugene Onegin.* Princeton, N.J.: Princeton University Press/Bollingen Foundation, 1964.

*Lectures on Literature.* New York: Harcourt Brace Jovanovich/Bruccoli, 1980.

*Lectures on Russian Literature.* New York: Harcourt Brace Jovanovich/Bruccoli, 1981.

*Lectures on Don Quixote.* San Diego: Harcourt Brace Jovanovich/Bruccoli Clark, 1983.


## BIBLIOGRAPHIES

Alexandrov, Vladimir E. "Bibliography." In *The Garland Companion to Vladimir Nabokov.* New York: Garland, 1995.

Field, Andrew. *Nabokov: A Bibliography.* New York: McGraw-Hill, 1973.

Juliar, Michael. *Vladimir Nabokov: A Descriptive Bibliography.* New York: Garland, 1986.

Schuman, Samuel. *Vladimir Nabokov: A Reference Guide.* Boston: G. K. Hall, 1979.

Zimmer, Dieter E. *Vladimir Nabokov: Bibliographie des Gesamtwerks.* Hamburg: Rowohlt, 1963.

## BIOGRAPHY AND SELECTED CRITICISM

BIOGRAPHY

Boyd, Brian. *Vladimir Nabokov: The Russian Years.* Princeton, N.J.: Princeton University Press, 1990.

———. *Vladimir Nabokov: The American Years.* Princeton, N.J.: Princeton University Press, 1991.

Field, Andrew. *Nabokov: His Life in Part.* New York: Viking, 1977.

———. *VN: The Life and Art of Vladimir Nabokov.* New York: Crown, 1986.

COLLECTIONS OF ESSAYS

Alexandrov, Vladimir E., ed. *The Garland Companion to Vladimir Nabokov.* New York: Garland, 1995.

Appel, Alfred, and Charles Newman, eds. *Nabokov: Criticism, Reminiscences, Translations, and Tributes.* Evanston, Ill.: Northwestern University Press, 1970.

Bloom, Harold, ed. *Vladimir Nabokov.* New York: Chelsea House, 1987.

———. *Vladimir Nabokov's Lolita*. New York: Chelsea House, 1987.

Dembo, L. S., ed. *Nabokov: The Man and His Work*. Madison: University of Wisconsin Press, 1967.

Gibian, George, and Stephen Jan Parker, eds. *The Achievements of Vladimir Nabokov*. Ithaca, N.Y.: Cornell University Press, 1984.

Page, Norman, ed. *Nabokov: The Critical Heritage*. London: Routledge and Kegan Paul, 1982.

Proffer, Carl R., ed. *A Book of Things about Vladimir Nabokov*. Ann Arbor, Mich.: Ardis, 1974.

Quennell, Peter, ed. *Vladimir Nabokov: A Tribute*. New York: Morrow, 1980.

Rivers, J. E., and Charles Nicol, eds. *Nabokov's Fifth Arc: Nabokov and Others on His Life's Work*. Austin: University of Texas Press, 1982.

Roth, Phyllis, ed. *Critical Essays on Vladimir Nabokov*. Boston: G. K. Hall, 1984.

CRITICAL STUDIES

Alexandrov, Vladimir E. *Nabokov's Otherworld*. Princeton, N.J.: Princeton University Press, 1991.

Appel, Alfred. *Nabokov's Dark Cinema*. New York: Oxford University Press, 1974.

Barabtarlo, Gennady. *Aerial View: Essays on Nabokov's Art and Metaphysics*. New York: Peter Lang, 1993.

———. *Phantom of Fact*. Ann Arbor, Mich.: Ardis, 1989.

Beaujour, Elizabeth Klosty. *Alien Tongues: Bilingual Russian Writers of the "First" Emigration*. Ithaca, N.Y.: Cornell University Press, 1989.

Grayson, Jane. *Nabokov Translated: A Comparison of Nabokov's Russian and English Prose*. Oxford: Oxford University Press, 1977.

Hyde, George M. *Vladimir Nabokov: America's Russian Novelist*. London: Marion Boyars, 1977.

Johnson, Donald Barton. *Worlds in Regression: Some Novels of Vladimir Nabokov*. Ann Arbor, Mich.: Ardis, 1985.

Nicol, Charles, and Gennady Barabtarlo. *A Small Alpine Form: Studies in Nabokov's Short Fiction*. New York: Garland, 1993.

Pifer, Ellen. *Nabokov and the Novel*. Cambridge, Mass.: Harvard University Press, 1980.

Proffer, Carl R. *Keys to Lolita*. Bloomington: Indiana University Press, 1968.

Rampton, David. *Vladimir Nabokov: A Critical Study of the Novels*. Cambridge: Cambridge University Press, 1984.

Tammi, Pekka. *Problems of Nabokov's Poetics: A Narratological Analysis*. Helsinki: Suomalainen Tiedeakatemia, 1985.

Toker, Leona. *Nabokov: The Mystery of Literary Structures*. Ithaca, N.Y.: Cornell University Press, 1989.

—MICHAEL WOOD

# *Ezra Pound*
## *1885–1972*

$E$ZRA LOOMIS POUND was born on October 30, 1885, in the frontier mining town of Hailey, Idaho, and died in Venice on November 1, 1972. He was buried in the Protestant cemetery on the nearby island of San Michele, surrounded by the graves of other expatriates who had made Venice their spiritual home. Pound first saw Venice in 1898 while on a European tour, and he returned to the city often, spending most of his last years there. His first book of poems, *A Lume Spento,* was published in Venice in 1908, and some of the most moving passages in *The Pisan Cantos*—written in 1945 while Pound was a prisoner in the U.S. Army's Disciplinary Training Center near Pisa—are formed from memories of the Venice he thought he might never see again. Recalling the Venice of 1908, Pound says: "Things have ends and beginnings."

### AN AMERICAN IN EUROPE

The poetic lives of Pound and T. S. Eliot would appear to follow a classic pattern of expatriation, a return to "beginnings" that antedate the American experience. At the start of their careers they, like Henry James before them, felt keenly the "thinness" and provinciality of American culture. For a young American poet, the first years of this century were especially dispiriting. The generation after Walt Whitman had produced no American poet with a distinctive voice, and the anthologies of the turn of the century are filled with poems written in a weak style one might call "academic romanticism." Looking back on this period many years later, Eliot remembered the irrelevance of contemporary British verse and then added: "There were no American poets at all." If we look at the verses that Pound and Eliot wrote at around the age of eighteen the lack of freshness is striking, although their models are quite different. Pound was, as he remarked later, "drunk with 'Celticism,' " as in this imitation of the early Yeats:

> I have heard a wee wind searching
> Through still forests for me,
> I have seen a wee wind searching
>     O'er still sea.

Eliot's style is more Tennysonian, but equally derivative:

> The flowers I sent thee when the dew
>     Was trembling on the vine
> Were withered ere the wild bee flew
>     To suck the eglantine.

Both Pound and Eliot came to feel that an escape from these stylistic prisons could not be accomplished unless they escaped from the American social and literary scene.

Those contemporaries of Pound and Eliot who chose to remain in America and create a native American modernism often spoke of the expatriates as enemies of this enterprise who had renounced the American inheritance. This was especially true of William Carlos Williams, who felt that the "academic" nature of Pound's early poetry threatened to stifle a more spontaneous American form based on "the local conditions," and who compensated for his own sense of isolation and belatedness by casting Pound and Eliot in the role of cultural traitors. In book 1 of *Paterson* (1946) Williams "envies the men that ran / and could run off / toward the peripheries—," leaving him and his companions to grapple with the task of creating a new poetic idiom out of American speech. The contest he set up between an international style and a native American modernism may have been necessary at the time in order for the young poets to define their aims, but from the perspective of over half a century we can now see that Pound and Eliot were in many ways just as "American" as Williams or Wallace Stevens, and that Williams and Stevens were as "international" as Pound or Eliot.

Pound chose Europe because he felt it offered the cultural stimulation he found lacking in America, but his personality remained quintessentially American throughout his life. Even the tragic and perhaps unforgivable errors of his later years were committed in the name of America. From his early essay on American literature and society called "Patria mia" (1912)—later revised for a book with the same title—through the autobiographical writing of *Indiscretions* (1923) to the American history cantos, Pound remained an American abroad, a man of only one country. The first section of the book *Patria Mia* (1950) opens with "America, my country" and ends:

If a man's work require him to live in exile, let him suffer, or enjoy, his exile gladly. But it would be about as easy for an American to become a Chinaman or a Hindoo as for him to acquire an Englishness, or a Frenchness, or a European-ness that is more than half a skin deep.

Pound resembles in many ways the great nineteenth-century poets who believed they had a social as well as a literary mission. His mission was "to drive Whitman into the old world . . . and to scourge America with all the old beauty."

Eliot's "Americanness" is less obvious, but no less profound. Pound makes this argument in a 1920 exchange with Williams, where he shrewdly turns the tables by saying that Williams is the newly arrived "outsider" who is objective enough to survive the American environment, while he and Eliot are so deeply infected with the American virus ("Eliot has it perhaps worse than I have—poor devil") that they must "fight the disease day and night." While Pound remained to the end a rambunctious American abroad, Eliot assimilated British culture until he became superficially an Englishman. He chose British citizenship in 1927, and it is said that he valued the Order of Merit conferred upon him by the Crown in 1948 (the highest civilian award for a British subject) more than the Nobel Prize he received that same year—possibly because Henry James had also belonged to the Order. But Eliot knew that he was, at he once said of James, "everywhere a foreigner," and just as he believed that no one but an American "can *properly* appreciate James" so no one can properly appreciate Pound without understanding those deep attachments to the American landscape and the American past that are the imaginative sources of much of his best work.

ORIGINS AND EDUCATION

Ezra Pound's father, Homer Loomis Pound, was the son of Thaddeus Coleman Pound, a prominent

Wisconsin businessman who once served as lieutenant governor of the state. Shortly before moving to Idaho, where he was register of the U.S. Land Office, he had married Isabel Weston of New York City. When Ezra Pound was two years old the family returned to the east coast, and in 1889 Homer Pound was appointed assistant assayer of the U.S. Mint in Philadelphia. Ezra Pound attended local schools and in 1901 entered the University of Pennsylvania, where a year later he met William Carlos Williams, a fellow student who was to become his closest "poet friend." In 1903 Pound transferred to Hamilton College, where he studied Romance languages and began work on some of the poems later published in *A Lume Spento*. While at Hamilton he read Thomas Lovell Beddoes's *Death's Jest-Book* (1850) and marked the following passage, which he would recall forty years later in *The Pisan Cantos*.

I utter
Shadows of words, like to an ancient ghost,
Arisen out of hoary centuries,
Where none can speak his language . . .

Pound's lifelong project was to translate into the modern world the speech of ancient ghosts, and it may have been at Hamilton that he first conceived the idea of a long poem "including history."

In 1905 Pound returned to the University of Pennsylvania to begin graduate work in Romance languages, and it was at this time that he met Hilda Doolittle ("H. D.") who would later join him as a member of the imagist movement: the effort among a group of English and American poets (1912–1917) to cast off contemporary, "sentimental" poetic conventions and create a precise new form of free verse. After receiving an M.A. in 1906 Pound spent the summer in Europe pursuing research on the Spanish playwright Lope de Vega (1562–1635), but when he returned to the University of Pennsylvania he found that he was more and more at odds with the narrow tests and philological interests of his teachers. In the sum-

mer of 1907 he abandoned graduate work and took up a teaching position at Wabash College in Crawfordsville, Indiana, where he soon began to think of himself as an "exile." The opening lines of "In Durance," written at this time, sum up his feelings:

I am homesick after mine own kind,
Oh I know that there are folk about me,
    friendly faces,
But I am homesick after mine own kind.

After a few months at Wabash his "Latin Quarter" behavior (which included befriending a stranded actress) led to his dismissal, and in early 1908 he sailed for Europe where after a summer in Venice he settled in London. A second volume of poetry, *A Quinzaine for This Yule*, was published in December 1908, and in the same month there appeared an announcement that a "Short Introductory Course on the Development of the Literature of Southern Europe" would be given at the London Polytechnic in early 1909 by Ezra Pound, M.A. At last Pound felt that he had found a congenial place in which to live and write, and he soon formed a productive friendship with William Butler Yeats, "the only living man whose work has more than a most temporary interest." "Am by way of falling into the crowd that does things here," he wrote to his friend Williams, "London, deah old Lundon, is the place for poesy."

In spite of his great admiration for Yeats, Pound knew that in order to become a modern poet he would have to cast off the influence of the Yeats of the 1890s, which had made so many of his early poems shadowy and diffuse. The story of Pound's remarkable poetic development from 1908 to 1914 is one of a struggle toward clarity, precision, and a direct conversational diction, and he was delighted to discover that Yeats was also moving in that direction. But the process was not an easy one, and many of the poems in Pound's first important volume, *Personae* (1909), did not survive in *Personae: The Collected Poems* (first published in 1926). Ironically, one of these casualties is entitled "Revolt, against the Crepuscular Spirit in Modern Poetry," which fails because the attack on "twilight" poetry is made in a diction equally outmoded. A brief excerpt will illustrate the point:

No! if we dream pale flowers,
Slow-moving pageantry of hours that languidly
Drop as o'er-ripened fruit from sallow trees.
If so we live and die not life but dreams,
Great God, grant life in dreams,
Not dalliance, but life!

In the poems Pound wrote before 1912 we find many of the ideas that inform his entire poetic career, but they are seldom expressed in language that would satisfy his post-1912 standards.

One of these ideas is that the modern poet can, from time to time, recapture the vitality of ancient myths, since the gods are still with us. "The Tree" (1908) begins "I stood still and was a tree amid the wood," and it is typical of Pound that he does not use a simile, suggesting that metamorphosis is still possible and that the modern poet can experience it and make us feel it. I am sure Pound did not retain this poem as the program piece of *Personae: The Collected Poems* (1926) out of admiration for its style, but rather because it was his best early statement of a belief that would guide his entire poetic life. Related to this belief is Pound's notion of personae or masks: the contemporary poet can sustain a dialogue between past and present by speaking through various personalities drawn from history or legend. A rudimentary example of this method is "Villonaud for This Yule" (1908), in which Pound speaks with the voice of the fifteenth-century poet François Villon (using Villon's favorite ballade form) but in a manner that reflects his own contemporary situation. Furthermore, the refrain of the poem ("Wining the ghosts of yester-year") is adapted from the refrain of Dante Gabriel Rossetti's famous nineteenth-century version of Villon's "The Ballad of Dead Ladies" ("But where are the snows of yesteryear?"); thus the poem plays off the experiences of Villon against those of Rossetti and those of Pound. This method of composition culminates years later in Canto 1, in which Pound retells the story of Odysseus' descent into hell (from book 11 of the *Odyssey*); Pound's version synthesizes the compressed narrative form of a Renaissance Latin translation with a style drawn from Anglo-Saxon epic verse. This fusion allows us to view the problems of the modern poet, a type of Odysseus, from a complicated historical and literary perspective.

Pound's obsession with the literary past, his desire to revive ancient ghosts and their languages, lies at the center of both his early poetry and his early criticism, and for a time it seemed as if the "archaeological" impulse might smother his drive to "Make It New." Although in the preface to his first volume of criticism, *The Spirit of Romance* (1910), Pound had anticipated the argument of Eliot's "Tradition and the Individual Talent" (1919) with his declaration that "all ages are contemporaneous" and his call for a literary criticism that will "weigh Theocritus and Yeats with one balance," in the book itself his fresh perceptions are often obscured by the language and methods of conventional scholarship. A similar difficulty is evident in *Canzoni* (1911), which is in many ways the most remote of all Pound's volumes, partly because at the last minute he succumbed to "hyperaesthesia or over squeamishness and cut out the rougher poems" about modern subjects. *Canzoni* is filled with examples of the stilted language that Pound would soon leave behind, partly due to the influence of the novelist Ford Madox Hueffer (later Ford) who insisted that poetry should have the economy and precision of the best modern prose. When Ford read *Canzoni* he literally rolled on the floor in helpless laughter, and according to Pound this therapeutic roll "saved me at least two years, perhaps more. It sent me back to my own proper effort, namely, toward using the living tongue (with younger men after me) though none of us has found a more natural language than Ford did." Pound's motto soon became "Poetry must be *as well written as prose,*" by which he meant the prose of Flaubert and James Joyce. It must depart "in no way from speech save by a heightened intensity (i.e. simplicity)."

CRITICISM AND IMAGISM

A drive toward a more contemporary speech and attitude was first evident in Pound's criticism. In 1911–1912 he published in the British Journal *New Age* a series of essays called "I Gather the Limbs of Osiris" in which he discussed the need to identify the essential "virtue" of a writer or literary period and to translate that "virtue" into contemporary experience. The format of "I Gather the Limbs of Osiris" blends discursive commentary with poetic demonstrations, and its center of gravity is Pound's splendid rendering of the Anglo-Saxon "Seafarer," a work that although imitative of an antiquated style has the urgency and intensity of a contemporary poem:

No man at all going the earth's gait,
But age fares against him, his face paleth,
Grey-haired he groaneth, knows gone companions,
Lordly men, are to earth o'ergiven,
Nor may he then the flesh-cover, whose life
  ceaseth,
Nor eat the sweet nor feel the sorry,
Nor stir hand nor think in mid heart,
And though he strew the grave with gold,
His born brothers, their buried bodies
Be an unlikely treasure hoard.

Translation for Pound is a dynamic act, a vital transaction between past and present in which both are affected. Robert Frost once remarked that "poetry is what is lost in translation." Pound believed just the opposite: he wished to discover "what part of poetry was 'indestructible,' what part could *not be* lost by translation."

As the form and substance of "I Gather the Limbs of Osiris" demonstrates, Pound believed that criticism and poetic creativity are inseparable. In a later essay he divided criticism into five "kinds," listing them in ascending order of importance. The first is "criticism by discussion," ranging from occasional reviewing of specific works to the formulation of general principles—everything we normally think of as literary criticism. This category would include Pound's thousands of reviews and essays and his vast correspondence, all of which has to be read against the background of contemporary literary needs as Pound saw them. The second category is "criticism by translation," and under this heading would come not only "The Seafarer" but all Pound's adaptations from Chinese and Latin designed to interpret one culture to another. The third, "criticism by exercise in the style of a given period," reflects Pound's belief that the final test of a poet is his ability to recognize and re-create traditional styles. Pound's major poems are a museum of re-created styles, and these imitations are essential means for renewing the past and defining the present. The fourth kind, "criticism via music," indicates the importance Pound attached to what he called "melopoeia," the music within words that directs their meaning. Whatever one may think of Pound's excursions into musical theory and composition (he wrote two operas, *The Testament of François Villon* in 1923 and *Cavalcanti* in 1932), these efforts were a form of criticism. Finally, the fifth and highest form of critical activity is "criticism in new composition." All Pound's major works fall under this heading, since everything he wrote was a form of creative criticism. The belief that it should be often lead Pound to adopt a pedagogic or hectoring tone in his writing; in his later career his critical impulse took monstrous shapes. But his critical views were also the source of the extraordinary unity that marks his poetic work.

Pound's talents as a poet-critic are on full display in the public and private history of the imagist movement. *Ripostes* (1912) is a transitional volume, containing some poems that would not be out of place in *Canzoni* but others that bear the unmistakable stamp of what we now call modernism. The conversational, direct syntax of "Portrait d'une Femme" and the lovely free cadences of "The Return" (which Yeats praised for its "organic rhythm") give *Ripostes* a distinctive voice lacking in Pound's earlier volumes:

> Great minds have sought you—lacking someone
>   else.
> You have been second always. Tragical?
> No. You preferred it to the usual thing:
> One dull man, dulling and uxorious,
> One average mind—with one thought less, each
>   year.
> Oh, you are patient, I have seen you sit
> Hours, where something might have floated up.
> And you pay one. Yes, you richly pay.
>
> ("Portrait d'une Femme")

> See, they return, one, and by one,
> With fear, as half-awakened;
> As if the snow should hesitate
> And murmur in the wind,
>               and half turn back;
> These were the "Wing'd-with-Awe,"
>               Inviolable.
>
> ("The Return")

In the appendix he announced that a new school of poets, *les imagistes,* had the future "in their keeping." This "school" was actually invented by Pound to publicize his new poetry and that of his friend Hilda Doolittle. When she submitted a group of her finely chiseled poems to *Poetry* magazine, which had recently named Pound "foreign correspondent," he insisted that she sign them "H. D., *Imagiste,* and, two months after they appeared in the January 1913 issue of *Poetry,* Pound followed with the essays "Imagisme" and "A Few Don'ts by an Imagiste" that sought to give the movement a theoretical underpinning. The slogans and rules laid out in these essays were to have a profound impact on the course of twentieth-century poetry.

1. Direct treatment of the "thing," whether subjective or objective.
2. To use absolutely no word that [does] not contribute to the presentation.
3. As regarding rhythm: to compose in sequence of the musical phrase, not in sequence of a metronome.

Imagism and its descendent vorticism were, like most critical theories, post facto explanations of tendencies already well developed in practice. This is clear in Pound's two descriptions of how he came to write his famous imagist poem "In a Station of the Metro":

> The apparition of these faces in the crowd;
> Petals on a wet, black bough.

The first account in June 1913 is a matter-of-fact history of how an intense visual experience was transformed into something resembling a Japanese haiku; the second and much longer account in the "Vorticism" essay of September 1914 provides an elaborate theory of the "one image poem."

Pound's interest in imagism culminated in 1914 with the publication of his anthology *Des Imagistes.* After that the movement became "popular," a negative development for a poet who under Yeats's influence was rapidly developing the notion that great art belongs to a chosen few. When the American poet Amy Lowell became the leading theorist of the movement, Pound labeled the diluted form "Amygism" and turned to other causes. But imagism had a lasting impact on his poetic language, as it did on Williams' and Stevens', and also on Pound's sense of the poet's mission. From the beginning of his career Pound had believed that the poet is the interpreter of the mystical forms that lie behind the physical world. Imagism gave Pound a way to ground this neo-Platonic belief in specific and concrete language, in the "luminous detail."

### THE INFLUENCE OF CHINESE POETRY

Imagism was, however, only one aspect of Pound's immensely energetic poetic life in the years 1912 to 1915. Scanning the contents of *Lustra* (1916) one is struck by the topicality of many of Pound's subjects, his engagement—usually satiric—with contemporary social and intellectual life. Also prominent is a new interest in Chinese poetry, which was brought into focus in late 1913 when the widow of Ernest Fenollosa, the pioneering American orientalist, entrusted her husband's literary manuscripts to Pound. She had met Pound and read some of his poetry, and she must have felt that his new style was ideally suited to the works her husband had studied. In Fenollosa's analysis of the Chinese ideogram Pound found not only support for his new belief in the power of the concrete particular but also a method for organizing images into larger patterns through juxtaposition. This method offered him the possibility of writing "a long imagiste or vorticist poem" that would exclude the transitional passages of lesser intensity usually found in the traditional long poem. Pound was impressed by the Japanese Noh plays, which are often organized around a single image "enforced by movement and music," and he began to translate Noh drama. He also began to translate Chinese poetry, using the notes Fenollosa had obtained from Japanese masters, and in 1915 collected his translations in *Cathay.* Many of the poems in *Cathay* have war, exile, and isolation as their themes and are oblique commentaries on World War I that threatened to destroy both the old social order and the "new Renaissance" in the arts.

In his introduction to Pound's 1928 *Selected Poems* T. S. Eliot called Pound "the inventor of Chinese poetry for our time," a phrase which implies that every age re-creates the past through its translations and that Pound had a special affinity for Chinese even before he mastered the rudiments of the language. When we compare a translation made by an early twentieth-century scholar, H. A. Giles, with Pound's version of the same poem (probably done before he received the Fenollosa materials), Eliot's point becomes clear.

> The sound of rustling silk is stilled,
> With dust the marble courtyard filled;
> No footfalls echo on the floor,
> Fallen leaves in heaps block up the door . . .
> For she, my pride, my lovely one, is lost,
> And I am left, in hopeless anguish tossed. (Giles)

> The rustling of the silk is discontinued,
> Dust drifts over the court-yard,
> There is no sound of foot-fall, and the leaves
> Scurry into heaps and lie still,
> And she the rejoicer of the heart is beneath them:

> A wet leaf that clings to the threshold. (Pound)

Giles's translation is a weak poem cast in the "period" style that Pound had finally purged from his own writing; it gives no sense of the original. Pound's free version, with its direct diction, its startling but precise use of the "unpoetic" word "discontinued," and its imagist closure, re-creates the sensibility of another culture. When we compare poems such as this with Pound's verses of five years before we get some measure of how far he had to travel in order to make himself into a modern poet.

### HUGH SELWYN MAUBERLEY

Two poems in *Lustra,* "Provincia deserta" and "Near Perigord," are tokens of Pound's continuing desire to write longer poems "including history." Narrative in development, they combine autobiography with a sense that the world of the Provençal troubadours can still be re-created out of the present-day landscape. This approach was employed at greater length in the original Cantos

1–3 (1917), which were later radically revised and rearranged, with the rendering of Odysseus' descent into hell moved from the third to the first canto. "Ghosts move about me / Patched with histories" might be the motto for these early cantos, where Pound rehearses the literary and personal experiences that had shaped his art. But if the subjects of *Three Cantos* point forward to his later work, the form is disconcertingly loose and Browningesque, making the cantos look curiously old-fashioned in comparison with the poems in *Lustra*. Between 1917 and his departure from London in 1920 Pound continued to draft further cantos, but much of his energy went into *Homage to Sextus Propertius* (1919), a free "translation" of the Latin poet's elegies in which Pound uses Propertius as a persona for expressing his own growing dissatisfaction with the society around him, and into *Hugh Selwyn Mauberley* (1920), his "farewell to London." Later Pound would draw on the lessons he learned in writing these poems when he virtually collaborated with Eliot on the rewriting of *The Waste Land*.

When we look at the poetic development of Pound between roughly 1915 and 1920, one of the most striking aspects is the thickening of conscious, orchestrated allusions. In his September 1918 "A Note on Ezra Pound" Eliot reflects on the method; he has been discussing the fusion of past and present, of literary, historical, and personal references, in Pound's "Near Perigord."

> This effect is all the more peculiar because of the deliberateness. James Joyce, another very learned literary artist, uses allusions suddenly and with great speed, part of the effect being the extent of the vista opened to the imagination by the very lightest touch. Pound's recent unfinished epic, three cantos of which appear in the American edition of "Lustra," proceeds by a very different method than that of Joyce in "Ulysses." In appearance, it is a rag-bag of Mr. Pound's reading in various languages, from which one fragment after another is dragged to light, and illuminated by the beauty of his phrase.... [There is] apparently no continuity. And yet the

thing has, after one has read it once or twice, a positive coherence; it is an objective and reticent autobiography.

*Hugh Selwyn Mauberley* falls into two parts: the longer first part is a series of related short poems that brilliantly dramatizes the plight of the Odyssean artist in the modern world and also traces the origins of the cultural attitudes that led to World War I and its aftermath. The second part, "Mauberley 1920," is a crisp and ironic commentary on the forms and themes of the first part. The opening poems of *Hugh Selwyn Mauberley* present a world in which the aggressive side of Pound's personality, "E. P.," can no longer function as it had in the hospitable prewar London. "Mauberley 1920" develops an alternative persona, Hugh Selwyn Mauberley, who embodies Pound's fears of what he might become if he remained in England as an isolated stylist. If E. P. is a thwarted Odysseus then Mauberley is a modern counterpart to Elpenor, Homer's man of "no fortune," who dies by accident and is left unburied (*The Odyssey,* book 10). At the most immediate level *Hugh Selwyn Mauberley* is, as Eliot later said, "the experience of a certain man in a certain place at a certain time," and paradoxically it is this deep engagement with the contemporary scene that gives the poem its lasting power. But *Mauberley,* like Yeats's "The Second Coming" and Eliot's "Gerontion," is also a more general expression of the historical moment, of postwar disillusionment, while on yet another plane it is a delicate reading of literary history from the Pre-Raphaelites (a mid-nineteenth-century group of English artists that aimed at a simple, "truthful" style) through the poets of the 1890s to the present. All these diverse interests reinforce each other in a work where every detail of rhythm and imagery seems exactly right. *Hugh Selwyn Mauberley* is an enduring monument to all that Pound achieved during his London years.

Pound's notions are brought into sharp focus

when we examine the manuscript of Eliot's *The Waste Land,* which was "lost" for many years but rediscovered and published in 1971. Reaching back to "The Death of St. Narcissus," a poem Eliot wrote sometime around 1914 but suppressed in proof, the false starts in the manuscript provide a record of Eliot's spiritual and psychological anguish during the early London years. In late 1921, while recuperating from a physical and nervous breakdown, Eliot began work on his long poem in earnest, piecing together some of the earlier fragments and writing new passages, sometimes in an almost trancelike state. He then turned to Pound for the kind of "editorial" help he had already provided with Eliot's *Poems* (1920); Pound's extensive cutting and revising of *The Waste Land* earned him the poem's dedication, which describes him as *il miglior fabbro,* "the better craftsman." It is a sign of Pound's genius that he saw the formal possibilities in Eliot's loose sequence. Under his hand the poem was transformed from a series of narrative and dramatic episodes into a "cinematographic" montage of images and incidents that is unified by a presiding sensibility. Whether we look at Pound's large structural changes or at his work on the details of language, we see the practical result of his long struggle to forge a modern idiom.

The tendency before the publication of *The Waste Land* manuscript was to read the poem as a magisterial critique of modern society; since the 1970s, with new evidence before them, critics have emphasized the poem's personal and lyric qualities. As with *Mauberley,* both types of readings are valid and reinforce each other. We might say that *The Waste Land* began as a personal confession and ended as a text for its time. Earlier critics, influenced by Eliot's comments on the "mythic method" in *Ulysses* (1920), stressed the importance of the Grail legend as a controlling point of reference; many readers in the 1990s would find Eliot's exact allusions to the topography of London just as important, since they enable him to intensify the power of the hallucinatory scenes by placing them against a familiar landscape. Reacting against the initial cry that Eliot was a poetic "Bolshevik" who had destroyed the tradition, Eliot's first defenders may have overstressed the poem's order and mythic unity while neglecting the distinctive voice that holds *The Waste Land* together. When Virginia Woolf heard Eliot read the poem in late 1922 she said that she had not yet "tackled the sense": "I have only the sound of it in my ears. . . . But I like the sound." Anyone who has heard Eliot's masterful reading of the poem will know that all the variations in tone and voice (many suggested by Pound) come from a single personality.

### THE MOVE TO ITALY

In the biographical sketch that Pound provided for his 1957 *Selected Poems* we find this entry: "1918 began investigation of causes of war, to oppose same." World War I was the decisive trauma in Pound's personal and poetic life. Some of his closest friends died in the trenches, most notably the philosopher T. E. Hulme and the young sculptor Henri Gaudier-Brzeska ("and they killed him, / And killed a good deal of sculpture" Pound lamented in Canto 16). These deaths became for Pound symbols of all the other disasters of the war, which had by 1919–1920, as *Mauberley* testifies, made him a marginal figure in London. In a sense, all Pound's later economic and political obsessions, including his anti-Semitism, date from this time. His prewar writings are remarkably free of the easy prejudices of his generation, but in the war elegies of *Mauberley* lines such as "usury age-old and age-thick / and liars in public places" foreshadow the future.

From 1921 until 1924 Pound lived in Paris, where he tried to play the same role of instigator and literary entrepreneur that he had brilliantly performed in the London of 1912–1918, when he helped to launch the careers of Frost, Eliot, Wyndham Lewis, and Joyce. The Paris years were exciting ones for Pound, including his discovery of Ernest Hemingway and work with artists such as Constantin Brancusi and Fernand Léger, but in 1924 Pound moved to Rapallo, and Italy was to be his home for the rest of his life. He may have left Paris because he once again felt "marginal," but *A Draft of XVI Cantos* (1930) shows that he was also lured by a growing interest in Italian art and history. Among the many subjects of these cantos—the myths of metamorphosis, the Odyssean journey, Confucian ethics—was the career of the Renaissance prince Sigismundo Malatesta (1417–1468), who in the midst of economic and historical chaos built the great Tempio in Rimini. With its interlacing of pagan, Christian, and humanist motifs, the Tempio might almost be a model for *The Cantos;* Pound admired Sigismundo as an "entire man" who, like Thomas Jefferson or Benito Mussolini, could impose his vision on history. (In 1935 Pound published a book called *Jefferson and/or Mussolini.*) Understandable as his admiration for Sigismundo might have been at the time, in the light of Pound's later support of fascism it strikes an ominous note.

George Kearns, in his *Guide to Ezra Pound's 'Selected Cantos,'* has argued that Canto IV opens with an "ideogram" of Pound's themes. Juxtaposition has replaced the narrative transitions of conventional poetry.

> *Destruction of a City* (Troy)
> *Anaxiforminges*
> (Poetry/Music)      *Aurunculeia*
> (Fertility, Love)
>
> *Foundation of a City* (Thebes)

The canto begins and ends amid the fallen stones of civilizations: Troy and its successor, Rome. From the image of the smoldering boundary stones (Odysseus has just departed after having sacked Troy's holy citadel), the canto moves through a series of vivid scenes at which we have the illusion of being present, until, in the last lines, we suddenly find ourselves removed watchers in an age that no longer supports such passionate, if sometimes destructive, encounters with gods.

### THE CANTOS

Pound's life in Italy from 1925 until 1945 is a history of the writing of *The Cantos;* all his other prolific literary, economic, and social writings were adjuncts to this enterprise. *A Draft of XXX Cantos* (1930) reflects his growing concern with modern avarice and usury, which is contrasted with the savage splendors of the Renaissance and the natural order celebrated in pagan myths and Chinese philosophy. In Cantos 31–41 Pound turns to American history, tracing Jefferson's and John Adams' original vision of a national bank and Martin Van Buren's opposition to it. *The Fifth Decad of Cantos* (1937) continues the argument against modern exploitive economics, and at its center we find Canto 45, Pound's magnificent denunciation of USURA as that which thwarts all natural processes.

> With usura hath no man a house of
>       good stone
>          each block cut smooth and well
>             fitting
> that design might cover their face,
> with usura
> hath no man a painted paradise on his church
>    wall . . .
> with usura the line grows thick
> with usura is no clear demarcation
> and no man can find site for his dwelling.

Pound believed that clarity and precision in life or art depend on a "clean" economy, and in the Old Testament measures of Canto 45 this conviction rings with ancient authority. But as the nature of European fascism became clear to others after Italy's invasion of Abyssinia and after the Spanish Civil War, Pound began to lose touch with the reality behind Mussolini's "dream." The Chinese and John Adams cantos of the late 1930s reflect Pound's growing disorientation, and during World War II Pound made hundreds of broadcasts over Rome Radio attacking the Allies and the economic conspiracy which, he thought, had caused another war. In 1945 he was arrested by the U.S. Army and spent nearly six months in the detention center at Pisa, confined for part of the time in a steel cage. He suffered a mental collapse, and when he was flown back to the United States to be tried for treason he was declared "mentally unfit for trial" and remanded to St. Elizabeths hospital for the insane in Washington, D.C. Pound lived in St. Elizabeths for twelve years, reading, writing, and receiving a host of visitors who ranged from famous writers to right-wing fanatics. In 1958 his friends finally obtained a release order and he returned to Italy, where he spent most of his remaining years in penitential silence.

## FINAL POEMS

During the time at Pisa and St. Elizabeths Pound continued to work on his long poem. *The Pisan Cantos* (Cantos 74–84) appeared in 1948, and when Pound received the Bollingen Prize for this work the controversy surrounding his imprisonment intensified. *Rock-Drill* (85–95) was published in 1955, followed by *Thrones* (96–109) in 1959 and *Drafts & Fragments* (110–117) in 1969. The poetry of *Rock-Drill* and *Thrones,* written out of the relative isolation of St. Elizabeths, often harks back to the attitudes of the 1930s. But *The Pisan Cantos* and *Drafts & Fragments* are filled with moving passages of great poetry that medi-

tate on the tragic arc of Pound's poetic life. The most famous of these occurs in Canto 81:

> The ant's a centaur in his dragon world.
> Pull down thy vanity, it is not man
> Made courage, or made order, or made grace,
>     Pull down thy vanity, I say pull down.

Yet at the end of this self-accusatory chant Pound recalls, as we must, the great accomplishments that make the word "tragic" possible:

> But to have done instead of not doing
>         this is not vanity . . .
>             To have gathered from the air a live
>                 tradition
> or from a fine old eye the unconquered flame
> This is not vanity
>         Here error is all in the not done,
> All in the diffidence that faltered . . .

The question that every reader of *The Cantos* must ask is the one that Pound himself repeats throughout *Drafts & Fragments:* Does it cohere? Pound has no doubt that the ideal world behind appearances "coheres all right," yet he is keenly aware that his own vision flares "fitfully and by instants." From the beginning of his work on his long poem he had called its sections "drafts," and in the last cantos he speaks of "my notes," "a tangle of works," a "palimpsest." Along the way Pound had thought of his poem as a fresco of many scenes, a fugue of intertwined melodies, an arena in which the drama of past and present is enacted. But in the end it turned out to be a personal voyage "as the wind veers," a record of the richest and most complex poetic life this century has witnessed. As Michael Alexander has said in *The Poetic Achievement of Ezra Pound* (1979): "For all their wrong-headed politics and confusing form," *The Cantos* "present simultaneously an heroic imaginative openness to actual living and to nature" and an access to "certain cultural possibilities that cannot be reproduced."

# Selected Bibliography

## WORKS OF EZRA POUND

*The Spirit of Romance.* 1910. Reprint. Norfolk, Conn.: New Directions, 1953.

*The Cantos.* 1917–1970. New York: New Directions, 1995. (Includes *The Pisan Cantos,* 1948; *Rock-Drill,* 1955; *Thrones,* 1959; and *Drafts & Fragments of Cantos* CX–CXVII, 1969.)

*ABC of Reading.* 1934. Reprint. New York: New Directions, 1960.

*Guide to Kulchur.* 1938. Reprint. Norfolk, Conn.: New Directions, 1952.

*The Letters of Ezra Pound, 1907–1941.* Edited by D. D. Paige. New York: Harcourt, Brace, 1950.

*Literary Essays of Ezra Pound.* Edited by T. S. Eliot. Norfolk, Conn.: New Directions, 1954.

*Selected Prose, 1909–1965.* Edited by William Cookson. New York: New Directions, 1973. (Includes "I Gather the Limbs of Osiris.")

*Personae: The Shorter Poems of Ezra Pound.* Edited by Lea Baechler and A. Walton Litz. New York: New Directions, 1990.

*Ezra Pound's Poetry and Prose: Contributions to Periodicals.* 11 vols. Edited by Lea Baechler, A. Walton Litz, and James Longenbach. New York: Garland, 1991. (Reprints items listed in Section C of Donald Gallup's 1983 bibliography.)

## CRITICAL AND BIOGRAPHICAL STUDIES

Alexander, Michael. *The Poetic Achievement of Ezra Pound.* London: Faber and Faber, 1979.

Bell, Ian F. A. *Critic as Scientist: The Modernist Poetics of Ezra Pound.* London: Methuen, 1981.

Carpenter, Humphrey. *A Serious Character: The Life of Ezra Pound.* London: Faber, 1988.

Gallup, Donald. *Ezra Pound: A Bibliography.* Charlottesville: University of Virginia Press, 1983.

Stock, Noel. *The Life of Ezra Pound.* New York: Pantheon, 1970.

Wellek, René. "Ezra Pound (1885–1972)." In Vol. 5 of his *A History of Modern Criticism: 1750–1950,* 152–169. New Haven: Yale University Press, 1986.

—A. WALTON LITZ

# *Wallace Stevens*
## *1879–1955*

WALLACE STEVENS WAS born in Reading, Pennsylvania, on October 2, 1879, the child of Garrett Barcalow Stevens and Margaretha Catherine Zeller Stevens. Garrett Stevens was a lawyer and a small businessman who attempted to provide the best possible education for his sons. After graduating from Reading Boys' High School in 1897, Wallace Stevens attended Harvard College as a special student. Although he did not take classes with either of the two famous philosophers, William James and George Santayana, Stevens' sensibility was shaped profoundly by James's "will to believe," the notion that human beliefs are profoundly useful though not necessarily true. Stevens came to know Santayana personally and actually exchanged sonnets with him: throughout Stevens' life, Santayana would epitomize both the wonder and the danger of a single-minded devotion to aesthetic concerns. Stevens' contributions to the *Harvard Advocate,* of which he became president, included not only fanciful lyric poems ("Where is the maid on the road in her gig, / And where is the fire-side cat?") but sternly practical essays, one of them called "Political Interests." In it the young Stevens wrote, "If there is one thing more desirable to our present relation to politics than another, it is that we should be informed openly and candidly just what the various parties stand for and how they run."

Stevens moved to New York City in 1900, where he attempted to make a living as a newspaper reporter. He covered the McKinley–Bryan election for the *New York Tribune* and worked briefly as an assistant editor for *World's Work,* a monthly magazine. But the work was neither emotionally fulfilling nor financially rewarding. The question Stevens asked in a journal entry for 1900 would echo throughout his career: "Is literature really a profession?" After a few months Stevens wrote to his father, saying that he planned to give up journalism and devote himself to the "literary life" full-time. Garrett Stevens returned the letter torn to pieces.

Acquiescing to his father's wishes, Stevens enrolled in New York Law School; he graduated in the spring of 1903. For the next five years he was employed by a variety of firms but found law no more satisfying than journalism had been. "Working savagely," wrote Stevens in his journal, "but have been so desperately poor at times as not to be able to buy sufficient food." Understandably, Stevens' interest in a "literary life" dwindled away. In 1908, after joining the American Bonding Company (the first of several insurance firms for which he would work), Stevens did write a small collection of poems for his fiancée, Elsie

Kachel. But by and large Stevens gave up writing poetry altogether. Because his parents disapproved of his relationship with Elsie, Stevens could not count on them for support, and his financial worries were not completely dissipated until 1914, when he was hired as a vice president of the New York office of the Equitable Surety Company of St. Louis. Two years later he would move to the Hartford Accident and Indemnity Company, where he would be employed until his death from cancer on August 2, 1955. His only daughter, Holly, was born in Hartford in 1924. After becoming a vice president of the Hartford Accident and Indemnity Company ten years later, Stevens was able to maintain a comfortable and sometimes extravagant suburban lifestyle for his family, even during the lean years of the Great Depression.

James Merrill once said that the poet Elizabeth Bishop sustained a lifelong impersonation of an ordinary human being; the same thing could be said about Stevens, except that one feels that his ordinariness was in no way an act. As I have told the story of Stevens' life so far, it sounds like a life that might have been lived by any number of young men who attended Harvard at the turn of the century, nursed halfhearted literary ambitions, and became successful businessmen. The fact that Stevens also went on to become one of the greatest poets of the twentieth century is not in itself remarkable; few poets make a living as poets, and just as T. S. Eliot worked as a banker and William Carlos Williams worked as a doctor, Stevens worked as an insurance lawyer. What distinguishes Stevens is that after 1914 he never gave the impression of feeling any tension between the different aspects of his life. His first relatively mature poems were published in 1914, and his first masterpiece, "Sunday Morning," appeared as if from nowhere the following year. After his first book of poems, *Harmonium,* was published in 1923, Stevens stopped writing poems again for almost a decade, and his letters never suggest that he felt any anxiety about his silence. *Ideas of Order* appeared in 1935, and it would be followed by five more major collections (and several small press editions), culminating in the *Collected Poems* of 1954. Stevens would receive virtually every honor that could be bestowed on an American poet, including the National Book Award and the Pulitzer Prize for the *Collected Poems* in 1955. But he continued to work at the Hartford Accident and Indemnity Company even after he passed the mandatory age of retirement.

Stevens once quipped that "money is a kind of poetry," but he more often emphasized that his daily life was in no meaningful way poetic. In "Surety and Fidelity Claims" (1938) he took pains to emphasize that his work was above all tedious: "You sign a lot of drafts. You see surprisingly few people. You do the greater part of your work either in your own office or in lawyers' offices. You don't even see the country; you see law offices and hotel rooms." Stevens embraced tedium—the world of what he called the "ordinary," the "normal," or the "humdrum": in order to write poems at all, he needed to feel that his most fanciful poetic flights were balanced by a clear, no-nonsense engagement with the ordinary world. Stevens could not write poems if he felt that the writing made him irresponsibly extravagant; his deepest desires always needed to be checked and balanced by denial. Neither could he remain content with a life so humdrum that it left no room for extravagance at all. Stevens spent his entire adult life reading about exotic places, buying exotic foods from Ceylon and exquisite paintings from France. But he never once visited Europe. Even Williams (a staunch advocate of American culture and writing) spent long periods of time abroad. Especially since most successful businessmen do travel, Stevens' disinclination to do so suggests that he needed to keep his pleasures at arm's length. Depending on how we look at him, Stevens can seem like the most worldly or the most otherworldly of the moderns.


## EXTRAORDINARY POETRY

The very texture of Stevens' poetry often embodies the same delicate system of checks and balances as his life-style. In "The Comedian as the Letter C" (1923), the long poem published in *Harmonium,* Stevens describes the imaginative wanderings of "Crispin" as a way of making sense of his own poetic development. Having begun with the proposition that "man is the intelligence of his soil," Crispin comes to feel that "his soil is man's intelligence," that we derive our identities from the place where we live. This position proves to be equally unsatisfactory, however: Crispin's new poetic notion contains "the reproach / That first drove Crispin to his wandering." Stevens' own poems also generate their own reproach. Not simply was his distrust of poetry as strong as his devotion to it; the more he distrusted it, the stronger his poetry became. The critic Kenneth Burke once said that poetry is preeminently of value because it is "a highly fluctuant thing often turning against itself and its own best discoveries." Stevens' highly equivocal poetry provides the best possible example of what Burke meant. "The poet represents the mind," said Stevens, "in the act of defending us against itself."

Stevens offered this paraphrase of the poem "To the One of Fictive Music" (1922), one of the last and most programmatic poems written for *Harmonium:* "After writing a poem, it is a good thing to walk round the block; after too much midnight, it is pleasant to hear the milkman, and yet, and this is the point of the poem, the imaginative world is the only real world, after all." On the one hand, "To the One of Fictive Music" does proclaim that "music is intensest which proclaims / The near, the

clear"; on the other hand, it asks the muse to save us from the merely apprehensible world.

> Yet not too like, yet not so like to be
> Too near, too clear, saving a little to endow
> Our feigning with the strange unlike, whence
>     springs
> The difference that heavenly pity brings.

As these lines suggest, Stevens' poems often enact a dialogue between the extraordinary and ordinary worlds, between midnight and the milkman, or between what Stevens more often (and somewhat blandly) called reality and imagination. "To the One of Fictive Music" does not suggest that the imaginative world simply is the real world; it shows the two worlds in tension, each one qualifying the other. As Helen Vendler has cautioned in *Wallace Stevens: Words Chosen out of Desire,* we must not reduce the play of reality and imagination to a dialectical opposition that progresses to a synthesis. Stasis and enclosure are what Stevens fears most; change and uncertainty are his highest values: "It can never be satisfied, the mind, never," he says in a poem from 1941, "The Well Dressed Man with a Beard." Some of Stevens' poems may suggest that the imaginative world becomes the real world; others may tip the scale toward one world or the other. But more important than any single conclusion is the ongoing project of Stevens' poetry—the "endlessly elaborating poem," as he says in "An Ordinary Evening in New Haven" (1949; collected in *The Auroras of Autumn,* 1950).

In "Insurance and Social Change" (1937), in which he uses parables to explain various kinds of insurance to a general audience, Stevens says that it "helps us to see the actual world to visualize a fantastic world." His poems often realize this strategy. As a poet Stevens' whole effort was, as he put it in "Effects of Analogy" (1948), to "press away from mysticism toward that ultimate good sense which we term civilization." But Stevens rightly understood that it is not a simple task to arrive at that good sense; our ordinary world is not easy to apprehend. In the final sentence of "Imagination as Value" (1948) he writes that "the chief problems of any artist, as of any man, are the problems of the normal." But at the same time he also emphasizes that the artist needs, "in order to solve [those problems,] everything that the imagination has to give." Like Ralph Waldo Emerson before him, Stevens wanted to embrace the common, the familiar, the low (as Emerson put it in *The American Scholar,* 1837), but he also understood that we require extraordinary means in order to see the ordinary.

In the late poem "The Plain Sense of Things" (1952) Stevens emphasizes that plainness was for him an achievement, the result of an ongoing struggle: "the absence of the imagination had / Itself to be imagined."

> The great pond,
> The plain sense of it, without reflections, leaves,
> Mud, water like dirty glass, expressing silence
>
> Of a sort, silence of a rat come out to see,
> The great pond and its waste of the lilies, all this
> Had to be imagined as an inevitable knowledge,
> Required, as a necessity requires.

These final lines of the poem equate the recovery of the "plain sense of things" with the assumption of a rat's low perspective on the world: viewed from a higher point of view, the surface of the water would be clouded by reflections. Yet Stevens' construction of this trope is itself a highly imaginative act: the poem both describes and embodies the notion that the absence of imagination must be imagined.

### "THE PRESSURE OF REALITY"

Despite the power of poems like "The Plain Sense of Things," it has sometimes been difficult for readers to understand what substantive or emotional issues are at stake in Stevens' "endlessly elaborating poem"; the themes preoccupying Stevens may too easily come to seem abstract and philosophical. For many years Stevens was known mostly as a poet of gorgeous nonsense, a poet who inherited the excesses of the aesthetes and symbolists of the later decades of the nineteenth century. His poetry was compared (usually to Stevens' disadvantage) to the earthier work of William Carlos Williams or Robert Frost; it did not seem to bear the cultural weight associated with the work of T. S. Eliot or Ezra Pound. Most critical narratives about Stevens' career consequently characterize the Marxist critic Stanley Burnshaw's review of *Ideas of Order* (which provoked the poem "Mr. Burnshaw and the Statue," one of the poems in *Owl's Clover,* published in 1936) as an aberration: they suggest that the poet of the ivory tower was dragged reluctantly into the real world of the 1930s, only to regain his tower in the later years of his career.

Since the 1980s however, Stevens' readers have maintained that his poems of the 1930s are paradigmatic rather than aberrational. While it would be wrong to stress Stevens' engagement with society at the expense of his extraordinary verbal mastery, Stevens is better served by a critical point of view that acknowledges the worldliness as well as the otherworldliness of his poetry. If only because Stevens himself so distrusted imaginative excess, always wanting to return to ordinary experience, we must pay attention to the ways in which his poems were provoked by or responded to the social events of his time. If only because Stevens so distrusted a complacent acceptance of the ordinary, we must also pay attention to the ways in which the poems erect (and dismantle) their own imaginative universe.

In "The Irrational Element in Poetry," an essay written to accompany a reading from *Owl's Clover* at Harvard University in 1936, Stevens argued that the poet must "resist" rather than "escape" what he called "the pressure of the contemporaneous" or "the pressure of reality." His essay is certainly a product of the social upheavals of the 1930s, but it is interesting to note that in it Stevens maintains that the thirties do not feel qualitatively different from the two preceding decades: "The pressure of the contemporaneous from the time of the beginning of the World War to the present time has been constant and extreme. No one can have lived apart in a happy oblivion."

These sentences seem all the more weighty when we remember that Stevens himself began his poetic career writing in response to World War I. "Phases," a sequence of poems about the war published in *Poetry* magazine in 1914, was Stevens' first major publication; a second sequence, "Lettres d'un Soldat" (inspired by the letters of a French soldier, Eugène Lemercier), appeared four years later. Stevens would not reprint these sequences, but several of the poems of "Lettres d'un Soldat" were shorn of their epigraphs from Lemercier's letters and reprinted in *Harmonium.* Unlike Eliot's *Waste Land* (1922) or Pound's *Hugh Selwyn Mauberley* (1920), Stevens' first book seems in no obvious way a product of the war. Yet these lines from "Lettres d'un Soldat" (retitled "The Death of a Soldier") seem perfectly at home in the world of *Harmonium:*

Death is absolute and without memorial,
As in a season of autumn,
When the wind stops,

When the wind stops and, over the heavens,
The clouds go, nevertheless,
In their direction.

### "THE SNOWMAN" AND
### "TEA AT THE PALAZ OF HOON"

As Harold Bloom observes in *Wallace Stevens: The Poems of Our Climate* (1977), in "The Death of a Soldier" one can see the "emergence of the

poet's most characteristic voice." It is true that, throughout his career, Stevens returns almost obsessively to a vision of the world that is untouched by human feeling, a world in which the plain sense of things grows not only stark but also oddly compelling. In "The Snow Man" (first published in 1921 and later collected along with "The Death of a Soldier" in *Harmonium*) Stevens emphasizes the difficulty of achieving this vision, insisting that "one must have a mind of winter" if one is

                    not to think
Of any misery in the sound of the wind,
In the sound of a few leaves,

Which is the sound of the land
Full of the same wind
That is blowing in the same bare place

For the listener, who listens in the snow,
And, nothing himself, beholds
Nothing that is not there and the nothing that is.

Stevens is surely relying on a conventional literary topos here. (Robert Frost reveals a similar interest in the wintery blankness of the natural world in poems like "Desert Places.") Stevens suggests in "The Snow Man," as he does in "The Plain Sense of Things," that the act of emptying the mind is a highly imaginative act: to "behold" nothing, rather than merely to "regard" it, is to acquire some kind of majesty. That said, it is important to register the fact that Stevens' "most characteristic voice" first came to him when he attempted, during World War I, to account for a kind of death that made any metaphor, any elegiac consolation, seem inadequate. In "The Noble Rider and the Sound of Words" (1941), written during World War II, Stevens would say that "when one is trying to think of a whole generation and of a world at war . . . the plainest statement of what is happening can easily appear to be an affectation." The poet tries to allow the world to speak for itself, recognizing that his effort to do so will inevitably be compromised.

Still, however characteristic "The Snow Man" may be, the poem manifests only half of Stevens' sensibility. For as often as Stevens wrote about the pressure of reality on the vacant mind, he wrote about imagination exerting an equal pressure on the recalcitrant world. In "Tea at the Palaz of Hoon" (1921), which was first published beside "The Snow Man," Stevens' "Hoon" exists completely in an imagined space of the mind:

> I was the world in which I walked, and what I saw
> Or heard or felt came not but from myself;
> And there I found myself more truly and more
>     strange.

As "To the One of Fictive Music" suggests, Stevens wove his endless elaborations between the poles epitomized by "The Snow Man" and "Tea at the Palaz of Hoon." Sometimes, as in "Tea," he emphasized the mind's ability to fabricate elaborate metaphors or structures of belief; other times, as in "The Snow Man," he cautioned us to remember that those structures inevitably collapse in the face of events that even our most cherished beliefs cannot encompass. Stevens eventually offered three prescriptions for a viable belief system in "Notes toward a Supreme Fiction" (1942), the most important of them being "It Must Change": however delightful the imagined palaz of Hoon may be, we must not be allowed to grow accustomed to it.

In "Esthétique du Mal" (1944) Stevens confessed that the "death of Satan was a tragedy / For the imagination." But Stevens was also adamant that this tragedy was "the imagination's new beginning": "we require another chant" to replace the outmoded fictions in which we no longer believe. In many ways the title of the long poem "Notes toward a Supreme Fiction" may stand for all Stevens' poetry: throughout his career (though less systematically at the beginning of it) he was attempting to satisfy what William James called the "will to believe" in a skeptical age. The supreme fiction was, for Stevens, something to which we assent while knowing it to be untrue. Like James, Stevens was interested in the usefulness of the stories we tell ourselves rather than in their singular truth: "The final belief is to believe in a fiction, which you know to be a fiction. The exquisite truth is to know that it is a fiction and that you believe in it willingly." Various poems, from "Sunday Morning" (1915) to "The Owl in the Sarcophagus" (1947; collected in *The Auroras of Autumn*) offer a fiction in which we might believe. But the only thing of which we can be certain in Stevens is that the fiction must change—midnight gives way to the milkman, the palaz of Hoon gives way to the snow man—since the world for which the fiction accounts is changing too.

## HARMONIUM

"Sunday Morning" consists of eight stanzas of fifteen blank verse lines. Like most of Stevens' longer productions, the poem moves by association and juxtaposition rather than by any linear narrative or argument. (Stevens published shorter versions of both "Sunday Morning" and "An Ordinary Evening in New Haven" in which the poems' sections appear in a different order.) In "a skeptical age, in the absence of a belief in God," Stevens once said, "the mind turns to its own creations and examines them . . . for the support they give"; the eight sections of "Sunday Morning" offer differing perspectives on this proposition. Dawdling luxuriously over coffee and oranges instead of attending church, a woman discovers that her earthly pleasures seem like "things in some procession of the dead": they are not immortal, and they consequently remind her of her own mortality. She longs for "some imperishable bliss," even though the oracular voice of the poem tells us that any meaningful notion of divinity "must live within herself" rather than in some obsolete fiction of heaven. Traditional notions of the after-life offer no real consolation, the voice continues, because a perfect, unchanging paradise would finally strike us as tedious and thin. "Death is the mother of beauty," the poem insists, recalling John Keats's "Ode on Melancholy" (1820): thus the fear of mortality with which the poem began is transmuted into the most powerful consolation available to human beings.

Mocking traditional piety in "A High-Toned Old Christian Woman" (1922), the first poem in which the phrase "supreme fiction" appears, Stevens insists that humans must "whip from themselves / A jovial hullabaloo among the spheres"; that is, they must create the mythology by which they live. The penultimate stanza of "Sunday Morning" shows a "ring of men" doing exactly that: they "chant . . . / Their boisterous devotion to the sun, / Not as a god, but as a god might be." Their act of fiction-making does seem exaggerated in its fervor; the vision of their masculine community pointedly excludes the woman who appears elsewhere in the poem. But this stanza must be understood as forming a dialogue with the other sections of the poem. "Sunday Morning" concludes with a far more generous and ambiguous vision of earthly beauty. The final lines, embracing change and mortality, strike Stevens' more authentically elegiac note:

> Deer walk upon our mountains, and the quail
> Whistle about us their spontaneous cries;
> Sweet berries ripen in the wilderness;
> And, in the isolation of the sky,
> At evening, casual flocks of pigeons make
> Ambiguous undulations as they sink,
> Downward to darkness, on extended wings.

Both thematically and structurally, "Sunday Morning" is Stevens' first great achievement; he would continue to spin variations on the poem for the rest of his career. In comparison to other poems in *Harmonium*, however, "Sunday Morning" can seem a little pious in its rejection of traditional piety; it lacks the self-mocking verbal energy of "Le Monocle de Mon Oncle" (1918) or "The Comedian as the Letter C," the two other major poems in the volume. Contemplating the ways middle age diminishes us in "Le Monocle," Stevens wants to "quiz all sounds, all thoughts, all everything" in order to "find / Bravura adequate to this great hymn." The poem's verbal extravagance embodies this ambition. But "Le Monocle" is even more quintessentially Stevensian because in it Stevens also checks his own poetic extravagance: while the "fops of fancy in their poems leave / Memorabilia of the mystic spouts," the poet himself is merely an ordinary man—"a yeoman, as such fellows go." Similarly, the power of "The Comedian as the Letter C" (which Frank Kermode—in his book *Wallace Stevens*, 1960—has justly called a "sustained nightmare of unexpected diction"), also depends on the conflict between its exuberant language and its dour subject matter. This most verbally extravagant of Stevens' poems describes the failure of poetry: Stevens' Crispin gives up poetic ambition for "social nature," a "shady home" in the suburbs, and "daughters with curls."

That is, of course, exactly what Stevens himself did after publishing *Harmonium,* and it is telling (as I have suggested) that another decade of silence caused him no visible anxiety: Stevens' social nature—his familial and civic commitments—were as important to him as poetry, and he never entertained the fantasy of "living apart" (as he put it in "The Irrational Element of Poetry"). It is also telling that, as a poet, Stevens sat out most of the 1920s—the most mythologized literary decade of the century—and returned to poetry during the 1930s, a decade that made most poets feel irrelevant. Just as the Great War helped to ignite the first phase of Stevens' career, the social upheavals of the Great Depression prodded him to write some of the most intelligent poems we have about the strengths and limitations of poetry in a time of social strife. Stevens was not much of a topical poet, but his poetry always emerged in dialogue with the events of his time.

## IDEAS OF ORDER

The poet of *Ideas of Order* (1935) does seem chastened in comparison to the poet of "The Comedian as the Letter C," however; gone are the exotic landscapes and the boisterous music that characterize much of *Harmonium*. The poems now speak of "besieging pain," of "sudden mobs of men," and of a "voice of angry fear"; the poet himself now seems like a "most inappropriate man / In a most unpropitious place." This discouragement is momentary, however, and does not descend into despair: the world has changed, and so must the poet's way of thinking about that world. Referring back to "Tea at the Palaz of Hoon" in "Sad Strains of a Gay Waltz" (1935) Stevens dismisses Hoon—"who found all form and order in solitude"—from his poetry; he wants instead to be a "harmonious skeptic" who will confront "these sudden mobs of men," "uniting" them in a music that "will be motion and full of shadows." Favoring the stark vision of "The Snow Man," Stevens insists in poems like "How to Live. What to Do" (1935) or "Evening without Angels" (1934) that "bare earth is best." In "How To Live" two men climb a rock, hoping to find "a sun of fuller fire"; instead, they discover that the massive, denuded rock is all there is: "There was neither voice nor crested image, / No chorister, nor priest." Having accepted that we have no priest—that is, no viable fiction—to explain this "bare earth," Stevens nonetheless insists in "Evening without Angels" that we must build the house in which we dwell and so construct a new consolation. Although our houses are "huddled low" beneath an intimidating firmament, "the voice that is great within us rises up, / As we stand gazing at the rounded moon."

Throughout *Ideas of Order,* Hoon's extravagance is not merely rejected in favor of the barrenness of "The Snow Man." While insisting that "bare earth is best," the Stevens of *Ideas of Order* is more interested in constructing a communal or collective vision—ideas of order—that might protect us from the sheer inhumanity of barrenness. In "The Idea of Order at Key West" (1934), the most important poem in the volume, a woman sings as she walks along a deserted beach. Listening to the song, Stevens feels that the voice is somehow something more than human, yet he cannot locate the source of its otherworldly power. Deeply skeptical of its own propositions, the poem considers and rejects the notion that the woman sings with the voice of the ocean or the firmament; it refuses to indulge in an easy animation of "bare earth." Once again recalling "Tea at the Palaz of Hoon" ("I was the world in which I walked"), Stevens proposes that the singer "was the single artificer of the world / In which she sang"; "there never was a world for her / Except the one she sang and, singing, made."

If the Wordsworthian meditation of "The Idea of Order at Key West" ended here, however, the poem would settle for a merely solipsistic vision of art's power; Stevens asks how poetry—even poetry that is made by and for the poet alone—may nevertheless help us to order our world. "Poetry is not the same thing as the imagination taken alone," wrote Stevens at around the same time he wrote "The Idea of Order": "Nothing is itself taken alone. Things are because of interrelations or interactions." In the penultimate stanza of "The Idea of Order" (a splendid example of Stevens' mastery of blank verse), Stevens addresses a hitherto unmentioned companion, Ramon Fernandez, and asks about the interactions between the place, the singer, the song, and the listeners.

Ramon Fernandez, tell me, if you know,
Why, when the singing ended and we turned
Toward the town, tell why the glassy lights,
The lights in the fishing boats at anchor there,
As the night descended, tilting in the air,

Mastered the night and portioned out the sea,
Fixing emblazoned zones and fiery poles,
Arranging, deepening, enchanting night.

The life of the song exists in its interaction with the landscape and its audience: even after the song has ended, even if the singer sang for herself alone, the song has altered the way in which its audience perceives the world. Nothing mystical has happened; the song has not embodied the transcendental spirit of the place. The interaction of song, place, and audience has brought a new sense of order and purpose to bare earth.

Although "The Idea of Order at Key West" seems to be a highly generalized meditation on the social function of poetry, it nonetheless shows that Stevens was far from unacquainted with the intellectual left in the 1930s: Ramon Fernandez, the silent auditor of the poem, was a highly political literary and social critic whom Stevens had been reading in *Partisan Review* and other magazines. In contrast to Fernandez, Stanley Burnshaw (who reviewed *Ideas of Order* in the Marxist periodical the *New Masses*) was no ideologue. Although he complained that one "can rarely speak surely of Stevens' ideas," Burnshaw presented Stevens as a middle-ground writer who might be persuaded to join forces with the left. Stevens' response to Burnshaw—"Mr. Burnshaw and the Statue"— was neither clearly defensive nor oppositional; Stevens spoke of the poem as a "justification of leftism," by which he meant that the poem's highest value is openness to change. Stevens juxtaposes "Mr. Burnshaw" with "celestial paramours" throughout "Mr. Burnshaw and the Statue," ultimately disclosing his view that the resolutely Marxist and the purely aesthetic perspective on art are both inadequate: "It is only enough / To live incessantly in change," says Stevens at the climax of the poem. Stevens feared the entropy of order as much as he feared the anarchic energy of disorder, and it is important to remember that his "ideas of order" are fleeting and provisional.

## OWL'S CLOVER AND THE MAN WITH THE BLUE GUITAR

"Mr. Burnshaw and the Statue" eventually came together with four other poems to make the long poem *Owl's Clover,* first published in 1936 and then reprinted in a shorter version in *The Man with the Blue Guitar and Other Poems* (1937). Each of the poems of *Owl's Clover* offers a new perspective on the "statue"—that is, on the social function of art—and the result is Stevens' most topical poem; he thought of calling it "Aphorisms on Society" and spoke of the poem as an effort to make poetry out of "the day's news." But though *Owl's Clover* represents a crucial stage in Stevens' development, Stevens remained dissatisfied with the effort, ultimately excluding it from his collected poems. When Elizabeth Bishop first read *Owl's Clover* in 1936, she praised Stevens for writing poems that display "ideas at work," in contrast to those poets who "write all their ideas in bad prose." Yet she complained about "the way [Stevens] occasionally seems to make blank verse *moo.*"

There is a kind of uncharacteristically bovine heaviness about the poems of *Owl's Clover;* its plodding verse often makes it sound dogmatic, even though the entire thematic thrust of the poem is away from certainty and toward the dynamics of change. In stark contrast to the long blank verse paragraphs of *Owl's Clover,* Stevens' next major effort, "The Man with the Blue Guitar" (1937), is written in clipped tetrameter couplets. Its thirty-three brief and highly aphoristic sections play off one another in ambiguous ways, suggesting that Stevens was searching for a more appropriate formal means to embody his thematic devotion to uncertainty and change. For although "The Man with the Blue Guitar" feels like a very different kind of poem, it displays many of the same ideas as *Owl's Clover.* Having given up the effort to write topical poetry (an effort which did not come naturally), Stevens was nonetheless able to offer more supple and convincing ways of thinking about the social function of poetry.

Recalling "Sunday Morning," Stevens writes in "The Greenest Continent" (the third poem of *Owl's Clover*) that there "was a heaven once," the "spirit's episcopate, hallowed and high, / To which the spirit ascended." In section 5 of "The Man with the Blue Guitar" (which was also published alone as "The Place of Poetry" in *Twentieth Century Verse* in 1937) Stevens rephrased the thought once again:

> The earth, for us, is flat and bare.
> There are no shadows. Poetry
>
> Exceeding music must take the place
> Of empty heaven and its hymns,
>
> Ourselves in poetry must take their place,
> Even in the chattering of your guitar.

These lines form the emotional center of "The Man with the Blue Guitar": having faced the poverty of all inherited beliefs, Stevens insists that poetry (or any act of the mind) must provide our consolation. Some sections of the poem stress the mind's inability to make sense of the barren world; other sections caution us against the mind's power to overwhelm the world completely. Throughout the poem, Stevens both describes and enacts a delicate interchange between the "imagined and the real, thought / And the truth, Dichtung und Wahrheit [poetry and truth]" (section 23) searching ultimately for a "balance" that "does not quite rest" (section 29). The gradual unfolding of the poem, one section modifying our sense of another, is more important than any of the poem's momentary conclusions.

Stevens did not yet use the phrase "supreme fiction" with any regularity, but when he looked back on section 10 of "The Man with the Blue Guitar" in 1953, he saw that the poem was a testing ground for the concept: "If we are to think of a supreme fiction, instead of creating it, as the Greeks did, for example, in the form of a mythology, we might choose to create it in the image of a man: an agreed-on superman." Increasingly throughout the 1930s and 1940s, Stevens explored the notion of the plausible hero—someone "beyond us, yet ourselves," to use the language of the opening section of "The Man with the Blue Guitar"—as the most useful fiction in which we might agree to believe. As he explains in the tenth section of "The Man with the Blue Guitar," Stevens is not interested in his culture's conventional hero, the political demagogue in "whom none believes, / Whom all believe that all believe." Although a note of Nietzschean arrogance sometimes creeps into Stevens' idea of heroism, his most convincing heroes are egregiously ordinary and even hapless human beings: the tramp of the Depression or the soldier of World War II—figures in whom all people might be able to discover the possibility of their own greatness. In the thirtieth section of "The Man with the Blue Guitar," Stevens asserts that he "shall evolve a man" out of "the old fantoche / Hanging his shawl upon the wind, / Like something on the stage."

> At last, in spite of his manner, his eye
>
> A-cock at the cross-piece on a pole
> Supporting heavy cables, slung
>
> Through Oxidia, banal suburb,
> One-half of all its installments paid.
>
> Dew-dapper clapper-traps, blazing
> From crusty stacks above machines.
>
> Ecce, Oxidia is the seed
> Dropped out of this amber-ember pod,
>
> Oxidia is the soot of fire,
> Oxidia is Olympia.

The unlikely figure of the "fantoche" becomes a lineman working on the electrical cables in the "banal suburb" of Oxidia; at the same time, he is also a godlike figure, hanging at the "cross-piece on a pole" in a newly imagined vision of Olympia. Both "soot" and "seed," both the residue of destruction and the promise of rebirth, the banal suburb is the only heaven we shall ever know.

### PARTS OF A WORLD

As "The Man with the Blue Guitar" suggests only briefly, Stevens' notion of the hero is deeply paradoxical: he must be both real and imagined, both ordinary and extraordinary, both a part of our world and a figment of a world beyond. In "Asides on the Oboe" (1940), one of the many hero poems collected in *Parts of a World* (1942), Stevens begins with the programmatic declaration, "The prologues are over. It is a question now, / Of final belief. So, say that final belief / Must be in a fiction." Stevens then discards the "obsolete fiction" of the wide river, the gods, and the "metal" (or merely earthly) heroes "that time granulates." In their stead, he proposes "The impossible possible philosophers' man":

If you say on the hautboy man is not enough,
Can never stand as god, is ever wrong
In the end, however naked, tall, there is still
The impossible possible philosophers' man,
The man who has had the time to think enough,
The central man, the human globe, responsive
As a mirror with a voice, the man of glass,
Who in a million diamonds sums us up.

Simultaneously possible and impossible, this hero represents both the potential for human greatness and the means by which we perceive that potential. "He is and in his poems we find peace"; in summer he "cries / 'Thou art not August unless I make thee so,' " suggesting that through him, we perceive both what the world is (August) and what it could be (august). But if this exclamation makes the hero's power over the world seem implausibly strong, Stevens challenges the "central man" with

the stark reality of war: "One year, death and war prevented the jasmine scent / And the jasmine islands were bloody martyrdoms." Like so many of Stevens' poems, "Asides on the Oboe" may seem generally philosophical, but its desperation for "peace" was conditioned by Stevens' acute awareness of the events of World War II:

How was it then with the central man? Did we
Find peace? We found the sum of men. We found,
If we found the central evil, the central good.
We buried the fallen without jasmine crowns.
There was nothing he did not suffer, no; nor we.

In "Like Decorations in a Nigger Cemetery" (1935), the long, fragmentary poem in *Ideas of Order,* Stevens had asserted that "union of the weakest develops strength / Not wisdom." In mature hero poems such as "Asides on the Oboe," the wisdom of greatness is ultimately defined through (and not in opposition to) the union of all people: "There was nothing he did not suffer, no; nor we." As David Bromwich suggested in his essay from 1987, "Stevens and the Idea of the Hero," Stevens moves "from the idea of a great man who carves a new image of life from the acquiescent human data, to the less brutal idea of a man or woman who is made great by an enterprise in which others have a part." This is why Stevens is so careful to prevent his contradictory notions of heroism from resolving into a dependable vision of human greatness: the possible hero must never be allowed to degenerate into the predictable tyrant.

Consequently, in "Examination of the Hero in a Time of War" (1942), also collected in *Parts of a World,* Stevens insists that the hero is a fiction of our own making, a fiction for which we are responsible and one which we must continue to revise. "There is no image of the hero," he asserts, for to give the idea of heroism a certain shape is to make it resistant to change. As important as the act of devising a plausible hero is the act of dismantling it: "Each false thing ends," says the final section of "Examination": "After the hero, the familiar / Man makes the hero artificial." These hero poems show Stevens' delicately self-critical poetics at its best. After assuming the imaginative power of "Tea at the Palaz of Hoon," we must measure our fiction against the stark reality of "The Snow Man." In the terms of "The Man with the Blue Guitar," the fiction of the hero must hover precariously between "the imagined and the real, thought / And the truth."

As A. Walton Litz has shown in his study of Stevens' poetic development "The Man with the Blue Guitar" marked an important turning point: "After its composition Stevens was a poet who reacted mainly to his own achievements and theories, building the self-referring world of the later poems." However superficially coherent the universe of Stevens' later poetry may appear, it is crucial to see that it resembles what William James called a "pluralistic universe"—a world in which unity is made rather than taken for granted, a world in which all values are highly contingent, in which there can be no centralized standard of truth. As the title of *Parts of a World* suggests, Stevens is more interested in the scattered pieces of his world than in any static vision of its wholeness. But while Stevens will offer only "notes toward" a supreme fiction, not any fully realized vision of it, he is not interested in settling for chaos. If, as he says in "Connoisseur of Chaos" (1938) we cannot return to a time when "bishops' books / Resolved the world," we must not merely accept the "squirming facts" as they are but perceive relations between them, building the facts into provisional structures: "relation appears, / A small relation expanding like the shade / Of a cloud on sand."

The very notion of "truth" is scorned throughout the poems in *Parts of a World* (many of which seem in retrospect like notes toward "Notes toward a Supreme Fiction"). "Where was it one first heard of the truth?" asks Stevens in the final line of "The Man on the Dump" (1938). His answer is "The the," suggesting that we crave a notion of

truth—*the* truth—only when we indulge in the vocabulary of certainty and centrality. "It was when I said, / 'There is no such thing as the truth,' " recalls the speaker of "On the Road Home" (1938), "That the grapes seemed fatter." Having "escaped from the truth," the protagonist of "The Latest Freed Man" (1938) is similarly aware of a more beautiful and satisfying world of change: "It was everything bulging and blazing and big in itself, / The blue of the rug, the portrait of Vidal." In contrast, while the protagonist of "Landscape with Boat" (1940) discards "the colossal illusion of heaven," he nevertheless continues to cling to the notion of a "truth beyond all truths" and cannot appreciate the fact that the imperfect world is his paradise.

> He never supposed
> That he might be truth, himself, or part of it,
> That the things that he rejected might be part
> And the irregular turquoise, part, the perceptible blue
> Grown denser, part, the eye so touched, so played
> Upon by clouds, the ear so magnified
> By thunder, parts, and all these things together,
> Parts, and more things, parts. . . .

Had he been able to discard not only heaven but also the desire for truth that heaven answers, he would have seen that the ordinary world—a world of disparate, unconnected parts—provides all the consolation we need. The power of this poem's quizzically generic title ("Landscape with Boat") becomes clear in its final lines: "He might observe / A yellow wine and follow a steamer's track / And say, 'The thing I hum appears to be / The rhythm of this celestial pantomime.' " If he could escape from the truth, then he would perceive the wonder of the most commonplace scene.

### "NOTES TOWARD A SUPREME FICTION"

Building on the pragmatist tradition of William James, the contemporary philosopher Stanley Cavell wonders throughout *In Quest of the Ordinary* why the most ordinary aspects of human life are often the most difficult topics for philosophers and poets. He concludes that ordinary experience is "always the subject of a quest and the object of an inquest"; in order to appreciate the wonder of the commonplace, we need to complicate and distort it. Growing out of the poems of *Parts of a World,* "Notes toward a Supreme Fiction" (1942) represents Stevens' most strenuous effort to embrace the ordinary; it is simultaneously (and, as Cavell would say, not paradoxically) Stevens' most fancifully elaborate poem—the poem toward which his earlier work seems in retrospect to prepare, the poem on which the many extraordinary poems of his prolific final phase depend.

"Notes" is divided into three parts—"It Must Be Abstract," "It Must Change," and "It Must Give Pleasure"—each part consisting of ten cantos of twenty-one lines. The supreme fiction must be abstract in the sense that it must be abstracted from experience—a constructed, not a given thing. It must change because the world for which it accounts changes; a fiction that is useful at one historical moment may not be useful at another. Finally, the supreme fiction must give pleasure in the most profound sense of the word: it must make our human condition tolerable. The woman in "Sunday Morning" yearns for "imperishable bliss," but in "Notes" Stevens speaks, less desperately, of "accessible bliss" and "expressible bliss": he wants to describe the pleasure that might be found even in the repetitive grind of our ordinary waking hours.

The first canto of "It Must Be Abstract" begins by instructing the "ephebe," or student, to "become an ignorant man again," discarding all outmoded fictions. He must attempt to see the sun not as Phoebus Apollo but purely and simply as itself. "The sun / Must bear no name," says Stevens, but as in "The Snow Man" or "The Plain Sense of Things," he also recognizes that it is difficult to achieve or maintain this purity of vision. In the

second canto Stevens consequently acknowledges that "not to have is the beginning of desire": old fictions must be discarded only so that we may begin the task of constructing new ones. "From this the poem springs," says Stevens in crucial lines from canto 4: "that we live in a place / That is not our own and, much more, not ourselves." We need fictions to make our lives bearable, and much of the remainder of "Notes" proposes and discards various fictions, moving back and forth between what Stevens calls an "ever-early candor" (the willed state of ignorance) to a "late plural" (the fullness of the achieved fiction).

In the eighth canto of "It Must Be Abstract" Stevens begins to propose a particular fiction. What he now calls "major man" is another version of the heroic ideal, and as in his other hero poems, Stevens insists that major man cannot be divined through "romantic intoning" or "apotheosis": the ideal of human greatness must never be divorced from our ordinary lives. Major man is given an ordinary name ("MacCullough"), but Stevens describes him only generally and says that we must "give him / No names"—as if the act of naming or too clearly identifying major man would compromise his usefulness as our supreme fiction. Yet the poem itself dramatizes our impatience ("Who is it?"), and Stevens finally offers us a glimpse of this "rabbi" or "chieftain" in the final lines of canto 10. Expecting a figure of magnitude, we meet instead a tramp "in that old coat, those sagging pantaloons," a single figure who unites "these separate figures one by one." Stevens makes the appearance of MacCullough seem like the Resurrection ("Cloudless the morning. It is he"). But like the "old fantoche" in "The Man with the Blue Guitar," MacCullough is simultaneously ordinary and extraordinary. Similarly, the poem itself has to use extraordinary means—great flights of metaphor— in order to make us feel the wonder of our everyday world.

Having offered us this heroic fiction, however, Stevens immediately drops the idea, never to return to it. Just as he dismissed his vision of the hero in "Examination of the Hero in a Time of War" ("Each false thing ends"), so does Stevens emphasize throughout the cantos of "It Must Change" that our supreme fiction must not be taken for granted. In canto 3 of "It Must Change" Stevens suggests that our hero could too easily become rigid and absurd, like the majestic statue of General Du Puy: "There never had been, never could be, such / A man." The general was "rubbish in the end," suggests Stevens, "because nothing had changed."

Throughout Stevens' poetry, statues often serve as emblems of fictions that have grown rigid and need to be changed. But in "Notes" even our changing world does not change enough. The first canto of "It Must Change" rejects seasonal change as merely predictable: "The distaste we feel for this withered scene / Is that it has not changed enough." "It is a repetition. . . . not broken in subtleties." Although birdsong in canto 6 ("Bethou me, said sparrow") recalls Percy Bysshe Shelley's west wind in "Ode to the West Wind" (1820), the birdsong, too, yields the "granite monotony" of mere repetition. Like the statue of the general, the living sparrow "is a bird / Of stone, that never changes." Stevens insists that meaningful change is something we do not merely observe but must help to enact; our fictions must be as rigorously dismantled as they are constructed.

Throughout "It Must Give Pleasure," the final movement of "Notes toward a Supreme Fiction," Stevens emphasizes that the work of change is the source of our most profound pleasure. "To sing jubilas at exact, accustomed times," he says in canto 1, is merely "common"—"a facile exercise." As an antidote to this vision of conventional religious piety, Stevens offers the "Canon Aspirin," the supreme individualist, the man of extravagant imaginative power. In canto 5 the Canon consumes an elaborate meal of "lobster Bombay with mango / Chutney" but observes the simple life of his sister and her daughters. Unlike the Canon, his sister lives in a world of other people; she holds her daughters "closelier to her by rejecting dreams." However attractive the Canon's extravagance may seem initially, he is finally an ineffectual dreamer—a fiction-maker who is content to live within his fiction, refusing to test his dreams against the ordinary world. "He imposes orders" on the world instead of discovering them, says Stevens in canto 7; the Canon "establishes statues" instead of keeping his fictions malleable.

Having rejected both the common ritual of religious observance and the uncommon Canon Aspirin (who initially seemed like the source of active change), Stevens reaches the crisis point of "Notes" in canto 8: "What am I to believe?" His answer—"I have not but I am and as I am, I am"—has several different important connotations: he stands alone with poetry (the repeated "I am" embodies the rhythm of the iambs in the iambic pentameter line); with imagination (which Samuel Taylor Coleridge defined in *Biographia Literaria* [1817] as "a repetition in the finite mind of the eternal act of creation in the infinite I AM"); and most importantly with the ordinary self ("as I am") in the ordinary world. In canto 9 of "It Must Give Pleasure," the climax of the entire poem, Stevens is now able to embrace mere repetition as the highest good. Once scorned as monotonous, birdsong is now presented as redeeming: "These things at least comprise / An occupation, an exercise, a work, / A thing final in itself and, therefore, good." Everyday experience that once seemed "common" is now treasured precisely because it is "common"—both ordinary and communal, a meal not eaten in solitude (like the Canon's) but shared with other people:

One of the vast repetitions final in
Themselves and, therefore, good, the going round

And round and round, the merely going round,
Until merely going round is a final good,
The way wine comes at a table in a wood.

And we enjoy like men, the way a leaf
Above the table spins its constant spin,
So that we look at it with pleasure, look

At it spinning its eccentric measure. Perhaps,
The man-hero is not the exceptional monster,
But he that of repetition is most master.

"Notes toward a Supreme Fiction" does not offer a vision of another world as our consolation. It goes to great length (as Cavell suggests we must) in order to display the most ordinary experience as being of the highest value: the heroic state of mind is exceptional only in as much as it allows us to take pleasure in the most common, everyday experience. In these lines of canto 9, Stevens the poet and Stevens the insurance executive (who emphasized the dull routine of his work in "Surety and Fidelity Claims") have each made the other possible.

In the final canto of "It Must Give Pleasure" the pleasure of embracing repetition ("the merely going round") is linked to the spinning of the earth. But if the final lines make Stevens' vision seem dangerously whole and complete (his "fluent mundo / . . . will have stopped revolving except in crystal"), the poem's coda jolts us back into the rough and savage time that provoked Stevens to write the poem in the first place—the time of World War II: "Soldier, there is a war between the mind / And sky." We need to feel this line as an intrusion into the dangerously beautiful world that "Notes toward a Supreme Fiction" offers us. "It is a war that never ends," Stevens continues, "Yet it depends on yours." Stevens wants to assert the importance of the poet's struggle in a time of war. Yet he is careful not to equate the two wars: they are "parallels that meet if only in / The meeting of their shadows or that meet / In a book in a barrack." Speaking here is the same Stevens who in 1939 responded to a *Partisan Review* questionnaire about the role of the writer in wartime by saying that a "war is a military state of affairs, not a literary one." This is not an aesthete's credo; Stevens knew that a socially responsible poet must acknowledge the limitations of poetry as well its strengths. And as "Notes" suggests, part of the strength of poetry is its ability to turn against itself, converting certainty into ambiguity.

### *TRANSPORT TO SUMMER* AND *THE AURORAS OF AUTUMN*

After publishing both *Parts of a World* and "Notes toward a Supreme Fiction" in 1942, Stevens would go on to write three more major books of poetry: *Transport to Summer* (1947), *The Auroras of Autumn* (1950), and the final section of *The Collected Poems,* called *The Rock* (1954). (*The Auroras of Autumn* won the National Book Award in 1951.) "Notes toward a Supreme Fiction" would be reprinted as the final poem in *Transport to Summer,* but it is more properly understood as the foundation of that book. If Stevens began in "The Man with the Blue Guitar" to piece together his "pluralistic universe," he achieved in "Notes toward a Supreme Fiction" a provisional consolidation. Throughout his later years, he would sometimes offer temptingly aphoristic lines, suggesting that his "fluent mundo" was whole and coherent; in "A Primitive like an Orb" (1948), collected in *The Auroras of Autumn,* he posited an "essential poem at the centre of things," a "huge, high harmony" which is "seen and known in lesser poems." But just as often, Stevens stood appalled by this totalizing vision; in "Things of August (1949), also collected in *The Auroras,* he spurned "the high and deadly view" from which "the particles became / The whole man" and "differences lost / Difference and were one." However "Stevensian" the themes of Stevens' late poems might seem, we need to pay attention to the particular ways in which they extend and complicate those themes. Like Stevens himself, we must resist the "high and deadly" view from which all differences are obliterated; we must remember that Stevens' "pluralistic universe" hovers in the space between its wholeness and its parts, and we must honor the provisionality of the poetry.

One important way in which the later poems reconsider the interplay between reality and imagination is by dwelling on metaphor—the particular language used by the mind to organize the world. "On an old shore," proposes Stevens in a poem from *Transport to Summer,* "Somnambulisma" (1943), "the vulgar ocean rolls / Noiselessly, noiselessly, resembling a thin bird, / That thinks of settling, yet never settles, on a nest." As the poem continues, this metaphor (the restless bird as a figure for the ocean) is extended so that we feel the presence of the bird more than the presence of the ocean. "Without this bird that never settles," Stevens concludes, "the ocean . . . / Would be a geography of the dead": without metaphors that make new sense of the world, the inhuman world would be inhospitable to human life.

But the fact that the poem dwells on the vehicle of the metaphor (the bird) at the expense of the tenor (the ocean) makes Stevens nervous. Standing beside "Somnambulisma" in *Transport to Summer* is "Crude Foyer" (1947), which begins with the assertion "Thought is false happiness." Stevens is worried, as he puts it in "The Pure Good of Theory" (1945), that "to speak of the whole world as metaphor. . . . is to stick to the nicer knowledge of / Belief." In the final lines of "Crude Foyer," Stevens seems to express relief that the mind is not always capable of producing metaphors that humanize the world: he admits that "we are ignorant men incapable / Of the least, minor, vital metaphor." By living exclusively within "the exhilarations of changes," as Stevens writes in "The Motive for Metaphor" (1943), we are in danger of ignoring the immitigable fact of mortality: blank reality, though "fatal," is as "vital" as metaphor itself.

> The motive for metaphor, shrinking from
> The weight of primary noon,
> The A B C of being,

> The ruddy temper, the hammer
> Of red and blue, the hard sound—
> Steel against intimation—the sharp flash,
> The vital, arrogant, fatal, dominant X.

In these lines, however self-critical they may be, Stevens does not intend simply to wipe away a poet's metaphors. He wants to judge their usefulness, making sure that they account for the world instead of obscuring it. In the dialogue poem "Saint John and the Back-Ache" (1950), collected in *The Auroras of Autumn,* the backache begins by asserting that the "mind is the terriblest force in the world"; Saint John counters that the "world is presence and not force," suggesting that the world is not so easily mastered by the mind: "The effect of the object is beyond the mind's / Extremest pinch." Saint John then offers a catalogue of metaphors (none of which are fully capable of accounting for the world), culminating in these lines:

> My point is that
> These illustrations are neither angels, no,
> Nor brilliant blows thereof, ti-rill-a-roo,
> Nor all one's luck at once in a play of strings.
> They help us face the dumbfoundering abyss
> Between us and the object, external cause.

It is important to face the limitations of our metaphors (they are not "angels") so that we do not become too perfectly at home in the world. At the same time, although our metaphors are inadequate, they are nevertheless useful in that they help us to face the stark otherness of the world. "Saint John and the Back-Ache" is a dense, difficult poem, but it seems quintessentially Stevensian: although lyrical and profoundly serious in its exploration of human fiction-making, its language (beginning with the title) is also playful and self-deprecatingly humorous, checking its own tendency toward portentousness.

Stevens insists throughout his later poems that we must be held responsible for our metaphors: since the world is shaped by our metaphors, we may become the victims of our metaphors, forgetting that we have created the terms of our own misfortune. Like Robert Frost, Stevens was especially suspicious of eschatological and apocalyptic metaphors. "It is immodest for a man to think of himself as going down before the worst forces ever mobilized by God," said Frost. Stevens was similarly troubled by the fact that exaggerated visions of catastrophe and revelation often serve to reinforce our complacency in the face of real disasters. From the beginning of his career, Stevens' sensibility was always more social and comic than alienated and tragic; consequently, in the age of Eliot's *Waste Land* and Yeats's "The Second Coming," Stevens' poems often appeared suspiciously disengaged from the fate of Western culture. In fact, Stevens' resistance to apocalyptic metaphors is one of the clearest marks of his sense of a poet's social responsibility. He wants to understand not only the strengths but also the limitations of our metaphors in shaping human history.

In two of the great long poems written after "Notes toward a Supreme Fiction," "Esthétique du Mal" (1944) and "The Auroras of Autumn" (1948), Stevens dramatizes the act of defusing apocalyptic metaphors. The two poems could not read more differently; the former unfolds at a leisurely, meditative pace while the latter presents ten compressed and emblematic tableaux. But each poem begins with an ominous image of the natural world (a groaning volcano and the aurora borealis), and each poem offers metaphors that make the opening image seem more and more threatening. In "The Auroras of Autumn" the uncannily lit sky becomes a snake, a deserted cabin, an aging mother, and a domineering father; the "scholar of one candle" watches this "theatre floating through the clouds" and "feels afraid" (canto 6). In contrast, the protagonist of "Esthétique du Mal" finds it "pleasant to be sitting" beneath the rumbling volcano; he reads a book about the sublime, finding time-honored metaphors for his apparently impending doom—making "sure of the most correct catastrophe" (canto 1).

Stevens indulges in no idealism about the fate of human history in these poems; he is adamant in "Esthétique" that "life is a bitter aspic. We are not / At the centre of a diamond" (canto 11). Still, he suggests in both poems that no matter how ominous the natural world seems, it is not necessarily an image of catastrophe unless our metaphors make it seem catastrophic. In "Esthétique" the protagonist must put down his book and observe the world in different terms: he "establishes / The visible" and (like the Old Testament creator) "calls it good" (canto 13). In "The Auroras" the scholar must see that the very changeableness of the auroras (their susceptibility to a variety of ominous metaphors) suggests that the unnaturally lit sky is not an inevitable sign of doom: the image can "move to find / What must unmake" itself (canto 7), and the maker of metaphors can learn to be similarly self-critical, unmaking his own apocalyptic designs. If it is possible that the auroras are not "a spell of light / A saying out of a cloud," it is also possible that they are an "innocence of the earth and no false sign / Or symbol of malice" (canto 8). This innocence is an achievement, not an evasion of harsher realities. Stevens wants to suggest that a vision of our ultimate demise may be as consoling and seductive as a vision of our infancy: positing the end of the world, we are relieved of our responsibility for it. "That greatest poverty," says Stevens in the final section of "Esthétique du Mal," is "to feel that one's desire / Is too difficult to tell from despair."

In "An Ordinary Evening in New Haven" (1949, in *The Auroras of Autumn*), the longest and most wayward of the later poems, "Professor Eucalyptus" faces a barren world that Stevens insists is "plain" rather than "grim": the world is never just grim but "grimly seen" by an "indifferent" eye. By describing our world with a more "commodious adjective," the professor discovers a sense of divinity within the plain sense of things (canto 14). As both Charles Berger and Eleanor Cook have suggested, Stevens plays with the word "eucalyptus" (meaning "well covered," in contrast to "apokalypsis," the extraordinary uncovering of things). And though "Esthétique du Mal" and "The Auroras of Autumn" might be called "eucalyptic" poems, they are not simply anti-apocalyptic: if they reject the notion that revelation comes only at the end of human existence, they do not assert that revelation is unavailable to us in our everyday lives. More sternly than ever before, Stevens locates the extraordinary within the ordinary. "We seek / Nothing beyond reality," he insists in "An Ordinary Evening in New Heaven," finding within reality the "pattern of the heavens and high, night air" (canto 9). At first reading, these long poems may seem frustratingly aimless. But since Stevens is fighting against all notions of the end (catastrophe, transcendence, revelation, apocalypse), the inconclusiveness of a poem like "An Ordinary Evening in New Haven" must be seen as a "part of the never-ending meditation" (canto 1). When Stevens asserts that a "more severe" master offers "more urgent proof that the theory / Of poetry is the theory of life," Stevens is not suggesting that he himself is incapable of such rigor; he is once again stressing the importance of dwelling within ambiguity—of rejecting the easier consolations of certainty for "the intricate evasions of as" (canto 28).

Characteristically, however, Stevens himself was skeptical even of this hard-won skepticism. He worried that the ambitious long poems collected in *The Auroras of Autumn,* however strategically open-ended, gave the impression of a self-contained and self-sustaining worldview. Consequently, in the brief, elliptical poems collected in *The Rock* or left uncollected at his death, Stevens both described and enacted the values of partialness and incompletion: "The great structure has become a minor house," he says in "The Plain Sense of Things," referring to both the world he sees and the poetry he has written. His luminous and almost weightless final poems are perhaps Stevens' finest achievement. Reading them, we feel the presence of a lifetime's work behind the deceptively simple lines. They are the poems of an old man facing the end of his life but refusing to value the end over the ongoing process, even when he recognizes that the process will continue without him.

## FINAL POEMS

Ever since he wrote "The Death of a Soldier" and "The Snow Man," Stevens had been fascinated by the wintry blankness of the inhuman world. In the late short poems this world seems blanker—and yet more uncannily beautiful—than ever before. While some poems (such as "The Rock," "Final Soliloquy of the Interior Paramour," or "To an Old Philosopher in Rome," all collected in *The Rock,* 1954) still tempt us with a vision of wholeness and plenitude, Stevens nevertheless cautions in "The Course of a Particular" (1951) that although "one says that one is part of everything, / There is a conflict, there is a resistance involved." Stevens is ultimately more fascinated by the conflict, the resistance, than by the feeling of wholeness. While some poets believe in "a universal poetry that is reflected in everything," Stevens writes in "The Relations between Poetry and Painting" (1951), he himself "is better satisfied by particulars." In "The Course of a Particular" he rejects all metaphors for the sound of dead leaves swept by the wind:

> The leaves cry. It is not a cry of divine attention,
> Nor the smoke-drift of puffed-out heroes, nor
>     human cry.
> It is the cry of leaves that do not transcend them-
>     selves,
> In the absence of fantasia, without meaning more
> Than they are in the final finding of the ear, in the
>     thing
> Itself, until, at last, the cry concerns no one at all.

The leaves "do not transcend themselves"; they offer no augury or image of a world beyond our own. Stevens wants us to feel the sublime wonder of particulars: he wants us to divest ourselves of all expectation, scrutinizing the ordinary world so meticulously that we discover its majesty.

In "The River of Rivers in Connecticut" (1953), Stevens speaks as a man who has seen the Styx, the river that divides this world from the afterlife. But he hangs back, focusing our attention on a river "this side of Stygia" that is just as "great":

> On its banks,
> No shadow walks. The river is fateful,
> Like the last one. But there is no ferryman.
> He could not bend against its propelling force.
>
> It is not to be seen beneath the appearances
> That tell of it. The steeple at Farmington
> Stands glistening and Haddam shines and sways.
>
> It is the third commonness with light and air,
> A curriculum, a vigor, a local abstraction . . .
> Call it, once more, a river, an unnamed flowing,
>
> Space-filled, reflecting the seasons, the folk-lore
> Of each of the senses; call it, again and again,
> The river that flows nowhere, like a sea.

In "The Idea of Order at Key West" Stevens listens to a woman singing beside the ocean; in "Sunday Morning" a "procession of the dead" seems to "wind" across "wide water." Here, in contrast, the earthly river seems sparsely populated even when compared to the afterlife; there is no shadow on its banks, no ferryman to take us across. The force of the river could not be mastered by Charon (who ferries the souls of the dead across the Styx), which suggests that the earth cannot be encompassed by any myth. The river is itself a "commonness"; it has no metaphysical depth beneath its appearance. The things of this world—even our images of transcendence (the steeple)—are merely reflected back to us in the river's shining, sway-

ing surface. Yet the river is a wonder (the "river of rivers") precisely because it holds us so firmly within our ordinary, earthly existence. Hanging on to a life that will soon end, Stevens finds the ultimate consolation in an image of meandering process, something that "flows nowhere." And he invites us to join in that process, a process that is at once the endless becoming of the earth and the endless project of his poetry: we must give the unnamed river its name "again and again."

### AN APPRAISAL

When Stevens began writing in his journal in the year 1900, he gave these lines from Keats a page to themselves: "But my flag is not unfurl'd / On the Admiral-staff, and to philosophize / I dare not yet." As both poet and insurance lawyer, Stevens was nothing if not cautious. He waited until he was almost forty-four years old to publish his first book; he weathered long poetic silences stoically in order to secure his economic future. Although he became perhaps the most important American poet of the century (his unmistakable influence is apparent in poets as radically different from each other as John Ashbery and Donald Justice), his enabling skepticism never left Stevens. The power of his poetry grows from the startling fact that it makes the largest possible claims for poetry at the same time that it subjects poetry to the most rigorous critique.

From the beginning of his career to the end, from "Sunday Morning" until "The River of Rivers in Connecticut," Stevens proclaims that the "imperfect is our paradise." He insists that we not only recognize our failures but also embrace them: "Note that, in this bitterness, delight," he writes in "The Poems of Our Climate" (1938; in *Parts of a World*), "Since the imperfect is so hot in us, / Lies in flawed words and stubborn sounds."

If Stevens is known as the poet who insisted most convincingly that we create the fictions by which we live, he must also be known as the poet who insisted most bracingly that we must discard even our most treasured formulas for living. "Some people always know exactly what they think," said Stevens late in his career. "I am afraid I am not one of those people. The same thing keeps active in my mind and rarely becomes fixed."

# Selected Bibliography

## WORKS OF WALLACE STEVENS

POETRY AND ESSAYS

*The Necessary Angel: Essays on Reality and the Imagination.* New York: Knopf, 1951.

*The Collected Poems.* New York: Knopf, 1954. (Includes *Harmonium, Ideas of Order, The Man with the Blue Guitar, Parts of a World, Transport to Summer, The Auroras of Autumn,* and *The Rock.*)

*The Palm at the End of the Mind: Selected Poems and a Play.* Edited by Holly Stevens. New York: Knopf, 1971.

*Opus Posthumous.* Revised, enlarged, and corrected. Edited by Milton J. Bates. New York: Knopf, 1989.

CORRESPONDENCE, JOURNALS, AND MISCELLANEOUS

*Letters of Wallace Stevens.* Selected and edited by Holly Stevens. New York: Knopf, 1966.

*Souvenirs and Prophecies: The Young Wallace Stevens.* Edited by Holly Stevens. New York: Knopf, 1977.

*Secretaries of the Moon: The Letters of Wallace Stevens and Jose Rodriguez Feo.* Edited by Beverly Coyle and Alan Filreis. Durham, N.C.: Duke University Press, 1986.

*Sur Plusieurs Beaux Sujets: Wallace Stevens' Commonplace Book, A Facsimile and Transcription.* Edited by Milton J. Bates. Stanford, Calif.: Stanford University Press, 1989.

"Letters to Ferdinand Reyher." Edited by Holly Stevens. *Hudson Review* 44, no. 3:381–409 (autumn 1991).

## BIBLIOGRAPHIES

Edelstein, Jerome Melvin. *Wallace Stevens: A Descriptive Bibliography.* Pittsburgh: University of Pittsburgh Press, 1973.

Serio, John N. *Wallace Stevens: An Annotated Secondary Bibliography.* Pittsburgh: University of Pittsburgh Press, 1994.

## CRITICAL AND BIOGRAPHICAL STUDIES

Bates, Milton J. *Wallace Stevens: A Mythology of Self.* Berkeley: University of California Press, 1985.

Berger, Charles. *Forms of Farewell: The Late Poetry of Wallace Stevens.* Madison: University of Wisconsin Press, 1985.

Blackmur, R. P. *The Double Agent: Essays in Craft and Elucidation.* New York: Arrow, 1935.

Bloom, Harold. *Wallace Stevens: The Poems of Our Climate.* Ithaca, N.Y.: Cornell University Press, 1977.

———, ed. *Wallace Stevens.* New York: Chelsea House, 1985.

Borroff, Marie, ed. *Wallace Stevens: A Collection of Critical Essays.* Englewood Cliffs, N.J.: Prentice Hall, 1963.

Brazeau, Peter. *Parts of a World: Wallace Stevens Remembered, An Oral Biography.* New York: Random House, 1983.

Bromwich, David. "Stevens and the Idea of the Hero." *Raritan* 7, no. 1:1–27 (summer 1987).

Carroll, Joseph. *Wallace Stevens' Supreme Fiction: A New Romanticism.* Baton Rouge: Louisiana State University Press, 1987.

Cook, Eleanor. *Poetry, Word-Play, and Word-War in Wallace Stevens.* Princeton, N.J.: Princeton University Press, 1988.

Doggett, Frank A. *Stevens' Poetry of Thought.* Baltimore: Johns Hopkins University Press, 1966.

Doggett, Frank, and Robert Buttel, eds. *Wallace Stevens: A Celebration.* Princeton, N.J.: Princeton University Press, 1980.

Filreis, Alan. *Modernism from Right to Left: Wallace Stevens, the Thirties, & Literary Radicalism.* Cambridge: Cambridge University Press, 1994.

Gelpi, Albert, ed. *Wallace Stevens: The Poetics of Modernism.* Cambridge: Cambridge University Press, 1985.

Grey, Thomas C. *The Wallace Stevens Case: Law and the Practice of Poetry.* Cambridge, Mass.: Harvard University Press, 1991.

Kermode, Frank. *Wallace Stevens.* Edinburgh: Oliver and Boyd, 1960.

Leggett, B. J. *Wallace Stevens and Poetic Theory: Conceiving the Supreme Fiction.* Chapel Hill: University of North Carolina Press, 1987.

Lensing, George S. *Wallace Stevens: A Poet's Growth.* Baton Rouge: Louisiana State University Press, 1986.

Lentricchia, Frank. *Modernist Quartet.* Cambridge: Cambridge University Press, 1994.

Litz, A. Walton. *Introspective Voyager: The Poetic Development of Wallace Stevens.* New York: Oxford University Press, 1972.

Longenbach, James. *Wallace Stevens: The Plain Sense of Things.* New York: Oxford University Press, 1991.

MacLeod, Glen G. *Wallace Stevens and Modern Art: From the Armory Show to Abstract Expressionism.* New Haven, Conn.: Yale University Press, 1993.

Miller, J. Hillis. *The Linguistic Moment: From Wordsworth to Stevens.* Princeton, N.J.: Princeton University Press, 1985.

Poirier, Richard. *Poetry and Pragmatism.* Cambridge, Mass.: Harvard University Press, 1992.

Richardson, Joan. *Wallace Stevens: A Biography.* 2 vols. New York: Morrow, 1986–1988.

Riddel, Joseph N. *The Clairvoyant Eye: The Poetry and Poetics of Wallace Stevens.* Baton Rouge: Louisiana State University Press, 1965.

Schaum, Melita, ed. *Wallace Stevens & the Feminine.* Tuscaloosa: University of Alabama Press, 1993.

Vendler, Helen. *On Extended Wings: Wallace Stevens' Longer Poems.* Cambridge, Mass.: Harvard University Press, 1969.

———. *Wallace Stevens: Words Chosen out of Desire.* Cambridge; Mass.: Harvard University Press, 1986.

*—JAMES LONGENBACH*

# John Updike
## 1932–

*I*T IS NOW possible to say of John Updike what he wrote about Vladimir Nabokov in his 1965 essay "Grand-Master Nabokov" collected in *Assorted Prose*: he is "the best writer of English prose at present holding American citizenship, [and] the only writer . . . whose books, considered as a whole, give the happy impression of an *oeuvre*, of a continuous task carried forward variously, of a solid personality, of a plenitude of gifts exploited knowingly." No other American writer of the later twentieth century has been so prolific, so consistent, so conscious a designer of his own *oeuvre complète*, nor so possessed of a plenitude of literary gifts as John Updike. If he was able to appreciate that Nabokov "writes prose the only way it should be written—that is, ecstatically," he was—it turns out thirty years later—only describing himself. Updike seems to have known from the time his first novel, *The Poorhouse Fair*, was published by Alfred A. Knopf in 1959 what his future work would be about (doubt, faith, transience), how it would be written (elegantly, confidently), and even how it would look—typeset in Janson and bound elegantly by the Haddon Craftsmen of Scranton, Pennsylvania, as if it were the first volume of a uniform edition. Appearances, in his case, have not been deceiving. As one reviewer foresaw in 1972, "He is putting together a body of work which in substantial intelli-

gent creation will eventually be seen as second to none in our time." When he published his first short story in the *New Yorker* at the age of twenty-three, he seemed a prodigy. Now after some forty books he has become simply prodigious.

At the structural center of his work is the figure of Updike himself, or what might best be called the narrative shape of his own life. Much of his best fiction draws upon his boyhood and adolescence, on the experiences of his parents and family, the places in southeastern Pennsylvania where he grew up, his marriage and adult life in northeastern Massachusetts, and on the intimate details of his infidelities, divorce, and remarriage. Yet Updike's autobiographical impulse has been curiously dispassionate, not confessional or narcissistic. He has no wish to perform or flaunt himself, but rather to be, as he explained in "Why Write?" (1974), "a means whereby a time and place make their mark." He sought, that is, selflessness: "Beginning with the wish to make an impression, one ends wishing to erase the impression, to make of it a perfect transparency, to make of oneself a point of focus purely, as selfless as a lens." Confident that his own time and place had to be significant and would express themselves through the lens of a scrupulous eye, Updike set about the investigation of his own life.

SHILLINGTON

John Updike was born in Reading, Pennsylvania, on March 18, 1932, the only child of Linda Grace Hoyer and Wesley Russell Updike, a junior high school teacher of mathematics. For the next thirteen years the family lived on Philadelphia Avenue in Shillington, the small town Updike would memorialize as Olinger in his fiction (the nearby city of Reading became "Brewer"). His mother had a master's degree from Cornell and literary ambitions. One of his earliest memories was recounted in "A Soft Spring Night in Shillington," in *Self-Consciousness*, of her "tapping away in the front bedroom at her unpublished stories." She subscribed to the *New Yorker* and by age twelve her son aspired to become a contributor there, too. He came to see her bookcase full of college texts as a symbol: "I didn't read them, but in the walls of my life the bookcase stood like the door to a secret passage."

Making ends meet was difficult on a teacher's salary during the Depression, particularly with Updike's grandparents, Katherine and John Hoyer living in the same house as well. Updike was especially aware of his father's hardships: "Life had given my father a beating," he wrote in *Self-Consciousness* (1989); "his own father's failures and sorrow and early death had poured through him like rain through a broken window." Updike memorialized his father in the moving characterization of George Caldwell in *The Centaur* (1963), a self-sacrificing and compassionate teacher who was ridiculed by his students and colleagues. The novel gives him mythic status as the "blameless" centaur Chiron, half man and half god, whose wish to die is at last granted by the gods.

In 1945 Updike's family moved, at his mother's urging, to a ninety-three-acre farm near Plowville, eleven miles from Shillington, and into the very sandstone farmhouse where his mother was born. For her it was a deliverance of sorts; for her son

in high school it was a form of exile and humiliation. "Agricultural enterprise," in *Self-Consciousness*, was "the most depressing activity, I felt, in the world." His father's reaction was similar, and is voiced by Caldwell to his wife in *The Centaur*: "I want to be frank with you because you are my wife. I hate Nature. It reminds me of death." Echoes of these feelings resonate in such stories as "Flight" (1959), "Pigeon Fathers" (1961), *Of the Farm* (1965), "Harv Is Plowing Now" (1966), and "A Sandstone Farmhouse" (1990). When Updike summons remembrance of things past, he recalls Shillington affectionately and Plowville with an ambivalence bordering on revulsion.

As a self-conscious adolescent Updike was plagued by psoriasis, stuttering, and anxieties about acceptance. "I was a homely, comically ambitious hillbilly," his fictional representative in the story "Flight" admits frankly. "Consciousness of a special destiny made me both arrogant and shy." He knew himself to be an outsider, set apart from the children of other middle-class families. But he did not feel socially inferior, exactly. He remembers his father insisting that "we were poor!" and joking grimly about ending up in the poorhouse—literally, since the large yellow County Home was at the end of their street. But as Updike recalled in his 1964 essay "The Dogwood Tree: A Boyhood," "I felt neither prosperous nor poor. . . . My father's job paid him poorly but me well; it gave me a sense of, not prestige, but *place*. As a schoolteacher's son, I was assigned a role; people knew me. . . . I had a place to be." A vivid expression of this fundamental recognition appears in his 1960 story, "A Sense of Shelter." Characteristically, Updike worked to solidify that sense of place through words. He won not just approval but identity by means of his writing and cartooning. Over the years he contributed to his high school newspaper some 285 stories, articles, light verse, and drawings. He attempted writing a mystery novel in his sophomore year, but his announced ambition was to be a cartoonist. By the time he graduated in 1950 he had become class president and co-valedictorian. Still he remained at a distance, as his classmates' wording about him in the yearbook testified: "the sage of Plowville hopes to write for a living."

Shillington has remained for Updike a microcosm of the middle-class America he declares the deepest love for, the place he has drawn upon most for his fiction. On a return visit in 1980 he declared (in "A Soft Spring Night in Shillington" in *Self-Consciousness*),

> I loved Shillington not as one loves Capri or New York, because they are special, but as one loves one's own body and consciousness, because they are synonymous with being. It was exciting for me to be in Shillington, as if my life, like the expanding universe, when projected backwards gained heat and intensity. If there was a meaning to existence, I was closest to it here.

From this perspective Rabbit Angstrom, the protagonist of Updike's four novels about a foolish failure of a husband and father who struggles through all the confusions of lower middle-class America, represents Updike himself "projected backwards." He stands for something that Updike once was, might have become (if he had remained in Shillington), and still is to some extent: a typical confused small-town American kid, decent but selfish, driven this way and that by his relentlessly secular society, an innocent who still believes it best to trust his own instincts. Loyalty to this figure runs throughout Updike's work. Ironically, since Updike's own adult sophistications are apparent, Rabbit embodies for him someone more authentic, closer to the "meaning of existence" than he feels himself to be. That sophisticated adult self he often designates, revealingly, as an impersonation. He recalls, on another return to Shillington (in "The Dogwood Tree: A Boyhood" in *Assorted Prose*) staring at a picture of himself as a boy:

> I stand before that photograph, and am disappointed to receive no flicker, not the shadow of a flicker, of approval, of gratitude. The boy continues to smile at the corner of the room, beyond me. That boy is not a ghost to me, he is real to me; it is I who am a ghost to him. I, in my present state, was one of the ghosts that haunted his childhood. Like some phantom conjured by this child from a glue bottle, I have executed his commands; acquired pencils, paper, and an office. Now I wait apprehensively for his next command, or at least a nod of appreciation, and he smiles through me, as if I am already transparent with failure.

## WRITING AS AUTOBIOGRAPHY

Meanwhile the Sage of Plowville was awarded a full tuition scholarship and went off to Harvard College in the fall of 1950. Except for two summers working as copy boy for the Reading *Eagle*, in 1951 and 1952, he would never again live at home. He launched a novel, wrote sketches and drew cartoons for the Harvard *Lampoon*, and studied enthusiastically. A glimpse of his first year in college may be conveyed in "The Christian Roommates" (1966) where Updike casts himself in the minor role of Kern: "A farm boy driven by an unnatural sophistication, riddled with nervous ailments ranging from conjunctivitis to hemorrhoids, Kern smoked and talked incessantly." Updike majored in English literature, wrote poetry, became president of the *Lampoon*, and on June 26, 1953, married Mary Pennington, a Radcliffe student two years older than he, and the daughter of a Unitarian minister in Chicago. After a honeymoon in Ipswich, Massachusetts, and a summer working with Mary at a camp in Vermont, Updike returned for his senior year at Harvard, wrote an honors essay on the poetry of Robert Herrick, graduated *summa cum laude*, and in the summer of 1954 sold his first short story ("Friends from Philadelphia") and first poem ("Duet, With Muffled Brake Drums") to the *New Yorker*. It marked the beginning of a lifelong association with the magazine that published most of his stories, poems, essays, and reviews.

Awarded a Knox Fellowship for 1954–1955, Updike went to Oxford, England, to study at the Ruskin School of Drawing and Fine Art. In April 1955 the Updikes' first child, Elizabeth, was born. A few stories offer autobiographical reflections on their Oxford experience, the best of which is "A Madman" (1966), about their struggle to find lodging. As he suggests in *Picked-Up Pieces*, the experience seems to have strengthened his appreciation of America: "For nine months in England I felt like a balloon on too long a tether." On their return to America in August Updike took a job as staff writer for the *New Yorker* that he had been offered by the editor Katherine S. White when they met in England. For a time he lived in what seemed an atmosphere of "dreams come true," he wrote in *Picked-Up Pieces*. " I was twenty-three, newly a father, newly employed. Since boyhood I had wanted to live in New York. I had wanted to work for the magazine that now I did work for. I had wanted to be a writer and now a few poems and short stories were filtering into print." In fact many of those poems ("Summer: West Side," for example) and stories ("A Gift from the City," for example) reflected the Updikes' happiness in Manhattan. Then a second child, David, was born in January 1957; Updike completed a six-hundred-page novel, *Home*, which he chose not to publish; and he decided to quit his job, move to the coastal village of Ipswich, Massachusetts, and devote himself full-time to his own writing.

Troubled though he still was by inhibitions and inferiorities, embarrassed by psoriasis and an unpredictable stutter, Updike remained superbly confident of his writing. Now responsible for a family of four, he had no employer and he had not yet published a book. Nevertheless success arrived promptly. Harper and Brothers published his first collection of poems, *The Carpentered Hen* in 1958; when they asked him to change the ending of his new novel, *The Poorhouse Fair*, he refused and sent it to Knopf, which published it in January. *The Same Door*, his first collection of stories, was published by Knopf later that year, shortly after a second son, Michael, was born in May. In 1960 *Rabbit, Run*, the novel many critics think his best, was published; *The Poorhouse Fair* won a prize from the National Institute of Arts and Letters, and a daughter, Miranda, was born in December. Evidently his career as writer and father was now well begun.

He later came to see Ipswich as a version of Shillington, except it was an hour north of Boston and higher up the social scale. His new neighbors reminded him, he wrote in *Self-Consciousness*, of "those Shillington residents who stood a step or two higher on the stairs of fulfillment than our somehow blighted, quixotic household, and they, perhaps, responded to the conscientious Shillington boy in me. In Ipswich my impersonation of a normal person became as good as I could make it." His life and career appeared to be exceptionally stable over the next decade. Apart from a steady stream of novels, stories, verse, essays, reviews, and prizes, not much changed on the surface. In 1961 he rented an office on South Main Street in Ipswich where he went to work every morning, six days a week. As a regular treatment for his chronic psoriasis he sunbathed in the dunes at Crane's Beach in summer and in midwinter vacationed alone in the Caribbean. In 1964 he traveled to Eastern Europe and Russia for the U.S. State Department.

However, signs of marital discontent began to appear in the stories of *The Music School* (1966), including episodes of infidelity, impending separation, obsessive guilt, unsuccessful therapy, and divorce. He discovered in the late 1960s that he could not side with his liberal neighbors in criticizing the United States' involvement in the Vietnam war. In 1968 he published his most shocking, sexually explicit novel, *Couples*, about wife-swapping and adultery in Tarbox, a thinly disguised version of Ipswich. The book quickly became a national best-seller, and his picture appeared on the cover of *Time* magazine, on April 26, 1968. On top of that Hollywood offered him five hundred thousand dollars for the film rights to the novel, and when he expressed disbelief they offered one hundred thousand dollars more. He marked the event with a sadly ambivalent essay, "Farewell to the Middle Class." Although it seemed a betrayal of his essential self, he knew everything had changed: he was rich.

Sensing himself at a turning point in his life and career, Updike wrote "Midpoint" in 1969, a long autobiographical poem about his origins and desires, beliefs and lack of belief. It concludes guardedly,

> Born laughing, I've believed in the Absurd,
> Which brought me this far; henceforth, if I can,
> I must impersonate a serious man.

Then he took his family to England for a year, escaping and avoiding some of the political, communal, and domestic conflicts he had become embroiled in. It proved to be a respite, but not a solution. The fact of the Updikes' disintegrating marriage kept appearing in his fiction, as a series of stories about Richard and Joan Maple. Updike invented these surrogate figures for himself and his wife, Mary, in "Snowing in Greenwich Village" (1956) and he completed two more stories about the couple in 1966. Then in *Museums and Women* (1972) suddenly there were five new stories about the Maples, all of them clearly transpositions into fiction of the Updikes' impending breakup. During 1973 they traveled together in Africa on a Fulbright grant (Updike lectured in Ghana, Nigeria, Kenya, and Ethiopia). And in 1974 the Updikes finally separated—the sorrowful, half-comic details are made into fiction in "Separating" (1975)—and he went to live in an apartment in Boston. They filed for a "no fault" divorce in 1976.

The remarkable fact about all these events is that Updike chose to chronicle them so openly. He changed the names but otherwise used fiction as virtual autobiography. When the stories were gathered into a sequence, *Too Far to Go: The Maples Stories* (1979), Updike acknowledged in the foreword, "Though the Maples stories trace the decline and fall of a marriage, they also illumine a history in many ways happy, of growing children and a million mundane moments shared." It would be hard to miss the personal message in that. These stories are also remarkable for their stylistic directness. Updike has sometimes been faulted for excessively self-conscious, ornately metaphoric language, but the manner of the Maples stories is, as they evolve, increasingly plain. In a moving final gesture of the book, as the judge grants their divorce, Richard and Joan Maple step back, "uncertain how to turn, until Richard at last remembered what to do; he kissed her."

Whether this occurred in Updike's own life hardly matters. The point is that Updike transformed his experience into something fine, a beautifully expressive gesture. He once declared to an interviewer, "I disavow any essential connection between my life and whatever I write. . . . The work, the words on the paper, must stand apart from our living presences." Indeed they do; the difference between life and art, actuality and its representation, is enormous. But it is also paper thin. To "disavow any essential connection" fools nobody.

Two months later Updike moved to Georgetown, Massachusetts, with Martha Bernhard and her three sons. When the divorce became final a year later he and Martha were married, on September 30, 1977, and now live in Beverly Farms, Massachusetts, a North Shore community not greatly different from Ipswich. Neither riches nor divorce and remarriage transformed him quite so much as might have been expected. For another notable fact about Updike's interwoven life and career is that he continued, through all the discord and guilt and domestic upheaval, to write. His fiction seems in fact to have been nourished and deepened from these experiences. He even became, if anything, more prolific in the late 1970s and 1980s than before. Many of the stories collected in *Problems and Other Stories* (1979) and *Trust Me* (1987) focus on versions of himself—men of a certain age, divorced husbands, remarried fathers, angry and ambivalent men who are feeling guilty about their children, regretful about the past, and conscious of their mortalities. If these are not so directly autobiographical as the Maples stories, they are still variations on that theme, continuations of that narrative.

Updike's mother died in 1985, an event that stimulated a significant number of new stories about home. Updike wrote the memoir, *Self-Consciousness* in 1989, part of which explores the more remote history of his father's family in New Jersey, New England, and Holland. In recent years his short fiction has turned increasingly to stories of death and physical deterioration, but also to new versions of his mother and father, many of which are collected in *The Afterlife* (1994). And his most important later novel, *In the Beauty of the Lilies* (1996), takes its point of departure from his grandfather's experience as a Presbyterian minister in Trenton, New Jersey, at the turn of the century. Rarely is Updike's fiction without some autobiographical design, some personal figure in the carpet. To Charles Thomas Samuels he admitted, reluctantly, that there was "a submerged thread connecting certain of the fictions, and I guess the submerged thread is the autobiography." It is clearly much more than a thread, and hardly submerged. Updike has come to admit that. "The autobiography of a writer of fiction," he said in a 1975 review, "is generally superfluous, since he has already, in rearrangement and disguise, written out the material of his life many times."

## NATURALISTIC DETERMINISM

An equally fundamental component of Updike's vision is his acceptance of naturalistic fact. From the naive boy, David, in "Pigeon Feathers" to the silenced grandfather, Wilmot, in *In the Beauty of the Lilies*, Updike's characters have been thrust against the daunting "truths" of post-Darwinian science. His essays and reviews, poems and lectures are no less studded with dismal recognitions of the impersonal forces that rule our existences. The laws of chemistry and biology, geology and physics are overwhelmingly powerful; human beings with their fragile systems of value and belief are weak, transitory, and groundless. "Who dares now doubt," Updike wrote in a 1975 review of *The Lives of the Cell* (in *Picked-Up Pieces*), "that empirical science is the only legally licensed hunter of truth and the one legitimate dispenser of information about reality?" Yet to accept such truth is no happy matter. He wrote in 1985,

> we shrink from what [modern science] has to tell us of our perilous and insignificant place in the cosmos. . . . our century's revelations of unthinkable largeness and unimaginable smallness, of abysmal stretches of geological time when we were nothing, of supernumerary galaxies and indeterminate subatomic behavior, of a kind of mad mathematical violence at the heart of matter have scorched us deeper than we know.

These scorching conceptions clearly underlie much of, if not all, Updike's writing. They are the basis of his skepticism and the impetus for his, and his characters', quests for faith. The brilliant first chapter of *The Centaur*, for example, presents Caldwell's classroom lecture on the history of the universe and its "sickening" numbers. When Caldwell reaches the climax of this narrative, with the appearance "one minute ago" of that tragic animal, man, "his very blood loathed the story he had told."

Updike may well share the feeling. His suggestively titled collection of poems, *Against Nature*, includes seven "Odes to Natural Processes"; three of which processes—growth, healing, and crystallization—are integrative, while four—rot, evaporation, fragmentation, and entropy—are disintegrative. If the world is so devoid of any intrinsic reassurances, taking positions "against nature" has a certain defensive logic. Similarly, at the midpoint of his philosophical poem, "Midpoint," Updike dwells on the elemental fludity of matter, in a section called "The Dance of the Solids." Nothing about solids is solid. Their every property dramatizes uncertainty, asymmetry, relativity, unpredictability, disintegration, and flaw:

> Textbooks and Heaven only are Ideal;
> Solidity is an imperfect state.
> Within the cracked and dislocated Real
> *Nonstoichiometric Crystals* dominate.

At a more personal level in the 1977 poem, "The Solitary Pond," Updike recalls attempting to skate on an uncooperative little pond in the woods when he was thirteen years old, beset by twigs and thorns, rough ice, cold weather, and his own clumsiness. When he gives up in disgust, "and thrashed home through the trees hating / the very scratches left by my experiment," it is as if that adolescent grievance against nature were renewed in the adult speaker, as hot as ever. He enlarges upon such feelings in "On Not Being a Dove" in *Self-Consciousness*: "I had become sore at the world—at its mud, its mess, its 'dirty talk,' its menace, its eventual victory over us in death. If a dirty war was being fought in Indochina, what was so unusual? What was worth protesting, decrying, getting self-righteous about? That was what the world was—a dirty war, somewhere or other, all the time." In a similar vein Updike concluded a review of Lewis Thomas' *The Lives of a Cell* (1985), collected in *Picked-Up Pieces*, with these grim observations:

> Every day, my well-fed cat brings as tribute to my back porch the mauled body of a field mouse or baby rabbit; one wonders how complacently the little corpses submitted to their part in our triune symbiosis. One does not have to live very close to nature to cringe at all the carnage and waste it contains. . . . Dr. Thomas' shimmering vision of a "fusion around the earth" that will spring from "more crowding, more unrestrained and obsessive communication" seems less a prognosis than a hope defiant of much we *can* observe about our increasingly crowded, irritable, depleted, de-institutionalized, and cannibalistic world.

Although Updike is determined to have no romantic illusions about nature and may loathe it and its "dirty war," its "carnage and waste," he is drawn to it nevertheless. He is moved again and again to marvel at its beauty, its fascinating intricacy, its depths of ambiguity and mystery. How can creation be so barbaric and chaotic and yet so beautiful—as if it were designed for us? In "Pigeon Feathers" the boy who shoots the birds because they are a nuisance discovers afterward the wonder of their plumage: each feather is "trimmed to fit a pattern that flowed without error across the bird's body." He is mesmerized by the sheer artistry of the creation: "across the surface of the infinitely adjusted yet somehow effortless mechanics of the feathers played idle designs of color, no two alike, designs executed, it seemed, in a controlled rapture, with a joy that hung level in the air above and behind him." So too the unnamed narrator of "Leaves" (1966) meditates on a "curiously beautiful" grapevine, with its perfect indifference to human suffering, its "casual precision" and "effortless abundance of inventive 'effect.'" At any moment in an Updike narrative such an epiphany may occur. Interrupting a tense moment in "The Christian Roommates," for example, a bell rings "like a heartbeat within the bosom of time" and suddenly "the walls of the room vibrated with leaf shadows, and many minute presences—dust motes, traffic sounds, or angels of whom several could dance on the head of a pin—thronged the air and made it difficult to breathe." Passages like these indicate Updike's unwillingness to surrender everything to science. He keeps discovering in nature hints of the same impulses that impell his art—the joy of pattern, intricacy, design, delicacy, inventiveness—as if the creator were revelling in it.

In his National Book Award acceptance speech of 1964 (for *The Centaur*) Updike registered his scientific skepticism, but made clear at the same time how he thought his art—"a tissue of literal lies"—could serve beauty, goodness, and truth. He reasoned that since reality "is—chemically, atomically, biologically—a fabric of microscopic accuracies," then the writer's responsibility is to "grapple for the shape and shade" of that fabric, not presumptuously or egotistically but "through a series of hesitations and qualifications," and with a "kind of timid reverence toward what exists." Peter Caldwell in *The Centaur* makes much the same point. Far from feeling revulsion at nature, "a patch of Pennsylvania in 1947," he "burned to paint it, just like that, in its puzzle of glory." Peter concludes, "it came upon me that I must go to Nature disarmed of perspective and stretch myself like a large transparent canvas upon her in the hope that, my submission being perfect, the imprint of a beautiful and useful truth would be taken." These attitudes go far toward explaining Updike's style, which ranges so freely from the warmth of metaphor to the chill of taxonomial Latin, from a sensuously nuanced detail to a high-flown abstraction, from learned allusion to a painterly aestheticism and austerity. It is a shape-shifting style, restlessly supple and full of surprise twists and turns, endlessly attentive to the "fabric of microscopic accuracies" that it would represent, the "puzzle of glory" it would evoke.

## VESTIGES OF CHRISTIANITY

Naturalistic determinism continued to influence Updike's writing. His sense of "the mad mathematical violence at the heart of matter" and the "abysmal" dimensions of time and space haunt his characters—whether they consciously recognize it or not—and form Updike's central subject. The "scorching conceptions" of modern science are what we have instead of God. After those shattering revelations, he asks, what belief is possible? What meaning or faith can there be? Updike's characters flounder in a secularized, commodified mid-American world; most of them, like Rabbit Angstrom, are only dimly aware of their disappointment in life. He saw his characters in 1967 as "the wistful citizens of a violent society desperately oversold, for want of other connectives, on love." They are trying the "experiment," as T. S. Eliot called it in "Thoughts after Lambeth" (1933), "of a civilized but non-Christian mentality." The experiment will fail, said Eliot, who wanted Christianity to be preserved "through the dark time ahead." Updike, of a later generation, finds no such hope in Christian belief. Although he was raised a Lutheran, attended a Congregational church in Ipswich, and is now an Episcopalian, his fiction remains devoutly skeptical. When questioned he denies being a "Christian writer," and only admits to being a writer who "happens to be Christian." In 1968 he told an interviewer that his subject was, "After Christianity, what?" Twenty years later in *Self-Consciousness* he put the matter somewhat differently. He remembers discovering early in his career ("as I set out") that what he had to say as a writer concerned "the whole mass of middling, hidden, troubled America," that it concerned some "terrible pressure of American disappointment." He saw his subject, he claimed in *Self-Consciousness*, summed up in an "odd and uplifting" line from "The Battle Hymn of the Republic": "In the beauty of the lilies Christ was born across the sea." It was the idea of a nation "severed from Christ by the breadth of the sea."

Thus when Updike came to write *In the Beauty of the Lilies* in 1994, it had a long foreground. Vestiges of Christian ideas and institutions, echoes of its traditional language and imagery, appear steadily throughout his works. But more often than not their presence signals an absence. Protestant ministers and theologians figure prominently, for example, in *Rabbit, Run, A Month of Sundays* (1975), and *Roger's Version* (1986), but they mainly serve to misguide the protagonist or are deeply hypocritical. Most of them are egotistical, like the divinity student in "Lifeguard" (1961) who conceives of faith as rescue from the sea; or profoundly ineffectual and passive, like Tom Marshfield in *A Month of Sundays*; or ludicrously insincere, like Roger Lambert, the preacher-turned-professor whose bad faith runs rampant in *Roger's Version*. One suspects that Updike, a great reader of Karl Barth and Paul Tillich in the 1950s and something of a lifelong divinity student himself, generated these men of the cloth as embodiments of his own faltering beliefs, as if to caricature the fraudulence or impossibility of such a role. Only the crusty old Lutheran minister Kruppenbach in *Rabbit, Run* embodies a respectable position. He is the sole figure—and a minor one at that—who offers an exemplary understanding of what faith might mean; but his piety is rigid, old-world asceticism, not something that Rabbit can understand.

*In the Beauty of the Lilies*, on the other hand, presents a new ministerial figure, the sympathetic Clarence Wilmot of Paterson, New Jersey, circa 1910, whose fateful act at the beginning of the novel is to fall silent. A scholarly and somewhat diffident man, Wilmot discovers he has lost his faith. Like Updike's grandfather, who surrendered the pulpit to his wife when a throat ailment silenced him, Wilmot uses a throat ailment as an

excuse. He surrenders his vocation because he can no longer resist the revelations of post-Darwinian science; God is no more than a fiction. In language subtly reminiscent of Theodore Dreiser, Frank Norris, and Stephen Crane, Wilmot discovers "what he had long suspected, that the universe was utterly indifferent to his states of mind and as empty of divine content as a corroded kettle." One can still detect Updike's style here, but the voice resonates with other turn-of-the-century texts, including Tennyson's *In Memoriam* and Matthew Arnold's "Dover Beach" as well as Stephen Crane's "The Open Boat" and Harold Frederic's *The Damnation of Theron Ware*:

> The former believer's habitual mental contortions decisively relaxed. And yet the depths of vacancy revealed were appalling. In the purifying sweep of atheism human beings lost all special value. The numb misery of the horse was matched by that of the farmer; the once-green ferny lives crushed into coal's fossiliferous strata were no more anonymous and obliterated than Clarence's own life would soon be, in a wink of earth's tremendous time. Without Biblical blessing the physical universe became sheerly horrible and disgusting. All fleshy acts became vile, rather than merely some. The reality of men slaying lambs and cattle, fish and fowl to sustain their own bodies took on an aspect of grisly comedy—the blood-soaked selfishness of a cosmic mayhem.

Never before has Updike so effectively historicized these issues, dissolving his own ideas into those of a character wholly unlike him. Coincident with Reverend Wilmot's spiritual surrender, in the novel's first chapter, is the rise of the American film industry. In a burst of documentary realism we are shown D. W. Griffiths directing Mary Pickford in a scene from *The Call to Arms*. Updike's design is not merely to trace the Wilmot family's spiritual and moral decline over the next three generations but to locate in the history of American films the creation of substitute deities—

stardom, publicity, technology, money—as the regnant gods of America.

That these gods are profoundly deceptive and inadequate to human needs is, of course, Updike's central point. But he also manages to show that Wilmot's granddaughter Essie survives rather well, as a movie star who manages to redefine her image for successive generations, a veteran of multiple roles. Like her novelist-creator she has learned to become transparent, a lens through which her audience sees beyond itself. Her son Clark, left to drift aimlessly in the margins of his mother's success, surrenders his pointless freedom to a religious cult group living in a commune in the mountains of Colorado, run by a Bible-quoting fanatic named Jesse. Bringing his story to a disastrous conclusion in the manner of the Waco, Texas, massacre, Updike dramatizes the fateful outcome of the religious abdication his narrative—and the twentieth century—began with: a pitched battle between Jesse and his desperate cohorts, who need to believe in something, and decent law-abiding citizens, who believe, complacently, in nothing.

Like many of Updike's novels *In the Beauty of the Lilies* gets its depth from religious questions, but provides no answers to the questions it raises. The beauty of Christ and the lilies across the sea seems to lie in their remoteness, in the breadth of the separation. Updike's critics have frequently mistaken him for a more religious writer than he is, especially in searching his books for "yea sayings" and epiphanies and bits of spiritual wisdom to be shored against the ruins—as in "The world is the host; it must be chewed" from "The Music School" or the cryptic epigraph from Pascal in *Rabbit, Run*: "The motions of Grace, the hardness of the heart; external circumstances." Engaging as these formulations can be, Updike remains detached from them. He entertains them, in his fiction, rather than believes in them. A revealing passage near the end of *In the Beauty of the Lilies* describes Clark/Esau, the uneasy conscript in

Jesse's commune who has become their public relations man, mulling over his go-between status:

> Returning then, besmirched by contact with the corrupt world, to put on his disciple's gown and sit and listen to Jesse rant upon the most ghastly passages of Ezekiel and Jeremiah and Revelation, pounding this desert lode of old grief into a present furious sword until his hoarse voice croaked shut, was no more strange, Esau told himself, than shifting from one to another of any of the layers that make up human existence—from wakefulness to sleep, from social dress and conversation to the mute nakedness of lovemaking, from eating blessed cereal at a ceremonial table to shitting in hunched solitude on a cold bowl. Man is a mixed bag, a landscape of swamps and caves as well as sunlit slopes.

So too Updike puts on his disciple's gown, after forays into "the corrupt world." He too shifts from one to another of the layers that make up human existence. He continues to listen, more bemused than compelled, to those who hunger for spiritual sustenance, to those who are still excavating "the desert lode of old grief." But human existence is too many-layered for him to praise it unequivocally. Human nature has too many swamps and caves.

What Updike offers instead is a religious sensibility. In fact there is some reason to understand it as a specifically Lutheran sensibility. The population of the area where Updike grew up German American was prevailingly Lutheran, so the church his family regularly attended was Lutheran as well. When Updike began to read theology in college he gravitated toward the Germanic Protestants of northern Europe, particularly Kierkegaard, Karl Barth, and Paul Tillich. About the latter he observed in 1966, as if he were describing himself, "His tolerance of uncertainty and of contradiction was perhaps specifically Lutheran," going on to quote Tillich's characterization of Lutheranism (in *On the Boundary*) as "a consciousness of the 'corruption' of existence, a repudiation of every kind of social Utopia (including the metaphysics of progressivism), an appreciation of the mystical element in religion, and a rejection of Puritanical legalism in private and corporeal life." Tillich was by no means Updike's favorite theologian, but it is curious to see how well Tillich's description accords with Updike's own sensibility at every point, not least the final, rather cryptic one about Puritanical "legalism." The phrase refers to the Puritan's extreme dissociation of the private self or "soul" from the merely public (corporeal, communal) self, as if the two really had nothing to do with one another. Updike's often surprisingly blunt references to sex, the genitals, copulation, or excretion, especially when they follow many an elegant phrase, may be symptomatic of a vigorous Lutheran rejection of the Puritan dichotomy rather than some shocking lapse of taste.

The theologian who most appealed to Updike over the years is Barth. In the foreword to *Assorted Prose* (1965) he recalls that "Barth's theology, at one point in my life, seemed alone to be supporting it." Despite the offhand terms Updike likes to use about "my curious hobby, Christianity" he takes very seriously the deep negativity of Barth's thought. "There is no way from us to God," Updike quotes approvingly from Barth as the opening of his essay, "Faith in Search of Understanding." Barth's contempt for the consoling God constructed from mere human needs and desires is scorching, and Updike clearly relishes that: "The real God, the God men do not invent, is *totaliter aliter*—Wholly Other. We cannot reach Him; only He can reach us." The off-putting ferocity of Kruppenbach in *Rabbit, Run* clearly owes something to Barthian theology; so too does the climactic destruction of the Tarbox church in *Couples* and the fiery holocaust at the end of *In the Beauty of the Lilies*. Even the sleazy Roger Lambert takes out his old Torchbook edition of Barth's *The Word of God and the Word of Man*, at the beginning of *Roger's Version*, to savor "the superb iron" and "seamless integrity" of Barth's prose.

The margins of his book are "marked again and again by the pencil of a young man who thought that here, definitively and forever, he had found the path, the voice, the style, and the method to save within himself . . . the Christian faith." Clearly that young man was as much Updike himself as his protagonist.

But as a writer Updike never found or wanted to find "definitively and forever," one path, one faith, or one theology. If he gravitates sometimes toward Barth, or toward Lutheran attitudes, or generally toward the traditional language and imagery of Christianity, he does it through his characters and through an acute consciousness of the things of this world. George Steiner once observed that Updike's style in *A Month of Sundays* reflects an "American spirituality . . . flesh-rooted and bound" wherein "grace is of this world or it is of none." Clearly Updike likes to hint at something transcendent—the "puzzle of glory" in nature, or some cryptic message, like the one at the end of "Midpoint": "Deepest in the thicket, thorns spell a word." But who can read what those thorns spell? So Updike always comes back again in his fiction to the fallen human beings and the perishable things of this world, without confidence there is anything else to believe in.

## LOVE, THE EXALTED ARENA

What we have left to believe in then is love. At one level Updike registers the futility of this, describing Americans as "desperately oversold, in the absence of other connectives, on love." But at another level he sympathizes, perhaps even sells the idea himself: "Only in being loved do we find external corroboration of the supremely high valuation each ego secretly assigns itself." Love is the "exalted arena" where men and women "choose that other being in whose existence their own existence is confirmed and amplified." Updike wrote these enthusiastic words in 1964 in "More

328 / AMERICAN WRITERS

Love in the Western World," reviewing a book by the Swiss essayist, Denis de Rougemont, whose famous critique of romantic love, *Love in the Western World*, first appeared in 1939. Summarizing Rougemont's thesis Updike found himself freshly persuaded by it: that romantic love celebrates passion, that it feeds on denial and not fulfillment, on narcissism and not reciprocity; that it prefers suffering to happiness, erotic sublimation to gratification; that it strengthens with distance and separation, and weakens with familiarity and accessibility. "Happy love has no history," says Rougemont. "Romance only comes into existence where love is fatal, frowned upon and doomed by life itself." And that is what our romantic myths glorify, Rougemont argues, not conjugal love or mutual understanding, but illicit or adulterous love, passion confirmed by the intensity of its risk and suffering. Updike was not only taken with Rougemont's thesis, which seemed to him in 1964 "increasingly beautiful and pertinent," he was also taken with the archetypal story, even going so far as to write a parody of it—"Four Sides of One Story" in *The Music School*. Since this material would have far-reaching effects on Updike's fiction for at least the next fifteen years, it is important to understand in more detail how Rougemont's arguments work.

Using the twelfth-century myth of Tristan and Iseult as an archetype, Rougemont traces from medieval times to the modern era the recurrent elements of a story that pervades our culture and generates fundamental problems in modern love and marriage. In brief outline, the story focuses on the knight Tristan who falls in love with Iseult, the woman King Mark has sent him to find and bring back to be his queen. On the return voyage they drink a potion that commits them to love each other until death. Iseult marries King Mark but she and Tristan remain secret lovers. After many trials, exposure, and punishments they run off together, but when their passion weakens they repent of their betrayals. Iseult the Fair, as she is called,

goes back to King Mark, and Tristan eventually marries another Iseult, whom he does not love, called Iseult of the White Hands. When he is wounded, only his first love can cure him, and he dies thinking (mistakenly) that his wife, not Iseult the Fair, is coming to succor him. Iseult the Fair arrives moments after Tristan's death, and she, too, dies—of a broken heart. So the story as Rougemont reads it glorifies and celebrates passion, suffering, separation, and love-unto-death. The fact that this love is adulterous only makes it, according to the myth, more sublime, because then it transcends (seemingly) such worldly and conventional concerns as propriety, duty, responsibility, marriage contracts, the safe and sanctioned realm of ordinary love. By flying in the face of these concerns, illicit passion confirms its own ultimate importance.

The effects of Rougemont's arguments on Updike's fiction were immediate. His typical middle-class American husbands began to acquire Tristanian guilts and longings, and the women they loved became Iseults, desirable insofar as they were unattainable. In "Four Sides of One Story" the first voice we hear is Tristan's on board a modern cruise ship, writing Iseult a long letter that revels in the anguish of their separation. Its second narrator is Iseult of the White Hands, cast as a suburban housewife whom Tristan has just left, writing a sardonic letter to a friend: "And through it all, making life a hell for everybody concerned, including the children, he wears this saintly pained look and insists he's trying to do the right thing." Iseult comes next, writing to Tristan a brief, fragmented letter (unsent) with phrases like "I dismay myself" and "you ravished me with absences." The final letter is written by King Mark to his lawyer, gloating that "the young man bolted" and his queen will be "tractable" now that he has compelled her into psychoanalysis. The story may be only a parodic sketch, a rewriting of the legend in half-modern guise, but it identifies a basic design Updike would use more subtly in many other fictions to come, most notably the later Maples stories, *A Month of Sundays*, some of the Bech stories, *Marry Me: A Romance* (1976), *Problems*, and *Brazil* (1994).

One of the best Henry Bech stories, "The Bulgarian Poetess" (which first appeared in *The Music School* and which was reprinted in *Bech: A Book*) for example, concludes with the protagonist's sad last attempts to convey his love for a woman he takes to be his soul mate, even though she barely speaks his language and he not a word of hers. Bech is a semi-famous Jewish novelist, representing his country on a cultural exchange tour abroad, but his career is sagging and he is hungry for approval. At a farewell party at the American embassy in Bulgaria he struggles to see Vera, the mysterious poetess, but is surrounded by brassy American diplomats' wives and a "rasping American female" who clutches his arm. When the hypothetical lovers manage to meet for a few seconds, she gives him a slim volume of her poems in a language he cannot read and in a copy of his own book he writes to her, "It is a matter of earnest regret for me that you and I must live on opposite sides of the world." Bech's "romance" is like Tristan's, predicated on its impossibility. The eloquence of his inscription arises from the same source. Underscoring the irony, Updike exposes the mechanism of Bech's failure to "see" his beloved: "The mirror had gone opaque and gave him back only himself." Thus always the narcissistic Tristan constructs an Iseult of his own longings.

But Updike is not consistently so critical of Tristan as Rougemont. As he puts it in "More Love in the Western World," "a man in love, confronting his beloved, seems to be in the presence of *his own spirit*, his self translated into another mode of being, a Form of Light greeting him at the gate of salvation." Imagery such as that plays through "Leaves" and "The Stare" and "The Morning," all meditations (in *The Music School*) of guilty and ambivalent husbands searching for

some blessing in illicit love, a form of light, a salvation. Ominously, none of them have names, as if they have given up that sort of identity. They merge in the narrator of the title story, "The Music School," who neatly sums up the issue: "We are all pilgrims, faltering toward divorce." It is worth reading Rougemont's chapter "Marrying Iseult?" for its uncanny anticipation of the typical Updikean issues. It begins:

> Now suppose that, in spite of everything, a man succeeds in plumping for a particular type as his type—a type which will be a cross between what naturally appeals to him and what the cinema has taught him to like. He meets a woman of this type, and identifies her. There she is, the woman of his heart's desire and of his most intimate nostalgia, the Iseult of his dreams! And of course she is already married. But let her get a divorce, and she shall be his! Together they will experience "real life," and the Tristan he nurses like his hidden daemon in his bosom will wax and bloom.

Apparently Updike read the chapter with a shock of recognition. So many of his protagonists—Richard Maple, Rabbit Angstrom, Joey Robinson in *Of the Farm*—already had that hidden demon. And Rougemont's most "provocative" phrase, Updike admits in his 1964 essay, was "the woman . . . of his most intimate nostalgia." It is as if he had found the key to his whole work. "What is it that shines at us from Iseult's face but our own past, with its strange innocence and its strange need to be redeemed?" He goes on, sounding more like a Tristan every moment, "What is nostalgia but love for that part of ourselves which is in Heaven, forever removed from change and corruption?" This was for Updike not only an explanation for his characters' deepest longings but a clue to his own motives as a writer:

> But the images we hoard in wait for the woman who will seem to body them forth include the inhuman—a certain slant of sunshine, a delicate flavor of dust, a kind of rasping tune that is reborn in her voice; they

are nameless, these elusive glints of original goodness that a man's memory stores toward an erotic commitment. Perhaps it is to the degree that the beloved crystallizes the lover's past that she presents herself to him, alpha and omega, as his Fate.

What were his own writings if not such stored and hoarded images, gathered in unconscious anticipation of "an erotic commitment," a woman who would "body them forth" and so "crystallize" his past?

## ECHOES OF ROUGEMONT

The Rougemont thesis continued to shape Updike's fiction after *The Music School*. But by the time he finished *Marry Me* in 1976 (he had begun it in 1968) he had learned to cast a colder eye on such nostalgia. He set the novel in 1962 "in a fiefdom of Camelot called Greenwood, Connecticut," and gave his Tristanian protagonist two Iseults whose desirability keeps interchanging and a King Mark who threatens to become another Tristan. Wryly, Updike subtitled it *A Romance*, as if to acknowledge the game he was playing. His later work is less personal and less nostalgic, but Tristan and his discontents remain. The 1975 story "Problems" offers a witty variation on the theme, a diagram of the domestic triangle as if it were a "story problem" in mathematics. It begins, "*A*, though sleeping with *B*, dreams of *C*." *A* turns out to be the would-be Tristan, sleeping with *B* whom he casts as Iseult, but he dreams of the now eroticized *C*, his estranged wife. "Which has he more profoundly betrayed, *B* or *C*?" While the story seems light, almost a joke, it clearly has its rueful side.

In *A Month of Sundays* the theme is transposed to a new key. Tristan's quasi-religious impulse to find alpha and omega in his beloved becomes the Reverend Tom Marshfield's quest—after betraying his wife and his congregation and being forced into exile in the desert (actually, to a comfortable motel-sanatorium, somewhere in the American west)—to write out his imperfect shame and guilt. Seeking a paradigm other than Rougemont's, Updike decided that Hawthorne's *The Scarlet Letter* would serve. It is probable that, after such sexually bold works as *Couples* and "Midpoint," Updike had emerged with a new attitude that ran counter to Tristanian sublimations and separations. He wrote in the *New York Times Book Review* in 1973, "Now we stand in a moment when sex again seems worth studying and celebrating. More, it now appears our last uncontaminated act, the sinuous passageway down into the womb where worship is possible, in a unifying darkness of instinctive purpose." So in the figure of a modern Reverend Arthur Dimmesdale, rather than another Tristan, Updike explores that "sinuous passageway" between sexuality and belief, the flesh and the spirit. Impelled to write penitentially each day for a month, Marshfield finds himself writing a sermon each Sunday. They become the heart of the book, some of the best writing Updike has ever done: a sequence of four sermons on adultery, on miracles, on the desert, and on the mystery of our existence—Pascal's "*Qui m'y a mis?*" Who has set me here? On other days of the week Marshfield may be a foolish and flippant man, merely playing with words, but on Sundays he comes near to voicing his author's deepest beliefs. "Yes—at last," he announces after the fourth, " a sermon that could be preached."

Echoes of the Rougemont thesis continue to appear in Updike's fiction, most notably in *Brazil* where Tristan and Iseult become Tristão, a poor black teenage boy from the slums of Rio, and Isabel, the rich white girl with whom he falls fatefully in love. But the Hawthorne paradigm largely replaced it, generating at least three more books: *The Witches of Eastwick* in 1984 as a modern version of Salem beset by witchcraft in the seventeenth century, *Roger's Version* in 1986 as an improvisation on *The Scarlet Letter*'s Roger Chillingworth, and *S.* in 1988 as a revision of the story from Hester Prynne's point of view. All these books are richly inventive and witty, but they lack the intensity of their progenitor, *A Month of Sundays*. While the Tristan myth compelled Updike's belief, even to the point of affirming what Rougemont criticized, he could only parody Hawthorne's tale of adulterous woe. Updike simply does not believe in what Hawthorne memorably called "that foul cavern, the human heart." The sense of sin so powerfully projected upon Hester by her relentless community has no weight whatsoever when Updike comes to write of witches and covens in Eastwick. The febrile energies of Dimmesdale's voice or the anguish and anger that Hester turns against herself are not, when Updike puts them in modern dress, symptoms of spiritual disease, but rather more like the opposite—proofs of strength. At best these Hawthorne parodies are ironic commentaries on a contemporary society that satirizes itself, unwittingly, by failing to measure up to the tragic past. It is hard not to find Updike's vision limited here, in that he refuses to imagine parallels between Hawthorne's "blackness of darkness" and some of the horrors of human evil perpetrated in our own time.

## WOMEN

With Updike's increasing willingness to regard sex as "our last uncontaminated act" comes—at long last for some readers—a greater curiosity about women, and a new interest in adopting their points of view. *The Witches of Eastwick* and *S.* are practically revolutionary in this respect. Heretofore female characters in his work were largely constructions of the nostalgic Tristanian male gaze. Or they were women—wives and mothers, mainly—who were always seen by male narrators and subordinate to their concerns. Updike's autobiographical impulse virtually guaranteed that. However daringly he stretched beyond his own experience—to the black African ruler Elleloû in

*The Coup* (1978) or to Updike's antithesis, the bachelor Jewish writer of only one novel, Henry Bech, or to the historical figure of President James Buchanan in *Buchanan Dying* (1974)—he did not attempt a woman's point of view. In fact Elleloû and Buchanan are distinctly patriarchal figures, the first a Muslim potentate with four wives and the second the only American president with none. Most of Updike's other male protagonists act out of patriarchal assumptions too, despite their conspicuous deficiencies in worldly power, notably Rabbit Angstrom, George Caldwell, Joey Robinson, and Richard Maple. They share, too, a tendency toward misogyny.

Both Caldwell and his son Peter associate women with nature. For the father, his wife and her farm tie him equally to mortality: "I hate Nature," he says. "All Nature means to me is garbage and confusion and the stink of skunk—*brroo!*" Peter veers to the opposite extreme: he "burns" to paint nature, to "stretch himself upon her" in worshipful, erotic expectation. He also idealizes the female as supremely maternal and domestic, not his own mother but the surrogate paragon of domesticity, Vera Hummel, whose "presence branched into every corner of the house." Similarly he worships Miss Appleton, his Latin teacher, as the deity who unaware of her divine purpose incarnates language with a sublime radiance: "there is *style* to divinity," she teaches him. "These lines brim with a sense of that radiance, breaking in upon the unknowing Aeneas." So strenuous are the abstractions defining women in *The Centaur* that their ordinary human existence, their power to act in the world, is virtually denied.

In Rabbit Angstrom the principle of masculine arrogance is exposed—he abuses his wife Janice, he is the indirect but ultimate cause of his daughter's drowning, he takes up with the prostitute Ruth and demands that she love him. But in the end *Rabbit, Run* asks us to grant him respect because he trusts his instincts. He is the only one who recognizes the paltriness of his world, the shabbiness of its false teachers, and the hollowness of its beliefs. Feminist critics have rightly wondered where that leaves Janice and Ruth. Eleven years later in *Rabbit Redux* (1971) Rabbit is trying to make another go of it as a breadwinner, muddling through, cutting his losses. This time Updike lets Janice narrate some of the story, as if to dramatize Rabbit's surrender of power. She is meant to sound a bit like Joyce's Molly Bloom, but Rabbit still tends to think of her critically and condescendingly. In fact the pathos of all the book's female characters—Rabbit's dying mother, Jill the desperate and depressed runaway from a wealthy family in Connecticut, and Janice with her tawdry illusions—becomes more powerful because Rabbit dimly knows of their suffering but always puts himself first. Despite various encroachments on his authority, he remains the novel's focus, a sad and troubled victim of forces beyond his control, clinging to conventionality as his home and nation come apart at the seams. Updike seems to endorse that conventionality as if it were precious, a touchingly blind faith in America. Rabbit and Sinclair Lewis' average man of the 1920s, Babbitt, are clearly relatives. Although he is implicated in the despair and death of three women, Rabbit still emerges at the end of the novel with his marriage put back to rights. Naturally then some critics have wondered whether Updike has not gone out of his way in *Rabbit Redux* to defend the indefensible. The only response must be that, defensible or not, Rabbit is authentic, an all-too-plausible representation of an ordinary man of that time and place. Rabbit's culpability is not Updike's concern. "I do not stand for anything," he warned an interviewer in 1993. "I . . . seek to describe the world as it is . . . the only social service a writer can perform."

However, there are still many occasions in Updike's fiction where the minds and emotions of women are justly represented. Joey's mother in *Of the Farm*, long-suffering Joan Maple in such stories as "Twin Beds in Rome" and "Giving Blood," and Sally in *Marry Me* are all good examples. But perhaps the most interesting proof of Updike's capacity to imagine a woman's point of view comes in a story of 1966, "My Lover Has Dirty Fingernails." An unnamed woman enters her psychotherapist's office, not for the first time evidently, but she is still acutely conscious of her every gesture and his. She feels anxious and apologetic, needing his help but fearful of his ambiguous and minimal responses. He brushes aside her tentative efforts to explain herself, and at last delivers an ingenious reading of her problem. Her lover, he decides, represents the "unbuttoned, unwashed" naturalness of the earth, but the "earth is death" to her. "By conquering him, by entangling him in your clothes, you subdue your own death; more exactly, you pass through it, and become a farm girl, an earth-girl, who has survived dying." But the woman instantly sees through this glib theory; and when she tells him feelingly "I want the truth" and "I need help," he feels threatened. Pointedly she asks whether by this time shouldn't something "have happened between us" (she obviously means transference but he will not supply the term). Then in a final burst of understanding she tells him, "I keep getting the feeling that you've fallen in love with *me*. . . . So I feel tender toward you, and want to protect you, and pretend not to reject you, and it gets in the way of everything. You put me into the position where a woman can't be honest, or weak, or herself." Every nuance of the story conveys the justice of this woman's complaint, the clarity of her recognitions. The story is a paradigm of how insecure men maneuver and betray the trust of women to get what they want.

When at last Updike came to write a whole novel from a woman's point of view, *S.*, in the first person, he did so with much the same critical purpose. Through Sarah Worth's eyes the lies and betrayals of men become transparent. Her narrative begins when she abruptly leaves her husband, a doctor, in New England and joins a commune in

Arizona led by a Hindu adept called the Ahrat. Like the woman in "My Lover Has Dirty Fingernails" Sarah is generous in her love, honest about her feelings, and not quick to condemn—unlike the men she must deal with. If she shares anything with her progenitor, Hester Prynne, besides a daughter named Pearl and a previous marriage she would like to forget, it must be her refusal to yield to patriarchal authority. Sarah signs her letters, since this, too, like *A Month of Sundays* is an epistolary novel, with the simple but sinuous letter *S.*, a sexy but not so scarlet a letter as the one Hester wore. The winning thing about her, however, is her brisk social energy: she has a flair for talk, and a different voice for each one of her correspondents. The run-on prodigality of her letters (plus a few audio tapes too) is infectious.

She may have left house and home in a sudden desperate bid for personal freedom at the age of forty-two, but she is no fool. American women who pay the bills and rear the children and see to the house repairs and lawn maintenance while their husbands go off to the cities all day, Updike attests, need not see themselves as helpless victims. Sarah's sensible first acts, before disappearing impulsively into the desert, are to raid the joint bank accounts and hide her family heirlooms from her soon-to-be wrathful husband. So the novel has little to do with adultery, guilt, or betrayal. It becomes a rueful social comedy, another domestic triangle in which a deathly conventional spouse is exchanged—theoretically—for a deeper belief, and the possibility of a life-enhancing soul mate. But Sarah discovers that the Ahrat is just as much a fraud (an American Jew from Watertown, Massachusetts) as her husband was, and the commune is little more than a front for capitalist enterprise. On her own once more at the novel's end, still cheerful and indefatigable, she seems as firmly anchored in her loquacious New England identity as when she began. In fact she emerges as the complete opposite of all those defeated and passive women in *Rabbit, Run* and *Rabbit Redux.*

Neither etherealized nor condemned to an identification with earthly mortality, sex, and death, she shrugs off the definitions others would place on her. In her capacity for role-playing she anticipates Essie/Alma in *In the Beauty of the Lilies*; as actresses and survivors their American prototype is not Hester at all but Huckleberry Finn.

## CELEBRATING THE ORDINARY

Their more covert prototype, however, is probably the role-playing novelist himself. How many voices can a writer be expected to "do"? Updike liked to emphasize that he felt most at home in the world of his boyhood in Shillington, that his subject is "ordinary" and "middling" America, that he felt "like a red-faced farm boy in the beautiful country club," and that he stuttered in the presence of "people of evident refinement or distinction." By defining himself as typically American, middle-class and small-town, Updike licensed himself to be representative. "Didn't I detect, . . . in his later work," says his alter ego Henry Bech, "an almost blunt determination to, as it were, sing America?" To which Updike replies, in this mock interview of 1975, "that he was married to America and did not wish a divorce." Thus Updike lays claim to a broadly democratic ambition, like Whitman's. The fact of the matter however is that Updike's social class is distinctly privileged, rarefied by his exceptional education, removed (by his choice) from urban masses, noise, and violence, isolated by the nature of his contemplative and aesthetic work, and exempted by his phenomenal success from the common anxieties about money and security. Most of Updike's fiction actually is not about the American middle class. Set against the four Rabbit Angstrom novels, the rest of his work concerns the wealthier and more privileged strata of American society—a realm Updike once said he was glad to leave to John Cheever, not recognizing that as chroniclers of East Coast suburbia and as writers for the *New Yorker* they were rivals. Updike is sometimes sublimely unaware of the difference between his own sophisticated and privileged consciousness and that of his ordinary American characters. Both *Rabbit Is Rich* and *Rabbit at Rest* are marred by the elegant sensitivity and metaphoric ingenuities of the style, which purportedly represents the shallow and egotistical Rabbit Angstrom thinking only of himself. In *Brazil* the consciousness of a black teenager—whose mother was a whore and who must steal and beg to survive—comes to us laden with the finely tuned elegance of a master stylist. Critics have often objected to stylistic excess in Updike's work, but the problem is actually one of decorum: does the style fit the mind and sensibility of the person whose thoughts are being represented? All kinds of "excess" are possible, valid, and interesting, when the protagonist is (say) an extravagantly paranoid and narcissistic writer like Henry Bech or a deposed African ruler beset by delusions of grandeur like Hakim Elleloû in *The Coup*.

Nevertheless Updike's achievement rests on his capacity to portray a "middleness" that might not be purely a matter of social class. It has more to do with ordinary people, like two girls wearing bikinis in a supermarket, or common things, like a flip-top American beer can, or listening to the songs on the radio:

> "Lah-vender blue, dilly dilly,
> Lavendih gree-heen;
> *Eef* I were king, dilly dilly,
> You would: be queen."

Nobody has rendered a pop singer's voice—Nat King Cole's, 1955—with more finesse than that. Updike told Charles Thomas Samuels in 1968, "My fiction about the daily doings of ordinary people has more history in it than history books." He was not bragging, merely stating a fact. He told Jane Howard (in an interview reprinted by James Plath) in 1966 that his subject was "the American small-town middle class" because "I

like middles. It is in middles that extremes clash, where ambiguity restlessly rules." For Updike clearly the ordinary is the extraordinary. In his earlier fiction one sees his debt to James Joyce for the principle that common things may suddenly shine forth, with a radiance beyond themselves, as in an epiphany. Joycean too, probably, is Updike's sense that the writer puts himself in a quasi-religious position, transforming the ordinary bread and wine of experience into immaterial and symbolic essences. But more recently he seems to have found a different sort of antecedent in William Dean Howells. In "Howells as Anti-Novelist" (1987; reprinted in *Odd Jobs*) Updike admires the principle that the ideal novelist does not meddle with reality but sets it down with, as Howells puts it, "the same voluntary and involuntary actions, the same unaccountable advances and perplexing pauses, the same moments of rapture, the same days and weeks of horrible dullness." Updike seizes upon that word "dullness" to define Howells' project, and his own: a "vision of bringing dullness and mixedness out of the rain of actuality into the house of fiction." He finds another, even more eloquent passage on the same theme in Howells' *Their Wedding Journey*. The words were written in 1871 but they clearly speak for Updike today:

> The sincere observer of man will not desire to look upon his heroic or occasional phases, but will seek him in his habitual moods of vacancy and tiresomeness. To me, at any rate, he is at such times very precious; and I never perceive him to be so much a man and a brother as when I feel the pressure of his vast, natural, unaffected dullness. Then I am able to enter confidently into his life and inhabit there, to think his shallow and feeble thoughts, to be moved by his dumb, stupid desires, to be dimly illumined by his stinted inspirations, to share his foolish prejudices, to practice his obtuse selfishness.

No better description could be written of the relation between Updike and Rabbit Angstrom, or Updike and ordinary American life, than this.

A DISTINCTIVE VOICE

Updike became a prolific writer in part because of simple dedication to the work. He wrote three pages or about a thousand words every day, six days a week, steadily since 1957. In addition to his fiction and poetry he wrote, according to Jack De Bellis' 1994 bibliography, some 520 articles, essays, and reviews. In an age of writers-in-residence and poet-professors attached to academic institutions, Updike remained on his own, a cottage industry unto himself. Naturally enough he maintained a certain professional detachment about his art, which sometimes puzzled interviewers and critics who wondered if he was sufficiently serious. They did not always like to hear that *Rabbit, Run* owes something of its inspiration to *Peter Rabbit*, that *The Coup* derives in part from Nabokov's *Pale Fire*, and takes some names—Klipspringer and Michaelis—from *The Great Gatsby*; that three of Updike's novels are spun, rather casually and playfully, out of *The Scarlet Letter*; that the form of *Bech: A Book* comes from Nabokov's *Pnin*. Ever since *Buchanan Dying*, a projected novel that turned into a play, most of Updike's novels were assiduously researched, and came equipped with substantial bibliographies—another sign that a productive writer may not wait for inspiration but plow ahead anyhow. Conversely, he recalled how quickly he was able to invent *A Month of Sundays* because its form was a daily journal. He took a day to write each section, revised everything, and finished the book in three months. Much of his poetry, for that matter, is light verse written quickly, purely to entertain. Then, too, he is practical about the value of suspense. In *Picked-Up Pieces* he differentiated "gnostic suspense" in fiction, which is waiting for the fine aesthetic moments as in Proust, from "the lowly appetite, aroused by even comic strips, to know the outcome." A good novel may have the former, but it must have the latter. He complained bitterly, in fact, about reviewers who

gave away the endings of his books, "blabbing . . . all the turns of my suspenseful and surpriseful narrative."

Yet for all this Updike remained an endlessly inventive writer, never formulaic (except insofar as he sometimes inevitably imitates himself), never derivative, never less than curious and attentive, elegant and restlessly inventive. His professional detachment did not detract at all from his art; in fact it helped him to use his own experience dispassionately, in the shaping of his genre scenes of American life that evoke the paintings of Jan Vermeer. The influence of Joyce, Proust, and Nabokov can be detected frequently in his language. But others contributed as well, both directly and indirectly. J. D. Salinger's presence is heard in such early stories as "Should Wizard Hit Mommy?" and in the fine technique of italicizing only the stressed syllable in a spoken word ("It must be *ter*rible to know so much"). E. B. White's example was followed in making poems out of funny lines in newspapers ("Miss Terriberry to Wed in Suburbs" or "Writing here last autumn of my hopes of seeing a hoopoe"). John Cheever's "O Youth and Beauty!" incited Updike—"goaded" him, he said—"to write a contrastingly benign story." The poetry of Wallace Stevens can be heard from time to time, notably in "Leaves" and "The Music School"; indeed anyone who thinks Updike is not a very good poet should study the rhythms and imagery of his fiction, not his verse. Father Mapple's sermon in *Moby-Dick* surely can be heard in the fourth sermon of *A Month of Sundays*. "Pale Fire," the poem in Nabokov's novel of the same name, probably influenced "Midpoint" more strongly than any passage by Alexander Pope or Oliver Goldsmith. But was it Joyce or Nabokov who prompted all the verbal play in *A Month of Sundays*? The truth is Updike's writing remained open to any number of voices because he was so sure of his own. If the mark of an important writer is the ability to invent a unique style, or a distinctive way of seeing, or if it is the capacity to invent new forms that change the shape of our understanding, then Updike made his mark. Only he could have invented such a disturbingly elegant monster as *The Centaur* or a character as embarrassingly real and American as Rabbit Angstrom. Only John Updike could have described a young black radical from the point of view of a nervous, fascinated "America-first" conservative—think of the difficulty!—in such supple and expressive style as this:

> The peculiar glinting lustre of his skin. The something so very finely turned and finished in the face, reflecting at a dozen polished points: in comparison white faces are blobs: putty still drying. The curious greased grace of his gestures, rapid and watchful as a lizard's motions, free of mammalian fat.

This is art of a very high order, and not many writers can reach it.

# Selected Bibliography

## WORKS OF JOHN UPDIKE

### NOVELS
*The Poorhouse Fair*. New York: Knopf, 1959.
*Rabbit, Run*. New York: Knopf, 1960.
*The Centaur*. New York: Knopf, 1963.
*Of the Farm*. New York: Knopf, 1965.
*Couples*. New York: Knopf, 1968.
*Rabbit Redux*. New York: Knopf, 1971.
*A Month of Sundays*. New York: Knopf, 1975.
*Marry Me: A Romance*. New York: Knopf, 1976.
*The Coup*. New York: Knopf, 1978.
*Rabbit Is Rich*. New York: Knopf, 1981.
*The Witches of Eastwick*. New York: Knopf, 1984.
*Roger's Version*. New York: Knopf, 1986.
*S*. New York: Knopf, 1988.
*Rabbit at Rest*. New York: Knopf, 1990.
*Memories of the Ford Administration*. New York: Knopf, 1992.
*Brazil*. New York: Knopf, 1994.

*Rabbit Angstrom: A Tetralogy*. New York: Knopf, 1995. (Reprints all four of the Rabbit novels, with an introduction by the author.)
*In the Beauty of the Lilies*. New York: Knopf, 1996.
*Toward the End of Time*. New York: Knopf, 1997.

### SHORT STORY COLLECTIONS AND STORY SEQUENCES
*The Same Door*. New York: Knopf, 1959.
*Pigeon Feathers and Other Stories*. New York: Knopf, 1962.
*Olinger Stories: A Selection*. New York: Vintage, 1964.
*The Music School*. New York: Knopf, 1966.
*Bech: A Book*. New York: Knopf, 1970.
*Museums and Women and Other Stories*. New York: Knopf, 1972.
*Problems and Other Stories*. New York: Knopf, 1979.
*Too Far to Go: The Maples Stories*. New York: Fawcett, 1979.
*Bech Is Back*. New York: Knopf, 1982.
*Trust Me*. New York: Knopf, 1987.
*The Afterlife and Other Stories*. New York: Knopf, 1994.

### POETRY
*The Carpentered Hen and Other Tame Creatures*. New York: Harper, 1958.
*Telephone Poles and Other Poems*. New York: Knopf, 1963.
*Verse*. Greenwich, Conn.: Fawcett, 1965. (A reprinting of the first two collections.)
*Midpoint and Other Poems*. New York: Knopf, 1969.
*Tossing and Turning*. New York: Knopf, 1977.
*Facing Nature*. New York: Knopf, 1985.
*Collected Poems, 1953–1993*. New York: Knopf, 1993.

### COLLECTED PROSE
*Assorted Prose*. New York: Knopf, 1965.
*Picked-Up Pieces*. New York: Knopf, 1975.
*Hugging the Shore: Essays and Criticism*. New York: Knopf, 1983.
*Just Looking: Essays on Art*. New York: Knopf, 1989.
*Odd Jobs: Essays and Criticism*. New York: Knopf, 1991.
*Golf Dreams: Writings on Golf*. New York: Knopf, 1996.

OTHER WORKS

*Buchanan Dying: A Play*. New York: Knopf, 1974.

*Self-Consciousness: Memoirs*. New York: Knopf, 1989.


BIBLIOGRAPHIES


De Bellis, Jack. *John Updike: A Bibliography, 1967–1993*. Westport, Conn.: Greenwood Press, 1994. (Coverage begins in 1967 where Taylor [see below] ends.)

Gearhart, Elizabeth A. *John Updike: A Comprehensive Bibliography with Selected Annotations*. Darby, Penn.: Norwood Editions, 1980.

Olivas, Michael A. *An Annotated Bibliography of John Updike Criticism, 1967–1973*. New York: Garland, 1975.

Taylor, C. Clarke. *John Updike: A Bibliography*. Kent, Ohio: Kent State University Press, 1968.


CRITICAL STUDIES


Bloom, Harold, ed. *Modern Critical Views: John Updike*. New York: Chelsea House, 1987. (Reprints ten of the best critical essays on Updike's fiction.)

Burchard, Rachael C. *John Updike: Yea Sayings*. Carbondale: Southern Illinois University Press, 1971.

Campbell, Jeff H. *Updike's Novels: Thorns Spell a Word*. Wichita Falls, Texas: Midwestern State University Press, 1987.

Detwiler, Robert. *John Updike*. Revised edition. New York: Twayne, 1984.

Greiner, Donald J. *The Other John Updike: Poems, Short Stories, Prose, Play*. Athens: Ohio University Press, 1981.

———. *John Updike's Novels*. Athens: Ohio University Press, 1984.

Hamilton, Alice and Kenneth. *The Elements of John Updike*. Grand Rapids, Mich.: Eerdmans, 1970.

Hunt, George W. *John Updike and the Three Great Secret Things: Sex, Religion, and Art*. Grand Rapids, Mich.: Eerdmans, 1980.

Luscher, Robert M. *John Updike: A Study of the Short Fiction*. New York: Twayne, 1993.

Macnaughton, William R., ed. *Critical Essays on John Updike*. Boston: Hall, 1982. (Reprints thirty-two of the best reviews and essays.)

Markle, Joyce B. *Fighters and Lovers: Theme in the Novels of John Updike*. New York: New York University Press, 1973.

Neary, John. *Something and Nothingness: The Fiction of John Updike and John Fowles*. Carbondale: Southern Illinois University Press, 1992.

Newman, Judie. *John Updike*. New York: St. Martin's, 1988.

O'Connell, Mary. *Updike and the Patriarchal Dilemma: Masculinity in the Rabbit Novels*. Carbondale: Southern Illinois University Press, 1996.

Ristoff, Dilvo I. *Updike's America: The Presence of Contemporary American History in John Updike's Rabbit Trilogy*. New York: Lang, 1988.

Schiff, James A. *Updike's Version: Rewriting* The Scarlet Letter. Columbia: University of Missouri Press, 1992.

Searles, George J. *The Fiction of Philip Roth and John Updike*. Carbondale: Southern Illinois University Press, 1985.

Tallent, Elizabeth. *Married Men and Magic Tricks: John Updike's Erotic Heroes*. Berkeley: Creative Arts, 1982.

Taylor, Larry E. *Pastoral and Anti-Pastoral Patterns in John Updike's Fiction*. Carbondale: Southern Illinois University Press, 1971.

Trachtenberg, Stanley, ed. *New Essays on Rabbit Run*. New York: Cambridge University Press, 1993.

Uphaus, Suzanne Henning. *John Updike*. New York: Ungar, 1980.

Vargo, Edward P. *Rainstorms and Fire: Ritual in the Novels of John Updike*. Port Washington, N.Y.: Kennikat Press, 1973.

Vaughan, Philip H. *John Updike's Images of America*. Reseda, Calif.: Mojave, 1981.


INTERVIEWS


Plath, James. *Conversations with John Updike*. Jackson: University Press of Mississippi, 1994. (Reprints thirty-two interviews, given between 1959 and 1993.)

Samuels, Charles Thomas. "The Art of Fiction XLIII," *Paris Review* 12 (Winter 1968). Reprinted in *Writers at Work: The Paris Review Interviews*, vol. VI, ed. George Plimpton. New York: Viking, 1976.

Updike, John. "One Big Interview" in *Picked-Up Pieces*, pp. 493–518. (A composite of passages from seven different interviews given between 1966 and 1971.)

———. "On One's Own Oeuvre" in *Hugging the Shore*, pp. 839–878. (A composite of interviews drawn from various sources.)

———. "Literarily Personal!" in *Odd Jobs*, pp. 833–872. (A composite of responses to interview questions in various formats—footnotes, informal remarks, reminiscence.)

## FILM, TELEVISION, AND OPERA BASED ON WORKS BY JOHN UPDIKE

*Rabbit, Run.* Feature film, 94 mins. Written and produced by Howard Kreitsek. Directed by Jack Smight. Warner Brothers–Seven Arts, 1970.

"The Music School." Videorecording, 69 mins. Adaptation by John Korty. Coronet/MTI Film and Video, 1976. (Tape also includes story by Richard Wright.)

*Too Far to Go.* Videorecording, 120 mins. Directed by Fielder Cook. Sea Cliff Productions, 1981. (Adapted for television on March 12, 1979, and later released commercially.)

"The Music School." Videocassette VHS, 30 mins. Produced as part of PBS's American Short Stories series. Chicago: Perspective Films, 1982.

"The Roommates." Videorecording, 96 mins. Television production. Directed by Nell Cox. Screenplay by Morton Miller. American Playhouse, Public Broadcasting System, January 27, 1984. (Based on "The Christian Roommates" from *The Music School.*)

*The Witches of Eastwick.* Feature film, 118 mins. Directed by George Miller. Screenplay by Michael Cristofer. Warner Brothers, 1988. (Also released in Warner videorecording.)

"Pigeon Feathers." Videorecording. Directed by Sharon Miller. Produced by Robert Geller. Coronet Films, 1988.

*S.* Opera composed by Ron Perera (music) and Constance Congdon (libretto). Directed by Mark Harrison. First performance: Smith College, Northampton, Massachusetts, September 21 and 23, 1995.

*—DEAN FLOWER*

# Eudora Welty
## 1909–

"*T*HE MYSTERY IN how little we know of other people is no greater than the mystery of how much," observes the title character of Eudora Welty's *The Optimist's Daughter* (1972). This mystery is at the heart of Welty's writing. Her "real subject," as she puts it in *One Writer's Beginnings* (1984), is "human relationships." "My wish, indeed my continuing passion, would be not to point the finger in judgment but to part a curtain, that invisible shadow that falls between people, the veil of indifference to each other's presence, each other's wonder, each other's human plight," she states in *One Time, One Place: Mississippi in the Depression, a Snapshot Album* (1971). As she unveils the relationships among her characters, Welty similarly dispels the barriers between author and reader since "inherent in the novel is the possibility of a shared act of the imagination between its writer and its reader," as she writes in *The Eye of the Story: Selected Essays and Reviews* (1978). This imaginative participation can transform readers and their own relationships, she continues, since

> great fiction shows us not how to conduct our behavior but how to feel. Eventually, it may show us how to face our feelings and face our actions and to have new inklings about what they mean. A good novel of any year can initiate us into our own new experience.

As her views of the human capacity for imaginative and compassionate growth indicate, Welty's attitude toward experience is ultimately optimistic and comic. In *Conversations with Eudora Welty* (1984), she tells an interviewer, "My tendency is to believe that all experience is an enrichment instead of an impoverishment." What she says in *A Writer's Eye: Collected Book Reviews* (1994) of her fellow Mississippian William Faulkner applies equally well to her writing:

> The complicated and intricate thing is that his stories aren't decked out in humor, but the humor is born in them, as much their blood and bones as the passion and poetry. Put one of his stories into a single factual statement and it's pure outrage—so would life be—too terrifying, too probable and too symbolic too, too funny to bear.

Her ability to find life comic and enriching is intricately linked with the emphasis on love in her craft. As she describes the novelist's "focus" in *The Eye of the Story,* Welty observes that it "means awareness, discernment, order, clarity, insight— they are like the attributes of love," a love that transforms tragedy into comedy. For Welty, "without the act of human understanding . . . experience is the worst kind of emptiness."

Welty's choice to see experience as enrichment, not impoverishment, is part of her strategy for artistic survival. Viewing her task as a fiction writer in universal terms is a means of resisting two labels that could diminish her achievement and denigrate her reputation: southern writer, which can mean ignorant and provincial, and woman writer, which can stand for trivial and sentimental. Although Welty does share southern fiction's emphasis on the importance of place, in *Conversations with Eudora Welty,* she rejects its obsession with the past, commenting, "I don't write historically or anything. Most of the things that I write about can be translated into personal relationships." To an interviewer in *More Conversations with Eudora Welty* (1996), she once avowed, "You know, I don't like reading anything about the Civil War. . . . I hate it. I never have read *Gone with the Wind.*" Similarly, despite the remarkable array of female characters and experiences in her fiction, Welty also rejects the identity of woman writer, asserting in *Conversations with Eudora Welty* that "writing is a profession outside sex." While one might attribute Welty's denials of regional and gendered identity to her well-known modesty and self-effacement, she herself would assert that such self-labeling would limit her imaginative scope as an artist. She writes in *One Writer's Beginnings,* "I wished to be, not effaced, but invisible—actually a powerful position."

### EARLY LIFE

Her relatively quiet and uneventful life has also been a source of strength for Welty, who declares in *One Writer's Beginnings:* "A sheltered life can be a daring life as well. For all serious daring starts from within." Eudora Alice Welty's outwardly sheltered but inwardly daring life began on April 13, 1909, in Jackson, Mississippi, the small but growing state capital where her father worked for an insurance company. She was named for her paternal grandmother, Alice Welty, and her maternal grandmother, Eudora Andrews. "Eudora"

means "good gift" in Greek, but as a child she did not find it much of a prize. As she recalled to an interviewer in *More Conversations with Eudora Welty,* "I cried because nobody could understand my name and they laughed at me for having such a funny name. I always had to spell it everywhere I went."

The young Welty's feelings of difference were exacerbated by her parents' status as non-natives of Mississippi. Her father, Christian Webb Welty, was from Ohio. He met her mother, Mary Chestina Andrews, a schoolteacher, while on a visit to her native state, West Virginia. The adventuresome young couple decided to move to what for them was an exotic but promising locale, Mississippi, where they always retained their outlanders' point of view. Welty's mother did not share the southern passion for "porch talk," storytelling as entertainment and bonding. In *One Writer's Beginnings,* Welty remembers,

> My mother let none of this idling, as she saw it, pertain to her; she went her own way with or without her calling cards, and though she was fond of her friends and they were fond of her, she had little time for small talk. At first, I hadn't known what I'd missed.

When she did realize what her lack of an extended southern family was causing her to miss, she joined the porch talk of her neighborhood, where "there were a lot of grand talkers that I used to sit at the feet of and listen to, telling not only family stories but just what went on in their own lives and interpreted in a dramatic way," as she recalls in *More Conversations with Eudora Welty.* Attentiveness to porch talk provided an excellent apprenticeship for a novelist known for her marvelous ear for the telling anecdote related in a uniquely personal voice.

Of her parents and her two younger brothers, Walter and Edward, Welty later commented in *More Conversations with Eudora Welty,* "We were a very reserved family. But passionate." A shared source of passion was books. In her memoir, *One Writer's Beginnings,* Welty avidly recalls her parents' steady accretion of books for children, despite their modest income. When at about age six, she was forced to stay in bed for a "fast-beating heart," Welty remembers that "an opulence of story books covered my bed; it was the 'Land of Counterpane.'" She was especially fascinated by a ten-volume set of fairy tales, myths, and legends entitled *Our Wonder World,* the initial source of the future writer's many allusions to such traditional stories. She supplemented the family library with as many books as the stern town librarian would allow her to take out at once.

Welty may have been a bookish child, but she was not a reclusive one. She has fond memories of the small-town Jackson of her youth, where children were considered safe when wandering throughout the downtown, to the grocery store, the ice cream parlor, the swimming pool, the park—sites for the future writer's intense people-watching. In *Conversations with Eudora Welty,* she recalls that with her friends she roller-skated "*through* the Capitol, skimming over the marble floors (very desirable echoes in the rotunda) and rounding a circle in the Hall of Fame." At the movies with her brother Edward, she gloried in the slapstick comedy. "My sense of making fictional comedy undoubtedly caught its first spark from the antic pantomime of the silent screen, and from having a kindred soul to laugh with," Welty comments in *One Writer's Beginnings.*

Across from her house was the Davis School, the public elementary school Welty attended, a strict environment where a child would be reproached for using the southern colloquialism "might could," but where a teacher would catch some of Jackson's rare snow on her outspread cloak to bring in for the children to enjoy. The principal of the Davis School, Miss Duling, was an imposing figure with a passion for teaching. Welty points out in *One Writer's Beginnings* that "she emerges in my perhaps inordinate number of schoolteacher characters," such as Miss Eckhart in

*The Golden Apples* (1949) and Julia Mortimer in *Losing Battles* (1970). Although Welty herself never wanted to be a teacher, Miss Duling served as a model of a professional woman totally dedicated to her art, pedagogy.

As early as elementary school Welty showed a budding dedication to her own art. She wrote stories for the children's magazine *St. Nicholas* and for the children's page of the newspaper *Commercial Appeal.* She composed comic poems for family and friends and even wrote plays that were produced in the garage for an audience of neighbors. In *More Conversations with Eudora Welty,* she recalls: "I won a prize at an early age. It was a patent something called 'Jackie Mackie Pine Oil,' and they gave me a prize for the best poem about it, and I won twenty-five dollars." In high school, she enjoyed what she calls her "early book reviewing": "I used to write the book reports of a good many others besides me, because they didn't want to read the book. That was fun."

After four years at Jackson Central High School, in 1925, when Welty was sixteen, two events of lasting significance occurred. Her father built the brick Tudor-style home on Pinehurst Street where Welty still lives. At that time, however, Welty enjoyed the new house only on vacations, since she started attending the Mississippi State College for Women, two hundred miles away in Columbus, the farthest her parents would allow a sixteen-year-old to go. At college, she began to accumulate the detailed knowledge of other regions of Mississippi so characteristic of her fiction. She was packed into her crowded dormitory room with girls "from every nook and corner of the state, from the Delta, the piney woods, the Gulf Coast, the black prairie, the red clay hills, and Jackson," she states in *One Writer's Beginnings.* To find some solitude, Welty walked and read; she purchased her first book for her personal library, Mississippi poet William Alexander Percy's *In April Once* (1920), a choice perhaps inspired by Professor Lawrence Painter, who awakened her to poetry as he read to her class. Welty recalls, "I had come unprepared for the immediacy of poetry." In a lighter vein, she wrote parodies and satires for the college newspaper in the manner of popular humorist S. J. Perelman, who remained a lifelong favorite of hers. In *Conversations with Eudora Welty,* she says, "I like to think I didn't take myself seriously then, but I did," and she quotes this opening sentence as an example of "how bad I was": "Monsieur Boule inserted a delicate dagger in Mademoiselle's left side and departed with a poised immediacy."

After two years at Mississippi State College for Women, Welty's parents allowed her to finish her college education at the University of Wisconsin, where she minored in art history and majored in English from 1927 to 1929. Welty had always been intrigued by painting, and the vivid descriptions of light and landscape in her works could be termed painterly. Of her art classes and her visits to the Art Institute of Chicago, she states in *More Conversations with Eudora Welty,* "It helped me to see more clearly." She found another inspiring English teacher, Ricardo Quintana, who taught her more than the contents of a reading list: "He really made us realize the strength and truth of poetic feeling and depth of feeling and emotional drive. . . . I had never realized that it was all right to be so wholly enraptured by things." He had given her permission to have what she later called in *The Eye of the Story* "every artist's secret—passion."

As a teenager, Welty needed these epiphanies for, in a 1941 letter to her literary agent, Diarmuid Russell, collected in *Author and Agent* (1991), she remembers:

> I was very timid and shy, younger than the rest and those people up there seemed to me like sticks of flint, that live in the icy world. . . . It was more than the pangs of growing up, much more, I knew it then, it was some kind of desire to be shown that the human spirit was not like that shivery winter in Wisconsin.

Her wish was granted when she discovered the works of the Irish poet W. B. Yeats, whose "Song of Wandering Aengus" later infused *The Golden Apples,* and the autobiography of another Irish writer known as "A. E.," who was George Russell, Diarmuid's father: "I would read every afternoon, hurry to read, it was the thing the day led to, and at night what I had read would stay as my secret heart, for I did not let anybody there really know me." In these writers, she found the mystical quality, the attention to spirit, not just matter, that she found so lacking in the pragmatic "sticks of flint" around her. She learned:

> What you look for in the world is not simply for what you want to know, but for more than you want to know, and more than you can know, better than you had wished for, and sometimes something draws you to a discovery and there is no other happiness quite the same.

By the time that she graduated from college, Welty knew that she wanted to be a writer, but her father wanted her to be able to earn a secure living, so she proceeded to New York City, where she studied advertising at the Columbia University Graduate School of Business during the academic year 1930–1931. She then got an advertising job, from which she was dismissed after two weeks; she later learned that this agency was running the scam of using new graduates as unpaid labor for a few weeks and then firing them. "I was so disillusioned," she recalls in *More Conversations with Eudora Welty.* Hard times continued when she was summoned back to Jackson by the diagnosis of her father's leukemia and his death in 1931 at the age of fifty-two. Welty needed to help support her mother and brothers, financially and psychologically, so she remained in Jackson, taking a part-time job at a radio station in the basement of the Lamar Life Insurance Building, where her father had worked for so many years, and freelancing for newspapers and as a publicist. From this time, Welty made her permanent home in Jackson, placing the needs of her family before her own desire to try new places. In *One Writer's Beginnings,* she remembers that when she made trips to New York City for business or entertainment, she felt "an iron cage around my chest of guilt. . . . I knew that even as I was moving farther away from Jackson [on the train], my mother was already writing to me at her desk, telling me she missed me but only wanted what was best for me."

The 1930s, the years of the Great Depression, tested Welty's philosophy that experiences enrich rather than impoverish. In *More Conversations with Eudora Welty,* she recalls that she enjoyed what she found in Jackson and remembers many happy social occasions with young friends and trips to a record store on Berry Street where they listened to "race records, that is, records all-black artists made really for themselves." This interest in African American music emerges in her fiction, particularly in her short story "Powerhouse," which appears in *A Curtain of Green and Other Stories* (1941). With another couple, she and her escort managed to get seats at a Bessie Smith concert that was meant for an all-black audience in those days of racial segregation. "I'll never forget when she came out on the stage, this absolutely all-embracing, big, happy-looking woman . . . you know, just opening her arms to the world." For Welty, Bessie Smith was the public version of her own private art of writing, embracing the world through the artist's gift of focused attention, a form of love.

## PHOTOGRAPHY AND FIRST WRITING

During the mid-1930s, Welty pursued the two interests that were her specialties in college, art and literature. From 1933 to 1936, she worked in Mississippi as a publicity agent for the Works Progress Administration, a federal agency established as part of Franklin Delano Roosevelt's New Deal to counteract the effects of the Depression. In *One Time, One Place,* she recollects:

> As publicity agent, junior grade, for the State office, I was sent about over the eighty-two counties of Mississippi, visiting the newly opened farm-to-market roads or the new airfields hacked out of old cow pastures, interviewing a judge in some new juvenile court, riding along on a Bookmobile route and distributing books into open hands like the treasures they were, helping to put up booths in county fairs, and at night, in some country-town hotel room under a loud electric fan, writing the Projects up for the county weeklies to print if they found the space. In no time, I was taking a camera with me.

The photographs she took on these trips became the basis of a one-woman show at Lugene's Gallery in New York City in 1936 and were later variously collected in *One Time, One Place* and *Photographs* (1989).

As Welty traveled the roads of Mississippi and took her photographs, she was acquiring knowledge and skill for what was rapidly becoming her major focus, the writing of fiction. In *Conversations with Eudora Welty,* she recalls that "that experience . . . was the real germ of my wanting to become a real writer, a true writer." The photographs are well worth careful attention for their revelation of the world of Welty's fiction with some of its now unfamiliar folkways and icons, such as bottle trees, bootleggers, and bird pageants. One can also recognize settings from her fiction, such as the church steeple in Port Gibson, topped by a hand pointing to heaven, that figures so prominently in her story in *The Golden Apples,* "The Whole World Knows." However, the most moving of her photographs are her portraits, with their direct but compassionate observations of men, women, and children, often in poverty but never lacking in dignity and integrity. These portraits are the embodiments of her artistic credo, as stated in the introduction to *One Time, One Place,* that "the sharpest recognition is surely that which is charged with sympathy as well as with shock—it is a form of human vision."

Although Welty gained myriad facts and settings for her stories on her WPA journeys, her most important advance was the development of a narrative stance. As a reticent but passionately inquisitive person, Welty needed to find a point of view that would gain her entry to a narrative situation and its concomitant relationships while still keeping herself as a writer relatively and safely detached. As a woman writer she needed a self-effacingly ladylike device to feed her devouring appetite for knowledge. At Mississippi State College for Women, she recalls in *One Writer's Beginnings,* "I was lucky enough to have found for myself, at the very beginning, an outside shell, that of freshman reporter on our college newspaper, *The Spectator.*" The camera was a more serious and probing version of that shell, simultaneously what she calls in *One Time, One Place* "a shy person's protection" and in *One Writer's Beginnings* "a hand-held auxiliary of wanting-to-know." In *More Conversations with Eudora Welty,* she recalls that from the literal device of holding a camera, she developed her characteristic narrative stance: "I nearly always write from the point of view of the stranger or the traveler because that is the only way I could vouch for what I say," and that point of view is not limited to that of a woman or a person of Welty's class or color.

A stranger and traveler is the central consciousness of Welty's first published short story, "Death of a Traveling Salesman," which appeared in *Manuscript* in 1936. R. J. Bowman has been a shoe salesman for fourteen years, and he thinks he knows his shoes and his roads. After a bout of influenza, however, the shaky convalescent takes a wrong turn, drives his car into a ditch, and seeks help and shelter at a remote cabin. As his physical condition deteriorates, he tries to make sense of the relationship of the man and woman living in the cabin. At first he thinks the shapeless and slow-moving woman is the man's mother, but later

he discovers that she is his young and pregnant wife. "He was shocked with knowing what was really in this house. A marriage, a fruitful marriage. That simple thing. Anyone could have had that," she writes—anyone willing to make the commitment, that is. Bowman, though, cannot accept that "the only secret was the ancient communication between two people." As he runs from the house and this knowledge toward his car and his life of alienated traveling, his heart, which he has betrayed through lack of use, betrays him. He dies, still clinging to his solitude. "He covered his heart with both hands to keep anyone from hearing the noise it made. But nobody heard it."

"Death of a Traveling Salesman" was later included in Welty's first collection, the seventeen short stories making up *A Curtain of Green,* and R. J. Bowman is typical of one end of Welty's spectrum of characters in that volume. In *The Eye of the Story,* Welty asserts that "relationship *is* a pervading and changing mystery"; how a character reacts to that mystery is the touchstone of value in *A Curtain of Green.* The title of the collection and the title story suggest that the curtain of green vegetation leads to life and hope if one penetrates it to reach other people. In the collection, however, some characters, like R. J. Bowman, are repulsed and frightened by relationships. Others, like the young girl who is the narrator of "A Memory," are torn between accepting realistic human relationships or losing themselves in romantic dreams. Although Welty is usually among the least directly autobiographical of writers, the young girl resembles her youthful self caught between her overprotective parents and her budding artistry. Like the young Welty, she took painting lessons and now forms "small frames" with her fingers "to look out at everything," much as Welty's use of a camera allowed her a focused detachment. But despite the safe frames of her fingers, the young narrator prefers to lose herself in the dream of a boy in her class at school who once accidentally touched her wrist. In response to less ephemeral contacts, she withdraws. When the boy gets a bloody nose, she faints. Only when she is older and narrates the "memory" can she confront reality unflinchingly.

On the summer's day at the beach that the narrator recounts in "A Memory," she is repulsed by a loud and active lower-class family, particularly their physicality, with its overtones of sexuality. She keeps closing her eyes in an attempt to shut them out and focus on her romantic dream.

> Once when I looked up, the fat woman was standing opposite the smiling man. She bent over and in a condescending way pulled down the front of her bathing suit, turning it outward, so that the lumps of mashed and folded sand came emptying out. I felt a peak of horror, as though her breasts themselves had turned to sand, as though they were of no importance at all and she did not care.

The result of a sexual relationship, the girl fears, is becoming all body; what interior self remains is turned inside out for the benefit of the family, as in this perverse version of breast milk. The "peak of horror," though, is that a woman could so lose her self in a sexual relationship that she is incapable of caring for her lost identity.

The narrator of "A Memory" refuses to go to the beach again. If she is to become the profound artist that Welty is, she needs to combine her love for the delicacy of spirit with a similar appreciation of the robustness of the physical world. In a 1941 letter to Russell, quoted in *Author and Agent,* Welty writes, "The time comes when I can't bear things on their immediate, ugly, unexplained level but have to look back at them through some vision or reason." As "A Memory" ends, there is some promise of this fulfillment when the narrator paradoxically looks forward to look back, using her memory: "I could imagine the boy I loved walking into a classroom, where I would watch him with this hour on the beach accompanying my recovered dream and added to my love."

Welty herself finds this merging of spirit and body easier in stories in which she uses as her artist's frame, or camera's eye, central characters who are ostensibly unlike herself. In two comic stories in *A Curtain of Green,* "Why I Live at the P.O." and "Petrified Man," she presents two women who are avid but frustrated gossips. Sister, who is postmistress of China Grove, moves from her family's home to the post office because her sister, Stella-Rondo, will not tell her the facts of her apparently failed marriage to Mr. Whitaker. Stella-Rondo is supported in her reticence by the other willfully blind members of the family, who prefer to believe that little Shirley-T. is Stella-Rondo's adopted daughter, not her biological daughter who was born a little too soon for conception in wedlock. The beautician in "Petrified Man," Leota, is miffed because she cannot penetrate the mysteries of human experience as does her quondam friend Mrs. Pike, who has first spotted the pregnancy of Leota's customer Mrs. Fletcher. Gallingly, Mrs. Pike has also identified the petrified man whom they both saw in the freak show as a rapist, earning a reward for herself alone. Both Sister and Mrs. Pike can recognize the truth beneath deceptive appearances, but only Mrs. Pike is rewarded for it because she is a stranger to the town and cares nothing for its carefully preserved facades.

As Welty comments in *The Eye of the Story:* "Human beings are unpredictable and spontaneous, apt to rise up anywhere without announcement." Sister and Mrs. Pike, however, do not want serendipity but rather control; Sister wants knowledge in order to gain power over Stella-Rondo and Mrs. Pike wants a monetary reward for what she knows. Welty's more imaginative and compassionate characters want to use knowledge to increase their ability to love, as do Phoenix Jackson in "A Worn Path" and Ruby Fisher in "A Piece of News." "A Worn Path" is one of Welty's most frequently anthologized stories and it won for her the second-place O. Henry Award for a short story in 1941. Part of its success lies in the inspiring character of Phoenix, an old African American woman who makes a long journey on foot across a rural landscape with its hazards of man, fauna, and flora and then through an equally treacherous urban landscape, in order to get medicine for her suffering grandson. It is the wisdom of her age and experience, her knowledge of physical and psychological terrains, that allows her to attain her goal and even find a toy for her grandson. As the title indicates, Phoenix has made the journey many times before, on the "worn path" of what Welty calls in *The Eye of the Story* "the deep-grained habit of love."

The other character who uses her imaginative knowledge of human relationships to enrich her life is Ruby of "A Piece of News." Ruby enlivens the boredom of her marriage to Clyde through liaisons in the empty shed of the cotton gin. After one such excursion, she returns to her cabin, where she reads in a newspaper left by one of her lovers that "Mrs. Ruby Fisher had the misfortune to be shot in the leg by her husband this week." Ruby proceeds to imagine Clyde so enraptured by her and so enraged with jealousy that he would shoot her and thus once again become the man she married: "He used to be very handsome and strong." She would be "beautiful, desirable, and dead," a comic version of the fear often expressed in Welty's work of a woman's death as an individual through marriage or a sexual relationship. When Clyde returns and Ruby shows him the paper:

> Slowly they both flushed, as though with a double shame and a double pleasure. It was as though Clyde might really have killed Ruby, and as though Ruby might really have been dead at his hand. Rare and wavering, some possibility stood timidly like a stranger between them and made them hang their heads.

Although they then notice that the news item concerns a Ruby Fisher in Tennessee, not in Mississippi, their imagined and somewhat farcical tragedy allows them to rekindle their relationship; it is no longer dead history but a living "piece of news."

Ruby and Clyde Fisher briefly act like artists in their imagined romantic melodrama and thus enrich their impoverished marriage. In "Powerhouse," the title character, an African American musician based on Fats Waller, uses the imagined adultery of his wife to try to understand her loneliness during his frequent absences for concert trips. He has called her on the preceding night to check if she is at home, and as his band plays, takes a break, then plays again, he imagines her death by suicide and her affair with a mythical "back-door man," Uranus Knockwood: "He come in when we goes out." When a waitress asks Powerhouse if these stories are true, he replies, "Truth is something worse, I ain't said what, yet. It's something hasn't come to me, but I ain't saying it won't." Truth comes to him through his songs, his art—a title like "Sent for You Yesterday and Here You Come Today" suggests his imaginative empathy with his wife. But truth, for Powerhouse, ultimately resides in his relationship with his art and his audience, which he uses his relationship with his wife to feed. The last song in the story is "Somebody Loves Me," and Powerhouse, as a "vast, impersonal and yet furious grimace transfigures his wet face," sings, "Maybe it's you"! The artist to Welty can be a kind of sacred monster, a monster to his partner in an individual relationship and to himself as he suffers loneliness and jealousy, but one who feels a sacred calling to his pursuit of "impersonal" truth and a commitment to convey it to his audience, with the possibility, but not the certainty, of their appreciative love.

Welty herself needed a similarly strong sense of artistic vocation because in the half dozen years preceding the publication of *A Curtain of Green* in 1941, many of her stories were repeatedly rejected, singly and in various collections. In 1940, Russell offered to become her literary agent, an association that lasted more than thirty years, but his initial attempts to publish many of Welty's stories in journals and magazines failed because editors often considered her work obscure; they were looking more for plot than for Welty's object of illuminating human relationships from within. Russell also had trouble placing Welty's collection of short stories with a publisher because, he told her, editors were most interested in novels. Welty, however, adamantly refused to put aside her short stories and write a novel, telling Russell in a letter collected in *Author and Agent,* "When I only think of a novel, it scares me. I never wanted to be contrary, but it is the natural thing for me to do what I can within a lesser space. I suspect that that comes from my being a female, and is permanent."

Although Welty did not want to write a novel and often disavowed any interest in writing about history, she did both in significantly modified ways in her next work, *The Robber Bridegroom* (1942). She may have feared encroaching on the turf of the male literary giant to the north of her in Oxford, Mississippi—William Faulkner, renowned as a novelist with a profound sense of history. Welty evaded this potential comparison by writing a novella, midway in length between a short story and a novel, and treating her history of the Natchez Trace from the frontier days to the antebellum plantation era with the magic and fantasy of a fairy tale, unlike the realism of her preceding works. In contrast to the stories in *A Curtain of Green, The Robber Bridegroom* is packed with action; Welty's approach to the characters is external rather than internal. The Natchez Trace, however, functions as a psyche in a waking dream or reverie in which the characters enact various subconscious needs, from the wicked stepmother Salome's extreme greed to the beauteous heroine Rosamond's compulsive lying (or unbridled composition of fiction). The other characters find it difficult to determine whether Rosamond is lying or telling the truth because, to a novelist like Welty, the truths of American history rival fairy tales in

strangeness and wonder. Thus, while *The Robber Bridegroom* seems to be a humorously rollicking tall tale, it is actually a portrait of the southern and, to some extent, the American mind; as it conquers Native Americans, African Americans, nature, and women; it retains some beautiful memories but also nightmares of collective guilt.

## THE WIDE NET

The atmosphere of reverie remains in Welty's second collection, eight short stories in *The Wide Net and Other Stories,* published in 1943. Her fiction is outwardly untouched by the vicissitudes of World War II, including her worries over her loved ones overseas: her two brothers and John Frasier Robinson, a writer from the Mississippi Delta with whom Welty was romantically and professionally involved through most of the 1940s though she never married. The war years, however, make a subliminal appearance as Welty goes back in time to early-nineteenth-century Mississippi to explore the motivations of those who shaped her world, public figures like Aaron Burr in "First Love," the bandit James Murrell, the evangelist Lorenzo Dow, and the naturalist and artist John Audubon in "A Still Moment." Despite passages of great descriptive power, these two stories are among Welty's least satisfying in that they are stories about incomprehension, which leave the reader puzzled. The deaf boy senses many of Aaron Burr's emotions as he watches Burr with the infatuation of "first love," but neither he nor the reader is enlightened about Burr's unsuccessful military and political stratagems; indeed, the reader must know some of Burr's history to fully comprehend the story. Although Murrell, Dow, and Audubon find "a still moment" in contemplating a lovely white heron, they are ultimately unaffected by it and continue on their various careers—good, bad, and artistic. Welty may be suggesting that love and beauty cannot provide insight into the motivations of those ruled by other passions and that private individuals remain ignorant of the stratagems of public figures like the statesmen and generals of World War II even though they are affected by their actions, as was Welty through the vulnerability of her loved ones at war.

In the title story, "The Wide Net," Welty explores the implications for women of men's desire for adventures like war, or drinking escapades, or dragging a river. In this outwardly humorous story, young and pregnant Hazel Jamieson is angry that her husband William Wallace Jamieson has been out all night drinking, and she decides to get her revenge by making him worry as much as she had: she leaves him a note that she plans to drown herself, but actually hides in their house. Although William Wallace knows that Hazel is terrified of water and is unlikely to choose that means of suicide, he and the men of the town use her note as an excuse to take old Doc's wide net and spend an entire day dragging the Pearl River for fish and treasures while ostensibly seeking Hazel's corpse. Hazel's plight is symbolized by a small rabbit that William Wallace captures and holds but eventually lets down, commenting, " She can go if she wants to, but she don't want to." His friend Virgil responds, "Anybody can freeze a *rabbit*." Hazel is found at home; apparently she could have gone if she wanted to, but she did not. Hazel, however, is frozen by her pregnancy and her economic and sexual need for William Wallace. "It was just as if he had chased her and captured her again. She lay smiling in the crook of his arm. It was the same as any other chase in the end." Hazel's only, and temporary, means of keeping herself captured—sex—is indicated in the last lines of the story: "She took him by the hand and led him into the house, smiling as if she were smiling down on him."

"The Winds," "At the Landing," and "Livvie," in the same volume, more directly address the question of women's roles in wartime, as represented by wind, flood, and spring. In "The Winds," the central character, the child Josie, persists in looking forward to leaving the safety and infinite precautions of her parents' house despite what she has seen on a night of hurricane-force winds: "There, outside, was all that was wild and beloved and estranged, and all that would beckon and leave her, and all that was beautiful. She wanted to follow, and by some metamorphosis she would take them in—all—every one." At the conclusion of the story, her fate, frustrated in waiting for a man, is foreshadowed by that of her neighbor, a young woman named Cornella, in a scrap of a letter written by Cornella that "the winds" blow to Josie: "O my darling I have waited so long when are you coming for me"?

In "At the Landing" and "Livvie," sexual relationships also serve as the wind or natural force that blows a woman out of childhood and the past to a future of waiting and hoping. In "At the Landing," a flood acts as a catalyst that parallels Jenny's sexual affair with Billy Floyd in that it makes her decide to leave the isolated, past-ridden world of her grandfather's house in which she has spent her entire life. As a woman, however, she ends the story in a passive posture, offering herself sexually to any man and "waiting for Billy Floyd," the flood who she presumes will move her. Similarly, in "Livvie," the title character, another young woman, is bound to the past in an old man's house, in this case that of her extremely old and bedridden husband, Solomon. They dwell in Solomon's isolated farmhouse, where he hopes to keep her to himself, immune from the lures of youth and the present. Despite his cautions, along comes young, handsome, zoot-suited Cash McCord on a riotously burgeoning spring day. Solomon realizes his defeat when, just before he dies, he hands Livvie his watch, a symbolic indication that he expects her to control her own time and make her own decisions. Her choice of Cash, however, simply puts her into another passive, silent position. The story ends as Livvie "rested in silence in his trembling arms, unprotesting as a bird on a nest." Despite *The Wide Net*'s ostensible detachment from World War II, Welty is making the sad comment that men act and women react; women wait and hope, but what they hope for may be as actively dangerous to them as the past was passively stultifying; in either case, they are caught by their gender and their sexual needs in the "wide net" of men's activities.

### DELTA WEDDING

In her first novel, *Delta Wedding* (1946), Welty continues to explore gender relations in a setting based on a plantation owned by the family of John Robinson, where Welty sometimes visited while he was away at war. She uses what appears to be a woman's topic, a wedding, and a woman's space, a plantation named Shellmound in the Mississippi Delta, with its suggestions of the goddess of love, Aphrodite or Venus—shells like that upon which Venus rose from the sea and female genitalia, as in the mound of Venus and Delta of Venus. As if further to emphasize female sexuality, in interviews Welty stated that she set the novel in the 1920s because it was a time when the men were not at war and the area was not in a crisis like the Depression of the 1930s; against a relatively uncomplicated backdrop, Welty clearly delineates the patterns of behavior of the Fairchild women, quite similar to those of the women of *The Wide Net*. Ellen Fairchild, the plantation mistress, is fixed in a seemingly endless round of pregnancies and childbearing, the prospect facing Hazel in "The Wide Net." Also like Hazel, Ellen's sister-in-law, Robbie, is a runaway wife, but she ends up running straight back to her husband, "caught in marriage" like a wide net. Like Livvie and Jenny, Dabney, the bride, becomes tamed by sex; at a family picnic following her honeymoon, she obeys her husband's injunction for silence and seems unable to sit up straight without his assistance. Robbie observes that "things almost never happened, almost never could be, for one time only," and we learn that earlier Fairchild women suffered through frontier life and the Civil War but remained dependent on their men; one ancient aunt even talks to her long dead husband and other dead male relations.

Two young female characters, however, suggest a resistance to the established gender relations of Shellmound. Young Laura McRaven is visiting from Jackson; her dead mother was one of the Fairchild girls of the preceding generation. Although Laura is seduced by the glamour of the aptly named Fairchilds, she decides she will decline Ellen Fairchild's offer to keep her at Shellmound; she will return to her father in Jackson with the wider possibilities of urban life in a world not controlled by female sexuality. Similarly, the oldest Fairchild daughter, Shelley, seems to be renouncing female sexuality by also leaving Shellmound, first for a trip to Europe, then college, and then, she hopes, a career as a writer. Her name's close identification with her place of birth, however, indicates the relentless pull of the female body's sexuality and fertility.

Welty had long resisted the literary world's demands for a novel and when she finally did write *Delta Wedding* she used some of the techniques of her short stories magnified and multiplied. The novel is linked by the preparations for and the aftermath of Dabney Fairchild's marriage to the Fairchild overseer, but it has little plot in the conventional sense beyond the suspense of whether the Fairchilds will succeed in assembling the family connection and completing preparations for the wedding. Instead, Welty again emphasizes the mystery of human relationships, but here with a large cast of characters in a plethora of relationships. Their moments of contact are the beads that are strung on the thread of the wedding plot. In a 1941 letter to Russell collected in *Author and Agent,* Welty's comment about "The Winds" shows her evolving technique for *Delta Wedding:*

> Every body exerts its influence & pull on every other body, no matter how far apart or how different they may be, stars on stars, or a falling flower on the motion of the universe—the pull is each upon the other, and it is only a difference in weight that keeps the rest of the universe from showing its disturbance and lets the flower float to the ground.

*Delta Wedding* ends with Laura McRaven lifting her arms as if to embrace not a falling flower, but a falling star, "both arms held out to the radiant night." This vision of a pattern, the connections between people and the universe, makes a dark night, the night of human sexuality, radiant for a young woman, but only if she is too young for sexuality or if she can detach herself from the pattern of gender relations enough to recognize that the wide net can be a spider's web for a woman.

### THE GOLDEN APPLES AND THE PONDER HEART

Welty's next book, *The Golden Apples,* is more optimistic about gender relations, though that is not its primary theme. In this sequence of seven short stories in which the characters are connected by their sometime residence in the small town of Morgana, Mississippi, Welty divides characters more by their attitudes toward experience than by gender. The book's title is taken from Yeats's "The Song of Wandering Aengus" and concerns those who seek the silver apples of the moon in contrast to the golden apples of the sun. The seekers of silver apples prefer to take their experience at second hand, as the moon takes its light from the sun. They are frequently attracted to the golden apple seekers but are ultimately afraid of the aura of adventure and danger that surrounds them. Miss Snowdie Hudson is attracted to King MacLain, marries him, and becomes pregnant by him in "A Shower of Gold," alluding to Danaë's rape by Zeus, but she is contented in a married life in which she is usually separated from him by his wanderings. Cassie Morrison is attracted to Virgie Rainey, who can follow their piano teacher, Miss Eckhart, into the realms of art's passion, but Cassie lives vicariously, dreaming behind closed doors and through her memories of golden apple seekers. Nina Carmichael is fascinated by the daring orphan Easter during their weeks of summer camp at Moon Lake, but she will never take the dangerous plunge into the depths of experience of Easter's immersion in the lake. The MacLain twins, Ran and Eugene, try philandering and wandering like their father, the golden-apple-seeker King MacLain, but they are never more than imitations or reflections of the sun's light onto their satellite moons.

Male seekers after golden apples like King MacLain or Loch Morrison seem to come and go at will, but such direct grasping of experience is more difficult for and dangerous to women. Easter nearly drowns in Moon Lake, but when she is resuscitated by Loch, a Boy Scout, in a parody of sexual intercourse, it seems as if she has escaped one danger for another. Cassie and Loch's mother, Mrs. Morrison, seems to have been a golden apple seeker thwarted by marriage, childbearing, and the women's bridge parties of Morgana; she commits suicide. Virgie Rainey, however, still keeps her potential for seeking. As a child, she had learned piano from Miss Eckhart, but when she felt that Miss Eckhart was trying to control her, she gave it up, despite her evident talent. She leaves Morgana for a life of freedom, including sexual freedom, but returns to stay with her widowed and ailing mother until her death. The night before she leaves Morgana after her mother's funeral, she swims, "hung suspended in the Big Black River as she would know to hang suspended in felicity." This suspension, this delicate balance, is what Virgie has successfully maintained. As her name indicates, she carefully maintains her relations with other people, sexual or familial, drawing the "reins" on her character, but remains a sort of "virgin" as she keeps inviolate her individuality and capacity for independent action.

It is not surprising that *The Golden Apples* is Welty's favorite work. A character like Virgie is as close to Welty's ideal as can be found in her fiction, but the book was also a joy to Welty in terms of her evolving technique. As Welty wrote many of these stories, she was unaware of their connections; in a flash of insight she realized that the characters of the stories could be drawn together by their place of origin, which she called Morgana as an allusion to the fata morgana, or illusions, that govern the characters. Welty was firm in her refusal to call the book a novel, and much of her pleasure was found in the way she could work in her chosen genre, the short story, while creating a work that in some ways resembles a novel. As in *Delta Wedding,* it is the myriad permutations of human relationships that give *The Golden Apples* its richness, but each story within the book has the gemlike integrity of a golden apple in a way that the episodes of *Delta Wedding* do not.

The late 1940s and early 1950s were successful years for Welty. Like Virgie Rainey, she kept her ties to home while making trips, in her case to New York and San Francisco. She even went abroad in 1951, where in Ireland she met the fiction writer Elizabeth Bowen, whose works she greatly admired. She began reviewing books frequently for the *New York Times,* some under the pseudonym Michael Ravenna, when it was believed that a woman would not be a credible reviewer of books about the war. She gave her first major critical lecture, "Some Views on the Reading and Writing of Short Stories" at a writers' conference in Seattle, Washington, in 1947. Recognition also came in the form of various awards. "Livvie Is Back" won the first-place O. Henry Award in 1943. She received one thousand dollars from the American Academy of Arts and Letters in 1944 in recogni-

tion of the body of her works. In 1949 she was awarded a Guggenheim Fellowship and in 1952 was elected to the National Institute of Arts and Letters. Her success continued into the mid-1950s, when her novella *The Ponder Heart* (1954) became a best-seller and the basis for a Broadway production in 1956.

In *The Ponder Heart,* Welty returns to some of the techniques and comedy of her early fiction. The novella's narrator, Edna Earle Ponder, is the proprietress of the little-used Beulah Hotel. When a rare guest arrives, she buttonholes him or her, the "you" addressed in the narrative, and tells the story of the Ponder family, particularly her Uncle Daniel. As in "The Petrified Man," Welty's masterly conveyance of character through voice is not only essential to the story; in many ways, it *is* the story. In *The Eye of the Story,* Welty could be writing of her own talent when she states that the novelist Henry Green has the "gift . . . of turning what people say into the fantasy of what they are telling each other, at the same time calling up out of their own mouths their vital spirit." As Edna Earle tells her visitor and the reader, "I size people up"; we see her fantasy of judgment and control at the same time that we realize Edna is a somewhat limited narrator since, for Welty, human beings tend to resist sizes and categories.

Edna Earle is ironically named after the heroine of one of the best-selling novels of the nineteenth century, Augusta Jane Evans Wilson's *St. Elmo* (1866). The original Edna Earle reformed the hero, the title character, so that she could convert, marry, and domesticate him. Countless little southern girls were named after her in the hope that they would emulate her self-sacrificing and loving womanly ideal. Edna Earle Ponder, of course, cannot marry her uncle, but she is determined to "save" him from himself and keep him with her in the less than perfect domestic setting of the Beulah Hotel. Welty's sardonic commentary on female self-sacrifice here arises from the fact that Uncle Daniel is much happier when following his own impulses. He loves to give things away, including money and property and, in that sense, he is the self-sacrificing one. He is much more like *St. Elmo*'s Edna Earle than his niece because his world is built upon love: "He's been brought up in a world of love," Edna Earle observes, and "he loves more people than you and I put together ever will." He is "the Ponder heart." When he has lost the perfect object of his love, Bonnie Dee Peacock, and is forced to dwell in the Beulah Hotel with Edna Earle, she has achieved her desire to save and protect him. Like the heroines of nineteenth-century novels, however, she realizes a Pyrrhic victory in that Uncle Daniel saved and protected is not the man that she wanted. Her comment to the townspeople is an unwitting reflection upon herself: "Not to know how to take what's offered shows your manners."

Welty had good reason to reflect upon the ideal of womanly self-sacrifice during the next fifteen years. Her brother Walter's death in 1959 left her with new responsibilities for his survivors and increased care for her mother, who was in failing health for over a decade before her death in 1966. Walter's death was followed a few days later by the sudden death of Welty's other brother Edward. Inevitably these cares and griefs affected Welty's ability to work. She wrote by cutting and pinning together scraps of paper until she achieved a satisfying whole, much as Virgie Rainey of *The Golden Apples* gets pleasure from cutting a dress pattern from a difficult print like a plaid. At that point in her life, Welty no longer had the necessary serenity nor the sustained blocks of time she needed for her work—for a time she drove an hour each way to visit her mother daily in a nursing home. Her short-story collection *The Bride of the Innisfallen and Other Stories,* published in 1955, was her last full-length book until the publication of *Losing Battles* in 1970.

Welty, however, tested her philosophy that experience is an enrichment, not an impoverishment, as she found satisfaction in a different kind of pattern-seeking, that of her own identity. In a 1972 interview, collected in *Conversations with Eudora Welty,* she reflected thus:

> The battle for identity is not even necessary. It's a sticking together. It involves both a submerging and a triumph of the individual, because you can't really conceive of the whole unless you *are* an identity. Unless you are very real in yourself, you don't know what it means to support others or to join with them or to help them. So it's a much more complicated business than identity-seeking.

In this comment, Welty is expressing not only the traditional view that a woman's identity is partly based on her commitments to others but also the southern ideal that identity is not based on inherent qualities but is largely formed by relations with others and reflects the views of the community.

### THE BRIDE OF THE INNISFALLEN

Perhaps Welty in some sense needed this enforced leave of absence from sustained writing. Considering her work before *Losing Battles,* Welty commented in a 1985 interview, collected in *More Conversations with Eudora Welty,* that she felt her work had become "overly" introspective, "too contemplative and slow-moving"; indeed, most of the stories in *The Bride of the Innisfallen* fit that description. Her two lengthy travel stories, the title story and "Going to Naples," emphasize leisurely contemplation and description over any compelling plot. The seven stories in this volume are, however, linked by the concept of marriage, as indicated by the title story, but in this collection, as in *The Wide Net,* brides, women who are potentially sexually active, are not happy: they are on the run, betrayed, ignored, violated without benefit of matrimony, abandoned, and, most cruelly, not wanted at all.

The men, though, are equally stuck in this endlessly repeating pattern, characterized by this pair of Irish ghosts in "The Bride of the Innisfallen":

> She comes first because she's mad, and he slow—got the dagger stuck in him, you see? Destroyed by her. She walks along, carries herself grand, not shy. Then he comes, unwilling, not touching with his feet—pulled through the air. By the dagger, you might say, like a hooked fish. Because they're a pair, himself and herself, sure as they was joined together.

In "Ladies in Spring," young Dewey's father might betray his mother, but he is drawn right back to her after his adventures. Extremely elderly Uncle Felix in "Kin" has the delusion that he is making an assignation in his youth with Daisy, but he is still firmly under the thumb of his wife, as represented by her "kin." The runaway woman in "No Place for You, My Love" finds her man waiting for her in her hotel lobby after her excursion, while the man with whom she journeyed is returning to his wife.

In "Going to Naples," the challenge faced by the female characters of *The Bride of the Innisfallen* is expressed through a young Italian American girl, Gabriella, whose mother is taking her to Italy in the hope of finding her a husband. For a moment, Gabriella is dancing by herself.

> It began to seem to the general eye that she might be turning around faster inside than out. For an unmarried girl, it was danger. Some radiant pin through the body had set her spinning like that tonight, and given her the power—not the same thing as permission, but what was like a memory of how to do it—to be happy all by herself.

To be happy all by themselves: that is what the suicidal sisters of "The Burning," Welty's only Civil War story, cannot learn. It is what the title character of "Circe," abandoned by Odysseus, must learn, as she builds on her reflection that "all men are swine." It seems to be what Miss Hattie of "Ladies in Spring" has learned as she calls down

rain for the town by sitting alone in nature; her solitary happiness is not selfish, for it allows her to benefit the town in the same way that Gabriella's dancing benefits the voyagers on the ship, by allowing them the refreshment of remembering their autonomy before rejoining the community. "For an unmarried girl, it was danger," but to refuse the challenge is to remain locked in the matrimonial hell of the ghosts in "The Bride of the Innisfallen."

In the fifteen years between *The Bride of the Innisfallen* and *Losing Battles,* Welty wrote a children's book, *The Shoe Bird* (1964), in which she reflects on some of the lessons of her years of artistic drought and familial challenges. Arturo, a parrot and the main character, is a "bookish bird" who unreflectingly parrots information, to the confusion of the bird world. Over the course of the story, he learns a new motto: If You Hear It, Think It Over. From the extinct Dodo, he learns the two gifts that are "stronger than extinction": love and memory. From the self-renewing Phoenix, he learns that "in your own questions lie the answers." *Art*uro is discovering Welty's evolving credo that art is a never-ending process of questioning; answers do not arrive ready-made but are refined in the memory through a process of loving contemplation. Truth is inward and individual, nothing a parrot can parrot.

## LOSING BATTLES

Arturo learns his individual lessons, but he masters them with the help of his community, and the themes of education and community are also prominent in Welty's *Losing Battles.* Welty herself, as she relates in *More Conversations with Eudora Welty,* was pursuing her artistic education; she wanted to discard her interior method and "see if I could do something altogether in action and conversation and still show the same thing." Her setting is a farm near the isolated community of

Banner in the hills of Mississippi, and her subject is the reunion of Granny Vaughn's descendants to celebrate her birthday and to learn from each other: to remember the past, enjoy the present, and hope for the future. The newcomer to the family, the bride Gloria Renfro, wants to persuade her husband to leave this intricately educative family connection so that they can have a little house all to themselves. But, as Welty comments in *Conversations with Eudora Welty,* Gloria "lacks imagination" because she is unable to learn what Welty did during her years of family service: that identity consists of the "submerging and triumphing" of the individual. Gloria's husband, Jack, in contrast, has the artist's ability to lose himself in loving contemplation of other people: "When he listened to Uncle Homer it was the same as when he listened to all his family—he leaned forward with his clear eyes fixed on the speaker as though what was now being said would never be said again or repeated by anyone else." Jack's identity is gained in this temporary immersion of himself in his family and his community, unlike the Banner community's longtime teacher, Miss Julia Mortimer, who must retain her separateness in order to criticize and correct the community.

In *More Conversations with Eudora Welty,* she refers to Miss Julia as "the heroine of the novel." Although Miss Julia can never entirely win her battle to educate the hearts and souls of Banner's children, even on her deathbed she keeps trying. As she writes to her former pupil and admirer, Judge Oscar Moody: "Things like this are put in your path to teach you. You can make use of them. . . . I haven't spent a lifetime fighting my battle to give up now. I'm ready for all they send me. There's a measure of enjoyment in it." Like Welty herself struggling with the shape of her art or Virgie Rainey with the pattern of her plaid, Miss Mortimer is fundamentally engaged in educating herself; only then can she teach others. Also like Welty and Virgie, Miss Mortimer remains single, despite her many suitors, in order to pursue her vocation. Her single status, particularly as a career woman, is regarded as a challenge and an affront to the community. As the family remembers at their reunion, "She never did learn how to please," but as Welty remarks in *The Eye of the Story,* "Real compassion is perhaps always in the end unsparing; it must make itself a part of knowing"; it is the real compassion of the artist who is a loving teacher and the memory for a community.

Welty was sixty-one years old in 1970 when *Losing Battles* was published, and after that her career took an increasingly reminiscent and retrospective turn. Honors rained down upon her, including being named to the American Academy of Arts and Letters and being given a Gold Medal for Fiction from the National Institute of Arts and Letters, the National Medal of Literature, the Presidential Medal of Freedom, the Modern Language Association Commonwealth Award, and many others. The Public Library of Jackson, Mississippi, was renamed in 1986 in her honor, as befitted the young girl who read so avidly there, and the Eudora Welty Writers' Center was founded in 1995 at her childhood address of 741 North Congress Street. The Eudora Welty Society was established in 1991. Her portrait was placed in the Smithsonian Institution's National Portrait Gallery in 1989. Even international recognition arrived with her induction into the French Legion of Honor in 1996.

Two collections in particular are an enduring source of interest to students of Welty's work: *The Eye of the Story: Selected Essays and Reviews* (1978) and *A Writer's Eye: Collected Book Reviews* from 1942 to 1984 (1994). As the many quotations from them in this essay demonstrate, they are treasuries of Welty's profoundly held convictions about her art. *A Writer's Eye* demonstrates Welty's range as well as her critical acumen. *The Eye of the Story* reveals Welty's close identification with her favorite authors: Jane Austen, Henry Green, Katherine Anne Porter,

Willa Cather, and Anton Chekhov. It also contains essays on fictional techniques, such as setting and time, as well as a section of charmingly written autobiographical "Personal and Occasional Pieces."

### COLLECTED STORIES

Welty's *Collected Stories,* her most enduring monument, appeared in 1980. In addition to *A Curtain of Green, A Wide Net, The Golden Apples,* and *The Bride of the Innisfallen,* the volume includes two previously uncollected works, "Where Is the Voice Coming From?" (1963) and "The Demonstrators" (1966). These stories seem to be direct answers to the charges leveled at Welty that she evades controversial current events. In "Where Is the Voice Coming From?," Welty's narrator is a lower-class white man, so-called white trash, who decides to shoot a black civil rights leader for what he claims is his "own pure-D satisfaction." In the course of the story, he recognizes that the civil rights leader "was like me" and "I was like him." By the end of the story, when he picks up his guitar and sings, "Sing a-down, down, down, down. Down," the reader realizes that all members of society are implicated in the civil rights struggle; we are like him and he is like us, and we are all going down together. In "The Demonstrators," Welty uses Dr. Strickland as her protagonist since, like an artist, he must diagnose the social ills that cause the physical ills presented to him. In the middle of the story he experiences a moment of nostalgia when he longs for the old patronizing days of noblesse oblige in race relations, "as though someone had stopped him on the street and offered to carry his load for a while." By the conclusion of the story, he acknowledges, through the symbolic gesture of picking up his medical bag, that though his task is "hard," he must eschew nostalgia and persevere.

With love but no sentimental nostalgia, Welty approaches what she calls "that most wonderful interior vision which is memory" in twin works: an autobiography of her development as an artist, *One Writer's Beginnings,* and an autobiographical novel, *The Optimist's Daughter. One Writer's Beginnings* originated when Welty was asked to deliver the William E. Massey Sr. Lectures in the History of American Civilization at Harvard in 1983. She decided to confront this daunting task by writing about what she knew, her craft. The book is divided into three sections that express Welty's stages of development from childhood to young womanhood: "Listening," "Learning to See," and "Finding a Voice." Welty's first subject as a budding writer was, of course, the mystery of human relationships, and as a child she focused on the relationship between her parents and their relationship with her. Beneath the many beguiling anecdotes of small-town life in an essentially happy family lies the drama of growth away from that family seen as a sort of betrayal. Welty writes:

> There is no wonder that a passion for independence sprang up in me at the earliest age. It took me a long time to manage the independence, for I loved those who protected me—and I wanted inevitably to protect them back. I have never managed to handle the guilt. In the act and the course of writing stories, these are two of the springs, one bright, one dark, that feed the stream.

In *One Writer's Beginnings,* Welty emphasizes the bright stream of love that fed her craft, but in *The Optimist's Daughter,* she reveals the dark stream of guilt, need, and betrayal that a woman must cross in order to become an artist. As Welty declares in *The Eye of the Story,* "Personal history may turn into a fictional pattern."

A widow, Laurel McKelva Hand, "the optimist's daughter," returns to Mount Salus, her childhood home, for the final illness and death of her father, Judge McKelva. As she confronts the views of the townspeople about her parents, Laurel tries to penetrate the mystery enshrouded in self-serving opinions and discover who her parents really were as individuals. Her happiest childhood memory was of her parents reading to each other as she fell asleep, "never letting a silence divide or interrupt them, combined into one unceasing voice and wrapped her around as she listened." This ideal memory of a marriage and family bound together with fictive words is undercut by her mother's factually unfounded feelings of betrayal in the blindness of her last illness and her father's remarriage to the lower-class, much younger Fay Chisom, a member of "the great, interrelated family of those who never know the meaning of what has happened to them." Laurel is in danger of joining that family of the uncomprehending as she initially clings to her idealized memories and rejects Fay.

Laurel, however, is an artist, and Welty's kind of artist, a fabric designer who learned her craft by putting together scraps of fabric from her mother's sewing basket, much in the way that Welty and Laurel stitch together childhood memories in an attempt to arrive at a viable truth. That truth, however, is only one truth of many, the best that can be divined from a plethora of facts and interpretations. For as Laurel observes, "the mystery in how little we know of other people is no greater than the mystery of how much." In the face of that mystery, Laurel must take the implied advice of her family's maid, Missouri, about Fay when she observes, "All birds got to fly, even them no-count dirty ones." Laurel accepts the mystery of human relationships, but she will return to Chicago and her art because without the attempt to fathom the mystery, "experience is the worst kind of emptiness," as Welty states in *The Eye of the Story*.

As Laurel and her parents are linked in a pattern by the words they read and as Welty's characters are held in the pattern of Welty's words, so the mystery of Eudora Welty herself can best be discovered in the pattern of her works. With a change of name and pronouns, what Welty said about William Faulkner in *A Writer's Eye* could be her challenge to her readers:

No [woman] ever put more of [her] heart and soul into the written world than did [Eudora Welty]. If you want to know all you can about that heart and soul, the fiction where [she] put it is still right there. The writer offered it to us from the start, and when we didn't even want it or know how to take it and understand it; it's been there all along and is more than likely to remain. Read that.

## Selected Bibliography

### WORKS OF EUDORA WELTY

NOVELS AND SHORT STORIES
*A Curtain of Green and Other Stories.* New York: Harcourt, Brace, 1941.
*The Robber Bridegroom.* New York: Doubleday, Doran, 1942.
*The Wide Net and Other Stories.* New York: Harcourt, Brace, 1943.
*Delta Wedding.* New York: Harcourt, Brace, 1946.
*The Golden Apples.* New York: Harcourt, Brace, 1949.
*The Ponder Heart.* New York: Harcourt, Brace, 1954.
*The Bride of the Innisfallen and Other Stories.* New York: Harcourt, Brace, 1955.
*The Shoe Bird.* New York: Harcourt, Brace, and World, 1964.
*Losing Battles.* New York: Random House, 1970.
*The Optimist's Daughter.* New York: Random House, 1972.
*The Collected Stories of Eudora Welty.* New York: Harcourt Brace Jovanovich, 1980.

LITERARY CRITICISM AND OCCASIONAL PIECES
*The Eye of the Story: Selected Essays and Reviews.* New York: Random House, 1978.
*The Norton Book of Friendship.* Edited with Ronald A. Sharp. New York: W. W. Norton & Co., 1991.
*A Writer's Eye: Collected Book Reviews.* Edited by Pearl Amelia McHaney. Jackson: University Press of Mississippi, 1994.

AUTOBIOGRAPHY
*One Writer's Beginnings.* Cambridge, Mass.: Harvard University Press, 1984.

PAPERS

Welty's papers are held at the Mississippi Department of Archives and History.

PHOTOGRAPHS

*One Time, One Place: Mississippi in the Depression, a Snapshot Album.* New York: Random House, 1971.

*Photographs.* Jackson: University Press of Mississippi, 1989.

## BIBLIOGRAPHIES

Polk, Noel. *Eudora Welty: A Bibliography of Her Work.* Jackson: University Press of Mississippi, 1994.

Swearingen, Bethany C. *Eudora Welty: A Critical Bibliography, 1936–1958.* Jackson: University Press of Mississippi, 1984.

Thompson, Victor H. *Eudora Welty: A Reference Guide.* Boston: G. K. Hall, 1976.

## CRITICAL AND BIOGRAPHICAL STUDIES

Appel, Alfred, Jr. *A Season of Dreams: The Fiction of Eudora Welty.* Baton Rouge: Louisiana State University Press, 1965.

Bloom, Harold, ed. *Eudora Welty: Modern Critical Views.* New York: Chelsea House, 1986.

Desmond, John F., ed. *A Still Moment: Essays on the Art of Eudora Welty.* Metuchen, N.J.: Scarecrow Press, 1978.

Devlin, Albert J. *Eudora Welty's Chronicle: A Story of Mississippi Life.* Jackson: University Press of Mississippi, 1983.

Devlin, Albert J., ed. *Welty: A Life in Literature.* Jackson: University Press of Mississippi, 1987.

Dollarhide, Louis, and Ann J. Abadie, eds. *Eudora Welty: A Form of Thanks.* Jackson: University Press of Mississippi, 1979.

Evans, Elizabeth. *Eudora Welty.* New York: Frederick Ungar, 1981.

Gretlund, Jan Nordby. *Eudora Welty's Aesthetics of Place.* Newark: University of Delaware Press, 1994.

Gygax, Franziska. *Serious Daring from Within: Female Narrative Strategies in Eudora Welty's Novels.* Westport, Conn.: Greenwood, 1990.

Harrison, Suzan. *Eudora Welty and Virginia Woolf: Gender, Genre, and Influence.* Baton Rouge: Louisiana State University Press, 1997.

Kreyling, Michael. *Author and Agent: Eudora Welty and Diarmuid Russell.* New York: Farrar Straus Giroux, 1991.

———. *Eudora Welty's Achievement of Order.* Baton Rouge: Louisiana State University Press, 1980.

Manning, Carol S. *With Ears Opening Like Morning Glories: Eudora Welty and the Love of Storytelling.* Westport, Conn.: Greenwood, 1985.

Manz-Kunz, Marie-Antoinette. *Eudora Welty: Aspects of Reality in Her Short Fiction.* Bern: Francke Verlag, 1971.

Mark, Rebecca. *The Dragon's Blood: Feminist Intertexuality in Eudora Welty's "The Golden Apples."* Jackson: University Press of Mississippi, 1994.

Mortimer, Gail L. *Daughter of the Swan: Love and Knowledge in Eudora Welty's Fiction.* Athens: University of Georgia Press, 1994.

Prenshaw, Peggy Whitman, ed. *Eudora Welty: Critical Essays.* Jackson: University Press of Mississippi, 1979.

Romines, Ann. *The Home Plot: Women, Writing and Domestic Ritual.* Amherst: University of Massachusetts Press, 1992. Pp. 192–291.

Schmidt, Peter. *The Heart of the Story: Eudora Welty's Short Fiction.* Jackson: University Press of Mississippi, 1991.

*Southern Quarterly Special Issue: The World of Eudora Welty.* 32 (Fall 1993).

Turner, W. Craig, and Lee Emling Harding, eds. *Critical Essays on Eudora Welty.* Boston: G. K. Hall, 1989.

Vande Kieft, Ruth M. *Eudora Welty.* New York: Twayne, 1962.

Westling, Louise Hutchings. *Sacred Groves and Ravaged Gardens: The Fiction of Eudora Welty, Carson McCullers, and Flannery O'Connor.* Athens: University of Georgia Press, 1985.

Weston, Ruth D. *Gothic Traditions and Narrative Techniques in the Fiction of Eudora Welty.* Baton Rouge: Louisiana State University Press, 1994.

Yaeger, Patricia S. "The Case of the Dangling Signifier: Phallic Imagery in Eudora Welty's 'Moon Lake.'" *Twentieth Century Literature* 28, no. 4 (1982): 431–452. Reprinted in *Faith of a (Woman) Writer.* Edited by Alice Kessler-Harris and William McBrien. Westport, Conn.: Greenwood, 1988. Pp. 253–271.

## INTERVIEWS

Prenshaw, Peggy Whitman, ed. *Conversations with Eudora Welty.* Jackson: University Press of Mississippi, 1984.
———, ed. *More Conversations with Eudora Welty.* Jackson: University Press of Mississippi, 1996.


## PERFORMING WORKS BASED ON THE WORKS OF EUDORA WELTY

*The Ponder Heart.* Play by Joseph Fields and Jerome Chodorov. Directed by D. Robert Douglas. First production: The Music Box, New York, 1956.
*A Season of Dreams.* Directed by Frank Hains. First production: Jackson, Mississippi, New Stage Theatre, 1968. Mississippi ETV, 1970. (Adaptation of several works.)
*The Robber Bridegroom.* Musical by Alfred Uhry (book and lyrics) and Robert Waldman (music). Directed by Gerald Freedman. First production: New York, 1976.
*Sister and Miss Lexie.* Scripts based on "June Recital," *Losing Battles,* and "Why I Live at the P.O." by David Kaplan and Brenda Currin. First production: Chelsea Theater Center, New York, 1981.
*The Ponder Heart.* Opera by Alice Parker. First production: Jackson, Mississippi, New Stage Theatre, 1982.
*The Wide Net.* Script by Anthony Herrera. First broadcast: Public Broadcasting System, American Playhouse, 1987.

*—VERONICA MAKOWSKY*

# Edith Wharton
## 1862–1937

ONE JULY AFTERNOON in 1925, F. Scott Fitzgerald set out in a speedy Renault to call upon Edith Wharton at the Pavillon Colombe, her home outside Paris. Although Wharton had written admiringly of *The Great Gatsby,* Mathew Bruccoli recounts in *Some Sort of Epic Grandeur* that Fitzgerald was reportedly so intimidated by her reputation as America's greatest living "literary aristocrat" that he stopped frequently along the way to steady his nerves with a number of stiff drinks. Arriving unfashionably late, Fitzgerald received a cool welcome—an inauspicious beginning to an evening that failed to improve after the younger novelist drunkenly launched into an autobiographical account of an American couple who had mistakenly spent three days in a Paris bordello. Wharton was apparently not amused: the story, she is said to have observed dryly, neither supplemented her knowledge of French brothels, nor ended with a good punchline. A mortified Fitzgerald returned to Paris and confessed to his wife, "They beat me! They beat me!" After his departure, Wharton turned to her friend Gaillard Lapsley and remarked, "There must be something peculiar about that young man." That evening, next to Fitzgerald's name in her diary, she scribbled one word: "awful."

This image of Wharton, the soul of seated poise, balancing a cup of tea as she quietly tolerates Fitzgerald's drunken boasts, epitomizes a prevailing impulse to depict her as a prim literary dowager, an outdated novelist of manners, and a member of what the playwright Thornton Wilder caustically called the "cardboard generation." Yet the writer whom Ernest Hemingway sought in Paris, T. S. Eliot called "the satirist's satirist," Virginia Woolf reviewed, and Ezra Pound actively solicited for the *Little Review,* was far from a staid literary relic. On the contrary, as Fitzgerald acknowledged in a 1924 letter to Thomas Boyd, "She's a very distinguished grande dame who fought the good fight with bronze age weapons when there were very few people in the line at all."

Indeed, despite her blueblood lineage, her elite social connections and her formidable, often intimidating intellect (the French writer Paul Bourget is said to have had Wharton in mind when he wrote of the American "intellectual girl," "'Oh, for one ignorance, one error, just a single one. May she make a blunder, may she prove not to know!' In vain. A mind may be mistaken, a mind may be ignorant, but never a thinking machine"), Wharton's writings reveal a richly complex and deeply personal assessment of the ambiguities of modern experience. In novels that chronicle the explosive impact of early-twentieth-century industrial capitalism, ghost stories that trespass into places of dangerous erotic knowledge, writings about incest and illicit sexuality, fictional detours into the desperate world of America's "other half," accounts of excursions across into battle lines tenuously separating war from peace, Wharton returns again and again to what she hinted in her autobiography, *A Backward Glance* (1934), were "regions perilous, dark and yet lit with mysterious fires, just outside the world of copy-book axioms, and the old obediences that were in my blood."

Curiously conflicting images became the staple of Wharton's fiction. If incisive social observation, a controlled precision of language, and a sly, ironic wit were her stylistic hallmarks, the heated contest between the often rigid codes of codes of societal expectation and the capricious, thrilling realm of the individual, the sexual, and the creative were her subject. Torn between the "grave endearing traditions" she extols in *The House of Mirth* and what Candace Waid, in *Edith Wharton's Letters from the Underworld* (1991), called the modern "underworld of experience," Wharton struggled throughout her career to reconcile the competing claims of ancestral reverence and individual transgression; she would imagine a long line of characters who confronted similar dilemmas. As such as Charity Royall, the heroine of Wharton's 1917 novel *Summer* reflects, "In the established order of things as she knew them she saw no place for her individual adventure."

### EARLY LIFE

Wharton's own early life was characterized by this conflict between the surface of a well-regulated existence and the possibilities of what she described in "Life and I," an unfinished autobiography that appears in *Novellas and Other Writings* (1990) as "Life, real Life" that rumbled beneath. Edith Newbold Jones was born on January 24, 1862 into an affluent New York family who traced its American lineage back almost three

hundred years to a prosperous generation of English and Dutch merchants, bankers and lawyers. She was the daughter of George Frederic Jones, a gentleman of leisure who dabbled (unsuccessfully) in real estate, and Lucretia Stevens Rhinelander Jones, an "indolent" (complained Wharton) though impeccably dressed society matron. "Pussy" Jones, as she was then known, had a dual existence. On one level, she was the intelligent though painfully self-conscious young girl at play among Roman ruins and along the Champs Élysées of Paris, where she spent the majority of her early childhood and where she developed a lifelong passion for European art, culture, and language (she spoke French, Italian, and German with considerable facility). On another level, however, she was also a wildly imaginative child who lived, she recalled, "in complete mental isolation," inventing stories and entertaining any number of unspeakable fears and "torturing moral scruples."

After returning in 1872 to the United States, where she lived alternately on West Twenty-third Street in New York and at Pencraig, the Joneses' expansive Newport "cottage" in Rhode Island, Edith Jones was raised according to patrician custom, characterized, she later complained in *A Backward Glance,* by "a blind dread of innovation, an instinctive shrinking from responsibility." She was reared in a milieu that cultivated a benign ignorance in its daughters: her formal education was the charge of a series of well-meaning, narrow governesses who valiantly tried to protect their charge from mental fatigue. Within this "intellectual desert," far removed from the experience of her two older brothers in cozy tutorials at Cambridge University, Wharton nevertheless devoured a daunting literary diet that included the Old and New Testaments, Plutarch, Dante, Johann Wolfgang von Goethe, John Milton, John Keats, Percy Bysshe Shelley, Thomas Carlyle, and John Ruskin.

"Whenever I try to recall my childhood," Wharton wrote in her autobiography, "it is in my father's library that it comes to life." Squatting on a thick Turkish rug, hidden in a "retreat where I wished no one to intrude," Edith Jones pored over volume after volume, each gingerly removed from her father's glass-enclosed bookcase, reveling in "a secret ecstasy of communion." Wharton always associated secrecy, passion, and transgression with the pleasures of reading and writing. Indeed, she identified the source of her creativity as a "secret garden" where "the vital interest begins." Wharton had described this *"giardino secreto,"* a flowering Renaissance space designed for "complete privacy" in *Italian Villas and Their Gardens* (1904); in its metaphoric sense, however, the secret garden became the place of transgression.

Wharton recalls in "Life and I" that as a child she would beg her mother to relieve her of onerous social obligations and allow her to "make up" in the seclusion of her own room. Clutching an upside-down edition of Anthony Trollope, she would pace the floor, enjoying "The rapture of finding myself again in my own rich world of dreams! I don't think I exaggerate or embellish in retrospect the ecstasy which transported my little body & soul when I shut myself in & caught up my precious [Trollope]. It was really the Pythoness-fury that possessed me!" As an adult, Edith Wharton often spoke of writing in this way—as a breathless joy, a consuming passion, an obsession. When Theodora Dace, the seventeen-year-old heroine of Wharton's 1905 short story "April Showers" (in *The Collected Stories,* 1968) discovers that her first story is to be published, she reacts with similar rapture: "Everything was crowding toward the light and in her own heart hundreds of germinating hopes had burst into sudden leaf. She wondered if the thrust of those little green fingers hurt the surface of the earth as her springing raptures hurt—yes, actually hurt!—her hot, constricted breast! . . . The brown earth throbbed with her joy, the treetops trembled with it, and a sudden star broke through the branches like an audible 'I know!' " What Shari Benstock, in *No Gifts from Chance,* calls Wharton's "ecstatic, almost orgas-

mic, responses" to writing belie the rather mundane constraints of the author's early life: as Kathy A. Fedorko argues, Wharton's inner world—the life of the mind—followed the plot of "a Gothic heroine."

FIRST WRITINGS AND MARRIAGE

In January 1877, at the age of fourteen, Edith Newbold Jones completed a self-described "novelette," suggestively entitled *Fast and Loose,* written under the unlikely nom de plume, "David Olivieri." The story is devoted to the sentimental rise and fall of Georgie Rivers, "a wicked, fast, flirtatious little pauper—a lazy, luxurious coquette," who casts aside her true love, Guy Hastings, to wed the "ancient" British nobleman, Lord Breton. A broad satire of English romance, *Fast and Loose* contained the seeds of what later became the trademarks of Wharton's adult work: a fine sense of irony and wit (Lord Breton's face conjures "the ghost of what some might recall as a fascinating smile; but which was more like a bland leer to the eye unassisted by memory"), the pairing of a restless young heroine and a weak though sensitive man, and a preoccupation with the social and intellectual restrictions imposed on women (Lord Breton ominously insists, for example, that the tomboyish "Georgie" accept the more conventionally feminine name "Georgina," foreshadowing Lady Breton's transformation from "lively, plump prettiness" to a face "so fragile, so sad & white" after her marriage). In one of three wonderfully parodic "reviews" that Wharton appended to the novella, a "critic" for *The Nation* flatly consigns *Fast and Loose* to obscurity: "Every character is a failure, the plot a vacuum, the style spiritless, the dialogue vague, the sentiments weak, & the whole thing a fiasco. . . . Is not . . . Mr. Olivieri very, very like a sick-sentimental schoolgirl who has begun her work with a fierce & bloody resolve . . . & has ended with a blush . . . ?"

Fortunately, not everyone shared "*The Nation's*" opinion. By 1878, Lucretia Jones had arranged to have a dozen of her daughter's poems privately published in a chapbook entitled *Verses,* and in 1880, five additional poems appeared in the *Atlantic Monthly,* after Allen Thorndike Rice (former editor of the *North American Review*) recommended the verses to Henry Wadsworth Longfellow, who then passed them on with warm praise to the *Atlantic's* William Dean Howells. Indeed, despite a broken engagement to Henry Stevens in 1883, the cause of which, whispered New York's *Town Topics,* was "an alleged preponderance of intellectuality on the part of the intended bride," the reportedly "ambitious authoress" married her brother Harry's friend, Edward Robbins Wharton, a likable if rather intellectually uninspired Bostonian, on April 27, 1885.

Wharton entered her marriage woefully ignorant of sexual matters, a state of naïveté that she blamed firmly on her mother, whose standard reply, "It's not nice to ask about such things," left her daughter with a permeating sense of "not-niceness." A few days prior to her marriage, "seized with . . . a dread of the whole dark mystery," Edith Jones begged her mother to tell her "what being married was like": "I'm afraid, Mamma—I want to know what will happen to me." Wharton later recalled in "Life and I" the "dreadful moment" when her mother responded with a coldness that "deepened to disgust": "I never heard of such a ridiculous question!" Had Edith not seen sculptures and drawn the appropriate conclusions? Lucretia's rebuke was sharp and humiliating: "Then for heaven's sake don't ask me any more silly questions. You can't be as stupid as you pretend!" The incident, Wharton bitterly concluded, "did more than anything else to falsify & misdirect my whole life."

As Henry James remarked in hindsight, the match between Edith Jones and Teddy Wharton was "an almost—or rather an utterly—inconceivable thing." According to Ogden Codman, Jr., the Boston architect with whom Wharton collaborated on *The Decoration of Houses* (1897), Teddy was "a sort of school boy in his tastes and in his mental development": the marriage, by all accounts intellectually inequitable and sexually empty, was Wharton's "greatest mistake." Teddy's father had committed suicide after being institutionalized for mental illness, and his son would suffer a similar series of nervous collapses throughout his married life. Moreover, it could not have been easy, as R. W. B. Lewis perceptively points out in *Edith Wharton: A Biography,* to withstand the strain of a life "everywhere and altogether dominated by an affluent and brilliantly successful wife of strong personality." Within the first four years of their marriage, Wharton had begun to establish her name as an emerging literary talent, publishing four poems in *Scribner's, Harper's Monthly,* and *Century Illustrated Monthly Magazine.* Years later, a bemused Teddy Wharton, walking a few paces behind his wife, would comment to Walter Maynard, "Look at that waist! No one would ever guess that she had written a line of poetry in her life!"

### EARLY FICTION

Wharton's first published fiction, a short story entitled "Mrs. Manstey's View" (in *The Collected Short Stories*) appeared in *Scribner's* in July 1891. The story, which describes a sick and aging widow whose one joy in life, the view she enjoys from her third-floor boardinghouse room, is threatened by the development of a nearby building, is a curious combination of the removed and the immediate. That Wharton could imagine a life so reduced, attenuated, and removed from her own world of affluence has surprised many of her critics. Yet Mrs. Manstey clearly shares the tastes of her prosperous creator. She is said to be "at heart . . . an artist" harboring an aesthetic repugnance for the "state of chronic untidiness," "the noisy slatterns" who work in nearby apartments, and the "statuettes and antimacassars" that clutter a room. In more important ways, however, Wharton's story reimagines her own constrained existence in a marriage that is intellectually stifling and, like Mrs. Manstey's view, rapidly contracting.

As many critics have noted, the analogy between a woman and the house in which she lives proved a consistent theme in Wharton's work. Two years after the appearance of "Mrs. Manstey's View," *Scribner's* accepted "The Fullness of Life," a remarkable story which imagines a woman sinking into a suicidal drug-induced stupor, contentedly reflecting that "she should never again hear the creaking of her husband's boots—those horrible boots." Wharton ultimately called "The Fulness of Life" "one long shriek" written "'at the top of my voice'" and would refuse to allow *Scribner's* to republish it in her first collection of short stories, *The Greater Inclination* (1899; it was included in *The Collected Short Stories*). Perhaps the story was too baldly autobiographical. As the narrator feels her consciousness slipping away, she meets the allegorical Spirit of Life, who asks if she has ever really experienced life. No, she replies; her marriage was "a very incomplete affair":

> But I have sometimes thought that a woman's nature is like a great house full of rooms: there is the hall, through which everyone passes in going in and out; the drawing room, where one receives formal visits; the sitting room, where the members of the family come and go as they list; but beyond that, far beyond, are other rooms, the handles of whose doors are never turned; no one knows the way to them, no one knows whither they lead; and in the innermost room, the holy of holies, the soul sits alone and waits for a footstep that never comes.

The architectural problem that provides the conflict in "Mrs. Manstey's View" here becomes the central image of a woman's intellectual, spiritual, and sexual identity. The narrator's husband, like Teddy Wharton, has never gotten beyond the sitting room, yet the woman ultimately rejects the prospect of spending eternity with a perfect, "kindred soul," dutifully choosing instead to await her husband's arrival.

Wharton likely had Walter Berry in mind when she imagined a "kindred soul." They had met in Bar Harbor in 1883 and courted without resolve, but as Wharton would recall in *A Backward Glance,* "the encounter had given me a fleeting hint of what the communion of kindred intelligences might be." Himself a son of Old New York—he was actually a distant Rhinelander cousin—Berry eventually became a respected international attorney and a judge on the International Tribunal in Egypt. From Wharton's point of view, however, he was "an expansion, an interpretation, of one's self, the very meaning of one's soul." In her memoirs, she credited him (hyperbolically) with teaching her how to write and acknowledged him (sincerely) for his unflagging and intelligent attention to her work: "No critic was ever severer, but none had more respect for the artist's liberty. He taught me never to be satisfied with my own work, but never to let my inward conviction as to the rightness of anything I had done be affected by outside opinion." Both during and after her marriage, Wharton and Berry traveled extensively together—many times to Italy, Switzerland, and once, quite memorably, to Morocco. Although critics have found traces of Berry, the noncommittal man about town, in Wharton's pale, tentative heroes, she later claimed that a love affair with Berry would have spoiled their intellectual and profoundly emotional meeting of the minds: as she wrote to John Hugh Smith after Berry's death in 1927, "I am proud of having kept such a perfect friendship after the great days were over."

Wharton's fascination with the metaphor of houses and their interiors culminated in her collaboration with Ogden Codman on *The Decoration of Houses,* a genteel study of interior decor and design. The book, an unanticipated success, articulates Wharton's response to what she saw as the tasteless excesses of ornamentation, mass production, and democratization in American culture. And perhaps more than any of her later writings, *The Decoration of Houses* most clearly locates Wharton's early class interests. While purportedly aimed at a middle-class audience, the manual instructs readers to emulate the classical and, above all, traditional tastes Wharton associated with a genealogically authentic elite. Thus, her comment on the function of doors is in many ways emblematic: "It should be borne in mind of entrances in general that, while the main purpose of a door is to admit, its secondary purpose is to exclude. The outer door, which separates the hall or vestibule from the street, should clearly proclaim itself an effectual barrier." While *The Decoration of Houses* invites its readers to copy the style it outlines, its loving descriptions of "gala" ballrooms, frescoed ceilings, and Louis XVI chairs suggest that it is less an instruction manual than a paean to Wharton's own aristocratic tastes—tastes that would bear fruit in The Mount, an expansive western Massachusetts mansion whose design she supervised in 1901. Situated on 113 rolling Berkshire acres, the Whartons would summer there until its sale—much to Wharton's dismay—in 1911.

### THE GREATER INCLINATION

Wharton's first collection of short stories, *The Greater Inclination,* met with enthusiastic reviews and brisk sales. The stories probe the tense dynamic between sexual passion and restrictive social conventions. In "The Muse's Tragedy," for instance, Mary Anerton, the "muse" of a great poet, Vincent Rendle, confesses that their famed intimacy was nothing but a literary invention. The poet's impassioned writings were mere "cosmic philosophy, not a love poem; addressed to Woman, not to a woman!" Her passion thwarted, Mrs. Anerton if left to crawl "into myself as into a snow

hut." Similarly, the wife in "A Journey," who must secretly convey her dead husband's body aboard a train to New York, recalls a stultifying marriage in which "she was never to be allowed to spread her wings": "Now their energies no longer kept step: hers still bounded ahead of life, preempting unclaimed regions of hope and activity, while his lagged behind, vainly struggling to overtake her." *The Greater Inclination* is preoccupied with what Elizabeth Ammons, in *Edith Wharton's Argument with America,* identifies as "the isolation and powerlessness of women, the failure of men to live up to women's expectations, the confinement of marriage for wives, . . . the suspect ideal of feminine self-sacrifice, the loneliness of the 'intellectual' woman." From Mrs. Amyot of "The Pelican," who has been forced to disguise her longing for a career as a "maternal sacrifice," to Lydia Tillotson in "Souls Belated," who escapes a confining marriage only to find that the liberating relationship she desired is equally conventional, Wharton's women are everywhere restricted by a "keep-off-the-grass morality." "Do you know, I begin to see what marriage is for," Lydia remarks. "It's to keep people away from each other."

If Wharton is interested in the ways in which socially sanctioned relationships mask frustration and deprivation, she is equally captivated by proscribed connections that mask a superabundance of transgressive passion. *The Greater Inclination* concludes with one such startling example—Wharton's first published incest story, "The Portrait." The tale describes a painter whose revealing portrait of a political boss, Alonzo Vard, betrays the "miserable secret" of Vard's relationship with his daughter and moves the "monstrous" father to commit suicide. The interest in the tale, however, lies not in the moral condemnation of the story's central "horror" (a word Wharton would throughout her career associate with incest), but rather in the daughter's tabooed pleasure. Miss Vard's heated admiration for her father ("Yes, she said, *wasn't* her father splendid, and didn't I think him one of the handsomest men I'd ever seen?") and her erotic possessiveness ("It was like carrying a guilty secret about with her: his friends, his admirers, would never forgive her if they found out that he kept all his best things for *her*!") seems to suggest that, for Wharton, one's "greater inclinations" could not always surmount one's baser desires.

### THE TOUCHSTONE AND *CRUCIAL INSTANCES*

Wharton's ensuing fictions played out the dialectic between the forbidden and the transgressive. *The Touchstone* (1900) describes a vibrant and brilliant woman writer, Margaret Aubyn, hopelessly in love with a lesser creature, Stephen Glennard. Like many of Wharton's heroes, Glennard cannot "rise to the height of [Mrs. Aubyn's] passion": "It was not that she bored him, she did what was infinitely worse—she made him feel his inferiority." After Mrs. Aubyn's death, Glennard publishes her love letters for profit, only to be mortified and embittered to discover that the letters reveal both his own simpering cruelty and his former lover's passionate potential. Mrs. Aubyn serves as an early incarnation of what Waid has called the Whartonian "Persephone"—the woman writer who "dwells in the underworld savoring the supernatural fruit of letters and books," and rejects the "pastoral earth of Demeter which represents cyclical timelessness and asexual reproduction." As a "gift from the grave," (the novella's title in England), ghostly voice of Mrs. Aubyn is embodied in her letters, whispering secrets from the underworld of intellectual and erotic experience.

Although the majority of Wharton's critics agree that her second short-story collection, *Crucial Instances* (1901), did not match *The Greater Inclination*'s achievement, the volume is noteworthy for its exploration of the gothic and its indebtedness to the American romantic tradition of Nathaniel Hawthorne and Edgar Allan Poe. Sev-

eral of the stories insistently return to a reversal of the Pygmalion myth: a woman is eerily trapped in a work of art. In "The Duchess at Prayer," for instance, the title character's liaisons with her lover in a saint's crypt come to a violent end when her suspecting husband gives her a sardonic gift: the sculptural image of the duchess at prayer. When the duke then seals off the entrance to the tomb where the lover is hidden, the duchess swoons and dies; only the Dorian Gray–like changes in the sculpture—a look of "frozen horror"—betray her secret. Similarly, the aging caretaker of "The Angel at the Grave," who rejects a marriage proposal in order to remain the high priestess of her grandfather's literary legacy, is said to have been born "as it were, into a museum, and cradled in a glass case with a label." Finally, in "The Moving Finger," the late Mrs. Grancy lives on in a portrait that her husband modifies as time and circumstances change. After Mr. Grancy's death, Claydon, the artist who was himself in love with Mrs. Grancy, restores the painting to its original youth: "'Pygmalion,' he began slowly, 'turned his statue into a real woman; *I* turned my real woman into a picture.'" The conflict between art and life and the ways in which art can imprison life, occupy a central place in these stories. Wharton, in her newfound role as an increasingly popular author, betrayed a growing anxiety with an existence devoted exclusively to art at the expense of "Life, real Life."

### THE VALLEY OF DECISION

In light of the deeply personal quality of Wharton's early fictions, her first novel—*The Valley of Decision* (1902)—appeared at first glance to be a radical detour into the rather arcane world of late eighteenth-century Italy. As Wharton explained to her editor at Charles Scribner's Sons, William Crary Brownell, "The Valley . . . is an attempt to picture Italy at the time of the breaking up of the small principalities at the end of the 18th century, when all the old forms & traditions of court life were still preserved, but the immense intellectual & moral movement of the new regime was at work beneath the surface of things." If the subject seems esoteric, the roots of its appeal date back to Wharton's concerns about class in *The Decoration of Houses*. In the character of Odo Valsecca, the reform-minded duke of Pianura, Wharton vividly depicts the consequences of a culture suddenly democratized, its political and cultural policies reformulated to give power to the people. After Odo's wife, Fulvia, is slain in a mass uprising, his subjects eventually join forces with Napoleon's troops, bringing what Wharton considered the anarchic horrors of the French Revolution to Italy. Wharton described *The Valley of Decision* in *A Backward Glance* as "saturated with the atmosphere I had so long lived in," and although she was referring to her long held passion for eighteenth-century Italy, she was equally describing the American climate in which she was immersed. Like Fulvia, who is "in spite of herself . . . a child of a new era," Wharton plays out her own anxieties about a rapidly expanding, heterogeneous American public in the early twentieth century. The angry mob in *The Valley of Decision* later became the "hoardes of the uninvited" hovering around the edges of *The House of Mirth*—waves of immigrants and working-class Americans who threaten to storm the traditional bastions of America's cultural elite. As Wharton's friend Gaillard Lapsley remarks in Percy Lubbock's *Portrait of Edith Wharton,* "She was to all appearance standing (in America) between two worlds, 'one dead, the other powerless to be born.'"

Yet it was precisely the dying traditions of blue-blood families and inherited wealth that Edith Wharton struggled to affirm. Indeed, despite Henry James's famous injunction in a 1902 letter urging Wharton to tackle "the *American Subject*. There it is round you. Don't pass it by— the immediate, the real, the ours, the yours, the novelist's that it waits for. Take hold of it and keep hold and let it pull you where it will . . . *Do New York!*" Wharton had arguably embarked on a career-long consideration of the American scene in *The Valley of Decision*. For all its immersion in the minutiae of eighteenth-century Italian life, Wharton's first novel was a profoundly American book, built out of the components of an American cultural landscape that preoccupied her throughout her long career.

It was to be a career that was frequently dogged by the long and imposing shadow of Wharton's dear friend, Henry James. She first met James in the late 1880s at a dinner party hosted by the artist Edward Boit, a friend of Teddy's. Despite the "pretty frock" she wore, however, Wharton recalls in *A Backward Glance* being defeated by her own shyness: the dress, "alas . . . neither gave me the courage to speak, nor attracted the attention of the great man." A subsequent meeting several years later in Venice, this time featuring *"a beautiful new hat!"* produced similar results: James later admitted that he could not recall meeting Wharton on either occasion. In *A Backward Glance,* Wharton implies that it was not until she could address James as a fellow author rather than a fluttery *femme,* when she was "no longer afraid to talk to Henry James of the things we both cared about," that their relationship blossomed. Indeed, it was as a critically acclaimed writer that she sent James a copy of *The Greater Inclination* and a subsequent story, "The Line of Least Resistance" (in *The Collected Short Stories*), which he criticized as being "a little hard, a little purely derisive."

Theirs was to be a friendship at once lastingly intimate and profoundly competitive. Wharton grew to find comparisons between their work wearisome and objectionable: "The continued cry that I am an echo of Mr. James (whose books of the last ten years I can't read, much as I delight in the man)," she complained to Brownell in 1904, "makes me feel rather hopeless." For his part, James seemed daunted by Wharton's meteoric energy and her popular success. She was, in the words of Lubbock, James's "dazzling intruder, *la femme fatale,* the golden pheasant invading the barnyard." Over the years, James portrayed his friend as the "Devastating Angel" or "Fire Bird" who, as a 1909 letter to their mutual friend Howard Sturgis reveals, suddenly announces herself "flashing down here . . . and culling me, as she passes, to present me as a limp field flower that evening." Trapped in her "coruscating claws," James has time only to "make you this small squirming sign" before being "hurled on your hospitality." If this image of Wharton suggests a degree of what R. W. B. Lewis identifies as "sexual panic," it equally betrays professional jealousy. After hearing that Wharton had purchased a new car with the profits from *The Valley of Decision,* James is said to have remarked, "With the proceeds of my last novel, I purchased a small go-cart, or hand-barrow, on which my guests' luggage is wheeled from the station to my house. It needs a coat of paint. With the proceeds of my next novel I shall have it painted."

Wharton's soaring "motor-flights," on which James was such a hapless victim, gave her ample opportunity to pursue her second passion after fiction—the study of architecture and landscape design. In *Italian Villas and Their Gardens,* she researched, analyzed, and described some eighty villa gardens in minute detail. Her fascination with these gardens sprung primarily from their synthesis of art and nature—"the subtle transition from the fixed and formal lines of art to the shifting and irregular lines of nature." The inherent beauty of the Italian garden, Wharton insisted, lay in its "deeper harmony of design." Such observations became crucial elements of Wharton's fiction. She explored Lily Bart's mesmerizing blend of the artificial and the natural in *The House of Mirth,* and would bring her rather austere notions of political and architectural design to the disorderly worlds of *The Fruit of the Tree* (1907) and *Summer.*

With the publication of *The Descent of Man and Other Stories* in 1904, Wharton revived an element of her craft that had been absent from both *Crucial Instances* and *The Valley of Decision*—a gift for comedy. The collection ranges from the title story about a brilliant professor whose broad scientific satire, *The Vital Thing,* is taken so seriously by the reading public that he is forced to continue writing fluff to finance his "real" research on beetles, to "The Mission of Jane," the story of a genteel though rather estranged couple whose adopted daughter grows into such a monstrously selfish adult that her departure brings the couple together. The comic tone, however, does not conceal Wharton's continued grievances—her sense of displacement as an intellectual woman (as Professor Linyard comments in "The Descent of Man," there are only two types of women—"the fond and foolish, whom one married, and the earnest and intellectual, whom one did not"); her imprisonment in a mentally and sexually bankrupt marriage (according to the narrator of "Expiation": "Though the trials of married life have been classified and catalogued with exhaustive accuracy, there is one form of conjugal misery which has perhaps received inadequate attention; and that is the suffering of the versatile woman whose husband is not equally adapted to all her moods"), and her fear that traditional patrician foundations of identity were giving way to a new, "corporate" self. (Waythorn, the hapless third husband in "The Other Two," thinks of himself as "a member of a syndicate. He held so many shares in his wife's personality and his predecessors were his partners in business.")

### *THE HOUSE OF MIRTH*

These concerns culminated in Wharton's first best-selling novel, *The House of Mirth*. The achievement of *The House of Mirth* is in many ways Wharton's mature ability to synthesize the most personal elements of her best short stories with a new, far-reaching political and economic critique of contemporary American culture. Lily Bart, much to the mitigated delight of Henry James, who pronounced her "very big & true," was a New York version of Odo Valsecca, stalled between two worlds. As Elaine Showalter noted in *Sister's Choice,* Lily is in "historical transition from one house of American women's fiction to another, from the homosocial women's culture and literature of the nineteenth century to the heterosexual fiction of modernism." If the opening of the novel finds the beautiful Miss Bart paused in the middle of Grand Central Station, itself the quintessential site of social movement and industrial transformation, then the narrative as a whole charts Lily's inability to keep pace with the rapid transformations that the train station represents. In the eyes of Lawrence Selden, the genteel though modestly situated lawyer who plays Lily's would-be lover, Miss Bart's "purity of tint" and perfect beauty, at once "vigorous and exquisite, . . . strong and fine," distinguish her from the common herd of humanity: "The dinginess, the crudity of this average section of womanhood made him feel how highly specialized she was." Yet Lily's specialization—the very fact that "the material was fine, but that circumstance had fashioned it into a futile shape"—ultimately doom her to Darwinian extinction. As her name suggests, she is a hothouse flower who can flourish only under artificial and carefully monitored circumstances. *The House of Mirth* envisions Lily's decline from debutante to pauper as at once an extinguishment and an apotheosis, the annihilation of a rare species and a stylized act of preservation.

Lily's path is marred by a seemingly unending series of failures and losses circulating around the theme of disinheritance. After her ineffectual father is ruined on Wall Street and subsequently dies, Lily's mother desperately struggles to arrange a "brilliant" marriage for her beautiful daughter but dies after realizing that the "dinginess" and so-cial isolation she associates with poverty are unavoidable. Lily is effectively severed from her nuclear family, the source, according to Wharton, of economic and genealogical stability. Wharton may have drawn on her own bitter experiences in the wake of her mother's death in 1901. Benstock notes that Lucretia Jones had sided with Edith's eldest brother, Frederic, after his divorce from Minnie Cadwalader Jones and had broken with her younger son, Harry, after he sought to adopt Frederic's daughter Beatrix to ensure her inheritance. Lucretia's will reflected her allegiances: after the equitable division of the family property, she left the lion's share of the remaining real estate and money to Frederic, putting Edith's sum in a life trust to be controlled by her eldest brother. Wharton was infuriated. Together, she and Harry insisted that Frederic agree to reallocate the properties and to dissolve the old trust, turning its control over to Teddy. *The House of Mirth* reflects Wharton's sense of an American woman's fragile and contingent economic status. Lily begins the novel without a reliable source of familial support, and her fate over the course of the narrative bears out the precariousness of her situation.

Thrown on the good graces of her prim widowed aunt, Mrs. Peniston, Lily carves out an existence financed by the whims of her wealthy friends, who invite her to their estates and yachts in exchange for her fluid social skills, her willingness to play high-stakes bridge, and her performance of menial secretarial tasks. And though she flourishes in the world of luxury, Lily proves curiously unable to make the choices necessary to sustain this affluent life. Her visit to Bellomont, the lavish home of her friends Judy and Gus Trenor, results in her abysmal failure to capture Percy Gryce, the eligible though socially inept son of a millionaire collector of antiquarian "Americana." Missing her opportunity to play the pious churchgoer with Gryce, Lily chooses instead to spend a crucial afternoon wandering the estate's manicured grounds with Selden, discussing his vision of an elusive "republic of the spirit" where one is free from "everything—from money, from poverty, from ease and anxiety, from all the material accidents." Lily, however, realizes that Selden's "republic" is really nothing more than "a close corporation"—a company that, because its shares are not traded on the stock exchange, can create "arbitrary objections in order to keep people out." Selden's "republic of the spirit" is closely aligned with Lily's notion of the inheritance-based family: both are essentially undemocratic and exclusive, grounded in economic structures that conserve money in the hands of the cultivated few.

Cast adrift in a world beyond Selden's republic, Lily finds herself battered by economic forces she at once embraces and rejects. She is unable to keep up with the extravagant pace at Bellomont; after losing a startling sum at bridge, she consequently pursues an arrangement in which Gus Trenor will "speculate" with her money. This scheme, however, as Lily plainly realizes, is based on inherently false assumptions: when Trenor begins to pay her regular monetary installments, he also begins to expect proportionate amorous attentions in return. Many critics, including Irving Howe, have seen Lily's conflict as "the problem of mediating between the expectations of a commercial society and the ideals of humane civilization." Yet as Walter Benn Michaels shows in *The Gold Standard and the Logic of Naturalism*, Lily embraces risks like her arrangement with Trenor at every turn, transforming the unpredictability of the marketplace into a morality of its own: whether gambling at bridge, speculating on Wall Street, paying an unchaperoned visit to Selden's apartment, or imbibing narcotics, Lily is inclined to "take the risk." In this sense, *The House of Mirth* does not critique the destructive evils of the corporate marketplace; rather, it is committed precisely to the opposite effect: "the passionate contingencies of the marketplace," according to Michaels, "are here rewritten as the fundamental criteria of ethical choice, as if the only morally im-

peccable acts are those whose consequences are unforeseen."

This argument, however, meets its limits in Simon Rosedale, the "glossy" Jewish arriviste, whose tasteless opulence embodies Wharton's fears of the "hordes of the uninvited" storming the gates of Old New York and America more generally. Marrying Rosedale would appear to be the ultimate social risk, a risk that, at least initially, Lily disdainfully rejects. In the words of Elizabeth Ammons, "The book is about the snow-white heroine, the flower of Anglo-Saxon womanhood, not ending up married to the invading Jew." Rosedale embodies both menace and appeal. After Lily has avoided a sexual assault by Trenor and gently but disastrously rebuffed the simpering attentions of George Dorset, the husband of her nemesis, Bertha Dorset, she attempts to renew Rosedale's attentions. As Michaels contends, Rosedale's suggestion that Lily blackmail Bertha, who socially ostracizes her in order to hide her own sexual indiscretions, represents a clear path and freedom from risk. Lily proves too morally fastidious, however, to blackmail Bertha with love letters that would force her to compromise Selden, who is curiously Bertha's former lover. At the same time, however, Lily cannot bring herself to take the ultimate risk—that of aligning herself with Rosedale.

Thus, Mrs. Peniston's decision to disinherit her niece puts the final nails in Lily's social coffin, depriving her of her only independent source of income. After her aunt's death, Lily quickly spirals down the social ladder—from the nouveaux riches Wellington Brys and the midwestern divorcée Norma Hatch to the milliner's shop where Lily lacks even the skill to trim fashionable hats. In her final moments, Lily pays her debt to Trenor with the small allotment left to her by her aunt and overdoses on chloral. Selden, "seldom" able to muster the courage to stand by her in the face of social adversity, arrives too late and can only admire her beauty in death.

Lily, in fact, only becomes what Selden calls "the real Lily Bart" when she has been "divested of the trivialities of her little world, and catching for a moment a note of that eternal harmony of which her beauty was a part." Only when Lily is utterly disinherited, that is, does she most completely and artificially embody the full potential of her racial and genealogical inheritance. Stripped of her worldly possessions, Lily is able to value the "slowly-accumulated past [that] lives on in the blood—whether in the concrete image of the old house stored with visual memories, or in the conception of the house not built with hands, but made up of inherited passions and loyalties." Lily's losses emphasize what she has retained: a belief in the "mysterious links of kinship" that Wharton associated with a rich, patrician ancestry.

In Lily Bart, Wharton realized a culmination of her previous heroines—those who had been disappointed by inadequate men, trapped by limiting social and intellectual circumstances and menaced by the larger forces of democratization. Although Wharton would continue to publish poems, reviews, and travel essays—*Italian Backgrounds,* a collection of sketches dating back to 1894 appeared in 1905—she had found her primary calling as a novelist.

### THE FRUIT OF THE TREE

Wharton followed up her great success in *The House of Mirth* with a new novel that seemed initially to be a radical departure. Set against the unlikely backdrop of industrial mill reform, *The Fruit of the Tree* describes the two ill-fated marriages of John Amherst, a progressive though patrician mill manager, who weds the owner's wealthy widow, Bessy Westmore, only to discover that his bride is more interested in parties and clothes than in the workers' welfare. Their subsequent estrangement is brought to a violent end when Bessy suffers a paralyzing riding accident and subsequently dies.

Amherst then falls in love with Justine Brent, the merciful and reform-minded nurse who, unbeknownst to him, helped his first wife end her suffering by euthanasia. Somewhat predictably, the hero's discovery of Justine's role in Bessy's death permanently poisons their marriage. Justine is forced to lower her expectations, realizing that "life is not a matter of abstract principles, but a succession of pitiful compromises with fate, of concessions to old traditions, old beliefs, old charities and frailties."

As Janet Goodwyn acknowledged in *Edith Wharton: Traveller in the Land of Letters,* the ambitious if fragmented plot of *The Fruit of the Tree* suggests that Wharton was attempting to attain "a larger relevance, through a wider social and demographic picture." Despite Wharton's obvious unfamiliarity with the industrial mill world she describes (readers wrote her with corrections while the novel appeared serially in *Scribner's Magazine*), the issues of the novel are clearly in line with those of *The House of Mirth*. Like Lily Bart, Justine Brent is disappointed by a man who cannot match her broader (albeit nascent) emotional, sexual, and moral vision. Amherst, as Louis Auchincloss observes in *Edith Wharton: A Woman in Her Time,* "takes his ultimate stand in the chilly line of Edith's heroes: men of good taste, good manners, and attenuated will power." A more fundamental similarity with its predecessor, though, is the novel's focus on the still, prone body of an upper-class woman, a woman whose misery ends only after the administering of a conclusive dose of narcotics. In both cases, Wharton suggests that larger national issues are at stake. Bessy Amherst, like her factories, is dangerously vulnerable to mismanagement: her poor, incapacitated body—kept in excruciating pain by a self-serving young doctor—becomes Wharton's symbol of an American upper class that might lose control of industrial and intellectual production, a fear she shared with her new acquaintance, President Theodore Roosevelt. Amherst laments his first wife's adherence to "the ancient ineradicable belief in the separable body and soul!" While the novel opens with Justine ministering to a worker who has lost his hand in a mill accident, it insists, by marked contrast, that the body and soul of the American upper classes must remain united and intact. The act of euthanasia thus becomes a gesture of preservation and containment: if Lily Bart achieves eternal youth by overdosing on chloral, Bessy is reintegrated and rehumanized by receiving an overdose of morphine.

## MORTON FULLERTON

Wharton's own bouts of asthma and her husband's deteriorating mental health surely contributed to her anxieties surrounding the loss of political and personal agency. In January 1907, however, she met a man who would significantly alter her belief in the orderly life by introducing her to the "regions perilous" of sexual passion. William Morton Fullerton, a handsome, dark-haired American journalist, was working in the Paris office of the *Times* of London when his friendships with his former Harvard professor Charles Eliot Norton and Henry James brought him into Edith Wharton's circle. "The moment my eyes fell on him," she later wrote, "I was content." Their relationship, however, was anything but a contented affair.

Fullerton arrived for his first visit to the Mount in October 1907, and as Benstock remarks, "His brief stay in Lenox opened an unbridgeable gulf with all that had gone before in Edith's life." A cosmopolitan man of the world (he had had many lovers—both women and, unbeknownst to Wharton, men), Fullerton introduced sexual passion into Wharton's inexperienced life. She characteristically marked their affair in writing, recording her feelings in an old leather-bound journal that she entitled "The Life Apart (*L'Ame Close.*)" At the age of forty-five, she brought all of her repressed passions, her sense of the "real life" she

had been missing, to their escalating relationship. Even before they became lovers, her expectant fantasies had almost completely mastered her, transforming her, she wrote, into a "ripple of flame": "If, wherever you touch me, a heart beats under your touch, & if, when you hold me, & I don't speak, it's because all the words in me seem to have become throbbing pulses, & all my thoughts are a great gold blur." Their affair alternately exhilarated and annihilated her: Fullerton's letters periodically dropped off altogether, and he would lapse into tormenting silence. "What you wish, apparently, is to take of my life the inmost & uttermost that a woman—a woman like me—can give, for an hour, now & then, when it suits you," Wharton wrote him desperately in 1910. "And when the hour is over, to leave me out of your mind & out of your life as a man leaves the companion who had accorded him a transient distraction. I think I am worth more than that."

Wharton was at once a painfully insecure, imperiously demanding, and anxiously solicitous lover. After the two finally consummated their affair in a prosaic hotel room at London's Charing Cross in June 1909, Wharton recalled the night—some argue the following morning—in a fifty-two-line poem entitled "Terminus": "Wonderful was the long secret night you gave me, my Lover," the poem begins, lyrically invoking a night of "unfathomed caresses" in a dingy bed "that has born the weight of fagged bodies, dust-stained, averted in sleep, / The hurried, the restless, the aimless—" Wharton encodes at once a feeling of sexual ecstasy and modernist anonymity in her evocation of an affair that, though still in its infancy, was, she realized, already at a "terminus." Her experience with Fullerton had awakened her to new sensual possibilities, but it had also reinforced for her the sense that the erotic only exacerbated the automatizing alienation of modern culture.

Wharton plays out various of these possibilities in *The Hermit and the Wild Woman* (1908). If "The Pretext" describes the deception and abandonment of the married heroine by her younger lover, the title story of Wharton's fourth volume of stories explores the opposite possibility. "The Hermit and the Wild Woman" describes two holy people, a hermit and a renegade nun, who heal the sick despite the nun's apostasy from her convent. Dwelling in considerable detail on what it means to be a "wild woman," Wharton somewhat fantastically links illicit sexuality with religious beatification. The "wild woman" of the story's title escapes her convent at night to bathe: "None, I think, could have surpassed in ecstasy that first touch of the water on my limbs. . . . Its ripples rose about me, first in furtive touches, then in a long embrace that clung and drew me down, till at length they lay like kisses on my lips." When the hermit eventually discovers the former nun naked and dead in a pool of water, her body mysteriously surrounded by a halo of light, Wharton effectively canonizes a woman for her willingness to be erotically "wild."

By 1910 the affair with Fullerton had come to an end. The romance, however, permanently altered the emotional landscape of Wharton's work. In the midst of their relationship, Wharton temporarily and uncharacteristically turned her full attention to poetry, collecting verse she had written since 1902 in a volume entitled *Artemis to Actaeon and Other Verse* (1909). As Candace Waid points out, the poems share language and imagery that are not only "erotically charged and often ecstatic" but also insistently preoccupied with "bodily pain and acts of physical violation." The desire to probe the interiors of the eroticized body in order to discover, according to Waid, "the secret of fertility and reproduction" complicates Wharton's ongoing reconceptualization of the changes occurring in American culture. Images of violent penetration in poems such as "Life" and "Vesalius in Zante" manifest not only Wharton's interest in the links between sexuality and writerly creativity, as Waid contends, but also an increasingly complicated vision of American reproductive politics and class displacement. By exploring the interiors of women's bodies (Fallopius, the scientist who discovered the connection between the uterus and the ovaries, is a character in one poem), Wharton probes the confusing interiors in which Americans of various classes are reproduced. As stories such as "Afterward," from her fifth collection of stories, *Tales of Men and Ghosts* (1910), attest, Wharton saw afresh that women, like the houses to which they are frequently compared, were often "haunted," that the female body, the American home, and even the nation as a whole could not always be mastered, ordered, and protectively designed. Wharton understood with sudden immediacy that chaos and disorder were possible within even the best-regulated spaces, and this realization produced two responses. On one level, she brought a finer, more subtle vision to her treatment of human frailty and indiscretion—as she demonstrated in *The Reef* (1912) and *The Age of Innocence* (1920). On another level, however, Wharton equally succumbed to a tendency to grow nostalgic for a more genteel time when such lapses were neither permitted nor tolerated. As she recorded in *A Motor-Flight through France* (1908), a collection of travel essays, she was surprised and reassured to find the home of George Sand, the sexually vibrant French author, so "dignified and decent, so much more conscious of social order and restraints, than the early years of the life led in it. . . . One beholds this image of aristocratic well-being, this sober edifice, conscious in every line of its place in the social scale."

## ETHAN FROME

It may seem ironic, then, that Wharton turned to an impoverished town in rural New England for the setting of her next and perhaps most enduring fiction. *Ethan Frome* (1911) was originally written in French as a language exercise in 1907, and if the novella initially appeared to be a linguistic stretch for a woman who spoke a formal French that was "the purest Louis Quatorze" (according to her friend Paul Bourget), then the story's plot seemed equally an example of cultural tourism. Louis Auchincloss has remarked that the characters in *Ethan Frome* "were as far removed socially from The Mount as they must have been geographically close." Indeed, Lubbock recalls Howard Sturgis one day reading aloud to Henry James a sentence from the novella—"I had been sent up by my employers"—upon which James immediately mocked "the suggested image—of Edith *sent,* and sent by *employers!*—what power of invention it implied in her to think of that!" However far afield Wharton seemed to be in what she later called "the derelict mountain villages of New England," she had clearly found a milieu that suited her imagination: *Ethan Frome* was widely regarded as Wharton's best work to date. Reviewers, Wharton exulted in a letter to Fullerton, "don't know *why* it's good, but they are right: it *is.*"

The story is framed by a first-person narrator, a city engineer, who comes to the bleak town of Starkfield, where he meets the enigmatic Ethan Frome whose "shrunken body" and scarred face betray a story that the painfully inarticulate farmer cannot tell. Caught in a snow storm, Frome agrees to take the narrator back to his "forlorn and stunted" house, "exposed in all its plaintive ugliness." There, the visitor hears a droning voice and encounters the chief horror of the tale: Ethan's sallow wife, Zenobia, preparing dinner for a paralyzed, "bloodless and shrivelled" younger woman, Mattie Silver. The engineer's ensuing narrative, "a vision of [Frome's] story," pieces together a tale that begins with the arrival of Mattie, a vivacious but poor cousin, who has come to keep house for the Fromes. When Mattie and Ethan fall in love, a suspicious Zeena vindictively banishes the young cousin. In desperation, Ethan takes his would-be lover on an erotic, suicidal sleigh ride—a ride that results in a living death. Their bodies painfully

distorted, Ethan and Mattie are forced to spend a hellish eternity with Zeena, invalids in a claustrophobic little house in the middle of an isolated New England wasteland. As a neighbor, Mrs. Hale, remarks, "The way they are now, I don't see's there's much difference between the Fromes up at the farm and the Fromes down in the graveyard; 'cept that down there they're all quiet, and the women have got to hold their tongues."

The central feature of *Ethan Frome* is its consuming fascination with failure. The novella, Carol Singley argues in *Edith Wharton: Matters of Mind and Spirit,* is "a modernist allegory about despair and irretrievably lost faith—in God, community and self," or, in Waid's terms, a "vision of unrelenting infertility." Wharton's biographers have pointed to the author's identification with Ethan, a man hopelessly tethered to a spouse whose perpetual illnesses, like Teddy Wharton's, make his life a prison. Mattie is alternately Morton Fullerton, a lover who promised joy but could deliver only despair, or Wharton herself, exhilarated by her affair but fearful that her intoxicating erotic ride would ultimately paralyze her. The novella, however, also serves as a curious coda to both *The House of Mirth* and *The Fruit of the Tree.* Like Lily Bart and Bessy Amherst, Mattie Silver is rendered prone and incapacitated, but unlike her cultivated predecessors, the working-class Mattie is utterly destroyed. Wharton seems to save her hardest fate for the radically sterilized poor who are kept in a torpor of physical suffering, pointless droning, and fruitless isolation.

## THE REEF

Wharton designed a better, albeit more equivocal fate for her next working-class heroine in *The Reef* (1912). Though this novel has been called the most "Jamesian" of Wharton's works (James himself praised its "psychologic Racinian unity, intensity and gracility"), it is not her best: it lacks the passion of *Summer,* the polish of *The Age of Innocence,* and the cynical sophistication of *The Custom of the Country* (1913). Yet *The Reef* is certainly one of Wharton's most ambitious and experimental works. Intricate, complex, and unresolved, the narrative documents the uneasy assembling of an expatriate American family. Not one of the four principal adult characters is related to the others by blood. Yet when George Darrow, an American diplomat, arrives in France to propose marriage to his childhood sweetheart, the widowed Mrs. Anna Summers Leath, he is clearly intent upon creating a family. Charmed at the prospect of adopting Anna's young daughter, Effie, Darrow entertains visions of future domestic bliss, a resolve Anna's stepson, Owen, shares when he seeks the hand of Effie's new governess, Sophy Viner. The family scenario seems complete: Darrow will play the "father," Anna the "mother," and Owen, Sophy, and Effie the "children." The novel derives its drama precisely from this deception. The entire structure collapses into a jumble of multiplying "passions" and sexual obsessions when the familial ship founders on an unexpected incestuous "reef": Anna and Owen discover, in the manner of Adam and Maggie Verver in James's *Golden Bowl,* that Darrow and Sophy have had a brief though intense love affair in Paris.

Sophy Viner becomes the central, "indeterminate" axis in the novel. A hanger-on to the world of wealth, she is independent, boyish, self-determined, and sexually direct. "Oh, I never mean to marry," she informs Darrow. "Besides, . . . I'm not so sure that I believe in marriage. You see I'm all for self-development and the chance to live one's life. I'm awfully modern, you know." Sophy, in the words of Rebecca Blevins Faery, is "the embodiment of the dark terrain of female sexuality," a destabilizing presence who underlines and challenges the strict moral taxonomy that Anna and Darrow are so desperate to preserve. If Darrow subscribes to a rigid system of oppositions that designate various "feminine types"—"the women he had frequented had either been pronouncedly 'ladies' or they had not"—then Anna has been similarly inculcated into "the well-regulated, well-fed Summers world [in which] the unusual was regarded as either immoral or ill-bred, and people with emotions were not visited." Sophy radically questions these oppositions: Darrow fears that she could dangerously prove to be "a shifting and uncrystallized mixture" of his previously systematized typology, and Anna sees Sophy as the embodiment of what Fedorko calls "the limitations of rationality as well as . . . the fearfulness of nonrational experiences." Anna marvels at Sophy's bold statement of sexual desire and agency—"I wanted it—I chose it"—and ultimately sexually surrenders to Darrow in the hope of being "to him all that Sophy Viner had been": "She wanted him to feel her power and yet to love her ignorance and humility. She felt like a slave, and a goddess, and a girl in her teens."

However, Wharton's narrative literally cannot contain the thoroughly sexualized woman: to the dissatisfaction of some critics who complain that the plot seems inconclusive, Sophy departs for India, leaving Anna in limbo. Wharton, however, amply prepares the reader for this unresolved resolution. As Darrow discovers, matters sexual are "a thing that no amount of arguing can make 'straight.'" Indeed, the final sequence of the novel takes place in the pink, indulgently sexual demimonde of Sophy's sister, "the much-married Laura," a world of masseurs, caramel-eating dogs, and prolific pillows. Anna departs in moral confusion. By staging an explicitly erotic interior at the end of the novel, Wharton implies that human sexuality is never "straight."

Like Anna, Wharton felt herself torn between a disorienting passion and the obligations incumbent upon a life of social rectitude. Her affair with Fullerton, himself an active writer, had enabled her to see what life with a compatible mind might be. Teddy Wharton, by comparison, seemed all the more intellectually and emotionally unsuited to his energetic and brilliant wife. Traveling aboard a train to Lenox in 1908, she had turned to Teddy to share a passage from Robert H. Lock's *Heredity and Variation,* a recently published study in evolution. "Read that," she said, pointing. Apparently bewildered, Teddy could only respond, "Does that sort of thing really amuse you?" "I heard the key turn in my prison-lock," Wharton wrote that evening in her love diary. "Oh, Gods of derision! . . . And you've given me twenty years of it! *Je n'en peux plus!* [I can't take it anymore!]" Suffering from what today would be diagnosed as clinical depression and alert, no doubt, to his wife's obvious disaffection, Teddy's health deteriorated and his behavior became increasingly erratic. The Whartons spent long periods apart— Edith at her fashionable new Paris apartment in the Faubourg St. Germain or traveling through central Italy with Walter Berry or her friends Mary and Bernhard Berenson (the art critic); and Teddy at various health spas and sanatoria in quest of a cure to complaints of pervasive pain and depression.

In December 1909, Teddy joined his wife in Paris and confessed to selling some of her trust holdings and speculating with the proceeds in order to set up a house in Boston for a mistress with whom he then lived for several months. The sexual details of the matter, including Teddy's exaggerated claims that he had sublet rooms to chorus girls, seemed prosaic by comparison with the full financial truth: Teddy had apparently embezzled and spent some fifty thousand dollars of his wife's trusts. Though he was able to make restitution by drawing upon some sixty-seven thousand dollars he had recently inherited from his mother, money remained a source of acrimony between husband and wife. Teddy resented his financial dependence on his successful spouse; their relationship, moreover, had been almost entirely sexless. He frequently accused her of seeking to "humiliate & wound" him. By 1911, Wharton told her increasingly volatile husband that she was

"tired out." "As nothing I have done seems to satisfy you for more than a few hours, I now think it is best to accede to your often repeated suggestions that we should live apart." In 1913, she sued Wharton for divorce on the ground of adultery. After the proceedings were finalized in April, James congratulated her with characteristic irony, "your definite liberation, signed & sealed (oh blest consummation!)."

## THE CUSTOM OF THE COUNTRY

Wharton's next novel reflected her self-reproaching thoughts on divorce and the American cultural decline it signified. *The Custom of the Country* (1913), a novel five years in the writing, introduced Wharton's most monstrous but captivating anti-heroine, the voracious Undine Spragg. Identified by one contemporary reviewer as "quite the most disagreeable girl in our fiction," Undine vividly embodies the nouveaux riches "Invaders" who, according to Wharton, had come from obscure places in upstart frontier regions like the Midwest and flagrantly plundered the most sacred bastions of Knickerbocker New York. Even more to her dismay, however, is the fact that Old New York, its quaint traditions and exacting observances rendered obsolete, had actively participated in its own self-destruction. Ralph Marvell, Undine's "first" husband and the doomed, romantic scion of the Washington Square Dagonets, embodies what Wharton sees as a Darwinian example of "race suicide." He and other Old New Yorkers are "Aborigines . . . likened . . . to those vanishing denizens of the American continent doomed to rapid extinction with the advance of the invading race." Wharton curiously reconfigures the annihilation of the Native American in order to animate Ralph's anthropological perspective on the defeat of his "indigenous . . . conquered race." Only after Undine has left him, dismissing his ancestral allegiances as inconsequential and mocking his literary aspirations, does Ralph realize "the uselessness, the irrelevance of all the old attitudes of appropriation and defiance." Indeed, confronted with the "epic" and "Titanic" Elmer Moffatt, a rising Wall Street magnate of Frank Norris proportions who we eventually discover to be Undine's first husband from Nebraska, Ralph realizes that he has been "stumbling about in his inherited prejudices like a modern man in medieval armor." He understands moreover that the woman he married was not Undine Spragg, but in fact "Undine Moffatt," a realization that fulfills both his and Wharton's fears about the slipperiness of American identity in the twentieth century. Realizing that he has permanently lost custody of his son, Paul, Ralph commits ("race") suicide, fulfilling his earlier prediction of imminent racial defeat in the battle for America's soul against Undine, the Invaders' "Warrior Queen."

Wharton's vision in *The Custom of the Country,* however, is not merely that of American cultural decline, what she called the "queer, rootless life" of modern New York; it is also a prediction of an emerging American cultural imperialism. Katherine Joslin points out in *Edith Wharton* that Wharton's "femme fatale" emerges from the American pioneer tradition: "Undine finds that there is always another 'beyond'; each new society offers further promise of vistas Undine has not yet imagined." Having devoured the American patriciate, Undine sets off for Europe where she conquers an authentic French aristocrat, Raymond de Chelles. Unlike her fictional predecessor the Marquise de Malrive (née Fanny Frisbee), the American heroine of Wharton's earlier novella *Madame de Treymes* (1907) who, like James's Christopher Newman, the main character in *The American,* falls victim to the evil machinations of the French aristocracy, Undine conquers and pillages Europe. Her decimation of the Marquis and his ancestral estate, Saint Désert, comes to be imaged in a set of ancient tapestries that represent "the huge

voracious fetish they called The Family." To Undine, however, the tapestries only signify potential cash in her pocket, money that will enable her to move among the expatriate glitterati, and free her from the oppressive world of aristocratic duty. Her attempt to sell the tapestries brings Moffatt, now "the greatest American collector," to the estate. An infuriated Raymond de Chelles seems to speak for Wharton when he famously indicts the new breed of Americans:

> You come among us from a country . . . you care for so little that before you've been a day in ours you've forgotten the very house you were born in—if it wasn't torn down before you knew it! You come among us speaking our language and not knowing what we mean; wanting the things we want, and not knowing why we want them; aping our weaknesses, exaggerating our follies, ignoring or ridiculing all we care about—you come from hotels as big as towns, and from towns as flimsy as paper, where the streets haven't had time to be named, and the buildings are demolished before they're dry, and the people are as proud of changing as we are of holding to what we have—and we're fools enough to imagine that because you copy our ways and pick up our slang you understand anything about the things that make life decent and honourable for us!

Chelles's savage charge proves to be an empty, impotent howl in a new Americanized wilderness. "Who cares what they do over here?" Moffatt challenges. "You're an American, ain't you?" In the final sequences of the novel, the new Undine Moffatt has captured the disputed tapestries and tacked them to the walls of her tacky new Fifth Avenue mansion, itself "an exact copy of the Pitti Palace, Florence." Wharton's broad satire comes to an end, like Theodore Dreiser's *Sister Carrie,* with Undine longing to conquer not just Europe, but the world: "She could never be an Ambassador's wife; and as she advanced to welcome her first guests she said to herself that it was the one part she was really made for."

## WORLD WAR I

Wharton's fears of a U.S. diplomacy engineered by Undine Spragg would be put to the test when war broke out in Paris in July 1914. The First World War at once fascinated and horrified Edith Wharton. She rushed back from the Humphrey Wards' estate in Buckinghamshire in September, writing breathlessly to Sara Norton that she regretted "very much not having been in Paris during the week of the panic," but that "as to the horrors & outrages, I'm afraid they are too often true." Caught up in the nationalist fervor sweeping her adopted home, Wharton seemed at once compelled and repulsed by her tourist's eye-view of the front. After a self-described "adventure" on the battlefield in Verdun, she wrote to Henry James in March 1915 that "once within the military zone, *every* moment is interesting." The same letter, however, reveals Wharton to be overwhelmed by "a Horror-of-War picture" in a makeshift hospital in the pews of a decrepit church: "The poor devils sleep on straw, in queer little compartments a dozen or so are crammed, in their trench clothes (no undressing possible)—with nothing that I could see to be thankful for but the fact that they were out of the mud, & in a sort of fetid stable-heat."

Wharton's fiction seems to absorb precisely this sensation of being at once seduced and repelled by an environment in which the distinctions between public and private, as Alan Price points out in *The End of the Age of Innocence*, were turned "inside out." She saw the Great War less as an international military conflict than as a systematic attack on the ancestral home. "It is not in the mud and jokes and everyday activities of the trenches that one most feels the damnable insanity of war," she remarked in *Fighting France; From Dunkerque to Belfort* (1915), a collection of wartime essays; "it is where it lurks like a mythical monster in the scene to which the mind has always turned for rest." The image she came to

associate with wartime and postwar civilization was that of a roofless house. "In these exposed interiors, the poor little household gods shiver and blink like owls surprised in a hollow tree."

If "home" denoted, for Wharton, a very tangible structure with walls and roof, it also connoted a more metaphysical location—a place "to which the mind has always turned for rest." Wharton's considerable wartime activities centered on this profound sense of domestic dislocation. In November 1914, she established the American Hostels for Refugees in an effort to aid civilians displaced by the war. What began as a single modest hostel quickly burgeoned into half a dozen Parisian houses and apartments providing food, clothing, medical supplies, coal, work, and childcare assistance to some 9,330 refugees in 1915 alone. Together with the energetic and organizationally inclined Elisina Tyler, the wife of the art historian Royall Tyler, Wharton founded the Children of Flanders Rescue Committee after witnessing, on a tour of Belgium, multitudes of children either huddled in the basements of shelled-out houses or wandering the cratered streets, farms, and charred villages. The committee established settlement houses of sorts, providing classes in lacemaking, French language, and industrial training. Finally, Wharton organized a cure program, modeled after American therapies, for tubercular soldiers who had contracted the disease in the homeless netherworld of the trenches.

In 1916, Wharton edited an elaborate international anthology significantly entitled *The Book of the Homeless*. In the preface, she emphasized that proceeds from the book were to finance a refugee aid project that was "first and foremost to *help a homesick people*." The elaborate gift book was self-consciously designed and constructed, moreover, as a metaphoric home: "You will see from the names of the builders," she noted, "what a gallant piece of architecture it is." The "builders" included Theodore Roosevelt, Joseph Conrad, Thomas

Hardy, William Butler Yeats, Jean Cocteau, William Dean Howells, Sarah Bernhardt, Henry James, Claude Monet, and Igor Stravinsky. Yet as Wharton's own contribution—a poem entitled "The Tryst"—suggested, the volume as a metaphoric wartime "home" hardly bore the hallmarks of a secure domestic space:

> My house is ill to find, she said
> For it has no roof but the sky;
> The tongue is torn from the steeple-head,
> And all the rivers run poison-red
> With the bodies drifting by.

World conflict had suddenly cast a glaring public light on what Wharton called in *Fighting France,* "a hundred signs of intimate and humble tastes, of humdrum pursuits, of family association." The world's family had been stripped bare: superficialities had been dismissed and taboos and transgressions exposed for all to see.

### SUMMER

In addition to *Fighting France* and a series of her magazine essays collected to form *French Ways and Their Meaning* (1919), Wharton published two novels that explicitly took the war as their theme. *The Marne* (1918), which describes a wounded American Red Cross ambulance driver, and *A Son at the Front* (1923), the tale of an expatriate painter who (wrongly, Wharton insists) wants to prevent his son from fighting, have both been largely dismissed by critics as propaganda pieces. Despite its seemingly distant setting and unrelated subject matter, Wharton's vision of the war arguably received its first full expression in *Summer,* a novel set in the Berkshires and fondly nicknamed "Hot Ethan." Unlike *Xingu and Other Stories* (1916), a collection of tales, ghostly and humorous, written primarily before the war, *Summer* was conceived, Wharton later recalled in *A Backward Glance,* "while the rest of my being

was steeped in the tragic realities of war." And it is here that Wharton's notion of homelessness becomes significant. The story chronicles the sexual awakening of Charity Royall, a rural New England girl brought down as an infant from the Mountain—one of those "grim places, morally and physically" that Wharton, in her autobiography, associates with "insanity, incest and slow mental and moral starvation." Raised by her adoptive father, the lawyer Royall, one of North Dormer's leading citizens, Charity finds herself forced to marry her guardian after she becomes pregnant by a visiting young architect, Lucius Harney. The novel is first and foremost a story about incest, and in this sense it is Wharton's most typical "war novel."

In Wharton's thinking, the fighting had not only unleashed unparalleled violence and destruction on the warfront, but it had also revealed a vast underworld of incestuous desires on the homefront. "The world since 1914 has been like a house on fire," she observed in *Fighting France.*

> All the lodgers are on the stairs, in dishabille. Their doors are swinging wide, and one gets . . . revelations of their habits . . . that a life-time of ordinary intercourse would not offer. Superficial differences vanish, and so (how much oftener) do superficial resemblances; while deep unsuspected similarities and disagreements, deep common attractions and repulsions declare themselves.

In this sense, housing imagery is central to *Summer.* Charity falls in love with Harney, who has come to North Dormer to study the "old houses." After serving as Harney's guide to local architecture, Charity eventually begins to meet her new lover in "a little abandoned house," crumbling but "as dry and pure as the interior of a long-empty shell." It is only at the town's Old Home Week celebration on a hot day in midsummer that Charity foresees the future. As she sings "Home, Sweet Home," she senses that "all the glow in her blood, the breath of the summer earth, the rustle of the forest . . . seemed to pass into her untrained voice, lifted and led by the sustaining chorus." Her unwitting paean to "home, sweet home" is climaxed by Royall's speech, in which he admonishes those young men who are tempted to turn their backs on the old homes to "come back to them for their good." Suddenly, Charity catches a glimpses of Harney with the affluent Annabel Balch and realizes "the bare reality of her situation." As the minister intones a prayer in praise of returning to the old home, Charity faints at Royall's feet.

Pregnant, Charity rejects the idea of an abortion and desperately flees to the Mountain to try to reclaim her former home. Her mother, however, is dead—and grotesquely so, "like a dead dog in a ditch." The novel closes with Charity's marriage to Royall and subsequent return to the same "red house" from which she emerges in the narrative's opening moments. Wharton here uses incest as a curiously protective image—an image of cultural restoration in which the fragmented family is returned to the rites and traditions associated with "old homes." Charity's affair with a student of bygone American architecture and her marriage to a man who urges a return to the old homes both underline and complicate Wharton's effort to restore genealogical and even incestuous integrity to a homeless world.

Incest became an increasingly tantalizing subject for Wharton in her later years. In 1919, she drafted a short story to be entitled "Beatrice Palmato," which she intended to include in a projected collection, "Powers of Darkness." The story, which Wharton outlined in detail, was to examine the marriage of Beatrice Palmato, the daughter of an incestuous father, who hysterically explodes at her mild husband when she discovers him innocently kissing their daughter: "Don't kiss my child. Put her down! How dare you kiss her?" The truth of Beatrice's past (and, perhaps, present) dawns on her husband "in a glance of horror," and

with a look of "supreme appeal and avowal," Beatrice runs upstairs and shoots herself.

What has intrigued critics, however, is not so much the plot of "Beatrice Palmato" as the curious self-proclaimed "unpublishable fragment" that accompanies it—a graphic description of father-daughter oral intercourse described in erotic, if not pornographic detail. Beneath her father's knowing touch, Beatrice experiences "new abysses of bliss": "Already lightenings of heat shot from that palpitating centre all over her surrendered body, to the tips of her fingers, and the ends of her loosened hair. . . . The sensation was so exquisite that she could have asked to have it indefinitely prolonged." The Palmato fragment clearly suggests that the true terror of incest lies not in its abhorrence, but rather in its irresistible appeal. While a number of critics—Cynthia Griffin Wolff, Barbara White, and Judith Fryer—among them, have suggested that Wharton's thematization of incest gave the form of fantasy to her own childhood attraction to, or even actual relationship with, her father, it seems equally relevant to acknowledge the extent to which incest represents what Walter Benn Michaels argues in *Our America* is a type of nativism. Like William Faulkner, Wharton strongly suggests throughout her fiction that incest *is* in fact alluring precisely because it promises a sort of genealogical stasis in which outsiders are kept out and the ancestral home remains erotically intact.

Such stasis was clearly the stuff of fantasy. Wharton suffered several losses during and after the war. The deaths of her old friend Egerton Winthrop in 1916, her estranged brother Frederic in 1918, and a young soldier, Ronald Simmons, in 1918 were sources of profound grief. Yet of these, the loss of Henry James in 1916 was perhaps the most devastating. "His friendship," she wrote Lapsley, "has been the pride & honour of my life." Despite being made a chevalier of the Legion of Honor by the president of France in 1916, it was in this spirit of sadness and irrevocable ruptures with the past that she turned in 1920 to her last great novel, the Pulitzer Prize-winning *Age of Innocence.*

## THE AGE OF INNOCENCE

Although it is set in the Old New York of Wharton's youth in the 1870s, *The Age of Innocence* offers a distinctly postwar perspective on the world Wharton knew. "Not until the successive upheavals which culminated in the catastrophe of 1914 had 'cut all likeness from the name' of my old New York, did I begin to see its pathetic picturesqueness," she wrote in *A Backward Glance.* "Social life, as in the rest of the world went on with hardly perceptible changes till the war abruptly tore down the old frame-work, and what had seemed unalterable rules of conduct became of a sudden observances as quaintly arbitrary as the domestic rites of the Pharaohs." *The Age of Innocence* projects precisely this tone of primitivism and prehistory onto the world of Wharton's youth. As Katie Trumpener and James M. Nyce observe in a chapter from *Literary Anthropology,* Wharton places the reader at two removes from the story—the remove of time and the "remove of the social sciences." The "present" of the novel is set some thirty years after the central action of the plot, yet that present itself is, for Wharton, some twenty years earlier and a world war away. Indeed, if *The House of Mirth* had staged a monumental act of historic preservationism, *The Age of Innocence* is consumed with the anthropology of cultural extinction. Saturated in the language of ethnography and archeology, *The Age of Innocence* represents with self-conscious detachment a world preserved only "as bodies caught in glaciers keep for years a rosy life-in-death."

The novel chronicles the filial ordeals of two families, the Mingott-Manson clan and the "Archer-Newland-van-der-Luyden tribe." Each group is scrupulously ruled by a sacred if prehistoric sovereign: on one side, a "venerable ancestress," the voluminous "Matriarch" Mrs. Manson Mingott, whose "immense accretion of flesh . . . had descended on her in middle life like a flood of lava on a doomed city," and on the other, Mr. and Mrs. Henry van der Luyden, the "mouth-pieces of some remote ancestral authority." The arrival of a renegade Mingott, the Countess Ellen Olenska, sets the narrative into motion. Her intention to divorce her corrupt European husband threatens to bring scandal and shame to the Family, but when she develops a mutual passion for Newland Archer, her cousin May Welland's fiancé, the Family closes ranks and, in a bloodless coup, expels her. Only Archer's eventual submission to "tribal discipline" will, in the end, prevent him from abandoning his wife to consummate his illicit passion for her cousin. May's strategic revelation that she is expecting a child seals his fate. Archer is forced to understand that the farewell banquet they throw in honor of the Countess is nothing less than "the tribal rally around a kinswoman about to be eliminated from the tribe," a rite of sacrifice performed according to strict custom: "It was the old New York way, of taking life 'without effusion of blood.' "

Wharton had recently described in lavish detail scenes of blood sacrifice and sanguine ceremonial self-mutilation in her travel account, *In Morocco* (1920). *The Age of Innocence,* with its pervasive language of ritualized violence, implicitly centralizes the blood rituals of the Great War and the seeming period of American purity that preceded it. Newland Archer feels oppressed by May's

> factitious purity, so cunningly manufactured by a conspiracy of mothers and aunts and grandmothers and long-dead ancestresses, because it was supposed to be what he wanted, what he had a right to, in order that he might exercise his lordly pleasure in smashing it like an image made of snow.

Virginity and marriage become violent battle-grounds in *The Age of Innocence*. Indeed, Wharton casts a cool and cynical eye on the soft trappings of nostalgia. Archer, like his Jamesian predecessors Isabel Archer (in *The Portrait of a Lady*) and Christopher Newman (in *The American*), realizes that "all this frankness and innocence were only an artificial product. Untrained human nature was not frank and innocent, it was full of the twists and defenses of instinctive guile." Wharton grasps the significance of the war in a flash: the militarized catastrophe had violently severed present from past, transforming the world before the war into an ancien régime, a seeming "age of innocence" to be classically revered like Pompeii or Troy. It had transformed the past into something it never was yet must become for the purposes of cultural memory. Archer understands that innocence is "factitious," yet he simultaneously clings to its simplicity as a source of permanence. When he meets Ellen for one of their final trysts, he appropriately chooses the room housing the "Cesnola antiquities" in New York's Metropolitan Museum. The lovers seat themselves on a divan and stare silently at a glass cabinet "which contained the recovered fragments of Ilium": "Its glass shelves were crowded with small broken objects—hardly recognisable domestic utensils, ornaments, and personal trifles—made of glass, of clay, of discoloured bronze, and other time-blurred substances." In the postwar "kaleidoscope where all the social atoms spun around on the same plane," the past had become a rarefied museum piece, and history itself an artifice. It is Ellen Olenska, then, who quietly utters the simple pathos of Wharton's postwar vision: "It seems cruel . . . that after a while nothing matters . . . any more than these little things, that used to be necessary and important to forgotten people, and now have to be guessed at under a magnifying glass and labelled: 'Use unknown.'"

## LATER WRITINGS

Wharton's later writings, though often considered disappointing in light of her earlier masterpieces, suggest an avid mind, restlessly attuned to the slightest shifts in popular culture. Although she lived for most of the year in the Pavillon Colombe, a house she had purchased in the village of St.-Brice-sous-Forêt outside Paris, her later works, with greater or lesser success, are conspicuously grounded in the land of her birth. Writing to Berenson, Wharton revealingly described *The Glimpses of the Moon* (1922) as "the adventures of a young couple who believe themselves to be completely *affranchis* & up-to-date, but are continually tripped up by obsolete sensibilities & discarded ideas." The book was quickly made into a film, with titles by F. Scott Fitzgerald, but Wharton's précis forms a prescient description of herself, unsure of her place in a new literary milieu. The novel was roundly criticized, but sales were brisk, moving Appleton's editor Rutger Jewett to remark, "the Young Intellectuals . . . like young terriers worrying a muff, have lashed themselves in idle rage over your novel." In novels such as *Twilight Sleep* (1927) and *The Children* (1928), Wharton aimed her satire not only at the follies and self-indulgences of the 1920s, but also, as Dale Bauer in *Edith Wharton's Brave New Politics* notes, at the politics of eugenics with which she grew increasingly uncomfortable. The novels were politically engaging but aesthetically unsatisfying.

*Old New York* (1924), a handsome boxed collection of four novellas, each set in a different decade from the 1840s through the 1870s, found Wharton on more familiar ground. The subjects range from dictatorial patriarchs ("False Dawn") to uncaring mothers ("The Spark"), from deceptively virginal aunts ("The Old Maid") to seemingly unconventional wives ("New Year's Day"). Wharton treads on well-worn terrain, but in notably modernist terms. "False Dawn," with its depiction of despotic resistance to racial and gendered otherness, anticipates Faulkner's Thomas Sutpen in *Absalom! Absalom!* Similarly, "The Old Maid" imagines a modern displaced woman whose sexual confidence and self-knowledge clearly make her kin to Willa Cather's Marian Forrester in *A Lost Lady.*

*The Mother's Recompense* (1925) marked not only Wharton's final sustained consideration of the war but also a significant change in her thinking. The story of a vain, middle-aged mother whose younger lover incestuously marries her own daughter operated, in one sense, as a reconception of *Summer.* Wharton traces the troubled homecoming of Kate Clephane, who has been summoned to New York eighteen years after deserting her husband and infant daughter for a meaningless love affair. Kate returns to find the Clephane mansion on Fifth Avenue a monument to nostalgia, a graceful contrast to the rest of "Babylonian New York." Despite her reservations about the pitfalls of sentimentality, Kate nevertheless commits herself to a homey fantasy of filial bliss, determined to "play the part of Anne's mother."

Incest, however, undermines Kate's idyll of home. The mother's dreams unravel when she discovers that Anne has become engaged to an American war hero, Chris Fenno, her *own* former lover. Overnight, an "incestuous horror" revises Kate's dream. The Clephane mansion is transformed from a timeless monument to intergenerational bliss to a locus of ambiguity. Wharton marshals her loaded wartime vocabulary in forcing Kate to admit that "I really *am* homeless. Or at least, in remaining where I am I'm forfeiting my last shred of self-respect." Indeed, Kate finds it impossible to sustain any "air of permanence" within the ancestral mansion: sitting at the Clephane dinner table, "again she had the feeling of sitting in a railway station, waiting for the train to come in."

*The Mother's Recompense* substantially revises *Summer*'s over-determined insistence on the re-

constitution of the prewar ancestral "home." Instead, a more mature, and perhaps wearier Wharton seems to reach Thomas Wolfe's conclusion that you can never go home again. Such old homes, she suggests in stories such as "Miss Mary Pask" from her collection *Here and Beyond* (1926) and "After Holbein" from *Certain People* (1930), are haunted by the living dead who cannot forget the past.

In the last ten years of her life, Wharton remained astonishingly prolific. She published her two most sustained, but in some ways least successful, meditations on the writer's craft in companion *künstleromans, Hudson River Bracketed* (1929) and *The Gods Arrive* (1932). Her final collection of stories, *The World Over* (1936), however, contained some of her best short fictions, among them "Roman Fever," a brilliant update of "The Old Maid," and two first-rate ghost stories, "Pomegranate Seed" and "The Looking Glass." She had begun work in 1933 on a comedy of manners about a group of marauding American girls with ambitions of marrying into the British aristocracy amusingly entitled *The Buccaneers,* but died before she could complete it. The novel was subsequently published in 1938, and many—among them, Shari Benstock—consider it "the most charming novel Edith Wharton ever wrote." Wharton embraces her female pirates with a comic sympathy that reflects her mellowing vision of America's future. She had apparently reconciled herself to the triumph of the Invaders.

In 1934, three years before her death on August 11, 1937, by a stroke, Edith Wharton dedicated *A Backward Glance* to "the Friends Who Every Year on All Souls' Night Come and Sit with Me By the Fire," and as her life drew to an end, she did, indeed, find herself increasingly surrounded by ghosts of dear companions now gone. In her last completed work of fiction, a ghost story entitled "All Souls'," Wharton imagines herself as an androgynous narrator listening to the story of Sara Clayburn, a woman who finds herself abandoned, injured, and wandering from room to room in a hauntingly empty house after her servants have been called to the woods to take part in a witches' coven. Wharton surely recognized her younger self in Sara, a woman who, paralyzed by loneliness and her fear of sexuality, is forced to confront the emptiness of the ancestral house. Significantly, though, Wharton seems to identify herself more strongly with the narrator—a mature, adaptive, and orienting figure who can tell the tale and nurture the fragmented self back to life.

# Selected Bibliography

## WORKS OF EDITH WHARTON

NOVELS AND SHORT STORIES
*The Greater Inclination.* New York: Scribners, 1899.
*The Touchstone.* New York: Scribners, 1900.
*Crucial Instances.* New York: Scribners, 1901.
*The Valley of Decision.* New York: Scribners, 1902.
*Sanctuary.* New York: Scribners, 1903.
*The Descent of Man and Other Stories.* New York: Scribners, 1904.
*The House of Mirth.* New York: Scribners, 1905.
*Madame de Treymes.* New York: Scribners, 1907.
*The Fruit of the Tree.* New York: Scribners, 1907.
*The Hermit and the Wild Woman and Other Stories.* New York: Scribners, 1908.
*Tales of Men and Ghosts.* New York: Scribners, 1910.
*Ethan Frome.* New York: Scribners, 1911.
*The Reef.* New York: Appleton, 1912.
*The Custom of the Country.* New York: Scribners, 1913.
*Xingu and Other Stories.* New York: Scribners, 1916.
*Summer.* New York: Appleton, 1917.
*The Marne.* New York: Appleton, 1918.
*The Age of Innocence.* New York: Appleton, 1920.
*The Glimpses of the Moon.* New York: Appleton, 1922.
*A Son at the Front.* New York: Scribners, 1923.
*Old New York.* 4 vols. New York: Appleton, 1924. Includes *False Dawn, The Old Maid, The Spark,* and *New Year's Day.*
*The Mother's Recompense.* New York: Appleton, 1925.
*Here and Beyond.* New York: Appleton, 1926.
*Twilight Sleep.* New York: Appleton, 1927.
*The Children.* New York: Appleton, 1928.
*Hudson River Bracketed.* New York: Appleton, 1929.
*Certain People.* New York: Appleton, 1930.
*The Gods Arrive.* New York: Appleton, 1932.
*Human Nature.* New York: Appleton, 1933.
*The World Over.* New York: Appleton, 1936.
*Ghosts.* New York: Appleton, 1937.
*The Buccaneers.* New York: Appleton-Century, 1938.
*The Collected Short Stories of Edith Wharton.* 2 vols. Edited by R. W. B. Lewis. New York: Scribners, 1968. Includes "April Showers," "Mrs. Manstey's View," and "The Fullness of Life."
*The Ghost Stories of Edith Wharton.* New York: Scribners, 1973.
"Beatrice Palmato." In *Edith Wharton: A Biography.* Edited by R. W. B. Lewis. New York: Fromm International, 1985.
*Novellas and Other Writings.* New York: Library of America, 1990. Includes "Life and I."
*Fast and Loose and The Buccaneers.* Edited by Viola Hopkins Winner. Charlottesville: University Press of Virginia, 1993.
*Edith Wharton Abroad: Selected Travel Writings, 1888–1920.* Edited by Sarah B. Wright. New York: St. Martin's, 1995.
*The Uncollected Critical Writings.* Edited and with an introduction by Frederick Wegener. Princeton, N.J.: Princeton University Press, 1996.

POETRY
*Verses.* Newport, R.I.: C. E. Hammet, Jr., 1878.
*Artemis to Actaeon and Other Verse.* New York: Scribners, 1909.
*Twelve Poems.* London: Medici Society, 1926.

NONFICTION
*The Decoration of Houses.* With Ogden Codman, Jr. New York: Scribners, 1897.
*Italian Villas and Their Gardens.* New York: Century, 1904.
*Italian Backgrounds.* New York: Scribners, 1905.
*A Motor-Flight through France.* New York: Scribners, 1908.
*Fighting France, from Dunkerque to Belfort.* New York: Scribners, 1915.
*French Ways and Their Meaning.* New York: Appleton, 1919.

*In Morocco.* New York: Scribners, 1920.

*The Writing of Fiction.* New York: Scribners, 1925.

*A Backward Glance.* New York: Scribners, 1934.

*The Cruise of the Vanadis.* Amiens: Presses de l'UFR Clerc, Université de Picardie, 1992.

TRANSLATION

Suderman, Hermann. *The Joy of Living.* New York: Scribners, 1902.

COMPILATIONS

*The Book of the Homeless.* New York: Scribners, 1916.

*Eternal Passion in English Poetry.* With Robert Norton and Gaillard Lapsley. New York: Appleton-Century, 1939.

CORRESPONDENCE AND MANUSCRIPTS

*The Letters of Edith Wharton.* Edited by R. W. B. Lewis and Nancy Lewis. New York: Scribners, 1988.

*Henry James and Edith Wharton: Letters, 1900–1915.* Edited by Lyall H. Powers. New York: Scribners, 1990.

The largest collection of Wharton's manuscripts and correspondence is housed in the Yale Collection of American Literature, Beinecke Rare Book and Manuscript Library, Yale University. Other major holdings include the Lilly Library, Indiana University; the Harry Ransom Humanities Research Center, University of Texas, Austin; the Scribners Archive, Firestone Library, Princeton University; Robert Frost Library, Amherst College; Houghton Library, Harvard University; Villa I Tatti, Harvard Center for Renaissance Studies, Florence, Italy.

*BIBLIOGRAPHIES*

Garrison, Stephen, ed. *Edith Wharton: A Descriptive Bibliography.* Pittsburgh: University of Pittsburgh Press, 1990.

Lauer, Kristen O., and Margaret P. Murray, eds. *Edith Wharton: An Annotated Secondary Bibliography.* New York: Garland, 1990.

Tuttleton, James W., Kristin O. Lauer, and Margaret P. Murray, eds. *Edith Wharton: The Contemporary Reviews.* Cambridge: Cambridge University Press, 1992.

*CRITICAL AND BIOGRAPHICAL STUDIES*

Ammons, Elizabeth. *Edith Wharton's Argument with America.* Athens: University of Georgia Press, 1980.

Auchincloss, Louis. *Edith Wharton, A Woman in Her Time.* New York: Viking Press, 1971.

Bauer, Dale M. *Edith Wharton's Brave New Politics.* Madison: University of Wisconsin Press, 1994.

Bell, Millicent, ed. *The Cambridge Companion to Edith Wharton.* Cambridge: Cambridge University Press, 1995.

———. *Edith Wharton and Henry James: The Story of Their Friendship.* New York: Braziller, 1965.

Bendixen, Alfred, and Annette Zilversmit, eds. *Edith Wharton: New Critical Essays.* New York: Garland, 1992.

Benstock, Shari. *No Gifts from Chance: A Biography of Edith Wharton.* New York: Scribners, 1994.

Bloom, Harold, ed. *Edith Wharton.* New York: Chelsea House, 1986.

Dwight, Eleanor. *Edith Wharton: An Extraordinary Life.* New York: Harry N. Adams, 1994.

Erlich, Gloria. *The Sexual Education of Edith Wharton.* Berkeley: University of California Press, 1992.

Faery, Rebecca Blevins. "Wharton's *Reef*: The Inscription of Female Sexuality." In *Edith Wharton: New Critical Essays.* Edited by Alfred Bendixen and Annette Zilversmit. New York: Garland, 1992.

Fedorko, Kathy A. *Gender and the Gothic in the Fiction of Edith Wharton.* Tuscaloosa: University of Alabama Press, 1995.

Fryer, Judith. *Felicitous Space: The Imaginative Structures of Edith Wharton and Willa Cather.* Chapel Hill: University of North Carolina Press, 1986.

Gilbert, Sandra M., and Susan Gubar. *Sexchanges,* vol. 2 of *No Man's Land: The Place of the Woman Writer in the Twentieth Century.* New Haven, Conn.: Yale University Press, 1989.

Goodman, Susan. *Edith Wharton's Inner Circle.* Austin: University of Texas Press, 1994.

———. *Edith Wharton's Women: Friends and Rivals.* Hanover, N.H.: University Press of New England, 1990.

Goodwyn, Janet. *Edith Wharton: Traveller in the Land of Letters.* London: Macmillan, 1990.

Howe, Irving, ed. *Edith Wharton: A Collection of Critical Essays.* Englewood Cliffs, N.J.: Prentice Hall, 1962.

Joslin, Katherine. *Edith Wharton.* New York: St. Martin's, 1991.

————and Alan Price, eds. *Wretched Exotic: Essays on Edith Wharton in Europe.* New York: Peter Lang, 1993.

Kaplan, Amy. *The Social Construction of American Realism.* Chicago: University of Chicago Press, 1988.

Killoran, Helen. *Edith Wharton: Art and Illusion.* Tuscaloosa: University of Alabama Press, 1996.

Lewis, R. W. B. *Edith Wharton: A Biography.* New York: Fromm International, 1985.

Lubbock, Percy. *Portrait of Edith Wharton.* New York: Appleton-Century-Crofts, 1947.

Michaels, Walter Benn. *The Gold Standard and the Logic of Naturalism.* Berkeley: University of California Press, 1987.

Nevius, Blake. *Edith Wharton: A Study of Her Fiction.* Berkeley: University of California Press, 1953.

Price, Alan. *The End of the Age of Innocence: Edith Wharton and the First World War.* New York: St. Martin's, 1996.

Showalter, Elaine. *Sister's Choice: Tradition and Change in American Women's Writing.* Oxford: Clarendon Press, 1991.

Singley, Carol J. *Edith Wharton: Matters of Mind and Spirit.* Cambridge: Cambridge University Press, 1995.

Trumpener, Katie, and James M. Nyce. "The Recovered Fragments: Archeological and Anthropological Perspectives in Edith Wharton's *The Age of Innocence.*" In *Literary Anthropology: A New Interdisciplinary Approach to People, Signs, and Literature.* Edited by Fernando Poyatos. Philadelphia: John Benjamins, 1988.

Vita-Finzi, Penelope. *Edith Wharton and the Art of Fiction.* New York: St. Martin's, 1990.

Waid, Candace. *Edith Wharton's Letters from the Underworld: Fictions of Women and Writing.* Chapel Hill: University of North Carolina Press, 1991.

Wershoven, Carol. *The Female Intruder in the Novels of Edith Wharton.* Rutherford, N.J.: Fairleigh Dickinson University Press, 1982.

White, Barbara A. *Edith Wharton: A Study of the Short Fiction.* New York: Twayne, 1991.

————. "Neglected Areas: Wharton's Short Stories and Incest." *Edith Wharton Review* 20:3–10 (Fall 1991).

————. "Neglected Areas: Wharton's Short Stories and Incest, Part II." *Edith Wharton Review* 32:3–12 (Spring 1991).

Wolff, Cynthia Griffin. *A Feast of Words: The Triumph of Edith Wharton.* New York: Oxford University Press, 1977.

—*JENNIE A. KASSANOFF*

# *Walt Whitman*
## *1819–1892*

WALT WHITMAN MAY be America's most uneven great poet. There is general consensus that *Leaves of Grass,* Whitman's gradually accreting collected poems, is better in its early incarnations than in its late ones. But from the beginning, Whitman could be maddeningly inconsistent. His prodigious variety is by no means always a defect. By turns highfalutin and slangy, abstract and quirkily concrete, the idiom of his early editions shows an unusual range that is one of Whitman's greatest strengths: his often brilliant idiomatic variety registers a potentially daunting range of mid-nineteenth century American life, which he sometimes appears content simply to celebrate. But the stylistic melange of Whitman's poetry is not always so successful or so convincingly accounted for. From its first publication, *Leaves of Grass* was by turns pithy and vague, incisive and baggy. Whitman is often trite and bombastic, effects characteristically associated with his notorious though sometimes brilliant "catalogs" or extended lists. In "Salut au Monde!" (1856) the poet is determined to "see" all the races and nationalities that people the earth. This perhaps laudable project leaves him badly overextended. Whitman's imagination cannot keep pace with his determination, and the resultant catalogs display an air of distraction, as if the poet had had time to do no more than quickly fill in the blanks, deploying the first thing that came to mind, which frequently was cliché:

> I see vapors exhaling from unexplored countries,
> I see the savage types, the bow and arrow, the poison'd splint, the fetich, and the obi.
> I see African and Asiatic towns,
> I see Algiers, Tripoli, Derne, Mogodore, Timbuctoo, Monrovia,
> I see the swarms of Pekin, Canton, Benares, Dehli, Calcutta, Tokio,
> I see the Kruman in his hut, and the Dahoman and Ashantee-man in their huts,
> I see the Turk smoking opium in Aleppo,
> I see the picturesque crowds at the fairs of Khiva and those of Herat,
> I see Teheran, I see Muscat and Medina and the intervening sands, I see the caravans toiling onward

There is material even in relatively weak passages like this one that will repay attention: the biblical parallelism; the obsessive fascination with place names, in whose sounds the audience is invited to revel; the implication that the poet, who is supposedly omniscient, may be omnipresent as well. Yet few would wish the poem longer than it is. Composed mostly of lengthy catalogs like the one from which the lines above are excerpted, "Salut au Monde!" continues on for 226 lines, some twelve pages. The poet himself, as he nears the finish line, seems slightly dazed by his prodigious effort:

> My spirit has pass'd in compassion and determination around the whole earth,
> I have look'd for equals and lovers and found them ready for me in all lands,
> I think some divine rapport has equalized me with them.

If the reader too emerges glassy-eyed, this stupor is not necessarily a sign of the poet's failure, as this state resembles meditative absorption, a condition Whitman might well have wished to produce.

But stretches like this hardly characterize Whitman at his finest. Just as he keeps his eye on unlikely detail in his strongest descriptive passages, so is his diction capable of unexpected idiomatic swerves, which serve to alter in dramatic ways the enunciatory situation, the public and oratorical or intimately conversational scene the audience is invited to imagine. Whitman is often at his brilliant best in short passages in which the poem's audience is talked to directly and personally, and talked to, moreover, in circumstances intriguingly difficult to pin down. In the early editions of *Leaves of Grass*, the audience, fuddled or made restive by one of Whitman's long lists, is regularly pulled up short by brief passages of a very different order. Addressed directly to the audience, these passages seem ambiguously sacramental or seductive, and the eerie way they seem to focus on the reader can both delight and discomfit. So in his 1855 masterpiece "Song of Myself" Whitman modulates his direct address from teasing questions to a characteristically disconcerting pair of assertions. The poet directs his attention intently to his audience:

> Do you guess I have some intricate purpose?
> Well I have . . . for the April rain has, and the mica on the side of a rock has.

> Do you take it I would astonish?
> Does the daylight astonish? or the early redstart twittering through the woods?
> Do I astonish more than they?

> This hour I tell things in confidence,
> I might not tell everybody but I will tell you.

Whitman's closing suggestion that he is talking to his audience in the here and now is not one which will likely be taken literally. In one sense it amounts to a kind of joke, trading on the contrast between the text that is literally being read and the whispering voice that invites each member of the poet's audience to imagine that he or she is being addressed, out of all the book's readers, alone. Yet the joke is a serious one, and the illusion it fosters is crucial to the imaginative economy of *Leaves of Grass*. Whitman said on more than one occasion that as a poet he "intended to throw together for American use, a gigantic embryo or skeleton of Personality, fit for the West, for native models." Yet the self that stands so magnificently at the center of his poetry is not merely a reflection of his times, a democratic identity finding its way in mid-nineteenth-century America—though it is surely that in part. In passages such as the one quoted above, which abound in the first two editions of *Leaves of Grass*, the poet seems able to single out for special intimacy the "you" to whom he whispers; he seems to speak to that special "you" right now. The outlook is simultaneously panoramic and local, public and intimate; it is as if the shared public space were being transformed into the place of a private communion. The self who could initiate such a transaction would be more than just a representative instance of nineteenth-century democratic identity. The transformative encounter Whitman claims to initiate indeed suggests something sacramental: a presence rises up as if by magic, whenever these words are repeated, deflecting linear time into the cycle of eternal return, extended space into the sacred spot defined by this manifestation.

The epiphany repeatedly enacted in Whitman's poems is erotic as well as religious. The presence that makes itself manifest is a desiring body as well as a transcendent spirit, as the lines immediately preceding those quoted above from "Song of Myself" make clear:

> This is the press of a bashful hand . . . . this is the
>   float and odor of hair,
> This is the touch of my lips to yours . . . . this is the
>   murmur of yearning,
> This is the far-off depth and height reflecting my
>   own face,
> This is the thoughtful merge of myself and the
>   outlet again.

Each repetition of the word "this" seems to suggest an act of pointing. The effect might seem to be unfortunately comic: Whitman declares a presence and, to prove it, points to a collection of body parts that turn out not to be there. But there is an upside to this gesture: pointing to a presence the reader cannot quite see, Whitman conjures up a body that seems elusive and fluid: "I effuse my flesh in eddies and drift it in lacy jags," the poet declares near the end of "Song of Myself." This liquid quality, which is seen throughout much of *Leaves of Grass,* is made to seem deliciously sexual. At the same time, however, such an elusive form may suggest a sacramental, barely material presence. The erotic and the religious are consistently confounded in Whitman's early editions.

These lines may also suggest that a presence is just now putting on flesh, just now becoming incarnate as these words are spoken. Perhaps the words themselves are generating the presence, the magical body. "And God said let there be light, and there was light." And Whitman said let there be Walt, becoming, as it were, the Word incarnate. Both Whitman's poems and his essays on language recur repeatedly to this sense of shamanistic speech, of performative utterance (language that does something, that makes something true) that is magical and not merely conventional. "I

now pronounce you man and wife," says the minister, not describing a marriage but performing one. Whitman wants to go the minister one better:

> It avails not, time nor place—distance avails not,
> I am with you, you men and women of a genera-
>   tion, or ever so many generations hence,
> I project myself, also I return—I am with you, and
>   know how it is.

If they work, these lines from the important 1856 poem "Crossing Brooklyn Ferry" make something seem to happen, not just in the symbolic, social realm governed by custom, but in the actual physical world shaped by literal action—or magic.

## EARLY YEARS

Whitman was born on May 13, 1819, in West Hills, Long Island. Buffeted by the economic instability of the period, his family moved numerous times during his childhood and adolescence, shuttling at irregular intervals from house to house in Brooklyn, and between Brooklyn and various other parts of Long Island. Walt's father, Walter Whitman Sr., was a carpenter, housebuilder, and sometime minor real estate speculator, who never quite found his way in the emerging entrepreneurial culture of early nineteenth-century America. Long Island, where the Whitman family had settled as far back as the early seventeenth century, was somewhat less susceptible to boom and bust than the rapidly expanding, bustling but economically precarious world of Brooklyn. Yet this place of partial retreat was by no means a stable haven for the Whitman family. Walt's father sold the last of the family holdings in West Hills in 1836. Walt left school and entered the printing trades as an apprentice at the age of twelve and thereafter shuttled among the thriving metropolis of Manhattan, the still somewhat rural but giddily growing city of Brooklyn, and various family homes on Long Island.

Whitman was the second of nine children, and while his younger brothers thrived the fates of many of his other siblings were grim. There were important countervailing sources of stability and strength within the family, however. In later years Whitman consistently described his mother, Louisa, to whom he was devoted, as the crucial figure in his life and a key influence on the values registered in *Leaves of Grass*. He spoke especially of her Quaker heritage. In his youth Whitman heard the radical Quaker leader Elias Hicks preach, and in his mind Hicks's inner-light theology dovetailed with the democratic radicalism that was the poet's crucial intellectual heritage from his father. Yet in the 1820s and 1830s, as this artisanal world progressively disappeared, such idealized portraits of the trades were matched by radical proposals for reform among the emergent working class; such relatively mild schemes as advocacy of mass public education vied with calls for redistribution of property and other radical measures. Walter Whitman knew the Revolutionary-era radical Tom Paine, and reform meetings and reform literature were part of Walt's upbringing. Like his father, he was also well read in the "freethinking" literature of France's revolutionary enlightenment.

Whitman entered the printing trade as an apprentice in 1831 and trained as a compositor, but soon began writing and editing copy. In 1842 he took over briefly as editor of the *Aurora*, a Manhattan daily, and in 1846 he became editor of the Brooklyn *Daily Eagle*. In the course of an active career in journalism that lasted well into the late 1850s, Whitman worked for countless papers as both writer and editor. Despite occasional charges of on-the-job loafing (training for his subsequent profession, perhaps), he enjoyed a career whose bumpiness was far from peculiar. Whitman lost his position as editor of the *Daily Eagle* in 1848, when the paper returned to the more conservative Democratic fold; Whitman, a more radical Democrat and Free-soiler, was left in the lurch.

The crucial issue that divided the New York Democratic party, like the rest of the nation, in the 1840s and 1850s was slavery, which intertwined in sometimes tricky ways with labor issues. Like Lincoln until 1863, Whitman resisted the abolitionist position, except for brief periods of waffling, arguing that attaining the goal of immediately freeing southern slaves was not worth endangering the survival of the union; like many, he believed that slavery would gradually disappear in the course of anticipated social, economic, and moral developments. Like Lincoln, he favored repatriation—sending those slaves who were freed back to Africa. But like much of New York labor culture and many northern reformers, he was a "free-soiler," staunchly opposing the introduction of slavery into the western territories and arguing that these should be admitted to the union only as "Free [labor] states." Whitman believed that the country was caught in a moral quagmire that party politics only exacerbated. Increasingly, he looked to populist energies as the best possible source for a moral and cultural, if not immediately political, national renewal. Undoubtedly he understood *Leaves of Grass,* at least in part, as contributing to this populist trend.

Whitman's demotic leanings were personal as well as political. His newspaper work and his recreational urban cruising—activities that tended to blend into one another—helped fuel the emerging poet's street-level populism. Whether covering stories or sauntering the city for pleasure, Whitman reveled in the surging and unregulated street life of Brooklyn and Manhattan. He seems to have been drawn particularly to working-class men. He loved to ride the city omnibuses and engage the drivers in talk; anticipating his later Civil War hospital visits, he used to frequent hospital wards to chat with injured or sick drivers. Whitman also admired, and wrote approvingly of, the working-class street culture of the tough-nut "Bowery B'hoys" and (with more ambivalence) the early urban "gang" culture of New York's "roughs" and "loafers."

When the spectacular Crystal Palace exhibition, a massive World's Fair, opened in Manhattan in 1853, Whitman became an enthusiastic and inveterate visitor. He trolled the crowds as well as the exhibits, mingling, meeting people, talking. Yet there is a haunted quality to the notes he made about these encounters, just as there is to a notebook entry he made somewhat later, probably in the late 1850s, adjuring himself to keep up his social researches:

> Talk to everybody everywhere—try it on—keep it up—*real* talk—no airs—real questions—no one will be offended—or if anyone is, that will teach the offender just as any one else

Here Whitman encourages himself to try on, as a salutary exercise, the role of hearty democratic comrade he elsewhere invites readers to imagine as naturally his. The diarist who reminds himself to engage in "*real* talk" (the emphasis is Whitman's) is not simply a happy conversationalist; rather, he appears intent on acquiring a skill, almost like someone striving to learn a foreign language. Although the passage focuses on what might be called professional research (it appears among notes Whitman made for a projected, never-completed book on the American language), it nonetheless sounds rather like an attempt to overcome inveterate personal isolation.

The running record Whitman kept of his Crystal Palace cruising has something of the same quality:

> Bill Guess—aged 22. A thoughtless, strong, generous animal nature, fond of direct pleasures, eating, drinking, women, fun etc. . . . Was with me in the Crystal Palace.
> Peter ——— ——— , large, strong-boned young fellow, driver. Should weigh 180. Free and candid to me the very first time he saw me.

Whitman kept similar records through the 1850s:

> Johny (round faced—in Dunbar's and engine house—full eyes) and liquid

John Kiernan (loafer young saucy looking pretty goodlooking.)

Such passages seem poignant: they read like memorials of unfulfilled desire, marking intimacy as a briefly glimpsed possibility. They might be regarded instead as a sort of brag sheet, a tally of conquests, which is how the critic Charley Shively reads them, citing notebook passages that seem to point to consummated assignations in the early 1860s, during the Civil War:

> William somewhat feminine [. . .] told me he had never been in a fight and did not drink at all gone in 2nd N.Y. Lt Artillery deserted, returned to it slept with me Sept 3d

The contemporary meaning of the poet's phrases is not always clear to the late-twentieth-century reader: the term "slept with" does not necessarily have a sexual meaning. This is particularly the case with what would now be categorized as homosexual relations. The very term "homosexual" did not come into use until the end of the nineteenth century. Until then, social historians have demonstrated, sexual acts were not linked to the notion of some essential or dominant sexual "orientation." It is apparently also the case that same-sex displays of physical affection, and same-sex sentimental attachments, were quite common and were regarded as entirely "normal." It is fairly certain that Whitman in later years had long-term sexual relationships, and formed deep emotional bonds, with men who later went on to marry. Whether his notebooks of the 1850s and 1860s are tallies of sexual assignations, rather than notations of casual meetings or "sentimental" but not overtly sexual intimacies, tinged with Whitman's own longing, is less certain.

The notebooks do not make mention of the sort of sustained erotic and affectional intimacy that Whitman apparently achieved in later years. Shively notes that "while there is considerable evidence of Whitman's homosexual liaisons as early as 1836, there were no lovers until [Fred] Vaughan [in the late 1850s]"—that is, no sustained love relationships so far as is known. Whitman's biographer, Justin Kaplan, in a similar vein, remarks on Whitman's "chronically objectless affections." "The completeness of object-erosion in him is striking," Quentin Anderson likewise notes of the Whitman of the 1850s.

Such judgments about Whitman's private life in the pre–Civil War years are admittedly somewhat conjectural. Toward the end of his career, Whitman assiduously pruned his massive personal archives, removing or revising many items that failed to jibe with the portrait of the "good gray poet" (his friend William O'Connor's brilliant polemical phrase) he was preparing for posterity. The 1850s in particular exist primarily as an extended blank in this revised record. Like the written archive, the photographic one is problematic but suggestive. The critic Ed Folsom notes the astonishing fact that, while Whitman preserved an elaborately plotted collection of personal photographs (a kind of iconography in progress), there currently exists no picture taken of Whitman before the Civil War in which he is seen with another person. Later pictures display him—sometimes in "marriage" poses—with lovers. It is possible that this oddity is the result of Whitman's archival tinkering. Yet the notebooks and photographic record suggest a personal impasse that the poetry tends to confirm: neither the 1855 nor 1856 editions of *Leaves of Grass* offers us even the hint of a particular intimacy, or even, for all their focus on the "self," of Whitman in anything like intimate biographical detail—the poet's self is insistently generic.

To read Whitman's poetry simply as a kind of versified political platform or populist social vision is thus to risk thinning out the work. Whitman's poems are in important respects also an imaginative grappling—sometimes triumphant, sometimes comic, sometimes desperate or forlorn—with intimate needs and desires. The poet

figure who can be viewed as the guarantor of a demotic social ideal or the solution to a political impasse serves also to assuage needs of a less public or universal order.

### LEAVES OF GRASS (1855)

There is still pretty general agreement that when *Leaves of Grass* first appeared in 1855 it marked a spectacular breakthrough for Whitman, as well as for American poetry. Ralph Waldo Emerson, for one, went on record immediately and resoundingly. Whitman, still largely unknown in national literary circles, had the temerity to send a copy of his cottage-industry first edition to the pre-eminent American man of letters, and Emerson responded:

> Dear Sir,
>     I am not blind to the worth of the wonderful gift of "Leaves of Grass." I find it the most extraordinary piece of wit & wisdom that America has yet contributed. I am very happy in reading it, as great power makes us happy. . . . I greet you at the beginning of a great career, which yet must have had a long foreground somewhere, for such a start.

This generous appreciation suffered an ungenerous fate. Whitman, well-schooled in the hucksterism of the New York newspaper world, had few qualms about recycling Emerson's personal letter in unauthorized forms, brandishing this and other excerpts from it as advertising copy for his book. Emerson, who was outraged, nevertheless generally continued to champion Whitman's work.

The mysterious "foreground" Emerson mentions has tantalized several Whitman critics and biographers. What is there, in Whitman's prior writings, that might anticipate the ungainly genius of his mature work? In most important senses, not much. His earlier poetry fits conspicuously into the category of juvenilia: published in newspapers and periodicals, his efforts are stilted exercises in rhyme and rhythm-making; their thematic burden, generally melancholy, is entirely conventional. In light of his mature career, Whitman's early attempts at fiction writing—several published short stories, as well as the commissioned temperance novel *Franklin Evans,* which sold some twenty thousand copies—are interesting as antecedents but not much more. Characterized by a lurid and violent undercurrent of the macabre despite their moralizing armature, they anticipate several of the sexual and familial anxieties explored more compellingly in *Leaves of Grass.*

In the absence of a visible and sustained apprenticeship leading clearly toward the sorts of expressive, social, and sexual values evident in *Leaves of Grass,* critics long tended to recur to one or another illuminationist model to account for Whitman's achievement. Whitman (who claimed he could "go negative" and stop the flow of his thoughts when he wanted) was a mystic whose ecstatic experiences transformed him from hack to genius; or he underwent a spectacular sexual initiation that changed him forever. This may be so. On the other hand, the breakthroughs that help make *Leaves of Grass* a revolutionary and exciting work are in part anticipated by short notebook passages, most likely dating from the late 1840s. These passages register not only erotic and visionary excitement, but also the political turmoil that engaged Whitman in his public and professional life. They also include several brief attempts to concoct a mythic poetic persona capable of subsuming the sectional, racial, and class conflicts provoked by the issue of slavery.

The dangers of invoking one or another illuminationist hypothesis to account for *Leaves of Grass* thus include the tendency to read the poems in a single register only (sexual *or* mystical) and, perhaps more important, the temptation to regard them as the retailing of an already fully achieved personal breakthrough—rather than as an ongoing, sometimes perilous grappling with a complex of recalcitrant issues, both personal and political, that

through his peculiar genius for language Whitman struggled to resolve. Several of Whitman's notebook entries seem to be testing the resources of a new sort of poetic idiom and a new sort of poetic line; they move haltingly toward the sorts of verbal textures that define the early editions of *Leaves of Grass,* breaking through the limits of iambic pentameter into longer, more loosely and irregularly measured lines aware of both American vernacular speech and prophetically cadenced biblical idiom, two limits between which the language of Whitman's poems often seems to play.

The 1855 edition as a whole violated decorum in a number of roughly congruent ways. It had a title on the cover and a title page inside, but no author's name on either. The copyright, however, belonged to "Walter Whitman," and in one of the poems the speaker refers to himself as "Walt Whitman . . . one of the roughs." Unlike later editions, the 1855 volume included no poem titles, no section numbers dividing the longer pieces into more manageable units, or absolutely clear demarcations indicating where one poem ended and another began. Designed by Whitman and hand set, partly by Whitman himself, it was published in an edition of 795 copies by the small firm of Rome Brothers and distributed by Fowler and Wells. Seeming partly austere and partly casual in its disregard of the proprieties, the volume's very appearance mirrors the strange mix of demotic and prophetic traditions already noted in Whitman's style: its appearance, like its apparently authorless condition, places it ambiguously as an anonymous casual production or a sacred text.

The mythic, annealing persona tried on in the notebooks turns up in several of the printed poems, perhaps most conspicuously in the piece subsequently known as "Song of the Answerer":

Every existence has its idiom . . . . every thing has
   an idiom and tongue;

He resolves all tongues into his own, and bestows
  it upon men

. . . . . . . . . . . . . . . . . . .

One part does not counteract another part . . . . He
  is the joiner . . . he sees how they join.

He says indifferently and alike, How are you
  friend? to the President at his levee,
And he says Good day my brother, to Cudge that
  hoes in the sugarfield;
And both understand him and know that his speech
  is right.

This transcendental ward heeler, a fantasized instrument of political consensus, grapples elsewhere in the poem with more recalcitrant obstacles to democratic fulfillment. He must not simply consult, but transform his constituency by (re)-embodying them:

The insulter, the prostitute, the angry person, the
  beggar, see themselves in the ways of him . . . .
  he strangely transmutes them,
They are not vile any more . . . . they hardly know
  themselves, they are so grown.

Toward the beginning of the poem, this remaking is made to seem magical, the "answerer" cast less as statesman than as shaman:

Him all wait for . . . . him all yield up to . . . . his
  word is decisive and final,
Him they accept . . . . in him lave . . . . in him
  perceive themselves as amid light,
Him they immerse, and he immerses them.

Here the poet's word—or is it his body?—becomes a kind of transfiguring baptismal fluid: poetry does not reveal the solution to political problems through some special insight; it makes it happen, magically, or aspires to. Claiming to activate an extreme power, these lines intervene in an imagined political or social crisis that is presented as correspondingly extreme. Yet they do more. The poet's ductile body itself may be a quirky figure for the solution to a political impasse, but that can also seem pretty delicious.

Might polymorphous sexuality serve as a figure for political resolution? Or as a literal political strategy? Or is it the other way round, the poem's political agenda serving primarily as respectable cover for a more urgent substratum of erotic fantasy and visionary erotic fulfillment?

It is worth noting, in this regard, that the space these bodies occupy is tricky to map: "Him they immerse and he immerses them." This ductile, illogical space in which we are inside what is inside us is the imaginative space of much of the poetry of Whitman's early editions. This does not mean that he had a deep-seated desire to return to the womb. But for powerful personal as well as urgent public reasons his work is haunted by images of division and self-division, separation, isolation, and fragmentation. And the poetry, where it is most like a shamanistic spell cast against these terrors, tends to conjure up a delicious (or stifling) fluid space in which bodies and selves mingle and blur. This polymorphous space is significantly regressive—it conjures up fleeting and partial visions of how, supposedly, the infant experiences body and world. This regression need not be a defect: "strong memory," often in the form of infantile or childhood material, frequently serves to figure utopian content; and sexual and political fulfillment not uncommonly figure, or enable, each other. In such highly charged and unstable terrain, it is probably unwise to read in one direction only: to regard visionary erotic material in *Leaves of Grass* as always simply an elaborate metaphor for political possibility—or the reverse.

"A Song for Occupations" and "I Sing the Body Electric" both make extensive use of Whitman's catalog technique: the former is largely a listing of the tools employed in various occupations; the latter, among other things, is a spectacularly extended list of big and small body parts. Both lists seem curiously poised between passive appreciation and apotropaic litany, an incantation intended to ward off something. The lists of gadgets, for example, might be celebrations of the glorious accouterments of industry; attempts to memorialize (or magically preserve) the tools of the workplace before mechanization sweeps them away along with the small artisan workshop; or desperate efforts to conjure away their dispiriting solidity, to redeem an increasingly cluttered world of things that threatens to control us. The poem, like much of Whitman's work composed during this period, accordingly seems to hover ambivalently amid reportage, didactic political intervention, and shamanistic spell. "I Sing the Body Electric" ranges among a similar variety of speech acts, ambivalently exploring the political and social control of the body, the eroticization of public and social space.

## "SONG OF MYSELF"

The volatile mixture of public and private concerns, political and sexual material, utopian content and regressive fantasy that characterizes Whitman's best work is managed with spectacular success in "Song of Myself." The poem as a whole is the sometimes buoyant, sometimes anguished, and ultimately unresolved attempt to turn these various preoccupations into facets of a single mystery, or vision. This tolerance for irresolution—or to figure it differently, Whitman's ability in "Song of Myself" to keep a lot of balls in the air at once, without dropping too many or fretting too much when one happens to fall—is similar to Keats's poetics of "Negative Capability," that is, the capability "of being in uncertainties, Mysteries, doubts, without any irritable reaching after fact & reason."

But as the critic Richard Chase points out, the resultant maddeningly open-ended poem is also crucially modern or modernist: nervous attempts to extract a neat plot or orderly pattern of development are bound to founder when negotiating Whitman's plotless epic, which profoundly engages and only partly resists the confusing, de-

centered, or polycentric, space of modernity; the critic needs to exercise some of the negative capability the poem displays. "Song of Myself" is loosely structured around a number of recurrent but by no means constant preoccupations; the relations among these foci of attention are likewise variable. A list of what might be called the poem's social concerns should include the following: American vastness as challenge or threat, danger or instigation; the panoramic variety of American life as auguring disunion or as enabling the resiliency of what would now be called multiculturalism; political turmoil and its ambiguous relation to populist upheaval; urbanization and modernization, and the breakup of closed communities that accompanies them, as potentially both alienating and liberating. To these concerns we should add the preoccupation with American nature as a healing force. If the poem also ponders the relation of the individual to such vast agents, it tends to do so by considering the force and fate of the body, especially the sexual body. To what extent is the body the medium through which social demands or social anxieties are internalized; conversely, to what extent might sexuality model or unleash an anarchic energy that challenges such constructions, or an agglomerative urge that can anneal social space?

If Whitman's language is sometimes the imagistic medium that cannily records social and sexual landscapes, it often aspires to a performative or shamanistic power to redeem what it names. The poet's own presence and body, likewise, are characteristically lent a power of sacramental or sexually based transfiguration. Such shamanistic urges toward redemption or control tend to assume one of two characteristic forms, in "Song of Myself" as well as in other major poems of Whitman's first two editions. The poet's word in his catalogs exercises a centripetal pull on what it names, sliding objects toward a sacred space or center ultimately indistinguishable from the poet's own presence. This presence, in the poet's apostrophes, tends to effuse outward, in a centrifugal movement that conveys a diffused and redemptive body. This imaginative pattern is repeated, in rather more schematic form, in such other major pre–Civil War poems as in "Crossing Brooklyn Ferry" (and "Salut au Monde!"). But part of the peculiar difficulty of "Song of Myself"—and a source of the poem's greatness—is Whitman's tendency, in this poem as in no other, to gum up the shamanistic works. The poem is virtually unique in Whitman's oeuvre in its willingness to include, at unexpected junctures, material that seems to call into question the poem's own overarching aims; "Song of Myself" slides toward delicate comedy or pathos as Whitman registers a vast variety of competing energies and claims that delay or disrupt the poet's project.

Though the poem does not begin with one, the extended list or catalog is a conspicuous feature of "Song of Myself." What is now known as section 15 of the poem begins:

> The pure contralto sings in the organloft,
> The carpenter dresses his plank . . . . the tongue of
>     his foreplane whistles its wild ascending lisp,
> The married and unmarried children ride home to
>     their thanksgiving dinner,
> The pilot seizes the king-pin, he heaves down with
>     a strong arm,

Sixty lines later, the proceedings are still in progress:

> Patriarchs sit at supper with sons and grandsons
>     and great grandsons around them,
> In walls of adobe, in canvass tents, rest hunters and
>     trappers after their day's sport.

It is difficult to know how to attend to such extended litanies, just as it is difficult to characterize what they are up to; Whitman's catalogs have occasioned a great deal of critical disagreement. It is clear that they are not imaginatively situated in any single scene or locale. The prodigious expansion of attention that characterizes such passages might be understood as an enacting of American populism (everything matters), and as the faithful, celebratory recording of the staggering variety of American life (merely listing its wonders is enough). Likewise the tendency to parallelism (most lines cued with an initial repetition, here the word "the") can be taken as encoding democratic values (one man, one vote; one person, one line). Yet the catalog's conclusion implies a more complex and ambivalent agenda:

> And these one and all tend inward to me, and I
>     tend outward to them,
> And such as it is to be of these more or less I am.

The second of these lines is the more modest (especially that "more or less"): stopping short of claiming one identity with all he records, the poet here settles for partial identification. The word "tend," in the prior line, might be read as similarly modest: a tendency need not be fully realized or universal. Yet the movement traced in this line is one that is imaginatively crucial to Whitman's work: things move in toward the poet, while the poet flows outward to meet and characteristically subsume them. The line also possesses a possibly disconcerting performative force: "these one and all tend inward to me," I make it happen, by saying so. The preceding catalog may likewise function as performative, or as a sort of shamanistic spell: not simply celebrating what is, but by imaginatively transfiguring it, the poet's naming would bring into being a world of other selves and an American space worthy of such celebration. If the vast panorama of American life and the doings of so many other selves, perhaps, provoke anxiety as well as pleasure—threatening to reduce the poet, as it were, to only a single mote in the prodigious array—the poem would thus be the private, but socially resonant, cure for the very anxieties it records.

A number of features of Whitman's list can be understood as contributing to the redemptive spell the poet weaves. There is the very extent of the litany; coupled with insistent patterning, this stretching of attention tends to produce a blurry receptivity, which suggests both the trancelike experience of ritual and the fluid space in which objects mingle that ritual might produce. The catalog's parallelism can likewise suggest shamanistic spell as much as democratic paean: if populist-minded readers are reminded of "one man, one vote," others might remember the substitution drills for learning foreign languages. Once the grammatical pattern is established, anything at all can be slotted into it. As the passage progresses, this insistently repeated operation increasingly suggests the substitutability of whatever is subjected to it. Everything is made to inhabit the same space or same position ("these one and all tend inward to me"), into which the poet's spell entrances it. The distended and difficult world of objects is gathered up into a ritual space and imaginatively controlled.

Similarly, time in Whitman's catalog is registered less as a series of discrete instants separated by intervals than as a collapsible continuum in which every moment can be superimposed on every other one: the linear time of profane historical change and action, as it were, turns into the cyclical time of the sacred. All Whitman's verbs in the catalog hover ambiguously between the "continuous" versus the "simple" present. To say that "the pure contralto sings in the organloft" might mean that she is doing so right now (dynamic), or it might mean that she habitually or repeatedly does so (stative). In context, this ambiguity works to collapse the simple and the continuous present, suggesting an odd sort of time in which all present actions are varieties of recurrent processes; what happens now is simply an instance of what happens forever. If things were truly so, the world would be less vertiginously complicated, more manageable; if the poet's word makes it so, he manages the world, for himself and for everyone.

While looking at Whitman's catalog technique,

a brief glance ahead will show how some catalogs in other poems vary the techniques displayed in this passage from "Song of Myself," pressuring perception more forcefully toward the ritual contours described. A brief excerpt from an extended catalog in "Crossing Brooklyn Ferry" can serve as an example:

> I too saw the reflection of the summer-sky in the
>     water
> . . . . . . . . . . . . .
> Looked toward the lower bay to notice the arriving
>     ships,
> Saw their approach, saw aboard those that were
>     near me,
> Saw the white sails of schooners and sloops, saw
>     the ships at anchor,
> The sailors at work in the rigging or out astride the
>     spars,
> The round masts, the swinging motion of the hulls,
>     the slender serpentine pennants,
> The large and small steamers in motion, the pilots
>     in their pilot-houses,
> The white wake left by the passage, the quick
>     tremulous whirl of the wheels

As this passage progresses, grammatical structure gets progressively attenuated, suggesting a world in which independent being and doing grow increasingly vestigial. The "I" of the first line is the subject of a massively distended sentence (there is no period until after six additional long lines): a world full of multiple agents is thus transformed into a more manageable one, in which everything becomes the object of the poet's organizing perception. That perception ("I too saw") is the only action to which the passage accords grammatical weight. Moving forward through the passage, the repeated verb "saw" is also omitted. Having dropped verb as well as grammatical subject, there are simply ten long object phrases, parallel instances of what the speaker "saw." This is a substitution drill with a vengeance: everything the speaker names drops into an identical grammatical space, another parallel instance of what the poet "saw." Here vision becomes visionary and the one who sees becomes a seer. And what, we may ask, are all these substitutable, superimposed people and objects doing? As the passage renders them, other acts have lost the initiatory power of finite verbs. Rendered by participles and verbals, what might well have been actions have instead become diffuse, continuous processes (the swinging, the whirl); no longer initiated by independent persons or things, they seem instead to flow through the entire scene, like manifestations of a single suffusing impulse which the poet's word traces, or propels. Such grammatical shamanism is a crucial attribute of several poems in Whitman's early editions.

In "Song of Myself" not only do things tend inward to the poet, as in Whitman's characteristic catalogs, the poet also tends outward to them. This flowing outward of a diffuse, transfiguring presence is often suggested most strongly in those moments where the poet addresses his audience directly, seeming to hover as a vaporous body conveyed on the accents of the poet's voice. One such moment constitutes the poem's beginning:

> I celebrate myself,
> And what I assume you shall assume,
> For every atom belonging to me as good belongs to you.

Whitman's "you" here is ambiguous, being simultaneously intimate and universal; the poet thus seems to flow outward (on the voice that announces his presence) in all directions at once, a godlike emanation. Since what is we are promised are the very atoms that make him up, the audience "assumes" what the poet assumes not simply in the sense of believing what he believes, but in the stranger one of putting on his disseminating body as its own. Political prospect (we are one because we share the same beliefs) jostles for imaginative priority with a more archaic transaction here (I have turned you into myself, or floated myself out to flow inside you). The complex of social and personal aspirations and anxieties that might mo-

tivate such an imaginative confounding is surely resistant to any single, neat formulation, whether couched in terms of politics or psychology.

The quirkier Whitman's depictions of the poet's presence, the more resistant they will be to didactic reduction. "Song of Myself" abounds in such peculiar formulations, many of them outlandishly sexual. In one passage, whatever the poet comes into erotic contact with becomes in effect part of him; yet he brushes up against some unlikely partners, his own sexual ebullience suggesting the sexuality of all he comes across. The confounding of self and other here, and of eros and nature, is truly wild:

> If I worship any particular thing it shall be some of
>     the spread of my own body;
> Translucent mould of me it shall be you,
> Shades ledges and rests, firm masculine coulter, it
>     shall be you,
> Whatever goes to the tilth of me it shall be you,
> . . . . . . . . . . . . . .
> You sweaty brooks and dews it shall be you,
> Winds whose soft-tickling genitals rub against me
>     it shall be you,
> Broad muscular fields, branches of liveoak, loving
>     lounger in my winding paths, it shall be you,
> Hands I have taken, face I have kissed, mortal I
>     have ever touched, it shall be you.

Elsewhere, the poet makes love to futurity in a consummation at once outrageously cosmic, comic, and tender:

> By my life-lumps! becoming already a creator!
> Putting myself here and now to the ambushed
>     womb of the shadows!

Just as the tone in these passages can change abruptly or glide almost undetectably from one register to another, so too these proclamations of the poet's godlike powers seem to shuffle unpredictably among gigantesque ambition, megalomanic euphoria, sexual bravado, and comic or wistful irony. The poet who could write them was surely a remarkable writer. Yet they suggest an odd mix of jaunty self-confidence, lurking anxiety, compensatory boasting, and lingering pathos that, in combination, make both the significance of these passages and the personal and cultural work they perform elusive. Such tolerance for irresolution, for Keatsian "negative capability," surfaces frequently in the poem as irony, whether wistful or ebullient, pathos-filled or playful. One moment of high comedy shows the absorptive body of the poet's innards as cluttered up with objects, while his hide is plastered with the stuff that apparently could not be taken inside him:

> I find I incorporate gneiss and coal and long-
> threaded moss and fruits and grains and esculent
> roots,
> And am stucco'd with quadrupeds and birds all
> over.

Likewise the catalogs, which tend to enucleate what they name, in "Song of Myself" frequently encounter the sort of recalcitrant peculiarity that resists such assimilation. Unlikely metaphor, typically, suggests the sort of quiddity that will stick in the shaman's craw: "Where the alligator in his tough pimples sleeps by the bayou"; "Where the ground-shark's fin cuts like a black chip out of the water."

Such moments perhaps suggest good humor more than self-doubt. It is as if Whitman, discovering his imaginative powers in this great early poem, took pleasure both in exercising them and in holding back—in letting things be, from time to time, rather than subjecting them right away to the newfound verbal and imaginative resources of his homemade ritual.

### LEAVES OF GRASS (1856)

The thorny issue of the status and possible meaning of such ritual powers seems to have preoccupied Whitman even before the first edition of

*Leaves of Grass* went to press. The 1855 preface (composed just before the volume was published) strenuously insists on the national provenance and function of the ensuing poetry; the poetry itself, as the critic John Kinnaird points out, mentions the United States far less often than the preface does. In keeping with Whitman's populist and largely anti-institutional sympathies, the preface, like "Song of the Answerer," casts the poet in the role of cultural healer, reconciling threatening differences which the president and political parties have been unable to absorb into the body politic of the United States: "Their Presidents shall not be their common referee so much as their poets shall. . . . . [The poet] is the arbiter of the diverse and he is the key. He is the equalizer of his age and land." Yet this political function, the solid and respectable public ground on which the volume is presumably being placed, blurs into the shamanistic role we found in the overdetermined universe of the poems.

In the 1856 edition of *Leaves of Grass,* large chunks of the preface turn up virtually unedited in the poem "By Blue Ontario's Shore." That this recycled material seems different in its new context is largely the result of the change of genre; the change nevertheless turns out to be symptomatic. In the ostensibly expository context of the preface, Whitman's manically distended sentences, with their agrammatical ellipses in place of more standard punctuation, deflect even hortatory pronouncements toward exuberant, comic excess. Set as poetry, by contrast, it is the hortatory insistence that comes through.

The 1856 edition of *Leaves of Grass* is not without its fine moments, and fine poems. But on the whole it lacks the unpredictable idiomatic and imaginative suppleness of its predecessor. In the new pieces Whitman composed, the poet's powers tend to be proclaimed more solemnly and less jauntily, and their exercise is more unremitting. Resistance and the doubt it can occasion tend to provoke, not wistful self-deprecation or outlandish comic bravado, but anxious insistence or momentary despair. This shift, which characterizes to a lesser extent the poems Whitman composed for the important 1860 edition as well, likely has several causes. In the mid to late 1850s, the political landscape of the country darkened as war loomed closer. Whitman's passional life, from the little we know of it during this period, seems also to have been intense but dark. *Leaves of Grass,* likewise, failed to fare as well as its author had hoped. In later years, Whitman wildly exaggerated both the success and the utter neglect of the 1855 edition, as occasion dictated. On the whole, however, despite Emerson's glowing acknowledgment, *Leaves of Grass* was probably more notorious for its sexual explicitness than admired for its poetic qualities, and it enjoyed neither the notoriety nor the admiration that would have propelled Whitman into the sort of national prominence to which he aspired.

The insistent quality of "By Blue Ontario's Shore" is evident as well in several of the other twenty-odd poems Whitman composed for the 1856 volume. It mars not only the minor "Salut au Monde!" but also the more important "Song of the Open Road," a poem whose declarations of American open-endedness and faith in adventurous wandering are belied rather than exemplified by the poem's relatively monochromatic diction and sometimes hectoring tone, as well as by a kind of programmatic tightening up of the digressive and meandering style of "Song of Myself"; the poem claims to revel in the glories of unexpected by-roads but in fact explores few of them.

The most important new poem of the 1856 edition is undoubtedly "Crossing Brooklyn Ferry," which recapitulates the crucial transactions of "Song of Myself" in a condensed and more consistently lyrical manner. Missing are the digressions, idiomatic shiftiness, and abrupt tonal variations that make the earlier poem such a challenge and triumph. Though a lesser achievement, "Crossing Brooklyn Ferry" is without doubt one of Whitman's most important poems, offering perhaps the best brief introduction to the imaginative universe of his crucial first two editions.

Missing, too, from "Crossing Brooklyn Ferry" is the giddy shifting of scenes and perspectives at work in "Song of Myself." Here the single locale of New York's East River where the ferry crossed between Manhattan and Brooklyn provides Whitman with an ideal site for enacting his characteristic vision of erotic and social blending: as several critics have pointed out, the river, the forms drifting on it, and the haze overhead proved especially congenial to Whitman's purposes, allowing the poet to enact what he elsewhere calls "the merge" without seeming to do violence to the objects of things his ritual acts upon. On this limited scene and in a comparatively compact performance, Whitman works his characteristic verbal ritual in an almost schematic fashion. Yet his typical ambivalence is also evident. On the one hand, from the outset the poem proclaims itself a celebration of the contemporary scene, which despite its welter of activity and sense of evanescence is declared to be the harbinger of eternity. On the other hand, the bulk of the poem works the sort of transformative shamanistic spell on this scene typical of Whitman's 1855 and 1856 poems. A convincing case might be made that it is only this imaginatively transfigured scene that Whitman's poem celebrates, and that the very urgency and scope of the transformation bespeaks an intense discomfort with the harbor world and the American conditions that this world typifies: the anonymity and "rushing and raging" activity, as Whitman calls it in a newspaper piece he earlier wrote on the ferries, of a great American city caught up in the throes of industrial development and breakneck urban growth.

The traces of Whitman's transformative project are evident in the poem's bizarre but effective, and altogether typical, temporal scheme, which stands out sharply. Beginning in the present tense, much of the poem is couched in the past. But it turns out that these two tenses refer to the same time span, the one in which the poem's speaker rides the ferry in what we might call the poem's "profane" present moment. The vantage he speaks the bulk of the poem from, and from which the time spent aboard the ferry may be said to be superseded, is not so much an imagined future moment as the eternal one of sacred time, in which ritual events repeat themselves and "now" becomes forever. Few of Whitman's poems evoke the poet's floating omnipresence so powerfully or insistently, and few declare so clearly the centripetal effects on profane time and space that this figure supposedly exerts:

> What is it, then, between us?
> What is the count of the scores or hundreds of
>    years between us?
>
> Whatever it is, it avails not—distance avails not,
>    and place avails not.
>
> Closer yet I approach you,
> What thought you have of me now, I had as much
>    of you—I laid in my stores in advance,
> I consider'd long and seriously of you before you
>    were born.
>
> Who was to know what should come home to me?
> Who knows but I am enjoying this?
> Who knows but I am as good as looking at you
>    now, for all you cannot see me?

The second of these passages owes its difficulty to the presence of both profane and sacred time: sliding into the past tense to describe the initially profane moment in which, supposedly standing aboard the ferry in 1856, he throws his voice to his audience (the present tense of the poem's opening) and using the present tense to refer to the future moment in which that audience will receive his word. He also proclaims the sacred "now" of his manifestation, a paradoxically eternal moment that conjoins the first two times and collapses the distance between them. The poem's catalogs work a complementary magic on both space and time:

while the poet's addresses evoke his effusing, centrifugal presence, his catalogs seem to collapse objects inward and lever them into the same sort of "eternal moment" as his proclamations of presence generate.

In one sense, the shaman's advent, proclaimed when Whitman addresses the reader, seems to lift both the poet himself and those who hear him out of anonymous, treacherous public space, conveying the audience to a redeemed realm that is also deliciously intimate:

> What is more subtle than this which ties me to the
>    woman or man that looks in my face?
> Which fuses me into you now, and pours my
>    meaning into you?
>
> We understand, then, do we not?
> What I promised without mentioning it, have you
>    not accepted?
> What the study could not teach—what the preach-
>    ing could not accomplish is accomplished, is it
>    not?
> What the push of reading could not start is started
>    by me personally, is it not?

Yet such imagined encounters can seem confining rather than liberating, and as oppressively abstract despite their air of private communion. Whitman's play with mode here—his proclamation of a personal presence, supposedly attested to and conveyed by the voice these lines want to make his audience thinks it hears, and his concomitant dismissal of reading—is a tenuous sleight of hand that can end up working either way. The poet claims to single "you" out from public space and usher you into a protected realm of magical intimacy; but the text of Whitman's book offers this salvation simultaneously to everyone, in a transaction every bit as abstract and anonymous as the public space from which it aspires to save us.

Since social conflicts and contradictions are as intractable as they are—and since imaginative writers grow up inside the cultures whose problems they often claim to solve—this double reverse is neither surprising nor wholly disabling. It is certainly not a sign that Whitman was not a good poet or a culturally resonant imaginative thinker. According to the critic Quentin Anderson, the peculiar bind here is indeed one Whitman shares with several other major American authors, including his contemporaries Thoreau and, most notably, Emerson. Their gigantesque claims of an inclusive and total power, which supposedly allowed them to achieve visionary possession of a world they thereby transfigured, are in Anderson's account a desperate defense against an inclusive social predicament they end up mirroring rather than solving.

Whitman, that is, despite his political commitments, is in the imaginative universe of the poems of 1855 and 1856 ultimately less concerned with political action than with a kind of visionary or magical transformation of the self and its objects, which ought to be available to a inclusive act of possession and transfiguration. The unlimited scope of this imagined transfiguration suggests, according to Anderson, at one and the same time: the sweeping nature of the transformation wrought by the emergent capitalist economy on antebellum America; the absence of noncapitalist social structures sufficiently well established and powerful to provide an effective counterforce to this change; the anxiety such a total transformation of the social scene provoked in individuals set adrift in the essentially anonymous and unmoored space defined by the impersonal laws of economic exchange; the desperate though seemingly triumphant status of an act of imaginative resistance that relied on the powers of the single self; and the peculiarly abstract or generic status of this self (Walt as shaman, devoid, in the poems, of personal history), an abstraction that, ironically, reproduces the very anonymity this figure has been designed to cure, so that his transformative acts replicate the impersonality of the law of exchange his advent supposedly supersedes.

One virtue of this account is that it lets us see the personal predicaments that helped shape *Leaves of Grass* as symptomatic in a cultural and not merely personal sense, as revelatory rather than merely idiosyncratic or disqualifying. The evidently unmoored quality of Whitman's personal life through the mid 1850s, that is, presents an extreme version of an increasingly common condition: in Whitman's case private sources of isolation dovetailed with contributing conditions which were shared and public, resulting, in *Leaves of Grass*, in an imaginative landscape at once intensely personal and socially resonant. Likewise Whitman's imaginative solutions, both in what they proclaim and in what they avoid, in their blindness as well as their insight, turn out to be an extreme version of a common cultural pattern.

### LEAVES OF GRASS (1860)

Surprisingly, the wholesale transformations of social and psychic space that characterize the 1855 and 1856 editions of *Leaves of Grass* turn out to be pretty much confined to this extraordinarily productive phase of Whitman's career. By the time Whitman published the third edition of *Leaves of Grass* in 1860, this intensely imagined universe had very nearly dissolved. The 1860 edition no longer centers on the figure of the poet as shaman; nor is language deployed so as to display or enact its supposed performative power to transfigure social and personal space. In part, public events were overtaking Whitman's redemptive project.

In the 1860 edition of *Leaves of Grass* shamanistic magic is superseded not only by a darkened mood appropriate to the times, but also by many moments of great tenderness, and by a feeling of emotional reconciliation rather than cataclysm. Such feelings, for the most part, surface in the poet's extended meditations on homosexual love. It has been argued, on occasion, that this turn to the world of intimate relations is itself a symptom of political malaise: Whitman writes about personal life, because he despairs of public life. Yet this surely accords political events too singular a role in the evolution of Whitman's career, and thus to risk reducing him to what the poet Wallace Stevens later called, not in reference to Whitman, "the lunatic of one idea." Though the hard evidence that remains in the aftermath of Whitman's assiduous archival prunings is somewhat scanty, Whitman biographers tend to concur that sometime before publishing his 1860 edition he had fallen in love and experienced a period of intense and apparently reciprocated romantic attachment. The most likely candidate is Fred Vaughan; like Whitman's other most serious partners he was a younger working-class man to whom Whitman was a mentor and quasi father-figure as well as a lover. Along with the changing course of American history, perhaps, this experience and the changed sense of personal possibility it seems to have inaugurated were responsible for the shifting contours of Whitman's poetry.

This love experience almost undoubtedly provided the crucial personal impetus for Whitman's "Calamus" sequence, one of the great achievements of the 1860 edition of *Leaves of Grass*. Oddly, despite their quality and their volatile subject matter, Whitman's "Calamus" poems pretty much escaped notice when they were published. The ire that might have been directed to them fell instead on the companion Children of Adam sequence, Whitman's labored attempt to do for heterosexuality what he had already done for homosexuality in the "Calamus" poems. Emerson, still in Whitman's corner despite the purloined letter, apparently argued long and hard with the poet, during a walk in Boston Common, that the Children of Adam sequence had to be excised or expurgated, so that *Leaves of Grass* could make its way without the already weighty indecency albatross continuing to hang around its neck. As it turned out, Emerson proved both right and wrong: while several reviews were vituperative, others praised Whitman for an essentially "healthy" or "natural" view of sex. On the whole the sequence's notoriety probably helped sales more

than it hurt them, keeping Whitman in the public eye. Thayer and Eldridge, Whitman's abolitionist Boston-based publishers, wrote the poet that their initial printing of a thousand copies had virtually sold out; unfortunately, their plans for a second run never materialized, as the firm went bankrupt in 1861. In retrospect it is hard to get very excited about the poems that stirred up this fuss: healthy-minded to a fault, they are certainly not prurient by present standards. Poetically, they are entirely unexceptionable, and curiously abstract or abstracted. The poet has a hard time working up credible enthusiasm for heterosexual intercourse; intended eroticism tends to collapse quickly into eugenicist cheerleading.

By contrast the "Calamus" sequence is intensely imagined and felt. Where the forced enthusiasm of Children of Adam produces frenetic or hectoring rhetoric, the tone in "Calamus" is both resonant and mobile. The poems glide between tenderness and poignancy, longing and regret, solemnity that is understated rather than overblown and erotic bravura tinged with wistfulness or self-deprecating humor. An early and shorter version of the sequence, called "Live-Oak with Moss," is more clearly narrative and presumably autobiographical than "Calamus" in its entirety, telling the story of the growth and then the decline and death of a love affair. Yet the public claims and concerns of "Calamus," which some critics see as merely an attempt to distance the sequence from these autobiographical intensities, are present in the earlier series as well. In one respect, then, "Calamus" rewrites the demotic populism of the 1855 and 1856 editions by tying it more clearly, perhaps even exclusively, to what we now call homosexuality. Whitman tended to use the phrenological term "adhesiveness" for both same-sex romantic passion and, more generally, friendship. As this term indicated, they had the power, in Whitman's view to knit the nation together as laws and politicians could not. Yet the sequence, published as war loomed nearer, seems to imagine these ties as enduring cataclysm rather than preventing it; part of the sequence's complex resonance derives from its insistent stepping aside from public space, its imagining of a kind of adhesive or homosexual shadow republic out of which the meaning of America might eventually be reconfigured, its promise reinvented and fulfilled beyond whatever disaster sectional strife would bring.

If the series escaped the notoriety that descended on Children of Adam, it is probably due not only to its political, even nationalist, strands, but also to the borderline relation it establishes between accepted traditions of same-sex friendship and homosexual love. Writing in an era before the notion of homosexuality as a distinct sexual orientation existed, Whitman both appeals to the aboveboard tradition of same-sex romantic friendship and slides it discreetly toward a range of overtly sexual expression and behavior less accepted and less openly discussed. One result of this blurring is that Whitman manages, in "Calamus," simultaneously to proclaim the political and cultural value of widespread homosociality and more furtively to celebrate (and strengthen) the rituals of an emergent community of what we would now call homosexuals. In effect, he establishes discreetly, for his era, a sort of "homosexual continuum," in some ways anticipating Adrienne Rich's later recent overt proclamation of the crucial social and political role played by a "lesbian continuum" in women's history and women's lives.

Yet at the same time "Calamus" enacts a tentative gay coming out, it acts as Whitman's coming into culture. If the 1855 and 1856 editions stage the poet as a shaman who stands above culture to transfigure and redeem it, the "Calamus" sequence envisions the personal and communal rituals, at once erotic and social, that might place him more firmly within culture, imagining gay history as America's secret history. This shift away from the huge imaginative claims of 1855 and 1856 can be criticized by characterizing the scope of Whit-

man's ambitions here as smaller than heretofore; but it can be praised by calling their scale more human. (Thoreau, apparently a bit unnerved upon meeting Whitman in 1855, noted that the poet "occasionally suggests something a little more than human.")

Whitman's own response to this shift in his life and work seems in effect to have been divided between these two hypothetical reactions. Among the 1860 edition's other major poems are "Out of the Cradle Endlessly Rocking" and "As I Ebb'd with the Ocean of Life." While the first celebrates the discovery or affirmation of human scale, the second explores the anxiety and near despair provoked by a shedding of the shamanistic stance of the earlier work and the psychological advantages that it provided. The latter poem has become the more widely praised. "Out of the Cradle," once much admired for the economy and consistency of its compressed system of symbols, has come to look a little dogmatically neat. Detailing an awakening to love and personal loss as the origin of his poetic calling, the poem's speaker recounts the genesis of the art of the 1860 "Calamus" sequence rather than the poems of 1855 and 1856. Telling a story in which love is cut short by death, Whitman both dramatically heightens the poem's situation and registers a fundamentally human recognition. Yet this heightening may be partly obfuscatory and melodramatic—obscuring Whitman's own loss of Fred Vaughan, who had not died but had simply moved out.

By contrast the extreme anxiety and bitterness of "As I Ebb'd with the Ocean of Life" seem wholly earned. The poem is an agonized appraisal of an apparent vanishing of powers, both personal and poetic. They are, as detailed in the poem, powers that seem very much like those of the shaman of 1855 and 1856. The diminished poet confronts an opposing self who might be the shaman: "I musing late in the autumn day, gazing off southward, / Alone, held by the eternal self of me that threatens to get the better of me, and sti-fle me." Further on, this earlier, grandly aspiring poet figure is bitterly excoriated as a preposterous sham:

> Oppress'd with myself that I have dared to open
> my mouth,
> Aware now, that, amid all the blab whose echoes
> recoil upon me, I have not once had the least
> idea who or what I am.

As he gazes down at the rows of sediment while he walks the Long Island beach, the poem's diminished speaker enumerates a catalog gone bust, naming a world of lifeless forms not gathered and reanimated by the poet's power, but dispersed and irretrievable:

> Fascinated, my eyes, reverting from the south,
> dropped to follow those slender windrows,
> Chaff, straw, splinters of wood, weeds, and the
> sea-gluten,
> Scum, scales from shining rocks, leaves of salt-
> lettuce, left by the tide.

The poet no longer capable of redeeming this detritus is now reduced to imagining himself part of it:

> I, too, but signify at the utmost a little wash'd-up
> drift,
> A few sands and dead leaves to gather,
> Gather, and merge myself as part of the sands and
> drift.

The poem is complex in its bitterness; "the merge," earlier Whitman's favorite name for the transfiguring process the poet was said to help propel, is bitterly echoed as the poet merges with "the sands and drifts." Turning partly against the grand claims of Whitman's earlier editions, now seen as pretensions, it also ambivalently mocks the self who has failed to fulfill them. Yet whether the poem blames the figure of the shaman or the lover who has foolishly bartered away his sacramental

vocation for a personal happiness that turned out to be elusive, the poem confronts the resultant anxiety and despair unflinchingly. In ensuing years Whitman apparently went on to find a personal happiness as well as a public fame that had hitherto eluded him; yet "As I Ebb'd with the Ocean of Life" may be the last great poem he ever wrote.

## POST-1860 POETRY

If the last is an arguable judgment, it is a fairly common one. Once praised fairly frequently, if by no means universally, for their supposed polish and imaginative consistency or their supposedly Hegelian doctrinal clarity, most of the poems Whitman added to *Leaves of Grass* after 1860 have for some time been widely dismissed as minor work. Their once-vaunted smoothness of idiom criticized as a retreat to gentility; their nicely manageable symbol systems judged as plodding; and their availability to neat doctrinal paraphrase seen as the sign of an imaginatively exhausted poet's lapse into not especially profound cogitation or tireless but tiring exposition. This severe judgment has been mitigated somewhat by the leveling tendencies of new historicist literary criticism and cultural studies, for both of which the socially symptomatic status of the poem or the cultural work it performs may outweigh other concerns. On the whole, however, the later poetry is not as well regarded and less frequently read and written about than the earlier work.

Since Whitman, as early as the 1860 edition, began to tinker with the ordering of the ever-expanding list of poems that made up *Leaves of Grass,* arranging them in various thematic "cluster" schemes rather than chronologically, the general falling off of intensity and quality in the later work can be difficult to discern from a quick perusal of the so-called "deathbed" edition (essentially the edition of 1881). A look at the three-volume *Variorum,* which arranges the poems by date of first appearance in *Leaves of Grass,* is therefore a useful exercise.

The poems first published in 1865 as a separate volume, *Drum-Taps,* display a shift of focus and scope that is altogether understandable: no longer the poet of mythic transfigurations in which present pleasure and anxiety are rewritten under the sign of utopian prospect, Whitman becomes first the cheerleader of the war effort and then the haunted but accepting chronicler of its costs and the typically quiet heroism with which these were borne. The bombast of the first strain is more than made up for by the understated dignity of the latter one; Whitman, much moved, commits himself to a modest and minor poetry of chronicle, eschewing both epic and the earlier visionary mode of his greatest work. *Sequel to Drum-Taps,* oddly dated 1865–1866, prints eighteen new poems, most memorably Whitman's elegy for Lincoln, "When Lilacs Last in the Dooryard Bloom'd," an undoubtedly important poem most resembling, perhaps, "Out of the Cradle" among Whitman's earlier works. Like the earlier poem, this one is both heartfelt and occasionally purple. Almost uniformly somber in tone, it shares with the earlier poem the exalted diction and sustained decorum appropriate to commemoration. Its public provenance and function likewise virtually necessitate the imaginative compression that a limited and consistently manipulated system of symbols can give. (As in "Out of the Cradle," Whitman gives birds pride of place.)

As with the tendency to oversimplify the powerfully overdetermined imaginative contours of the triumphant early editions of *Leaves of Grass,* it is necessary to be on guard against the temptation to posit some single cause for the sustained decline of Whitman's poetry. Age and illness are assuredly important factors. Beginning in the 1860s Whitman sustained a number of strokes from which he never fully recovered. For a poet

who made such grand claims for the body and reconfigured America in his poems as the agglomerating space an extravagantly polymorphous sexuality suggests, such difficulties must have been especially disabling. Increasing artistic caution, an eye increasingly trained on fame and thus surreptitiously glancing at propriety, also surely played a part. At the same time, the Civil War affected Whitman so intensely that the poetry of myth and possibility seems to have given way to the less ambitious poetry of chronicle. By contrast the Gilded Age appears to have thoroughly discomfited him as a writer. The world of industrial and social rationalization that grew out of the Civil War's massive mobilization of the American citizenry and economy was one to which he responded ambivalently, but not poetically. His later poetry seems often to fly as high above American space, and as close to some timeless empyrean as possible, an ascent for which his earthy talents and intense if ambivalent immersion in American social and political life left him ill-suited.

By contrast, his poetic imagination had been deeply and perhaps irrevocably engaged by the pre–Civil War period, the decades in which American capital and attendant social organizations emerged from the precapitalist artisanal and social forms that Whitman's strongest poetry evokes, and the passing of which it marks. Perhaps as important as all this, however, are Whitman's own changed circumstances: his emergence from a largely rootless condition into public fame, a domestic life in which he both lived once more among family and hosted a growing circle of friends who were also admirers, disciples, and acolytes; and a passional life apparently marked by sustained if stormy intimacies. It may seem odd that such settling in should have proved detrimental to his poetry. But it may well have been the case. Perhaps rootlessness—provoking as it did the peculiar combination of open-ended possibility, grandiosity, poignant self-doubt, and largely compensatory comic bravado that characterizes the early editions of *Leaves of Grass*—was as important a stimulant to Whitman's imagination as quirky erotic material and populist turbulence.

## LATER YEARS

If the new poetry Whitman produced in the years after 1860 grew less intense and interesting, his life assuredly did not. His brother George, who had enlisted in the Union army in 1861, was wounded in late 1862 during the debacle at Fredricksburg. Whitman traveled south to Virginia to tend to him; returning to Washington for an indeterminate period, he ended up staying for the duration of the war and well beyond. What drew him, powerfully enough to be called mesmerically, were the war hospitals. Beginning as an unofficial visitor, Whitman became an unpaid "delegate" of the Christian Commission, a kind of volunteer companion and nurse to wounded and dying soldiers. By the time the war ended, Whitman had made some six hundred visits to army hospitals, several of these lasting for days at a time. He brought special items of food and other small gifts to those in his care, wrote letters and read to them, stayed to soothe and to talk, and often to kiss and embrace. In a consummation at once horrific and wondrous, Whitman seems to have found among this community of the wounded an unlikely fulfillment, at one and the same time, of the heroic populism *Leaves of Grass* had promulgated, the homosocial republic imagined in "Calamus," and, to some degree at least, the passionate intimacy he had begun to experience in the late 1850s. Whitman's attachment to some of these young men was extremely intense, a feeling that seems at least in part to have been reciprocated in more than one instance.

Yet the intense and turbulent world of the war hospitals was partly offset for Whitman, during his Washington years, by the growing stability he came to enjoy. He was appointed to a government clerkship in the Office of Indian Affairs early in 1865. When he was fired later that same year as part of a supposed moral purge engineered by the new secretary of the interior, James Harlan (who had supposedly read Whitman's working copy of *Leaves of Grass* while ransacking the poet's desk), that turned out to be a piece of great good fortune too. Before the ruckus had cleared Whitman had been transferred to a better job in the Attorney General's office. More important, his abolitionist friend William O'Connor came to Whitman's defense. O'Connor was a brilliant and spirited polemicist, and his invective—originally planned as a letter of protest to be delivered to Harlan but published instead as a privately printed pamphlet, *The Good Gray Poet*—stirred up a storm and played an important role in changing the footing on which Whitman's reputation was based. O'Connor argued that the work of this supposedly notoriously prurient poet was in fact surpassingly moral.

After Whitman moved to Camden, in declining health in 1873 (he lived first with his brother George and later in a small house of his own on Mickle Street, which is now maintained as a sort of Whitman museum), his circle of friends and admirers widened, coming to include, among others, the Canadian alienist Richard Maurice Bucke, who also wrote a book on Whitman. But the welter of feverish activity on Mickle Street was increasingly matched by burgeoning interest in centers of cultural power, in England as well as in the United States. A selection of Whitman's poems published in England in 1868, edited by William Michael Rossetti, secured his reputation in England, and in subsequent years Whitman's rising stock in America was to some degree sustained by the backwash from England. Famous visitors, both English and American, trooped to Camden, and the American press took note. By the time he died, following a lingering last illness, on March 26, 1892, in Camden, he was a public figure and person of letters of general renown if of disputed stature.

This burgeoning of both public attention and devoted attendance by an inner circle of acolytes seems to have been matched by a brightening of Whitman's intimate life. Beginning with the former Confederate soldier and streetcar conductor Peter Doyle, several younger men—mostly working class—seem to have reciprocated Whitman's affections and entered into sustained and intense intimacies with him.

### PROSE WORKS

Whitman's most important work during this long period was done not in poetry but in prose—not as utopian myth-making but as memoir, or as frequently cogent social criticism essentially untinged by the exuberant imaginative excess characteristic of the early editions of *Leaves of Grass*. *Specimen Days,* published in 1882, is an odd but often affecting conglomeration of writings from several occasions, part diary or daybook and part episodic memoir of Whitman's Civil War experiences.

*Democratic Vistas,* combining essays written in 1867 and 1868 and published in pamphlet form in 1871, is probably the most significant piece of writing Whitman did during the last thirty years of his life. Responding to Thomas Carlyle's scathing attack on democracy in "Shooting Niagara; and After?" (1867),Whitman both admits the force of Carlyle's criticisms, indeed offering his own bill of particulars, and turns his indictment into the occasion for a renewed declaration of faith in American democracy. Part cogent denunciation of the unchecked triumph of greed and commercialism in the Gilded Age, the essay is also a striking instance of what Sacvan Bercovitch calls the American jeremiad, a culturally pervasive pattern of castigation and call for recommitment that helps both to instigate and to limit the scope of

reform in United States political and cultural debate. Both a paean to American individualism and a critique of it, the essay ponders the ways in which polis and person may be mutually reenforcing rather than at loggerheads. Perhaps not surprisingly, Whitman finds his answer in culture, in a double sense: literature, or cultural production, is both to grow out of and knit together American culture in the broader meaning of that term. Culture's crucial function is to encourage a superb, redeemed individualism.

Some politically oriented criticism of Whitman's work has ably drawn out the ways in which his imaginative vision of a transfigured America ironically extols as virtues and resources some of the very habits and strategies that, in hindsight, can be seen to have exacerbated the problems they were called on to cure. Yet such limitations certainly do not vitiate, though they may qualify, the achievement of *Leaves of Grass*—notably its utopian hopes and energies and the peculiar, mobile, and nearly always eroticized imaginative constellations that sometimes support but often remain irreducible to the book's political ambitions. If Whitman is our most uneven great poet, he is also arguably our greatest uneven one. That at least has been the judgment of countless twentieth-century poets, major as well as minor, for whom Whitman has been a crucial resource despite his notoriously slack stretches. While each poet undoubtedly has his or her own Whitman, it is probably safe to say that it is the poet of the first three editions who has proved to be a crucial challenge or enabling instigation. And if it is in a way a joke to call the poems of this period peculiarly timeless, the joke is peculiarly Whitmanian, and serious. We can end with it:

> Whoever you are, now I place my hand upon you,
>     that you be my poem,
> I whisper with my lips close to your ear,
> I have loved many women and men, but I love
>     none better than you.

# Selected Bibliography

## WORKS OF WALT WHITMAN

### POETRY

*Leaves of Grass.* Brooklyn, 1855. (Printed by Rome Brothers.)

*Leaves of Grass.* Brooklyn: [Fowler & Wells], 1856.

*Leaves of Grass.* Boston: Thayer and Eldridge, 1860.

*Drum-Taps.* New York, 1865.

*Leaves of Grass.* New York, 1866. (W. E. Chapin, Printer. This is the so-called 1867 edition.)

*Leaves of Grass.* Washington, D.C., 1871. (Printed by J. S. Redfield, New York.)

*Leaves of Grass.* Boston: James R. Osgood, 1881–1882. (Copyright is 1881. Modern Whitman editors regard this as the final edition of *Leaves of Grass.* The plates from this edition were used for all later printings, including the so-called "death-bed edition" of 1891–1892. Various annexed poems were appended to *Leaves of Grass* proper in subsequent printings.)

### PROSE WORKS

*Democratic Vistas.* Washington, D.C., 1871.

*Specimen Days and Collect.* Philadelphia: Rees Welsh, 1882.

### FACSIMILES AND REPRINTS

*Leaves of Grass: The First (1855) Edition.* Edited by Malcolm Cowley. New York: Viking, 1959.

*Leaves of Grass: Facsimile of the First Edition of Leaves of Grass, Published by Whitman in Brooklyn in 1855.* New York: Eakins Press, 1966.

*Leaves of Grass: Facsimile of 1856 Edition.* With an introduction by Gay Wilson Allen. Norwood, Pa.: Norwood Editions, 1976.

*Leaves of Grass: Facsimile Edition of the 1860 Text.* With an introduction by Roy Harvey Pearce. Ithaca, N.Y.: Cornell University Press, 1961.

### COLLECTIONS

*The Complete Writings of Walt Whitman.* Edited by Richard Maurice Bucke, Thomas B. Harned, and Horace L. Traubel. 10 vols. New York: Putnam, 1902.

*The Uncollected Poetry and Prose of Walt Whitman.* Edited by Emory Holloway. 2 vols. Garden City, N.Y.: Doubleday, Page, 1921.

*The Poetry and Prose of Walt Whitman.* Edited by Louis Untermeyer. New York: Simon & Schuster, 1949.

*Whitman's Manuscripts:* Leaves of Grass *(1860): A Parallel Text.* Edited by Fredson Bowers. Chicago: University of Chicago Press, 1955.

*The Collected Writings of Walt Whitman.* Edited by Gay Wilson Allen and Sculley Bradley. 22 vols. to date. New York: New York University Press, 1961–. (Among the volumes in the New York University edition are the following: *The Correspondence.* Edited by Edwin Haviland Miller. 6 vols. 1961–1977. *The Early Poems and the Fiction.* Edited by Thomas L. Brasher. 1963. *Prose Works 1892.* 2 vols. Edited by Floyd Stovall. 1963–1964. [Volume I is *Specimen Days.*] *Leaves of Grass: Comprehensive Reader's Edition.* Edited by Harold W. Blodgett and Sculley Bradley. 1965. *Daybooks and Notebooks.* Edited by William White. 3 vols. 1978. *Leaves of Grass: A Textual Variorum of the Printed Poems.* Edited by Sculley Bradley et al. 3 vols. 1980. *Notebooks and Unpublished Prose Manuscripts.* Edited by Edward F. Grier. 6 vols. 1984.)

## BIBLIOGRAPHIES AND CONCORDANCE

Eby, Edwin Harold. *A Concordance of Walt Whitman's* Leaves of Grass *and Selected Prose Writings.* Seattle: University of Washington Press, 1954.

Myerson, Joel. *Walt Whitman: A Descriptive Bibliography.* Pittsburgh: University of Pittsburgh Press, 1993.

## CRITICAL AND BIOGRAPHICAL STUDIES

Allen, Gay Wilson. *The New Walt Whitman Handbook.* New York: New York University Press, 1975.

———. *The Solitary Singer: A Critical Biography of Walt Whitman.* New York: New York University Press, 1967.

Anderson, Quentin. *The Imperial Self: An Essay in American Literary and Cultural History.* New York: Knopf, 1971.

———. *Making Americans: An Essay on Individualism and Money.* New York: Harcourt, 1992.

———. "Whitman's New Man." In *Walt Whitman's Autograph Revision of the Analysis of* Leaves of

Grass *(For Dr. R. M. Bucke's Walt Whitman).* Text notes by Stephen Railton. New York: New York University Press, 1974.

Asselineau, Roger. *The Evolution of Walt Whitman.* 2 vols. Cambridge, Mass.: Harvard University Press, 1960–1962.

Burroughs, John. *Notes on Walt Whitman as Poet and Person.* New York: American News Co., 1867.

Chase, Richard. *Walt Whitman Reconsidered.* New York: William Sloane Associates, 1955.

Erkkila, Betsy. *Whitman the Political Poet.* New York: Oxford University Press, 1989.

Erkkila, Betsy, and Jay Grossman, eds. *Breaking Bounds: Whitman and American Cultural Studies.* New York: Oxford University Press, 1996.

Folsom, Ed. "Whitman's Calamus Photographs." In *Breaking Bounds.* Edited by Betsy Erkkila and Jay Grossman. New York: Oxford University Press, 1996.

Hollis, C. Carroll. *Language and Style in* Leaves of Grass. Baton Rouge: Louisiana State University Press, 1983.

Kaplan, Justin. *Walt Whitman, A Life.* New York: Simon & Schuster, 1980.

Kinnaird, John. "*Leaves of Grass* and the American Paradox." *Partisan Review* 25:380–405 (1958). Revised and reprinted in *Whitman: A Collection of Critical Essays.* Edited by Roy Harvey Pearce. Englewood Cliffs, N.J.: Prentice-Hall, 1962.

Larson, Kerry C. *Whitman's Drama of Consensus.* Chicago: University of Chicago Press, 1988.

Lawrence, D. H. *Studies in Classic American Literature.* New York: T. Seltzer, 1923; New York: Viking, 1961.

Matthiessen, F. O. *American Renaissance: Art and Expression in the Age of Emerson and Whitman.* New York: Oxford University Press, 1941.

Miller, Edwin Haviland. *Walt Whitman's Poetry: A Psychological Journey.* New York: New York University Press, 1968.

Miller, James E., Jr. *A Critical Guide to* Leaves of Grass. Chicago: University of Chicago Press, 1957.

Moon, Michael. *Disseminating Whitman: Revision and Corporeality in* Leaves of Grass. Cambridge, Mass.: Harvard University Press, 1991.

Nathanson, Tenney. *Whitman's Presence: Body, Voice, and Writing in* Leaves of Grass. New York: New York University Press, 1992.

O'Connor, William Douglas. *The Good Gray Poet: A Vindication.* New York: Bunce and Huntington, 1866.

Pease, Donald E. "Blake, Crane, Whitman, and Modernism: A Poetics of Pure Possibility." *PMLA* 96: 64–85 (1981).

———. *Visionary Compacts: American Renaissance Writings in Cultural Context.* Madison: University of Wisconsin Press, 1987.

Reynolds, David S. *Walt Whitman's America: A Cultural Biography.* New York: Knopf, 1995.

Shively, Charley, ed. *Calamus Lovers: Walt Whitman's Working-Class Camerados.* San Francisco: Gay Sunshine, 1987.

Thomas, M. Wynn. *The Lunar Light of Whitman's Poetry.* Cambridge, Mass.: Harvard University Press, 1987.

Traubel, Horace. *With Walt Whitman in Camden.* 6 vols. [Various places and various publishers], 1908–1983.

Warren, James Perrin. *Walt Whitman's Language Experiment.* University Park: Pennsylvania State University Press, 1990.

Zweig, Paul. *Walt Whitman: The Making of the Poet.* New York: Basic Books, 1984.

—TENNEY NATHANSON

# William Carlos Williams
## 1883–1963

WILLIAM CARLOS WILLIAMS was a physician in Rutherford, New Jersey, for more than forty years, until forced to retire by the heart problems that finally killed him in 1963 at the age of seventy-nine. But despite his full-time career as a doctor, he published forty-nine books, a remarkable testament to his energy and determination, even if some of those books do represent collections of previously published material. In addition, his bibliography lists almost a hundred contributions to books edited by other people and more than six hundred publications in periodicals. These numbers include not only Williams' poetry but also his novels (he published four), his essays, a history, numerous reviews of books and art exhibitions, and even an opera libretto. But for all this output, Williams did not begin to gain the kind of recognition accorded such contemporaries as T. S. Eliot, Ezra Pound, and Wallace Stevens until the last dozen years of his life. When that recognition finally came, though, it brought with it the attention of such younger poets as Allen Ginsberg, Robert Creeley, Denise Levertov, and even Robert Lowell, all eager to learn from Williams' lifetime of writing and his ways of articulating what he saw as the necessary direction for American poetry. An indication of what Williams meant to the more radical poets of the 1950s comes from Amiri

Baraka's account of his own education in Greenwich Village, in *The Autobiography of LeRoi Jones* (1984). Among the various people who sought:

> a point of departure from the academic, from the Eliotic model of rhetoric, formalism, and iambics. . . . Williams was a common denominator because he wanted American Speech, a mixed foot, a variable measure. He knew American life had outdistanced the English rhythms and their formal meters. The language of this multinational land, of mixed ancestry, where war dance and salsa combine with country and Western, all framed by African rhythm-and-blues confessional.

### EARLY LIFE AND POEMS

Williams often explored his own mixed ancestry in his poetry. He was born on September 17, 1883, in Rutherford, the older of the two sons of William George and Raquel Hélène Rose Hoheb Williams. His father was born in England of English parents but accompanied his mother to the New World in 1856 at the age of five, where they lived on various Caribbean islands, finally settling in Santo Domingo. William George married Raquel, of Puerto Rico, in 1882, when the couple—along with William George's mother—moved to

New York and then to Rutherford. William Carlos' younger brother, Edgar, went on to become a noted architect. (In the 1950s he contributed to the design of the Rutherford Public Library, which now houses a rich collection of the papers of the town's famous poet-doctor.)

The record of the relationship between the two brothers has been preserved more in their extensive correspondence than in the poems of William Carlos. But Williams' views of his father and mother and also of his paternal grandmother form the subject of a number of his poems. Even more extensive are the poems that come out of his life with Florence (Flossie) Herman, whom he married in 1912 (after being turned down by her sister). The poems that focus on these close family members are informed by ideas of marriage and cultural and gender identities that are central to Williams' poetry. These poems also reflect Williams' belief that the poet must concern himself with local material as an essential first step toward reaching for more universal issues.

Williams' early education took place in local public schools, and he attended the town's Unitarian church, with which his father was closely associated. The family sent William Carlos and Edgar to Geneva and Paris for just over a year from 1898 to 1899, before the two brothers continued their education at Horace Mann School in New York City. Despite what Williams' biographer Paul L. Mariani characterizes as Williams' "mediocre record" at Horace Mann, three years later he began studies at the University of Pennsylvania, initially in the School of Dentistry, before switching to the School of Medicine. There the nineteen-year-old Williams met the seventeen-year-old Ezra Pound, then a sophomore at the university, and began a lifelong, if sometimes frustrating, friendship. In this same year, 1902, Williams met Charles Demuth, who was to become one of America's foremost modernist painters. Williams dedicated his volume of poetry and prose *Spring and All* to Demuth in 1923. In 1902 Williams also met a friend of Pound's, Hilda

Doolittle, the poet who later signed herself H. D. She was to follow Pound to London and be a central part of the imagist movement that had such an impact on Williams' poetics.

Williams' poetry in the first decade of the century reflected his strong admiration for John Keats, although he also harbored an admiration for Walt Whitman, a writer who was to exert a much more lasting influence. One reminder of Williams' Keatsian phase is an unpublished and unfinished epic poem based on *Endymion* (1818). As Williams described the poem in his autobiography:

> it was a narrative in that vague area of thought that associated itself with a romantic past. . . . It opened with a Keatsian sonnet for prologue, followed by an 'Induction' that recounted in blank verse a tragic story.

Keats is the central figure behind the shorter poems Williams wrote during his three years of internships at New York City hospitals following his graduation from medical school in 1906. His second European trip included six months of studying pediatrics in Leipzig and meeting up with the now London-based Pound in 1910. In December 1912 he married Florence Herman, and the couple went on to have two sons, William Eric and Paul Herman.

In 1909, before leaving for Leipzig, Williams published his first book, *Poems,* with a local journeyman printer. The title page was designed by Williams' brother Edgar, and the book was published at the poet's own expense. Here were the results of his writing while interning in New York City. A small pamphlet of twenty-seven poems, the book, Williams soon came to recognize, was stuffed with the clichés and poetic diction of the most conventional verse of the previous century. He would never reprint the poems in any of his collections.

One of the sonnets in *Poems* celebrates what its title calls "The Uses of Poetry" (or "poesy" as the poem itself refers to verse). The imagined situation involves the poet reading to "a lady . . . /

The while we glide by many a leafy bay." The trees, boat, and poetry produce a mood that lifts the gliding couple out of the everyday world; poetry, the poem argues, can "close the door of sense" and allow one to escape to a peaceful landscape that holds no "anguish." In a similar poem, "On a Proposed Trip South," the poet anticipates leaving the harsh winter landscape surrounding him and taking "a southern flight" to a landscape that contains many of the familiar trappings of scenes in late Romantic poetry: "lush high grasses . . . / Gay birds and . . . bees." The genre is that of W. B. Yeats's "Lake Isle of Innisfree" (1890), but in that poem the conventions are freshly realized, and the longing behind them more than the merely rhetorical gestures that one finds in these early poems by Williams.

In almost every feature, the verse in *Poems* goes against what would be the characteristics of Williams' later poetry. His mature verse would stress direct engagement with the local landscape and world of objects in Williams' New Jersey, not the conventions of an imagined world inherited from Romantic poetry. In his later poems Williams would seek to achieve the immediacy and directness of everyday speech, rather than the artificial diction of his 1909 *Poems*. His open-ended line breaks and stanza forms would emphasize the syntactical energy of the poem itself and the moment that it expresses simultaneously. Following *Poems*, many years would pass before Williams published another sonnet.

### THE TEMPERS

Pound's response to *Poems* was to send Williams one of what were to be many reading lists over the years. (Forty years later, Williams included a representative sample of these reading lists from Pound in his long poem *Paterson*.) In response to this first book, Pound gently informed Williams that although the volume demonstrated that the writer had "poetic instincts," he was writing in a form perfected in the early part of the previous century. He was simply out of date and out of touch. In London, Pound argued, Williams would realize this and would acquire some standards against which he could judge his own work.

This letter was one of a number Pound sent to Williams at this time suggesting recent and contemporary writers that Williams should read. In addition, Pound introduced Williams to some of the journals in London that were publishing modern writing. The most important of these was the *Egoist,* which H. D. and later T. S. Eliot helped to edit. Williams' poetry began to appear in it beginning in 1913. His first journal publication, the year before, was in the London *Poetry Review,* and his second book, *The Tempers,* was also published in London, in 1913. Like Robert Frost, another poet often particularly associated with American characteristics, Williams found his earliest publishers in London. With Pound's help, in 1913 Williams' work made its first appearance in the new journal *Poetry,* in Chicago.

*The Tempers* shows that Williams had taken Pound's advice to heart, even a little too much, for the writer mirrored in this work is the Pound of *Canzoni* (1911) and *Ripostes* (1912, dedicated to Williams). Such opening lines as those from Williams' poem "An After Song" ("So art though broken in upon me, Apollo, / Through a splendor of purple garments—") and "First Praise" ("Lady of dusk-wood fastnesses, / Thou art my Lady") set alongside Pound's "Erat Hora" or "Quies" show the debt. But a poem from the 1913 group that appeared in *Poetry* reveals some characteristics of Williams' mature voice. "Sicilian Emigrant's Song" (1913), although still containing some of the archaic diction one finds in *Poems* and *The Tempers,* puts such diction into the mouth of a person from the old world emigrating to the new. This tactic anticipates how Williams will locate the source of such diction in his later poetics. It also constitutes an attempt to justify such diction: in terms of characterization, this is a character's voice, not the poet's voice.

One of the poems that appeared in *The Tempers,* "Hic Jacet," comes out of Williams' professional duties as a doctor; it is the first example of his use of what became an important source of material for his writing. "The coroner's merry little children" who prosper from death, and are far enough from old age to laugh at it, come out of Williams' observation of the local scene. Williams' profession both brought him to that scene and lent him, as a doctor, some shared characteristics with the subjects of his poem, even as he emphasizes his role as spectator. Nevertheless, "Hic Jacet" contains the kind of syntactical inversions that Williams would soon reject, and it is titled with a Latin tag that is a legacy of Pound's continuing influence.

Williams wrote a number of poems at this time that function more as announcements of his intentions in poetry than as realizations of those intentions. "On First Opening *The Lyric Year*" (1913) compares the contents of the poetry journal *The Lyric Year* to a graveyard and rejects the comforts of rest and relative anonymity for the challenge of engaging the contemporary world, but the world is only implicit in this poem. In the longest and most important of these poems, "The Wanderer" (1914, revised 1917), Williams asks himself, "How shall I be a mirror to this modernity?" "The Wanderer," which Williams chose to lead off his *Collected Earlier Poems* in 1951, is his fullest early confrontation with the contemporary. In this poem the poet is guided around the local landscape by an aged muse, identified in Williams' autobiography as his grandmother. The journey includes a visit to the city of Paterson and concludes with a ritual, presided over by the muse, in the nearby "filthy" Passaic River. In the ritual the poet gives part of himself to the river. "The Wanderer" ends with a gesture characteristic of many of Williams' poems: it initiates a new beginning, one connected to the landscape, to the potential of American poetry, and to the present. This present has its source not in the kind of transatlantic culture that interested Pound, Eliot, and

H. D. over in London but in the hidden springs and accumulative strength represented by the Passaic River, even in its soiled, commercially exploited condition. That, too, Williams suggests, has to be included and embraced.

## WILLIAMS' NASCENT POETICS AND THE AVANT-GARDE ABROAD

The poems of 1914–1917, including those of Williams' third book, *Al Que Quiere!,* reflect his attempt to find expression for his nascent poetics. The poems of this phase of Williams' career have an exhortatory tone, often instructing his "townspeople," as in the often anthologized "Tract," how to view the local world around them, spelling out implicitly or explicitly the associations with the kind of poetry that needs to be written. In this poem, for example, the call to remove superfluous decoration and euphemistic ceremony from the burial ritual parallels the paring down that Williams was attempting in his writing.

The biggest impact on Williams' poetics in these years once again came out of London, from the imagists, especially Pound. The imagists' emphasis on the "direct treatment of the 'thing'" that is the subject of the poem justified for Williams the elimination of such mediating factors as a past—too often contaminated with inherited ways of thinking that were not pertinent to current American needs—and all kinds of poetic (artificial) diction. The imagists' call for innovative rhythms justified throwing out a good deal of other poetic conventions, while their demand for eliminating superfluous words reinforced Williams' impulse to move toward a poetics of immediacy.

The shift in Williams' poetry after 1913 that emphasized the contemporary moment and personal experience, and the consequent shift in language necessary to express this emphasis, can be studied through two poems with characteristic sexual themes. A poem collected in *The Tempers,* "Postlude," which was much admired by H. D., frames its presentation of what is apparently a postcoital tension within a range of classical allusions—to Venus, Mars, Carthage, Philae, Jason, and Poseidon, among others. Inasmuch as these allusions are part of the poem's subject matter, they highlight the lack of such personifications in the modern world and the poet's problem in the "postlude" of the present: how to write poetry without them. The postcoital moment is expressed in terms of language and associations linked to a distant and generalized past. Three years later, with "The Young Housewife" (1916) Williams' mocks such language and associations and returns his poetry emphatically to the present.

"The Young Housewife" is also revealing of some ways that Williams' work has been read. In the poem the poet sees, or imagines, a "young housewife" behind the walls of "her husband's house" as he drives by. Then on a later occasion, or one recalled in the present, or one completely imagined, she comes "shy, uncorseted" to the curbside to meet with tradesmen, upon which the poet compares her to a fallen leaf. The temporal ambiguity is conveyed simply by "Then again":

> Then again she comes to the curb
> to call the ice-man, fish-man, and stands
> shy, uncorseted, tucking in
> stray ends of hair, and I compare her
> to a fallen leaf.

In the concluding stanza of this short poem, the wheels of the poet / observer's car take him past the house, accompanied by the crackling sound of dried leaves, and he bows with the gesture of a modern version of a medieval courtly lover to the contemporary muse encountered on his rounds.

Commentators interested in the gender issues in Williams' poetry sometimes suggest a reading of "The Young Housewife" that sees the poet defining the woman on his own terms and moving her from one form of entrapment ("the wooden walls of her husband's house") to another: the particular vision of her realized in the poem. Such a reading emphasizes that the car passes over the fallen leaves that the woman is compared to, and they interpret the poem as a fantasy of dominance. A biographical reading of the poem, such as that offered by Barry Ahearn in his book *William Carlos Williams and Alterity* (1994) emphasizes the sexual restraint that Williams felt his marriage put upon him in these early years. Ahearn notes that it is the tradesmen who actually meet the housewife, rather than the professional man who must consider his status in the community, if not his role as a husband, and who merely fantasizes about the housewife. The suggestion that the housewife, in the eyes of the poet at any rate, is "fallen," is a crucial part of both readings.

But while such readings are clearly supportable both in terms of the specific language of "The Young Housewife" and in terms of the context of Williams' work overall, they are not denied by another reading. We may see the poem as being about what is at some level the subject of every Williams' poem—poetry itself: the poet playfully compares the housewife he sees on his daily journey to a fallen leaf, but then his car moving over the actual leaves in the street returns him to the object-world. And the object-world must be his subject according to his new imagist-directed poetics. Thus "The Young Housewife" dramatizes the making of a poetry that treats actual rather than metaphoric leaves, leaves that are part of a poetic whimsy. Basic to this reading, as well as the other two, is the observation that Williams focuses on the immediate, contemporary world, including his daily professional life, in this poem. He does so in particularly direct language. "The young housewife" may remain more distant from the poet than the "lady of dusk-wood fastnesses," but she is an actual contemporary figure whose degree of presence and absence for the poet is directly examined.

FURTHER DEVELOPMENTS:
THE AVANT-GARDE AT HOME

The years 1914 to 1917, a period of fast-paced development in Williams' poetics, saw him taking up and responding to movements and ideas from various sources. In the pages of the *Egoist* he laid out a gender theory arguing that women were concrete thinkers, rooted to the soil, and that men, who were more abstract, had a tendency to float skyward. (This theory came out of Williams' reading Otto Weininger's *Sex & Character,* published in 1906, and the contemporary writings of Dora Marsden in the pages of the *Egoist.*) Whatever the value of such ideas beyond Williams' own poetics, they indicate how sexual attraction in Williams' volume *Al Que Quiere!* (1917) is linked metaphorically to writing and to everything Williams meant by "local": the local landscape, the surrounding community, his own life and that of his family, and in a larger sense America itself, especially as contrasted with Europe. For example, in "A Portrait in Greys," which many years later Williams said was a poem about his marriage, or in "Spring Strains," male and female forces appear antagonistic but essential to each other. The full recognition of these sexual issues becomes for Williams both the basis for poetry in general and a way to ground his own poetry, to move from the flights of fancy and escape represented by such work as the romantic fantasies of *Poems* or the ethereal world of *The Tempers* to the concrete world of reality. In numerous poems Williams associates this shift with sexual attraction and sometimes even fulfillment.

The pictorial elements in Williams' work that came out of his interest in imagism reinforced his early and lifelong interest in the visual arts. His poetic experimentation with the visual received further impetus during World War I when he became involved with the explosion of avant-garde activity in New York City and the nearby artists' colony of Grantwood. Artists such as Francis Picabia and Marcel Duchamp moved to New York and joined the writers, photographers, and painters loosely grouped around Walter Arensberg and Alfred Stieglitz. Although Williams' interest in avant-garde art movements may not have begun as early as the 1913 Armory Show, as he claimed later in his career, by 1915 he was certainly involved in the ferment of ideas those movements produced. A photograph from the spring of 1916 often reproduced in studies of Williams shows a group including Williams, Duchamp, Arensberg, and Man Ray on the lawn of Williams' house in Rutherford. Such work as Duchamp's "Nude Descending a Staircase," with its emphasis on the materials of its own construction—particularly the photographic reprint of that painting that Williams saw in Arensberg's apartment—entered into Williams' developing ideas about the necessary form and function of contemporary American poetry. So, too, did Duchamp's "ready-mades," in which Duchamp took an everyday, mass-produced object such as a snowshovel or dishrack and with minimal or no alteration beyond the conceptual one, declared the object a work of art. Such a claim raised challenging questions about the subject matter of art, the artist's role in composition, and the status of a viewer's expectations. Williams discusses a number of Duchamp's works explicitly in his prologue to his book of improvisations *Kora in Hell* (1920) published at the end of the decade.

The artists who surrounded Arensberg and frequented the Grantwood colony in New Jersey produced the journal *Others,* and Williams became centrally involved with it. The title of the journal reflected the group's general identification with New York as opposed to Chicago or London, where other members of the avant-garde were publishing magazines also promoting the new poetry. The pages of *Others* included poems by T. S. Eliot, Wallace Stevens, and Marianne Moore. By the final issue in July 1919, edited by Williams, and including two aggressive, angry, and iconoclastic editorials by him, Williams had moved a considerable distance from the tone of patronizing good manners with which he had addressed his "townspeople" in the *Al Que Quiere!* poems.

Along with Williams' growing insistence upon the importance of writing rooted in and expressive of the writer's locality went an ambivalence, which sometimes became the subject of his work, toward whether this writing should be expected to meet international standards. Williams emphasized what he saw as basic, incontrovertible facts about the American condition that he believed American writing needed to acknowledge: the culture, including its literature, was just beginning to realize its potential; therefore it sometimes produced tentative, fragmented work; and entrenched ideas and commercial values had made America a country with a hostile, even dangerous culture for its native artists. Williams was always ready to insist that the American writer learn from other cultures. He discussed non-American artists and writers in his prose. At various times he published translations from French, Latin American, and Chinese sources, in the latter two cases with assistance from specialists in the languages. For Williams, the highest international standard the American writer had to follow was to infuse the characteristics of his or her local culture into the language, form, the very subject matter and shape of the work produced. Such an insistence lies behind the problems Williams struggled with in selecting the title *Al Que Quiere!* and also figure in the "Prologue" to *Kora in Hell.*

### AL QUE QUIERE! AND KORA IN HELL

The Spanish title of *Al Que Quiere!* ("To Him Who Wants It"), like the copy on the dust jacket of the book (a sample sentiment: "neither the author nor the publisher care much whether you like it or not"), point to Williams' disdain for an audience whose demands, he felt, had restricted the possibilities of American poetry. But as Williams told Marianne Moore in a letter, he had also wanted to include an alternative title: "The Pleasures of Democracy." If this alternative title was partly an ironic comment on the tyranny of the majority behind the limited audience for innovative poetry, it also represented the side of Williams that saw himself as the heir to Whitman's populism. For this side of Williams, what distinguished American poetry was its attempt to reach out to large numbers of readers rather than limit its accessibility only to an educated elite. Williams the doctor literally went out to the community, and he wanted his poetry to extend itself similarly. Williams' unflagging optimism about reaching out to a larger audience is captured in a comment of Mrs. Williams' to an interviewer, some years after her husband's death: she said that despite her attempts to restrain him (because of so many past failures) Williams never tired of trying to convince his fellow citizens in Rutherford of the importance of the ideas behind his poetics and of the vital importance of poetry generally.

In the "Prologue" to *Kora in Hell* Williams makes his fullest plea for his brand of modernism, setting himself against the internationalism of Pound, Eliot, H. D., and even Wallace Stevens. Williams aligns himself with his Grantwood colleagues Alfred Kreymborg and Maxwell Bodenheim, while being careful to note their limitations. The classical myth that Williams appropriated for his title, of Kora/Persephone's banishment to the underworld of Pluto for three months of the year, during which the earth experiences the barrenness of the winter season, mirrored his version of America: it offered the potential for a new spring but within the context of a hell of violence and infertility. In his essay Williams links the example of Duchamp's "ready-mades" to *his* call for a poetry that would emphasize its own constructedness—and thus minimize the mediation between itself and its subject matter. This poetry would draw attention to the fact that it, too, formed a part of the object-world. For Williams, this concept of poetry entailed redefining what he increasingly came to call in the 1920s the "imagination." Like Duchamp's projects it demanded a reevaluation of the assumptions behind the definitions of and the creation of "art."

Many of the pronouncements in Williams' "Prologue" concern the new kinds of energized relationships between elements in a poem, between a poem and its subject, and between cultures, that might result from such a reevaluating. For example: "Given many things of nearly totally divergent natures but possessing one-thousandth part of a quality in common, provided that be new, distinguished, these things belong in an imaginative category and not in a gross natural array." Consequently "a poem is tough by no quality it borrows from a logical recital of events nor from the events themselves but solely from that attenuated power which draws perhaps many broken things into a dance giving them thus a full being." As for those poets "who have . . . the conventionality" to take off for London, "where the signposts are clearly marked," the roads clearly laid out by tradition and common usage, Williams wants to "confine them in hell for their . . . assumption that there is no alternative but their own groove."

The prose improvisations that follow the "Prologue" proved important to Williams' continuing attempt to shake his poetry free from the established conventions of syntax and grammar. They helped him discover a flexible line that allowed him to emphasize as much as possible that a given poem's arrangement was not predetermined but arose directly from the pattern shaped by the particular words of that poem. As Williams tells the story of the improvisations in his own autobiography, he set down these short prose pieces after he came home exhausted each night during the influenza epidemic of 1917–1918. At the end of a year he rearranged and numbered the pieces in a loose order and also wrote some commentary on a few of them. These improvisatory pieces, like the prose included with the twenty-seven poems of *Spring and All,* are for Williams a direct engagement of his imagination with the world of his experience—hurried, automatic, not preshaped in any way. Thus Williams turned the constant interruptions and the physical and emotional demands of his medical practice to advantage. Such interruptions and demands left Williams no time to construct formulaic patterning for his language and gave it instead, for him, the authenticity of unmediated experience. In the poems of his next book, *Sour Grapes* (1921), Williams engaged aspects of his world—among them, family ("Waiting"), patients ("Complaint," "The Cold Night"), the landscape ("The Desolate Field"), and writing ("March")—in situations of various degrees of extremity.

### SPRING AND ALL

Williams explained years later that the title *Sour Grapes* reflected his being disappointed that New York had lost to Paris not only the European artists who had made New York such a vital center during World War I, but also the American artists. (One consequence was that Williams was faced in the 1920s with advocating his poetics largely through books and journals published in Europe.) A particular blow to Williams was the exodus of Robert McAlmon, with whom Williams had edited *Contact,* the journal that succeeded *Others.* McAlmon went on to play his part in American publishing and literary history by setting up *Contact* editions in France, putting out books by Williams, Pound, Ernest Hemingway, Ford Madox Ford, and Gertrude Stein, among others. But Williams' attitude toward such a compromise as McAlmon represented to him is captured in his novel from 1928, *A Voyage to Pagany,* which came out of his own six-month trip to Europe in 1924. The doctor-protagonist of *A Voyage to Pagany* holds a genuine but ambivalent affection for the character modeled on McAlmon, Jack Murry, but Murry is finally irrelevant to the protagonist's sense of what he must do when he returns to the United States, alone.

McAlmon published Williams' prose and poetry sequence *Spring and All* (1923), a book which is now regarded by many critics as one of Williams' finest pieces of sustained writing. Only about three hundred copies were printed, and this indicates how small Williams' audience was at this time. "If anything of moment results," the book begins, "—so much the better. And so much the more likely will it be that no one will want to see it." Pound, writing an essay on Williams a few years later, had to ask for a copy. The twenty-seven poems collected in this book represent what Williams had developed with his radical experiments with syntax in *Kora in Hell*, while the prose in *Spring and All* imagines, and argues for, a physical and cultural American landscape in which the poems could not only appear but also take root.

The first poem in *Spring and All*, one of Williams' best-known, depicts such a landscape:

> By the road to the contagious hospital
> under the surge of the blue
> mottled clouds driven from the
>
> northeast—a cold wind. . . .
>
> . . . . . . . . . . . .
>
> They enter the new world naked,
> cold, uncertain of all
> save that they enter. . . .

This poem, later titled "Spring and All," is on one level an account of a professional trip to a local hospital. But it is also a portrait of the New Jersey swampland at the moment when the dormancy of winter gives way to the first stirring of spring, and it is a celebration of a number of other births and beginnings, some barely implied: a newborn child, the beginning of the poem sequence in the book and figures arriving in the New World wholly open to its newness, not imposing on it fixed categories imported from Europe. All enter "the new world naked," part of the inclusive and ambiguous antecedent of the line's "They." This line gave Paul Mariani the title for his biography of Williams, *A New World Naked.*)

When one reads "Spring and All" in the rich context of prose that surrounds it in the book of the same title, and when one understands the significance of the poem's being first, one realizes how much readers lose if they know it as an isolated selection. Context and sequence make a difference to the meaning of all the components of *Spring and All*. But many readers only know the poems from anthologies, or perhaps from the 1938 and 1951 collected editions, where circumstances allowed Williams no space to reprint the prose as well. Poems such as the much anthologized "The Red Wheelbarrow" (poem 22 in *Spring and All*), "To Elsie" (poem 18), and "The Rose" (poem 7) are all enriched by their original context.

Part of what Williams was trying to accomplish in a sequence such as *Spring and All*, and in later sequences such as *The Descent of Winter* (1928; also a poetry/prose sequence) and "Della Primavera Trasportata al Morale" (1930; in which he originally intended to include prose) was the creation of a broad design within which poems could be placed without compromising their individual strategies of immediacy. The idea is expressed by Williams' title: "Spring" suggests energy and movement *within* the season; "and All," all the particular forms that spring may take. These sequences, like his later works *Paterson* and "Pictures from Brueghel," emphasize the immediacy of the encounter between the poet and his world that produces the poem. But various devices undermine the temporal aspects of reading—such as foregrounding death, using pictorial strategies, or contextualizing a particular time within the cycle of seasons.

The sequences allowed Williams access to the range of structural and thematic possibilities open to the writer of a long poem, including locating a shorter piece within a specific and accumulatively self-referential set of contexts. For example, when the final poem of *Spring and All*, number 27, later titled "The Wildflower," celebrates the "rich . . . savagery" of the "black eyed susan," the promise of the landscape depicted in the first poem is fulfilled in a multitude of ways: that landscape flowers and becomes associated with an untamed, fertile, female sexuality.

### IN THE AMERICAN GRAIN
### AND *A VOYAGE TO PAGANY*

Williams' foregrounding of the New Jersey landscape in *Spring and All* has led some readers to speculate that one of his intentions was a response to T. S. Eliot's *The Waste Land*, published the year before and already becoming a significant text. Certainly Eliot's poem came to represent for Williams a benchmark against which he measured the wrong direction, as he saw it, that American poetry took for the next twenty-five years. The apparent pessimism of *The Waste Land,* its multiple international allusions, and its return to symbolist techniques were for Williams a denial of the promise of a still nascent American literature; they were a denial of a landscape with a rich potential subject matter that had barely been touched by American writers. For the next three decades Williams came to define himself against "Eliot," by which he meant a poetics incorporating the kind of international modernism embodied by *The Waste Land*: "Eliot had turned his back on the possibility of reviving my world," Williams wrote of these years in his autobiography. "And being an accomplished craftsman, better skilled in some ways than I could ever hope to be, I had to watch him carry my world off with him, the fool, to the enemy."

Williams could not deny Eliot's talent or the pull and fascination of Europe. But the travels and writing that resulted from the twelve-month sabbatical Williams took from his medical practice beginning in the summer of 1923 reflect the full complexity of his response to what Eliot and the challenge of Europe represented. Williams spent the first six months researching and writing his series of historical essays, *In the American Grain* (1925). In these essays Williams looked anew at some of the major figures of schoolroom history to reveal them—through various strategies, including using their own words—in a context that released them from the clichés of conventional histories. The second six months Williams spent in Europe with Flossie, where as well as meeting up again with McAlmon and Pound, he met James Joyce and generally sampled the expatriate scene. In the following months Williams and his wife traveled to the south of France, to Italy, Austria, and Switzerland, before returning to Paris.

Williams has left two complementary records of his journey. One is a series of raw, improvisatory, sometimes obscene notes, composed largely in Italy and Vienna and published posthumously as "Rome" in 1978. The writing of these notes is described in the other version of the trip that Williams published, *A Voyage to Pagany*, in which a thinly disguised Williams (Dr. Dev Evans), through a series of failed sexual relationships, tries to come to terms with a European heritage that challenges and threatens to overwhelm him. Europe in this novel has a greater openness to the qualities of creativity and sexual liberation than America, luring away the kind of woman who would mitigate Evans' isolation in his home country. In a significant development that brings the two sides of Williams' year together, in Vienna Dr. Evans gives his lover Grace Black, who will not return with him to New York, "a copy of a book he had once published upon some characters from the American History." With the parting gift of *In the American Grain* to his lover in Vienna, a book arguing that America is a culture marked by sexual repression and fear, Evans acknowledges why an American woman would find the United States an impossible place to live in. Such a recognition and its full implications become part of what Evans must confront in taking up the challenge at the end of *Voyage to Pagany* to return home, to make another of Williams' beginnings.

*In the American Grain* has often been compared to D. H. Lawrence's *Studies in Classic American Literature*, published in book form in 1923 but first appearing in *The English Review* some years before. In a generous review of *In the American Grain* in 1926, Lawrence praised Williams for embarking on "the really great adventure in the New World" to "touch America as she is; dare to touch her!" This Lawrence opposed to what Williams, and Lawrence himself, defined as recoiling, "the Puritan way." (The admiration Williams felt for the British writer is expressed in his poem on Lawrence's death, "An Elegy for D. H. Lawrence," 1935.)

In his historical essays Williams sets up a dialectic between those figures whose response to the New World was to recognize its indigenous potential (Montezuma, Père Sebastian Rasles, Daniel Boone) and those whose interests in it were merely exploitative (Christopher Columbus, Hernán Cortés, Hernando de Soto, Benjamin Franklin). But then Williams complicates this polarity in a number of ways. De Soto, for example, is drawn further and further inland by a search for gold, not realizing that his journey is actually driven by the seductive call of a female voice ("She" in the essay), and his body itself, cast by his followers into a river, enacts a ritual fertilization of the landscape. In another essay Williams reverses the chronology of Columbus' diaries to end by describing Columbus' sense of wonder at the New World landscape on his first arrival; thus Williams emphasizes Columbus' initial sense of awe rather than his disappointments or his motivations for later voyages. In the essay on Boone, Williams tells the explorer's story while simultaneously exposing as false an eighteenth-century document by John Filson supposedly dictated by Boone himself. In another essay, Williams quotes Franklin at length, before offering a "commentary" on Franklin that accuses him of drawing back in fear from his knowledge of America's potential. Edgar Allan Poe's life and writings, for Williams, reveal the cost of facing and dramatizing America's repressed condition, both in terms of the writer's personal fate and the later categorization of his writings by a culture afraid to accept the truth about itself.

Lawrence, in his review of *In the American Grain,* points to Williams' characterization of the continent as

> a woman with exquisite, super-subtle tenderness and recoiling cruelty. It is a myth-woman who will demand of men a sensitive awareness, a supreme sensuous delicacy, and at the same time an infinitely tempered resistance, a power of endurance and of resistance.

Such qualities are characteristic of the female figures in Williams' poems, from the aged muse of "The Wanderer" on. They are the qualities possessed by the women in *A Voyage to Pagany* who refuse to live in America, since the culture's denial of the essential forces of the New World, its full generative possibilities figured by Williams in sexual terms, amounts to the denial of their place within it. But a number of critics who have studied cultural and gender issues in Williams' work have noticed that *In the American Grain* itself treats few female figures, and that those who do appear are largely constructed by Williams, the very complaint he has against the dominant culture. Williams' treatment of women, and similar critical responses to it, come up again with *Paterson*, where in the poem's telling of the history of the city, the role of documents, habit, history itself, and the implications for language used as historical record and as contemporary expression are central.

DEVELOPMENTS OF THE 1930s

Williams' work in the 1930s included an association with the "Objectivist" group, which included Louis Zukofsky, Basil Bunting, and Charles Reznikoff. As Williams explained the Objectivist movement in his autobiography, the intention was to build upon the clearing operation undertaken by imagism, emphasizing as the imagists had the status of the poem as object: "but not as in the past. For past objects have about them past necessities—like the sonnet—which have conditioned them and from which, as a form itself, they cannot be freed." To use a past object, such as the sonnet form, is not to recognize the contemporary need for forms that parallel the qualities of the present age. Williams acknowledged the role of Gertrude Stein's work in the thinking of the Objectivists.

His association with the Objectivists allowed Williams the chance for his first retrospective collection, *Collected Poems, 1921–1931* (1934), which opened with an introduction by Wallace Stevens in which he argued that Williams brought into his poetry the "anti-poetic." But an irritated Williams ("not so hot" he wrote at the foot of the essay in a copy he inscribed for Sylvia Beach of Shakespeare and Company) rejected Stevens' distinction. For Williams there was no such thing as the anti-poetic: everything was material for poetry; poetry itself was part of the object-world. The difference between Williams and Stevens on this point marked the divergent paths these two poets had taken since the days when both were contributors to *Others*.

Their responses to each other in print over forty years—which include Stevens' elaboration on a Williams poem in his "Nuances of a Theme by Williams"; Williams' mixed review of Stevens' *Man with the Blue Guitar* (1937); an exchange in the 1940s when Williams responded to Stevens' "Description without Place" with his own "A Place (Any Place) to Transcend All Places", and Williams' respectful appreciation of Stevens when he died in 1955—reveal the distant but ongoing admiration each poet had for the other. They admired each other despite their quite different views on the place of traditional poetic devices in modern poetry, the role of the imagination, and the particular importance of place.

The 1930s also saw Williams publish the fine short sequence "Della Primavera Trasportata al Morale," which contains one of the important poems Williams wrote about his parents in these years. Williams incorporates pictorial signs into his poetic language in the first poem, "April" (as he also does in two other poems from this period, "The Attic Which Is Desire" and "Brilliant Sad Sun"). "Della Primavera Trasportata al Morale" concludes appropriately with a thematic fusing of Williams' poetry with visual art, here that of Botticelli (always associated in Williams' mind with the birth of Venus and with spring), invoked in the poem "The Botticellian Trees."

The penultimate poem of the series, "Death," articulates in lines that veer between emotional extremes the speaker's response to the death of an unnamed "he." However, details in the poem's first published version clearly identify that "he" as Williams' father, who had died of colon cancer on Christmas Day 1918. (Williams sometimes blamed himself for hastening his father's death by administering an enema to him some hours before.) In the final version of the poem Williams does not link his father, as he often did, to England and the cultural heritage toward which the son was almost always hostile. But the details cut from the revised version of "Death," which concern his father's South American business trips, reappear in the more broadly ranging poem "Adam," written during the mid-1930s. In this later poem, Williams makes explicit, through language that incorporates Spanish, the ambiguity behind his father's courage and never complete commitment to the New World:

But being an Englishman
though he had not lived in England
*desde que tenía cinco años*
he never turned back
but kept a cold eye always
on the inevitable end
never wincing—never to unbend—
God's handyman
going quietly into hell's mouth
for a paper of reference—
fetching water to posterity
a British passport
always in his pocket—
muleback over Costa Rica
eating pâtés of black ants . . .

. . . . . . . . . . . .

He never had but the one home. . . .

In contrast, the companion poem, "Eve," in which Williams addresses his mother, then in her eighties, presents his mother as furiously fighting against time and creating an imagined world of her own that she inhabits and insists upon with a physical strength and presence that leaves the poet astonished:

those fingers
which cannot hold a knife
to cut the meat but which
in a hypnotic ecstasy
can so wrench a hand held out
to you that our bones
crack under the unwonted pressure—

In the poem the son promises to help his mother to live on by writing a book about her. *Yes, Mrs. Williams* was finally published in 1959. Williams' joint translation with his mother of Don Francisco de Quevedo's *The Dog & the Fever* was published earlier, in 1954. (Around 1915 Williams had also worked with his father on translating a short story by Rafael Martínez.) In a series of poems written in the 1940s Williams recorded his mother's battle with age and infirmity and finally his response to her death: "The Horse Show," "Another Old Woman," "Two Pendants: For the Ears," and "An Eternity." After Flossie, Williams' mother is the most important female figure in his work.

### NEW DIRECTIONS

Williams' problems in finding a publisher for his books became acute in the mid-1930s, and the volume containing "Adam" and "Eve," *Adam & Eve & the City* (1936), as well as the previous year's *An Early Martyr and Other Poems* were issued in printings of only 167 and 165 copies, respectively. But in 1936, once again through Pound, Williams began an association with James Laughlin and New Directions. The immediate result of this collaboration was the appearance of Williams' *White Mule* (1937), the first novel of a trilogy based on the experiences of Florence Herman's family soon after she was born. The other two novels are *In the Money* (1940) and *The Build-Up* (1952). The three novels are more conventional in execution than *Voyage to Pagany* but always lively and perceptive. The prose focuses sharply on concrete details. The syntax shifts in rhythm, the narrative has sudden ellipses, and the author offers sometimes cryptic comments.

For some readers these qualities show to better advantage in Williams' short stories. James Laughlin soon published *Life along the Passaic River* (1938), the second of Williams' three story collections. In the stories, as in the novels, Williams often used characters and events directly out of his own experience. He had to pay a five-thousand-dollar out-of-court settlement for a story, "The Five Dollar Guy," published by *New Masses* in 1926, in which he had absentmindedly forgotten to change the real names. And he had to delay publication of one of his last stories, "The Farmers' Daughters," for some years because it concerned an actual, and perhaps not accidental, shooting.

For some readers Williams is at his finest as a short story writer when retelling events that come out of his medical experience. These stories have been posthumously collected as *The Doctor Stories* (1984). Included are the frequently anthologized "The Use of Force," in which the doctor and a determined child patient become increasingly furious with each other as he uses physical force to get her mouth open so that he can check on the possibility of her having diphtheria. The doctor becomes so furious that he "could have torn the child apart . . . and enjoyed it." "It was a pleasure to attack her," the narrator admits, even as a part of an effort to heal her. There is also the haunting "A Night in June," which conveys the exhausting routine of a doctor, the long waiting and necessary patience, through the night, of a difficult pregnancy. In both stories, as in all *The Doctor Stories*, Williams conveys his deep concern for and love of the lives that made up the community he served as a physician.

The good fortune of New Directions coming on the scene allowed Williams to publish a comprehensive collection of the poems that had appeared over the previous twenty-five years, the somewhat misleadingly titled *The Complete Collected Poems of William Carlos Williams, 1906–1938* (1938). The early first date may reflect a Williams defensive about his late start as a modernist, for the book does not even contain the 1909 *Poems*; it begins with poems from *The Tempers*. In the 1940s Williams also continued to make occasional forays into playwriting, which he had begun even before the period when he edited *Others*. This interest in playwriting would result in one notable commercial success, at the end of Williams' life: the Living Theater production of *Many Loves* ran for 216 performances in 1959 and was revived for another successful run in 1961 by the same group. Williams' approach to drama is summed up in his "Writer's Prologue to a Play in Verse" (1940):

expresses something of
the things, to your knowledge, that
take place in the mind and in the world
but seldom on the lips.

### PATERSON

Williams' main preoccupation from the end of the 1930s was with the formal problems of his projected long poem *Paterson*, and he began to publish scattered sketches from the poem in various magazines. In 1939 he sent James Laughlin what turned out to be a false start, an eighty-seven-page typescript titled "Detail & Parody for the poem 'Paterson'" that contained none of the prose that the final poem was to incorporate. Many of the poems in this early version represented fragmentary details of the world he heard and saw around him. Others parodied various literary styles and genres as part of Williams' search for what could be a usable language and form. This search remains central in the final version of *Paterson* but the role of parody is put less in the foreground, and the various details more thematically integrated.

What remains in published form of this early conception of *Paterson* is a truncated fifteen-poem sequence published in *The Broken Span* (1941), titled "For the Poem *Patterson*" (*sic*). Many of the "Detail & Parody" poems eventually appeared piecemeal in magazines and were subsequently collected in *The Wedge* (1944). For that book Williams at one point planned an elaborate, largely autobiographical arrangement that reflected the development of his own poetics, beginning with his earliest published poems. He originally intended to title the collection "the Lang\wedge."

By the mid-1940s, after more than fifteen years of trying, Williams finally found a satisfying form for *Paterson*. He originally intended that the poem have four major sections, and these were published separately from 1946 to 1951. Williams added a fifth book in 1958 and then even began a sixth. The central figure of the poem, Dr. Paterson, has a shifting identity but variously embodies the city and his poet/creator. He seeks in the landscape around Paterson, in its history and its people, in the letters he receives while writing and publishing the poem, and in the process of composition itself the language by which he can articulate the poem and represent the local world from which it arises.

The endings of book 4 and 5 are beginnings. At the end of book 4 recorded history has been problematized so that it no longer has the status of authority; it is just a part of what Dr. Paterson must read, acknowledge, incorporate, and finally transcend by means of the record of struggle that is the poem. Book 5 ends with a continuing dance ("to dance to a measure / contrapuntally, / Satyrically, the tragic foot"), which suggests the promise beyond the end of the poem and beyond the death of the poet/Paterson himself, now in old age.

Williams explained in comments on the poem that he chose nearby Paterson because he needed a city with a complex past and one that was, for his purposes, representative of his view of the major currents in American history. He observed that his home town of Rutherford was too small, while nearby New York City was too large. Paterson's history as it is presented in the poem includes accounts of cruelty toward the original Native American inhabitants; events from the pioneer life of the early Dutch settlers; and incidents from Paterson's dominant position in the late nineteenth century as a silk manufacturing center. It includes the story of Alexander Hamilton's idealistic plans to harness the water power of the city's spectacular falls (the central motif of *Paterson*) so that the city could serve as the manufacturing center of the thirteen colonies. The poem also takes up the history of the falls as an early tourist attraction. The verse in *Paterson* is juxtaposed with passages of prose, sometimes reproduced documents, from various sources, including material from turn-of-the-century histories and newspapers, newspaper reports that appeared while Williams was writing the poem, letters to Williams himself or to others, transcriptions of oral testimony, and other kinds of documents. Thus the prose builds up a comprehensive account of the city and its surrounding area, as well as a history of the poet himself and even of the process of the poem's composition.

All this history informs *Paterson* as a whole, both the poetry and the prose, and the falls come to represent the hidden, ignored, or commercially exploited source of a potential way out of the failures of the past. The continuing sound of the crashing falls, the dominant language of the landscape, acts as a counterpoint to the failures of language recorded and presented in the prose documents the poem quotes or paraphrases. The sound of the falls also serves as a reminder to Dr. Paterson of the necessary grounding for the language of the poem. Poem and language are often associated specifically with the falls, especially in the earlier books of *Paterson*:

> That the poem,
> the most perfect rock and temple, the highest
> falls, in clouds of gauzy spray, should be
> so rivaled

And the poet listens:

> Caught (in mind)
> beside the water he looks down, listens!
> But discovers, still, no syllable in the confused
> uproar: missing the sense (though he tries)
> untaught but listening, shakes with the intensity
> of his listening

The precipitous drop of the falls also represents a "descent" that Williams believed the culture and the poet must undergo in order to achieve the rebound that would constitute renewal. In this sense *Paterson* reimagines a key concept from Williams' earlier work, the "edge." The term, which appears relatively frequently in Williams' poetry, includes among its meanings the effect produced by line breaks that interrupt grammatical units or even break up single complete words. The connotations of sharpness and clarity that "edge" implies also remind us that *Paterson* is an object. "Edge" suggests the importance of careful observation and delineation, and a contrast to the lack of specificity in the romantic landscapes that Williams understood as failures of vision and language. In *Paterson* the edge is the place of poised counterforce before the waters crash onto the rocks below. But this place, signifying a moment of potential discovery, is characterized by the same qualities of violence and danger that Williams insisted accompanied the discovery of new space in *Paterson* and in the imagination. The histories in *Paterson* include accounts of those who come to look over the edge of the falls, filled with fascination and wonder, and are pulled in or jump to their deaths.

Three of the most important correspondents whose letters are incorporated into the poem were themselves poets: Ezra Pound, Allen Ginsberg (who lived in Paterson, and was then writing his first poems, years before *Howl*), and the far less well-known Marcia Nardi. (Williams also includes communications from Edward Dahlberg and Gilbert Sorrentino.) To various degrees he hides the identity of his correspondents, who come to represent various positions on the social and expressive problems (i.e., problems of expressions, of articulating matters through the medium of language) of being a writer, on the role of the past, on gender issues, and on the progress and impact of the poem itself.

The letters from Marcia Nardi, which first appear in book 1 but appear mostly in book 2, have probably received more discussion than all the other documents in the poem put together. Nardi, a published poet who introduced herself to Williams in his Rutherford office, began the largely one-sided correspondence in 1942 following the visit. What began as a discussion of her poetry, some of which Williams wrote an introduction for when it was published in the *New Directions* annual for that year (*New Directions Number Seven*), soon broadened to include the particular difficulties of being a writer, or searching for any kind of job, for a single mother with no financial resources or even access to a typewriter. In early 1943, after Williams had made some efforts to find Nardi employment, and forwarded a little money to her, he abruptly ended the correspondence, producing two remarkable letters from Nardi, which are inserted at various points in book 2.

The book closes with a long extract from one of the letters, in which Nardi accuses Williams of holding one set of values in his writing and another when it comes to dealing with the actual person who writes. The letter charges:

> And how were you, a man of letters, to have realized it when the imagination, so quick to assert itself most powerfully in the creation of a piece of literature, seems to have no power at all in enabling writers in your circumstances to fully understand the maladjustment and impotencies of a woman in my position?

Williams recognized, as he began to piece *Paterson* together, that Nardi's letters provided him with one way to dramatize the divorce of male and female that he wanted to argue mirrors the divorce of Americans, including Dr. Paterson, from their own landscape. And through the words of the final letter from Nardi, Williams cast Dr. Paterson himself as both a contributor to and a victim of the culture's silencing of the female voice.

The long extract that closes book 2 is signed "La votre C," recalling the correspondence of Criseyde (Cress), the victimized and faithless lover of Troilus in Chaucer's *Troilus and Criseyde*. The meaning of this allusion, and Williams' use of the letters generally, has been much debated. For some readers Williams' use of Nardi's letters, probably without her permission, amounts to an appropriation of her voice; it constitutes an attempt to blunt her attack and represent it on his own terms as a part of Dr. Paterson's experience. The editing and arranging of Nardi's letters within *Paterson,* equal, to some critics, to rewriting them, is in this view a further act of appropriation. To other commentators, and to Williams himself (who made this argument to a correspondent) the inclusion of Nardi's letters represents an acknowledgement of Nardi's case against the poet/protagonist. Some respond that this answer only validates Nardi's charge further, that Williams offers only literary, not actual, resolutions. From another perspective, the determination of the then unknown Allen Ginsberg whose letters appear later serves for some readers as an answer to Cress's failure of nerve. But whatever Williams intended by the juxtaposition within the poem of these two poets (and the juxtaposition is within the context of many other prose documents, including letters, and many other thematic levels), Ginsberg's letters to Williams point out the patriarchal associations of one level of the title, Pater/son. One could argue, however, that continuity is achieved through the poet's inclusion of the female voice within the poem through Nardi's letters and elsewhere. Ginsberg's letters, importantly, are a response to reading the poem as it was published in separate books. The son and his letters are born out of the associations of the earlier books of the poem, themselves an attempt to confront and heal the "divorce" of male and female. But no resolution in *Paterson* remains stable, for, as the patriarchal associations of the title also suggest, no place has yet been found in the city, poem, and history that is *Paterson* for the female, and the poem's search continues.

Nardi's letters prepare for the central figure of book 3: a violated woman, the victim of a gang rape, whom Dr. Paterson tries to comfort in her pain and fear. The scene takes place in the context of an account of a number of acts of destruction, including the fire, flood, and heavy winds that struck Paterson in 1902–1903. As for the powerful letters of Marcia Nardi, readers can now ex-

amine the full surviving correspondence between Nardi and Williams, which was resumed when a surprised Nardi discovered her letters in the poem: *The Last Word: Letters between Marcia Nardi and William Carlos Williams,* edited by Elizabeth Murrie O'Neil, was published in 1994. The letters are worth reading for their own sake as well as for a glimpse of how Williams worked on some of the documents, and experiences, that went into his poem.

For some commentators *Paterson* is Williams' major achievement, while for others the poem is a late and derivative response to *The Waste Land,* Pound's *Cantos* (from 1919 to 1959), and Hart Crane's *The Bridge* (1930). A number of reviewers complained as the later books of the poem were published that they failed to match the achievement of the earlier books, and nearly fifty years later some critics still feel that way; the view was occasionally even suggested by Williams. *Paterson* has also been discussed in terms of the way it developed the relationships between poetry and prose that had interested Williams as early as *Spring and All.* Critics have assessed the place of *Paterson* among other long American poems, especially its relationship to the work of Whitman. Some have focused on the characteristics of the poem's main protagonist. A suggestive approach comes out of the work of Michael André Bernstein, who focuses, in his book from 1980, on the tension created by *Paterson's* repeatedly refusing closure (as in the addition of book 5 and even of the projected book 6), and other forms of limitation while at the same time offering multiple myths, historical narratives, and formal patterns: the latter seem to invite closure. They are imbued with romantic assumptions about poetic unity that run counter to the emphasis upon the fragmentary, the concrete, and the moment summed up in the poem's early assertion of "no ideas but in things." As for *Paterson,* book 5, which represents some of Williams' strongest writing, critics debate whether it is more usefully compared to Williams' triadic line poems from the 1950s or, as Williams intended, seen as a continuation of *Paterson*. Again, the problem of assessing the unity of a poem like *Paterson* is that in many ways it resists the kinds of terms and assumptions that are brought to such a discussion.

## A TIME OF SUMMATION AND A NEW BEGINNING

With the publication of the individual books of *Paterson* Williams achieved a wider recognition; this increased in succeeding years. In 1950, at the age of sixty-six, Williams won the National Book Award's first Gold Medal for Poetry. The same year the first book-length study of his work appeared (Vivienne Koch's *William Carlos Williams*), and he was elected to the National Institute of Arts and Letters. But in 1950 Williams also broke with James Laughlin and New Directions, dissatisfied on the whole with the marketing of his books. The financial consequences of his limited sales were compounded for Williams by his impending retirement from medicine: a stroke in 1951 finally forced him to give up his practice. Williams was never one to write for the commercial market, although as far back as the double title he proposed for *Al Que Quiere!* he had wanted as wide an audience as possible without compromising his work. The powerful influence of T. S. Eliot over his own and the next generation of poets—while Williams was being published in limited editions—only contributed further to Williams' sense of being ignored. Finally receiving attention, and facing the loss of his major source of income, he followed a New Directions editor to Random House, and for the first time in his career Williams was published by a major commercial publishing house.

Thus the years 1950 and 1951 were a time of summation for Williams. He produced his *Collected Later Poems* (1950) and *Collected Earlier Poems* (1951), published his autobiography (1951), and completed *Paterson* (according to his original plan) with book 4. The early 1950s was also a time when Williams, who always resisted endings, looked forward to another new beginning, with recognition, time to write, and the possibility of a wider readership. But his stroke changed this new beginning in ways Williams had not foreseen. The physical difficulties and self-doubt brought on by his condition received expression in the poem, "The Desert Music," the result of a commission by Harvard's Phi Beta Kappa society. Williams read the poem at Harvard in May 1951, six weeks after the stroke. The poem asserts Williams' determination to face the difficulties confronting him and to reassert his identity as a poet. But over the next eighteen months, during which he suffered another and more serious stroke, Williams fell into a state of depression, wrote very little poetry, and briefly entered a mental hospital. (One poem that resulted was "The Mental Hospital Garden.") To compound Williams' difficulties, there was a building resistance to his appointment to the prestigious position of Consultant in Poetry to the Library of Congress. In the McCarthy years Williams ran into some opposition generated by his treatment of the Soviet Union in such poems as "Choral: The Pink Church" (1949) and "A Morning Imagination of Russia" (from *The Descent of Winter*) and to his generally left-wing (although never doctrinaire) sympathies in the 1930s.

In 1954 Williams published another volume of poems, *The Desert Music*, including the poem of that title. Williams led off the volume with a poem that represented the renewal of his creative energies. "The Descent" is actually an extract from book 2 of *Paterson* that describes a stage of Dr. Paterson's searching. While "The Descent" articulates Williams' career-long theme of despair leading to renewal, it offered him a new form, a triadic line. He realized that the form provided not only a visual counterpart to the idea of descent but also allowed for flexibility in the line and meter—what he called "the variable foot". The triadic line, Williams argued, enabled him to write in lines whose "measure" was that of the speaking voice. In a series of critical essays and statements that followed, in which Williams never argued a consistent set of principles to his full satisfaction or that of many others, Williams insisted that his new line allowed him to measure the American speaking voice, what he termed "the American idiom." "The Descent" begins:

> The descent beckons
>              as the ascent beckoned.
>                          Memory is a kind
> of accomplishment,
>              a sort of renewal
>                          even
> an initiation, since the spaces it opens are new
>      places
>              inhabited by hordes
>                          heretofore unrealized,
> of new kinds—

With the exception of "The Desert Music" itself, all the poems in *The Desert Music* and in the book of poems that followed, *Journey to Love* (1955), are written in the triadic line. In all these very accessible poems, which introduced Williams to a wider audience, the poet, unable to make the physical journeys that are so much a part of his earlier poetry, engages the past experiences that have been categorized by memory. But the experiences reencountered are now realized with a fuller recognition of their significance, seen within the context of a full life and the limitations that have forced this reexamination. When the subject is not memory, the housebound Williams explores the view from his window or looks carefully at his sons, at their marriages, or his own marriage, turning his physical passivity to advantage by dramatizing the activities of his engaging, reflecting, questioning mind. In long, probing lines Williams

seeks to avoid, as much as he did in his earlier poems, sanctioning the imposition of meaning upon experience. The best-known of his triadic line poems, "Asphodel, That Greeny Flower," is addressed to Florence Williams. It comes out of the tensions caused in the Williams' marriage when Williams, thinking he was dying following his strokes, confessed to having had affairs. Begun as a continuation of *Paterson*, and sharing the marriage theme with the yet-to-be-written book 5, "Asphodel" emerged as a poem about defeating time through memory, love, a shared life, and a shared despair.

### PICTURES FROM BRUEGHEL

Williams' poetics shifted again for his final book, *Pictures from Brueghel* (1962), for which, posthumously, he was awarded his only Pulitzer Prize. The degree of his shift has been debated, but certainly by the middle of the 1950s Williams began to feel that the triadic line had itself become something of a mold. He broke out of it with some poems that contained, in contrast, prose-like stanza blocks: "The High Bridge above the Tagus River at Toledo," which concerns a memory from his 1910 trip to Spain; "Tapiola," a commemoration of the composer Sibelius; and—as he often did when uncertain of his direction—some translations, this time from the Chinese, working with English versions supplied by David Wang. The poems that make up the bulk of Williams' final volume are usually written in short lines reminiscent of Williams' work in the 1920s and 1930s, but they retain the casual, reflective speaking voice of the triadic line poems.

The title sequence of *Pictures from Brueghel* celebrates Brueghel's engagement with his landscape and its people, and his powers of sight and composition, all qualities Williams sought a verbal equivalent for in these poems. Thus Williams made another gesture toward transcending time, aligning himself with the painter across four hundred years. Williams' pictorial emphasis in the *Brueghel* poems has been usefully compared to other poems on the same paintings, most often with W. H. Auden's "Musée des Beaux Arts" (on Brueghel's "Landscape with the Fall of Icarus"), and John Berryman's "Winter Landscape" (on Brueghel's "Hunters in the Snow.") Williams stays closer to pictorial detail than either Auden or Berryman do. Williams' argument is implied through his selection of that detail and the overall arrangement of the poems, rather than through the more generalized statements on the human condition that the two younger poets took from Brueghel's paintings.

Williams' strokes handicapped him to the extent that he could barely type a line in the last two years of his life, and his physical condition made him uncomfortable about seeing the many writers who wanted to make the pilgrimage to Rutherford. His wife took over much of his correspondence, and Williams finally gave up trying to write. But the last poem of his last book, "The Rewaking," characteristically anticipates the revival of spring, while the penultimate poem, "Heel & Toe to the End," celebrating Yuri Gagarin's pioneer space flight, begins with a stanza that reflected Williams' sentiments about his life:

Gagarin says, in ecstasy,
he could have
gone on forever

Williams wrote to James Laughlin at the end of 1962, when the two had reconciled and Williams had returned to New Directions, "You have been very faithful, it is deeply appreciated." He added "I wish I could write as I could formerly."

Williams died on March 4, 1963, in the house in Rutherford. Florence Williams died on May 19, 1976, but 9 Ridge Road remained the home and office of a Dr. Williams, son William Eric, until his death in 1995. In 1996 the house passed out of the hands of the family.

THE CRITICAL RESPONSE

In the years since 1963, Williams has retained his position of importance in twentieth-century American writing, although all too often he is known to casual readers only as the author of "The Red Wheelbarrow" and one or two other short, frequently anthologized pieces. New Directions has kept his major works in print, published some of the previously uncollected essays and reviews, and brought back into print such important books as the full poetry and prose text of *Spring and All* and also *Kora in Hell* with its original "Prologue." The *Collected Poems* volumes that appeared in 1986 and 1988 gather many of the poems that appeared only in magazines, and they include notes that report a number of Williams' late comments on individual poems. The revised edition of *Paterson,* prepared by Christopher MacGowan (1992), returns the book to its original format and notes many of Williams' sources. Volumes of correspondence that supplement John Thirlwall's 1957 edition of Williams' *Selected Letters* continue to appear, including a selection of Williams' correspondence with Pound and also a volume of his correspondence with James Laughlin.

Vivienne Koch's 1950 book was just the first of many studies of Williams to appear. Two of the earliest remain the most useful introductions, Mike Weaver's *William Carlos Williams: The American Background* (1971) for the complex of ideas and personalities surrounding Williams' work, and James E. B. Breslin's *William Carlos Williams: An American Artist* (1970) for a broad overview of the work itself. A number of critics have looked at Williams from the perspective of his interest in the visual arts, examining the pictorial strategies in his work and the influence of visual artists on his ideas, including Marsden Hartley, Charles Demuth, Charles Sheeler, Juan Gris, Marcel Duchamp, and Brueghel. Other studies, most notably Stephen Cushman's *William Carlos Williams and the Meanings of Measure* (1985), have looked at

Williams' poetics; more specialized studies have looked at the prose and at individual books.

Some of the issues arising from discussions of gender in Williams' work have already been noted. The important role of Williams' mother in his general treatment of gender themes has been explored, as has the place of the Spanish heritage that Williams often set against the Anglo-Saxon characteristics of his father and English literature generally. Other studies have examined Williams' interest in orientalism and also the relationship of his work to the Transcendentalists' and to African-American writing. Critics have also continued to be interested in the intersection of Williams' writing and medical careers. James Laughlin has published a record of his long, important association with Williams.

Such studies are invaluable guides to this complex man and his multiple interests. But readers who want to move beyond the familiar anthology pieces could not do better than to let Williams himself be a first guide: to enter the local but never narrow world of this writer through the full text of *Spring and All*, the "Prologue" to *Kora in Hell*, Williams' lively, sometimes exasperated letters to Pound, or the comments and readings by Williams captured on the tapes that make up the *Collected Recordings*.

# Selected Bibliography

## WORKS OF WILLIAM CARLOS WILLIAMS

### POETRY

*Poems*. Rutherford, N.J., 1909. (Printed by Reid Howell for the author.)
*The Tempers*. London: Elkin Matthews, 1913.
*Al Que Quiere!* Boston: Four Seas, 1917.
*Sour Grapes*. Boston: Four Seas, 1921.
*Spring and All*. Paris: Contact, 1923.
*Collected Poems, 1921–1931*. New York: Objectivist Press, 1934.

*An Early Martyr, and Other Poems*. New York: Alcestis Press, 1935. (Includes "An Elegy for D. H. Lawrence.")
*Adam & Eve & the City*. Peru, Vt.: Alcestis Press, 1936.
*The Complete Collected Poems of William Carlos Williams, 1906–1938*. Norfolk, Conn.: New Directions, 1938.
*The Broken Span*. Norfolk, Conn.: New Directions, 1941.
*The Wedge*. Cummington, Mass.: Cummington Press, 1944.
*Paterson*. Book One. Norfolk, Conn.: New Directions, 1946.
*Paterson*. Book Two. Norfolk, Conn.: New Directions, 1948.
*Paterson*. Book Three. Norfolk, Conn.: New Directions, 1949.
*The Collected Later Poems of William Carlos Williams*. Norfolk, Conn.: New Directions, 1950.
*Paterson*. Book Four. Norfolk, Conn.: New Directions, 1951.
*The Collected Earlier Poems of William Carlos Williams*. Norfolk, Conn.: New Directions, 1951.
*The Desert Music, and Other Poems*. New York: Random House, 1954.
*Journey to Love*. New York: Random House, 1955. (Includes "Asphodel, That Greeny Flower.")
*Paterson*. Book Five. New York: New Directions, 1958.
*Pictures from Brueghel and Other Poems*. Norfolk, Conn.: New Directions, 1962.

### PROSE

*Kora in Hell: Improvisations*. Boston: Four Seas, 1920.
(Reprinted in Williams' collection *Imaginations*.)
*In the American Grain*. New York: Albert & Charles Boni, 1925.
*A Voyage to Pagany*. New York: Macaulay, 1928.
*White Mule*. Norfolk, Conn.: New Directions, 1937.
*Life along the Passaic River*. Norfolk, Conn.: New Directions, 1938.
*In the Money*. Norfolk, Conn.: New Directions, 1940.
*The Autobiography of William Carlos Williams*. New York: Random House, 1951.
*The Build-Up*. New York: Random House, 1952.
*The Dog & the Fever*. By Francisco de Quevedo. Translated by William Carlos Williams and Raquel

Hélène Williams. Hamden, Conn.: Shoe String Press, 1954.

*Selected Essays.* New York: Random House, 1954.

*Yes, Mrs. Williams.* New York: McDowell, Obolensky, 1959.

*The Farmers' Daughters: The Collected Stories of William Carlos Williams.* Norfolk, Conn.: New Directions, 1961. (In addition to the new title story, collects Williams' three books of stories. Reprinted in 1996 as *The Collected Stories of William Carlos Williams.*)

*Many Loves, and Other Plays.* Norfolk, Conn.: New Directions, 1961. (Collects four of Williams' plays and his opera libretto.)

"Rome." *Iowa Review* 9, Summer 1978.

CORRESPONDENCE

*The Selected Letters of William Carlos Williams.* Edited by John C. Thirlwall. New York: McDowell, Obolensky, 1957.

*William Carlos Williams and James Laughlin: Selected Letters.* Edited by Hugh Witemeyer. New York: Norton, 1989.

*The Last Word: Letters between Marcia Nardi and William Carlos Williams.* Edited by Elizabeth Murrie O'Neil. Iowa City: University of Iowa Press, 1994.

*Pound/Williams: Selected Letters of Ezra Pound and William Carlos Williams.* Edited by Hugh Witemeyer. New York: New Directions, 1996.

COLLECTED WORKS

*Imaginations.* Edited by Webster Schott. New York: New Directions, 1970. (Collects a number of Williams' important prose works and prose/poetry arrangements from 1918–1932, including *Kora in Hell* and *Spring and All.*)

*A Recognizable Image: William Carlos Williams on Art and Artists.* Edited by Bram Dijkstra. New York: New Directions, 1978.

*The Doctor Stories.* New York: New Directions, 1984.

*The Collected Poems of William Carlos Williams.* Volume 1: 1909–1939. Edited by A. Walton Litz and Christopher MacGowan. New York: New Directions, 1986. (Includes "The Young Housewife," *The Descent of Winter,* "Della Primavera Trasportata al Morale," "The Attic Which Is Desire," and "Brilliant Sad Sun.")

*Something to Say: William Carlos Williams on Younger Poets.* Edited by James E. B. Breslin. New York: New Directions, 1985.

*The Collected Poems of William Carlos Williams.* Volume 2: 1939–1962. Edited by Christopher MacGowan. New York: New Directions, 1988. (Includes "Choral: The Pink Church," "The Horse Show," "Another Old Woman," "Two Pendants: For the Ears," and "An Eternity.")

*Paterson.* Revised edition prepared by Christopher MacGowan. New York: New Directions, 1992.

BIBLIOGRAPHY AND RECORDINGS

Baker, Richard J., and Richard Swigg. *William Carlos Williams: The Collected Recordings.* Keele, England: Keele University. Twenty audiocassette tapes.

Wallace, Emily Mitchell. *A Bibliography of the Works of William Carlos Williams.* Middletown, Conn.: Wesleyan, 1968.

## CRITICAL AND BIOGRAPHICAL STUDIES

Ahearn, Barry. *William Carlos Williams and Alterity: The Early Poetry.* New York: Cambridge University Press, 1994.

Bernstein, Michael André. *The Tale of the Tribe: Ezra Pound and the Modern Verse Epic.* Princeton, N.J.: Princeton University Press, 1980.

Bremen, Brian A. *William Carlos Williams and the Diagnostics of Culture.* New York: Oxford University Press, 1993.

Breslin, James E. B. *William Carlos Williams: An American Artist.* New York: Oxford University Press, 1970.

Callan, Ron. *William Carlos Williams and Transcendentalism: Fitting the Crab in a Box.* New York: St. Martin's Press, 1992.

Conrad, Bryce. *Refiguring America: A Study of William Carlos Williams' "In the American Grain."* Urbana: University of Illinois, 1990.

Crawford, T. Hugh. *Modernism, Medicine, and William Carlos Williams.* Norman: University of Oklahoma Press, 1993.

Cushman, Stephen. *William Carlos Williams and the Meanings of Measure.* New Haven: Yale, 1985.

Davie, Donald. "William Carlos Williams." *New Republic,* vol. 196: 16, pp. 34–39. (A dissenting view of Williams' poetry in a review of the *Collected Poems.*)

Diggory, Terence. *William Carlos Williams and the Ethics of Painting.* Princeton, N.J.: Princeton University Press, 1991.

Dijkstra, Bram. *The Hieroglyphics of a New Speech: Cubism, Stieglitz, and the Early Poetry of William Carlos Williams*. Princeton, N.J.: Princeton University Press, 1969.

Driscoll, Kerry. *William Carlos Williams and the Maternal Muse*. Ann Arbor, Mich.: UMI, 1987.

Fedo, David. *William Carlos Williams: A Poet in the American Theatre*. Ann Arbor, Mich.: UMI, 1983.

Fisher-Wirth, Ann W. *William Carlos Williams and Autobiography: The Woods of His Own Nature*. University Park, Pa.: Pennsylvania State University Press, 1989.

Frail, David. *The Early Politics and Poetics of William Carlos Williams*. Ann Arbor, Mich.: UMI, 1987.

Kinnahan, Linda A. *Poetics of the Feminine: Authority and Literary Tradition in William Carlos Williams, Mina Loy, Denise Levertov, and Kathleen Fraser*. New York: Cambridge University Press, 1994.

Koch, Vivienne. *William Carlos Williams*. Norfolk, Conn.: New Directions, 1950.

Laughlin, James. *Remembering William Carlos Williams*. New York: New Directions, 1995.

Mariani, Paul L. *William Carlos Williams: The Poet and His Critics*. Chicago: American Library Association, 1975. (Summarizes contemporary responses to Williams in reviews and early books and essays.)

————. *William Carlos Williams: A New World Naked*. New York: McGraw-Hill, 1981. (The most complete biographical study.)

Miki, Roy. *The Prepoetics of William Carlos Williams: "Kora in Hell."* Ann Arbor, Mich.: UMI, 1983.

Miller, J. Hillis. *Poets of Reality: Six Twentieth-Century Writers*. Cambridge, Mass.: Harvard University Press, 1965. (Includes an influential essay on Williams.)

Qian, Zhaoming. *Orientalism and Modernism: The Legacy of China in Pound and Williams*. Durham, N.C.: Duke University Press, 1995.

Riddel, Joseph N. *The Inverted Bell: Modernism and the Counterpoetics of William Carlos Williams*. Baton Rouge: Louisiana State University Press, 1974.

Sankey, Benjamin. *A Companion to William Carlos Williams' "Paterson."* Berkeley: University of California Press, 1971.

Sayre, Henry M. *The Visual Text of William Carlos Williams*. Urbana: University of Illinois, 1983.

Schmidt, Peter. *William Carlos Williams, The Arts, and Literary Tradition*. Baton Rouge: Louisiana State University Press, 1988.

Tapscott, Stephen. *American Beauty: William Carlos Williams and the Modernist Whitman*. New York: Columbia University Press, 1984.

Weaver, Mike. *William Carlos Williams: The American Background*. Cambridge: Cambridge University Press, 1971.

Whitaker, Thomas R. *William Carlos Williams*. New York: Twayne, 1968. Rev. ed. Boston: Twayne, 1989.

INTERVIEWS

Wagner-Martin, Linda. *Interviews with William Carlos Williams: "Speaking Straight Ahead."* New York: New Directions, 1976.

Williams, William Carlos. *I Wanted to Write a Poem. The Autobiography of the Works of a Poet*. Reported and edited by Edith Heal. Boston: Beacon Press, 1958.

*—CHRISTOPHER MACGOWAN*

# Index

*Page numbers in boldface refer to the
main entry on a subject*